# "THE HEATHEN IN HIS BLINDNESS…"

# "THE HEATHEN IN HIS BLINDNESS..."

*Asia, the West and the Dynamic of Religion*

S.N. BALAGANGADHARA

MANOHAR
2024

First published 1994, by E.J. Brill, Leiden, The Netherlands
Second edition 2005, with corrections
Paperback edition 2013
Reprinted 2019, 2020, 2021, 2022, 2023, 2024

ISBN 978-93-5098-008-8

*Published by*
Ajay Kumar Jain for
Manohar Publishers & Distributors
4753/23, Ansari Road, Daryaganj,
New Delhi-110002

*Printed at*
Replika Press Pvt. Ltd.

*Two women. From two cultures. One an Indian, and the other from Europe. The one is my mother and the other, my wife. Neither has met; I do not know if they ever will. But without either I would be a never-has-been.*

*All of us need a dream. Mine is this: to tell my mother what I write and think about. In my language and in her idiom. At this stage, I cannot; that is what this essay is about. "Perhaps, one day, some day..." so I dream. To that extraordinary woman, without a peer or parallel, I dedicate the first fruit of my project. In memory, because she is not there anymore. So, now I know that I merely dream. But what of it? We all need a dream...*

*To her, my mother, I wrote of the other, my wife, and said: "A Gift from the Gods." Gods may give; but we humans must learn to receive. Oftentimes, a gift is easier given than graciously taken. More so, when the drudgery of daily life and the problems of living corrode and erode both style and grace. Yet... To my wife, Anne, in love and gratitude, this essay is dedicated.*

# CONTENTS

ACKNOWLEDGEMENTS     xi

INTRODUCTION     1

I. SOME PUZZLES AND PROBLEMS     10
1.1. On Some Strange Sentiments     11
1.2. About Mystery and Mystifications     18

II. "NOT BY ONE AVENUE ONLY ..."     31
2.1. On the Cobbled Streets of Pagan Rome...     31
   2.1.1. Romans and Their 'Religio'     39
   2.1.2. From Demonstratio Evangelica...     44
   2.1.3. ...to Praeparatio Evangelica     47
2.2. ...en Route to *De Civitate Dei*     54
   2.2.1. "Will the True Pagan Stand Up, Please?"     56
   2.2.2. From Augustine to Calvin and Beyond     60

III. THE WHORE OF BABYLON AND OTHER REVELATIONS     65
3.1. A Modern Photo Album     66
   3.1.1. What is 'Modern' About Sexual Liberation?     71
   3.1.2. The Heathens and Their Irreligion     76
   3.1.3. Snapshots Superimposed     78
3.2. All Roads Lead to Rome     79
   3.2.1. Some Four Reference Points     80
   3.2.2. On the Eve of a Reasonable Age     83
3.3. "What has Paris to do with Jerusalem?"     89
   3.3.1. On the Banks of the Seine     91
   3.3.2. About the Pagans and the Primitives     95

IV. MADE IN PARIS, LONDON, AND HEIDELBERG     103
4.1. Evangelical Quandaries     103
   4.1.1. A Conceptual Quandary     104
   4.1.2. A Social Quandary     107
4.2. The Oriental Renaissance     119
   4.2.1. 'Vile Hindus'? The Other Face of the Coin     122
   4.2.2. Buddha, the Saviour of People     129
4.3. A Conceptual Interregnum     138

V. REQUIEM FOR A THEME     143
5.1. A Methodological Consideration     144
5.2. The Metaphysical Speculations     154
   5.2.1. Angst, Nature and Man     155
   5.2.2. Fear Theory and Fear from Theories     161

5.3. The Psychological Speculations    165
5.4. On Explaining Religion    171

VI. Shall the Twain ever Meet?"    174
  6.1. A New Development and Some New Concerns    175
    6.1.1. Development on Two Levels    175
    6.1.2. Grouping the Concerns    178
  6.2. A Pagan Prosecution of Christianity    180
  6.3. A Christian Persecution of Paganism    185
    6.3.1. Delineating Some Protestant Themes    186
    6.3.2. Tracing the Themes Further    201
  6.4. "J'Accuse"    204

VII. "Guilty as Charged, My Lords and Ladies?"    206
  7.1. The Prosecution's Case    207
    7.1.1. "Tell Me, Sonadanda, Who is a Brahmin?"    207
    7.1.2. "Tell Me Again, Brother Jacob, Who is Religious?"    219
    7.1.3. "Who is Religious, Dear Reader, Who Secular?"    221
  7.2. "The Prosecution Rests, M'Lords ..."    227
    7.2.1. Raising a Problem    228
    7.2.2. A Problem Illumined    231
    7.2.3. "What Say You, the Jury, Guilty or Not Guilty?"    235
  7.3. About One Half of an Argument    238

VIII. A Human Tragedy or the Divine Retribution?    243
  8.1. Because the Story Must Go On    245
    8.1.1. What is the Dispute About?    247
    8.1.2. ...de Gustibus Non Disputandum Est    252
    8.1.3. Interminable Disputations    255
    8.1.4. Classificatory Problems    258
    8.1.5. A Confusion of Issues    263
    8.1.6. On the Nature of a Meta-problem    267
  8.2. Switching the Tracks    270
    8.2.1. "Religion is...    271
    8.2.2. ...what Christianity, Islam, and Judaism Are"    274
    8.2.3. Linguistic Constraints Elaborated    277
  8.3. "Thou Shalt Resist Temptation ..."    279
    8.3.1. Misunderstandings and Temptations    279
    8.3.2. From a Simple Answer to a Complex Query    282

IX. Blessed are those who seek..."    289
  9.1. The Epistemology of Intolerance    290
    9.1.1. Historical Constraints Elaborated    292
    9.1.2. Religion and Doctrine    295
  9.2. "Our Father, which Art in Heaven"    298
    9.2.1. No Gods, but Lord God Alone    300
    9.2.2. Seek, and Ye Shall Find    304

9.3. "Thy Kingdom Come" 307
 9.3.1. "When the Son of Man Cometh... 308
 9.3.2. ...will he Find Faith on Earth?" 310
 9.3.3. "It is Absurd, therefore I Believe..." 313
 9.3.4. Ye Shall be as Children 316
9.4. On Religious Experience 318
 9.4.1. Atheistic Religiosity 320
 9.4.2. Controversies Illumined 324
9.5. "Hallowed be Thy Name" 326
 9.5.1. "The Heathen in his Blindness... 326
 9.5.2. ...bows Down to Wood and Stone" 331

X. "IMAGINE, THERE IS NO RELIGION..." 339
10.1 On the Very Idea of a Worldview 340
 10.1.1. A First Line of Defence 340
 10.1.2. A Second Line of Defence 345
 10.1.3. Religion and Worldview 351
10.2. Worlds Without Views 353
 10.2.1. A Metaphysical Impossibility 357
 10.2.2. The Sociological Impossibility 371
10.3. Views Without the World 380
 10.3.1. A Conceptual Fragment of the Answer 381
 10.3.2. The Depth of the Deep Questions 385
 10.3.3. Proselytisation and Secularisation 389

XI. PROLEGOMENA TO A COMPARATIVE SCIENCE OF CULTURES 395
11.1. Cultures as Configurations of Learning 396
 11.1.1. Learning Processes and Cultural Differences 396
 11.1.2. Religion as the Root Model of Order 400
 11.1.3. Science and the Root Model of Order 406
11.2. Conceptualising Cultural Differences 411
 11.2.1. Another Configuration of Learning 412
 11.2.2. A Different Kind of Knowledge 415
11.3. How a Difference Makes the Difference 424
 11.3.1. Raising a Naive Question 425
 11.3.2. An Encounter of Cultures 429
 11.3.3. Traditio, Knowledge, and the Religious Culture 433
11.4. The Dynamic of Religion 437
 11.4.1. Proselytisation and Secularisation 438
 11.4.2. Idolatry and the Sin of the Secular 440
11.5. About the Other Half of an Argument 446

XII. AT THE END OF A JOURNEY 447
12.1. The Different Rest Houses 447
12.2. About the Argument 452
12.3. Epistemic Questions 454

,REFERENCES                                        460

NAME INDEX                                         496

SUBJECT INDEX                                      499

# ACKNOWLEDGEMENTS

Before any other acknowledgement is made, it would have been nice to provide the arguments in this essay with an impeccable pedigree. Surely, many ideas have been anticipated before; thoughts have been better expressed by others elsewhere – these are the inevitable doubts of an author about to present a book under his name to a cultured public. I should like to hereby acknowledge any and all intellectual debts I may have incurred: if they are not explicitly recognized as such, it is not due to a moral failing. I hope that the informed reader will place footnotes as and when they are needed – heaven knows there are not enough of them; in so doing, express her/his goodwill – God knows I am in need of it.

My immediate environment has had a great influence on this book. Through its many versions, including its previous incarnation as a doctoral dissertation, several friends went through it – either fully or partially – taking the trouble to discuss their responses with me. The extent to which their criticism has helped is expressed by the fact that each version was new or different by a third. The final version is no exception either.

Prof. Dr. Diderik Batens, Prof. Dr. Jean-Paul van Bendegem, Prof. Dr. Karel Boullart, Prof. Dr. Arie de Ruijter, Prof. Dr. Dominique Willems – to each my thanks for the criticisms and suggestions. Similar help was given by Roland Cottoir, Guido Mareels, Carlos de Vriese and Pieter Welvaert, all of whom went through the entire essay.

Bob Carlier, Prof. Dr. Ronald Commers, Georg Hooreweg, Joke Meijering and Marc Poriau have commented on parts of the essay. The book has evolved mainly in discussions with Karel Arnaut, Tom Claes, Willem Derde, Filip Erkens, Yvan Houteman, Kris Muylaert, and Toon Tessier.

Harry van den Bouwhuijsen, a special friend from Holland, has been the kind of reader and critic that writers always dream of. Thorough and meticulous, he has constantly showered me with problems and questions, arguments and counter-arguments. If the essay has won on clarity, improved on substance (especially in the ultimate two chapters), a great deal of it has to do with his intelligent, creative, and sharp remarks.

A special kind of help was rendered by Willem Derde. He has helped me in indexing this essay, re-indexing and re-re-indexing as the chapters got rewritten, until they started flowing out of his ear. And yet, he has persisted. Added to this, in the last months, he has also been the first reader of several versions of a few chapters. As though this is not enough, he has helped me out with typing the manuscript; by running consistency checks in an enviably professional manner...all these with an unfailing cheer and friendliness. Such magnanimity, in these days of cynicism and calculation, is as refreshing as it is touching.

Prof. Dr. Rik Pinxten has been my constant support and encouragement. He has been a good friend, more than just that, a critic and a counsellor too. He was more disappointed than any that this essay has been so late in coming, but I hope he will continue to agree that it has only become the better for that.

To them all, my greatest thanks are due and are hereby rendered.

There is, finally, Prof. Dr. Etienne Vermeersch, who was also my doctoral supervisor. An extraordinary human being, whose kindness and generosity can only be acknowledged in this way: if it was not for his willingness and help, neither this essay nor the project of which it is a part would ever have matured. He gave me shelter when I needed one, while letting me free to explore the subject in my own way. From correcting my English through helping me to delve into the forest of theological discussions to forcing me to amend and improve my arguments – in all these ways and more – his help has been invaluable. His acuity and intelligence, openness and tolerance, have been a source of wonder and inspiration for me. The debt I owe him is overshadowed by only one other. That which I owe to my mother and my wife, to both of whom this essay is dedicated.

# INTRODUCTION

In this book, my object of study is the western culture or, at least, one element influential in its formation: religion. Today, it is a commonplace, in anthropological theorizing in any case, that the anthropologist describes other cultures using concepts native to one's own culture. Truths in truisms often hide problems – and the above is no exception. How does the culture of the describer reflect itself in his or her descriptions of other cultures?

The present essay is a partial answer to this question. By looking at the way members of the western culture have described religions in India, I try to decipher what such portrayals tell us about the western culture, about western religions, and about religion itself. That is, I attempt to specify how much of what the West says about India is rooted in the western culture, and why it is so. Such an attempt – one that seeks to cover all the important dimensions of culture – is, of course, a large and ambitious programme. In the present work, I carry out the programme focusing on one facet of the western culture: religion.

There is a further tightening of focus. I pick out one particular theme as a guiding thread to this work: the claim that religion is a cultural universal. I will argue that this idea and others related to it (we will come across many of them during this book) have more to do with the western culture than with what human cultures are.

## The Conventional Wisdom

Within the western culture, and among the intellectual layers of non-western cultures, it is widely believed that religion is a cultural universal. While accepting this is to entertain a truism, the common-sense wisdom of the contemporary West further assures us that, equally indubitably, many people in different parts of the world are irreligious. Atheism, agnosticism and ignorance of religious matters are widespread among the various cultures that constitute the humanity of today. Consequently, the claim about the universality of religion merely implies that native to each culture is some or another religion: Christianity to Europe; Islam to the Middle East; Hinduism, Buddhism, Jainism, and Sikhism to India; Shintoism to Japan; Taoism to China; Buddhism – due to both its antiquity and the modifications it has undergone – to South and South-east Asia... and so on.

Perhaps, we come nearer to describing this common-sense idea if we reformulate it thus: characteristic to cultures, and characterising their differences from one another, is their religion. Therefore, to some extent, differences between cultures can be explicated by speaking about the differences in their religion. Because religion is not merely a part of human cultures but also one of their constitutive moments, it makes sense to describe (though not exhaustively) cultural differences along the lines of religious differences. Religion is a cultural universal in the sense that some religion or another lends identity to a culture.

None of the above prevents one from acknowledging differences between religions. It appears to me that two types of differences are acknowledged in both common-sense talk and the intellectual parlance in the West. First, there is the kind of difference that exists among the Semitic religions (Judaism, Christianity, and Islam) themselves. The difference between a Muslim and a Christian (for example, believing that Muhammad is the prophet or that Jesus is the Son of God) is said to be analogous to that between a Christian and a Hindu. The Hindu's belief in the incarnations of Vishnu parallels the beliefs of the Christian. More abstractly, different doctrines and practices distinguish religions from one another.

Partly overlapping with this idea, but also partly differing from it, is the recognition of a second type of difference. This allows one to speak of different *kinds* of religion. In one religion, say Christianity, holy books and churches play an important role. In another, say the Native American religions, both may be absent. Buddhism does not merely appear different from Islam because it is another religion; it also seems to be another kind of religion to the extent it denies the existence of gods. It is, however, not always clear what makes something not merely a different religion (in comparison with some religion or another), but also a different kind of religion. Nevertheless, I do not think that I am far off the mark in summarising the common-sense wisdom in the following way: not only are different religions present in human cultures, but also different kinds of religion.

*The Theoretical Edifice*

This common-sense wisdom appears to rest on the results of generations of anthropological fieldwork: after all, have not centuries of ethnography proved that 'Religion' favours no single culture but, like God, treats all the children of Adam alike? Two anthropologists, one rather famous and the other less well known, are sufficient to buttress this observation. Raymond Firth in his *Elements of Social Organization* (1951: 216) says:

Religion is universal in human societies. This is an empirical generalization, an aggregation of a multitude of specific observations (cited in Smith 1962: 203; n. 2).

Or, as Saliba (1976: 22) puts it bluntly:

Since religion is a universal phenomenon, any study of a society or a culture which aims at taking a holistic approach cannot ignore it.

Such claims are not limited to the anthropological domain alone. Just think of those scholars and their specialised journals devoted to the comparative study of religion. From the meaning of the corn pollens for the Navajo Indians (Raitt 1987) through the problem of evil and the existence of God (*e.g.* Johnson 1984), through the evidential foundations for miracle (*e.g.* Odegard 1982) to the role of the teacher in Indian traditions (Mlecko 1982), many themes grace the pages of journals like *Religious Studies, The Journal of Religion, Religion, Numen,* and so on.

Anthropologists and scholars from the century-old field of religious studies are not the only ones to believe in the universality of religion. Philosophers and social scientists – from yesteryears and contemporaneous – share this belief too. During the eighteenth and the nineteenth centuries, for example, the origin of religion in human civilizations was a major issue that preoccupied thinkers from several domains – from philosophy to psychoanalysis. Today, many more domains participate in deciphering the mystery that religion confronts us with. Sociobiologists provide speculative hypotheses about the genetic basis of religion (Wilson 1978; Wenegrat 1990); cognitive neuroscientists meditate about the nature of the human brain that creates religion (see Gazzaniga 1985); psychologists, sociologists and anthropologists have generated mountains of literature about the psychology (*e.g.* Thouless 1961; Byrnes 1984), the sociology (*e.g.* Wach 1944; Wilson, B. 1982; Wuthnow 1988) and the anthropology (*e.g.* Van Baal 1971; Morris 1987) of religion.

Let me sum up the consensus – and the concordance between theory and common sense – in a negative way thus: today it is almost *sacrilegious* to suggest that there might be cultures that do not have religion. However, this consensus has not been won without battle. In one sense, this issue has been alive for nearly two thousand years. In the debate about the existence or non-existence of religion in other cultures, many souls have participated by taking all imaginable positions. Even today, there is no universal consensus but it is not clear where the disagreement lies. In this work, I would like to examine both the nature of the existing consensus and the issues and questions that undergird the dispute. As a consequence, I hope that a new and different light is thrown on a topic that is in need of a great deal of clarification.

### The Nature of the Journey

In the literal sense of the word, this essay is a journey in both space and time. Geographically, it flits between the two continents that Asia and Europe are. Temporally, it broadly picks out two thousand years of human history. Given the scope of the travel and its ultimate destination, a road map is perhaps needed to enable travellers to get off and on as they wish to. I will provide one very soon by describing the structure of the essay. Before that, however, a word or two from the guide may prove useful about such things as the entrance-fee, the travel routes, and the baggage one needs to bring along.

As it befits an organised tour, the baggage requirements are minimal. One needs merely to begin with the common-sense idea that Christianity, Judaism, and Islam are religions, as are Buddhism and Hinduism. This is a very reasonable demand, because it is what we intuitively take to be the case. Any further baggage, such as some or another explicit definition of the concept of religion, is going to be strictly superfluous for the travel; it will not bring any additional comfort along the way. To those among you who would prefer to begin with a clear definition, I would suggest patience. All things have their place and time; definition is no exception either.

Secondly, despite organisation, the planning is not rigid. We will mostly travel the highways, but, when interesting, make forays into the by-lanes and the meadows, and at times even fare along the tributaries. Even though the sights that we will see are important, the journey itself is no less so. The nature of the journey is important enough to suggest a travel requirement – that one is prepared to enjoy the travel as much as visiting the landmarks.

The entrance fee is minimal too. It merely requires a willingness – to think along, to enjoy the journey, and to lend an ear to your guide.

What, then, is our destination? What routes shall we travel? Where are the rest houses, and where the sights? To answer these questions, I need to talk of...

### The Structure of the Book

Consider the following three statements: (a) Christianity has profoundly influenced the western culture; (b) members from different cultures seem to experience many aspects of the world differently; (c) the empirical and theoretical study of culture in general and religion in particular emerged within the West.

In the present study, I try to show that these generally accepted truisms have implications for the conceptualisation of religion and culture. More specifically, I argue two interdependent theses: first, the constitution and identity of the western culture are tied to the dynamic of Christianity as a religion; second, because of this, it is possible to provide a different description of non-western cultures and 'religions' than those prevalent in the West. I plan to do this, among other things, by taking Indian culture as an empirical example not only because I myself belong to this culture, but also because India is supposed to rank first in terms of the number of religions it is alleged to have (Wilson 1978: 170).

My strategy will be the following. First, I will argue that the common-sense wisdom about the universality of religion does not just rest on the results of research – it also supports them. That is, the idea that religion is a cultural universal is the foundation for empirical and theoretical enquiries into religion. I will suggest too that this peculiar circumstance has hardly caught the eye of the students of religion. Second, I try to shed light on this state of affairs: why have generations of brilliant thinkers overlooked what, at first sight, looks like a massive exercise in *petitio principii*?

I hope to accomplish my task in the twelve chapters that make up the essay. Each chapter is a postulated landmark, signalling a shift in the kind of argument to follow. They are, in a manner of speaking, guest houses built for the travel-weary.

Chapter 1 introduces the theme and the general issues underlying it. By looking into the way contemporary authors describe different religions in several cultures, I attempt to specify questions that require satisfactory answering ere the investigation is closed. Even a random sampling of the literature points to the unease of modern-day writers; our problem is to localise it. An argumentative chain helps us here, because these authors appear to follow an inconsistent line of reasoning. In search of avenues to render them consistent, the subsequent three chapters set out in a historical direction.

In chapter 2, I take up the question of the dynamic of interaction between Christianity and the Roman *religio*. Through a contrast between the two, I lay the groundwork for tackling a whole set of issues and problems that will occupy us over the course of the essay. Neither here nor in the chapters to come, do I undertake a semantic analysis of 'religio' or 'religion' as concepts. My focus is on the object or the process referred to by these words. My aim is to begin the process of building a theory. Therefore, I look at the growth of Christianity, its relationship to the Roman *religio*, and the manner of its accommodation to the pagan milieu.

In chapters 3 and 4, we meet a mature Christianity and a confident European culture encountering Indian religions and people. Our sources are the well-known travel reports on the one hand, and the well-documented developments within European culture on the other. Again, my interest lies in deciphering Europe's image of itself and the other, as I see it revealed in the literature of the time. Together, these two chapters provide an outline sketch of Europe's discovery of religions in India. How did they find Hinduism and Buddhism? What did they find in them? Which were the multiple contexts of this interreligious encounter?

Taken together, these three chapters lay bare multiple questions – all of which require resolution. Regarding the *theme* of universality of religion, I argue that at least one conclusion is inescapable. By the time the German Romantic period draws to a close, we observe that the belief about the existence of religion in all cultures is not a result of empirical research. It is theoretically so certain that no empirical enquiry appears necessary.

To find out whether this is indeed the case, the next three chapters make a selection from the relevant literature. In this part, the tale changes tone: it is more thematic and less narrative in nature. The story shifts to the plane of anthropological theorising. It not only looks into the question of the origin of religion but also considers the theme of relating religion to experience. The naturalistic approach to the study of religion as initiated by Hume is the focus of the chapter 5. Authors like Schleiermacher, Söderblom, and Otto make their appearance in chapter 6.

Chapter 7 bundles the theoretical themes together. In doing so, a space is created for tackling yet another question: is the contemporary European culture itself, where religious dominance is on the wane and secular ideologies (atheism, freethinking) are more dominant, an example of a culture without religion? Answering this question depends on how one appreciates the process of 'secularisation'. Here, I slice this process in a fashion that is relevant for the theme of my essay.

At the end of chapter 7, many of the problems encountered in the earlier parts of the book begin to take a clearer shape. The theme about the universality of religion turns out to be a strand in a much bigger pattern, namely the extent to which religious theses have the status of uncontested and uncontestable certainties. Although this is the global problem, to which the second half of the book attempts to provide a solution, the theme itself never disappears. The general problem is also posed in the following way: why have intellectuals continued to believe in the universality of religion when there is neither theoretical nor empirical evidence in favour of it?

As an answer, one could trot out thousands of monographs that have studied religion elsewhere (see Firth's citation above). Before doing so, one needs to be sure that *what* they have studied in other cultures – surely, they have studied much – is also religion and not, say, an elaborate ceremonial preparation for some kind of dinner feast. Demanding such a guarantee requires a definition of the concept of religion – or so it appears.

Chapters 8 through 10 collectively tackle the problem of definition. They also move beyond it by providing a hypothesis that has empirical and theoretical consequences. My proposal not only helps us go forward in our quest to build a theory about religion, but also in tackling the issues that the first seven chapters have brought to light.

In chapter 8, the plot of the earlier chapters is picked up and is conceptually carried well into the last decade of the twentieth century. This period is the theatre where stories from the earlier centuries end up meeting. The meeting point also helps raise and answer the question of how to go about studying religion without providing an explicit definition first. I focus on the definitional problem from two perspectives. The first one shows that the definitional issue, in fact, has several sub-issues. The second perspective locates each of these within the framework of my story. The problem of defining religion is solved in this chapter. At the same time, a platform is also provided for building a rudimentary hypothesis about religion.

Because of my stance that a study of religion should not begin with presuppositions specific to the object under investigation – that is, with some or another explicit definition of religion – we are confronted with the issue of identifying the object of study. Chapters 2 through 4 come to our rescue in chapter 9. What had appeared as an empirical narration of the relation between Christianity and pagan Rome, and that between the West and India, carries a solution to an epistemological problem. Using this solution, I formulate a hypothesis about religion and spell out the conditions of adequacy that any such hypothesis has to meet. Having shown why religion is a particular kind of account, my proposal sheds light on the many dimensions considered vital to religion: faith and its relation to belief; interreligious rivalries as well as ecumenism; the nature of religious experience; worship; atheistic religiosity and the claim that one cannot study religion without being a believer oneself.

The truth in the last claim forces us to go looking for a more neutral description of religion. 'Worldview' is the nearest candidate we have for the job. Chapter 10 scrutinizes the fitness of this candidate. At this stage, we see *what* is interesting about the theme of universality of religion. Our question becomes: Do all cultures have or need worldviews to navigate themselves in the world? In one sense, answers to this question complete our investigation into the theme. However, the arguments used to provide the answer make the resolution of the global problem ever more urgent.

Chapter 11, although hypothetical and tentative in nature, expands the thesis about religion much further. Such an elaboration also generates testable consequences. The relationship between religion and the formation of the western culture is the problem to investigate; a comparative science of cultures is on the agenda of the future. In many senses, this chapter takes us beyond the confines of the present essay. However, what makes it a part of the essay is that, besides being programmatic, the proposed hypothesis also generates questions and tentative answers as they relate to the theme under discussion.

Chapter 12, the concluding chapter, reflects upon one facet of the methodological issue that comparative enterprises confront. This consideration helps clean the Aegean stables: it hints at what a comparative science of cultures must look like – and what it means to ask for one. By the end of the essay, I hope to have shown *why* the question about the universality of religion is an important question – and *what* its importance is.

The above paragraphs are meant as a rough sketch of both the travel route and the end of the journey. It might not be out of place to prepare you further for the coming travel by saying a word or two regarding the style employed in the essay. To this task, I now turn.

*Voices and Minds*

The entire essay is a sustained meditation on the theme of universality of religion and has the form of one continuous and extended argument. Like most arguments, this essay is addressed to an audience. The convention, or the presupposition, accepted while writing scientific treatises is that one writes impersonally – in the third person as it were – for what Perelman (1977: 14) calls 'the universal audience'. That is, one addresses those who are competent and reasonable. I should like to state at the outset that I am not speaking to the 'universal audience' but to a smaller subset: western intelligentsia and western-trained intellectuals from other cultures. They claim that religion is a cultural universal; they come with arguments and proofs. If my ideas bear up to scrutiny, most of the 'competent and reasonable' people from cultures other than the West cannot make much sense of the pronouncements of this smaller group. Therefore, my disputation will be with a specific kind of audience, irrespective of whether it fancies itself as 'the universal audience' or not.

I have tried to signal this state of affairs throughout the essay by eschewing an impersonal style. I am not addressing 'the reader' but you who belong to this subgroup; the 'we' in the text refers neither to the royal 'we' nor to an abstract group, but to 'you' and 'I'. Some among you might find it both annoying and insulting that I treat 'the reader' with a great deal of familiarity. My only answer is that I am indeed familiar with this group and hence the familiar mode of addressing.

This is not merely a question of style, but also of content. My aim is to show that a provincial experience of a small segment of humanity does not become universal by decree. Nor does a specific group become 'the universal audience' by merely pretending to be one. In terms of a metaphor, *contra* Perelman, one disembodied mind is not addressing other disembodied minds in this essay. Nor is there any striving for a 'meeting of the minds.' In this essay, a voice speaks while allowing other voices to join in a disputation. What you have on your hands is an argument, in the full sense of the term, between people who speak and vocalise their ideas. As is inevitable in disputations conducted by people, at times the discussions get heated up. In the process, now and then, voices are raised – human, all too human.

Even though this particular work has been in the making for quite a few years now, its significance lies in the project of which it is but a part. That unconcluded project, on which I have been working even longer, is within the broad domain of comparative anthropology. This study in its entirety is part of a broader project that seeks to provide a partial description of the West against the background of an Asian culture. Consequently, though the essay can stand alone, it is neither self-sufficient nor complete. Therefore, it keeps implicitly pointing to empty spaces and unbuilt structures. It is my hope to return to the work-site, with a larger crew if possible, alone otherwise – if not tomorrow, then at least the day after.

CHAPTER ONE

# SOME PUZZLES AND PROBLEMS

The focus of this chapter is upon raising questions that the subsequent chapters must investigate. I formulate these questions in a dialogue with the dominant ideas, partly because these ideas themselves constitute a problem. That is, I argue that the way contemporary authors look at religion in other cultures is itself a problem, in addition to problems that pertain to the nature of religion as such. In this sense, arguments developed in this chapter have a heuristic function – they do not settle the case one way or another.

The most important reason for writing this chapter has to do with the impact that the pioneering work of Cantwell Smith (1962) has had on the study of religion. Many people have begun to argue that the concept 'religion' requires jettisoning because, instead of helping us in understanding the phenomenon of religion, it merely hinders. There is merit to this suggestion: if a concept has pernicious effects on building a theory, let us get rid of it sooner rather than later. However, there is still the object of study. By refraining from using the word 'cancer,' or even rejecting the concept, we will not make the disease in question any less malignant or, if you prefer, any more benign. Of course, I am not implying that Cantwell Smith's suggestion amounts to a mere linguistic reform. Nevertheless, I do want to argue that the questions we confront while studying religion are not spurious but genuine, and that the absence of self-evident or obvious answers warrants further enquiries. Our problems persist irrespective of whether we use 'faith,' 'cumulative tradition,' 'religion,' or whatever else to designate the phenomenon we are investigating. That is why in the following discussion, until further notice, the word 'religion' (or the associated concept) carries no specific or technical meaning. It merely refers to what our daily language assures us it does. We use the word, albeit unreflectively, to designate a multitude of phenomena – from Christianity through Islam to Buddhism. Of course, it is possible that the term has no reference; I will take up this issue in chapter 8. For now, I will follow the practice common to writers in domains such as religious studies, anthropology and others. The task here is to reflect upon just what this practice either presupposes or implies.

## 1.1. On Some Strange Sentiments

Even a quick perusal of modern writings on the subject of religious traditions in 'other' cultures is sufficient to mystify any reader. On the one hand, these writings come close to suggesting that one could not possibly say what is constituted *as* religion in these cultures. That is, they imply that what investigators identify as religion in other cultures may not be religion at all. On the other hand, not only do these authors study other cultures, but they also claim that they are studying religion in these cultures. In terms of an analogy, it is as though these scientists are inviting us to study cooking processes in a culture in order to understand the phenomenon of jet propulsion. To appreciate that this analogy is not as exaggerated as it looks at first sight, let us listen to them directly.

Sam Gill, a specialist in Native American studies, confronts the following problem when he wants to study the religion of these cultures.

> ...(I)n terms of my training as a student of religion, I had no text, no canon upon which to base an interpretation of...highly complex events. There is no written history, no dogma; no written philosophy, no holy book (Gill 1987: 6).

The consequence of this situation, as Gill tells us a couple of pages later (*ibid*: 8), is nothing short of disastrous.

> Our very way of looking at religion is such that these cultures have nothing that we are trained to see as religion.

Faced with such a state of affairs, at least two possibilities open up: either the Native Americans do not have religion, which is why one cannot see religion there; or they do have religion, but one that we cannot see because of 'our' training. Convinced as he is that the Native Americans do have a religion, Gill tries to develop a *theory* of religion that makes the invisible visible. His conclusion with respect to the existing theories of religion, correspondingly, is that *"Our usual approaches to the study of religion...(are) largely unusable and inadequate"*. As readers, we are merely left with puzzles: how did Gill 'see' what is invisible? From whence his conviction that the Native Americans have religion too? How do we know that, in fact, he is studying religion and not something else?

Sir Moses Finley would quite sympathise with Gill's difficulty. He too confronts a similar problem regarding the Ancient Greek religion, which appears "fundamentally alien to our eyes". How fundamentally

alien it is, says Sir Finley (1985: xiv-xvi), can easily be shown by a simple listing:

> (1) Greek religion had no sacred books...no revelation, no creed. It
> also lacked any central ecclesiastical organization or the support of central
> political organization...
>
> (2) Although large numbers of men and women were involved in the
> administration of religion, in the case of temples and altars or sacred sites,
> in the conduct of festivals and sacrifices, and so forth, and though we call
> them 'priests' in the modern languages, a priesthood as that vocation is
> understood in many post-ancient religions simply did not exist. The great
> majority of the so-called priests were simply public officials whose duties
> in whole or in part, usually the latter, included some responsibility for
> some portions of the religious activity of the community. More often than
> not, they were selected by lot and they held office for only a year or even
> six months...There was no special training, no sense of vocation.
>
> Greek 'priests', in sum, were customarily not holy men; they were also
> not particularly expert or qualified in matters pertaining to their duties
> in office...
>
> (3) It follows as a matter of simple logic that places of worship were also
> radically different from anything known in later ages – despite the fact that
> the temple was the most extensive and imposing building of the Greek
> city...the temple was hardly ever 'a place for congregational worship.'

In other words, Greek religion does not look as though it were a religion; nonetheless, it requires to be made sense of, says Sir Finley. Need
one add, as a religion?
    John Gould (1985: 7-8) attempts to do precisely that and he does so
by suggesting, of all things, that it is easier to understand Greek religion
if we look at the Dinka religion – the religion of a tribal people in southern Sudan – but not at the 'better-known' religions. Why?

> Greek religion is not 'revealed' as Christianity is; there is no text claiming
> the status of the 'word of God,' not even of His prophets; no Ten Com-
> mandments, no creed, no doctrinal councils, no heresies, no wars of reli-
> gion in which the 'true believers' confront the 'infidel' or heretic. Central
> terms of our religious experience such as 'grace,' 'sin' and 'faith' cannot be
> rendered into the ancient Greek of the classical period: the central *Greek*
> term, *theous nomizein*, means not 'believe in the gods,' but 'acknowledge'
> them, that is, pray to them, sacrifice to them, build them temples, make
> them object of cult and ritual. There is never an assumption of divine omni-
> potence, nor of a divine creation of the universe, except in philosophical
> 'theology,' nor any consistent belief in divine omnipresence. There is no
> church, no organized body persisting through time comprising those with

dogmatic authority, able to *define* divinity and rule on what is correct and incorrect in religious belief...Greek religion is not theologically fixed and stable, and it has no tradition of exclusion or finality: it is an open, not a closed system. There are no true gods and false, merely powers known and acknowledged since time immemorial, and new powers, newly experienced as active among men and newly acknowledged in worship (italics in the original).

Even if one does not take exception to this description of the Greek religion, our problem is not solved. The Dinka religion, according to Rinehardt who studied it and upon whose material Gould bases his analogy, does not look like religion either.

For a more succinct summary of our problems regarding the Ancient Greek religion (for longer discussions, see Guthrie 1955; Burkert 1977), one need go no further than Adkins (1969: 377). Discussing the nature of Greek religion in the multi-volume *Historia Religionum*, he writes

Greek religion was a phenomenon far different from the religions called to mind (by the categories that reflect the questions which the modern reader naturally asks)...The data of Greek religion *do not fit into any given category* (italics mine).

Even though the data of the Greek 'religion' do not fit into any given category, we are to assume that this phenomenon fits into the category of religion. However, this category of 'religion' contains, as Adkins tells us, such subcategories as the existence of a creed, the existence of God and such like. Even when some practice (or a set of practices) does not fit any of the subcategories of religion (and thus, one would have thought, the category 'religion' itself), Adkins tells us that this should not *"prevent the exposition of the nature of Greek Religion"*. He goes on to do precisely that in the rest of the article. Again, we are left with puzzles regarding the identity of the subject matter. What phenomenon is being described here? Is it *one* phenomenon (the 'Greek religion') or sets of phenomena unrelated to each other? If the former, what is the difficulty in saying what Greek religion is? If the latter, how can we understand religion better by studying what does not look like religion? Perhaps, the Greeks had no religion at all...

In the second volume of the same work, an Indian (Dandekar 1969: 237), this time talking about Hinduism, says that

Hinduism can hardly be called a religion in the popularly understood sense of the term. Unlike most religions, Hinduism does not regard the concept of god as being central to it...Hinduism does not venerate any particular person as its sole prophet or as its founder. It does not...recognize any particular book as its absolutely authoritative scripture.

These observations do not prevent Dandekar from claiming that *"Hinduism has persisted through centuries as a distinct religious entity"* and from talking at great lengths about 'Hinduism' without showing how or why it is a distinct religious entity.

Similar thoughts occur in a handbook written by experts in the area, aimed also at a more general public:

Hinduism displays few of the characteristics that are generally expected of a religion. It has no founder, nor is it prophetic. It is not credal, nor is any particular doctrine, dogma or practice held to be essential to it. It is not a system of theology, nor a single moral code, and the concept of god is not central to it. There is no specific scripture or work regarded as being uniquely authoritative and, finally, it is not sustained by an ecclesiastical organization. Thus it is difficult to categorize Hinduism as 'religion' using normally accepted criteria.

It is then possible to find groups of Hindus whose respective faiths have almost nothing in common with one another, and it is also impossible to identify any universal belief or practice that is common to all Hindus. Confronted with such diversity, what is it that makes Hinduism a single religious tradition and not a loose confederation of many different traditions? (Weightman 1984: 191-192.)

A good question, one would say. What is Weightman's own answer?

The common Indian origin, the historical continuity, the sense of a shared heritage and a family relationship between the various parts, all these are certainly important factors. But these all equally apply to Buddhism, Jainism and Sikhism, each of which arose within the Hindu tradition but separated from it to become an independent religion. *Crucial*, however, *is the fact that Hindus affirm it is one single religion.* Every time a Hindu accepts someone as a fellow Hindu, in spite of what may be called radical differences of faith and practice, he is making this affirmation (*ibid*; emphases mine).

If Hinduism is one religion because the 'Hindus'[1] call it so, one would like to know whether the terms 'Hindu' and 'Hinduism' do make sense in India. Are we allowed to conclude that Hinduism is *not* a religion if

---

[1] Who, then, are the 'Hindus'? Presumably, those who belong to 'Hinduism.' What is 'Hinduism'? Perhaps that which is called so by the 'Hindus'?

the Hindus do not call it one? This could be dismissed as a rhetorical query, if not for the fact that the question 'Are you a Hindu?' does not make much sense to an Indian. To illustrate this, consider the following interview conducted by the Belgian Thierry Verhelst with a 'Hindu-born' intellectual in a   village in the southern state Tamil Nadu, where he records (1985: 9) the following question and answer:

> Q: Are you still a Hindu?
> A: No, I grew critical of it because of Casteism...Actually, you *should not ask to people* if they are Hindu. *This does not mean much.* If you ask them what their religion is, they will say, "I belong to this caste" (italics mine).

This answer is interesting for two reasons. First, the interviewer is told that he should not ask 'Hindus' what their 'religion' is, because it is almost a meaningless question. That is to say, what the respondent says about his 'fellow Hindus' is consistent with the way he himself understands the question. (His stance, I would like to add, is the normal and not the exceptional.) Second, this 'Hindu' says that he has ceased being one because he is critical of 'casteism'. That is, he effectively identifies 'Hinduism' (a 'religion') with the caste system, which is a social organisation. In other words, this 'Hindu-born' intellectual is replacing 'Hinduism' by 'casteism.' I have yet to come across writings that say, "Casteism, Judaism, Christianity and Islam are major world religions".

It is indicative of how strange the situation is. Weightman makes his answer depend upon what a majority of people say at some specific moment, as though an opinion poll could help solve the problem. Yet, he does not provide us with empirical data about precisely how many 'Hindus' call 'Hinduism' a religion.

Collins, a Buddhologist, is not so sanguine about the fact that Buddhism is an 'independent religion' unlike Hinduism. Speaking of the mistake of using emic categories of Christian thought as though they were etic categories of description and analysis in the academic study of religions, Collins adds (1988: 103) in parentheses, *"perhaps the most pervasive example of this is the concept of 'religion' itself"*. Of course, it is not clear what the implications of this stance really are.

In 1959, a phenomenologist of religion was complaining that his European Christian heritage made it difficult for him to understand non-Christian religions. He identified three presuppositions, which "we are frequently, in most cases even totally, unconscious of ...":

> 1. Our Western Christian thinking is qualified in its deepest philosophical and methodological ideas by a personalistic idea of God. This concept makes it particularly difficult to understand the fundamental disposition of Buddhism, which knows of no personalistic idea of God. The tradition-

al Western reaction, in Christian theology as well as in Western philosophy, is to characterize Buddhist theology as 'atheistic.' It is difficult for a Westerner to comprehend the specifically Buddhist form of the approach to the transcendent...the *basic difference between the two is not one of abstract theological concepts. It goes deeper than that...*

2. Hindu and Shinto polytheism confronted me with still another problem. I simply felt incapable of understanding why a believer preferred just one god or goddess among the vast pantheons...Christian theology itself has screened the Christian doctrine of trinity, sometimes interpreted in a polytheistic sense, *in such a way that an understanding of genuine polytheism was no longer possible.*

3. The third point is that Hinduism, like Buddhism and Shintoism, lacks one other distinction that is so fundamental for our Christian thinking: the basic essential difference between creation and Creator. For our Western Christian thought this absolute discontinuity between Creator and creation is normative, but it does not exist in Buddhism and Shintoism.

Another basic assumption...is the common preference we attribute to theology, the doctrinal part of our religion, when it comes to the interpretation of the forms of religious expression. But this preference is a specific sign of Christianity...(Benz 1959: 120-124; my italics.)

If the difference between Buddhism and Christianity is 'deeper' than the level of abstract concepts, what are the consequences? Could we presume that if an understanding of 'genuine' polytheism is no longer possible, the same applies to polytheism itself? (Unless one is to speak of 'fake' and 'genuine' versions of polytheism, of course.) If this is the case, then how could Hinduism be called p olytheistic at all? How could one say that Shintoism knows of any kind of theism? In any case, these and allied difficulties make Benz (*ibid*: 126) draw the following lesson:

The Western Christian...must beware of transferring to the Eastern religions his own ideas concerning the organization of religion. We always assume more or less consciously the ecclesiastical model of Christianity when analysing other religions. This approach suits neither Hinduism nor Buddhism nor Shintoism. The Japanese Buddhists do not form a Buddhist 'Church.'[2]

---

[2] Compare Emile Durkheim's (Schneider 1964: 35) definition of religion which was intended to allow Buddhism to remain a religion:

A religion is a unified system of beliefs and practices relative to sacred things, that is to say, things set apart and forbidden – beliefs and practices which unite into one single moral community called a Church, all those who adhere to them.

In *Le Corps Taoiste*, Schipper tries to evoke a picture of Taoism as it is practised in China. One of the difficulties that westerners face in understanding this phenomenon, says Schipper (1982: 12-13), is the religious language and practice of the West.

> To begin with, the concept 'religion' as we define it is itself a stumbling block…In our times…it has already reached the stage where the good Chinese have learnt that they are Buddhists, or Confucianists, or syncretic, or even quite simply superstitious…
>
> For a long time, Chinese language did not have a word to express our concept of religion. To translate this concept from foreign texts, there exists a word in modern Chinese, *zongjiao*, which literally means: 'the teaching of the sects.'

This is an unhappy formulation for several reasons. It is not clear whether we are talking here of a translation problem, or something quite different altogether. We need not attach a great weight to Schipper's observation if it is simply a question of translating across two different languages. If it is another kind of problem, namely, the inability of the Chinese language to *refer* to a phenomenon familiar to European culture, what precisely does it indicate? If, as Schipper says, the problem is with our definition of religion, the obvious counter-question requires to be noted as well: would another 'definition' make the problem go away? Having raised all these problems, Schipper ends lamely – with a warning note to the reader.

> When we apply this term to China's *own religion*, which wants to be truly a bond between all creatures without doctrines, without creeds, and without dogmas, misunderstandings are inevitable (my italics).

Surely, the problem is not one of using a newly coined Chinese word to refer to something that antedates it by a couple of thousand years. The problem is one of talking about China's "own religion", the home-grown variety, in terms of Taoist Canon, Taoist holy texts, Taoist Liturgy, as Schipper does. And this in order to explicate a 'religion' that lacks doctrinal teachings, dogmas and credos!

So we could go on and on, multiplying citations indefinitely by looking into the descriptions, claims and counter-claims made about other peoples and cultures in Africa, the Americas, and Asia by those who 'studied' them. However, the list above is enough to support the observation I made at the beginning of this chapter – writings of modern authors about religious traditions of several cultures are sufficient to mystify any reader.

## 1.2. About Mystery and Mystifications

At a phenomenological level, these multiple citations illustrate the common-sense wisdom I spoke of in the introduction. First, these authors assure us that Hinduism, Taoism, *etc.*, are different religions. However, if that is all they want to say, it is trivial: if one religion speaks about the Christ and the other about the Buddha, they are different from each other. Second, unable to find a unifying property that makes Hinduism and Shintoism into religions, they seem to say that these are different kinds of religion, even though they are not able to specify what the difference in kind consists in. Third, an obvious inference: because Hinduism, Taoism, Christianity, *etc.*, are conceived of as religions, the stance is that there is something 'common' to them (even if it is solely at the level of our language-use).

All these are familiar and obvious remarks. However, they cloak and conceal many problems. I would like to invite you to join me in building a chain of arguments to bring the problems to the fore. In the process, it will also become clear why these multiple citations contain enough elements to mystify any reader. Before identifying the factors responsible for the mystification, however, it would perhaps be best to use an analogy to illustrate the strange situation we are in.

Consider a locomotive and a photocopier. They both have their respective purposes. Even though they differ from each other in several respects, we consider both as machines. Hence, it is perfectly sensible to say, "although the locomotive and the photocopier look very different from each other, they are machines nonetheless." The reason why this statement is sensible is not far to seek. We feel that, in principle, we can continue the above statement with, "because they have the property(ies) of..." Of course, this 'in principle' possibility does not require that we are also in fact able to specify the set of relevant properties.

Imagine someone from another culture who has never seen any machine other than a locomotive. On a visit to the West, he sees several kinds of instruments including a photocopier. Quizzing his acquaintances about how photocopiers could also be machines, he gets the answer: "Even though the photocopier has no furnace, no wheels for locomotion and does not emit exhaust fumes, it is a machine nonetheless."

It could be the case that this visitor does not have a word in his language for machines and has merely an identifying description for locomotives. Therefore, he may be unwilling to accept that the word which translates 'locomotives' could also be used to identify a photocopier. This complication does not prevent a clarifying discussion about machines and their variety.

With respect to our theme, this is the analogue: "Even though in some tradition there is no New Testament, no belief in Jesus as The Saviour, no acceptance that God sent His only Son to save humanity, such a tradition is a religion nonetheless." There is nothing implausible about this, of course.

If we look at our authors and their claims again, we see that they are saying and doing something more. They are not telling us what makes something into a locomotive or a photocopier, but what makes something into a machine. That is, not what makes some tradition into Christianity or Islam, but what makes something into a religion at all. In other words, they are working at the level of distinguishing machines from other phenomena. Bearing this in mind, let us return to our analogy.

Imagine someone from the West returning the courtesy by visiting the other culture and holding an oration to a captivated audience. "Though lacking in an internal combustion engine and an external source of energy, though definitely not a human construct..." Here, our visitor pauses for a second, casts an anxious glance around and dramatically waves his hand: "...*it* is a machine nonetheless..." The audience looks around and sees *many* things that fit this description: trees, flowers, mountains, rivers, the sky, the animal refuse...Though eager to learn, they are puzzled by the speech of their learned visitor. Which is the 'it' referred to by the speaker? All of what they see? Only some? Or none of what they see, because the 'it' is invisible? The audience, of course, is thrilled to its soul. They may have a homegrown machine, but it would help them a great deal to know which of those things is a machine. Indians may have 'Hinduism,' but this appellation does not make sense to them; the Chinese may have 'Taoism,' but they have only just managed to learn that word; the Greeks may have had a religion, but who is going to interrogate them now? As far as the Native Americans are concerned, well, only Sam Gill appears to see the invisible...

*Issues in a Discussion*

I should like to draw attention to *four* striking aspects of this mystifying situation. The *first* has to do with the very intelligibility of these and similar enterprises: if the Native Americans, the Hindus, and the Ancient Greeks do/did not have what one could 'properly call' religion, why insist that they do/did have religion? Why not simply declare that these cultures do/did not have religion at all? If Buddhism and Taoism are not 'really' religions, why not simply say so?

The *second* aspect has to do with the ease with which these authors assume the identity of their subject matter. Despite the fundamental differences between these traditions, we are to suppose that they are all members of the same class. How do we know that they are indeed members of the same class? It could well be that they are not: the concepts, the practices and the organisations of these traditions are all so different from one another that one has a greater warrant to assume the contrary. That is to say, in order to believe that Buddhism, Hinduism and Shintoism are also religions, we need some compelling argumentation, because at first sight they do not look like religions. However, as the citations make it clear, the authors not only assure us of the truth of this *prima facie* appearance but also assume that they are studying another, different sort of religion.

If we shift our attention from the enterprise and the object of study to the authors themselves, we are confronted with the *third* aspect to our mystification. Clearly, each of these authors is working with some notion of 'the religious.' They point out the absence of creeds, prophets, scriptures, notion of God, *etc.*, in some traditions in order to say that "properly speaking" they are not religions. Could we, because of this, assume that, when they talk of these other traditions, each of them is using a definition that lays down the necessary and sufficient conditions for calling something a 'religion'? We cannot make that assumption because, if they were using such a definition, they need express no hesitation in their formulations. They would simply say, "according to this definition, the Native Americans, the Hindus and the Greeks have (or had) no religions," or whatever else is appropriate. Instead, all their statements have the following characteristic form: "Some traditions have neither X, nor Y, nor Z, but they are religions *nonetheless.*"

This gives birth to the *fourth* aspect that must mystify us. Not only do these authors appear to have a notion of what it means for something to be a religion, but they also appear to possess some criteria for identifying and distinguishing religion from other phenomena. Why, otherwise, call Hinduism a religion and not 'psychotherapy,' 'philosophy,' 'magic,' or 'proto-science'? Yet, what makes Christianity into a religion is apparently not what makes Hinduism into a religion.

Consider just what is being asked of us. The Hindus, the Native Americans, and the Greeks have (had) a set of traditions that lack the following: creeds, beliefs in God, scriptures and churches. Despite these, these traditions are not only 'religions,' but also distinguishable from one another as religious traditions. The religion of the Hindus is different from that of the Native Americans and both from that of the Greeks. This means that these three share only some properties in common – even if, one grants this with goodwill, one cannot say what these properties are. (Of course, a follower of Wittgenstein need not subscribe to this thought. It will become clear very soon that one's philosophical proclivities make very little difference to the case.) So far so good. Now we need to extend this argument: if these three traditions retain their identity as distinct religions even when they lack some properties, the same must hold elsewhere too.

Let us build the argument in two distinct steps, which ought not to be conflated with each other. Consider a tradition in the Middle East with the following properties: it does not believe in Allah or in Mohammed as His Prophet; it does not have the Koran or the Mosques. Could such a tradition be still a religion? Of course, it could – Judaism and Christianity lack these properties. Yet not only are they religions but they are also distinguishable from each other as religions. In other words, even where the traditions of the Hindus, the Native Americans and the Greeks do (did) not speak of Allah or of Mohammed as His prophet, they remain distinguished and distinguishable from each other as religions, because these properties are *not necessary* to being a religion. This shows that the properties that make some tradition into Islam are different from those that make Islam into a religion.

Now comes the second step. Our question is not what makes some tradition into an Islamic, Christian, or Judaic religion, but what makes Judaism, Christianity, and Islam into religions. What makes Hinduism into a religion must also make Islam into a religion. What makes a locomotive into a machine must also make a photocopier into a machine.

We have found that creeds, *etc.*, are irrelevant for some traditions to be religions. So, suppose we bracket away creeds, belief in God and prophets, existence of scriptures and churches from Judaism, Christianity and Islam. What would be left over? For one thing, we could not even tell the difference between these traditions, let alone distinguish them from Hinduism or Greek religion or whatever else. We would get an amorphous whole that could not be even called a religion. Obviously, these properties are absolutely necessary for these three religions if they have to remain not just as distinct traditions but as religions as well.

Consequently, we are left with a glaring inconsistency: (a) existence of creeds, *etc.*, are not necessary conditions for some traditions to qualify themselves as religions; and (b) existence of creeds, *etc.*, are necessary conditions for some other traditions if they have to be religions at all.

It will not do to say, to return to the locomotive and photocopier argument, that a locomotive without an engine, wheels, *etc.*, is neither a locomotive nor a machine and that my argument is fallacious for this reason. Of course, *Christianity* without the Christ figure, etc.; *Islam* without the prophet Mohammed, *etc.*; would cease being Christianity and Islam, respectively. Why should this affect their status as religions? After all, Hinduism has neither and yet it is supposed to be a religion. Similarly, there is no reason why a locomotive should not be able to cease being a locomotive, and yet remain a machine. Does the absence of wheels affect the status of the locomotive as a locomotive or its status as a machine? In this sense, does the absence of the Christ figure affect the status of Christianity as Christianity or its status as a religion? Suppose we are willing to accept that having an engine is a property that a locomotive shares with all other machines and that without an engine, nothing could be a machine. Then, indeed, a locomotive without an engine is neither a locomotive nor a machine. Which property of Christianity is analogous to this? Is having the Christ figure a specific property of Christianity alone or one it shares with other religions? Surely, no one suggests the latter today. Our problem, I repeat, is not what makes something into Islam or Christianity (a locomotive or photocopier) but rather what makes something into a religion (a machine) – in other words, what is involved in identifying 'religion' and distinguishing it from other phenomena.

Let me summarise the dilemma. Some properties are necessary for some traditions (Judaism, Christianity, Islam) to be religions. If one accepts this, the threat is that other cultures appear not to have religions at all. For some reason or another (I discuss the reasons in chapters 3 through 7), other cultures are said to have religions too. However, the conditions under which other cultures are to have religion are precisely those that make it impossible for the Semitic religions to be religions. That is to say, if the Semitic religions are what religions are, other cultures do not have religions. If other cultures have religions, then the Semitic religions are not religions. The inconsistency lies in insisting that both statements are true.

This appears to me as good an example of inconsistent reasoning as any other that one could think of. Yet, the authors are as gifted and brilliant as they come. Thus, we are confronted with an intelligibility problem: is there an inconsistency in their reasoning or is there a fallacy in the argumentative chain that we have built up? If the former, why have they not seen the inconsistency in their reasoning? I will be preoccupied with the last problem during the course of this entire essay, because I do think that there is an inconsistency in their reasoning. For now, let us briefly entertain the alternatives open to us to render them consistent.

*Some Avenues and Answers*

(1) The first possible way of rendering the above inconsistency harmless is to suggest that these authors are not taking any one religion as an example. Instead, one could argue, they are working with some kind of definition. However, we have already seen how they cannot be working with a 'definition' of religion that lays down necessary and sufficient conditions. Could they, then, be working with a definition that lays down only necessary conditions? Let me just mention here that this could not be the case. The characteristic hesitation in the formulations

would then not be present. Instead, one would get an unambiguous formulation with the proviso that some condition or the other should be seen only as a necessary condition.

Alternatively, could they be just reporting the consensus of scholars, that is, working with an 'ostensive consensual definition'? They could be, but it does not solve the problem. An inconsistent argument cannot be made consistent by invoking some fictitious consensus of scholars. Besides, an appeal to established practice – be it of laymen or of scholars – is hardly a justificatory argument in our context. In sum, none of the three definitional manoeuvres appears to work, leaving us with the unpleasant task of having to explain the mystery of how these scholars could designate anything as religion at all. It appears to me that the wisest course would be to drop this avenue of defence entirely. Yet, I will return to these issues (chapter 8) and examine them in a different light.

(2) The second avenue of making an inconsistency harmless is to affirm the truth of only one of the conjuncts: either the existence of creeds, belief in God etc., are not necessary conditions for some traditions to qualify themselves as religions; or they are necessary conditions. Suppose one says that the existence of creeds etc., is irrelevant for some phenomenon to be a religion. If one does this, the account is both wrong and inadequate. It is wrong because the divisions within Judaism, Christianity and Islam have historically and factually turned around prophets, churches, beliefs and creeds; it is inadequate because it cannot make sense of the experience of any of these traditions. If, on the other hand, one claims that creeds, belief in God etc., are essential, it means that one has to embrace the following conditional statement: if the Semitic religions are what religions are, then 'Hinduism', etc. are not religions. In chapters 8 through 12, I will explore the latter avenue more thoroughly. Here, we need to keep the global problem sharply before our eyes.

Either the properties like belief in the existence of god(s), the necessity of creeds, *etc.*, are not important. For instance, being colourless, odourless and tasteless are not important for some compound substance to be water. Consequently, two liquids with different mineral traces could be samples of water even if they taste, smell and look different from each other.

Or, God(s), prophets, creeds and churches play a role analogous to the molecular structure of water. A liquid which does not have the chemical composition of $H_2O$ is not water, whatever else it may be (for example, an acid).

As I noted earlier, belief in God, existence of holy books, *etc.*, are so important to Judaism, Christianity and Islam that in their absence it is impossible to recognise the latter as religions. Consequently, if we have to consider Judaism, Christianity and Islam as religions at all, we are compelled to accept the idea that God, holy book, *etc.*, are the central, determining properties without which no phenomenon could be religion. For the same reason, Hinduism and Buddhism are not religions and the ancient Greeks and the Native Americans did/do not know of religion either.

Could we not be mistaken, then? Is it not possible that we have erred in attributing such a great importance to scripture(s), beliefs about God, *etc.*? Could we not, in other words, see Hinduism and Christianity as sharing another vital property that we have not yet discovered?

Some scholars of religion see in 'holiness,' or in the 'sacred-profane' distinction precisely such a common property. The problem is that this does not help us: 'holiness,' 'sacred-profane,' do not distinguish one religion from another. As categories not common to different traditions, they cannot even distinguish 'religion' from other phenomena. (I return to this point in chapters 6 and 7.) Nor is the problem solved by suggesting that the dispute is about the use of a word. Call Judaism, Christianity and Islam as 'Pif Paf' and Hinduism as 'Paf Paf,' for all that matters. The question remains: is 'Pif Paf' the same phenomenon as 'Paf Paf'? Without some specifiable properties 'Paf Paf' continues to be 'Paf Paf,' whereas 'Pif Paf' becomes an amorphous whole. Therefore, 'Paf Paf' cannot be 'Pif Paf.'

(3) There is a third avenue open to us, which could help eliminate the inconsistency. One could appeal to our linguistic practices, inspired by the pronouncements of Wittgenstein. A term like 'religion,' one might wish to say, is akin to a term like 'game.' We do not know what is common to games like chess, football, solitaire and the Olympics (except that there is 'family resemblance'), but our linguistic community teaches us the use of such and similar words. The inconsistency arises because we have assumed that all religions share some properties. If we give up this assumption, but instead 'look' at all these diverse religions, we see that they do not have common properties but share, instead, a family resemblance. Therefore, the alleged inconsistency vanishes. Would this answer help us?

Perhaps it could, if it were an answer. However, it is not; it merely unravels a nest of problems. Linguistic practices of our communities, which teach us the use of words, have a cultural history. This history is the history of a community that has learnt to speak *this* way and not *that* way. For the West, this cultural history happens to be the history of Christianity. Therefore, our question becomes this: why are the people influenced by this cultural history convinced that other cultures have religion too? To say that this is a "language game" and, consequently, to say this 'why?' question is inappropriate, is to miss a crucial point: *religio* comes from Latin, used by the Romans first, but appropriated later by Christianity. This point raises two historical questions: what was the nature of the Roman *religio*? How was this 'language game' appropriated (and modified) by Christians and others? (Chapter 2 addresses these questions.)

Because we can talk both intelligibly and, hopefully, intelligently about these two historical questions, references to linguistic practices and language games merely raise further problems. How much of this cultural history has influenced people into believing that the Hindus, the ancient Greeks and the Native Americans also have religion? (A beginning is made in chapters 3 and 4 to investigate this question.) Further, why are the people influenced by this cultural history convinced that Buddhism, Taoism, Jainism, *etc.*, are religions as well, even when they differ so radically from the Semitic religions? Wherefrom this unshakeable certainty? (Chapter 7 explores this problem.)

What is the upshot of this Wittgensteinian answer to the problem at hand, namely, the inconsistent reasoning of these several scholars? A charitable response would be the following: this attempt to render the inconsistency harmless has the virtue of shifting our attention from the nature of the investigated phenomenon to the culture of the investigators. By doing so, it has enabled us to realise that historical and conceptual problems lie under these inconsistencies. Only when we have satisfactorily articulated and resolved these problems will it be possible for us to appreciate the reasons for this inconsistency – or even whether there is one.

Thus, we have our first cluster of questions. Do all cultures have religions? What is involved in attributing religion only to some cultures? Why have people over the centuries found it important to discuss this issue and to dispute with each other about it? Is the question about the existence of religion susceptible to empirical enquiry? What is the importance of these questions to comparative anthropology? I will argue that, paradoxical as it may seem, these and other related questions have not found any adequate treatment. Giving satisfactory answers to them would require of us not a mere rethinking of the questions, but a quasi-total reconceptualisation of the theme itself. Making this idea plausible is the burden that this essay assumes.

*Multiple Themes*

There is also another kind of question, which is more historical in nature. The earliest missionaries and explorers, some of whom recorded their first impressions in an honest way, appear to have seen things differently: the cultures in Africa, Asia and the Americas did not strike them as possessing 'religion' in any of the senses they were familiar with.

For example, this is what two Dutch civil servants,[3] on a tour through the island Enggano off the West coast of Sumatra during the middle of nineteenth century, had to say:

> *The Enganese do not have the vaguest notion of religion*; all our attempts to make them understand that somebody lived above...were in vain.

If we move further eastwards, we encounter China. The contradictory descriptions of its thought and culture, including the claim that the Chinese knew of no religion, created a debate that lasted nearly a century. Since we are going to encounter it in chapter 3, let us leave China aside for now and take note of a few of the descriptions provided of the Black Africans. Antonio Velho Tinoco declared of the blacks of the coast of Upper Guinea, in a report included in a letter of 1585 sent by the Jesuit priests of Coimbra to the Jesuit General in Rome, that

> All the people of the land along the seacoast are black. They are a harmless people... although...tend to be attached to magical practices *(inclinada a feitiços)*...They have no organized religion, and do not worship the Sun or the Moon or any other idols *(nem outros idolos alguns)*. (Cited by Pietz 1987: 37.)

With respect to the Hottentots, Dapper and van Riebeeck were to go further and declare that the former had no religion – organised or otherwise.

> Much to the surprise of those who came into contact with the Hottentots, there was no question of a religion among them. Never had "anyone, however diligently (he) researched, been able to detect any sign of religion among them; they worshipped neither God nor the Devil. Not withstanding the fact that they know there is one, whom they call *'s Humma,* who makes the rain fall on earth, moves the wind, provides warmth and cold, they do not pray to him. Because, they say, why worship this *'s Humma,* who gives a double drought once and double the required rains at another time where they would rather have seen it in moderation and appropriately..." *(Dapper)*...Abraham van Riebeeck found no ideas about God or the Devil among them. Rain, storm and such like were ancient that came habitually...(In Molsbergen, Ed., 1916: 19, n. 1.)

---

[3] Straaten van der, J. and Severijn, P. "Verslag van een in 1854 bewerkstelligd Onderzoek op het Eiland Enganno." *Tijdschrift voor Indische Taal-, Land- en Volkenkunde,* III, 338-369. Cited in Koentjaraningrat 1975: 19, n. 45.

Some among such travellers were even uplifted by this, because it meant that converting the 'natives' into Christianity would be so much more of an easy job. Columbus wrote in the journal of his 1492 voyage about the religion of the people he called "los indios":

> "They should be good servants and very intelligent, for I have observed that they soon repeat everything that is said to them, and I believe that they would easily be made Christians, for *they appear to me to have no religion*."

> And in a letter he wrote shortly after his journal entry, he referred again to the religion of these people. His single sentence on the subject is preceded by his observations on fish and followed by a detailed description of the trees. He wrote,

> "*They have no religion and I think that they would be very quickly Christianized,* for they have a very ready understanding." (Gill 1987: 174; my emphases.)

Such descriptions raise an intriguing question. Why did the early explorers and missionaries not see 'religion' if it was a ubiquitous phenomenon in all cultures? In this essay, I would like to probe an answer to this question too. I will do this by taking the Indian culture as a point of reference and by examining the arguments for maintaining that India knows of religion and the implications for a comparative study of cultures when the opposite stance is defended.

# PART I

This part groups the next three chapters around a single theme, *viz.* the confrontation of Christianity with the Roman *religio* and the Indian religions. The narrative is cast in historical terms and is crucial for what is to follow in the subsequent parts of the book. The thrust of the story is that the relation of Christianity to the outside world – *i.e.* the Roman milieu it grew in and the heathen religions of India – has to be understood in terms of the internal problems of Christianity. The story will merely touch upon and illustrate the way in which Christianity transformed and domesticated what it saw but could not comprehend. In the subsequent parts, my task will be to enlarge on this theme and explain it.

CHAPTER TWO

# "NOT BY ONE AVENUE ONLY ..."

Our historical journey begins at a beginning: in this beginning, some tell us, there was the Word, that Word was God, and God said... In a rather peculiar sense of the term, this chapter could be seen as a commentary on this thought. I believe that this idea about the beginning is true: neither because the Genesis is the truth about the creation of the Cosmos, nor even because Christianity is the true religion as it is alleged to be, but because our world – our intellectual world – happens to be a Christian world. Whether a Jew, a Dinka or a Brahmin, whether a theist, an atheist or a Muslim, our questions have a common origin. Here, I want to briefly trace the broad outlines of the issues and characterise their recognisable Gestalt. What you encounter in a germinal form in this chapter will be in view throughout the book. The themes outlined in this chapter will return repeatedly, albeit in new forms and in extravagant clothing.

I will tell some kind of a story in these chapters, so I will refrain from interrupting its flow to provide regular summaries. At the end of the fourth chapter, we will have time enough to pause and reflect on the distance travelled, the landmarks visited, and the sights seen.

## 2.1. On the Cobbled Streets of Pagan Rome...

The eclipse of the Graeco-Roman world by Christianity has been a matter of intense dispute and debate over the centuries (Gibbon 1776, Dodds 1965, Fox 1986). It is not my intention to add my two bits' worth to this controversy. My interest lies at the intersection of the following three questions:

(a) What was *religio* to the Romans?

(b) How did the Romans look at Christianity?

(c) What was the attitude of Christianity toward the Roman *religio*?

Answers to these questions help us triangulate the milieu in which Christianity grew: in the confines of a Graeco-Roman world, against the background of the Judaic community in the Roman Empire. It is thus that we will come to grips with the dynamic of Christianity's relation to its environment and gain a better understanding of the nature of the Christian religion itself.

*An Ancient Puzzle*

To someone from another intellectual and cultural world, what is striking about the various descriptions of the Roman world of the first century B.C.E. onward (MacMullen 1981, Wilken 1984, Fox 1986) is the extraordinary emphasis they place on the presence of a multiplicity of associations, philosophical schools, cults and cultic practices in understanding the Roman social life. Many of these associations were also the harbingers of political intrigues, as successive emperors were to find out. The associations of specific professions (butchers, tailors, undertakers, etc.) regularly supported candidates for political power. The activities of these associations – their ceremonies and ritual practices – often overlapped with those of the cults.

> The Roman empire was made up of about 1200 city units, plus a considerable number of ethnic groupings which we label 'tribes' and/or 'client kingdoms'. The divine forces worshipped in each of these units might be seen as similar, analogous, or parallel; one obvious example is the Juno, the cohesive force which gives life to any social unit, whether a family or a city-state. The Romans worshipped not only the Juno who had once belonged to their own kings – Juno Regina – but also the Junones of other states whom the Romans had invited to abandon their original communities and settle at Rome...These Junones were parallel, but not identical, in the same way as the many Jupiters and Zeuses worshipped throughout the empire were parallel but not identical. Each cult honoured its own god. (Wiedemann 1990: 69.)

This colourful variety and bewildering profusion was underpinned by a toleration of differences – a toleration that bordered on indifference toward the difference. Even though attempts to suppress the activities of this or that imported cult were not unknown (Frend 1965: 104-126), a peculiar kind of tolerance permeated the Roman cultural world. For example, the cult of Isis existed for a long time in Rome without being 'licensed', and was suppressed thrice in Rome during the 50s BCE. Very soon, it came to be tolerated again, enjoying a certain amount of protection under Augustus. We see Agrippa and Tiberius drive it away from the city, only to have it come back and flourish by the time of Nero. Domitian was apparently planning to rebuild its temple after it was burnt down during the period of Titus. One reason for this tolerance bordering on indifference, at least during those periods when things went well for the emperors and the citizens of the city-state, was the unanswerable question: who is to say which gods are to be celebrated, and which gods not?

One reason, probably accepted as self-evident, why the question was unanswerable had to do with the fact of diversity. The many cults, some flourishing and some not so prosperous, the numerous theories and disputations concerning the nature and existence of gods and the many philosophical schools and their differing theories about Man and Nature – these indexed two truths about human beings. First, that it is in the very nature of human existence to entertain multiple perspectives; second, because of this, diversity and difference was inevitable in human communities. Menucius Felix, a Christian writer from around 210 C.E., has Caecilius – the pagan protagonist in *The Octavius* – express the above thoughts in the following way:

> (A)ll things in human affairs are doubtful, uncertain, and unsettled, and all things are rather probable than true... [It is difficult to determine with]... any certainty concerning the nature at large, and the (divine) majesty, of which so many of the multitude of sects in all ages (still doubt), and philosophy itself deliberates still. (Roberts and Donaldson, Eds., n.d.,Vol. IV: 175.)

About some forty years earlier, Athenagoras the Athenian had to enter *A Plea for the Christians*. This remarkable document, written around 177 C.E., is addressed to the Emperor with the request that the Christians be allowed to practice their worship. The argument for 'tolerance,' although coming from a Christian writer, begins by noting that diversity is a fact in the Roman Empire.

> In your empire... different nations have different customs and laws; and no one is hindered by law or fear of punishment from following his ancestral usages, however ridiculous they may be...In short, among every nation and people, men offer whatever sacrifices and celebrate whatever mysteries they please...And to all of these both you and the laws give permission so to act, deeming, on the one hand, that to believe in no god at all is impious and wicked, and on the other, that it is necessary for each man to worship the gods he prefers... (Roberts and Donaldson, Eds., n.d., Vol. II: 129.)

Those wont to believe in One Supreme God had little problem in respecting the many deities that were part of the Roman landscape, because these gods were merely different manifestations of the supreme divinity or specific agencies subordinated to the supreme god or whatever else. For those who celebrated native and familiar deities, it was never too late to import exotic gods (Nock 1933: 66-76) from other cultures and far-off places.

Amidst all of these, certain practices were zealously preserved: residents of cities 'had to' participate in the religious practices and ceremonies celebrating the deities of the cities. I place 'had to' in scare quotes because it is surely a puzzle for all students of the Roman culture how this participation was secured. From whence the participation of nearly the entire populace and the intolerance toward those who did not? There were those who refused to celebrate the Roman gods: the Jews early on, and later the Christians. As Wiedemann (1990: 73) puts it:

> The persecutions of the third century AD have, I believe, to be seen in the context of the wider problems affecting the city, and the imperial government's response to that crisis…what is essential is that we should not conceive of an imperial 'religious policy' divorced from other aspects of imperial policy. Emperors felt that they were responsible for ensuring that the cities did not 'decline', i.e. that the basic public ceremonies of the city community continued to be performed with due regularity: and those ceremonies were pagan. Decius' edict, issued in December 249, ordered that sacrifices be performed in every city of the empire, supervised by commissioners chosen by the local councils. Decius' legislation should not be explained in political terms, as a reaction against supposed Christian support for his predecessor Philip the Arab.

Modern-day writers on Ancient Rome are reluctant to explain the religious intolerance of the pagan Rome in political terms. In addition, they are unable to agree upon the legal grounds for prosecuting religious crimes there. Apparently, there is some controversy among legal scholars about the existence or non-existence of religious crime in Roman Law. Most scholars appear to urge against the existence of religious offence on the following grounds: (a) the apparent lack of any provision in Roman criminal law for testing when such an offence has been committed; (b) the lack of competence of the religious tribunals; (c) the theory implied by the words of Tiberius, "the gods avenge their own wrongs"; and (d) the apparent absence of trials in cases of suppression (Guterman 1951; de Ste. Croix 1963, 1964; Sherwin-White 1964, 1966: 772-787; Barnes 1968; Janssen 1979; Keresztes 1979a). Not being competent or well informed about Roman Criminal Law, I do not want to enter that domain. Besides, what interests me is not whether a case could be made for finding legal bases in Roman law for prosecuting a 'religious crime,' but how the participation of Romans in their religious practices was secured.

The issue becomes intriguing when we consider the relation between the Roman and Greek intellectuals and the religious practices of their day. Clearly, there was no dearth of books, tracts, and philosophical schools, decrying, denigrating, and dismissing the importance of gods or even denying their existence. Though dangerous, even individuals dared to do it. For example, Lucian, the famous satirist from the second century, openly challenged the Cult of Glycon – visiting its chief priest, poking around its shrine, asking questions with a grin on his face. The danger – Lucian's life was endangered – lay not so much in challenging as in mocking. Even mockery, if directed against the credulous, was welcome, like Plutarch's *On Superstition* (MacMullen 1984: 15).

The intriguing feature of this relation is that many leading intellectuals participated in religious activities but did not believe in their gods! We do not need to go further than Cicero to be convinced of this fact. The social, psychological, and epistemic speculations put across in *De Natura Deorum* to account for the origin of religion have not been bettered to this day. Even those inclined to treat this evaluation as an exaggeration will have to admit that the arsenal of arguments that supported the attack against religion by the eighteenth-century European intellectuals came primarily from this one single work. Yet, Cicero himself was a priest. Though a sceptic and a critic of augury, he retained his membership in the Board of Augurs of the Republic.

Cicero was not the only one. Plutarch, the author of the famous essay against superstition, spent his later life as a priest in Delphi composing tracts on divine punishment and evident terrors of the next world. In Greece, Epicurus urged his followers to take part in sacrifices; he himself participated in the religious festivals of Athens and was initiated into the Eleusinian mysteries. His follower, Lucretius, followed the master's example in venerating ancestral gods.

From today's optic, this curious division between what they said and what they did is beautifully exemplified by Gaius Cotta – the Academic sceptic in Cicero's dialogue *On the Nature of Gods* – who is himself a priest:

> I, who am a high priest, and who hold it to be a duty most solemnly to maintain the rights and doctrines of the established religion, should be glad to be convinced of this fundamental tenet of divine existence, not as an article of faith merely but as an ascertained fact. *For many disturbing reflections occur to my mind, which sometimes make me think that there are no gods at all.* (*De Natura Deorum*, I, xxii: 61; my italics.)

How shall we understand this phenomenon, almost prototypical for the Graeco-Roman world, of participating in religious activities, sacrifices (oftentimes even leading them) while not believing in gods and the

deities to whom such sacrifices were offered? How could one deny the
existence of gods and yet officiate at the religious ceremonials? Let us
pick out at random some answers given by the Enlightenment thinkers,
to whom this appeared a problem.

*An Enlightened Solution?*

To Montesquieu, the disparity simply reflected the genius of Roman
politics: Rome used rational means to govern irrational masses. Neither
fear nor piety was at its foundation, but simply the recognition that all
societies need religion -- a mechanism required to govern the masses
by taking advantage of their credulity. Perpetuation of cults and the
manipulation of myths enabled the enlightened senators and others to
control the superstitious masses of people (Wade 1977). Diderot varied
this theme a bit: he suggested that Cicero was irreligious but then, in
his time,

> the people hardly read at all; they listened to the speeches of their orators,
> and the speeches were always filled with piety toward the gods; but they
> did not know what the orator thought and wrote about it in his study.
> (*Encyclopédie*, "Aius-Locutius"; cited in Gay 1973: 156.)

Hume was even more explicit, suggesting a fear of persecution if not
downright dishonesty:

> if there was ever a nation or a time, in which the public religion lost all
> authority over mankind, we might expect, that infidelity in ROME, dur-
> ing the CICERONEAN age, would openly have erected its throne, and
> that CICERO himself, in every speech and action, would have been its
> most declared abettor. But it appears, that, whatever sceptical liberties
> that great man might take, in his writings or in philosophical conversation;
> he yet avoided, in the common conduct of life, the imputation of deism
> (!) and profaneness. Even in his own family, and to his wife TERENTIA,
> whom he highly trusted, he was *willing to appear a devout religionist;* and
> there remains a letter, addressed to her, in which he seriously desires her
> to offer sacrifice to APOLLO and AESCULAPIUS, in gratitude for the
> recovery of his health (1757: 347; my italics).

Gibbon, in his magisterial *Decline* (1776: 13), accepts the theme whole-
heartedly. With an ease that can only surprise the modern mind, he
transforms the pagan thinkers into actors in a charade:

How, indeed, was it possible, that a philosopher should accept, as divine truths, the idle tales of poets, and the *incoherent traditions of antiquity;* or, that he should adore, as gods, those imperfect beings whom he must have despised, as men!...

In their writings and conversation, the philosophers of antiquity asserted the independent dignity of reason; but they *resigned their actions to the commands of law and of custom.* Viewing, with a smile of pity and indulgence, the various errors of the vulgar, they diligently practised the ceremonies of their fathers, devoutly frequented the temples of the gods; and sometimes condescending to act a part on the theatre of superstition, they *concealed the sentiments of an Atheist* under the sacerdotal robes... It was indifferent to them what shape the folly of the multitude might choose to assume; and they approached, *with the same inward contempt, and the same external reverence,* the altars of the Libyan, the Olympian, or the Capitoline Jupiter (my italics).

Or, again, this time on a larger canvas:

The policy of the emperors and the senate, as far as it concerned religion, was happily seconded by the reflections of the enlightened, and by the habits of the superstitious, part of their subjects. The various modes of worship, which prevailed in the Roman world, were all considered by the people, as equally true; by the philosopher, as equally false; and by the magistrate, as equally useful (*ibid:* 12).

These are not merely the opinions of the old masters. Peter Gay (1973: 155), our contemporary, endorses them. To him, the attitude of Cicero was a conscious compromise:

Cicero was urging the Romans to stand fast against new cults and oriental superstitions, but Cicero did not see, or did not say, that his policy sanctified practices which he scorned privately as vulgar and absurd.

Whichever way one twists and turns, no matter whether one appeals to prudence or expediency, this explanation attributes inauthenticity to the intellectuals of the Graeco-Roman world: even when they did not believe in the divinity of their deities or in the latter's existence, an Epicurus, a Cicero and a Plutarch not only participated but actually led religious practices. Of course, the Enlightenment thinkers did not call the Ancients 'inauthentic'. On the contrary: Diderot considered Cicero as the first Roman philosopher; Voltaire thought that *De Natura Deorum* was "perhaps the best book of all antiquity"; with a unanimity that is rare among the philosophers of the enlightenment, all were agreed upon the assessment of Diderot and Voltaire. Yet...

There is something very odd about the situation. In terms of philosophical or theoretical sophistication with respect to the socio-psycho-epistemic origins of gods and religion, the intellectuals of the classical age are on par with, if not better than, their counterparts of the age of enlightenment and beyond. However, the very same arguments, which moved many during the past three centuries to accept atheism and reject religion, God and gods, do not appear to have had the same effect on the Ancients.

If you are suspicious of the whole-scale condemnation of a culture as inauthentic, as I am, let us reverse the terms of the issue and ask why the very same arguments were decisive to the inheritors of the Graeco-Roman culture 1800 or so years later. The texts and their arguments did not change, but the cultural matrix, which understood them, had. In other words, this situation says more about what the European intellectuals thought religion was than it does about the Roman *religio*. What does it say? That beliefs and doctrines must have been extremely crucial in the sense that they formed the basis for religious practices.

Thus, at least one conclusion is inevitable: the Roman *religio* could not have been similar to the religions of Europe in the eighteenth century; it could only have been different. Different in *which* way? In the way that, whatever their philosophical predilections, the intellectuals of Antiquity did not counterpose their beliefs and doctrines to the religious practices of their day. That is, such was the Roman *religio* that its practice was *indifferent* to any given (in the sense of fixed) set of theological doctrines.

## A Methodological Orientation

That understanding the texts of a period and a culture requires coming to grips with the period and the culture is a truism today. It hides a problem nonetheless: How can one do the latter, when the only route to it is the former? A proper understanding of the texts requires an explication of their contexts. The latter, in turn, are texts as well.

The intellectuals of the eighteenth century took a particular path in understanding the Ancients and their texts (see Chapter 3). Instead of following them, I will adopt a different methodological precept: a problem for one generation or culture need not be so for another. Thus, if a Cicero and a Plutarch write presumably atheistic books and yet officiate as priests in religious ceremonies, we have a fact about the culture we are trying to understand, and not a moral problem about the behaviour of the individuals.

Of course, recognition of the facts of a culture requires that they strike us as problems: how could Epicurus be an Eleusinian initiate and write tracts against deities? How could Cicero decry augury and be a member of the board of augurs? Or – to shift across time and culture abruptly – how could an Indian communist or an Indian scientist participate actively in the religious festivals, marriage and funerary rituals, while remaining a communist or a scientist?[1]

One could answer these problems in such a way that they cease to appear as facts about a culture. Here are a few of the so-called explanations: because most Romans could not read, one wrote what one thought; it is the nature of the Roman genius to have recognised that religion is the "opium of the masses"; it is simply a testimony to the fact that superstition has a stronger grip on the human imagination than reason. Not only are these 'explanations' *ad hoc*, but they merely push the problem one step further without resolving them. As we have seen, this is the road travelled by many of our illustrious scholars.

The other alternative is to realise that these facts are reference points as well: they are the conditions of description. Any description of Roman religion – in order to be adjudged passable or plausible – must exhibit them as *its* facts; that is, it must lend intelligibility to them. In the rest of what follows, I'll defend this alternative not by arguing for it at the meta-level, but by practising it at the object-level.

### 2.1.1. Romans and Their 'Religio'

Our facts, then, tell us that the Roman culture appears to have allowed for two distinct 'things': theoretical disquisitions about gods and *religio* on the one hand, and religious practices on the other. If the former were not the reasons for the latter, how was the participation of the people ensured? What was, or could have been, religion in the Roman world? Again, the participants in Cicero's dialogue give us the best answer. Here's Cotta, the sceptic:

> I am considerably influenced...by the plea...when you exhorted me to remember that I am both a Cotta and a pontiff. This is no doubt meant that I ought to uphold beliefs about the immortal gods which have *come down to us from our ancestors*, and the rites and ceremonies and duties of religion. For my part, I shall always uphold them and have always done so,

---

[1] Speaking of the "labyrinth of contrasts, contradictions, and paradoxes" that India is, Sasthi Brata (1985: 21) treats us to one such "stupendous contrast":
> One thousand year old temples may be sitting next door to modern satellite communications complexes (in Thumba, South India), while nuclear scientists may start the day by offering *puja* (devotional offerings) to a clay god.

and no eloquence of anybody, learned or unlearned shall ever dislodge me from the belief...*which I have inherited from our forefathers*...Balbus...you are a philosopher, and I ought to receive from you a proof of your religion, *whereas I must believe the word of our ancestors even without proof* (*De Natura Deorum*, III, ii: 290-291; my italics).

Though the citation speaks for itself, two points are worth emphasising: first, some things are retained because they have been transmitted over generations and they require no other legitimation; second, philosophical argumentation may establish or prove some opinion, but it is irrelevant to traditional practice. Later in the dialogue, the last point is made even more strongly:

Although I for my part cannot be persuaded to surrender my belief that the gods exist, nevertheless you teach me no reason why this belief, *of which I am convinced on the authority of our forefathers,* should be true (*ibid,* III, iii: 293; my italics).

It is important to note how Cotta argues. Quintus Lucillus Balbus, the stoic opponent of Gaius Cotta, the Academic sceptic, feels a need to prove the existence of gods. Our sceptic uses this fact to show that his opponent is looking for wrong things in the wrong place.

You did not really feel confident that the doctrine of the divine existence was as self-evident as you could wish, and for that reason you attempted to prove it with a number of arguments. *For my part a simple argument would have sufficed, namely that it has been handed down to us by our forefathers.* But you despise authority, and fight your battles with the weapon of reason. Give permission therefore for my reason to join issue with yours (*ibid,* III, iv: 295; my italics).

The permission is given and the battle joined, but Balbus is truly lost. Cotta is a formidable mind (incidentally, so are his opponents). His central thesis is that one's beliefs about the existence or non-existence of gods are irrelevant to religion because religion is handed down over generations. It is not that religion is transmitted along with other things, but *that* which is transmitted is religion. As Plutarch puts it:

Our father then, addressing Pemptides by name, said, "You seem to me, Pemptides, to be handling a very big matter and a risky one – or rather, *you are discussing what should not be discussed at all,* when you question the opinion we hold about the gods, and ask reason and demonstration about everything. *For the ancient and ancestral faith is enough, and no clearer proof could be found than itself*...it is a common home and an established foundation for all piety; and if in one point *its stable and traditional character* be shaken and disturbed, it will be undermined and no one will trust it...If you demand proof about each of the ancient gods, laying hands on everything sacred and bring your sophistry to play on every altar, *you will leave nothing free from quibble and cross-examination*...Do you see, then, the abyss of atheism at our feet, if we resolve each of the gods into a passion or a force or a virtue?" (Cited in Glover 1909: 76; my italics.)

In *The Octavius*, Caecilius the pagan argues his case thus:

[It is better] as high priest of truth, *to receive the teaching of your ancestors, to cultivate the religion handed down to you*, to adore the gods whom you were first trained by your parents to fear...*not to assert an opinion concerning the deities, but to believe your forefathers,* who, while the age was still untrained in the birth-times of the world itself, deserved to have gods either propitious to them, or as their kings. (Roberts and Donaldson, Eds., n.d., Vol. IV: 176; my italics.)

Religion, then, appears to fall together with tradition – *religio* is what *traditio* is all about. Continuing a tradition does not require any reason other than itself: what is being continued is tradition itself. That is to say, no theoretical justification was needed to practise and uphold ancestral customs. (See also 11.2.3.)

The primary test of truth in religious matters was custom and tradition, the practices of the ancients...In philosophical matters one might turn to intellectuals and philosophers, but in religious questions one looked to the past, to the accepted practices handed down by tradition, and to the guarantors of this tradition, the priests (Wilken 1984: 62).

Ramsay MacMullen (1981: 2) makes an analogous remark:

(T)here was very little doubt in people's minds that the religious practices of one generation should be cherished without change by the next, whether within one's own community or another's. To be pious in any sense, to be respectable and decent, required the perpetuation of cult, even if one's judges themselves worshipped quite other gods.

Graeco-Roman intellectuals are not dogmatic traditionalists defending this or that particular practice by appealing to the fact that their fathers and ancestors performed them too. After all, as our history books never tire of mentioning, the Ancients pioneered the spirit of scientific enquiry – the spirit of ruthlessly questioning every belief. The Romans and the Greeks questioned practices too – the very existence of juridical institutions would have been impossible otherwise. Yet there was a sphere, the *religio*, not affected by critical questioning, practised because it was *traditio*.

> The late republic was an age of rationalism, certainly as far as the Roman nobility was concerned. But this tendency was never taken to its logical conclusion, rejection of traditional religious practice...Such respect for ancestral authority would assure the continuity of traditional ritual, just as the childhood associations, family tradition, and the peculiar nature of pagan beliefs would tend to preserve traditional mental attitudes. (Liebeschuetz 1979: 31-32.)

As Cicero puts it in *De Divinatione* (II, 77)

> It is wise and reasonable for us to preserve the institutions of our forefathers by retaining their rites and ceremonies. (Cited in Gay 1973: 155.)

Whose tradition is it? Obviously of a people. Which people? Why, those that belonged to a city, of course. Consequently, an identifiable people – identified by their relation to a city, with a language and a history – had tradition. Different groups would have different traditions: besides practising their own traditions, however, they had to respect the traditions of the peoples among whom they lived. Of course, this did not mean that the populace was 'tolerant' in religious matters, as we understand the term today.

> Again, because of people's narrowness of curiosity and loyalty the beliefs of some neighbouring region or city might have no reality; and such indifference could be simply accepted: 'all men do not worship all gods, but each, a certain one that he acknowledges.' (MacMullen, 1984: 12.)

There is the following famous passage of Plutarch (67.377) in *On Isis and Osiris*, which, in the words of Molly Whittaker, "would have been acceptable to any religious and educated Pagan, especially to a stoic":

> We do not conceive of the gods as different among different peoples, nor as barbarians and Greek, nor as southern and northern; but just as sun and moon and sky and earth and sea are common to all men, but have dif-

ferent names among different people, so for that one Reason which sets all things in order and for that one Providence which has oversight over them and for the attendant powers, which are set over all, different honours and names have come into being among different peoples according to their customs (Whittaker 1984: 268).

Similar thoughts are expressed by Quintus Aurelius Symmachus, a pagan prefect of Rome. In a justly famous letter to the Emperor, pleading the cause of the pagan cults within the framework of a bellicose and aggressive Christian march to power, Symmachus says:

> Grant, I beg you, that what in our youth we took over from our fathers, we may in our old age hand on to posterity. The love of established practice is a powerful sentiment...
>
> Everyone has his own customs, his own religious practices; the divine mind has assigned to different cities different religions to be their guardians. Each man is given at birth a separate soul; in the same way each people is given its own special genius to take care of its destiny...If long passage of time lends validity to religious observances, we ought to keep faith with so many centuries, we ought to follow our forefathers who followed their forefathers and were blessed in so doing...
>
> And so we ask for peace for the gods of our fathers, for the gods of our native land. It is reasonable that whatever each of us worships is really to be considered one and the same. We gaze up at the same stars, the sky covers us all, the same universe compasses us. What does it matter what practical system we adopt in our search for truth? Not by one avenue only can we arrive at so tremendous a secret. (Barrow, Trans., 1973: 37-41; my italics.)[2]

When you look at religion as tradition, that is, as a set of practices transmitted over generations, then the term appears as a minor variant of *our* intuitive notion of culture: to have religion is to have culture. Wherever there are people with a history, identifying themselves as a people, there traditions exist too. In other words, they have *religio* too. This is how the pagans seem to have seen the issue. As Balbus the Stoic, comments:

---

[2] When St. Ambrose heard of this petition, he wrote a letter (Epistle XVII) to Valentinian II threatening to excommunicate him if he even thought of giving in, and requesting a copy of the petition. His Epistle XVIII is the reply to the 'Memorial of Symmachus,' all three of which are in Schaff and Wace, Eds., Vol. 10, 1896: 411-422. Ambrose's vulgar polemic hardly touches the issue; neither does the full-length poem of Prudentius (Trans. Eagan) *Against Symmachus* written a few centuries later.

...(I)f we care to compare our *national characteristics* with those of foreign peoples, we shall find that, while in all other respects we are only the equals or even the inferior of others, yet *in the sense of religion*, that is, in reverence for the gods, we are far superior. (De Natura Deorum, II, iii: 131; my italics.)

Which 'national characteristic' is Balbus referring to? Perhaps the feature that each people has its local gods and national rites, whereas the Romans worship all divinities. According to Caecilius, it even accounted for the supremacy of the Roman empire:

[The Romans adore all divinities]...in the city of an enemy, when taken while still in the fury of victory, they venerate the conquered deities...in all directions they seek for the gods of the strangers, and make them their own...they build altars even to unknown deities...Thus, in that they acknowledge the sacred institutions of all nations, they have also deserved their dominion. (*The Octavius*, in Roberts and Donaldson, Eds., n.d., Vol. IV: 177.)

Thus the tolerance of different traditions and 'respect' for tradition, actually demonstrated by practising the tradition of the other, where and when necessary, appear to characterise the Roman *religio*.

*2.1.2. From* Demonstratio Evangelica...

How could one place the persecution of the Jews, and later the Christians, within such a context of tolerance? An answer to this question would involve many aspects I will not touch upon. However, one thing should be obvious: the fundamental objection that the Romans had against the Jews and the Christians would have been that Judaism and Christianity are not *religiones;* that is, they are not traditions. Consequently, they refuse to recognise that the traditions of other peoples and places are valid (see Wardy 1979).

The Jews appear to have met this charge in two ways: first, by showing that the Jews were a people with history; second, by laying claims to great antiquity. The many apologetic texts written by the Hellenic and Alexandrian Jews, including the famous one by Philo of Alexandria, attempted to argue that Judaism and Israel were more ancient than the Ancients were. Greek legislators, claimed Philo, actually plagiarised the Mosaic Law, and Heraclitus stole his theory of opposites from Moses "like a thief" (Wolfson 1947). This need to establish the antiquity of Judaism, I would like to suggest, is aimed at showing that Judaism was a '*traditio*'. When it comes to traditions, especially where a group claims exemption from practising the traditions of others, the most important 'property' is their antiquity. The Jews could argue that theirs was the most ancient of all traditions, therefore a '*religio*' *a fortiori*, allowing them not to follow the traditions of others in matters of conflicting injunctions.

It is important to recognise the novelty of the Jewish apologetics: with varying degrees of success, they tried to provide theoretical justifications why their traditional practice did not allow them to "seek the gods of the strangers." It was not sufficient to show that the Jews followed an ancient custom given to them by Moses. They had to justify that their ancestral practice forbade them from worshipping the various deities that littered the Roman landscape. That is to say, they had to provide a 'philosophical' underpinning to their ancient custom. That is what the Jewish apologetic texts attempted: explain why, if the Jews had *traditio*, they would not venerate the ancestral customs of other peoples. Their explanation, of course, centred around their scripture – more precisely, around its truth.

The uneasy recognition that the Judaic tradition had obtained in the Roman Empire can be observed in the way Celsus, one of the first Roman critics of Christianity, speaks about the Jews. Even though he is supposed to have despised many of the Jewish customs, he nevertheless notes (Origen, 5.25: 283):

> The Jews became an individual nation, and made laws according to the custom of their country; and they maintain these laws among themselves at the present day, and *observe a worship which may be very peculiar but is at least traditional.* In this respect they behave like the rest of mankind, because *each nation follows its traditional customs,* whatever kind may happen to be established. This situation seems to have come to pass not only because it came into the head of different people to think differently and because it is necessary to preserve the established social conventions, but also because it is probable that from the beginning the different parts of the earth were allotted to different overseers...In fact, the practices done by each nation are right when they are done in the way that pleases the overseers; and *it is impious to abandon the customs which have existed in the locality from the beginning* (my italics).

Cornelius Tacitus, the Roman historian, is not known for his sympathies toward the Judaic tradition either. Speaking of the Jews – to whom "all things are profane that we hold sacred", and who "regard as permissible what seems to us immoral" – he nonetheless acknowledges:

> Whatever their origin, these observances are *sanctioned by their antiquity.* (*The Histories*, 5.5, Wellesley, Trans., 273, my italics.)

*The Christian Quandary*

The Christians could not follow the route taken by the Jews, although they had to lay claim to the Judaic tradition. As Christians, they had to reject the Mosaic Law, but they had to show that they too had *traditio*.

It is likely that in the very early phases, it did not seem important to the Christians. Anticipating the end of the world any moment (Fredriksen 1988) and projecting the second coming of Christ onto the immediate future as they did (see Hill 1992 for a very good analysis of early Christian chiliasm), the zeal of the Christians tended to ignore the cultural matrix within which they were functioning. When it became clear, however, that the world would not end so soon, their problem became obvious: they were 'a people' without tradition.

Porphyry (Eusebius, *Praeparatio Evangelica*, 4.1.) for example, is said to have alleged that the Christians are guilty of

> the *greatest impiety* in taking no account of powers so manifest and so beneficent, but directly breaking the laws, which require every one to *reverence ancestral customs*, and not disturb what should be inviolable, but to walk orderly in following the religion of his forefathers and not to be *meddlesome through love of innovation*. (Gifford, Trans., 141-142; my italics.)

In the light of what I have said, it is evident that those who had no tradition would have been accused of atheism. Such indeed was the criticism levelled against the Christians by the pagans. That is, as the pagans of that period saw it, the early Christians were 'atheists' lacking religion (Grant 1973; Benko 1980, 1985; Meredith 1980). In a long passage, which is supposed to derive from Porphyry (as Wilken 1984: 156 surmises), Eusebius summarises the charges thus:

> (H)ow can men fail to be in every way impious and atheistical, who have *apostatized from those ancestral gods* by whom every nation and every state is sustained? Or what good can they reasonably hope for, who have set themselves at enmity and at war against their preservers, and have thrust away their benefactors? For what else are they doing than fighting against the gods?
>
> And what forgiveness shall they be thought to deserve, who have turned away from those who from the earliest time, among all Greeks and Barbarians, both in cities and in the country, are recognized as gods with all kinds of sacrifices, and initiations, and mysteries by all alike, kings, lawgivers and philosophers, and have chosen all that is impious and atheistical among the doctrines of men?...

(They have not adhered) to the God who is honoured among the Jews according to their customary rites, *but (have) cut out for themselves a new kind of track*...that keeps neither the ways of the Greeks nor those of the Jews (*ibid*, 1.3, Gifford, Trans., 5-6; my italics).

Tatian, in his *Oratio ad Graecos*, tells his pagan public not to think that he

aspiring to be above the Greeks, above the infinite number of philosophic inquirers, *has struck out a new path*, and embraced the doctrine of Barbarians. (Roberts and Donaldson, Eds., n.d., Vol. II: 80; my italics.)

We can now see the challenge the Christians faced: they were not Jews; nor were they Romans. The Christians could not see themselves as a people with a history, a tradition, a language – that is, they could not trace themselves back to any particular people. The Jews could; the Romans could; even the Egyptians who worshipped "cats, crocodiles, serpents, asps and dogs" could. However, the Christians alone could not. They had to show that Christianity was a *religio* even though their enemies accused them of not being a *traditio*. *That* they set out to do.

*2.1.3. ...to* Praeparatio Evangelica

*The Pagan Question*

As we have already seen, one of the fundamental charges against Christianity was its novelty and youth. No nation had ever heard of the Jesus heralded by the Christians; Christianity was not the ancestral custom of a people; they were "meddlesome through love of innovation."

During its first five centuries, writer after writer from the Christian Church tried to establish the antiquity of Christianity. Here, they followed the lead given by the Hellenic and Alexandrian Jews. Tatian, for instance, in his *Address to the Greeks*, deems it proper

to demonstrate that our philosophy is older than the system of the Greeks. Moses and Homer shall be our limits, each of them being of great antiquity;...Let us, then, institute a comparison between them; and we shall find that our doctrines are older, not only than those of the Greeks, but *than the invention of letters.* (Roberts and Donaldson, Eds., n.d., Vol. II: 77; my italics.)

Having 'established' this to his satisfaction, he goes on:

> But the matter of principal importance is to endeavour with all accuracy
> to make it clear that Moses is not only older than Homer, but than all the
> writers that were before him... (*ibid*: 81).

During the second century, Theophilus of Antioch, after an equally
thorough exposition of the Biblical chronology, makes it obvious that

> one can see the antiquity of the prophetical writings and the divinity of
> our doctrine, that the doctrine is not recent, nor our tenets mythical and
> false, as some think, *but very ancient and true*. (*Theophilus to Autolycus*. In
> Roberts and Donaldson, Eds., n.d., Vol. II: 121; my italics.)

Such arguments were not limited to one or two names; the roll call
reads like a who's who of the early church fathers: Justin, Origen,
Tertullian, Clement of Alexandria, Eusebius and, much later, even St.
Augustine. Each of them tried to show, as Eusebius says in *The History
of the Church*, that Christianity had long existed as "the first, most ancient, and most primitive of all religions" and, therefore, "shown not to
be modern and strange but, in all conscience, primitive, unique, and
true". (Williamson, Trans., 47, 49.)

There are two things of crucial importance to the Christian apologetics regarding the antiquity of Christianity. The first is the *question*
itself. The pagans challenged the Christians to show that they followed
ancient, and hence venerated, customs and practices of their forefathers. The Jews had met this challenge by arguing not only that Moses
was 'older' than Homer, but also that, and this is crucial, they were
faithful to this ancient custom. In contrast, the Christians, when they
appropriated the Jewish apology, *transformed* the very question: instead
of showing that they were true to ancestral *practice*, they argued that
their *doctrine*s were ancient and therefore true.

The second thing of importance is a problem generated by this
transformation of the pagan question. How could adherence to a doctrine be equivalent to following a practice? Let us look at each of these
points more closely.

*A Jewish Theme*

The ground for thus transforming the question was prepared during
the first century C.E. During this period, Christianity was embroiled in
a polemic with Judaism (Pelikan 1971; Rokeah 1982). The Christians

had to argue a number of points: that the Messiah had come and that he was the prophesied one; that the refusal of the Jews to acquiesce had to do with their inability to understand and interpret the Scriptures properly; that God's promise to His 'elect' was fulfilled in the coming of Christ in flesh, but the sons of Israel – who were God's elect – refused to see Jesus as the Christ. The Old Testament made Christianity sensible, but the refusal of the Jews to heed 'their' scriptures, as interpreted by the Christians, threatened to make Christianity senseless. To some extent, the problematic relation of the early Christians with the Jews is captured in the ambiguity of the Gospels themselves: the conflicting injunctions that one ought to and ought not to preach among the gentiles.

> Give not that which is holy unto the dogs, neither cast ye your pearls before swine, lest they trample them under their feet, and turn again and rend you. (*The Holy Bible*, King James' version, Matthew 7.6.)

And further, as instructions to the Apostles,

> These twelve Jesus sent forth, and commanded them, saying, Go not into the way of the Gentiles, and into *any* city of the Samaritans enter ye not: But go rather to the lost sheep of the house of Israel. (Matthew, 10.6-7)

Or again, as Jesus answered his disciples:

> I am not sent but unto the lost sheep of the house of Israel. (Matthew, 15.24.)

On the other hand, the same evangelists record Jesus saying:

> And they shall come from the east, and *from* the west, and from the north and *from* the south, and shall sit down in the kingdom of God. (Luke, 13.29; see also Matthew 8.11-12.)

Reflecting on these ideas,[3] Vermes (1984: 54-55) asks himself:

---

[3] See also Mark 7.27; Matthew 15.26 for similar colourful descriptions of the non-Jews.

However did the evangelists manage to record such sayings as these, and at the same time attribute to Jesus the view that the Gentiles were soon to displace the 'sons of the kingdom,' the Jews, as the elect of God?

I do not want to embroil myself in this controversy, over which much ink has been spilt, but I do want to draw your attention to the conclusion of the discussion: the Christians saw their religion as the fulfilment of Judaism. They alone were the followers of the true message of the scriptures. As Ignatius of Antioch, the Apostolic Father, formulated the thought in *The Epistle to the Magnesians,*

> To profess Jesus Christ while continuing to follow Jewish custom is an absurdity. The Christian faith does not look to Judaism, but Judaism looks to Christianity... (Staniforth, Trans., 90).

The theme of the elect of God survives but not the way Judaism saw it. Because they follow the doctrine, the Christians are the elect now. When Christianity entered into polemics with the pagan thinkers, it saw itself as having superseded Judaism, as its fulfilment. The Old and the New Testaments, together, formed the Christian scriptures. Because these were the most ancient of all doctrines, Christianity was also ancient.

## The Christian Answer

Though it would take a few centuries for our story to take shape, we can follow a straight line to come to the point quickly. In their dispute with the Jews, the Christians had implicitly severed the tie between being a nation and having religion by arguing that Christians were the followers of the 'true' doctrines. As a result, their religion was everything the Jews were waiting for. In their polemic with the pagans, Christians could travel much further along this path. Moreover, now there is an extra sting in the tail of the tale they were to tell: Christian religion was the fulfilment of the expectations of not merely the Jews, but all peoples. As Ignatius of Antioch continued the sentence in the epistle cited above (*ibid*),

> ...[In Christianity], every other race and tongue that confesses a belief in God has now been comprehended.

All that was 'good' and 'noble' in pagan thought has anticipated and expected the coming of Christ. The Christians were merely announcing the Good Word that the 'expectation of nations' had now been met.

Thus, the process of establishing the antiquity of Christianity took a new turn: many early Christian writers tried to show that Socrates, Plato, Virgil and even the Sibylline Oracles had implicitly anticipated and prepared for the advent of the Gospels. (For example, see chapter 3 of Pelikan 1985.) In very simple terms: all human nations and cultures, as Eusebius made it clear, were merely *Praeparatio Evangelica*. After Christ came in flesh, the preparatory work was finished finally: Christianity was the religion of the humankind.

Such a claim must have shocked the Roman sensibilities doubly: first, though manifestly no *traditio* of any nation, Christians claimed that they were *religio;* second, as *'religio'* of all peoples (a contradiction in terms, if my claim about *religio* and *traditio* is correct), Christians claimed exemption from following the traditions of the cities because all of them were wrong.

How could they show this? Only by opposing their *beliefs* – that is, their theology – to the prevalent *practices*. Thus, a fundamental shift was wrought: religion was countered to tradition.

In order to make their claims stick, Christians had to build a respectable theology. Moreover, because of the emphasis laid on doctrines, they had to enter into disputes with 'philosophers.' Unfortunately, Christians were hardly the intellectual equals of their opponents (but see Osborn 1981). In the early stages, Celsus charged, the Christians avoided all debates and discussions with intellectuals:

> We see that those who display their trickery in the market-places and go about begging would never enter a gathering of intelligent men, nor would they dare to reveal their noble beliefs in their presence; but whenever they see adolescent boys and a crowd of slaves and a company of fools they push themselves in and show off. (*Contra Celsum*, III: 50, p. 162.)

Or, even more pictorially:

> In private houses also we see wool-workers, cobblers, laundry-workers, and the most illiterate and bucolic yokels, who would not dare to say anything at all in front of their elders and more intelligent masters. But whenever they get hold of children in private and some stupid women with them, they let out some astounding statements...And if just as they are speaking they see one of the school-teachers coming, or some intelligent person, or even the father himself, the more cautious of them flee in all directions; but the more reckless urge children on to rebel. They whisper to them that in the presence of their father and their schoolmasters they do not feel able to explain anything to the children, since they do not want anything to do with the silly and obtuse teachers who are totally

corrupted and far gone in wickedness and who inflict punishment on the children (*ibid*, III: 55. p. 166).

It is interesting to note that Origen does not deny this charge:

> If you were accusing us of drawing away from philosophy those who have been previously interested in it, *you would not be speaking the truth,* though your argument might have some plausibility (*ibid*, III: 57, p. 167; my italics)

Instead, he enters into silly polemical rhetoric. As an example, consider this reply:

> What kind of father do you mean, sir, and what kind of teacher? If you mean one who approves of virtue and turns away from evil and welcomes that which is good, take notice that *we would be very bold* in telling our doctrines to his children, *since we would be approved of by such a judge.* If, on the other hand, we are silent before a father who has become notoriously opposed to virtue and goodness, and before men who teach doctrines contrary to sound reason, this is no charge against us, and it is not reasonable that you should make it so. (*ibid*, III: 58, p.167, my italics.)

Celsus' charge appears extremely plausible: the early Christian converts did not come from intellectual circles. As such, they could hardly take on the theoretical might of the Roman World.

> Latin-speaking Christianity in the West did not acquire a philosophical mind of any considerable quality before the middle of the fourth century, with the conversion of the Roman Neoplatonist Marius Victorianus, to whose difficult and reputedly obscure writings Augustine was to owe a little in constructing his own synthesis of Christianity and Platonism (Chadwick 1966: 3)

For my purposes, Chadwick's assessment is a side issue. The important point is that the Christian religion, in its polemic with the Jews and pagans alike, counterposed its doctrines to the prevalent customs. When such great store is set on beliefs, two things are inevitable: growth of different interpretations, and a critique of the tenability of these beliefs. The so-called 'heresy' is a phenomenon that grew along with Christianity itself (Snell 1982; Christie-Murray 1976). Already during the first three hundred years of its existence, Christianity knew of the following heretical offshoots: Paulicianism, Arianism, Montanism,

Marcionism, Apollinarianism, Origenism, Gnosticism, *etc.* Persecution and liquidation are also the ineluctable outgrowths of such a religion – at least when and where it is unable to show its strength against its intellectual opponents: Porphyry's books were burnt (Hulen 1938); heretics, liquidated.

We are now in a better position to understand what was entailed by the Christian transformation of the pagan question. Christianity was ancient not because it was the practice of any nation, but because of its doctrines. It was *religio* precisely because it was not *traditio.* No wonder, pagans had difficulties in understanding this alien growth.

## Christians and the Pagans

As noted earlier, the transformation of the pagan question generates a problem: how could adherence to a doctrine be equivalent to following a practice? It would be, if the practice embodies or expresses the doctrine, that is to say, if the practice of the Christians expresses the teachings they accept. If the teachings they accept are "primitive, unique, and true," it follows that their practices are likewise.

With this in mind, if we look at either the Christian defence in the face of persecutions (Benko 1985; Keresztes 1979b) during the first three centuries, or if we look at the Christian criticisms of 'paganism' then and in the centuries to follow, at least one thing is odd and striking: the criticisms were directed at pagan *practices* but the object of criticism were pagan *beliefs.*

As is well known, criticisms neither of beliefs nor of practices were new to the intellectuals of the Roman world. The early (or, for that matter, late) Christian critique of paganism did not go much beyond the pagan critiques of their *religio* either. The criticism of the Roman intellectuals did not challenge *tradition,* it merely restrained *superstitio*; that is, it functioned as a constraint on the excesses of human practice. The tradition handed down was not to be supplanted by 'reason' but to be held in check whenever contemporary practices threatened to run wild.

What Christianity did then – and was to repeat centuries later during the Reformation – was to criticise practices by criticising beliefs. That is to say, it postulated a link between *practices and beliefs.* A link of a type that (I claim) was unknown in Antiquity: practices express or embody the beliefs that human beings entertain. In this manner, Christianity further reduced *religio* to 'religion.' The former became a variant of the latter: paganism was an expression of a set of false or corrupt beliefs.

'Paganism as an expression of a set of false or corrupt beliefs'? What on earth enabled Christians to say this? An answer to this question requires a bit of a detour...

## 2.2 ...En Route to *De Civitate Dei*

Anyone who contrasts *The City of God* of St. Augustine with, say, *Summa Contra Gentiles* of St. Thomas Aquinas cannot but be struck by the different attitudes exhibited by these two great minds of the Catholic church with respect to 'other religions.' In the pages of St. Augustine, the 'religions' of the Greeks and the Romans are constantly present. His polemics are directed against the 'survivals' of the Roman cults and associations. They are living presences, constantly reminding Christianity of an *otherness*, irrespective of what St. Augustine called them and how the Church looked at them. In contrast, in a work written against the gentiles, Aquinas's tone is abstract and distant, not so much because of his rational approach, but because of the subject matter. In his history of the Christian doctrine, Pelikan (1971: 39) notes the situation as follows:

> The *Summa against the Gentiles* of Thomas Aquinas was written at a time when there were certainly very few "Gentiles," that is, pagans, left in western Europe and when those for whom it was ostensibly composed *could not have understood it* (my italics).

This observation, while true, masks a very important question: how could Aquinas understand what paganism was like?

Western Christendom had just recently 'rediscovered' pagan writers through the Arabian sources. Though respected, the Ancients were just that: Ancients – not living contemporaries. The pagan gods and the cultic practices, against which the early church fathers had fulminated, were transformed and absorbed into the Christian culture but not as pagan cults with distinct identities. In the early phase of the domestication of the pagan gods, the Greek poet Euhemerus played an important role for, we are told, he was one of the first to discuss the origin of religion. Of course, he was not really doing deep anthropological fieldwork but merely proffering a suggestion about the origin of gods. In a work called the *Sacred Inscription*, but translated by Ennius as *The Sacred History*, to which we owe the preservation of some fragments from Euhemerus' writings,

> he formed a theory of the origin of religion and gave it to the world in the form of an imaginary journey to a kind of Utopia or Erewhon... Euhemerus' theory was that all gods whose cults can be identified were originally human beings who so impressed themselves on the memory of their contemporaries that on their death they were deified. They made this

impression by their benefactions and achievements during their lives...
(Hanson 1980: 934-935)

This argument (see also Gamble 1979), current to this day, was to perform many a service to the Christians later: it allowed them to understand the pagan deities (Contreras 1980; Cooke 1927) and many pagan
and heathen religions and, as Seznec (1940) convincingly demonstrates,
it even allowed them to retain some pagan gods during the Middle Ages,
albeit not as gods but as meritorious and wise human beings.

The slow manner in which Euhemerism lost the polemical edge it
had in the early phases of Christianity is perhaps best illustrated in the
*Historia Scholastica* of Peter Comestor – the chancellor of Notre Dame
of Paris. Written in 1160, this book penetrated all parts of Europe and
enjoyed tremendous popularity.

> As an appendix to his sacred history, Peter condenses the mythological
> material furnished him by Isidore and his predecessors, Orosius and St.
> Jerome, into a series of short chapters, or *incidentiae*. The parallelism be-
> tween the two narratives, sacred and profane, is presented with curious
> precision: clearly, the figures from the world of Fable, though of differ-
> ent lineage, have now achieved a basis of strict equality with the Biblical
> characters. In both groups Peter recognizes men of superior stature, gen-
> iuses endowed with profound and mysterious wisdom. Zoroaster invented
> magic and inscribed the seven arts on four columns (Gen. XXXIX); Isis
> taught the Egyptians the letters of the Alphabet and showed them how to
> write (LXX); Minerva taught several arts, in particular weaving (LXXVI);
> Prometheus, renowned for his wisdom, is reputed to have created men, ei-
> ther because he instructed the ignorant or perhaps because he fabricated
> automata. All these mighty spirits are worthy of veneration, exactly as are
> the patriarchs, and for the same reason: they have been the guides and
> teachers of humanity, and together stand as the common ancestors of civi-
> lization. (Seznec 1940: 16; see further Hanson 1980 and Cooke 1927.)

Consequently, when Aquinas composed his *Summa contra Gentiles,*
there was not much to go by. How, then, did Aquinas know what paganism was like? Because his religion is true, variations of it cannot be anything other than 'heresies' and 'errors.' It is self-evident to St. Thomas
that only one true religion exists, the Christian religion; everything else
expresses the confusion and decay since the first religion of Man. The
religion of the gentiles was one such. Such was the theological certainty
of Aquinas.

St. Augustine, by contrast, was trying to demonstrate the truth
of such a theological stance in *The City of God.* In this single book,
Augustine would bring to completion what his Christian brethren had

been struggling to accomplish during the first 400 years: to transform the pagan 'other' into an image that Aquinas could recognize: a pale and erring variant of the Christian religious 'self.'

### 2.2.1. *"Will the True Pagan Stand Up, Please?"*

As we have seen above, the Christians claimed that their religion followed the most ancient of all doctrines. The Jews as well as all other nations on earth had anticipated the coming of Christ. By saying this, the Christians began the process of constructing the history of humanity itself. In appropriating the Old Testament, they also appropriated the past of humankind. The Old Testament was not just the past of humanity as the Jews envisaged it, but a true chronicle of events on earth. The real or imaginary past of the Jews became the framework for describing the history of humanity.

Of course, the Jews also treated the Old Testament as a historical chronicle. With Christianity, we see the emergence of an additional dimension: the coming of Christ in flesh that gives a greater concreteness and determination to human history; it was the fulfilment of God's promise. As a result, a philosophy of history also came into being – not merely in the sense that chronicles that traced and rediscovered the truth of Biblical events on earth were penned (Momigliano 1963), but also in the sense that the Christians experienced the worldly happenings as the execution of the divine plan. 'Human history' supposedly embodied this divine plan. (Latourette 1949; Dawson 1951; essays in McIntire, Ed., 1977.) In the words of Cameron (1991: 116-117):

> [The Christian] narratives are...important in terms of their relation to time, that is, the way they join with the canonical books and other early Christian writings to place the developing Christian mythology within a chronological worldview, by "an embedding of the present in a total time-sequence." Since Christian discourse was based on events perceived to have happened in historical time, it was itself inescapably anchored in time, and furthermore, in a concept of time that united worldly events with the mythic past and future...The stories in the Gospels, and the stories with which the bareness of the Gospel narratives was filled out, serve to bind the Christian discourse ever more closely to linear time, and thus to an appropriation by the present of the past and the future.

What took place was not just an appropriation of the "past and the future" by the present. Rather, it was an appropriation of the multiple pasts and histories of peoples on earth within the framework of one past of one people. This single history exhibited an order and pattern because God's promise was fulfilled in the present. In this process, the direction of the future was also clearly indicated. Let me recount the simplest version of a story that was to masquerade as nothing less than human history. There was once a religion, the true and universal one, which was the divine gift to all humankind. A sense or spark of divinity is installed in all races (and individuals) of humanity by the creator God himself. During the course of human history, this sense did not quite erode as it was corrupted. Idolatry and worship of the Devil – the false God and his minions – were to be the lot of humankind until God spoke to Abraham, Isaac and Jacob, and led their tribe back onto the true path. I cannot tell you with any great certainty what has happened since then: the Jewish, the Christian and the Islamic religions are yet to arrive at a consensus (for example, see Hick and Meltzer, Eds., 1989).

Irrespective of whether there is a consensus or not, two aspects of this story are important. We have already come across the first aspect: the 'best' among the pagans, by anticipating and preparing the advent of the Gospels, were now a part of the world history as the Christians wrote it. The second aspect is this: within the broad framework of the Christian (including Old Testament) philosophy of history, the *religio* of the Romans became the prototypical false religion of humankind.

How could this be? The Old Testament story was pressed into service here as well, not merely to explain the 'errors' of the gentiles but also to give them a permanent place within the Christian philosophy of history. The pagans were seduced into accepting false beliefs as true. Seduced by whom or what? By the Devil and his machinations, of course. The Devil and his minions tempt people into worshipping the false god, namely, himself. After all, that is why the God of Abraham, Isaac and Jacob made His appearance in the Arabian Desert. Consequently, the Roman deities were absorbed into the Christian framework as 'demons' and their worship was nothing but idolatry. From the innumerable writings of the early Church fathers about this issue, a citation at random:

> There are some insincere and vagrant spirits degraded from their heavenly vigour by earthly stains and lusts. Now these spirits, after having lost the simplicity of their nature by being weighed down and immersed in vices, for a solace to their calamity, cease not, now that they have ruined themselves, to ruin others; and being depraved themselves, to infuse into others the error of their depravity; and being themselves alienated from God, to separate others from God by the introduction of degraded superstitions. The poets know that those spirits are demons; the philosophers discourse of them; Socrates knew it, who, at the nod and decision of a demon that was at his side, either declined or undertook affairs. The Magi, also, not only know that there are demons, but, moreover, whatever miracle they

affect to perform, do it by means of demons; by their aspirations and communications they show their wondrous tricks...These impure spirits... consecrated under statues and images, lurk there, and by their status attain the authority as of a present deity...Thus they weigh men downwards from heaven, and call them away from the true God...and constrain men to worship them... (*The Octavius.* Roberts and Donaldson, Eds., n.d., Vol. IV: 189-90.)

That is why, the Christians argued, it was of primordial importance to follow the true doctrine in matters of faith. The 'antiquity' of a practice, in most matters, cloaked erroneous doctrines and seduced men into travelling false paths. Hence, the antiquity of a custom was no authority in so far as religion was concerned. Consequently, all the pagan cults, with their multitude of practices, ceremonies and rituals, all these *others,* became mere exemplifications of another religion – the false one, which worshipped the prince of darkness.

### The Philosopher's God?

Today, among intellectuals of different persuasions, one often hears complaints about the baneful influence of the pagan philosophy (especially the Hellenic thought) upon the Christian religion. This theme, however, is not new: from the early church fathers (*e.g.,* Tertullian) through the Protestant Reformation (*e.g.,* Luther), the same refrain has accompanied the growth and development of Christianity. The 'Hellenisation' of primitive Christianity is accountable for any of the ills that one cares to identify within the Christian tradition. How valid is this accusation? In drawing all the threads together by way of a summary, we shall also answer this question.

From its very inception and in its polemic with Judaism, Christianity was forced to emphasise its doctrinal loyalty and purity: the Christians were the only true followers of the doctrine, whereas the Jews were not. This attitude towards doctrine was carried forward, when challenged by the pagan milieu. The antiquity of Christianity was 'demonstrated' on grounds of the age of the Christian doctrine. Consequently, an extraordinary emphasis was placed on written texts and their correct interpretations.

This attachment to written texts was remarkable in itself, even if it did not penetrate far down the social scale; there was *little or nothing in Roman culture as a whole to induce such a development,* and many features in this highly traditional society in fact worked against it. (Cameron 1991: 110; my italics.)

The Christians answered the pagan question by arguing that their actions (or practices) were embodiments of their beliefs. If the beliefs they held were ancient, so too were the practices that embodied them.

Because their doctrines were true, it also meant that the story of their scriptures was not mythical, but factual. In turn, this implied that the pagan *religio* – which was at odds with Christianity – was *false:* it merely expressed the false beliefs of the gentiles. That is why paganism was an expression of a set of false or corrupt beliefs.

To the pagans, by contrast, *religio* had to do with following ancient practices. The philosophers and the philosophical schools disputed about all kinds of doctrines: the existence and non-existence of gods, their nature, and so on. Irrespective of such disputations (or even because of them), one continued the traditional practices because they were those of one's forefathers. Variations in such ancestral customs among nations were not only recognised, but were also inevitable, because they were human products. As Symmachus said so long ago, "What does it matter what practical system we adopt in our search for truth? Not by one avenue only can we arrive at so tremendous a secret."

If religion has to do with practising the true doctrine, then there can only be *one avenue,* because there can only be one true doctrine. Everything that deviates from it can only be false. That is what the Christians maintained.

When looked at this way, we can see something un-Hellenic about the 'Hellenisation' of Christianity. Christianity and Judaism felt compelled to do what their religious rivals, the cults, never did. The pagan religions were part of the very same Hellenic milieu in which Christianity grew. Yet, it was the latter and not the pagan cults that developed a theology to justify practices. Pagans never felt compelled, even when under attack, to develop a theology of the Isis cult, a kerygma of the Sibylline oracles or whatever else.

Tatian the Greek, when he became a Christian, did indeed "aspire to be above the Greeks." His religion did what the pagans never thought of doing: inscribe 'philosophical' disputations (or theology) into the very heart of religious practice. Only thus, and no other way, could Christianity become a religion. To overlook this, and to blame Hellenic thought for corrupting the allegedly pure *Urchristentum,* is equivalent to wishing that there was no Christianity – primitive or otherwise.

*The Nature of the Invitation*

The well-known fact that no Greek or Roman thinker defended his theory on the grounds of its antiquity underscores how the Christians were answering a transformed question. Neither Plato nor Aristotle, let alone other lesser luminaries, ever suggested that their philosophical doctrine ought to be accepted *because* it was "ancient, most unique, and therefore true" but the Christians, in their battle to establish themselves as *religio,* did precisely that.

An inevitable outcome of this transformation of the question – and the shift in both the reference and meaning of *religio* – is a parallel shift in the reference and the meaning of *traditio.* By the time Christianity had a bite, there were already disputes and discussions about the apostolic tradition itself. Here, 'tradition' referred to the line and process of transmission of the *messages* by the Apostolic Fathers. The Gnostic tendency within the Christian religion fed itself precisely on this pivotal issue: was there a 'truer' doctrine, which the Apostolic Fathers entrusted only to a select group? Consequently, when one talks of the Catholic, Christian, or even the apostolic tradition (*e.g.,* Pelikan 1984), the reference is to the transmission of some or another set of doctrines.

This parallel shift is a further indicator, I submit, of the fact that *religio* and *traditio* were coextensive within the Roman milieu. It is the transformation of the pagan question that enabled the Christians to raise two further problems, which must have sounded like absolute nonsense to the pagan ears: is your *religio* true? Is your *traditio* true? Let me use an anachronistic example and terminology to try to understand how Christians could have shocked the pagan sensibilities. In effect, this is my example, the Christians asked, 'Do green ideas sleep furiously?' That is, and this is the terminology, they were committing a fundamental category mistake. A pagan could understand the question, 'are you faithfully following your ancestral practice?' However, no pagan could answer the charge that his ancestral practice itself was false. How could tradition be true or false? Neither of these two predicates is applicable to *traditio* or *religio* (see #9.5.1). That the Christians nevertheless thought so, after having absorbed the pagan 'other', surely indicates the gulf separating the pagan and the Christian worlds.

How, I repeat, could Aquinas understand the Gentiles nearly a thousand years later, when even St. Augustine had difficulties in understanding the pagan world? "Will the true pagan stand up, please?"

### 2.2.2. *From Augustine to Calvin and Beyond*

None of what has been said implies that pagan thought had no influence on the growth and development of Christianity. Many pagan ideas were transformed and absorbed into the Christian framework, and yet others were taken over to reside uneasily with the Christian tradition over the centuries.

One such idea, which brings us closer to the theme of the book, is about the existence of gods. Cicero, propounding the Epicurean doctrine, has this to say in *De Natura Deorum* (I. xvii; 45):

> [Epicurus] alone perceived first that the gods exist, because nature itself has imprinted a conception of them on the minds of all mankind...(T)he belief in the gods has not been established by authority, custom or law, but rests on the unanimous and abiding consensus of mankind; their existence is therefore a necessary inference, since we possess an instinctive or rather an innate concept of them.

Balbus, the stoic, agrees with this claim:

> (T)he main issue is agreed among all men of all nations, inasmuch as all have engraved in their minds an innate belief that the gods exist (*ibid*, II. iv; 135).

Cotta, the sceptic, doubts the adequacy of this *consensus gentium* argument to prove the existence of gods:

> You said that a sufficient reason for our admitting that the gods exist was the fact that all the nations and races of mankind believe it. But this argument is both inconclusive and untrue. In the first place, how do you know what foreign races believe? For my part I think that there are many nations so uncivilized and barbarous as to have no notion of any gods at all (*ibid*, I, xxiii; 61).

Cotta goes on to refer to 'civilized' men, who deny the existence of gods and are guilty of sacrilege and impiety. Remember, however, that this is the same pontiff who believes in gods "because it has been handed down by the ancestors."

There is no better way to appreciate the persistence of this 'stoic theme' in the Christian tradition over the centuries than to let some of the proponents speak for themselves. As St. Augustine puts it in *Retractationes* (i. 13), summarising an argument in *De Vera Religione* (10, 19) ["That is the Christian religion in our time. To know and follow it is the most secure and most certain way to salvation." Trans., Burleigh: 19],

> This I said, bearing in mind, the name [religion] and the reality underlying the name. For the reality itself, which is now called the Christian religion, was already among the Ancients. It had never been wanting from the

beginning of mankind until the incarnation of Christ, and from then on the true religion, which had already been in existence, began to be called Christian. For when the Apostles began to make him [Christ] known after his resurrection and the ascension into heaven, and when many believed in him, his disciples were called Christians...That is why I said: 'This is the Christian religion in our times', not because it did not exist formerly, but because it received this name only later on. (Cited in D'Costa 1990: 137.)

Not only did the Romans not think that they were Christians, but they also thought that the latter were all 'atheists.'

Exactly the same sentiment occurs in Calvin:

*There is no nation barbarous, no race so brutish, as not to be imbued with the conviction that there is a God.* Even those who, in other respects, seem to differ least from the lower animals, constantly retain some sense of religion...Since...there has never been, from the very first, any quarter of the globe, any city, any household even, without religion, this amounts to a tacit confession that a sense of deity is inscribed on every heart. (*Institutes*, Beveridge, Ed., Vol. 1.: 43; my emphasis.)

Alexander Ross, in his *Pansebia: Or, A View of All Religions in the World* (Sixth edition, 1696) declares that, because both religion and rationality are the distinguishing features of humanity,

no Nation hath been so wretched as to deny a Deity, and to reject all Religion (cited in Pailin 1984: 27).

If to Augustine and Calvin, these were (evidently) matters of theological certainty, not so to Abrahamus Rogerius, an explorer and a missionary. To him, it was the result of empirical discoveries. Even though the editor of the French translation qualifies what Rogerius had to say about sea-voyages and empirical discoveries, to the author the matter was as evident as could be. Speaking of the Brahmins on the Coromandel coast, Rogerius tells us (1651: 85):

*None need think that these individuals are so much like beasts that they do not know of God or Religion* ...Sea voyages have also taught us that there lives no people so beastly, deprived of all reason, *that it does not know that there is a God; thus it also has a religion* (my italics).

By the time we reach 1900, this sentiment has taken the status of un-shakable certainty. Nor was this the case only among the missionaries. Sir Edward Tylor (1873, Vol. 2: 1), the anthropologist, repeats Calvin and Rogerius almost to a word:

> Are there, or have there been, tribes of men so low in culture as to have no reli-gious conceptions whatever? This is practically the question of the univer-sality of religion (my italics).

There is something very, very odd here. Between Augustine and Calvin, we know that no empirical investigations were done to find out whether all peoples had religion. Between Calvin and Rogerius, some 'explora-tion' did occur, but Rogerius' work was almost the first one to give Europe some idea of 'Brahman religion'. Further, 'sea voyages' showed nothing of the sort that Rogerius thought they did. Columbus had writ-ten a hundred years earlier that the Native American did not appear to have religion. The travel reports from Africa and China suggested similar findings.

If we look at Rogerius' travel report to India carefully, we notice some-thing extraordinary. His work was apparently important to the process of Europe's discovery of India. The entire book consists of descriptions with few personal comments by the author himself.[4] A model for con-temporary ethnographers, Rogerius meticulously records what he has seen and heard. He tells us who his informants are, shares with us what he has been told about the belief of Brahmins on the Coromandel coast. Though the book is extremely interesting and worthy of careful analy-sis, more important for our purpose here is to find out how he could have discovered the existence of 'religion' in India. Not knowing any In-dian language, preaching for over ten years in Portuguese in the coastal town in India, how did this missionary find out whether religion existed among the Brahmins of Coromandel? This is how:

> Because where there is a God, a religion *must exist* too; it is thus that we shall approach our investigation (my italics).

The language is illuminating: "there *must* be" a religion – the 'must,' *nota bene*, of logical consequence. Interestingly enough, this is the only place in the entire work where a logical inference is made in this fash-ion. That is to say, he needed to 'deduce' the existence of 'religion' be-

---

[4] This could also be the result of the posthumous publication of Rogerius' work. See the interesting analysis in Ouvry 1979. I am indebted to Pieter Welvaert for bringing this dissertation to my attention.

cause its existence was not evident. He is surprised that there are no 'observable' holy days; there are no public places of worship for the faithful, *etc.*

> In those ten years that I lived in *Paliacatta*, in which city they have erected a *pagoda* in honour of *Vishnu*...I could never observe a single gathering of people there, and I could find no traces of them having reserved any days specifically meant for people to worship God.

There have not been drastic changes in India since the days of Abrahamus Rogerius. Yet, today, almost all intellectuals in the West know that 'temples' (pagodes, as Rogerius called them) are the 'public places' of worship of the Hindus. Each tourist in India sees almost at once what Abrahamus Rogerius did not see even after ten years of missionary activity. Unless evolutionary growth has provided today's Westerners with sharpened eyesight denied to Rogerius and his contemporaries, this manifest presence of religion in India today, given its glaring absence yesterday, becomes quite a mystery to comprehend.

The difference between Abrahamus Rogerius and a tourist from, say, Belgium does not reside in the sharper eyesight of the latter. Should there be a difference in knowledge or information about Indian 'religion,' Rogerius would win easily: most tourists do not know a fraction of what Rogerius knew. Yet, an intellectual from Belgium can pontificate endlessly about the 'religion' of the Hindus, whereas Rogerius had to deduce its existence.

My suggestion must be obvious: today, your average German and the average Belgian believe that Hinduism is quite obviously a religion. They have less evidence to go on than Rogerius had, but they believe it a proven fact – or, worse still, a fact that needs no proof at all. Between Rogerius and Tylor, did empirical investigations take place? Did, perhaps, the European intellectuals come to an empirical conclusion, which was based on non-empirical considerations in Augustine and Calvin?

To answer these questions, we need to take a brief look at the intervening period. In the next two chapters, I will not merely investigate the way western writers looked at Indian religions, but go further: I will also suggest that their results can be better appreciated if situated within the context of the internal problems of Christianity – and within the context of the European culture of the time.

CHAPTER THREE

# THE WHORE OF BABYLON AND OTHER REVELATIONS

*A Medieval Dissertation*

Imagine a medieval monk at the turn of the fifteenth century – or, if you will, a student in a university, which would at that point be nearly four hundred years old as an institution of learning – writing a *status quaestionis*. The subject of the treatise, on the eve of discoveries and exploratory journeys into the Asian continent, is the knowledge the Europeans had of these nations, cultures, and peoples. What would have been its content? Though an exercise in imagination, the constraints on such a *status quaestionis* are objective enough to identify its probable skeletal content.

While composing such a treatise, the first thread that would have gone into the tapestry would have been about the exotic nature of the far-off lands. Even if our medieval monk and the university student disagreed about the geographical location of Asia – hardly a unique medieval disease, it appears – they would unanimously agree that Asia was exotic: besides normal creatures and unknown animals, they would write, weird and quixotic monsters live in these parts of the world. People with one monstrous foot (I doubt that they would have had the lame in mind), no head at all but with eyes in their chest...Thus would the list of oddities have gone on. Restrained only by their imagination, the authors would have referred to writers from the Ancient world – both Greek and Roman – as sources of information. Our pious monk might even cite *De Civitate Dei* of St. Augustine while discussing the question of the attitude that Christians should take with respect to such fantastic creatures.

The second thread in the tapestry would be about the great quantities of wealth available in these countries. Vast amounts of gold and precious stones were easily recoverable; ants were trained to recover golden nuggets from the soil; the great variety of spices in Asia, not to mention its silk production...Again, the list would have been limited only by imagination.

The third aspect of the *status quaestionis* – our monk might have gone into it at greater length – would be about a kingdom in Asia ruled by a devout and pious Christian king: powerful and mighty, he was ever ready to march towards Europe in order to join his Christian brethren and deal a deathblow to the 'Moors.' The 'lost' Christians of Asia, converts and the followers of the Apostle Thomas, had built a peaceful Christian kingdom, where milk and honey flowed on streets paved with gold. (Apparently, it is not just today's 'immigrants' to Europe and America who entertain such fancy dreams.)

In brief, both our monk and the university student would have entertained a recognisably similar picture of Asia. How could they not? They would have culled their information from the same sources – the nearly 1,600-year-old writings of the Ancients. The picture would also have been partially defined by the exigencies of the period our writers lived in. This was the picture that the early travellers and missionaries carried with them, when they ventured forth in search of new sea routes to the fabled lands collectively called 'Asia.'

## 3.1. A Modern Photo Album

*The Frame in the Early Snapshots*

To an interested observer from our times, two other elements that went into constructing this horizon of expectations would be important: the Biblical framework and the sources. The first of these would have been self-evident to both our monk and the student: it was obviously true that the people of Asia were the descendants of Noah. Though it was not clear which of Noah's sons went to Asia and populated its empty lands, there was little doubt that it happened exactly the way the Book and its commentators described. In other words, European travellers and missionaries knew the origin of and the truth about the Asian people even before they set sail eastward. There was, however, a question regarding the extent to which the Asian people knew of this truth: did they know that they were the descendants of Noah? There was also another question, which could only be answered empirically. It had to do with the religion of these people: had they preserved the 'true' religion or had they succumbed to heretic influences?

The second important aspect is the sources: histories and conquests of Alexander, the writings of Strabo and Ptolemy, the travel reports of Megasthanes and Pliny, and such.[1] If these hardly excite an anthropologist or an ethnographer of today, the reason is not far to seek: these consist mostly of reports about geography and the lay of the land (discussions about the size of the river Ganges, for example), accounts of the heroic feats of Alexander, some descriptions of animals (including camels and elephants), and so on. Regarding the mores of the people who inhabited the plains of the Indus, these Ancient authors appear almost totally devoid of curiosity. Of course, there is a mention here and there of the existence of different social layers (anachronistically translated as 'caste' groups), of a group of sophists or gymnosophists, identified as 'philosophers' (*e.g.* Philostratus), of the 'admirable' courage of women who immolated themselves on the funeral pyre of their husbands. Then, of course, there are several reports of monstrous beings. Most of the reports are based on hearsay: Megasthanes is generally the source for the reports about society (*e.g.* Arrian's *Indica*, Strabo's *Geography*) and Ctesias of Cnidus – a critic of Herodotus – is the authority on fabulous races and monstrosities (see Lach 1977: 87-99). As I say, nothing to get excited about.

What is interesting about this situation is not the absence of curiosity and fascination about the cultures and practices of Asians on the part of the Ancients. (To be sure, our histories prattle on endlessly about the Ancients as embodiments of human curiosity, but I will let that pass). These sources were nearly 1,600 years old when Europeans took them as ethnographic descriptions of Asia of their own time. Of course, I do not mean to imply that the Europeans mistakenly thought that a Strabo or a Pliny was their contemporary. Nevertheless, the Europeans did treat the writings of Strabo, Pliny, *et al*, as though they were contemporaneous. It did not occur to them that many changes could have taken place in Asia in those many centuries that separated them from Pliny. I grant that this duration is insignificant on a cosmic scale, but I am sure we all agree that it is not a negligible interval in terms of human history. Observing this, Hodgen (1964: 34) says:

> …(I)n the take-over of anthropological tradition from Antiquity, the feeling for elapsed time was lost. Medieval scholarship seemed to have no realization that a people described by the ancients one thousand years before might no longer exist; that it might have moved out of its earlier homeland, or have been swamped by an invading culture, or, as the result of a cloud of circumstances, lost its old name and altered its old way of life.

Of course, several hypotheses spring to one's mind for rendering this state of affairs intelligible. At least one such would be familiar to us

---

[1] A convenient collection in English is Majumdar (Ed.) 1960.

from our textbook histories of the origin and growth of scientific theorising in the West. Briefly, this story would say that empirical observation and experimentation to test received truths became a generalised
attitude after the Renaissance and that, before this period, people were
content to accept the words of the authorities as truth. Though there
is some validity to this caricatured representation of historical developments in the West, I prefer to isolate another aspect.

My candidate is the epistemic orientation that is common to both
medieval scholarship and modern citizenry. Though implicit, it postulates a peculiar relation between knowledge and text: knowledge is
textual in nature. Given that the late medieval and early Renaissance
scholarship had access only to the texts authored by the writers from
Antiquity, it does not create a great deal of wonder that they made
use of these texts without worrying about empirical circumstances that
might have changed the fortunes of some groups of people. Now it is
a commonplace that since the fifteenth century, knowledge of other
cultures and groups has steadily accumulated by means of 'fieldwork'
and firsthand reports. Given that, how plausible is it to maintain that
the same epistemic orientation persists even today? In the following
chapters, I will attempt to make the claim acceptable even with respect
to modern-day ethnography.

Let us, then, outline the horizon of expectation of those intrepid
fifteenth century Europeans who knew something of Asia:

1. It was an exotic land – one had to anticipate the presence of strange creatures and even stranger customs.
2. It was a wealthy land – a great deal of profit could be made.
3. There were Christian communities – one needed to establish
   contact and, if need be, win them over to the Roman Catholic
   Church, away from any heretic influences.
4. There would also be pre-Christian groups and communities, descendants of Noah, perhaps sunk in pagan practices and erring
   ways – conversion would be necessary to save their souls.

The travel reports and the missionary tales that found their way
back to Europe and enjoyed immense popularity were written within
this horizon of expectations. The European populace that avidly con-
sumed such writings shared the same framework. To see whether this
claim is even approximately true, let us look at a few of those classics.
We will have time enough later in the chapter to meditate on the implications.

*The Picture in the Early Snapshots*

One of the earliest travel reports – by an anonymous Franciscan friar
from the middle of the fourteenth century, titled the *Book of Knowledge*

*of all the Kingdoms, Lands and Lordships that are in the World* (Markham, Ed., 1877) – is a good place to start a brief survey of the travel and missionary reports. This report is important to us because of its structure. As we will see, the way this friar structures his description of other countries and peoples has remained invariant across generations and centuries. That is to say, between this friar's report and typical modern-day ethnography, a surprising similarity is to be found.

In this report, we come across a medley of information: geography, climate, the coat of arms, physical description of the inhabitants (like their skin-colour), their achievements, and so on. Often a connection is made between the intellectual and psychological prowess of a people and the climate of the land they inhabit. Consider, for instance, the following paragraph about India and Tibet:

> In th(e) empire of CATAYO there is a kingdom called SÇIM which bor-
> ders on the kingdoms of SARMAGANT, BOCARIN, and TRIMIC...
> The Kingdom of Trimic is all surrounded by mountains which give rise to
> many fountains and rivers. This land has a very healthy climate...so that
> those who are born and live here have very long lives. They are men of
> clear understanding and good memories, learned in the sciences, and live
> according to law...That is because they are at the birthplace of the east,
> and the rest of the towns and great cities, and the root of this kingdom
> are all due to the temperate climate which tempered their bodies and the
> good extended to their spirits, and gave them better understandings and
> good memories...Beyond these are the people of India who are near the
> equinoctial line. Their land is very hot. Most of their towns are on the sea
> shore and there are many islands. So that the air receives moisture from
> the sea, and tempers the dryness and heat. In this way are formed beauti-
> ful bodies and graceful forms, with fine hair; which are not produced by
> heat, except that it produces dark colour...(Markham, Ed., 1877: 49.)

What makes this citation important for our purpose is the fact that the author makes no distinction between *geo*-graphy and *ethno*-graphy. Both *graphein* are at the same level of description; epistemically speaking, knowledge of both *ethnos* and *gè* share the same status; that is, there is no distinction (either in principle or in practice) drawn between the knowledge of flora and fauna and the knowledge of other peoples and cultures. As knowledge, what distinguish them are the objects they talk *about:* in one case, it is about alien environment; in another, it is about alien groups. Because of this, in the same paragraph, he will talk arbitrarily about the flags and coats of arms, the location of the land, and the achievements of the people. Further, this anonymous Franciscan friar assumes that knowing another people and culture is equivalent to gathering information about them.

As time progressed and the number of travellers and missionaries multiplied, the ensuing reports retained the same structure. What changed, however, was the space allocated to the different items: instead of just a few lines, geography is accorded several paragraphs; the achievements of the peoples – whether laudatory or defamatory – take pages; new paragraphs about the structure of the houses, clothing of the people, the nature of the currency, the shapes of the animals, and more, make their appearance. Despite this, the general structure remains the same.

Today's anthropology and ethnography are the heirs of our Franciscan brother, except that they are far more systematic than he ever was. Today, we are treated to a neatly organised and ordered medley of information: the first chapter will be about the geography of the land with an accurate map of the region. This is followed, normally, by a chapter about the demography of the region, the sex distribution of the population, the division of labour, the festivals and seasons, the housing pattern, *etc.*, of the particular village or tribe, which the anthropologist intends to study. Only after these chapters will our ethnographer begin with his ethnography (*e.g.* Rohner and Chaki-Sircar 1988). While this 'scientific' orientation distinguishes our modern-day anthropologist from his religious brother, what unites them is the idea that *ethno*-graphy is on par with *geo*-graphy. To know a people and their culture is to have a descriptive acquaintance with them, in the same way that knowing the flora and fauna of a region requires a descriptive acquaintance. If you are a botanist or a zoologist, you need to go to the areas where the specimens are located, so that you may meticulously observe and record. If you are an anthropologist, then the same practice is called 'doing fieldwork.'

When contrasted with the writings of the Ancients, the novelty of the sixteenth and seventeenth century travel reports consists mainly in the two new domains they highlight: morality and religion. This is not to suggest that they imparted no new information or that they were merely reproducing tales from the Antiquity. In so far as they were describing the kingdoms they visited, the courts of the kings (both indigenous and Muslim), the structure of the houses, the clothing and eating habits of the populace, and so on of the sixteenth and seventeenth century India, they were after all providing facts absent from the records of the Antiquity. For example, when Duarte Barbosa described 18 different 'caste' groups of South India in the second volume of his *Account of the Countries Bordering on the Indian Ocean and their Inhabitants* written in 1610-20 (Dames, Ed., 1812b), he was ahead of Megasthanes, who described only five. For the purposes of this essay, however, none of the above is relevant; they are just details, elaborating, embroidering, and filling out the categories of information outlined by the writers from

Antiquity. Hence, I will speak only of the two novel domains mentioned above – morality and religion.

### 3.1.1. What is 'Modern' about Sexual Liberation?

Morality first. Running as a red thread throughout these reports is a description of the sexual mores of the Indians. Generally, they present a picture of these peoples as sexually loose, "much addicted to licentiousness," as the sixteenth century Venetian Nicolò Conti (Major, Ed., n.d.: 23) formulated it. In what way? *First,* there are reports about the wives that the indigenous kings – specifically the South Indian kings of Vijayanagara during the sixteenth and seventeenth centuries – were supposed to have had. The numbers are astronomical, varying from a mere thousand to a phenomenal twelve thousand. Conti speaks of twelve thousand wives of the king of Vijayanagara, which he calls 'Bizenegalia' (Major, Ed., n.d.: 6); Tomé Pires speaks of the king of Cambay having "up to a thousand wives and concubines" in his *Suma Oriental* (Cortesão, Ed., 1944: 41)

*Second,* there are stories about weird practices of deflowering virgins. Duarte Barbosa, for instance, speaks of one such practice in Vijayanagara, referred to as 'Bisnagua' by him, in the following terms:

> And another sort of idolatry is practised in this kingdom. Many women, through their superstition, dedicate the maidenhead of their daughters to one of their idols, and as soon as they reach the age of twelve years they take them to the monastery or house of worship where that idol is, accompanied with exceeding respect, by all their kindred, holding a festival for the maid as though she were to be married. And outside the gate of the monastery or church is a square block of black stone of great hardness about the height of a man, and around it are wooden gratings which shut it in. On these are placed many oil lamps which burn by night, and these gratings they decorate for the ceremony with many pieces of silk that they may be shut in and the folk outside may not be able to see them. On the said stone is another stone as high as a stooping man, in the middle of which is a hole in which is inserted a sharp stick. The maid's mother then goes inside the grating with her daughter and some other women of her kin, after great ceremonies, have been performed, "as to which I have scant knowledge by reason that they are concealed from view", the girl with the stick *takes her own virginity and sprinkles the blood on those stones,* "and therewith their idolatry is accomplished." (Dames, Ed., 1812a: 222-223; my emphasis.)

As a footnote to this text, the editor adds the following comment:

It is improbable that the practice described here was in any way universal, or widely spread among all classes. It was evidently connected with *the phallic worship* denoted by *linga*, and was probably considered as equivalent to marriage of the girl to the god Siva (*ibid*, 222).

The editor then goes on to cite other 'authorities,' like a certain Mr. Nicholson, who mention similar practices and suggests that the account given by Linschoten was perhaps taken from Barbosa.

However, there were other ways, more pleasurable ones, of achieving the same goal. The only catch, in 'Choromandel' any way, was that you had to be a Brahmin – as Thomas Bowrey tells us in his *Geographical Account of Countries Round the Bay of Bengal, 1669 to 1679* (Temple, Ed., 1905: 24). Bowrey's subjects are "young girls of about 10, 11, 12 years of age", whom the Brahmins in the temple of Jagannath wish to deflower. These 'priests', continues Bowrey's narrative,

> perswadeinge theire parents that they must, Upon Such a night, be Entertained in the Pagod, and that theire Patron Jno. Gernaet will appear to them and embrace them, makinge them Sensible of many transcations, which they must be very attentive too, not declareinge any thine to man, Woman, or Child, Save to the Brachmanes; and *thus Seldome or never passeth away one night but one young Virgin or more are Soe robbed of their Virginities by Some of these insatiable Idolatrous Priests*... (my italics).

One can easily picture the moral outrage this English gentleman must have felt when confronted with such abominable practices.

Obviously, not all Brahmins found the task of deflowering virgins pleasurable. In Calicut, Ludovico Di Varthema tells us (Badger, Ed., n.d.: 141)

> when the king takes a wife he selects the most worthy and the most honoured of these Brahmins and makes him sleep the first night with his wife, *in order that he may deflower her. Do not imagine that the Brahmin goes willingly to perform this operation. The king is even obliged to pay him four hundred or five hundred ducats* (my italics).

The editor cites two other writers to confirm that this was indeed the practice of the king of Calicut. But the king of Tarnassari, a place about whose identity there is some controversy, does not cause his wife's virginity to be taken by the Brahmins as the king of Calicut does, but he *causes her to be deflowered by white men*, whether Christians or Moors, provided they be not Pagans (*ibid*: 202; my italics).

*Third*, there was another interesting feature to the sexual practices of the Indians: wife swapping. Varthema, who tells us of this story, must have been a phenomenal person, a living refutation of everything that Linguistic science tells us about language learning. He could pick up language of the territories in a snap, and understood their conversation so well that he gives us a transcription of intriguing negotiations. The place is Calicut.

The Pagan gentlemen and merchants have this custom amongst them. There will sometimes be two merchants who will be great friends, and each will have a wife; and one merchant will say to the other in this wise: "Langal perganal monaton ondo?" that is, "So-and-So, have we been a long time friends?" The other will answer: "Hognam perga manaton ondo;" that is, "Yes, I have for a long time been your friend." The other says: "Nipatanga ciolli?" that is, "Do you speak the truth that you are my friend?" The other will answer, and say: "Ho;" that is, "Yes." Says the other one: "Tamarani?" that is, "By God?" The other replies: "Tamarani!" that is, "By God!" One says: "In penna tonda gnan penna cortu;" that is, "Let us exchange wives, give me your wife and I will give you mine." The other answers: "Ni pantagocciolli?" that is, "Do you speak from your heart?" The other says: "Tamarani!" that is, "Yes, by God!" His companion answers, and says: "Biti Banno;" that is "Come to my house." And when he has arrived at his house he calls his wife and says to her: "Penna, ingaba idocon dopoi;" that is "Wife, come here, go with this man, for he is your husband." The wife answers: "E indi?" that is, "Wherefore? Dost thou speak the truth, by God, Tamarani?" The Husband replies: "Ho gran patangociolli;" that is, "I speak the truth." Says the wife: "Perga manno;" that is, "It pleases me." "Gnan poi;" that is, "I go." And so she goes away with his companion to his house. The friend then tells his wife to go with the other, and in this manner they exchange their wives...(*ibid*: 145-146).

The editor, Rev. G. P. Badger, regrets that he could not reduce these native phrases into readable 'Malayalim,' perhaps because it is not 'Malayalim' at all – as one of the experts whom he consulted informed him.

In any case, his marvellous linguistic ability stood our traveller in good stead, for in Taranassari, the city we have already come across before, Varthema and others faced a deep problem. Very much like the habits of their king, the pagan populace had developed some strange tastes. They also, we are told, before they conduct their wives to their house, find a white man, of whatever country he may be, and take him into their house for this particular purpose, to make him deflower the wife. And *this happened to us when we arrived in the said city.* We met by chance three or four merchants, who began to speak to my companion this wise: "Langalli ni pardesi," that is, "Friend, are you strangers?" He answered: "Yes." Said the merchants: "Ethera nali ni banno," that is, "How many days have you been in this country?" We replied: "Mun nal gnad banno," that is, "It is four days since we arrived." Another one of the merchants said: "Biti banno gnan pigamanthon ondo," that is, "Come to my house, for we are great friends of strangers;" and we, hearing this, went with him. When we had arrived at his house, he gave us a collation, and then he said to us: "My friends, Patanci nale banno gnan penna periti in penna orangono panna panni cortu," that is, "Fifteen days hence I wish to bring home my wife, and one of you shall sleep with her the first night, and shall deflower her for me." *We remained quite ashamed at hearing such a thing.* Then our interpreter said: "Do not be ashamed, for this is the custom of the country." Then my companion hearing this said: "Let them not do us any other mischief, for we will satisfy you on this;" but we thought that they were mocking us. The merchant saw that we remained undecided, and said: "O langal limaranconia ille ocha manczar irichenu," that is, "Do not be dispirited, for all this country follows this custom." Finding at last that such was the custom in all this country, as one who was in our company affirmed to us, and said that we need have no fear, my companion said to the merchant that he was content to go through with this fatigue. The merchant then said: "I wish you remain in my house, and that you, your companions and goods, be lodged here with me until I bring the lady home." Finally, *after refusing,* we were obliged to yield to his caresses, and all of us, five in number, together with all our things, were lodged in his house. Fifteen days from that time this merchant brought home his wife, and my companion slept with her the first night. She was young girl of fifteen years, and he did for the merchant all that he had asked of him. But after the first night, it would have been at the peril of his life if he had returned again, *although truly the lady would have desired that the first night had lasted a month.* The merchants, having received such a service from some of us, would gladly have retained us four or five months at their own expense... (*ibid*: 202-204; my italics).

The editor, in a footnote to this text, adds among other things:

I find nothing to confirm the flagrant profligacy described...Nevertheless, revolting as the custom appears to us, and difficult as it may be to account for so strange an illustration of human depravity, *I see no reason to doubt the veracity of Varthema's narrative* (*ibid*: 204; my italics).

Neill (1984: 396) makes a more general point about Varthema's accounts. He finds that this work is of immense importance and gives 'epistemological' reasons why we should believe the truth of his reports.

> Varthema was an excellent observer, and there *is no reason to doubt the veracity of what he writes;* indeed the naiveté of his account of various events and activities gives strong reason to believe that he is recording and not inventing (my emphases).

Apparently, the rest of Europe thought the same way too, for Varthema's writing attained immense popularity. For scores of years, it remained one of the main sources of information about India in Europe. Having appeared in Italian in 1510, it was translated almost immediately into Latin in 1511. In 1520 a Spanish translation appeared which was reprinted several times. In 1534 came a German translation, followed by a Dutch translation, printed in Antwerp in 1563. In 1577, it was translated into English.

While I do not want to quarrel with the taste of the European public of the sixteenth century, it appears to me that issue can be joined with the twentieth-century scholar on epistemological grounds. If naiveté is to be the criterion for the veracity of ethnographic claims, one wonders what to make of the equally naive belief that people in many cultures entertain regarding European and American women – that they are all whores.

In any case, I cannot tell you with any great certainty whether any or all of these ethnographic descriptions are true. But I must confess that the image projected, most beautifully expressed in the following 'anonymous' narrative from the sixteenth century, strains one's credulity even in these days of 'liberal' sexual mores:

> (In 'Calichut', men) marry one wife or five or six women, and those who are their best friends gratify them by sleeping with their wives, so that among them there is neither chastity nor shame. And when the girls are eight years old they begin to secure their gain by this means. These women go nude almost like the men and wear great riches. They have their hair marvellously arranged and are very beautiful, *and they entreat men to deprive them of their virginity, for as long as they are virgins they cannot procure a husband.* (Greenlee, Ed., 1937: 79; my emphases.)

*3.1.2. The Heathens and their Irreligion*

From sex to God then. All the travel reports are unanimous in agree-
ing that Indians were heathens and idolaters. As Barbosa puts it, "The
Kings of Malabar are heathens and worshippers of idols" (Dames, Ed.,
1812b: 7); he speaks of each 'caste' having its "own separate idolatry"
(*ibid*: 60-65). Pires says that the entire province is "full of idolatry and
witchcraft and every other heathen practices" (Cortesão, Ed., 1944:
73) and that the "heathen of Cambay are great idolaters and soft, weak
people" (*ibid*: 39). Conti speaks of "Gods" which are "worshipped
throughout all India" and of the feasts for the gods, performed "after
the manner of ancient heathens" (Major, Ed., n.d.: 27). An Indian
convert, a certain Priest Joseph, speaks of the people of 'Guzerat' as
"idolaters who worship the sun and the moon and cows" (Greenlee, Ed.,
1937: 111) and says that Christians and Gentiles populate 'Calichut'.
Continuing, he says

> And in order that this name of Gentiles may be known to every one, those
> are called Gentiles, who in ancient times worshipped idols and various
> kinds of animals...(*ibid*: 99).

Bowrey has the following to say of the native inhabitants of 'Choromandel,' whom he calls the Gentiles:

> They are a Sort of harmless idolatrous people; they Worship many Gods
> of Sundry Shapes, and metles, as Gold, Silver, brasse, Coppar, Iron &c.,
> many alsoe of Stone, clay, or the like, but theire Chiefe God of all is in
> forme of a man Somethinge deformed, and is Set up in theire great Pa-
> gods, or temples, and is very circumspectly and with great adoration at-
> tended and prayed Unto at all hours of both day and night, and many
> Others Set up in theire Pagod Courts and small Stone buildings thereunto
> adjoyneinge, beinge of most hideous Shapes, as Satyrs, Cows, bears,
> Rhinocerots, Elephants, &c.,...worshippinge them with Strange and ad-
> mirable reverence. (Temple, Ed., 1905: 6.)

Many also identify Brahmins with the clergy, calling the former explicitly as "priests." Speaking of the Brahmins, Varthema says, "you must
know that they are the chief persons of the faith, as priests are among
us" (Badger, Ed., n.d.: 141). Barbosa identifies them as the "priests of
the heathen" who manage and rule their houses of prayer and idol-wor-
ship (Dames, Ed., 1812a: 115) and compares them explicitly with the
"clergy among us" (*ibid*: 33). Bowrey has a firm opinion too.

The Brachmans are theire Priests, but I am Sure, and without all controversies, very Diabolicall Ones. (Temple, Ed., 1905: 13.)

Even more categorically:

As for those Seduceinge and bewitchinge Brachmans, they beare great
Sway over the Gentues in Generall, causeinge all (or most of them) soe
much to confide in theire Sorceries and faire Stories, as if they onely were
the true Worshippers of a Deity, and noe Other Sect to live Eternally save
theire Owne (*ibid*: 23).

Again, it is Varthema who spells out things very clearly:

The king of Calicut is a Pagan, and worships the Devil...They acknowledge that there is a God who has created the heaven and the earth and all
the world; and they say that if he wished to judge you and me, a third and a
fourth, he would have no pleasure in being Lord; but that he has sent...his
spirit, *that is the Devil*, into this world to do justice: and to him who does
good he does good, and to him who does evil he does evil. Which Devil
they call Deumo, and God they call Tamerani. And the king of Calicut
keeps this deumo in his chapel...(which has) a wooden door covered with
Devils carved in relief. In the midst of this chapel there is a Devil made
of metal, placed in a set also made of metal. The said Devil has a crown
made like that of the papal kingdom, with three crowns; and it also has
four horns and four teeth, with a very large mouth, nose, and most terrible
eyes. The hands are made like those of a flesh-hook, and the feet like those
of a cock; so that he is a fearful object to behold. All the pictures around
the said chapel are those of Devils...(Badger, Ed., n.d.: 37).

Such descriptions cannot stand alone without an appropriately diaboli
cal mode of worship. The pagans pray in this manner, Varthema tells
us:

They lie with their body extended on the ground and very secret, and they
perform certain *diabolical actions* (or motions) with their eyes, and with
their mouths they perform certain *fearful actions* (or motions); and this
lasts for a quarter of an hour...(*ibid*: 149; my emphases).

Bowrey also gives us a description of a temple and a feast:

The Bengalas (viz. the Idolatrous people of the Countrey) have very
Strange ways of worshippinge their Gods (or rather Devils) they Set up

in their Pagods, as alsoe in theire owne houses, which images are of a most hideous Shape, that these poore Ignorant Souls doe soe much diefie, and torture theire owne persons for the Silly humors they hold adoreinge them, one of which as followeth:–

In the Month February, they publickly Shew theire Earnest devotions, and what they will Suffer for the Sake of their *Irreligious Molten Gods...* (Temple, Ed., 1905: 197; my emphases.)

To some, even the daily practices of the Jains appeared to be an expression of abomination and idolatry. The unwillingness or the refusal of the Jains to hurt or kill animals was, of course, idolatry:

This people eats neither flesh nor fish, nor anything subject to death; they slay nothing, nor are they willing to see the slaughter of any animal; *and thus they maintain their idolatry and hold it so firmly that it is a terrible thing.* (Dames, Ed., 1812a: 111; my emphases.)

And there are people today, who go around arguing for vegetarianism on moral grounds, oblivious to what our learned Barbosa has to say on the subject. Finally, some others mention the practice of immolation of widows at the funeral pyre of their husbands, which was highlighted as an illustration of the immoral practices of the heathens of India.

### 3.1.3. Snapshots Superimposed

In sum, these travel reports do not deviate in any fundamental sense from the early framework that guided their journeys. Next to the fabulous wealth that one could accumulate, there was the added incentive (one supposes) of free, easy, and uncomplicated sex. Alongside this was the confirmation that these people were mere heathens and idolaters, which made it obvious that there was little that one could learn from them.

Again, I cannot claim that all travel reports of the period are of the same kind or quality. I have not been able to study them all. But those that I have – some are cited in the body of the text – do present the picture sketched above.

There is, it appears, another series of reports (mostly in the form of letters) produced by the missionaries: *Lettres édifiantes.* From what I have been able to glean about them, they paint the same kind of image about the Indians – as heathens and idolaters who are immoral.

This relation between religion and morality is not a surprising connection. One of the beliefs of people of this period was that morality required grounding in religion. Where such a foundation was lacking

– after all it was lacking in idolatrous cultures because they only had 'false' religion – it was evident that morality would be absent.

It should not come as a surprise either that morality was described in terms of sexual mores. One can easily find out, especially if one is a genius like Varthema, whether and when the commandment "Thou shalt not commit adultery" is violated. How to find out when "Thou shalt respect thy parents" is fulfilled or violated? These travellers, in case you feel like donning the Freudian hat, were not really so much obsessed by sex as they had a problem; not a sexual problem, as the philosopher explained to the policeman, but an epistemological one: how to observe the fulfilment of a moral norm.

Whether I am right in identifying the kind of problem these travellers confronted or not, I think that the general picture that emerges from the foregoing does provide us with an idea of the image of the other that was beginning to crystallise in the Europe of that period. Though I would like to, it cannot be my intention to sketch the outlines of that image in this essay. What is more relevant to my concerns is to emphasise that none of these travellers asked the question whether there was religion in India. As I said at the beginning of this chapter, their assumption was that heathens and idolatrous populated the continent of Asia. The facts, of course, did not falsify it.

This was the first phase. In the coming periods, people were to ask more probing questions: What kind of beliefs guided these idolatrous practices? What were the 'varieties' of idolatry prevalent in the Indian subcontinent? In other words, the following generations began to fill in the details. By then, however, the framework was set. To appreciate this situation and these generations better, however, we need to move back across the oceans and into the heartland of Europe itself. It does not matter where this heartland was situated, because as one knows only too well...

## 3.2. ALL ROADS LEAD TO ROME

It is a platitude to suggest that to understand the spirit and the times of the sixteenth-century Europe, one has to come to terms with the schismatic movement within Christianity. Lutheran and Calvinist reformation had just begun to shake the foundations of the Papal authority and the Catholic practices. It is neither my intention nor is it in my capabilities to discuss the origin and causes of this religious and social turmoil. It is sufficient to note the terms of the debate and dissension regarding the nature of true religion.

### 3.2.1. Some Four Reference Points

*The first* pillar on which the debate rested was the question of idolatry and the immense importance of battling against it. The *second* pillar supporting the edifice had to do with the degeneration and corruption of religion. The *third* spoke of the relationship between Man and God, while the *fourth* raised the issue of truth. Though it is a simplification to put it that way, these four points of reference are all we need to appreciate the way in which the age of Reformation defined the terms of the debate forcing all to respond likewise.

To begin with, the battle against idolatry assumed great importance. Within the Catholic Church, the role of icons and images in the lives of the faithful had often been a contested issue. Both the iconoclasts and the anti-iconoclasts had clashed swords regularly over the centuries on this matter. What happened in the sixteenth century, however, went beyond anything Catholicism had known before – in depth, in ferocity, and in scope. From images to relics, from church altars to the blessed saints, and ultimately the ritual celebration of the Catholic Mass itself – all of these came under vicious and pulverizing attack. There was little difference, as the learned laity and some of the members of the clergy argued, between the Catholic rituals and those of the early pagans. Miracles belong to yesterday and cannot be performed by the images of the saints venerated by the masses. Catholicism was corrupt; the Church belonged to the Anti-Christ; idolatry ruled over the faithful.

Such a criticism of Catholic Christianity requires to be made plausible. The Reformation appealed to the Apostolic and early Christianity to speak of the fall and corruption of the Catholic variety. How to account for this degeneration? The Medieval thinkers had prepared the intellectual ground much earlier by utilising the Euhemerian and Epicurean doctrines to 'explain' pagan religions. Now, the Protestants attempted an account of Catholicism along similar lines. The newly discovered theorists from Antiquity fanned the dormant and half-forgotten 'theories' awake. Pagan criticisms of 'religion' was pressed into service by friends and foes alike. Did Christian rituals show surprising similarities with pagan rituals? In the eyes of the Catholics, it merely confirmed the long-known fact that all peoples had a common religion 'once upon a time.' While the majority of mankind fell prey to the machinations of the Devil, the memory of this common religion was preserved in their rituals (albeit in an impure form); this accounted for the 'similarities' that the Protestants made so much of. To the Protestants, of course, this similarity testified to the fact that Catholicism had taken over the idolatrous rituals of the pagan religions. In brief, Catholic Christianity was merely 'Christian paganism.'

If the Euhemerian theory was used by the Catholics to account for the pagan deities, the Protestants utilised it to explain the veneration of the saints by the Catholics. Egyptian and Delphic priests held the masses under the sway of ignorance and superstition, cried the Catholics; that is what Papal Rome and its clergy have done, denounced the Protestants. Thus, the story went on. (For details, see Manuel's excellent 1959.)

Third, to make matters worse, the Reformation thinkers postulated a more intimate relation between Man and God. Though Zwingli (e.g. Stephens 1992; see also Preus 1977; Locher 1965) was more restrained, Calvin (Grislis 1971) provided us with a picture of Man who could not but bear witness to God. For Zwingli, religiosity was selectively scattered among men and was not a universal achievement. Yet, by suggesting that a 'thirst after God' existed in virtue of the fact that man was made in His image, Zwingli appeared to postulate this thirst as a universal drive. Calvin differed on this score. He suggested that both Nature and the Book made it impossible that one could not see the revelation of God. Cicero, the "eminent pagan," came in handy too: after all, had he not himself said that all men had an innate sense of divinity? Consequently, argued both Zwingli and Calvin, God ought to be worshipped properly, that is, one had to return afresh to the Book in order to find the scriptural grounds for worship. In fact, what distinguished human beings from beasts was the relation between Man and God: Man knows that he is a servant of God, whereas the beasts lack this awareness. Calvin formulates it thus in his *Institutes* (1.3.3):

> Thus Gryllus, also, in Plutarch (*Lib. quod bruta anim. ratione utantur*) reasons most skilfully, when he affirms that, *if once religion is banished from the lives of men*, they not only in no respect excel, but are, in many respects, *much wretched than the brutes*...the only thing, therefore, *which makes them superior* is the worship of God, through which alone they aspire to immortality. (Beveridge translation, Vol. 1: 45; italics mine.)

As Preus (1977: 200) suggests,

> Zwingli could allude to the same idea, but instead of referring it to man's nature, he linked it to God's specific action: in order that *man might not fall into a bestial condition*, God kept calling him back when he lapsed into forgetfulness of his Creator (emphases mine).

Within the context of the Roman *religio* and its relation to culture, it is obvious why Man is but a beast if he does not revere the gods. Calvin appropriates this idea and makes it into a theological truth. Formulated simply, the Reformation suggested that religious sense was deeply ingrained in human consciousness.

Of course, this alone is not sufficient for human salvation. This brings us to the fourth reference point. Between the 'natural' religiosity and human salvation, there exists both a chasm and a bridge. The chasm was the degeneration into idolatry; the bridge was provided by the 'true' religion. How to know which was the bridge, and which, merely an illusion? The question, in other words, of *the religious truth*. One had to choose, at the risk of eternal damnation for failing to do so, between apparently competing Christian groups. From Bern through Bavaria, Christians began to define their loyalty along different axes than the ones before.

The details, both theological and social, are not important for us now, but two fundamental consequences are. First, this period defined the way in which the European intellectuals would approach the question of religion from then on. Second, in doing so, it posed the question about the truth of religion in an excruciatingly sharp form.

In a nutshell, and to redescribe it in different terms, paganism became an issue during the Reformation. The reappearance of this issue does signal that it was actual once upon a time: as we have seen in the previous chapter, the milieu within which Christianity grew was pagan in nature. It also does more. The resurfacing of this theme nearly 16 centuries later is deceptive from the beginning. It is not the 'same' paganism despite the fact that the same figures (Cicero, Plutarch, *et al.*) and the same protagonists continue to speak the same words. Now it is paganism not just with sacerdotal robes, but with a Christian soul as well. The arguments of the early church fathers against the Roman *religio* were now used as a weapon against Catholic Christianity. For example, Plutarch's *On Superstition* was wielded as a weapon against the Catholics. These indicate not only the distance separating the European intellectuals of that period from their own cradle, but also the extent to which the 'other' had now become a domesticated variant of one's own 'self': paganism becomes a recognised and recognisable deviation in Christianity.

In the previous chapter, I alluded to this process of domestication. What we see in the Reformation period is merely a confirmation of the depth of this process. To use a biological metaphor, the conception of Christianity occurred within the womb of another – the Judaic and Pagan milieux. The development of a foetus depends very much on its environment, *viz.* the womb of the mother. Unable to separate the contribution of the milieu from those processes internal to the foetus, biologists speak of an interaction of the organism with its milieu when conceptualising the growth of such an entity. In a way, such is also the case with Christianity. Thus, when the Reformation thinkers appealed to 'primitive Christianity', they had to appeal at the same time to the milieu, which housed it. That is, an Apostolic Christianity comes together with its apologetics, criticisms, and defensive postures against the pagan environment it grew in. In this sense, Protestantism had to transform Catholicism into paganism. The dissemination of the Ancient texts among a wide layer of the intellectuals, which the Italian Renaissance had inaugurated, together with the appeal made by the Reformation leaders to the early Christian movement, allowed the crystallisation of an extraordinary situation. One could not reappropriate 'primitive Christianity' without embracing its enemy -- the Ancient paganism. The polemic of early Christianity against the pagans was both modified and reproduced by the Protestants. The 'revival of Classical learning' lent a special poignancy to the whole episode: the texts of the Ancients had found a second birth.

One wonders what might have happened if the circumstances did not so fortuitously come together the way they did. In any case, the pagans and the Christians could now continue their interrupted debate a full 1,600 years later -- with the Pope playing the Pagan in Rome and a Calvin playing the Christian in Geneva. With the crucial difference, however, that when Protestantism challenged Catholicism, it was not really challenging the pagan 'other' that the early church fathers contended with: it was, above everything else, a confrontation of Christianity with its own childhood and past. In the process of transforming their own history into paganism, the European Reformation thinkers were sending out a signal that they were now, truly, unable to understand paganism. They had rediscovered the texts of the Ancients, but were unable to understand the messages. In the wings, waiting for their cue to confound matters further, were the ideologues of the 'Enlightenment' -- men who would utilise both of the discoveries of their previous generations: the discovery of the pagan texts and the discovery of the pagan cultures.

To see what they made of it – again not in detail but in outline – we need to move toward Paris, the "New Athens of Europe" as Peter Gay calls the Enlightenment Paris. Before we do so, let us take stock of the situation, as Europe stood poised to enter the "Age of Reason."

### 3.2.2. On the Eve of a Reasonable Age

The religious schism within Europe had many consequences for the study of the newly rediscovered cultures. The earliest of them was in the domain of human resources. The battle with the Protestants reduced both the number and the quality of the missionaries available to visit and stay for a long period among the heathens. Those who were nonetheless dispensable to the Orders were very reluctant to learn the languages of the natives because proficiency in the native tongues most certainly meant that they would be grounded for a long time on foreign soils:

> India was the first high culture that the missionaries encountered in the sixteenth century, and they soon found that it had within it as many or more regional linguistic, religious, and social divisions as Europe itself. Because of their limited numbers, their dependence upon the Portuguese, and their reluctance to compromise with the native cultures of India, the missionaries had only limited success in evangelizing the heathens or in understanding the people with whom they worked. *The most important first step in the penetration of India, the learning of the native languages, they were very slow to undertake.* The Franciscans, the earliest in the field in significant numbers, appear to have been particularly reluctant to apply themselves to language study...(N)o evidence exists to show that the Franciscans seriously began language study until near the end of the century, after they were admonished to do so by papal brief, royal declarations, and a direct command of their Custos and Commissary-General. They generally communicated through lay interpreters, though a few of them knew an Indian language by 1600. (Lach 1965: 278-279; italics mine.)

Or, as Neill (1984: 127) portrays the refusal of the Portuguese to learn Indian languages:

> One of the major problems that had to be faced was the almost pathological refusal of the Portuguese to learn any Indian language. In the second half of the century some went so far as to recommend the elimination of the Indian languages and their total replacement by a *lingua franca*, in this case of course Portuguese.

In effect, the result was that during the early centuries of contact between the Europeans and the Asians, the 'knowledge' the former had of other 'religions' in India was based on what those natives of India proficient in European languages could or would tell the missionaries. Their answers depended on how they understood the questions raised by the Christian missionaries. The latter's queries would have been constrained by their horizon of expectations, which we have had an opportunity to notice. Consequently, we can compress the 'knowledge' the European missionaries had of India thus: heathens and idolaters populated most parts of the Indian continent.

This situation would not have been so bad, were it not for the Protestant challenge to Catholic Christianity. As we have seen, by raising paganism from the dead, the Protestant reformation posed the question of religion as a relation between the false and the true: the false worship of the pagans as contrasted with the true worship of the Christians. During the early phases of the religious controversy, however, the living pagans and contemporary heathen cultures did not influence the discussion. When Calvin, for example, railed against the Pagan Rome, his pagans were still the Ancients. As I have already suggested, the rediscovery of the Ancient texts and an appeal to the pure and 'primitive' Christianity mutually reinforced the tendency to reproduce the old battle of Christianity against Pagan Rome – 1,600 or so years later.

*Knowledge of the Natives…*

Earlier (chapter #2.2), I spoke of the way Christianity appropriated the history of humankind in terms of the past of one people. The missionaries and travellers who started rediscovering countries and cultures of Asia, I suggested above, gave flesh and blood to this picture: the heathens and the pagans were the descendants of Noah who had somehow managed to retain vague memories of their past. Among other things, this belief meant that the Europeans had knowledge about the people of Asia that the Asians themselves did not have. One of the implications of this belief was the implicit or tacit acceptance of the idea that there was little for the European Christians to learn from the heathen and idolatrous societies.

Consequently, the only kind of knowledge that Europeans could extract from their renewed contacts with other cultures and peoples was knowledge about these natives – both in form and in content no different from the kind of knowledge they acquired about the fauna, flora, weather, geography, *etc.*, of these countries. Hence, as we have already had an occasion to notice, the information that these reports gave about the people of other cultures was sandwiched between descriptions of weather, the currency, the elephant, the structure of the houses, and such.

Quite obviously, as time progressed, the demand grew for a more accurate knowledge about the natives. Belatedly, European missionaries began to discover that the conversion of the natives would not produce the desired fruits unless one understood the natives. It was not sufficient simply to describe the people as heathens and idolaters, which they surely were. One also needed to make *sense* of their hideous and abominable practices. How to go about doing this?

In the previous chapter (#2.2.1), I also suggested that Christianity, already in the early centuries, had established a specific relationship between beliefs and practices: actions expressed or embodied the beliefs the individuals had. Protestantism revitalised and revivified this idea not merely by establishing a direct relation between man and God – without intermediaries – but also made it necessary that actions really did express what one believed in. One could not, argued Calvin, participate in Catholic Rituals – not even for the sake of preserving one's life – even though one had a pure faith in God and was not 'really' worshipping the idols by indulging in such ceremonies. The outer trappings of worship must be congruent with the inner reverence that one had toward God. Calvin's criticism of the Nicodemites (mostly of the French Protestants) was the theological argument against simulation. As far as Calvin was concerned, even feigned idolatry was false worship. Irrespective of the intentions of the worshippers, false worship is objectively evil and misdirected. Even though the service of God, argues Calvin, is located primarily in one's heart, external actions are the public confessions of faith. Consequently, to conform to the idolatry of Papal Rome, even if conceived as deceit, is an affront to God:

> The Christian man ought to honour God, not only within his heart, and with spiritual affection, *but also with external testimony*...(A)fter both body and soul in man have been consecrated and dedicated to God, it is necessary that his glory shine forth just *as much in one as it does in the other*. (Calvin, *Petit Traicté*. Cited in Eire 1986: 258; my emphases.)

In other words, acquiring knowledge about the natives – that is to say, to understand other cultures and their practices – meant finding out what the native believed in. To describe the belief systems of the heathens was to understand and make sense of their actions. More importantly perhaps, it would enable the Christian missionaries to spread the Gospel by suitably 'reinterpreting' it using the languages and belief systems of the natives.

### ...and the Problems of Proselytisation

The problems that the Christian missionaries faced in India were the eternal problems faced by any proselytising religion: how best to root out erroneous beliefs and replace them with correct ones? Christian missionaries tried the only two routes that they knew: persecution and criticism of beliefs. The Portuguese, for example, declared an all-out war on the Brahmins, who apparently offered the greatest resistance to conversion: exile, deprivation of their livelihood, *etc*. In 1545, King John III of Portugal produced a series of detailed instructions for the Governor of Goa, D. João de Castro:

> In this brief the king orders that neither public nor private "idols" be tolerated on the island of Goa and that severe punishment must be meted out to those who persist in keeping them. The houses of people suspected of

keeping hidden idols are to be searched. Heathen festivals are not to be tolerated and every Brahman is to be banished from Goa, Bassein, and Diu. Public offices are to be entrusted to neophytes and not to heathens; Christians are to be freed from heavy labour at the port of Goa, such tasks in the future being reserved exclusively for heathens. Portuguese, under pain of severe punishment, are forbidden to sell heathen slaves to Muslims, since heathens are converted more easily to Christianity under the Portuguese and to Islam under Muslim ownership. Revenues previously used for the support of mosques and temples should be diverted to aid in spreading the gospel. The governor should help the vicar by building churches and schools, by limiting the anti-Christian activities of the King of Cochin...heathens everywhere should be prevented from painting pictures of Christ, the Virgin, and the Saints, and from peddling them from door to door. Many of these directives soon acquired the force of law, and on occasion the viceregal law was more severe than the king's instructions (Lach 1965: 239-240).

The persecution of the heathens, however, was apparently neither consistent nor thoroughgoing enough to satisfy the blood lust of the Jesuits and the missionaries in Goa. For example, Francis Xavier wrote a letter (January 20, 1548) to King John III complaining "about the failures of the governor to support the mission and reproaching the king for not being more severe with his servants" (*ibid.*):

All that is needed for everyone in India to become Christian is for your Majesty to punish a Governor severely. (See Lach 1965: 236-286 for more details.)

They also tried to reward the heathen converts by providing jobs. However, the Portuguese administration began to suffer from the induction of incompetents purely on grounds of their Christian conversion.

The Orders had apparently been assured that most of the menial posts in the administration at Goa would be given to neophytes and orphans in their charge...This was an important arrangement...(Nevertheless, an) honest administrator probably preferred a Hindu of influence and experience to a neophyte whose only claim to a job was his Christianity (Lach 1965: 237).

Notwithstanding persecution, 'paganism' appeared difficult to eradicate. One could, and did, ban festivals, burial of the dead according to 'heathen' practices, *etc.* As Massarella (1990: 44) formulates it:

> In Goa...the destruction of temples and attempts by ecclesiastical councils to eradicate the rites and the ceremonies of the Hindu and other religious communities, as well as efforts to convert the local population to Christianity met with no...(great) success.

Lach (*ibid*: 243) again:

> Long experience with the...(Jews and Muslims) had convinced most churchmen that no quarter could be expected or given in the struggle of the monotheistic faiths. In India, where the gods were many, the Churchmen expected that compromise might be more easily worked out, but in this they underestimated the strength of the Brahmans and their control over the deeply rooted Hindu ways of life. Although temples were destroyed, baptisms forced, and religious leaders exiled, the church found that conversion to the ideas, values, and practices of Christianity was impossible to effect quickly. Clearly it took more than baptism, a European suit of clothes, and a new job to make a Hindu desert the customs of his fathers and take up foreign practices of the Christians.

But Goa was not the Roman Empire, the Portuguese governor was not the Emperor Constantine and Paganism in India was not the same as that of Rome. Neither was the Christian God so willing: after all, the ways of the Holy Spirit are said to be mysterious. Thus, an important weapon in Christianising the Roman Empire – the backing of political power with its attendant economic and coercive power – did not now deliver the goods that it did once.

Forced thus to take the second route – criticism of beliefs – Christianity began creating the Gestalts that we recognise today: Hinduism, Buddhism, Shintoism, Taoism, Confucianism, *et al.* These Gestalts were built up initially by reporting the beliefs that Indians held about their gods: the most popular ones were those about the ten 'incarnations' of Vishnu. Convinced as the Europeans were that these beliefs were all scripturally sanctioned (Hindu scriptures, of course), the hunt was on to locate the 'Holy Book' (to begin with, in singular) of the Hindus. The Augustinian majesty of criticising the 'inconsistent' myths of the Ancients and the 'immorality' of their gods was reproduced with a mind-numbing monotonicity and inanity on an ever larger scale: missionaries began to 'debate' with the Brahmins on the consistency of their scriptures. Given the lack of mastery of the 'holy language' of the heathens (Sanskrit) or even of the vernaculars, the 'texts' had to be acquired by the connivance of the natives through theft, browbeating and even downright forgery. However, these 'translations' did not alter the picture of what was known about the religion of the Indians; they merely began to fill in the details. Of course, it did not occur to these missionaries or to the readers of their exploits – how could it? – that they could be creating religions (to be subsequently called Hinduism, Buddhism, *etc.*) around the texts that they so feverishly began to search, translate and study. To make sense of the pagans, of this they were quite convinced, one needed only to find their 'theology.'

Of course, having texts is not enough. One needs to understand these texts as well, that is, interpret these texts. Again, knowing a language does not automatically guarantee an understanding of the texts or of the cultures whose texts they are. This elementary truism confronted the European intellectuals with respect to the texts of the Ancients too: did they, could they, understand the pagan authors, their civilization and culture, because they had Latin translations of their texts? What could they make out of Cicero's *De Natura Deorum* or Plutarch's *On Superstition?* How could they understand what was *religio* to the Romans by reading a dialogue or two?

Europe, on the eve of *Aufklärung*, was a confluence of all these (and more) crisscrossing threads, undercurrents and problems. To see what they made of it is to understand how and in what sense Tertullian's battle cry of centuries ago retains its validity even in the Paris of the eighteenth century.


## 3.3. "What has Paris to do With Jerusalem?"


*About the Porch of Solomon*


In the third century, Carthage was a principal theological centre for the Latin-speaking world. At the beginning of the century, one of the most prominent speakers for the Carthagian Church was Tertullian, a convert into Christianity. A lawyer by profession, a believer by conversion, and a heretic at death, Tertullian was a tireless defender of Christianity and a valiant battler of heresies like Gnosticism. In a tract titled *The Prescription Against Heretics,* he exclaimed:

> What has Jerusalem to do with Athens, the Church with the Academy, the Christian with the heretic?

What Indeed? Nothing at all, affirmed Tertullian (full text in an old translation in Roberts and Donaldson, Eds., n.d., Vol. III):

Our principles come from the Porch of Solomon...I have no use for a
Stoic or a Platonic or a dialectic Christianity. After Jesus Christ we have
no need of speculation, after the Gospel no need of research. (Alternate
translation cited in Dulles 1971: 43.)

Many modern writers are not so convinced that Tertullian is right. They
do believe that Christianity was influenced by the Stoic doctrines and
that research is needed even after the Gospel. Yet there are others (one
thinks of Kierkegaard in this connection) who are not very sure that
such influences were all for the good. In a very different way, during
the past two decades, a similar question has come to the fore: What has
Jerusalem to do with Paris? Both Cantwell Smith (1962) and Buckley
(1987) believe that the French Enlightenment sealed the way some
questions have been raised about religion ever since: believing or not
believing in the existence of God, they suggest, was never really a hallmark of being religious until the *Philosophes* appeared on the scene. To
Buckley, this indicates the extent to which Christianity has become a
theism having removed Christology from its centre; to Cantwell Smith,
it indicates the extent to which 'belief' has replaced 'faith' in the discourse about religion *tout court*. In other words, Jerusalem (they might
say) does not need the "Modern Athens" any more than it needed the
"Classical Athens".

This is not the place to get embroiled in the old controversy between
'faith' and 'belief.' We will have an occasion to brush against it elsewhere
(chapter 9). However, this is the place for us to mix our metaphors a
bit. It is the orthodoxy today to suggest that the French *philosophes*
were the 'fathers' of criticism of religion. Let us, therefore, invent a
modern Tertullian in defence of this 'church' of reason and put the
following question in his mouth: What has Paris to do with Jerusalem?
Our modern-day Tertullian would give the same answer as Tertullian of
yesteryears: he would say, "nothing!" That is, he would suggest, though
if it was not for Jerusalem, Paris could not have launched its critique
of religion, the contribution of the Enlightenment period neatly breaks
with the religious doctrines and dogmas that held men in bondage for
centuries. As I say, this answer is the orthodoxy.

What would a heretic answer to the question be? Paris has everything to do with Jerusalem, which is to say, the answers of Paris are the
answers of Jerusalem too. The Enlightenment period did not break with
either the questions or the answers of Jerusalem. In other words, as a
heretic, I would say that I do not see any great gulf between the Porch
of Solomon and the banks of the Seine.

Before going any further, a warning requires reiteration. The outline
sketch I am providing of the historical developments in less than a paragraph a century should not be confused with a historical explanation

or with a summation of historical happenings. In the vast tapestry that history is, all I am after is *one thread*. Tracing such a thread threatens to transform the figure into the ground. While inevitable, it also tends to project a magnified image of the thread as the *locus* of all events and happenings. This, however, is not my claim: neither what went before nor what follows should be seen as anything other than just one element in an extremely complex period and process. This said, let me return to the point at hand – how I could be right against a modern-day Tertullian.

### 3.3.1. On the Banks of the Seine

Let us begin with the question that Protestantism raised: the relation between Paganism and Christianity. Because this modern day paganism had paraded for centuries as the Christian religion, the question was really about the truth claims of Christianity. Which of the Christian religions is the true religion? Both the formulation of this question and the process of answering it required some understanding of what paganism was. That is to say, Protestantism enabled paganism to testify in the religious battle about truth. The evidence that paganism provided became vital for settling the question of religious truth. To the Enlightenment thinkers, this issue was also the starting point.

*Second*, as a corollary to the above, the Enlightenment thinkers accepted the evidence that paganism presented. Before asking what they made of it – an issue around which these thinkers built up their formidable reputation – let us ask what kind of paganism testified in the courts. Earlier on, I spoke of the double problem with which paganism confronted the European intellectuals: to understand the Ancient pagan texts and to make sense of the living pagan cultures. The period solved this problem in the most evident way – by making use of one to illumine the other. The Ancients (*i.e.* their texts) rendered the religious practices and beliefs, ceremonials and rites, of both the savage and civilized parts of the world meaningful. In exactly the same way, the contemporary pagans helped Europeans to understand the Ancients better (Manuel 1959; McGrane 1989). That is to say, over the generations, Europeans began to see a common, human experience in these 'congruencies.'

Histories of the Enlightenment period never tire of mentioning the challenges to religion posed by the thinkers of that period. However, not many of the very same histories mention that the problem had already taken a very insidious form by then. The claim Christianity made about the universality of religion – that each human being carries a sense of divinity in him (to put it in characteristically Calvinistic form) – was, to be sure, challenged by the *philosophes*. Yet they accepted as a datum that

all cultures had religion in some form or another. That is, they accepted
the existence of a domain of religious experience that was universal
across cultures. How could one use the Greek and Roman texts to
understand the meaning of Egyptian, Indian and Native American ceremonies, rites, *etc.*, and the latter to understand those very texts of the
Ancients? Only by presupposing that they had to do with the same kind
of experience. It can hardly be called an extraordinary achievement: all
that happened to a religious claim was merely a restriction in its scope.
Instead of all individuals having an innate sense of divinity inscribed in
their hearts, it would now appear, all cultures have an identical experiential domain – the religious.

It is here that one observes an epistemic superiority of the religious
claims over the 'theories' of our Enlightenment thinkers: Christianity
insisted that there was a difference – a very big one, in fact – between
being 'religious' (which meant being a Christian, to be sure) and being
a 'heathen.' Irrespective of the grounds on which such a claim was made,
Christians did not like to generalise their experience across time, space
and culture. Our Enlightenment thinkers had no such qualms: sitting in
their salons, over a bottle or two of good red wine, they had entered that
phase of intoxication where one is gripped and seized by the feeling of
universal brotherhood. Why retain the religious domain as the exclusive
property of the Jews and the Christians, they must have thought. The
claim of the Christians was testable: after all, it was a universal statement. The *philosophes* pounced on it with glee precisely for this reason.
Their own alternative, however, was a singular statement: all cultures
know of one common domain – the religious.

By saying this, I do not want to suggest that the *philosophes* were
blind to the possibility that Nations could survive not knowing of any
kind of religion. After all, Bayle and Voltaire had their famous controversy precisely with respect to the possibility of a Nation of Atheists.
However, the difficulty lay in conceptualising such a society: how, in
the absence of a conception of God, could such a Nation survive at all?
Why would people keep the promises they make, if they did not fear
punishment in the hereafter? How could a culture emerge in such a
society, where people could never rely on each other's word? Neither
commerce nor industry would be possible; ruin and desolation would
be the fate of such a nation of atheists.

Even here, the ground was prepared by the Christian missionaries.
Almost a century before the famous debate between Bayle and Voltaire,
the Jesuits were embroiled in a controversy with the Franciscan and
Dominican orders about this issue. To these Christians, as well as the
massive reading public that followed these disputes avidly for nearly
a century, it was not a debate about a hypothetical society. Instead, it
was about an old and civilized culture: China. The accumulating travel
reports about the Africas and the Americas were suggesting that most

of the native peoples there knew neither of God nor of the Devil. When the Christian missionaries met the Chinese culture, however, the issue took on an explosive form. The Confucian thought did not appear to countenance either God or the Devil. If this 'doctrine' was native to the Chinese culture, how was the nation to be characterised before 'Buddhism' came there? The latter, a religion of the illiterate masses, was mostly written off as gross idolatry. What about the Confucian doctrine?

Fuelled partially by the rivalry between different orders within the Catholic Church (the Jesuits on the one side and the Franciscans and the Dominicans ranged on the other), and partially by the genuine need to understand an alien culture, the conflict and the dispute required the intervention not merely of Sorbonne but of the Holy See itself. (See the brilliant work of Kors 1990, which should be read as a correction to Manuel 1959, 1983.)

What was at stake in this discussion, which lasted a century, conducted both in the pages of the popular press and through scholarly tracts? Let me allow two Jesuit fathers from the eighteenth century to come forward and testify. The first is Louis Le Comte:

> Would it not be...dangerous [for religion] to [say] that the ancient Chinese, like those of the present, were atheists? For would not the Libertines draw great advantage from the confession that would be made to them, that in so vast, so ancient, so enlightened, so solidly established, and so flourishing an Empire, [measured] either by the multitude of its inhabitants or by the invention of almost all the arts, the Divinity never had been acknowledged? What would become thus of the *arguments that the holy fathers*, in proving the existence of God, drew from the consent of all peoples, in whom they claimed that nature had so deeply imprinted the idea of Him, that nothing could erase it. (Italics selectively retained.) And, above all, why would they have gone to all the trouble of assembling with so much care all the testimonies that they could find in the books of the gentile philosophers to establish this truth, if they had not believed that *it was extremely important* to use it in that way...? (Cited in Kors 1990: 171-172; second italics mine.)

Almost a hundred years into this furious debate, Joseph Lafite wrote a tract summarising the discussion. Pleading the cause of the Jesuits, he warns his fellow-brethren to take heed:

> One of the strongest proofs against [the atheists]...is the unanimous consent of all peoples in acknowledging a Supreme being...This argument would give way, however, if it were true that there is a multitude of nations...that have no idea of any God...From that, the atheist would seem

to reason correctly by concluding that if there is almost *an entire world of people that have no religion*, that found among other peoples is the work of human discretion and is a contrivance of legislators who created it to control people by fear, the mother of superstition (*ibid*: 177; my italics).

Lafite sought to "reestablish the proof," as Kors emphasises (*ibid*),

however, not against the arguments of any atheists, but against a whole seventeenth-century tradition of his fellow learned Christians.

### On the Nature of a Hybrid Beast

Such a paganism, subpoenaed to testify in the ecclesiastical court, however, was a hybrid beast: it was a paganism that lived among the peoples and cultures of Asia, but one that came to the witness box clothed in the sacerdotal robes of the Ancients. Antiquity rendered meaningful the contemporary paganism, which, in turn, threw light on the texts of the Ancients. Consequently, both kinds of 'pagans' could be assimilated into each other as expressions of heathendom. The multiple gods of the Indian subcontinent were just like the pantheon of the Greeks and the Romans. Both were witnesses to idolatry and polytheism. In charitable moments, one was even willing to reconcile the 'worship' of animals as a way of allegorising virtues: after all, had not some of the Ancient thinkers themselves said so? Many decades later, in the hands of Sir William Jones, the father of British Orientalism, this identity between the Graeco-Roman paganism and the contemporary heathendom was to take a grotesque form stimulated by the newly emerging domain of linguistic science conceived at that time as comparative linguistics. (See Olender 1989 for some details.) In a series of lectures published in the *Asiatick Researches*, Jones (1789) argued on etymological grounds that the Ancient pagans and the Indian heathens not only expressed the same kind of religiosity but also that they worshipped the same gods.

The claim that the pagan religion was an invariant phenomenon across cultures is not limited to missionary reports, the Enlightenment thinkers, and the Victorian Orientalists. In the authoritative *Encyclopaedia for Religion and Ethics*, only recently supplanted by *The Encyclopaedia of Religion* under the editorship of the late Mircea Eliade, one discovers that Cicero is able to 'explain' the theological orientation of an Indian peasant:

The Hindu villager has no conception of the reign of law in the natural world. The occurrence of miracles is a matter of daily observance. He appeals to minor rather than the greater gods, because the latter have, in his belief, in a large measure lost touch with humanity, and no longer interest themselves in the petty details of his ordinary life ('Magna di curant, parva neglegunt' [Cicero, *De Natura Deorum*, II, 66, 167]) (Crooke 1913: 710).

Better still, one could simply mix up the Roman civilization with that of India as the following delightful paragraph from the same entry evidences. Speaking of the fact that religion in India has "often been compared with Gibbon's account of the state of religion in the Roman Empire," Crooke goes on to say:

'The various modes of worship which prevailed in the Roman world were all considered by the people as equally true; by the philosopher as equally false; by the magistrate as equally useful'. Like the brahmin vedantist 'the devout polytheist, though fondly attached to his national rites, admitted with implicit faith the different religions of the earth. Fear, gratitude, and curiosity, a dream or an omen...perpetually disposed him to multiply the articles of his belief, and to enlarge the list of his protectors.' The modern semi-educated Hindu resembles the 'ingenious youth...alike instructed in every school to reject and to despise the religion of the multitude'. There is, again, a philosophic class who 'viewing with a smile of pity and indulgence the various errors of the vulgar, diligently practised the ceremonies of their fathers, devoutly frequented the temples of the gods.' Lastly, the Anglo-Indian magistrate 'know and value the advantages of religion, as it is connected with civil government' (*ibid*: 712).

It must be obvious, which parts come from Gibbon and which do not.

Even though it took a while, this assimilation of Ancient Greek and Roman 'religions' into Asian paganism was an accomplished fact by the time the Enlightenment was into full swing. A neat division of the world into heathens, Christians, Jews and, in some cases, Muslims (often called Mohammetans) came into being by virtue of this assimilation. This is not the only legacy of the Enlightenment. The world was neatly divided in other ways too.

### 3.3.2. About the Pagans and the Primitives

Ancient paganism, as one well knew, antedated Christianity. In the Age of Reason one felt that the 'moderns' were far ahead of the Ancient civilizations of Greece and Rome. The various traveller and missionary reports had laid bare the superstitious, licentious and barbaric practices of the contemporary pagans as well. The idolatry and zoolatry of the Indians that demeaned the dignity of Man; the 'Sutti' tradition of burning widows in the funeral pyre of their deceased husbands; the adultery and wife-swapping that ran through the daily life of the Indian people, *etc.*, were parts of the same picture, as we have seen. These images were painted with colour when one discovered half-naked savages running around in Africa and the Americas, cannibalising each other, lacking script or culture, leading a life fit only for the beasts and – oh, Lord! – their souls lost for ever because they were yet to hear of The Saviour. The time, in other words, was now ripe for a developmental ordering of the human history with paganism representing the 'childhood' of Man.

One cannot accuse the *philosophes* of not living up to intellectual challenges, whatever else they may be guilty of. Indeed, they responded magnificently: seated in their salons, impressing ladies and the laity alike with their fire and eloquence, they spun out splendid tales of growth of Man from childhood to maturity. Pagans, whether dead or living, were indubitably at a lower rung of the ladder, separated by the brutish savages from the Africas and the Americas by just that – a rung. It is no fault of the *philosophes* that they pictured it in this fashion. There was, and is, objective ground for it: a ladder, after all, is made up of rungs.

You must not, however, think that all Indians shared this singular honour of being placed alongside the pagans from the Graeco-Roman world. There were whole groups of people in what is now Sri Lanka, for example, who did not even have a language. Poor souls, they went around grunting to each other like the animals that they were. Today, mistakenly one supposes, we call the same grunts a language – the Sinhalese.

> Max Müller quotes Sir Emerson Tennent to the effect that the Veddahs of Ceylon have no language: "they mutually make themselves understood by signs, grimaces, and guttural sounds, which have little resemblance to definite words or language in general." In fact they speak Sinhalese (an Indo-European tongue) (Evans-Pritchard 1965: 106).

Hence came into being the tale of the 'primitive': a man, a psychology and a society. Human history also achieved a developmental ordering, stretching from the primitive to the modern. The first person to formulate this thesis explicitly was the French thinker Bernard Fontenelle. Consider, for example, his claims about the primitive man: the 'order' in nature could not be apprehended by the primitive man. And why ever not? The answer is obvious: one could experience the order, said Fontenelle, only if one knew that the universe embodied the 'divine plan.' The primitive man did not experience the world this way because he could not think 'abstractly'. Instead, what characterised the primitive man was his 'concrete' thinking, because of which he did not arrive at the idea that the universe was governed by the plan of God. Of course, Fontenelle is correct when he says that the primitive man did not look at the universe the way the Jews, the Christians and the Muslims do: after all, the primitive man did not know of these religions. However, this is not how it appeared to Fontenelle; for him, the perception of harmony as divine plan indexed the extent to which humankind had progressed from its primitive days. To make this otherwise inane argument acceptable, he appeals to the picture of the 'primitive', which is as pathetic as his discourse. One needed to have developed the capacity for 'abstract' thought and ability to 'reflect' in order to perceive that there is a harmony and that it evidences a divine plan. By definition, the primitive man was incapable of it. It cannot be otherwise: this way of experiencing the world is more typical of the Semitic religions than other cultures and other religions. Nevertheless, for Fontenelle and many others who followed his example, this 'theology' exhibits the ability to think abstractly.

Hume in *The Natural History of Religion* accepted this argument. He believes too that 'personification' of natural forces accounts for the origin of religion. It is idolatrous in nature, and those who have idolatry in their midst are barbarous and ignorant also because of their defective cognitive development:

> In the very barbarous and ignorant nations, such as the AFRICANS, and INDIANS, nay even the JAPONESE, who *can form no extensive ideas of power and knowledge*, worship may be paid to a being, whom they confess to be wicked and detestable; though they may be cautious, perhaps, of pronouncing this judgement of him in public, or in his temple, where he may be supposed to hear their reproaches.
>
> Such rude, imperfect ideas of Divinity adhere long to all idolaters; and it may be safely affirmed, that the GREEKS *themselves never got entirely rid of them*. (Hume 1757: 353; emphases mine.)

Contrasted with this is the 'higher' and the 'more advanced' notion of the deity. This God of the Semites is undoubtedly an advance, or so the argument goes, because it evidences that man has begun to form 'abstract' conceptions. In this context, consider the following passage from Hume:

> But (to) a barbarous, necessitous animal (*such as a man is on the first origin of society*), pressed by such numerous wants and passions...an animal, compleat in all its limbs and organs, is...an ordinary spectacle...Ask him, whence that animal arose; he will tell you, from the copulation of its parents. And these, whence? From the copulation of theirs. A few removes

satisfies his curiosity, and set the objects at such a distance, that he entirely loses sight of them. Imagine not, that he will so much start the questioning, whence the first animal; much less, whence the whole system or united fabric of the universe arose (*ibid*: 312; my italics)

There is a delicious irony to this passage. To appreciate the irony, however, we first need to provide a possible interpretation. The primitive man does not go far enough in the procreation series. Consequently he cannot raise – leave alone answer – those questions that are indicative of his advanced and abstract concept formation. The primitive man is satisfied with the answer that some few members have an ancestor; he does not persist in following it through until he reaches the absolute beginning. In both theology and philosophy of religion, there is an argument that does precisely this. Called the 'cosmological argument' for proving the existence of God, it argues that since each member in such a series has an ancestor, there must be a single beginning for the entire series. However, this is not a logical consequence but a fallacy. The characteristic of infinite series is that at any arbitrary point, a given member could have an ancestor without it being true that there is one absolute beginning for the entire series. Nor is it a logical truth that different such series (animals, human beings, inanimate objects, *et al*) have the same unique ancestor. Because we are talking about events, processes, and objects within the universe that encompasses us, it is not evident what kind of series we are dealing with. As Bertrand Russell put it in his discussion with Father Copelston so long ago:

> I can illustrate what seems to me your fallacy. Every man who exists has a mother, and it seems to me your argument is that therefore the human race must have a mother, but obviously the human race hasn't a mother – that's a different logical sphere (Russell and Copelston 1948: 479).

The delicious irony is this: the primitive man, who cannot reason abstractly, is nevertheless being logical when he loses 'interest' in pursuing the question of the beginning. The 'civilized' man, allegedly more advanced in abstract thinking, commits a logical fallacy. Hume, in other words, makes such a logically perceptive thinker into a primitive.

What makes this situation even more intriguing is that such ideas survive to this day in several domains – in psychology, in anthropology, and elsewhere. In psychology, it is axiomatic today that children and the 'primitive' think concretely; whereas the hallmark of adult and scientific thinking is that it is abstract. In anthropology, the fieldwork of the last two centuries was in and about 'primitive' societies. It is interesting to note that the reputed anthropologist Adam Kuper recently wrote a book (Kuper 1988) tracing the origin of the 'myth of the primitive' in anthropology, convincingly demonstrating that the object of these field-works simply did not exist. Even if most anthropologists are rid of this myth today, it is canonised in the writings of Piaget, Vygotsky, and their followers as attributes of thought. Fascinating -- is it not? - how a religious and theological idea - the distinction between 'concrete' and 'abstract' thinking - has acquired universal currency in a secular mantle.

## The Enlightenment of the World History

I have already called your attention (chapter #2) to the fact that a universal human history came into existence by appropriating the past of all human groups into an imagined past of one group – the Jews. During the Enlightenment, a new twist is added to the old story. Even though the ground was being prepared from the days of Giambattista Vico, it is said that the notion of a secular universal or human history comes into being during the Enlightenment. Not having done any research into the question myself, I will accept this claim as true. If true, it is important to know how this new sense of history comes into being. If false, it is merely a question of what happened to the old sense of history.

It appears to me that the conceptual requirement for writing the universal history of humankind is that multiple stories about real or imagined pasts of different peoples are mapped on to at least two constant factors: a shared beginning and an underlying pattern. These two are not sufficient for writing such a universal history, as made clear by discussions about "evolutionary direction" and "evolutionary progress" (see Nitecki, Ed., 1989). They are, nevertheless, necessary. The fictitious 'primitive' man – with both a psychology and society – provided such an absolute beginning during the 17th and 18th centuries. As I have already suggested, the assimilation of Ancient Graeco-Roman cultures and the contemporary non-Christian cultures into 'paganism' enabled the Enlightenment thinkers to continue along the lines of their Christian predecessors: the empirical history of Europe became identical to the history of humankind. The movement from 'ancients' to the 'moderns' was the framework of such a universal history. Contemporary cultures of Africa, the Americas and Asia – being pagan and idolatrous – were where the 'ancient' pagans were some 1,800 years ago. No matter *how* one ordered the 'epochs' – a term coined by the French Bishop Bossuet – of human history, be it a Comtean or a Marxian periodisation, the point is that the pasts of other peoples and cultures were mapped onto the empirical history of the European Christendom. There is but one history, the Human history, which somehow happens to be coextensive with the European history.

The identification of human history with European history is hardly novel, of course. Biblical chronology had already performed this feat long ago. After all, human beings were the descendants of Noah directly and of Adam indirectly. When this provincial history of a fragment of humankind was *the* history of the Cosmos, how is it possible to leave the rest of humankind out?

One of the first writers from within Europe to challenge this identification was Isaac La Peyrère in 1640-41 with his *Prae-Adamitae*. His heresy, which he was forced to recant, included among other things the claim that man existed before Adam and that the Bible was the history of only the Jews and not the whole of humankind. Consequently, he argued, the Flood was a local event in Palestine and the world might have been going on for a long time. (See Popkin 1979, chapter XI and, for the evolution of the debate, Livingstone 1987.)

Fully two decades before that, Fabian Fucan, a Japanese 'apostate' was making a similar point in a notorious polemical tract *Ha Daiusu* (*Deus Destroyed*). In 1636, an ex-Jesuit Christovão Ferreira wrote *Kengiroku* (*Deceit Disclosed*) showing the implausibility of Biblical chronology. (Translation of both these Japanese texts, with an exhaustive and illuminating introduction, is to be found in George Elison 1973.) What is interesting about these episodes is the self-evidentness they manifest: the Biblical chronology was quite obviously wrong in one culture, whereas it was self-evidently true in another. (See Olender 1989; Aarsleff 1982 for its impact on linguistic science.)

The Biblical chronology was to exercise an intellectual dominance for another 200 years. What happened afterward is a secularisation of this religious identification of human history with Christian history. Western history becomes human history now. So deep is this identification, that a writer could write in 1987:

*When humanity was liberated from tyranny by the French revolution...*

Humanity liberated? The colonisation of Asia and Africa postdates the French revolution and the genocide of the Native Americans was already well into its first phase when "humanity was liberated." (Unfortunately, I am unable to find back the reference at this moment.) This was an inevitable consequence, as well as the conceptual presupposition, of a developmental ordering of human history.

Where did 'religion' fit in this history? Again, Protestant polemic against Catholic Christianity was taken over and secularised: instead of Catholicism being a 'degeneration,' religious developments represented the 'human error'. Whether all religions were expressions of human error or not, it was obvious that polytheism or – its synonym in that period – idolatry was. *The* human history shed some light even on this phenomenon: the frailty of the recently developed ability of humankind to think abstractly.

## How Does One Get to Jerusalem?

The claim of this subsection must be clear enough by now: the Enlightenment *philosophes* simply travelled further along the road to Jerusalem. They were as far away from Ancient Athens as is possible: "Modern Athens" is closer to the Old Jerusalem than it is to Classical Athens or Rome. In other words, a whole series of beliefs that are typically Christian was secularised by the sons of the Age of Reason. True, they fought battles with 'religion,' but their own contribution was simply to strengthen the grip of religious ideas by giving them a secular mantle. In this sense, it appears to me, Jerusalem has everything to do with Paris – no matter what a modern-day Tertullian may claim.

Remarkably enough, when the Catholic Church was raising problems about the issue of the universality of religion and when, as a conclusion to a dispute, the Pope was willing to acknowledge that a nation without religion (whether true or false) could exist, then the sons of the Age of Reason began to construct their theories of religion, which tried to explain why religion had to be a cultural universal. In doing so, these progressive intellectuals took a step sideward and backward – sideward in so far as they did not address the issue at all and backward because they naturalised a theological theme in the sense that they made God's gift to humankind (as the Christians saw their own religion) into nature's gift to humanity. Formulated slightly differently, an empirical question about the origin of Christianity became a theoretical question about the origin of religion pure and simple. 'Why did Christ emerge amidst the Jews?' became 'Why did gods emerge in human communities?' The Enlightenment thinkers universalised a religious theme by secularising it. We will soon see (chapter 5) what this move amounts to; for now, let us merely record what happened.

Within the cultural matrix of the post-Reformation period, mostly the partisans fought wars: the reports and representations of others were tailored to answer the vexing problems of their period. All parties began to create a picture of the 'other' on at least one common assumption: to know their 'religion' is to know the 'other.'

The sixteenth- through eighteenth-century travel reports began to build up a series of images and pictures of other cultures in two distinct, if interrelated, ways: on the one hand, a description of cults, religious practices and beliefs; on the other, interpreting and explicating the former by reference to 'similar' phenomena involving the Ancients. Both aspects were to be found in these travel reports, and they were assimilated thus as well. Here are some of the consequences:

1. The universality of religion was soon to be challenged during the French enlightenment, but the problem had by then taken on a more insidious form: a universal domain of religious experience.

Such a domain is but a mere restriction in scope of the earlier Christian belief in the universality of religion.

2. This enabled a reorganisation of the division between modes of thinking. One could distinguish between a 'superstitious' and a 'rationalist' mode of thinking.

3. With this division, the problem of 'progress' could be formulated differently, the answers to which were to colour the intellectual outlook in Europe for a long time. How did this superstitious mode come into being? What sustains it? How could one make a transition to a rational way of cognition?

4. As Ancients became assimilated with the other 'savage' and civilized groups, the notion of the primitive man and his society began to crystallise. The invention of the primitive was the counterfoil against which the 'progress' of Europe could be recorded and measured.

5. The emergence of a secular domain of human history was to describe this movement from the barbaric to the civilized: the European history became *de facto the history of humankind.*

Even though the seventeenth-century traveller's reports of exotic cultures came formatted and ready for immediate digestion, the eighteenth-century intellectuals laid the first framework for its ingestion and subsequent dissemination. One of the most important characteristics of this movement was its indulgence and obsession with the question of the origin of religion. The Biblical chronology was sacrosanct, although challenges to it were incipient. This meant that most discussions took place within the biblical history – including the origin of religion. Speculations regarding the latter focused upon paganism and primitive man. This contributed to the birth of the primitive and to assimilating the Asian culture with those of the Ancients. The distance between the two was bridged by the 'evolution' of mankind – from the primitive to the modern through the pagan.

# CHAPTER FOUR

# MADE IN PARIS, LONDON, AND HEIDELBERG

So far, we have concentrated mainly on the developments in the European continent while tracing the history of the evolution of our theme. This was necessary because these developments were primarily responsible for defining the way the Europeans would approach the question of understanding religions in India. The framework and the questions were decided in Europe; the answers could only be provided in India. Let us pick up our story somewhere at the end of the eighteenth century – the tail end of the French Enlightenment – by looking at the two fundamental problems that Christian missionaries confronted in bringing God's word to the heathens of India.

## 4.1. EVANGELICAL QUANDARIES

As I have suggested several times during the course of the last two chapters, Christianity postulated a specific relation between beliefs and actions. The Christian understanding of Man suggested that actions mostly expressed the beliefs held by individuals. The post-Reformation period laid a great weight on this relation. Appropriate beliefs were not only necessary in order to save one's soul from eternal damnation, but it was also important that these beliefs found an adequate and proper expression outwardly. A 'true' Christian is one who has learnt to bring these two aspects together; that is, he has developed an attitude, which allows him to act as a Christian. Never absent from Christianity, this theme resurfaced under the banner of 'piety'. This theological orientation, like others of its kin, bristles with delicious and intriguing dilemmas that hold most of us spellbound to this day: what is the relationship between willing (or 'intending' in contemporary idiom) and acting? What could one say about the intentions by looking at the actions of individuals? Why and what kind of a gap exists between intending and acting? If the characteristic property of human action is its intentionality, what kind of gap could possibly exist between one and the other? These questions arose in the religious and moral contexts of Christianity. Their generalisation across other contexts need not detain us here, either with respect to their applicability elsewhere or with respect to their validity.

## 4.1.1. A Conceptual Quandary

When intellectuals and/or missionaries of one culture approach another within this framework, some kinds of problems are bound to arise – as the Europeans were soon to find out. To begin with, the stock of concepts the Europeans used to understand the other was poor: 'heathens' or 'pagans'; 'idolaters' or 'devil worshippers'; 'zoolaters' – these three concepts just about exhaust the intellectual richness of the European cultural framework and its theory for understanding the other. As Richard Baxter, in *The Reasons of the Christian Religion* (1667), formulates it regarding "the several religions which are in the world",

> Four sorts of Religions I find only considerable upon earth: The meer Naturalists, called commonly Heathens and Idolaters: the Jews: the Mahometans: and the Christians. The Heathens by their Oracles, Augures and Aruspices, confess the necessity of some supernatural light; and the very Religion of all the rest consisteth in it. (Extracted in Pailin 1984: 154-157.)

For more than two centuries, these notions proved adequate as far as the Europeans were concerned. These concepts apparently enabled the Europeans to understand the cultures and peoples of Asia, Africa, and the Americas (not to mention the Greece and Rome), by classifying them under these two or three categories. As Sharpe summarises (1965: 25-26) the attitude of the Evangelical Protestants of the nineteenth century:

> Non-Christian religions (in this case Hinduism) were a piece with the corrupt world, and were summed up as "heathenism" or "idolatry". Early Evangelical missionaries were normally convinced as a matter of theological fact that the individual "heathen" in his darkness was doomed, unless he turned in faith to the sole remedy for his sin, the atoning death of Jesus Christ...Hinduism was a "false religion" *a priori*, the work of the prince of this world, not of God. Thus it was typical that Alexander Duff should call Hinduism "an old, pestilent religion" and that his fellow-Scotsman John Wilson should characterize Hinduism as "the grandest embodiment of Gentile error". Such terms of opprobrium might be multiplied almost indefinitely from the missionary literature of that period.

That they succeeded in understanding the 'other' based on these impoverished concepts is a fundamental achievement under any criterion but, please, do not ask me how this "European miracle" occurred. Not being a European, I cannot tell you much except to suggest that Europe must have really understood the other based on such flimsy categorisation. My evidence? The dominant writings of the period did not protest – or even indicate that a minority protested – that these concepts hardly helped them to understand other cultures. As though this was not enough, the theoretical 'sophistication' of the Enlightenment criticisms of religion was based on the 'data' provided by the missionary and travel reports. One assumes with good reasons that the intellectuals would have developed other notions if the above were not useful.

However, there are idolaters and idolaters – as the Bishop sighed into the ear of the Actress – whereas the problem is to distinguish between them. As a practice, there was little to distinguish one idol worship from another – unless it was with respect to the form, shape, and texture of the idols and the ceremonies that accompanied such acts of worship. Duarte Barbosa had already confronted this problem with respect to the several Indian 'castes' he had met. Though he appeared to have recognised the differences between them, his conceptual framework allowed him only to note that each of these groups "practised its own idolatry". Consequently, the only way of distinguishing idolaters from each other would have to consist of identifying the differences in their beliefs. That is to say, the differences in the practice of idolatry could be charted out according to the different kinds of beliefs held by the heathens.

*Sources of Belief and the Belief in Sources*

How to discover these beliefs? The initial attempt of the European merchants and the clergy is also the standard practice of anthropologists and ethnographers of today: eliciting information from the natives. While this often satisfies many an ethnographer and makes him believe that he has 'understood' (albeit partially) the natives, the Christian missionaries were well ahead of such anthropologists. They felt that they needed to understand the natives better, if they had to succeed in converting the natives into Christianity. Consequently, they began to search for the source of these beliefs.

What, however, could be the source of such beliefs? Again, to the Christians, it could not be anything other than texts. What kind of texts did they have to seek? After all, the Indian culture – being a literate one – had many, many texts. Clearly, reasoned the evangelisers, they will have to search and locate the 'religious texts'. Again, how could they recognise texts as 'religious' texts?

The only possible way open to them was to ask the natives. Which were their religious texts? Easier said than done, because how to be really understood by the natives? Christian missionaries, much like the ethnographers of today, are not the best equipped to raise and answer such epistemological questions. They knew that there must be a holy book or scripture – after all, the Bible assures us that God gave religion to all – and that they would merely have to find it. The heathens, afraid or suspicious, would not show them their holy book so easily.

Through their ethnological practice, they discovered that Indians often spoke of the 'incarnations of Vishnu'. Clearly, Vishnu had to be a heathen god, and the source of this story had to be a holy book. (*E.g.* Maurice devotes most of his massive two volumes *History* to depicting this story; Baldaeus records it as diligently as Dapper.) Besides, references were often made to 'Shastra', which actually means something like *Wissenschaft* and thus, they concluded, Indians had a holy book called 'Shasta'. Slowly, it became clear that there was yet another holy book – or was it a series of them? – called the 'vedam'. It was now obvious that the 'holy book' of the Indians was called 'vedam'.

This alone was not sufficient. Though many people had heard of the 'vedam' and spoke of its authority, not many knew what was in them. This state of affairs confirmed to the missionaries not only that the 'vedam' was a holy book but also, precisely because of its 'holiness', a secret book. After all, this was both expected and explainable: the books of 'magic', which the worshippers of the Devil relied upon, were secret and only in the possession of the few. To the 'libertines' of that period, the same secrecy confirmed yet another truth they knew all along: the real 'religion' survived only among a select few and the rest of the masses were sunk in deep error, prejudice, and superstition.

It is thus that the first translations of the Indian 'holy texts' began. Heathens were to be distinguished according to the beliefs sanctioned by their scriptures. That is to say, the Europeans believed that communities were united and differentiated from each other according to the beliefs they entertained.

To be sure, this was the experience of Europe. However, the applicability of this stance across other contexts and other cultures depends upon the truth of the other premises in the reasoning. If any/all of these premises are false, logical deduction does not guarantee the truth of the conclusion. In other words, this is a question for empirical enquiry. Yet, how many books on religion do not begin by defining religion as a mechanism of social integration? How many people do not definitionally decide the issue that religion transforms a set of individuals into a community? How many anthropological/ethnographic treatises do not describe the lives and practices of the Buddhist, Hindu, Shinto, Confucian, *etc.*, communities? Alas, indefinitely many. The line between the Christian missionaries guided by their religious beliefs and the modern day anthropologists guided by their 'sciences' appears continuous and unbroken.

In other words, faced with the empirical problem of transmitting God's word to the heathens, the Christian missionaries provided a series of theological solutions. Some kinds of 'texts' were 'holy', practices were guided and sanctioned by these scriptures, and communities were divided according to the 'scriptures' they apparently accepted. Only thus, and no other way, could the Holy Spirit animate the heathens of India – He/She/It also needed familiar landmarks of the Christian road in order to travel the heathen coast of Malabar.

### 4.1.2. A Social Quandary

The task of converting heathens into Christianity is a rewarding but difficult job – so tell(s) us the Public Relations department(s) of the Church(es) of God. This was definitely true in India anyway: materially rewarding for the marginalised heathens of India to become Christians, and socially difficult for the Christians to make headway and inroads into the Indian society. The reasons were double, as astute observers of that period accurately recorded: on the one hand, it had to do with the indigenous people and, on the other, with those who brought Christianity into India for the second time. You would be right to object that this is a banal observation. However, even profound truths are banal at times.

There were three fundamental obstacles for the conversion of natives into Christianity: the nature of Hinduism; the structure of social life; the role of the 'priests' of Hinduism, *viz.* the Brahmins. Let us briefly look at each of them by turn.

### "The Monkeys and their Playsome Whimsies"

Hinduism, the 'religion' of the Hindus, was amorphous. It was very difficult for the Christian missionaries to target their attack:

> ...Hinduism has never prepared a body of canonical Scriptures or a Common Prayer Book; it has never held a General Council or Convocation; never defined the relations of the laity and clergy; never regulated the canonization of saints or their worship; never established a single centre of religious life, like Rome or Canterbury; never prescribed a course of training for its priests. This is not due to the fact that war, or civic tumult, or foreign domination prevented the growth of institutions of this kind; but simply to the fact that all such action is essentially opposed to its spirit and traditions (Crooke 1913: 712).

Such a Hinduism appeared to 'resist' the onslaught of foreign religions, "anarchy and persecution", and hold grounds for ages. Crooke cites another author (Lyall, *Asiatic Studies*), who testifies:

> Taking things as they are now, and looking upon the actual state and movement of religions in India, an eye-witness would still be justified in affirming that this religion, although powerfully affected by social and political changes so strong and sudden that they would try the constitution of any national creed, is nevertheless not yet dead, nor dying, nor even dangerously ill... (*ibid*: 713).

Why is that? Because "it possesses wonderful powers of adaptation to novel conditions"; because it "has a fully organised and articulate social system" and so on.

However, long before this, Hume had pointed to an analogous difficulty involved in describing the nature of pagan religions. He thought that there was an important difference between a traditional, mythological religion and a systematic, theological one. This is the way he formulates the problem in his *Natural History:*

> The pagan religion...seemed to vanish like a cloud, whenever one approached to it, and examined it piecemeal (1757: 349).

About ninety years later James Mill was writing in *The British History of India,* a book that was extremely influential in defining the colonial policy in India, that

> Whenever indeed we seek to ascertain the definite and precise ideas of the Hindus in religion, the subject eludes our grasp. All is loose, vague, wavering, obscure, and inconsistent. Their expressions point at one time to one meaning, and another time to another meaning; and their wild fictions, to use the language of Mr. Hume, seem rather the playsome whimsies of monkeys in human shape than the serious asservations of a being who dignifies himself with the name of the rational. (In Schweinitz, Jr. 1984: 49.)

It did not occur to people then, as it does not seem to occur to people now, that this amorphous nature of Hinduism might have little to do with its "amazing capacities". It is more likely that the absence of structure has something to with the fact that Hinduism is an imaginary entity. For obvious reasons, the Christian missionaries could not swallow this possibility, as it was, literally, inconceivable.

To attack Hinduism as a false religion, they were thus compelled to criticise its doctrines. These doctrines could only be found in the texts. Thus, by default, all the texts they came across – from Vedas through Upanishads to Puranas – became religious texts.

Even more to the point, unless one could explicitly show that a text was not religious – because, say, it talked about rules of grammar – it was a part of the 'holy books'. This may be a convenient strategy, if not a useful one. To appreciate this point better, consider the texts and their variety: they discuss rituals or provide instructions to carry them out; they put across speculations about the structure of the Cosmos or instruct people how to live on earth; they tell stories or melodiously string names together. Now, if all of them were religious texts, then this 'religion' would dominate the totality of social life and human existence. If everything is a part of 'religion', the very word loses its meaning and becomes trivial. Yet, our scholars deny this implication by suggesting that it is very typical of 'Hinduism' to pervade all aspects of social, intellectual, and emotional life. In the coming pages (see also chapter #11.4.2.), we will discover the historical roots of this sentiment. For now, let me just say that this convenient strategy is a confession of ignorance. The tragedy lies in the fact that this confession has become the truth about 'Hinduism'.

### The Monkey as a Mirror?

There was a slight hitch to all of this though. Most people were either ignorant of or oblivious to these doctrinal cores identified by the European intellectual. As Chatfield (1808: 212-13) summarises the prevailing opinion in his time:

If...(we consider) the general ignorance of the Brahmins of the present age, the force of their prejudices will be found the more difficult to subdue...

In confirmation of this opinion of the general ignorance of the Brahmins, it is recorded, *that they cannot even read the books which contain their sacred records,* but are altogether immersed in such deep sloth and depravity, that immoral practices, which the most barbarous nations would have feared to adopt, are at this hour, openly allowed and sanctioned, in the most public places and polished cities of Hindoostan. Of the people, the description is generally degrading; *uninformed,* and only careful of their ablutions and the particular customs of their caste, they are said to *have as little acquaintance with the moral precepts of their Sastras,* as the Samoeides, and Hottentots, with the elegant arts of sculpture and painting. (Italics mine.)

The inconsistency between the different texts did not upset them as much as it did the "logical and rational mind of the West". This indifference no doubt confirms the immortal words of Geden (1913: 283), in the authoritative *Encyclopedia of Religion and Ethics,* when he says, "The East cares little for logic or consistency in the strict Western sense of the term."

Consequently, attention had to be paid to denouncing the practice of Hinduism. These practices disgust and raise the hackles of any civilized person:

> The Evangelical missionary's unfavourable impression was strengthened in practice by what he regarded as being a fatal cleavage in Hinduism between religion and moral behaviour. Part of the eighteenth century heritage in the Evangelical Awakening was of course the emphasis on morals...Hinduism fell short of the missionaries' ethical ideal. Much of what they saw disgusted them. The caste system, with its hard-and-fast barriers between man and man; the practices of *sati;* the zenana; infant marriage; hook-swinging and Hindu ascetic practices generally...all this, and more, seemed incommensurate with what they understood as being the purpose of religion...A religion which countenanced, and even recommended such practices degraded its adherents, rather than uplifting them; they spoke of the "loathsome link between Indian piety and Indian impurity" (Sharpe 1965: 26).

This way of drawing a distinction between the 'doctrinal cores' and common practices of the people meant creating a difference between a doctrinal or philosophical Hinduism and a popular Hinduism, which represented the current practice. In the words of Marshall (1970: 20):

> (C)omparatively soon Europeans had begun to make the distinction, which was to have so long a life, between what they regarded as 'popular' Hinduism and 'philosophical' Hinduism. Popular cults were described to be condemned or ridiculed, but most writers were also prepared to admit the existence of metaphysical assumptions and ethical doctrines in Hinduism of which they could approve because they seemed to be similar to western concepts, *although the similarities which they found now seem to depend largely on the inability of the Europeans to describe a religious system except in Christian terms* (my italics).

While it may have been convenient to draw this distinction, it was not very conducive to understanding 'Hinduism'.

They invariably made a distinction between 'popular' Hinduism, which they did not deem worthy of study, and 'philosophical' Hinduism, which they tried to define as a set of hard and fast doctrinal propositions and to place in current theories about the nature and history of religion. All of them wrote with contemporary European controversies and their own religious preoccupations very much in mind. *As Europeans have always tended to do, they created Hinduism in their own image* (ibid: 43; italics mine).

In any case, the conclusion of the period was that Hinduism is immoral as well. It was the "idolatry of the basest kind, represented by numberless idols and symbols of the most revolting Character" (Urwick 1885: 132). As the late lamented Reverend M. A. Sherring formulated it, after having lived thirty years among the Hindus at the 'headquarters' of Hinduism, *viz.* Benares,

(Here) idolatry is a charm, a fascination, to the Hindu. It is, so to speak, the air he breathes. It is the food of his soul. He is subdued, enslaved, befooled by it. The nature of the Hindu partakes of the supposed nature of the gods whom he worships. And what is that nature? According to the traditions handed about amongst the natives, and constantly dwelt upon in their conversation, and referred to in their popular songs...which perhaps would be sufficient proof...yet more especially according to the numberless statements and narratives found in their sacred writings, on which these traditions are based, it is, in many instances, vile and abominable to the last degree. Idolatry is a word denoting all that is wicked in imagination and impure in practice. Idolatry is a demon...an incarnation of all evil...but nevertheless bewitching and seductive as a siren. It ensnares the depraved heart, coils around it like a serpent, transfixes it with its deadly fangs, and finally stings it to death. (In Urwick 1885: 133.)

*The System of Caste*

If Hinduism melted away into thin air whenever one stared at it long enough, its social organisation promised greater solidity as long as one did not look too closely at it. Indian society was controlled and governed, it appeared to the foreign eyes, by a system of caste hierarchy with the Brahmins at the top. The problem faced by the Christian missions with this social setup had little to do with the socio-economic inequalities, which they found in Indian society. Not only because, in the immortal words of the Gospel, "there will be poor always", but also because socio-economic poverty must have been a very familiar experience to the foreign eyes. Besides, the cultural and social gulf between the nobility and the common folk was a matter of daily experience to the Europeans – especially the British. Rather, the penetration and the acceptance of Christianity were stifled by the 'caste system'. Unable to convert the higher echelons of Indian social life into Christians, the missionaries had to rest content with the induction of lower 'caste' groups. In effect, this meant that Christianity was identified with the lower 'caste' groups and began to be socially marginalised. Even those few Brahmins who became converts found themselves getting isolated and Christianity had not faced this difficulty elsewhere, including in other continents. Even the converts into Christianity continued their old practices of 'caste' discrimination *(e.g.* Sharpe 1965).

It is one thing to take note of this phenomenon but quite another to be able to do something about it. Much like the social theorists of today, the Christian missionaries of yesterday had very little idea of what they were confronting: people appeared to follow some rules without, however, being clear what these rules were. Caste system appeared to rest on authority – but on whose or, better still, *which* authority? Again, the Europeans had but two guesses: the 'holy books' of the heathens must have sanctioned such a social organisation; the 'priests' of the heathens must be responsible for the continued sway of this 'caste system'. Unable or impotent to bring God's word to the heathens in a successful manner – after all, converting heathens was said to be a walkover – the rage and fury of the Europeans turned against the two things, which appeared impermeable to the Christian message: the 'caste' system and its 'priests', *viz.* the Brahmins.

### *The Duplicity of the Devil's Messengers*

I have already drawn your attention to the fact that Brahmins were identified as the 'clergy' or the 'priests' of Hinduism. The Reformation period had launched a crusade precisely against this group, albeit of the Roman Catholic variety. While to the Roman Catholics this vocation was both important and sacred, the post-Reformation period had succeeded in making this clerical position into a debatable issue: irrespective of which side of the divide one stood, Roman Catholic clergy had achieved the limelight, which it might have chosen not to be in. While Protestants would leave no stone unturned in attacking this clergy, including emphasising the similarities between the heathen priesthood and the Catholic priesthood, Roman Catholics would have to defend the institution by showing the great difference between themselves and the heathens. Both these positions ended up generating a sharp attack on the heathen priests – their immoral character, their devilish practices, *etc.*

This explicit hostility towards the heathen priesthood was not helped by the inability of the messengers of God's word to convert Brahmins into Christianity. In Brahmins, they found a literate group, which was able to read, write, do arithmetic, conduct 'theological' discussions, *etc.* During the first hundred years or so, this group was also the only source of information about India as far as the missionaries were concerned. Schooled to perform many administrative tasks, the Brahmins were mostly the only ones well versed in the European language(s) – enough, at least, to communicate with the Europeans. In short, they appeared both to be the intellectual group and the most influential social layer in the Indian social organisation. Conversion of the heathens of India, as the missions painfully discovered, did not depend so much on winning the allegiance of a prince or the king as it did on converting the Brahmins. As Xavier saw the Brahmins:

> These are the most perverse people in the world...they never tell the truth, but think of nothing but how to tell subtle lies and to deceive the simple and ignorant people, telling them that the idols demand certain offerings, and these are simply the things that the Brahmans themselves invent, and of which they stand in need in order to maintain their wives and children and houses...They threaten the people that, if they do not bring the offerings, the gods will kill them, or cause them to fall sick, or send demons to their houses, and, through the fear that the idols will do them harm, the poor simple people do exactly as the Brahmans tell them...*If there were no Brahmans in the area, all the Hindus would accept conversion to our faith.* (Neill 1984: 146; my italics.)

Here, the Christian missionaries failed abysmally. They could not persuade the Brahmins to give up their 'religion'. Why is that? As I have already pointed out, Christianity believed that practices were guided by beliefs and that criticism of the former was identical to criticising the latter. The Brahmins were mostly unimpressed by the theological sophistication of the Christian critique of paganism. They also agreed with the Christian priests on several issues. As Abbé Dubois, the nineteenth-century missionary chronicles at large (1816), Brahmins clucked at the foolishness of the masses who worshipped in the temples (297), shaking their heads sadly at the credulity of the gullible folk for 'idol worship', (293-94) *etc.*; agreed enthusiastically that there was one God, the Supreme One, and that was that; exhibited no fear and little respect towards those very same idols in whose temples they officiated as 'priests' (295-96); and had little problems in saying that the 'gods' – whose stories they themselves were telling – were indeed immoral and definitely not worthy of supplication...In other words, the polemic of St. Augustine did not appear to perturb the 'priests' of this pagan religion.

In the first quarter of the eighteenth century, B. Ziegenbalg, a Protestant missionary, had the occasion to record thoughts similar to those expressed by Abbé Dubois. In this document, published as a series of letters in 1718, the Tamil-speaking Malabarian 'priests' (*i.e.* the Brahmins) spoke through the pen of Ziegenbalg on a variety of issues, including, for example, the morality of their gods:

> Such and such Actions are related of the Gods which would be criminal and sinful in any Man to do the like...Yet the Gods are subject to no Law or Precepts...and we are no more allow'd to withdraw from them the useful Religious Worship paid to them for so many Ages by our Forefathers, than we are to deny our Allegiance to our Lawful King. (Excerpted in Young 1981: 24.)

With respect to the Hindu 'polytheism', this is what they had to say:

> We teach the People to worship One only, and not many Gods...God is variously represented under different Attributes and forms; yet he is still but one God, as Gold is but one, as to its kind, tho' wrought into a Thousand different Figures (*ibid*).

As though this is not disconcerting enough, the Brahmins were also the most enthusiastic endorsers of any critique of their gods.

> (O)f all Hindus,...(the Brahmins) care the least and have the smallest amount of faith in...(their gods). It is by no means uncommon to hear them speaking of their gods in terms of the most utter contempt. When they are displeased with their idols they do not scruple to upbraid them fiercely to their faces, at the same time heaping the grossest insults upon them...
>
> The histories of their gods are so ridiculous that it is not surprising that the Brahmins are at heart conscious of the absurdity of worshipping such beings. There is, therefore, very little danger incurred in ridiculing the gods in the presence of Brahmins. Very often they agree with the scoffer, and even enlarge upon what he has said...
>
> There is another factor which must be taken into account in estimating the scanty veneration that they pay their gods...and that is the clear knowledge which most of them must have gleaned from their books of a 'God who is the Author and the Creator of all things...' (Dubois 1816: 295-297.)

Why would they not convert to Christianity then? François Bernier, in his famous *Voyages,* recounts a conversation that he had with some Brahmins. Discussing the frequency of ablutions, which they maintained,

> when I told them that in cold countries it would be impossible to observe their law during the winter, which showed that it was nothing but a pure invention of men, they gave me this rather amusing reply: that they were not claiming that their law was universal, but that God had made it for them alone, which was why they could not receive a foreigner into their religion;…they were not in the least claiming that our religion was false, but that it might be good for us and that God might have made several different paths to heaven; but they would not agree that as ours was general for the whole world, theirs could be but fable and pure invention. (In Dumont 1966: 402-403.)

As Chatfield (1808: 324) records, partially referring to Bernier,

> When the Brahmins have been pressed by the arguments of the Christians, that their law could only be observed in their own country, on account of its peculiar ordinances, their answer has been uniform, "that God had only made it for them, and therefore they did not admit into it strangers; that they pretended not that Christianity was false; and since God could make many roads to heaven, it was not thence to be presumed that their religion was mere fable and invention."

In other words, they were Brahmins who knew of these kinds of criticisms and arguments, and yet remained Brahmins despite, or precisely because of, these very same arguments.

How could Europeans, with their fixation on belief-fixation, even begin to understand this? In the same way the Enlightenment and post-Enlightenment thinkers suggested that the pagan writers from Antiquity were unauthentic (see chapter #2), the Brahmins were suspected of unauthenticity too. With this crucial difference, however, that the restraint imposed on the European intellectuals with respect to the intellectuals of Antiquity was removed when it came to the Brahmins of India.

Holwell (1767) a more sympathetic writer of this period, for example, wrote that the modern Hindus were

> as degenerate, crafty, superstitious, litigious and wicked a people, as any race of beings in the known world. (In Marshall, Ed., 1970: 27.)

After all, there was little to learn from these idolatrous priests. The hatred of heathen priesthood, and/or priesthood in general; impotence to convert the Brahmins; an identification of the latter as the 'priests'; inability to understand the culture they were functioning in; a supercilious arrogance born out of a bottomless ignorance – these were the ingredients that went into concocting the charges of duplicity, double standards, unauthenticity and immorality, against the heathen priestly caste. (See also Lach 1965: 258-59.)

As time progressed, this attack would also target the 'caste' system.

> Missionaries united in condemning the caste laws – "a lie against nature, against humanity, against history" – as being contrary to the spirit of Christian brotherhood; they declared caste to be the "bane of India", and demanded that caste should be utterly rejected by all converts to Christianity (Sharpe 1965: 31).

The 'caste system', together with the priestly caste of the Brahmins, epitomised all that was wrong with this nation of idolaters – and there were plenty of wrongs to talk about.

*On the Semantics of Talking and Shouting*

Talk they did, right down to the twentieth century. In 1882, William Hastie spoke of the *Hindu Idolatry and English Enlightenment* (1882: 30) by describing India as "the most stupendous fortress and citadel of ancient error and idolatry...Its foundations pierce downwards into the Stygian pool". Hinduism itself was, as he saw it, a mass of

> senseless mummeries, loathsome impurities...every conceivable form of licentiousness, falsehood, injustice, cruelty, robbery, murder...Its sublimest spiritual states have been but the reflex of physiological conditions in disease. *(Ibid:* 27; Cited in Maw 1990: 8.)

But, *nota bene*, this attack was born out of the inability of Christianity to gain a serious foothold in the Indian society. What has changed, as time and tastes have, is the set of 'wrongs' identified by the intellectuals: yesterday it pertained to saving the souls of the masses, today it pertains to saving their bodies; yesterday it was impervious to the message of the Gospels, today it is impervious to the message of social and economic progress. Christian priesthood moralised the discourse about the Brahmins and the caste system; their heirs, the social scientists of the twentieth century, faithfully continue it oblivious to anything else but their own sanctimony. This is not the only continuity between priests of yesterday (and today) and the social scientists of the twentieth century: something else unites them too, if not in Christ then elsewhere, namely, ignorance of what they were/are talking about.

Similar difficulties were encountered by the triumphant march of Christianity across the Asian continent as well. In Japan and China too, this 'irresistible force' met with an immovable object. The 'Holy Spirit' can move much but not, apparently, this immovable object. You do not need me to tell you who or what to blame: the heathens and their duplicity, of course. (Massarella 1990: 242, qualifies this description with respect to Japan and the European and English visitors during the early seventeenth century.) As the Mission Superior of Japan, Padre Francisco Cabral in 1596, voiced his thoughts about the induction of Japanese into the Jesuit Order:

> If one does not cease and desist admitting Japanese into the Society...that will be the reason for the collapse of the Society, nay! of Christianity, in Japan, and it will later hardly prove possible to find a remedy...I have seen no other nation as conceited, covetous, inconstant, and insincere as the Japanese...they are educated to be inscrutable and false. (In Elison 1973: 16.)

The 'red race' was primitive – it could be decimated; the 'blacks' were backward – they could be enslaved; the 'yellow' and the 'brown' were inferior – they could be colonised. How to convert them? One could persecute resistance and opposition. How to respond to indifference? Because, if there is one word to capture the attitude of these heathens towards Christianity, it is this: indifference. The shrill and strident tone of the Christian Gospels – leave alone those of the messengers – is itself suspect: if the missionary position is all that superior, as the actress sighed tiredly at the Bishop, why the need to shout?

*Criticism and Self-criticism*

This was only one side of the dialectic. Let me not overlook the second side either. The Christian missionaries were not beyond 'self-criticism' either – a formidable achievement, as Chairman Mao was yet to be born. How could the native heathens display any great enthusiasm to-wards the Gospels, when they see the Christian whites behaving so im-morally? From the earliest days, the European clergy were confronted with this problem. In the seventeenth-century Goa already, the good Father Lancilotto of the School of Jesuits was bemoaning:

There are innumerable Portuguese who buy droves of girls and sleep with all of them and this is known publicly. This is carried to such excess that there was one man in Malacca who had twenty-four women of various races, all his slaves and all of whom he enjoyed...But other men, as soon as they can afford to buy a female slave, almost always use her as a girl friend...beside many other dishonourable proceedings in my poor understanding. (In Neill 1984: 97.)

This state of affairs is hardly surprising given the picture the early travel reports paint of the Indian society. As time progressed, these complaints merely increased – no doubt, one assumes, in proportion with the attitudes and actions of the whites in India. As Abbé Dubois (1816: 300) was to put it:

...(I)t must be confessed that if, in these latter days, idolatrous Hindus have shown a greater aversion to the Christian religion as they became better acquainted with Europeans, the result must be attributed solely to the bad conduct of the latter. How could the Hindus think well of this holy religion, when they see those who have been brought up in it, and who come from a country where it is the only one that is publicly professed, openly violating its precepts and often making its doctrines the subject of sarcasm and silly jests? It is curious to note that the Brahmin does not believe in his religion, and yet he outwardly observes it; while the Christian believes in his, and yet he does not outwardly observe it. What a sad and shameful contrast!

A few years earlier, Chatfield (1808: 318) was speaking in a similar vein:

How then could either the Hindoo or the Mussulman believe a people, whose sacred books described a being, that delighted in a pure and spiritual worship, and in pious and generous actions, whilst persecution, theft, murder, drunkenness, and profanation of all that is just and good, were the common practice and distinguishing marks of its followers.

John Wesley exhorted Christians that they should live in such a way that

The Malabarian Heathen will have no more room to say, 'Christian man take my wife, Christian man much drunk: Christian man kill man! *Devil Christian!* Me no Christian.' (Cited in Pailin 1984: 146.)

These two quandaries of Christianity in India formed the local context within which the first translations, first texts, first discoveries, were to filter down to the European continent. The broader context, as it remained for a long period, was the preoccupation of the European intellectuals with their own religious feuds and controversies. More requires to be said about both these contexts than what I have said so far, but it is impossible to do so within the confines of my task.

The Portuguese referred to the Indians as '*gentues*' which the British made into *Gentoos*. This eighteenth-century word allowed one to speak of the 'religion of the gentoos', the 'law book of the Gentoo people' (*e.g.* Halhead 1776) and such like. The same gentoos were also known as the 'Hindus' to the Persians because the former lived on the other side of the Sindhu river. This name was adopted in the nineteenth century, and 'the religion of the gentoos' became 'the religion of the Hindoos' in order to achieve full recognition later as 'Hinduism'. In the initial stages, this 'Hinduism' merely signified the idolatrous religion of the Hindoos, so-called by the Moguls to designate the people, who lived on the banks of the Sindhu River. That this Hinduism metamorphosed into an independent religion has to do with some conceptual requirements ere the Europeans could make sense of other peoples and cultures. However, there are historical accidents as well, a brief sketch of which may not be out of place now.

## 4.2. THE ORIENTAL RENAISSANCE

The year is 1783. The man is William Jones. Son of a mathematician, this man is a gifted linguist: he wrote and published poems in Greek by the time he was fifteen; produced a remarkable Persian grammar and translated it into French when he was twenty-five; and before his death at the age of forty-eight, he would thoroughly know thirteen of the twenty-eight languages that he would study. This brilliant and well-read jurist is at the moment on his way to India. On a ship en route to Calcutta, he is going to join two other gifted minds – H. T. Colebrooke and Charles Wilkins – to serve the East India Company under the guidance of another splendid figure, Warren Hastings. The troika – Jones, Colebrooke, Wilkins – will set up the famous Asiatic Society very soon and bring out the celebrated *Asiatick Researches*. The intellectuals from London to Rome will be indebted to them, for the arrival of Jones in Calcutta would almost mark the end of one era and the beginning of another.

This period was to be known as the "second renaissance", anticipated to be as productive as the first one. It was also dubbed the "Oriental Renaissance" to distinguish it from the "Italian" variety. Today, not much is known about the second renaissance perhaps because, as Eliade remarks (1969: 55), it did not deliver the goods that were anticipated of it:

> The "discovery" of the Upanishads and Buddhism at the beginning of the nineteenth century had been acclaimed as a cultural event that presaged considerable consequence. Schopenhauer compared the discovery of Sanskrit and the Upanishads to the rediscovery of the "true" Greco-Latin culture during the Italian Renaissance. *One expected a radical renewal of Western thought as a consequence of the confrontation with Indian philosophy.* As is known, however, not only did this miracle of the "second Renaissance" not take place, but...the discovery of the Indian spirituality did not give rise to any significant cultural creation (my italics).

These words summarise the context and result of the second European encounter with India. Further, as the citation makes it amply clear, not only was there an anticipation of a renewal in the European culture that the second contact with India would bring, but also a yearning and desire that it would effectively take place. Schwab's (1950) masterly account of this period leaves little room to doubt that both the term – 'Oriental Renaissance' – and the longing were part of an age, and not a retrospective description projected by intellectuals of a later period.

*Let a Hundred Flowers Bloom?*

The Protestant Reformation, which split the Catholic Christianity, began to undergo divisions in its ranks. The same movement also gave birth to deism, the latter subdividing itself further. None of these variations on the Christian theme escaped the iron grips of the questions as they were formulated in the latter part of the sixteenth century. One may, anachronistically speaking, look upon this profusion of sects and movements within Christianity with a Mandarin-like equanimity and suggest to 'let a hundred flowers bloom'. Not an easy thing to argue in those periods when one thought that ninety-nine of these flowers were poisonous and deadly and only one invigorating and healthy. Caught amid persecutions and polemics, many intellectuals began to seek commonalities among the competing Christian groups with the hope of finding a foundation for their religious quest.

The earliest attempt was that of Lord Herbert of Cherbury. He sought to discover a shared way for getting out of the problems that confronted the seventeenth-century believers.

Standing at the head of a trend, which was then only emerging but was later to bloom into various shades of deism and natural theology,

Herbert of Cherbury wrote his *De Veritate* (1624) where he argued that there were certain 'Common Notions' concerning religion which were not only self-evidently true but also innate in all men. (More details in Bedford 1979; Preus 1987.) These common notions included the existence and nature of God, the duty of worshipping Him, the connection between virtue and piety, reconciliation through repentance, and the threat of punishment and reward in an afterlife. While in the initial stages this attempt was oriented towards Christian communities, very soon it spilled out to incorporate Judaism *(e.g.* Eilberg-Schwartz 1990), Islam (called Mohammetanism) too. (See the sublime dialogues of Bodin 1857, published nearly 260 years after the composition of the book.) As information about the heathen religions began to filter through and accumulate, based albeit on the traveller's tales in the early stages, it was inevitable that the attempt to catch all religions in one net should be extended to them as well.

This extension could not be accomplished without serious modifications because of the background of Christian theology and the necessity to demonstrate its superiority against other religions (*e.g.* Harrison 1990). As the battle within Christianity became complicated, so too did the problems. As Pailin suggests, in the eighteenth-century theology that provided the background for the treatment of other religions, at least four distinct ways of talking about other religions can be discerned:

> First, some appealed to other religions as providing evidence for their position. For example, there were those who affirmed the possibility of a natural knowledge of God and appealed to other religions as showing that an authentic knowledge of God was available before and outside the Christian revelation. Secondly, other religions were used as theological 'mud' to sling at opponents. To indicate the similarity of an opponent's beliefs and practices with those of a 'heathen' religion was considered by some theologians to discredit the former. Thirdly, there was a need to show that the arguments advanced to confirm a set of beliefs could not be held to confirm, perhaps even more strongly, the beliefs of another religion. This need arose particularly when Christian and Islamic claims were compared. Finally, it was widely felt that the truth of one's set of beliefs could be significantly confirmed by showing the rational unsatisfactoriness of the other religions (Pailin 1971: 85).

As though these alone were not sufficient, it was not always clear that the proponents and opponents spoke the 'same language' while conducting their disputations. A term that often kept resurfacing in the discussions was that of 'natural religion', and it was all but clear that it meant or referred to the same thing. Pailin (*ibid:* 86-87) again:

For some 'natural religion' referred to the religious beliefs which all men could in theory determine from nature and mankind by the use of their reason; for others it meant the beliefs which were innate in all men; for others 'natural religion' was religion which God revealed to Adam and, from Adam, was transmitted in theory and practice to all mankind; for others it denoted the beliefs and practices of those who were 'natural' men – unaffected, that is, by civilization; for others it meant the religion of those who were unaffected by divine revelation – that is, usually, those outside the influence of Judaism, Christianity and Islam (since Mahomet was held to have adopted many of his ideas from Jewish and Christian teaching). For some, talk about natural religion has a theoretical context, while for others it has primarily an empirical use. For some, natural religion was the pure and sufficient religion for all men; for others it was a human product which showed that valid religion can be derived only from a divine revelation accepted by faith.

This complexity in the dispute, which stretched over centuries, and the complications that ensued from it, should not blind us to that one issue which was at its origin: paganism was raised from the dead to testify in a battle about religious truth. The only problem was that this evidence was inherently ambiguous. Speaking through the voice of the living, the dead could only say what the living themselves could. Perhaps this indicates that what happened after the Protestant Reformation was not so much a séance around the ouija board as it was a ventriloquist's soliloquy. If, as the Protestants kept insisting, miracles belonged to yesterday and only Jesus could raise Lazarus from the dead, the paganism that would speak from the 'Orient' would merely be an illusion or, at best, a voice-displacement. Should this be true, we need not wonder that a 'radical renewal' in the West did not take place due to a contact with Indian philosophy and religion. Perhaps, the best-known example to illustrate this state of affairs is the use Voltaire made of "*Ezour-Vedam*" – a translation of an alleged 'holy book' of the Indians. This book, which Voltaire made so much use of in his battle against Christianity, was actually a fake document created by the Christian priests in Pondicherry with the intention of battling the idolatry of the Indians. To Voltaire, this document showed the subtlety and the sublime nature of Indian thought – refuting and criticising the grossness of Christianity. To the Christian priests who created it, it showed the subtlety and sublime nature of Christianity – refuting and criticising the grossness of heathendom.

*4.2.1. 'Vile Hindus'? The Other Face of the Coin*

The issue that Protestantism raised had enabled several people to collect several different kinds of evidence by the time William Jones set sail to Calcutta. For example, the Dutch, French, Danish, Italian, and English missionaries discovered and announced the existence of a language in India which was,

> a dead language, sacred, liturgical, and erudite, restricted to a high priestly caste, renowned for an immense and mysterious body of literature, and written in a script to which the key was missing. Formidable barriers defended this treasure from the impurity of the Europeans, who called it by various names, according to the dialect in which they first encountered it. For Abraham Roger it was *Samscortum*. Bernier employed the curious form *Hanscrit* which, with two exceptions, Voltaire also used. *Sahanscrit*, and worse, can be found in the *Lettres édifiantes*. Anquetil called it *Samscroutam* or *Samcretam* at first. Sonnerat called it *Sanscroutam, Samskret, Hanscrit* and *Grandon* (after *Grantham*). In 1806, Adelung termed it *Samscrada*. (Schwab 1950: 31)

Kircher, Roe, Lord, Rogerius, Baldaeus, Dapper, and other missionaries and travellers had amassed evidence about the existence of a holy book called 'Shaster', 'Shastah'; 'Beed', 'Bede', 'Bedam' and 'Vedam'. Some, like Rogerius, Baldaeus, and Ziegenbalg (Caland, Ed., 1926), wrote and published books about heathen tales, practices, and idol worship. The Enlightenment thinkers, as we have already seen, collected evidence about the evolutionary history of humankind with heathendom representing the infancy of humanity. So the list goes on. All this evidence for what? You may well ask.

Into this rich background fell the rain of the first authentic translations that Jones, Colebrooke, Wilkins, and others were to undertake. Though I would like to, this is not the place to discuss either the earlier translations of Indian texts from Persian (Holwell 1767; Dow 1768), or the background to the British Orientalism (*e.g.* Kopf 1969) or even the impact and importance of a figure like Jones for the emergence of the science of comparative linguistics which Bopp was to officially inaugurate (Aarsleff 1967). With respect to the theme of my essay, there are only two aspects of relevance: one regarding the continuity between Enlightenment and Romanticism, and the other about the legacy of Romanticism.

In the earlier chapter, I have drawn your attention to the emergence of the domain of universal history concomitant to the absorption of living heathen culture into the paganism of Antiquity. Generally, the eighteenth-century thinkers argued that the origin of religion – especially the primitive or the heathen ones – had to do with the fact that they, the 'others', hypostatised natural forces into gods with human and semi-divine attributes and embellishments, and thus inventing their pantheon. Not yet capable of rational and abstract thinking, the Early

Man used the fanciful imagination that he was endowed with. This was at the root of those fantastical creations and absurd stories that constituted his religious world. These mythologies – as some philosophers suggest to this day – are the products of 'mythical thought', standing opposed to which is the 'rational' or 'scientific' thought.

The Romantics from Herder through Schlegel and beyond accepted this Enlightenment legacy. They accepted the identification of the living heathens with the Ancient pagans. Consequently, the rediscovery of India and its culture meant a discovery of an ancient culture, which was contemporaneous with the modern one. The ancients were living in another part of the world. These ancients, as writer after writer testifies, represented the childhood of Man. Thus, as Romantics projected the image of India (see Willson 1964 for more details), India was the cradle of the world civilization. Fictitious gentle people of noble and simple souls appeared to inhabit the plains of the Ganges; its poetry was to be the last word on the subject as Goethe was to remark in the early days of the discovery of its language; and so on.

A slight bit of an unpacking of this notion of 'childhood' and 'the cradle of civilization' is necessary to understand what the German Romantics were really saying. Irrespective of what any single thinker said or did not say, each of them had accepted the framework of a universal history of humankind. Whether they liked it or not, there was a consensus that the European culture had matured. One may mourn the absence of innocence and spontaneity of childhood; one may long to rediscover the absence of affectation and deceit in the childhood; but it remains incontrovertible that this is how an adult looks back. By calling the Indian culture the childhood of Man, the Romantic thinkers did not go beyond or against the Enlightenment tradition – but merely extended it with a fanciful twist.

The same reflections are applicable to the appellation 'cradle of civilization'. To use that with respect to a culture long dead and gone, like the Greek or Roman, might be construed as a way of paying homage, tribute, or just acknowledgement to the contributions of the past. What does it mean when used to characterise a living culture? It can only mean that those who live in this culture are still in their cradles – and have been there during the last thousand years – unlike their European counterparts.

### The Enlightened Heirs of the Romantic Visionaries

That German Romanticism accepted the legacy of the Enlightenment – despite the alleged antagonism between Enlightenment and Romanticism – is best evidenced in the way they looked at and treated the theme of this essay, *viz.* religion.

Herder, the recognised leader of German Romanticism, places the cradle of humankind in the Orient. It is the land of gold and precious stones mentioned by Moses, the cradle of human desires and of all religion. As he exclaims in his *Auf eine Philosophie der Geschichte zur Bildung der Menscheit* (1774):

> Dort *Morgenland!* die *Wiege* der Menschengeschlechte, Menschlicher *neigungen* und aller religion. (In Willson 1964: 51.)
> [There, *Land of the east!* The *cradle* of human race, human *drives*, and all religion.]

As Willson further (*ibid:* 60-61) remarks:

> Herder believes that the first faint stirrings of religion were to be found in the worship of natural phenomena, *in reverence and awe before its revelations*...Herder points out that he considers the mythology of India older than that of any other land...He looks upon the mythology of the Hindus as *first, childlike attempts* to arrange objects systematically in ideas or images...(my italics).

Georg Forster, in his German translation of *Sakontala* from the English version rendered by Jones in 1789, recommends in the introduction

> (the) Indic literature as represented by *Sakontala* for the simple relationship the Hindu, *in a childlike and unspoiled state*, has with nature. The Modern European, *living in a highly civilized culture*, he says, has lost this intimate identification of himself with nature. He reminds his reader that, disposed by scientific refinement in skills and customs to an artificially gauged and rationalized way of life, the European could easily lose sight of an ingenious feeling for nature, *if he did not still encounter it in less sophisticated peoples* (*ibid:* 73; italics mine).

Eulogising further about this piece of poetry:

> Forster emphasizes that the *childlike imagination* of the Hindu personified all of nature, even the plants; the animating powers of the trees were divine creatures...Very closely connected with this belief is the sanctity and inviolability of the woods and groves in which those men favored by God reside (*ibid:* 75-76; my italics).

How far is this from the explanation about the origin of religion that the Enlightenment thinkers gave? Did they, after all, not also say the same things with respect to the origin of religion among the primitives? (See the next chapter.) Except that the primitive is nearer home, if we listen to the Romantics, than is the case according to the thinkers of the Enlightenment.

If we look at Novalis, it is easy to recognise his affinities with this strain of thought. He believed that at the beginning of history, the priest and the poet were one. Only much later did they become separate. Paradoxically enough (see chapter #11), there is some truth to this story but not in the way Novalis thinks. In any case,

> (s)uch a unity...existed in India, where the religious precepts were stated poetically in the mythology of the Hindu gods (*ibid:* 84).

Friedrich Ast suggests that there are three periods in the history of human civilization:

> that of the Hindu, in which the root of religion falls, where nature and love were intimately reciprocal, the period of golden innocence, of undivided religion, philosophy, and art; ...India...is an idyllic paradise where nature is entwined with love; the emotion and the object are inseparable, each includes the other. *In India there was a pure, golden innocence, the innocence of childhood* (*ibid*: 89; my italics).

To sum up all these different images in one succinct paragraph,

> India was an ancient land watered by a holy river, the Ganges, the river of Paradise, which came to symbolize for the Romanticists the idyllic existence they saw reflected in the Hindu culture. A protean spirit served and guarded by a superior class of holy men, implanted into every denizen of that land a simplicity and peace of soul which made for balanced virtues and ease of living. It was a land where poetry permeated every aspect of human wisdom, creating a sublime harmony of all knowledge. Here philosophy was one with religion, and a Universal Spirit was immanent in every creature and in every creation of nature. A mellow kinship pervaded all things. A marvellous magic was the companion of ordinary reality...This was the kernel of the mythical image of India (*ibid*: 71).

So could one go on and on, but my point is made I trust. India – *nota bene,* the Indian culture of the eighteenth and nineteenth century – represented not merely the childhood of Man, but was itself the child-

hood of Man. Its people were naive, innocent and good. They had retained intimations of a primal religion, which permeated all aspects of
their existence: religion, philosophy, poetry, knowledge, was all one. As
Hegel put it in less flattering terms, "fantasy makes everything into a
God here" (Halbfass 1981).

Based purely on the texts they read in translations, people built
these images. The first obvious conclusion that we can draw is: German
Romanticism did not go any further than their predecessors in empirically investigating into the existence or non-existence of religion in
India. They merely strengthened the grips of the Biblical story of an
original religion by painting India as the seat of such a primal religion.

With respect to the theme of this essay, something else must
strike our attention in this story. That has to do with the legacy of the
Enlightenment-Romanticism period to the generations that have followed them. All the subsequent writings in social sciences have accepted
these images created by these periods as facts about the Indian culture
and society. Two non-trivial examples should drive this point home.

Consider the image of the people of India constituting the childhood of Man. If, say, a few thousand years ago they were the childhood
of the human race and remain in that phase, how would you describe
their development over these years? Obviously, because they are in the
same stage, which they were in four thousand years ago, no development has taken place. That is, you would say, India is a static society
and a stagnant civilization. As Stevenson, a missionary in Madras was
to put it in his *Hinduism and Christian Religion* (1875: 15, 23):

> The implements of trade and agriculture have been unchanged for ages;
> there are no changing fashions even in women's dress; little original has
> been produced in literature or philosophy worth speaking of; and religion
> has become…a tremendous fossilized organism, dead at the core, yet
> standing strong by its vast mechanical solidity and hoary antiquity. (Cited
> in Maw 1990: 1-2.)

From Hegel through Marx and beyond, is this not the description of
India? Once this image is accepted as a fact about India, the next question is as obvious as its solution. What caused stagnation in Indian society? Your choices, of course, are limited: either it is the geographical
climate of India; or it is the psychological character of the Hindus; or it
is the characteristic property of that particular race; or it has to do with
the social structure. Each of these avenues has been explored during
the last centuries, but if you are a twentieth-century liberal (or Marxist)
your choices are extremely limited: you can only identify the social
structure as a cause for the social stagnation over the centuries. That
means, why, the 'caste system' of course. Thus, from Marx through

Weber and beyond, we hear incessant chatter about the obsolete 'caste system', which has caused stagnation in India.

While this is one element of our inheritance, there is another treasure waiting at the doorstep as well. As must be clear, the Romantics identified the primal religion in India and one consequence of an extended childhood is the dominance of religion in all aspects of human life. This longing of German Romanticism has ended up becoming the truth about Indian (Asian) society and culture today. From the 'scholar' to the 'street sweeper', from the 'tourist' to the 'television reporter' (*e.g.* Boenders and Coppens 1981), everyone insists that religion pervades everything in India. Here, at random, is one such example:

> There can never be a clear-cut understanding of the East on the part of the West until Westerners realise that *all* Asian thought is religiously conditioned...I can think of no single department of human activity in Asian lands that is not encompassed by religious concepts. (Abbot Sumangalo 1972: 19-20.)

If religion is everywhere in India, one feels like asking, what is the problem about saying what it is? (See further #11.4.2.) Yet, apparently, these 'religions' defy description. Perhaps, as a 'dialectical' philosopher-friend of mine once remarked, because religion is everywhere in India, it is also nowhere.

Such mythical images can never survive the onslaught of facts for long. Herder may have sighed about the childlike Hindus, all noble and good, dripping honey and sugar. Not so our intrepid Abbé Dubois, who lived for thirty years in India. No, he gives us facts about them. Speaking about the childlike innocence, candour, and honesty of the Hindus, the revered Dubois (1816: 662) says:

> Certain it is that there is no nation in the world who think so lightly of an oath or of perjury. The Hindu will fearlessly call upon all of his gods – celestial, terrestrial, infernal –to witness his good faith in the least of his undertakings; but should fresh circumstances demand it, he would not have the smallest scruple in breaking the word that he had so solemnly pledged...
>
> The unscrupulous manner in which Hindus will perjure themselves is so notorious that they are never called upon to make a statement on oath in their own courts of justice...

In case you feel that the words of a Catholic missionary hardly constitute facts, let me provide you with another random citation – this time from a non-Catholic:

...(C)ould I transplant my reader...to the purely native circle by which I am surrounded...and could he understand the bold and fluent hindostanee which the Hindoo soldier speaks, he would soon distinguish the sources of oriental licentiousness, and how unprincipled is the Hindoo in conduct and character.

In nothing is the general want of principle more evident, than in the total disregard to truth which they show; no rank or order among them can be exempted from the implication. The religious teachers set the example, and they are scrupulously followed by all classes. Perjury and fraud are as common as is a suit of law; with protestations of equal sincerity will a witness stand forth who knows the falsehood of his testimony, and he who is ignorant of what he professes to testify. No oath can secure the truth; the water of the Ganges, as they cannot wash away the filth of lying and deceit, so they cannot preserve the court of law from being the scene of gross and impious contradiction. No task is so difficult as is he who would elicit truth from the mouth of a witness. Venality and corruption are universal; they are remarkable, too, for their ingratitude. (Massie, Vol. 1, 1840: 466-467.)

Now, I am sure, you will agree with me that under the harsh sunlight of truth, the misty image of German Romanticism justly faded away. Apart from such facts, there were also other historical realities: the tighter control of the British over colonial India, the dissipation and dissolution of the Asiatic Society, the determined effort to spread the English education, and so on. However, the circle is not complete yet. At the beginning of this chapter, I identified two quandaries for the spread of Christianity in India. I did not tell you how these two quandaries eventually were sorted out. I shall do so now, again irritatingly briefly, because the time is exactly ripe – we are somewhere in the middle of the nineteenth century – for us to meet...

## 4.2.2. Buddha, the Saviour of People

You might be wondering why it has taken so long for you to meet this legendary figure, and why it is that I have hardly referred so far to Buddhism while discussing the question of investigating the existence or non-existence of religions in India. The reason is simple: the creation of Hinduism antedates that of Buddhism. By this, I do not imply that Hinduism existed in India before Buddhism came into being – this claim, after all, is a standard textbook trivium – but that the Europeans created Buddhism after they had created Hinduism. I do not intend to argue this thesis about the creation of Buddhism because Almond has done it superbly in his book (Almond 1988). Instead, as it is fit for a subsection *based* on his book, I will let Almond speak in his own words (1988: 4) to state the thesis:

> (T)here was an imaginative creation of Buddhism in the first half of the nineteenth century, and…the Western creation of Buddhism progressively enabled certain aspects of Eastern cultures to be defined, delimited, and classified…(T)he discourse about Buddhism…was created and sustained by the reification of the term 'Buddhism'…which, in its turn, defined the nature and content of this entity.

And further, suggests Almond (*ibid:* 12-13), what we witness

> in the period from the later part of the eighteenth century to the beginning of the Victorian period in the latter half of the 1830s is the *creation* of Buddhism. It *becomes* an object, is constituted as such; it takes form as an entity that 'exists' over against the various cultures which can now be perceived as instancing it, manifesting it, in an enormous variety of ways. During the first four decades of the nineteenth century, we see the halting yet progressive emergence of a taxonomic object, the creation of which allows in turn the systematic definition, description, and classification of that congeries of cultural 'facts' which instance it, manifest it, in a number of Eastern countries.
>
> The creation of Buddhism took place in two more or less distinct phases. The first of these coincided with the first four decades of the nineteenth century. During this period, Buddhism was an object which was instanced and manifested 'out there' in the Orient…
>
> This would subtly change in the first twenty-five years of the Victorian period. Originally existing 'out there' in the Oriental *present,* Buddhism came to be determined as an object the primary location of which was the West, through the progressive collection, translation, and the publication of its textual *past.* Buddhism, by 1860, had come to exist, not in the Orient, but in the Oriental libraries and institutes of the West, in its texts and manuscripts, at the desks of the Western savants who interpreted it. It had become a textual object, defined, classified, and interpreted through its own textuality. By the middle of the century, the Buddhism that existed 'out there' was beginning to be judged by a West that *alone* knew what Buddhism was, is, and ought to be. The essence of Buddhism came to be seen as expressed not 'out there' in the Orient, but in the West through the West's control of Buddhism's own textual past.

None of these developments should come as a surprise to the reader who has followed my arguments so far. Nor is there any necessity for me to repeat and reproduce the details from Almond's book. Instead, what I will do is to highlight the contexts in which this creation took place – both the European and the Indian ones.

## The Contexts of Creation

To begin with the European context first. As we are well aware by now, even though the mythical images that the German Romantics projected on India disintegrated very soon, one of the dissatisfactions that lay behind it did not. Though caused initially by the schismatic movement within Christianity, the 'spiritual solace' (as people formulated it) could not be found within the existing Christian traditions. The Christian worldview was increasingly incapable of giving satisfactory answers to the questions, which it itself had spawned, regarding the meaning and purpose of life, the goal and origin of human beings, and such like. It was unable even to resolve moral conflicts and problems of modern life, let alone answer existential questions like what it means to lead the life of a Christian industrialist, Christian plumber, or a Christian intellectual. It is one thing to shout from the treetops that one has to continue to live like a Christian in a secular world, but quite another to say what such a life consists of. The growth of 'secular' ethics appeared to sever the relation between religion and morality. To reduce Christianity to a variety of ethics appeared not only blasphemous but a downright degradation of the very idea of religion itself. This unsettling, if vague, disturbance with Christianity was one of the strands that lived on even after the disintegration of the Romantic mythical image and longing.

This disquiet was further fed by the evangelising work of Christianity itself. The discovery that the conversion of heathens required an understanding of their experiential world implied digging into the culture of India – albeit with European instruments and expertise. The work of British Orientalists, translation of the Gita and other texts, began to create an audience faintly receptive to the 'Oriental wisdom'.

Finally, both the East India Company and the British Crown were resistant to and suspicious of missionary activity. After 1858, when India became a colony of the British Empire officially, the Royal proclamation by the Queen of England read in part:

> Firmly relying ourselves on the truth of Christianity, and acknowledging with gratitude the solace of religion, we disclaim alike the right and the desire to impose our convictions on any of our subjects. We declare it to be our royal will and pleasure, that none be in anywise favoured, none molested or disquieted, by reason of their religious faith or observances; but that all shall alike enjoy the equal and impartial protection of the law. And we do strictly charge and enjoin all those who may be in authority under us, that they abstain from all interference with the religious belief, or wor-

ship, of any of our subjects on pain of our severest displeasure. (Cited in Thomas 1988: 287.)

Of course, this did raise the hackles of militant evangelisers. Many were to bitterly complain of the paradox of a Christian country supporting and sustaining heathen religions. (See, for example, the fifth chapter of Reverend Duff's 1839, or chapters thirteen through sixteen in part two of Chatfield's 1808 to get some idea of the discussions.)

The Indian context next. Actually, this is not so much about the Indian culture of that period as it is about the context of the Christians and Europeans in India. At the beginning of this chapter, as well as in the previous one, I have spoken of the impasse Christianity boxed itself into. I also alluded to the fact that both the Brahmins and the ubiquitous 'caste system' appeared to impede the progress of Christianity in India or, even worse, threatened to marginalise it.

As information accumulated about the different parts of Asia, it became evident that there was also another idolatrous practice – often referred to by the Brahmins in India, albeit not as an idolatrous practice – which appeared to be dominant in Ceylon (Sri Lanka), Siam (Thailand), Cathay (China) and Japan. Various people had spoken variously of this variety of heathendom. Maurice (1795), for example, had spoken in detail of the original Buddha and a second Buddha – whose name was softened by the Chinese into Fo. The latter, he claimed, was actually a fake Buddha

Of the elder Boodh...the reader will be presented with the history. It will then become evident that he could not be the source of these nefarious doctrines, which tend to deprive man of the glorious hope of immortality. Of the second Boodh, whose name the Chinese have softened into Fo, astonishing prodigies are related, and such contradictory accounts are given, as convince me that his disciples, to do him honour, have artfully blended the two histories; and confounded together the holy and benevolent personage, who humanely forbade the sanguinary sacrifices of men and beasts on the altars of India, with the guilty parricide, who, on his death-bed, summoned around him his numerous disciples, and with a dagger, more tremendous than the sacrificial knife, attempted to give the final stab to every hope with which he had inspired mankind, of future happiness and dawning heaven...(Maurice 1793-1800, Vol. 1: 398).

The definitive breakthrough in the 'scientific' study of Buddhism, according to the consensus of the scholars, (besides Almond 1988, see also Clausen 1975; Brear 1975), was the appearance in 1844 of the *Introduction à l'Histoire du Buddhisme Indien* by the French scholar Eugène Burnouf. Published by the Imprimerie Royale, this volume apparently provided the standard and set the guidelines for the further study of Buddhism. To this day, it is reckoned as an exemplar to follow (Staal 1989). Burnouf's colleague, Philippe Édouard Foucaux, apparently followed it up with an edition and translation of a Tibetan life of Buddha.

While this signalled the beginning of the deluge of translations of Buddhist texts from Sanskrit, Pali, Tibetan, Chinese, *etc.*, it is to the credit of E. Arnold to have made 'Buddhism' popular in the West. In 1879, his poem *The Light of Asia* fell amid an audience, which swallowed up more than a hundred editions in England and America, and had it translated into several foreign languages. From then on, the deluge became a veritable flood.

What is important to notice about this entire episode is that a religion – called Buddhism – was built around those many texts that found their way to the various institutions of learning in Europe. The different kinds of Buddhism that flourished in Asia were discovered and reconstructed through the translations and commentaries; the outline, feature, and Gestalt – nay, the very identity – of Buddhism was captured and delineated by the translations of these texts; the 'doctrinal core', the history, the evolution, and the transformation of the religion were decided by means of deciphering the texts. Most of these texts, *nota bene*, were old: sometimes a thousand years old, at other times even older than that. The only difference between the creation of Buddhism and Hinduism is: in the case of the former, it is easily discernible because it was spectacular – occurring in less than seventy years; whereas it was more drawn-out, but no less insidious for it, in the case of Hinduism. In short, as Almond convincingly argues (1988: 37),

> Buddhism had become by the middle of the nineteenth century a textual object based on Western institutions. Buddhism as it came to be ideally spoken of through the editing, translating, and studying of its ancient texts could then be compared with its contemporary appearance in the Orient. And Buddhism, as it could be seen in the East, compared unfavourably with its ideal textual exemplifications contained in the libraries, universities, colonial offices, and missionary societies of the West. It was possible then, as a result of this, to combine a positive evaluation of a Buddhism textually located in the West with a negative evaluation of its Eastern instances.

The creation of Buddhism went hand-in-hand with the interpretation and the appreciation the West showed for it. For my story, not all aspects are equally relevant. Therefore, I shall concentrate my attention on elucidating a couple of its features only.

*On How Buddha Saved Souls*

I have already drawn attention to the fact that the Brahmins – conceived as a priestly caste – and the 'caste system' frustrated the messengers of God in saving the lost souls of the idolatrous heathen. This resulted in moralising a discourse – inevitably in the name of such moral principles as equality and dignity of man – about phenomena the Europeans had no understanding of. Most of the British missionaries shared little love either for Roman Catholicism or for the 'Romish' priests or for the Catholic 'rituals'. After all, as we have seen in the previous chapter, the rituals of Catholic worship were one of the foremost targets of anti-Catholic or Protestant polemics.

Buddhism, as the European savants viewed it, was a reaction against Brahmanism. In no time at all, Buddha became the Martin Luther of India rebelling against the 'Roman catholic' Brahmanic priestly caste:

> ...'Original' Buddhism...was often called the Protestantism of Asia. (The lamaism of Tibet, on the other hand, was frequently compared by English writers to Roman Catholicism and regarded as a priestly, ritualistic corruption of original Buddhism.)...Max Müller gave broad currency to the view that Buddha was another Luther who, sweeping away the superstitions and rituals with which the Brahman priesthood had enshrouded India, took religion back to its simple and pure origins. (Clausen 1975: 7)

In 1886, H. C. DuBose was writing in *The Dragon, Image and Demon, or the Three Religions of China*, that Buddha

> was not so much the founder of a new sect as the Martin Luther among the Brahmans...The Brahmans opposed him throughout his career, and several times he was summoned to discussions before the Oriental Diet of Worms. (Cited in Brear 1975: 143)

In 1850, *The Prospective Review* declared that "Gotama was a Protestant against the Religion of his Country"; *The Christian Remembrancer* argued in 1858 that the comparison of Protestantism to Catholicism and Buddhism to Brahmanism held, even down to minute points of resemblance. *The Journal of Sacred Literature* exclaimed in the 1860s:

> Gautama did for India what Luther and the reformers did for Christendom; like Luther, he found religion in the hands of a Class of men who claimed a monopoly of it, and doled it out in what manner and what measure they chose; like Luther, he protested that religion is not the affair

of the priest alone, but is the care and concern of every man who has a rea-sonable soul; both laboured to communicate to all the knowledge which had been exclusively reserved for the privileged class...And as Europe bestirred itself at the voice of Luther, so India awakened heartily to the call of Gautama. (All details from Almond 1988: 73.)

The Unitarian James Freeman Clarke, in his "Buddhism: or, the Protestantism of the East", asked in 1869

Why call Buddhism the Protestantism of the east, when all its external fea-tures so much resemble those of the Roman Catholic Church?...Because deeper and more essential relations connect Brahmanism with the Romish Church, and the Buddhist system with Protestantism...Buddhism in Asia, like Protestantism in Europe, is a revolt of nature against spirit, of human-ity against caste, of individual freedom against the despotism of an order, of salvation by faith against salvation by sacraments (*ibid*: 74).

Almond continues to cite further evidence:

Such polemics were not absent from *The Westminster Review* of 1878 either. There it is observed that the Buddha's reformation bore to Brahmanism the same relation as Protestantism to Roman Catholicism. Buddhism, it went on, was a protest against the sacrificialism and sacerdotalism of the Brahmans: "it rejected all bloody sacrifice, together with the priesthood and social caste so essentially bound up with them" (*Ibid*).

It is no wonder that such a Martin Luther would receive applause from an appreciative audience, especially when we realise what they thought of Hinduism. Even though I have spoken about the subject ear-lier, it is beneficial to note the theme once again. One or two citations might prove salutary here, because they provide us with an overview of the context for the Indian Luther. "There is an universal agreement," claimed James Mill in *The History of British India*,

respecting the meanness, the absurdity, the folly, of the endless, child-ish, degrading, and pernicious ceremonies, in which the practical part of the Hindu religion consists...Volumes would hardly suffice to depict at large the ritual of the Hindus, which is more tedious, minute, and burthen-some; and engrosses a greater portion of human life than any ritual which has been found to fetter and oppress any other portion of human race (*ibid*: 71).

William Knighton sketches a world that surrounded the Buddha with
an *Einfühlung* that should provoke the jealousy of the best hermeneutic
practitioner one can think of:

> He saw Brahmanism in active operation around him, and of all creeds,
> Brahmanism is the most foul and soul-polluting. The frenzied widows,
> shrieking on the funeral pile of her husband under the scorching flames...
> the devotees cracking beneath the wheels of Juggernaut's car, their dying
> groans drowned in the horrid music of the Brahmans...Gotama saw all
> this, and a thousand times more than European public could be told, or
> would believe (*ibid*: 71-72).

Thus, to Liddon, Buddhism appeared a conscious rebellion against the
entrenched sacerdotalism of the Brahmins. It was a

> social and doctrinal rebellion...Socially, it rebelled against the system of
> caste; it protested in the name of Justice that all had a right to the knowl-
> edge and the privileges which were monopolized by the Brahmins. Doc-
> trinally, it attempted to provide an escape for the human soul from the
> miseries of transmigration to another body after death. (In Brear 1975:
> 143.)

This is not the only way Buddha came to the rescue of the European
intellectuals in finding an answer to the riddle of Brahmins and the
caste system. In the previous chapter, I have argued that one of the issues, which Protestantism formulated, had to do with the corruption
and degeneration of religion. The texts of Buddha and the textual Buddhism now allowed the same question to be put to 'Buddhism'; the answer confirmed the providential role played by Europe in civilizing the
Asian peoples and cultures. The practice of Buddhism in all countries of
Asia, as everyone knew, had degenerated into gross idolatry and superstitious idol worship. This corruption, dubbed the 'popular Buddhism',
was very different from the pure, simple, and original Buddhism of the
founder himself – to be called 'philosophical Buddhism'. Of course, this
'philosophical' Buddhism was captured and delineated in the texts of the
Buddhist tradition known to the European savants. Consequently, they
could now measure and pronounce upon what they found as a practice
in the Asian continent. In this sense, they did not have to depart from
the descriptions provided by the travellers and European missionaries.
These remained true of Asians; after all, 'popular' Buddhism was corrupt and degenerate.

How to account for this degeneration? Both the Enlightenment and
German Romantic thinkers had prepared the grounds. With this dif-

ference that in the period we are talking about, a certain 'nuance' was added: the 'doctrine' of the founder was pure, but it fell on dead ears; or, even better, among a people known for their unbridled imagination incapable of entertaining lofty thoughts. Almond (1988: 44) again:

> A Buddhist cosmology...signalled the Oriental tendency to the fanciful, the fantastic, and the grotesque...William Bryant declared that it is well known that the Hindus have been characterised from the earliest times by an excess of imagination.

The best formulation, perhaps, comes from Oldenberg (*ibid*):

> Whatever is, appears to the Indian worthless compared to the marginal illuminations with which his fancy surrounds it, and the images of his fancy grow in tropical luxuriance, shapeless and distorted, and turn eventually with terrific power against their creator. To him, the true world, hidden by the images of his own dreams remains an unknown, which he is unable to trust and over which he has no control.

That is to say, one could now wonder at the good things that the Indian civilization had, without having to admire its current state, living inhabitants, and the actual culture. Rather convenient, what?

You must not, of course, think that the European intellectuals were all equally drawn to Buddhism or that those who spoke of it favourably were unanimously positive about it. Our intellectuals reasoned in a far more subtle and 'nuanced' manner than my portrayal lets you suspect. There was, to begin with, a great diversity of opinion concerning the nature of Buddhism. As Robert Childers said in the *Contemporary Review* in 1876

> Much diversity of opinion appears to exist respecting the teaching of Buddhism. According to one it is a system of barren metaphysics, according to another it is sheer mysticism; a third will tell you that it is a code of pure and beautiful morality; while a fourth looks upon it as a very selfish abstraction from the world, a systematic repression of every impulse and emotion of the heart. (In Clausen 1975: 7.)

More importantly, even those sympathetic to Buddhism like Max Müller or Rhys-Davids felt compelled to contrast it with Christianity only to find the former inferior. Buddhism might have been one of the best pagan religions they encountered, but in the end it was "almost, but not quite" as good as Christianity.

Such, then, was the Buddhism as the West created it by the time we reach the turn of the century: moral, repellent and fascinating, pure and corrupt, it was a religion which came into being in Paris and London. Almond (1988: 140) once again:

> It was the Victorians who developed the discourse within which Buddhism was circumscribed, who deemed it a worthy focus of Western attention; it was they who brought forth the network of texts within which Buddhism was located. And it was they who determined the framework in which Buddhism was imaginatively constructed, not only for themselves, *but also in the final analysis for the East itself.* (Italics mine.)

## 4.3. A Conceptual Interregnum

In the course of the last three chapters, we have moved with a breathtaking rapidity across the centuries: from the Pagan Rome to the Modern India. Before we reflect about the wisdom, which this journey has imparted us with, let us very briefly recapitulate what we have learnt from the chronicle penned in the previous two chapters.

Truncated though my recounting of the history has been, even this potted history helps us isolate *three* important features of the 'rediscovery' of India by the West. There is, *first,* the image of India as the missionaries and explorers built it up. *Second,* there are the superimposed images and corrections arising out of the initially corrupt and unreliable translations of Indian texts. *Third,* there is the exigency of the European cultural situation, the need to do battle within the religious field, which adds nuances and subtleties.

Why are these features important to us? For the reason that the later descriptions do not alter the framework or outline of these many images, but merely modify the details. Common to them is this single belief: *to know and understand Indian culture is to study the relevant texts.* To understand a culture or a people is to find out what they believe in. Abraham Rogerius wants to know what Hindus believe in; Jones wants to translate the Hindu 'texts' so that he may help the world understand the Hindu culture; Max Müller translates *The Sacred Books of the East,* a formidable achievement by any standard, in order that he may ask what India could teach the West (Müller 1883). Indologists and Buddhologists multiply by the thousands, the one providing us with *A Survey of Hinduism* (Klostermaier 1989); another with *A History of Buddhism* (Warder 1980). Not to be outdone or left behind, Asians join the fray too: stories are told of *Indian Buddhism* (Nakamura 1980),

Sri Lankan and Japanese Buddhism; Thai and Tibetan Hinduism (Daweewarn 1982). This is a convenient travelogue of the Asian continent, no doubt, but hardly as illuminating. An image of Hinduism and Buddhism is built up – with the immoral 'popular' counterposed to the immortal 'philosophical' isms – culled out of the interpretation of texts.

Consider just how ridiculous this really is by indulging in the following thought-experiment. What could one say about European culture and its people of the eighteenth century by studying The Bible? How could one understand even the Middle Ages by reading the Gospel of St. Matthew? Just imagine a group of 'scholars' in India, none of whom know either the classical or modern languages of Europe, studying some gibberish translation in their vernacular of a fragment of the Bible only to make pronouncements about, say, fifteenth-century Europe. Even the French Enlightenment thinkers would find it absurd. Yet, this happened in Europe with respect to India for over two hundred years. What makes the absurdity a total farce is its continuation today. How many treatises do not refer to The Laws of Manu in order to talk about Hindu ethics? How many 'ethno-graphic' (ugh!) works talk about the 'caste-system' without solemnly mentioning the four Varna's? How many Brahmins have ever read the laws of Manu? How many have been told what the Dharma Shastra discusses about?

This farce has assumed tragic proportions because the Indian (Asian) intellectuals have made this attitude, this posture, and this stupidity their own. Protestant criticisms of Catholic priesthood which were used to describe and attack the 'Brahmanic priestly' caste by the ignorant West is a stock-in-trade of any 'progressive' intellectual you would meet in India.

Europeans' understanding of their own religion made them believe that all cultures had a set of religious beliefs, which guided religious practices. Their religious terminology – Paganism – helped assimilate Asia with the Ancient 'Pagans'. This fusion provided the notion of the 'primitive' – a man, a psychology, a society. The Christian arrogance, the economic and military expansion, and imperial consolidation lent greater weight to a periodisation of history. A hallucinatory concept – the primitive – became the foundation for building delirious theories about the origin of religion (see the next chapter). This self-evident set of notions becomes 'obvious' due to its long currency; the ideas become truisms and trivia to most anthropologists, philosophers, students of religion. The circle is complete when the intellectuals of other cultures accept these ravings as 'scientific' truths.

To summarise the claim of the last two chapters in its sharpest form: the reason for believing that India knows of religion is religious in nature. This was not an empirical question, ever: both the question and the answer are theological. That is why an Augustine can coolly declare

Socrates a Christian; a St. Thomas can 'deduce' the true religion from the 'natural light of reason' itself; and a Calvin can begin his *Institutes* with a declaration of impossibility. As I noted, this is an article of *faith* – no less, but no more either.

Why do people in the twentieth century accept this idea as well? One part of the answer is this: the theme has become an unexamined trivium due to its long currency. Besides, to deny 'religion' to a people is to deny them 'culture' and 'civilization'. This is partly the old association between *religio* and *traditio,* and partly the not so-old legacy of the relation between being 'not-primitive', thus having the "ability to think abstractly", and having a "home-grown religion". The intellectuals of Asia (India) accept this because of their peculiar attitude to their old colonial masters. This is a part of an answer, which is more historical in nature. There are other parts too – something which I will tackle later.

*A Summary*

The last three chapters as a whole have introduced several themes. As such, they have a double status: they are answers to some questions and yet stand in need of explanation themselves.

First, we observe the virtue as well as the weakness of the Wittgensteinian appeal to language games (in #1.2). Even if 'religion' is a language game, its appropriation by the Christians radically transformed what it was to the Romans. The consequences were immense: both for the pagan world and for the Christian communities.

Second, we have seen how Christians succeeded in domesticating the pagan 'other' of Rome. By the time Europe encountered the culture of India, the theological framework was set so rigidly that neither the missionaries nor the Enlightenment thinkers escaped its grip. Both themes require an explanation about their 'why'. The answers will come in the course of parts III and IV (*viz.* chapters #8 through #12).

There is also a third theme. If, as it has been described in these three chapters, the theological framework is so strong, what could we say about the secular theories of religion since the Enlightenment? If the story told hitherto were true, then these theories should carry definite theological burdens. In the subsequent part, we shall see the extent to which this observation is true.

In this way, we have introduced several themes, which will continue to recur throughout the rest of this book. We shall come back to them again and again, with the resources accumulated at that stage, to deepen our insight and formulate them as problems. At the end of a historical journey, we have begun a conceptual movement. It is a spiral – going from one chapter to the subsequent one – that brings us to the themes picked up here, while carrying us further at the same time.

# PART II

In the same way the last three chapters formed a group, the next three chapters form a unit. Building upon the results arrived at, they too tell the story of a period, its striving, and the consequences. The narrative picks up at the end of the eighteenth century and its destination is the middle of the twentieth century. Unlike the previous chapters, a potted history makes way for a thematic story. Together, they look at the phenomenon of theory formation about religion in the West. Cumulatively, they argue and demonstrate the following theme: the Christian theological framework has gone on to guide and embrace the naturalistic studies of religion. That is to say, 'scientific' theories about religion presuppose the truth of Biblical themes, which have received secular translations. In this sense, the charge is made that our secular world is a secularised religious world and the case is carried to its conclusion.

Taken together, parts I and II of the book set both the agenda and the problems that the next part addresses itself to.

# CHAPTER FIVE

# REQUIEM FOR A THEME

In the first chapter, we encountered two remarkable things both of which require careful noting. First, a *way* of speaking about other religions was an issue: Why *call* 'Hinduism' a religion and not a 'proto-science'? This manner of formulating a problem is not productive because it is not clear what would count as an answer. For instance, one answer could be: "It has to do with some or another definition of religion". Yet another answer might be the counter-question: "What else should we call it?" and so forth. Though this issue will be tackled later (in chapter #8), let us notice a few things now. By drawing attention to the existing *convention* of speaking about other religions, I hope to look at its grounds. I would like to argue that these multiple descriptions of religions in other cultures transcend any one definition of religion and that they have their roots in the nature of religion itself. That is to say, I will use a historically evolved convention as an entry-point to investigate the nature of the object in question, *viz.* religion.

A natural question at this stage would be about the circuitous route. This brings me to the second observation, *viz.* the questions raised in the first chapter are not sharply formulated.

One of the ways of generating questions is to transform an assertive sentence into an interrogative one. If you observe that the grass is green, you could always add a 'why' and arrive at a question: why is the grass green? In the presence of theories about colours, vision, chlorophyll, and sunlight, *etc.*, it is possible to give some kind of satisfactory answer to this question. Suppose that we have no such theories at our disposal. Then the same question admits of several kinds of answers: "Because it is in the nature of grass to be green"; "Because God made it so"; "Because Angels paint it green every night"; *etc.* That is to say, in this case, the question does not put any constraint on the process of seeking answers; it is not even clear where we have to look to discover an answer. Conceived as a cognitive problem, we would say that it is ill-defined.

The more we know about a phenomenon, the sharper and more focused our questions will become. When we have a theory about an object at our disposal, the problems we can raise in that theory will get a sharp formulation. The relevance of this methodological point to our theme is the following: the cluster of questions that I have formulated is ill-defined because we have no theory of religion that could enable us to pose sharp problems.

This may appear a preposterous claim to those familiar with several 'theories' of religion. Preposterous or not, I will defend the claim in the present and the subsequent two chapters.

More specifically, in this chapter, I will try to show that the claim about the universality of religion is pre-theoretical in nature. In the first section, I provide methodological arguments to this effect. In the next two sections (#5.2, and #5.3), I look at two influential versions of a 'theory' that account for the origin of religion in human cultures. The focus of the argument is neither to falsify the 'theories' in question nor to provide an alternative but to discredit their status. That is, I will try to show that they could not possibly be serious theories because one could argue for opposite conclusions with equal plausibility.

The next two chapters, whose concerns are also theoretical, carry the conclusions of this chapter much further. Their foci of attention are theories that try to characterise religion in terms of a specific kind of experience.

## 5.1. A Methodological Consideration

Samuel Preus, a professor of Religious Studies at the University of Indiana, wrote a book (Preus 1987) outlining the historical and theoretical contours of the eighteenth- and nineteenth-century arguments concerning the origin of religion. He is interested in tracing the emergence of a new 'paradigm' (in the Kuhnian senses of the term) in the field of religious studies, the 'naturalistic' paradigm as he calls it. Speaking of the fortunes of a discussion from Bodin through Hume to Freud, he records its unfortunate fate:

> The very abundance of contemporary literature about how religions and their study ought to be conceived and organized amounts to evidence of an identity crisis in the field; yet there is little indication today that the question of the cause and origin of religion is, or should even be, a topic of interest. It is worth reflecting on this remarkable and unfortunate fact. For about a hundred and fifty years, from David Hume to Emile Durkheim and Sigmund Freud, the issue was pursued and debated with the greatest urgency. *Now it is virtually ignored, and even demeaned as a futile question or worse.* (Preus 1987: xvii; my italics.)

As Preus himself notices, not everyone interested in the phenomenon of religion finds the demise of the question of origins a tragic event. Many authors, from anthropologists to historians, feel it a cognitive gain – as a random collection of the following few citations shows.

Ninian Smart, another scholar in the field of religious studies, lends approval to the current state of affairs in the Macropedia of the fifteenth edition of the *New Encyclopaedia Britannica* under the entry "Religion, Study of" (619) thus:

> The search for a tidy account of the genesis of religion in prehistory by reference to primitive societies...was hardly likely to yield decisive results. Thus, the anthropologists have been more concerned with functional and structural accounts of religion in society and relinquished the *apparently futile search for origins.* (*Ibid*, my italics.)

A recently published introductory text about the anthropological studies of religion confirms the opinion of Smart with the following words:

> The high-level questions about the origins of religion that...(the) Victorian scholars posed...have long since ceased to interest or guide anthropologists (Morris 1987: 91).

One such anthropologist is Evans-Pritchard, who makes clear what the situation is like:

> The great advances that social anthropology has made in and by field research have turned our eyes away from *the vain pursuit of origins,* and the many once disputing schools about them have withered away. (Evans-Pritchard 1965: 104; my italics.)

Historians of repute could not agree more with anthropologists on this question, it appears:

> Historians of religion have for the most part avoided the old controversy about the origin of religion. Most will agree with contemporary anthropology that *this is a dead issue.* (Penner 1968: 53; italics mine.)

As another historian puts it:

> Historical thought, as applied to the study of religion, has often concentrated attention on two questions which history is incapable of answering – those of the origin and nature of religion (Smith 1968: 8).

One reason for the dismissal of the question of origins could be due to misunderstanding and misinterpretation. Many conceive the issue in terms of providing a precise localisation (in time and space) of the beginnings of religion. This is the view, for instance, of the sociologist Vernon talking about the subject matter of his book:

> ...(I)t is important to recognize that we are not concerned here with the origins of religion. For all practical scientific purposes it is safe to assume that the origins of religion are lost in Antiquity. We merely accept the fact that religion exists and affects human behaviour (Vernon 1962: 43).

However, there are other intellectuals who do understand the thrust of the question properly. Despite viewing it as an issue that requires a specification of the *causes* of religion – why does religion come into being? Why does it survive? – they too fight shy of the question. Preus' explanation for the dearth of interest takes the following route:

> It seems that lack of interest in explaining religion stems from a combination of personal commitments, apologetic interests, and political convenience as much as the "scientific" modesty often expressed by religious writers. "Religious studies" as it is normally carried on seems comfortable with a quasi-theological or metaphysical "solution" (or paradigm), by which the origins or causes of religion are placed beyond investigation on the ground that the source of religion is "transcendent". From such a perspective it is both unnecessary and impossible to advance any further in explaining religion (Preus 1987: xviii).

A harsh indictment, surely. If true, a shocking state of affairs. Unauthenticity, bad faith, apologetic motivations – are we to take that generations of intellectuals have exemplified these rather dubious virtues in the field of religious studies? A total dismissal of an issue from the one side seems to bring forth a sweeping condemnation from the other. This situation is sufficient to make us pause and raise our suspicions. Our historical excursion has already warned us to be weary of assuming that there is a valid question here. Let us proceed, however, without prejudging the issue.

*What is the Naturalistic Paradigm About?*

Before we tackle the theme of the origin of religion, it would be best to get a handle on the nature of the 'naturalistic' paradigm that Preus talks about. What he means by the term is not at issue here. What is the paradigm about? In brief, the idea is the following: instead of appealing to the 'supernatural' to account for the origin of religion, the practitioners of the naturalistic paradigm appeal to 'natural' causes. That is to say, they break with theological assumptions and explanations in order to provide a secular account for the origin of religion. Beginning with Jean Bodin, Preus locates many luminaries in the tradition: Herbert of Cherbury, Bernard Fontenelle, Giambattista Vico, David Hume, Auguste Comte, Edward Tylor, Emile Durkheim, and Sigmund Freud. While the earlier authors began the process of paradigm construction, it is to the credit of Hume to have completed the shift.

> If there is one person...whose achievement might be marked as the completion of a paradigm shift, it is Hume...(who) produced a thoroughgoing naturalistic critique of all available theological explanations of religion... (He) not only undercut all appeals to supernatural or transcendent causes of religion, but went on to propose alternative paths of explanation of the available data – paths that are travelled still by scholars of religion (*ibid*: xiv-xv).

If we follow Preus' account, it would appear as though that at least from Hume onwards (including such writers as Feuerbach and Nietzsche), we are not likely to stumble across any theological residues in the 'naturalistic explanations'. In order to assess the truth-value of this claim, we need to be clear about their problem and their answers.

*The Nature of the Problem*

In so far as these several authors constructed theories to solve problems or explain phenomena, what was the problem or the *explanandum?* Preus (1987: xv) again:

> (I)f "God is not given," how is one to explain religions – that is, their universality, variety, and persistence until now? Without taking that next step, criticism would remain parasitic on established theological models – a mere exposure of old anomalies without providing alternatives. Alternative explanatory theories had to be constructed, and this is what the naturalistic program undertook to do; its specific agenda, insofar as it broke decisively with theology, unfolded as an address to that fundamental problem.

While the *explanans* identified the 'natural' causes, what required explanation was the universality of religion. It is important to note that these several theories did not undertake to study the historical causes for the origin of individual or specific religions. What they did was to account for the emergence of the phenomenon of religion as such. That is, the naturalistic paradigm undertook to explain why religion is a cultural universal or why humankind had to invent religion.

Two points require to be borne in mind at this stage. One is about the relation between the *explanans* and the *explanandum*; the other is about the stage of our knowledge of cultures and religions. The first point is simply this: because we are talking about theories, there is some logical relation between the *explanans* and the *explanandum*. These theories purported to explain why religion was *necessarily* a cultural universal – irrespective of what kind of 'necessity' is involved, whether social, psychological, epistemic, or metaphysical. If we have to consider the explanations provided by these thinkers as theories, if we have to take their participation in a paradigm seriously, then we are compelled to assume that they did not presuppose the *explanandum, viz.* the universality of religion. Because if they did, the probability is very great that we have an *ad hoc* explanation on our hands that identifies some alleged causes. An *ad hoc* 'naturalistic' explanation would not be any better or worse than an equally *ad hoc* 'supernatural' explanation.

It is equally essential for us to note that the ethnographic data about other cultures was neither complete nor exhaustive during this period. As we have already seen, they were not even free of ambiguity or inconsistencies. During the period of Bodin or Hume or even Freud, anthropological investigation had not come up with indisputable evidence showing that religion was a cultural universal. Consequently, we are not justified in assuming that these several authors tried to provide an explanation for an established fact.

For these two reasons, one is entitled to look at the naturalistic paradigm as a succession of theories that explained why religion *had to* exist in all cultures, why religion is a cultural universal, and why humankind had to create religions. The question of the origin of religion is important for this reason. It would indeed be shocking if the twentieth-century intellectuals have turned away from a "vain pursuit of origins" without having a better theory. Preus would then be right in accusing them of apologetic motivations.

*What if We are Wrong?*

Theories that explain the origin of religion make assumptions either about human nature (Feuerbach 1841); or about the human society (Durkheim 1912); or about the human psyche (Freud 1913, 1939); or about the human cognitive abilities (Hume 1757), *etc.* For the time being, let us leave aside the question whether these assumptions are true or plausible. Instead, let us first focus on the following issue. What are the consequences to these theories if it turns out that there are cultures that have no religion?

Let us suppose that we come across some culture (either living or dead), which does not appear to have religion. This situation is doubly hypothetical: (a) that we are able, today, to recognise the absence of religion in a culture; (b) that we do come across cultures that have no religion. What, precisely, would the importance of such a discovery be? Spiro (1966: 88), for example, tells us that such a situation would be very fascinating, but fails to tell us what the fascination consists of:

> Does the study of religion become any less significant or fascinating – *indeed, it would be even more fascinating* – if in terms of a consensual ostensive definition it were discovered that one or seven or sixteen societies did not possess religion?...Why should we be dismayed if it be discovered that society X does not have 'religion', as we have defined the term? For the premise 'no religion' does not entail the conclusion 'therefore superstition' – nor, incidentally, does it entail the conclusion 'therefore no social integration', unless of course religion is defined as anything which makes for integration (italics mine).

Although Spiro is 'open' to the idea that there might be societies and cultures that do not have religion, he is unable to find them empirically. Hence the reason, perhaps, why he does not reflect about the consequences of such a discovery. However, we need to do so because it is important for our purposes.

*What Issues are at Stake?*

In the literature (from anthropological to philosophical) that I have consulted, this question is not even raised much less discussed. In personal discussions with scholars on religion, I have experienced a strange reluctance on their part to enter into a dialogue on the matter. "It is a meaningless, hypothetical question", snapped one scholar in irritation when I pressed the point, "it is impossible for cultures to exist without religions and, besides, it is a fact that all cultures have some or another kind of religion". The question might be hypothetical, but meaningless it certainly is not. The latter not only because this question can be answered in several different ways but also because each of these answers has definite consequences to our theories of religion. The methodological importance of the question is best illustrated by looking at three such possible answers.

(i) Theories that postulate religion as a cultural universal turn out to be false;

(ii) They turn out to be inadequate because some cultures will not have religion, as this term is defined in such theories;

(iii) Such cultures lack a vital dimension.

Let us look at these possibilities by turn.

(i) Theories that postulate religion as a cultural universal turn out to be false.

So what? It is no doubt important to know that one had entertained false beliefs. This is a general cognitive argument, which holds for any and every claim we make about the world. What is the specific importance of discovering that religion is not a cultural universal? That is, what do we learn either about ourselves or about the world when we find out that some culture does not have religion?

Consider, for example, the Freudian theory of religion (see also his 1927) that relates the origin of religion to the emergence of a clan totem with a taboo on marriages within the clan. What conclusions could we draw if we come across a culture that does not have religion? Not many: either Freud's theory is false or this culture does not have that particular form of neurosis.

Let us enlarge our net. Consider theories that say that religion is an experience of the holy; or that it is a human response to the transcendent; or that it is an expression of human alienation; or that it is the cementing bond of the community, *etc*. What do we learn from our empirical discovery if we were to arm ourselves with these theories? Either these theories are false or: the members of such a culture do not have the experience of the holy; they have no response to the transcendent; they are not alienated; they lack a cementing bond of the community, *etc*. Even though we approach the same entity with different empirical theories, the lessons are logical in nature. These theories turn out to be false. So what? Are there consequences other than the realisation that we had entertained false beliefs and that we better find another theory?

(ii) Our theories turn out to be inadequate.

One might not be willing to accept the conclusion that our theories are false. One might suggest that the culprit is really our inadequate definition of religion. That is, one might insist that even this hypothetical culture does have religion and we cannot see it because of our 'definition' of religion. This ploy does not work, of course, because our assumption is that this hypothetical culture does not have religion. Nonetheless, it appears to me that we can accommodate this sentiment without making it look ridiculous by weakening the claim just a little bit.

Consider those theories that define religion as a "mechanism for social integration" (*e.g.* the functionalists) or as an "experience of the sacred" (*e.g.* the phenomenologists). Should we come across societies that do not know of religion, we could conclude, for instance, that these societies will be using other 'mechanisms' of social integration or have something else that replaces the 'experience of the sacred'. At this point, one could say that our definitions, as embedded in these theories, are inadequate because one had hitherto wrongly assumed that these specific mechanisms and these typical experiences were somehow necessary.

Let us accept this conclusion at face value without enquiring into its validity. Again, so what? We have learnt a methodological lesson that one ought to give adequate definitions. However, this is a general cognitive argument that would hold for any and every inadequate definition that theories provide. That a general 'methodological' lesson can be learnt in such cases, however important a lesson it might be, tells us very little about the issues at stake in the particular case.

Let us now look at the third possibility. (iii) Some specific culture will either not have the 'mechanism for social integration' or lacks the 'experience of the sacred' or is 'superstitious' or whatever else.

This specific consequence hinges entirely on the stipulative definition of religion. Such a result is cognitively uninteresting, because a discovery of major importance does not give birth to any serious problem; no rethinking of any major issue, except that of a stipulative definition, is entailed by a momentous discovery.

*Suspicious Circumstances*

This situation is rather odd, to put it mildly. It is self-evident to most that all cultures have religion, and yet one does not know what the consequences of its absence are. Surely, if the belief about the universality of religion has greater weight than my quixotic belief that Martians exist, one ought to be able to spell out the consequences that follow from the discovery of its falsity. Let us appreciate the importance of this issue to 'theories' of religion by assessing the consequences of similar answers. What if *modus ponens* is an invalid argument scheme in those logics where it is a valid rule of inference? What if there was no gravitational force on some planet in our universe? What if the mathematical set theory, which is believed to be consistent, is shown to be inconsistent? In each of these cases, one is able to spell out the major problems that would face us.

That is to say, in each of these cases, one can trace a rich and semantically relevant set of false beliefs. The point is not simply that they are false beliefs but also that they have consequences. These, in their turn, will not be tautologies. In other words, these discoveries would generate a wide and varied set of empirical and conceptual problems. Equally important for the purposes at hand is our ability to specify today (even if incompletely) what these problems will be. As we have seen, we are unable to do precisely this with respect to our theories of religion.

From this contrast, it must be clear that there is something suspicious about the claim regarding the universality of religion. Though held to be true and often fervently defended, it is a statement whose implications are all but clear. Of course, what Holmes finds suspicious hardly strikes Dr. Watson as significant. What is sauce for the gander is not sauce for the goose. Is this how one should understand John Hick when he makes this deplorable state of affairs into a virtue of our theories by appealing to the ambiguity of the universe? Speaking of the various interpretations of religion, for example, from Feuerbach through Freud to Durkheim he states:

> It is evident that each of these is more convincing in some areas than in others; but although severally limited they are in principle capable of being combined into comprehensive theories of religion as a self-regulating response of the human animal to the pressures generated by its particular niche within the biological system. *The impossibility of refuting such interpretations is an aspect of the pervasive ambiguity of the universe.* So also is the equal impossibility of refuting the interpretation of religion as our varied human response to a transcendental reality or realities – the gods, or God, or Brahman, or the Dharmakaya, or the Tao, and so on (Hick 1989: 1; my italics).

I do not know whether these several approaches can be developed into comprehensive theories of religion; but if they can, it is wrong to say that it is impossible to refute them. Theories have consequences, and if the consequences are falsified then the theories are refuted as well. However, John Hick is correct in maintaining (I suggest that this is what he has in mind) that these 'interpretations', *viz.* 'religion as a response to the transcendent' or that it is 'a self-regulating evolutionary response', cannot be refuted in the form they are now. This does not have anything to do with the "pervasive ambiguity of the universe" but with the fact that they are quite simply stipulative definitions.

There is another way of formulating this suspicion, which I have raised on methodological grounds. These several theories appear to presuppose the universality of religion. They assume that religion is a cultural universal; that humankind had to discover religion; assume its diversity too in so far as all cultures have some or another religion. Having assumed the truth of the *explanandum*, they then fish around to find a set of plausible looking claims which might 'explain' the phenomenon in question. Laudan (1990: 20) describes such a procedure and the problems involved with it succinctly:

> Suppose that I find some puzzling fact that piques my curiosity, may be I find a massive fossilized bone while digging in my backyard. I may develop a low-grade "theory" to explain this fact: perhaps I conjecture that God put it there to test my faith in the literal reading of the Scripture. Now although my hypothesis arguably explains the fact of a fossil bone in my backyard, that hypothesis is not *tested* by the fossil bone. On the contrary, my hypothesis was specifically constructed to explain the bone. My hypothesis might be testable but I would have to look further afield to find something which counted as a genuine test of it...
>
>     (A)n observation or set of observations is a "test" of a theory only if the theory or hypothesis might conceivably *fail* to pass muster in the light of the observations. If, as in my hypothetical case, the theory was invented specifically to explain the phenomenon in question, and was groomed specifically so as to yield the result in question, then there is no way in which it could fail to account for it. *Where there is no risk of failure, there is no test involved.* (Italics in the original.)

If the naturalist explanation of religion has followed such a path, then our situation becomes understandable. The only way we can test these theories is by assuming the *negation* of the *explanandum* – showing thereby that these theories were groomed to explain the universality of religion. The absence of empirical consequences to our theories of religion – if we discover a culture without religion – has to do with the fact that no genuine test of these theories is possible.

In other words, the claim about the nature and universality of religion is not part of any one theory of religion: if it were, we could immediately see what the consequences of its falsity were. Rather, it appears to be a statement, which undergirds all (or most) 'theories' of religion. It is a claim that appears to precede theory formation about religion. I would like to submit that this is indeed the case.

If my suggestion is true, some interesting consequences follow. *First,* it follows that judgements about religion are pre-theoretical in nature. That is to say, they must undergo all the vicissitudes that such intuitions are subject to. Consequently, there must be observable variations in the inter-generational and, to some extent, even inter-individual judgements regarding the same phenomenon. Prima facie, this consequence appears true: at times, the native Americans are said have religions (like our contemporary Sam Gill says, for example) and at other times not (Christopher Columbus); at times 'Buddhism' is a religion, at other times it is not, and yet at other times it is 'devil's worship' and so on. *Second,* not being a term of the art, nor a 'primitive' concept in an axiomatised theory, the 'definition' of religion will show all the consistency (or arbitrariness) of a stipulative definition. That is to say, the 'theory' of religion must include a cemetery of the definitions. In the words of Lott (1988: 15):

> Any attempt at an anatomy of religious life immediately faces the vexed question of a definition of religion. The field of religious studies is bestrewn with corpses of rejected definitions, found to be either too vague to be of any foundational value, or too specific to include types of religion that are found at the other end of the spectrum; or perhaps too cumbersome to be anything other than a summary description of typical features found in traditions which by general consent are part of comparative field of religious studies.

*Third,* my suggestion must be susceptible to historical enquiry, *i.e.* it must be possible to demonstrate that the ideas about the universality of religion are based on grounds other than serious factual investigation of cultures and peoples. This has been accomplished in the previous chapters. What we now see is their evidential value to our enterprise. *Fourth,* it must be possible to account for the persistence of the stubborn superstition (because that is what this belief will turn out to be, if the above three consequences can be shown to be true) among modern-day scholars that cultures without religions could not possibly exist.

I believe that each of these consequences is true and will endeavour to exhibit their truth at the appropriate place and time. Given the nature of the subject matter, however, the 'proofs' I can provide will be indicative rather than conclusive.


## 5.2. THE METAPHYSICAL SPECULATIONS

Cultures, it is often said in a semi-jocular and semi-serious vein, are driven to create religions if they do not have one. This statement, or its analogues, makes claims about the nature and needs of human beings and groups. That is to say, they provide us with speculative reconstructions of the origin of religion. The early discussions about the universality of religions took this form.

In the next two subsections, I shall look at the general structure of the explanations, which account for the origin of religion by appealing to the nature of the human experience of the natural world. In the next section, I shall look closely at Hume's explanation of the origin of religion. More specifically, I want to look at the explanatory robustness of the 'paradigm' that locates the origin of religion in the way the primitive man experienced his world. I shall examine both the general version of the paradigm as well as its specific variant, *viz.* the fear theory of the origin of religion. My aim is not to show that these theories are false but to see whether they are anything more than theories groomed to explain a particular phenomenon. In the process of exhibiting their *ad hoc* nature, I also hope to hint at the possible reason why these and assorted theories appear plausible at all.

### 5.2.1. Angst, Nature and Man

To the question, 'why does religion come into being?' I have been able to find but one basic answer with many variants: confronted by a chaotic world, the 'primitive' man had to impose some order on his experience. Experiencing phenomena that were both random and inexplicable, the primitive man devised 'mythical', 'magical' or 'natural religious' explanations. This enabled him to survive in a hostile world. From the beginning, man was confronted with two great mysteries: birth and death. The explanations he gave to make 'sense' of these experiences grew into elaborate religious explanations. So goes this basic account with many embellishments that constitute the different variants. As illustrations, consider the following claims:

> Primitive man's life is a life of great uncertainty combined with little knowledge. His universe confronts him with an unpredictable alteration of abundance and dearth, prosperity and famine, life and death. He *necessarily* experiences it as whimsical and unreliable, *threatening* him on vital points of subsistence and survival with far greater frequency than it does modern man. More often than the latter, primitive man has *reason* to experience events as intentional, as carrying hidden messages of some sort. (Van Baal 1981: 155-56; my italics.)

As James (1969: 23-24) puts it with respect to the prehistory of man,

> So far as Early Man is concerned, the three most arresting situations with which he was confronted were those of birth, propagation, subsistence and death. These, in fact, have been the fundamental events and experiences in the structure of preliterate society at all times, creating a *tension* for the relief of which ways and means had to be found. In the palaeolithic period, when life depended largely on the hazards of chase and of the supply of roots, berries and fish, the vagaries of seasons, and so many unpredictable and uncontrollable circumstances by the available human means, the emotionable *strain and stress* was endemic. To sublimate this a ritual technique was devised and developed to meet these requirements

and to maintain equilibrium in an expanding social and religious organization (my italics).

## Chaotic and Ordered Experiences

How sensible are these explanations? How plausible are they really? As I see the issue, not very. The claim that the 'primitive' man experienced the world as a chaotic entity borders on the incredible. If anything, he should have been impressed by the orderliness of the world: seasons, astronomical regularities, or even just the plain constancy and stability of the world around him. Water did not change into wine, streams never flowed uphill, objects always fell when let go, tigers and leopards never ate grass...the list is both varied and huge. Where would he have experienced chaos? Could he have seen 'random' events, such as unexpected thunder, and postulated gods to account for them? It is improper to speak of randomness with respect to early man, but only of unexpectedness. That is, certain events took place unexpectedly. However, if his experience of the world was such that it allowed unexpected events to take place, he need not postulate gods.

Besides, even if he did postulate gods to account for unexpected thunder, by virtue of this postulation alone, he cannot now anticipate and 'predict' at all: it would remain unexpected. In other words, the postulation of gods does not render his phenomenal world more orderly than before. One might be tempted to argue that this postulation does not make the world more orderly, but that it merely removes the fear arising from confronting the unexpected. I shall very soon return to this argument, which locates the origin of religion in fear. For now, let us leave it aside to look at another argument.

Could not the very existence of this ordered world have been the reason for the postulation of gods? Is it not plausible that the primitive man sought an entity (or several entities) to explain how (or why) this order came into being? Again, this is not plausible. Why should he assume that it is in the nature of the divine being to impose order? Why should it be self-evident to him that the principle of order is God? This assumption is characteristic of religions based on the Old Testament, but how could one possibly argue that the primitive man necessarily accepted this theological assumption? After the Flood, as the book of Genesis (8: 22) tells us, comes the guarantee of the order and constancy of nature:

While the earth remaineth, seed time and harvest, cold and heat, and summer and winter, and day and night shall not cease.

Not only is God the guarantor but, as the Genesis story has told us by now, He is also the principle of order separating light from darkness, day from night when the earth was "without form and void". For those who grow up in such a culture, it might appear obvious that the only way of explaining the natural order (before the scientific theories came into being) is to say that it either reveals or requires God or gods. I submit to you that it was not so obvious to the primitive man who did not have a handy exemplar of the Old Testament and had never heard of Christianity.

## Hostile and Unfriendly Experiences

Could we say that the natural world of the Early Man was hostile? Or that he experienced uncertainty because he lived in a world of 'scarcity' while longing for security? Caution is called for when one begins to speculate about the psychology of peoples from other times (or other cultures). Let us begin with the latter question.

The claim is that the primitive man experienced the world as scarcity. To assess the plausibility of this claim, we need to realise that his world gave him droughts and famines, floods and diseases, and plentiful supplies every now and then. That is to say, it would have been in the nature of the world to be this way. When there was scarcity at any one time, there was plenitude at another time. Both scarcity and plenitude would be parts of his experience of the world. The world of a poor man is not the world of a rich man minus his wealth; the world of the Early Man is not our world minus its wealth. To experience *the world-as-scarcity* – not merely as a world containing scarce resources – requires that he had experienced *the world-as-plenitude* and not merely as a world containing bountiful seasons. Even if scarce seasons were numerically more frequent than bountiful ones, he could not experience the world as scarcity. To the primitive man, that would be the normal way of the world. Of course, it is true that no prior experience of pleasure or plenitude is required to experience either pain or hunger. My point is that having hunger does not lead to experiencing the world-as-scarcity. For the Early Man, the experience of the world includes being hungry most of the time. This would be the way of the world, as far as he is concerned. If you or I were to be teleported back in time to *his* world, *we* would experience the world-as-scarcity. That is, his normal world would be our world of scarcity. Why should the Early Man long for security in an 'uncertain' world? The only plausible answer would refer to the typically human way of reacting to situations involving uncertainty. That is, it would appeal to human psychological make up. Do we not react in similar ways to situations involving uncertainty and insecurity? Perhaps we do; but this armchair psychologising, in the style of the en-

lightenment thinkers, could turn out to be true only under additional
assumptions.

The backward extension of our psychology to the psychology of
the primitive man can be true only if cultural evolution over the last
thousands of years has not had any significant impact on the nature
and structure of human emotions. Even the most rabid socio-biolo-
gist would have some difficulty in swallowing such a claim (but see
Lorenz 1971), as would some psychologists (e.g. Harrè 1988). We need
not enter into a controversy here, so let us continue. What, then, has
changed because of cultural evolution? Presumably, our ways of thinking. That means to say that emotions are primarily biological in nature
and are subject only to the laws of evolutionary development. This is
how our backward extension could become true.

Because neither ethology nor socio-biology has decided the issue
one way or another, we can press ahead and point out the implication
of this stance. We need to assume, then, that human beings have two
distinct 'aspects': the rational, which is subject to cultural change and
the emotional that does not undergo change. One of the characteristic properties of human beings is their capacity to develop culture
and change along with changes in the latter. What does change, as we
have seen, is our 'rationality'. Therefore, the "typically human" in us is
'rationality', which evolves and not the 'emotions' that are biologically
determined. This picture is very familiar to us, especially from those
days when men chose other words to express the theme. This bipartite
division of human beings into the rational and the bestial is a centuries-
old legacy. (It is interesting to note that most authors who describe the
origin of religions in terms of 'insecurities' etc., are also fervent critics
of this 'ratio' and 'affect' distinction.) One might want to accept this
legacy, but the only point I want to make is that without such an assumption and without accepting such an implication, it is very difficult
to see how the claims about the early man's psychology could carry
plausibility at all.

*Mysteries Galore*

The same can be said of the 'great' mysteries. What is mysterious about
either birth or death? They were the most banal happenings: people
were born and they died. Animals are born and they die. The primitive man would have accepted these events as the most 'natural' things.
There were no exceptions to death: all organisms he knew died at one
time or another. In fact, one could suggest with greater plausibility that
both birth and death constituted one of the regularities of the world
he lived in. They were part of the order of the world; instead of being

'mysteries' that generated fear or awe, they lent stability to his experience of the world.

It is again important not to confuse issues. I am neither affirming nor denying that the Early Man felt 'emotionally' involved in the birth and death of his 'loved' ones. Whatever his emotional involvement, there is no psychological necessity why the phenomenon of birth and death could not be seen as a regular occurrence. Even if elated by birth and depressed by death, the Early Man could still accept that they were as 'natural' as anything else was and attribute no special cognitive status to them as 'great mysteries'. Birth and death may be salient facts to *us;* but why should this be equally true of the Early Man as well?

On the other hand, even if they were 'mysterious', why does he need to 'solve' them? I mean, why not simply shrug his shoulders and say 'who knows?' and not indulge in some utterly fantastic speculations about them? To realise the flimsiness of these arguments that attribute religion to the primitive man on the grounds of some alleged experience of nature, consider now the 'theory' that neatly reverses the conclusion.

That man invents gods when confronted by his fragility before the terrors of nature or horror before death is an old idea, which stretches back to the Greeks. Popularly known as the 'fear theory' of the origin of religion, it is attributed to Democritus. In the seventeenth century, an influential and productive theologian at the Louvain University, Leynard Leys, Latinised into Lessius, argued in his *De Providentia Numinis et Animi Immortalitate. Libri duo Adversus Atheos et Politicos* (reference and some details in Buckley 1987) that fear lies at the origin not of religion but of atheism. Here is his argument briefly. Why, asks Lessius, does man want to deny religion? Quite obviously, he fears the punishment that will be meted out to him on the day of judgement. Unable to live with the fear and terror gnawing at his vitals, he invents atheism, which denies the existence of God. Atheism, thus, alleviates his fear by removing the cause of that fear.

Here is where one can choose: invention of gods removes the fear, and thus religions come into being; denial of God removes the fear, and thus atheism comes into being.

*Hostile World Revisited*

Clearly, one of the problems of these 'theories' is the fact that 'chaos', 'hostile nature', 'mystery', and such other terms are not descriptions of some 'primal' or 'primitive' experiences, but concepts that structure them. These concepts are the by-products of a culture, which experiences the world this way and not another way. To appreciate the significance of this statement with respect to the 'hostile' nature that the primitive man allegedly confronted, let us look at one element within that experience, *viz.* wildness. Wild animals and wild nature generate fear in man when he confronts them both: the former because they are unrestrained and unruly, the latter because it is untamed and uncultivated by man. While these are the dictionary explications of the term 'wild', our common-sense psychology tells us that the wild is something that we, human beings, are afraid of.

This common-sense psychology is a matter of history too: the spread of Christianity in the West involved, among other things, a pacification of nature:

> ...Christianity...taught...that hills, valleys, forests, rivers, rocks, wind, storm, sun, moon, stars, wild beasts, snakes, and all other phenomena of nature were created by God to serve man and were *not haunted (as the Germanic peoples believed) by hostile supernatural deities,* and that therefore it was possible...to *settle on the land without fear.* This was both preached and lived out in the fifth, sixth, seventh, and eighth centuries by tens of thousands of monks, who themselves settled in the wilderness...(Berman 1983: 62; my italics).

Or, as Berman puts it later (*ibid*: 75),

> Christianity opposed a peaceful and harmonious natural order against the experience of the Germanic peoples, whose natural order was *haunted by demonic forces.*

That is, until Christianity, the 'true religion', came to the Germanic peoples, they lived in fear and terror. Nature was a hostile force, populated by daemonic powers and malignant spirits. The coming of religion removed this fear from man. The 'secular' theories about the origin of religion turn out to provide a historical narrative of the spread of Christianity in the West and, as though not content with this, contain a theological message strong enough to warm the cockles of the hearts of diehard, born-again Christians. Could it be that the acceptance and popularity – ever since the eighteenth century – of the fear theory of religion reveals to us one of the basic trends in the contemporary intellectual scene, *viz.* a tendency to equate the European history with human history? Perhaps, the following story about the Buddha's conception will clarify the force of this question:

> Once it came to pass that a noble and beautiful woman...conceived. At this...moment, the elements of the ten thousand world-systems quaked and trembled as an unmeasurable light appeared. The blind received their

sight. The deaf heard. The dumb spoke with one another. The crooked became straight. The lame walked. Prisoners were freed from their bonds and chains. In hell the fire was extinguished. In the heaven of the ancestors all hunger and thirst ended. *Wild animals ceased to be afraid.* The illness of the sick vanished. All men began to speak kindly to one another as this new being was conceived in his mother's womb. (Herman 1983: 1; italics mine.)

Consider the italicised part of the story. Wild animals cease being afraid. Both in common-sense psychology in India and in the indefinitely many stories about the sages who bring 'peace' to the animals in the jungles by their presence and penance, the idea is the same: the wild is what is afraid of man. In one culture, the wild is what man is afraid of; in another, the wild is what is afraid of man.[1] In the first case, one experiences nature as a hostile force and is afraid. How can that sentiment carry conviction in the second case?

Let me sum up: the problem with the naturalistic paradigm is that the concepts it makes use of, *viz.* 'chaos', 'hostile nature', 'mystery', *etc.*, are not the experiential presuppositions for the development of religion. Rather, they appear to be the results of the development of religion.

### 5.2.2. Fear Theory and Fear from Theories

What appeared a respectable candidate has turned out to be a sorry-looking specimen of an explanation intending to render our human folly or the 'human response to the transcendent' intelligible. However, duty demands saying the funeral mass for its soul. In fact, we are yet to focus on the 'soul' of this paradigm, *viz.* that religious explanations are a way of reducing our fear. Speaking of this idea, and commenting on Hume's philosophy of religion, Gaskin (1988: 185) says,

To the twentieth century reader this may seem *so obvious* as to be scarcely worth insisting upon (my italics).

Let us assume that the Early Man did have a fearful attitude towards the world: fear of 'natural' events, fear of the future, fear of birth and death, and so on. Would the postulation of God (or gods) remove this fear? I do not see how it could.

---

[1] This contrast is intended to highlight the issue, which does not depend upon the meaning of 'wild'. As we well know, both in English and other European languages, one of the meanings of the term 'wild' picks out the fear that untamed animals have of man.

Consider the tales told by the Ancient Greeks about their gods. Or those told by the Indians as many thousands of years ago. Or even the tales of those tribes and groups, which the anthropologists are so fond of studying, about gods and creation, thunder and lightning, birth and death. In short, pick up any of these religious explanations (as our intellectuals call them) and look at it carefully. What do you see? You see an extremely rich and enormously complex explanation, which populates the world with all kinds of beings and entities. Intricate and devious intentions battle with unintended courses of events; divine and semi-divine beings vie with each other in choosing sides with the mortals; oftentimes crudely, and at others subtly, they influence the course of a war, the fortunes of a people and, now and then, even the banal actions of an unsuspecting person. In sum, these religious explanations create another world, which is even more complex than the events they are purported to explain.[2]

Religious explanations, it is said, reduce fear by making strange events appear familiar and thus render them more manageable. To see how these early explanations could do no such thing, consider a banal happening like unexpected thunder (or even an expected one) and a possible explanation from a Greek peasant around the time of Homer: is Zeus quarrelling again with Athena? Were not some people saying that the procession of the gods last week took place at an inauspicious moment? There is that greedy merchant Leondros who, as everyone knows, used tampered weights to measure out his offerings to the gods. Or, may be, it has something to do with the impiety of this Greek peasant...And so it would go on and on. If this alone is not enough, there is still the problem that this peasant faces regarding his course of actions. Our peasant, in other words, has more problems now than if he was simply afraid of the thunder and hid his face under the blankets or ran to his goats or sheep for comfort. Not only does he continue to fear the (unexpected) thunder, but he also piles up additional fears in a kind of masochistic glee and wild abandon. If religious explanations are supposed to reduce fear, and these early tales give us an inkling of the pattern of early explanations, then the early religions would not decrease but increase these fears. In our cultures, we are familiar with certain kinds of pathological individuals who do precisely that. In this sense, it is of course possible that the Early Man was a neurotic being so thoroughly under the grips of an illusion that he thought he was getting rid of his fears when he was really accumulating them.

The ground of this additional fear must be obvious: because his 'explanations' are to reduce the fear of natural events and happenings, he has allowed the divinities (construed as causal forces) to constantly interfere in the natural world. By doing so, he has introduced arbit rary,

---

[2] I would like to thank Marissa Vermaete for this insight.

punishing forces into his universe. This is not merely a matter of 'logic' but also of psychology – to stay with the Ancients a while longer – as Rist (1972: 177) tells us:

> As Lucretius and Plutarch, in his treatise on superstition, make clear, fear of the intervention of the gods was a factor in ancient life which could not easily be ignored, *and many individuals appear to have lived their lives in constant dread*...It was a fact of life for many, and Epicurus...*regarded it as a matter of primary importance* (my italics).

That is to say, this kind of fear of the gods was superstitious (*superstitio* in Latin also means the excessive fear of the gods), and one way of reducing it is to say that the gods do not interfere in the affairs of humankind. While this option was open to Epicurus (and to Lucretius, his follower), it is not open to us: after all, the development of religion is alleged to reduce the fear of natural events.

On second thoughts, why would this option not be open to us in the form of some variant or another? Which other concept has a force in Latin that is the opposite of *superstitio?* Why, *Religio* of course. (Obviously, we have left both the Early Man and the Greek peasant behind in time now.) How could religion oppose superstition, when the latter was the only religion known to the Early Man?

Here is how: the religion of the Early Man was not really religion (because it was, after all, superstition), or it was not the 'real' religion. A true and real religion would reduce fear and do away with superstition. Is this not a claim that Christianity made and continues to make?

There is one way a religious explanation could plausibly reduce the fear of the Early Man: it would reduce every event, every happening, and every misfortune to the same cause. Questions about how this cause does all these things are placed beyond the scope of human explanation and declared as a miracle. Such an explanation would be both simplistic and simpleminded, of course; but then, that is the explanation of Christianity and Judaism. Everything was the Will of God and the Will of God itself was a mystery. This is not a simplistic rendering of either of these two religions on my part, but the stance of Jews and the early Christians as late as second century C.E. (Common Era) much to the irritation and annoyance of figures like Galen, the famous physician. Discussing the problem of why eyelashes are of equal length, and speaking of the Platonic demiurge as well as the Mosaic God, Galen asks:

> Did our demiurge simply enjoin this hair (the eyelashes) to preserve its length always equal and does it strictly observe this order either from fear of its master's command, or from reverence for the god who gave

this order, or is it because it itself believes it better to do this? Is not this Moses' way of treating Nature and is it not superior to that of Epicurus? The best way, of course, is to follow neither of these but to maintain like Moses the principle of demiurge as the origin of every created thing, while adding the material principle to it. For our demiurge created it to preserve a constant length, because this was better. When he had determined to make it so, he set under part of it a hard body as a kind of cartilage, and another part a hard skin attached to the cartilage through the eyebrows. For *it was certainly not sufficient merely to will their becoming such:* it would not have been possible for him to make a man out of stone in an instant, by simply wishing so.

It is precisely at this point in which our own opinion and that of Plato and the other Greeks who follow the right method in natural science differs from the position taken up by Moses. For the latter it seems enough to say that God simply willed the arrangement of matter and it was presently arranged in due order; for he believes everything to be possible with God, even should he wish to make a bull or a horse out of ashes. We however do not hold this; we say that certain things are impossible by nature and that God does not even attempt such things at all but that he chooses the best out of the possibilities of becoming. We say therefore that since it was better that the eyelashes should always be equal in length and number, *it was not that he just willed and they were instantly there; for even if he should will numberless times, they would never come into being in this manner* out of a soft skin; and, in particular, it was altogether impossible for them to stand erect unless fixed on something hard. We say that God is the cause both of the choice of the best in the products of creation themselves and of the selection of matter. For since it was required, first that the eyelashes should stand erect and secondly that they should be kept equal in length and number, he planted them firmly in a cartilaginous body. If he had planted them in a soft and fleshy substance he would have suffered a worse failure not only than Moses but also than a bad general who plants a wall or a camp in marshy grounds. (Galen in Walzer 1949: 11; italics mine.)

To say that religion removes man's fear of the natural events is another way of suggesting that '*religio*' replaced '*superstitio*'. Put in historical terms, it is about how the '*vera religio*' defeated the pagan '*superstitio*'. Authors as varied as Dodds (1965) and Fox (1986) tell us that this is one of the major reasons for the triumphant spread of Christianity that eclipsed the pagan 'religions' in the Mediterranean world.

Even if one is willing to accept this as a historical truth with respect to the spread of Christianity, what does it have to do with the Early Man and other cultures? Nothing, unless one identifies human history with the European history. I submit to you, again, that this is what has happened: fear theories of the origin of religion effectively identify religion with Christianity and human history with the European history.

## 5.3. THE PSYCHOLOGICAL SPECULATIONS

If, in the above picture, we shift our emphasis from the experience of nature to the result of that experience, we arrive at the second popular explanation about the origin of religion. Though he is not the originator of this 'theory', its classic exponent is David Hume, the Scottish philosopher of the Enlightenment period. For him too, fear was at the origin of religion: the fear of unknown events.

Of course, Hume did not believe that all cultures have religion even though he believed that the "belief of invisible, intelligent power was generally diffused over the human race, in all places and in all ages" (1757: 21). Nor did he claim that monotheism was the 'original' religion of humankind that degenerated into polytheism. (Both claims were in vogue during that period as 'explanations' for the heathen and pagan polytheism, and as accounts for some of the similarities between pagan rituals and those of Catholic Christianity.) These differences and nuances between Hume and his contemporaries, important though they are for a fine-grained analysis of the Humean philosophical system, are irrelevant for our purposes. What joins him to our theme is his insistence that the origin of religion lies in fear of the unknown.

David Hume is an apt choice, because his *Natural History* has had an immense impact on later theoretical, historical, and even theological considerations on religion as Peter Brown records:

> The religious history of Late Antiquity and the early Middle Ages still owes more than we realize to attitudes summed up so persuasively in the 1750s by David Hume in his essay, *The Natural History of Religion*...(H)e provided historians with an imaginative model whose influence has remained all the more pervasive for having entered so imperceptibly into the tradition of historical learning...It is by...stages that Hume's model came insensibly to permeate the great tradition of liberal Anglican and Catholic scholarship that has fostered so much of learning on which ecclesiastical history of the Late Antiquity and medieval world is based (Brown 1982: 8-11).

This is high praise indeed, coming as it does from a reputed historian of Late Antiquity and the early medieval religions. I will not try to delineate the elements of Hume's 'theory', which have so imperceptibly seeped into the consciousness of a period that is dismissive of the question of the origin of religion. Let us just note that our choice of Hume's theory is defensible and that we can proceed further without having to face the charge of setting up a straw man. Let us listen to him now:

> No wonder, then, that mankind, being placed in such an absolute ignorance of causes, and being at the same time so anxious concerning their future fortune, should immediately acknowledge a dependence on invisible powers, possessed of sentiment and intelligence. The *unknown causes*, which continually employ their thought...are all apprehended to be of the same kind or species. Nor is it long before we ascribe to them thought and reason and passion, and sometimes even the limbs and figures of men, in order to bring them nearer to a resemblance with ourselves. (Hume 1757, III: 317)

Several significant things strike us if we look carefully at this citation, which outlines Hume's views on the *causes* (!) of religion. Two claims are entertained about human psychology: that we are ignorant of causes and that we are anxious about our future fortune. I suggest that we let these claims stand as they are and not discuss them further. Instead, let us focus on the result of this human psychology, *viz. religious explanation, which is characterised by five properties:*

(a) Religious explanations postulate invisible powers;
(b) Religious explanations acknowledge the dependence of human beings on such powers;
(c) These invisible powers are construed as (unknown) causes;
(d) All these causes are apprehended to be of the same kind;
(e) Finally, these causes are modelled after human beings.

If we look at any scientific theory, it is obvious that it has the *first four* properties too: postulation of invisible powers and relations; the claim that we are dependent upon them; the idea that they are causal forces and powers, which are of the same kind. Many philosophical theories –from metaphysical to ontological ones – possess these four properties too. Consequently, these four properties, severally or in conjunction, do not help us to say that the Early Man had 'religious', as against 'scientific', 'proto-scientific', or 'philosophical' explanation. Thus, the weight falls entirely on the *fifth* property. Its presence *must* transform some explanation into a religious explanation. Let us, therefore, look at it more closely.

*Religious Explanation*

The claim that causes are modelled after human beings is making two points: one about the activity and the other about the product. The former is a methodological or procedural feature involved in creating religious explanations, and the other is a semantic or substantial feature regarding theories.

The methodological aspect is this. Human beings provided an explanation or constructed a theory, which involved the activity of creating a model for that explanation. Alternatively, the Early Man made use of analogies in the process of constructing religious explanation. Both are unexceptionable points, because neither the activity of drawing analogies nor that of constructing models makes some theory into a religious one. This point is hardly worth belabouring in a period where cognitive science, philosophies and sociologies of science are studying the role of not just models but also of metaphors and analogies in the development and propagation of scientific theories. That leaves us with just one possibility to explore: according to a religious explanation, the causal forces operating in the universe are personalised entities, endowed with intention, "thought and reason, and passion".

Before we delve deeper into this point, let us remind ourselves that Hume was an enlightenment thinker who not only believed that religious explanations were the antipodes of rational explanations but was also busy trying to figure out how this 'weakness' in human spirit could be comprehended and made intelligible. With this in mind, if we look at the leftovers of Hume's 'theory', the first thing that we could say is this: the alleged 'anthropomorphising' on the part of the Early Man is in the best tradition of scientific theorising and rationality. The reason is obvious: the only thing, about which the Early Man had any knowledge, if he had knowledge at all, was himself. Consequently, when he developed an explanation about another domain, he cast it in terms of the 'theory' he already had. That is to say, he was explaining the unknown in terms of the known. Is this not the activity of scientific theorising under at least one description? In this sense, how could the emergence and origin of religion exhibit anything but human pride and strength, *i.e.* human rationality?

As we have seen Hume arguing, before something becomes a religious explanation, appeal has to be made to personalised entities as the governing powers of the universe. That is to say, divinity not only assumes a human form but it also regulates the universe according to its plans, intentions, goals and sentiments. This notion of divinity, however, is typical of the Semitic religions but not of Asian traditions: from Hinduism through Buddhism to Shintoism, none of them suggests that the universe is held together by one or even several deities – let alone that their thoughts, reasons and sentiments, regulate and govern the Cosmos. Consequently, the conclusion is inescapable: either Hume is explaining the origin of, say, Judaism or that he does not consider religions in Asia as religions at all. However, Hume does neither: he is telling us how humankind could have discovered religion.

*Explanatory Problem*

Further commentary and disputation are not relevant for our purposes. Let me compress the result of the earlier arguments thus: even if these theorists believed that they were explaining the universality of religion, it is not evident from their explanations that they were indeed doing so. They could well have been explaining the origin of stories, of theories, of philosophies, of proto-sciences...

There are two kinds of difficulties. If we look at their explanations in terms of their *explanandum, viz.* the universality of religion, there is no logical relation between it and the *explanans.* One could draw the opposite conclusion on exactly the same grounds with equal plausibility. This suggests that the claim about the universality of religion is not explained by the identified causes. The second difficulty reinforces the same impression. If we look at the *explanans* alone, we do not know what the *explanandum* is. It could be the emergence of any intellectual product whatsoever, including some variety of 'evolutionary epistemology', *viz.* the ways in which nature forces us to think.

The problem lies in seeing how the *explanandum* (as these theorists claim and as is claimed on behalf of these theorists) is connected to their *explanans.*

*Religion and Explanation*

Let us recast the issue in a more general form. Knowing as we do that there are several kinds of explanations the issue is this: Why are these early explanations religious and not philosophical? Or 'proto-scientific'? That is, the immediate problem is that of identity and individuation: along what lines could one distinguish between the class of religious explanations and those that are not? What distinguishes one religious explanation from another?

The problems have to do with the nature of explanations. Since Hume attributes 'religion' to the primitive man because he transforms natural forces into 'explanatory' units, the question is one of distinguishing 'religious' explanations from other types of explanations. Let us look at the possibilities open to us in answering this question.

One possibility is to differentiate between these two types (*i.e.* religious from scientific explanations) on formal (*i.e.* logical) grounds. That is, one could analyse the logical structure of different explanatory statements and try to establish that 'religious' explanations have a form that, let us say, 'scientific' or 'philosophical' ones do not have. However, the analyses of this issue as we have them in the philosophies of sciences (*e.g.* Achinstein 1983; Wilson 1985; Pitt, Ed., 1988) are neither fine-grained nor rich enough to permit such an argumentation.

The second possibility is that their content makes them into religious explanations. In that case, the desideratum for attributing religion to primitive cultures is that, in some non-trivial way, their explanations involve notions that are irreducibly religious in nature. The problem of identity and individuation recurs here again, but with respect to the 'religious' concepts now: what makes some concept, any concept, into a religious as opposed to 'proto-scientific', 'philosophical' *etc.*, concept?

Suppose we say, overlooking the circularity involved in this attempt and ignoring the conceptual quandaries that such a position would land us in, that concepts like 'God' *etc.*, are religious in nature, whereas concepts like 'proton' and so on are 'scientific' in nature. Would that help us? It could, provided we realise that not any kind of 'god' will do: to identify 'chichak' as a synonym for the notion of God, one needs to be able to show that 'chichak' and 'God' refer to one and the same entity. One way of doing this would be to establish that both share all properties, *i.e.* that they are identical in nature. However, this does not appear a realistic course because it requires knowledge about God, which many religions deny to human beings.

As an alternative, one could enumerate some 'properties', which allow us to recognise the entity talked about. For instance, "that which created the Cosmos" (appropriately hedged so as to exclude the big bang and such like) could help fix the reference of the term 'God' without entailing that it explicates the meaning of the term. That is to say, one could treat 'God' as a proper name for the sake of identification. Consider, for instance, a God who creates the Cosmos and is 'outside' it. Surely, this entity is not identical to creatures that are creations of an uncreated Cosmos no matter what their 'superhuman' powers are. Consequently, if references to such an entity within an explanation make it religious, none of the primitive 'religions' qualify as religions. Not merely that: Hinduism, Buddhism, Taoism, Shintoism, *etc.*, fall out of consideration as well.

The price that one has to pay for not facing up to the fact that this would be an *ad hoc* distinction between 'religious' as against other forms of explanation is the following: one has to effectively acknowledge that there are no religions outside Judaism, Christianity and Islam because they alone countenance this 'God'.

One could try to get out of this difficulty by making an epistemological appeal. In that case, we are faced with the embarrassing problem of having to provide methodological criteria to solve semantic problems. Not all souls, as is evident from our experiences in the world, are embarrassed by the same thing and some hardier ones among them have tried this route as well. Van Baal (1971: 3), an anthropologist, defines the religious as:

> all explicit and implicit notions and ideas, accepted as true, which relate to a reality which cannot be verified empirically.

In many other writings on religion, the above citation is but one example, we often come across claims that religion deals with the 'empirically unobservable', the 'scientifically unobservable', and with 'that which cannot be perceived by the senses' and so on. For our purposes, it is of no consequence whether these 'unobservables' and 'imperceptibles' are terms like 'God' and/or 'sacred'. It is relevant to notice, however, that this attempt at distinguishing the semantic content on methodological grounds fails for two interrelated reasons.

The first reason is that the 'empirically verifiable' terms and concepts ('observational terms', as they are called in the philosophy of science) are not absolute terms but are relative to some given theory. Not all empirically unverifiable 'entities' or 'terms' are religious either: many 'basic' concepts of theoretical physics as well as metaphysical and logical concepts are that too. Therefore, the problem of distinguishing religious from non-religious explanation is not solved.

The second reason has to do with the development of both science and technology. Not only do they make 'visible' what was 'unobservable' before; not only do they make 'perceptible' some entities, whose existence we did not know of until the event; but, what is more important, the very notion of 'observability' also changes as our knowledge of the world evolves. The problem of some clerical contemporaries of Galileo with the telescope had to do with what they were 'observing': were they seeing what was 'there' on the moon, or an illusory image projected by the telescope which had nothing to do with the so-called mountains on the moon?

The attempt to distinguish the religious from other classes of explanation fails on several counts. Even though one would like to distinguish between the different classes of explanations, the distinction cannot be drawn at a formal level (i.e. at the level of the logical structure of the arguments). One has to appeal to the meaning of these concepts. At this point, we bump against the fact that different 'religions' contain different concepts.

So if neither of these two ploys works, what have people explained when they thought they were explaining the origin of religion? How could they have maintained that the Early Man had religion? Appeal to archaeological evidence such as burial sites, practices of burying the dead, *etc.*, are so many icings on a rotten cake: one has to show that funeral practices are religious practices as well. Is that not, as the Bishop sighed to the Actress, the question at stake? Actually, even this will not do: one has to argue that funeral practices cannot be anything other than religious practices. The general archaeological consensus is hardly unambiguous on this score:

> Neanderthal graves represent the best evidence for Neanderthal spirituality or religion…but, more prosaically, they may have been dug simply to remove the corpses from habitation areas. In sixteen of twenty well-documented Mousterian graves in Europe and western Asia, the bodies were tightly flexed (in near-fetal position)…which could imply a burial ritual or simply a desire to dig the smallest possible burial trench. Ritual has been inferred from well-made artifacts or once-meaty animal bones found in at least fourteen of thirty-three Mousterian graves for which information is available…but there are no Mousterian burials in which the "grave goods" differ significantly from the artifacts and bones in the surrounding deposit…In sum, the Neanderthals and possibly their contemporaries clearly buried their dead, at least sometimes; but it does not follow that the motivation was religious…(Klein 1989: 328-329).

Thus, we have a puzzle on our hands. The 'naturalistic' explanations transform the empirical history of the Christianisation of the West into a 'theory' about the origin and universality of religion. They transform the Semitic theological ideas into the characteristic properties of religion. They presuppose a theme while claiming to be its *explanandum*. They have a theory, which has only trivial consequences…The list of defects is more varied than the existing number of explanations of the origin of religion. What has gone wrong with the naturalistic paradigm?

## 5.4. ON EXPLAINING RELIGION

As we have seen, the naturalistic paradigm suffers from several debilitating diseases. It is hardly obvious what is being explained; it is hardly evident what counts as evidence and what does not; assumptions are made whose truth-values can be legitimately disputed; one could, with equal plausibility, argue for the opposite stance on exactly the same grounds…

The problem with the naturalistic paradigm is its *explanandum, i.e.* what the practitioners thought they were explaining. As we have seen, one can derive many other conclusions – including the negation of the *explanandum* – from the 'causes' they identify. In this sense, the naturalistic 'explanation' does not appear groomed *even* to explain the universality of religion.

Consider a question of the following sort: Why did the primitive man invent religious explanation instead of philosophical or scientific theories, ballet dancing, or banging on drums? Why did he not do a pirouette, stand on his head, or simply go and invent cookies? Why, from all the possibilities open to him, did he have to go and invent religious explanation?

Throughout the chapter, my argument probed the naturalistic paradigm to see whether it can answer the question: 'Why religion rather than...?' That is, the argument tried to assess whether the explanatory theories embedded in the paradigm provide us with a contrast set. (For a discussion of this notion see van Fraassen 1980; Lipton 1990 and 1991; articles in Ruben, Ed., 1993.)[3] While contrastive explanation may not be all there is to being a theory, it is very important for our purposes. Otherwise, we could as well use the theories from the naturalistic paradigm, as many have done, to explain not just the origin of religion but also the emergence of ritual, music, dancing, mythologies...

The naturalistic paradigm is a latecomer in the field. Theological doctrines and religious beliefs, which constitute the "supernaturalistic" paradigm, had accounted for the origin of religion long before Bodin or Hume or Freud tried to do so. Therefore, if a choice has to be made between the paradigms on epistemic grounds, there are simply no good arguments for deserting the older paradigm. The reason for this is simple: the 'naturalistic' paradigm makes theological assumptions too – less explicitly, less honestly, and thus loses 'explanatory' force. In this sense, the 'naturalistic' paradigm does not force any kind of paradigm shift, no matter what is said on its behalf.

The harshest indictment that one could level against the naturalistic paradigm is not that it is incoherent but that it smuggles in theology as the science of religion. Preus and many others are so blinded by the talk of 'natural causes' that they fail to reflect on what is being explained. These theories – those from Bodin to Freud – are merely sets of claims, which are only *prima facie* plausible. Three quarters theology and a quarter of illiterate ethnology, such is their nature. They are not challengers to the 'supernatural' explanations of religion; they have never been that. Therefore, the real question is not about the universality of religion but about the intellectual belief that it is so.

---

[3] I would like to thank Erik Weber for drawing my attention to this aspect of my argument and to the relevant literature.

That such a hybrid, incoherent beast has met its 'natural death' due to indifference is not an occasion to accuse the twentieth-century intellectuals of duplicity, deceit, or apologetic motivations. Rather, it is time to look anew at our intellectual heritage to determine what we have really inherited.

## By Way of a Summary

Are we justified in writing off all those theorists who have tackled the question of the origin of religion as wrong, muddleheaded, and silly to the extreme? Today's orthodoxy strongly advocates this course: it is best that these theories are left where they are, say the contemporary scholars, *viz.* in yellowed tomes gathering dust in some forgotten corner of the library shelves.

I suggest that in these writings on the origin of religions a golden nugget of insight is still to be found. Even though I will refine this insight only much later in this essay (chapter #9.2), this is the place to mention at least what that insight of the thinkers from yesteryears is.

It is the belief that there is a very tight and intimate relation between 'being a religion' and 'being an explanation'. Therefore, to have a religion is to possess an explanation. An explanation is always an explanation of something or the other. Consequently, what does it explain? It explained, as these writers suggest, many events and happenings: birth and death; the meaning and purpose of life and Cosmos; the beginnings and ends of man and the world, etc. In short, these thinkers grasped religion-as-explanation. Even though this is not what they actually said, I suggest that their insight consists in seeing religion not as this or that sort of explanation but as explanation pure and simple. Cryptic though this formulation is, I will leave it here for now.

# CHAPTER SIX

# "SHALL THE TWAIN EVER MEET?"

In the first chapter, I identified an inconsistent line of reasoning in the writing of contemporary authors. It had to do with the question of what religion was, and the criteria used by them to identify their object of study. At that stage, we saw that several avenues were open to us to lend intelligibility to their quest. One such, which I shall take up in this chapter, was an appeal to the nature of religious experience.

What is interesting about such or similar accounts is the use they make of concepts like 'holy', 'sacred', *etc.*, to denote a particular kind of experience, which they would like to identify as characteristically or even typically religious. The emphasis shifts from an organised entity – be it as a set of doctrines, a movement, a structure – to an experience, which an individual could have. Of course, it is not easy to circumscribe experiences. No one claims that he has done it exhaustively with respect to religious experience either. Nevertheless, they suggest that we try to identify a recurring feature of religious experience; recurring in the sense that such an experience cuts across spatio-temporal and cultural boundaries of different organised and not-so-organised religions.

We can see what is interesting about such attempts. If successful, it will provide us with a criterion, using which we could idenify the 'the religious' in terms of an experience, and 'religion' by referring (in whichever way) to the religious.

In this and the subsequent chapter, I would like to look at this attempt rather closely. I shall do so in two phases: textual and conceptual. The textual phase (#6.3) involves analysing the arguments of influential authors advocating such an approach: Schleiermacher primarily, Otto and Söderblom secondarily. We shall also briefly encounter Durkheim and Eliade in this process. The conceptual phase sets both the background to the question (#6.2) and carries the argument to another level (chapter #7). I shall first outline the contexts: the historical context in which appeal was made to religiosity; the argumentative context of the book in which my dialogue with these authors takes place.

## 6.1. A NEW DEVELOPMENT AND SOME NEW CONCERNS

Even though I have just spoken of the historical context, it does not mean that I shall be able to trace it in evolutionary terms. It is a historical context only in the sense that it is a temporal location, which saw the birth of attempts to characterise religion by talking about a certain kind of experience. Paradoxically enough, the absence of history at this stage of the argument has to do with the fact that the developments in the late nineteenth-century thought are of fundamental importance to twentieth-century scholarship.

At the end of 1890s, there emerged a movement in Germany which acquired the label *Religionsgeschichtliche Schule*. Its platform (see Sharpe 1990) may be decomposed along three axes: *firstly,* this school (or its members) focused on religion and not on theology; *secondly,* as a consequence, doctrinal statements about religion interested them less than popular religion did; *thirdly,* as they saw the issue, an adequate appreciation of the Hellenistic world, as it formed the background to Christianity, was indispensable to understanding Christianity. Albert Eichhorn, William Wrede, Hermann Gunkel, Johannes Weiss, Wilhelm Bousset, Ernst Troeltsch, Wilhelm Heitmüller, and Hugo Gressmann were some of its prominent members. Curious is the fact that no full accounts of either these people, or their methods and approaches exist in English. What makes it curious is that their contributions are very important to the study of religion on at least two levels.

### 6.1.1. Development on Two Levels

The first level relates to what must have struck you already about my essay, *viz.* my constant use of the word 'religion' in the singular. As Hermann Gunkel wrote in 1913, describing the origins of the *Religionsgeschichtliche Schule:*

> From the beginning we understood by *Religionsgeschichte* not the history of religions, but the *history of religion*...Our work was permeated by the idea that the ultimate objective of the study of the Bible should be so as to look into the heart of the believers of the time as to enter into their innermost experiences and give them adequate description. We desired not so much to think about the books of the Bible and their criticisms as to attempt to discern in them living religion. (Cited by Sharpe 1990: 102; italics in the original.)

Commenting on this, Sharpe further remarks (*ibid*: 103):

In English we hardly know even what to call it, though most writers have opted either for "the history of religions school" (which is wrong) or the "religiohistorical school" (which is imprecise). It is far too easy to miss the point made by Gunkel, that in its label – apparently coined by Wilhelm Bousset in 1903 – the word "religion" is in the singular, and not in the plural. (In English, we have the semantic carelessness in respect of "comparative religions" versus "comparative religion" as shorthand for "the comparative study of religion" in the singular.)

Or, again, amplifying this statement somewhat later (*ibid*: 151):

(I)n the scholarly vocabulary of the time "religion" occurs almost always in the singular, in *Religionsgeschichte, religionshistoria,* "comparative religion," and the other more or less interchangeable terms. All religion is in the last resort one, however wide its range of variants. The Judeo-Christian tradition does not operate according to rules different from all the rest... All religion is one, and all religious traditions in some degree represent a human response to divine revelation...

Of course, why I speak of 'religion' in the singular has little to do with this school. It is, however, important to note that those who placed emphasis on the *subjective* experience of religion initially used the word in the singular. Such experiences vary across individuals. This being the case, how to make sense of their talk of 'religion' instead of 'religions'?

At the second level, as the earlier citations already make it clear, the emphasis on the unity of religion also meant an ability to investigate relations between religions. Believing that "the place of Christianity among the religions of the world cannot be seen in terms of a divinely protected enclave, immune form outside influence" (*ibid.*), this group began an investigation into the nature of religion itself. Sharpe (*ibid:* 103) again:

Certainly the members of the school began with the Judeo-Christian tradition, moving outward from there into the hinterland of the Ancient Near East on the one hand and Hellenism on the other. Their intention, however, was more ambitious: in illuminating a historical problem, that of the interplay of traditions in the ancient world, they sought to penetrate to the heart of religion itself.

For now, let us appreciate how important these developments are, and what their importance is.

*On the Two Levels*

What we must realise about this school and its members is their openly declared religious affiliation. Without exceptions, they were all firm believers – Protestant Christians, to be precise. This situation did not make them into the darlings of the Protestant Establishment. On the contrary. The school was frowned upon, its claims looked at with suspicion, and it was not always obvious to the outsider what the school was really aiming at. Notwithstanding these objections and resistance, it is important to note that the school was a nucleus of Protestant intellectuals.

As the earlier citations have made clear, there are at least three fundamental claims and some of their consequences that should strike us important.

The *first* is their refusal to speak in terms of the 'true' religion and the 'false' ones. Unanimously, they all suggest that the difference between religions is one of degree. All religions form a continuum, as one might wish to put it. However ecumenical this idea might be, an issue comes to the fore when the theme is formulated in this way. Degree of what? A continuum of what? A continuum of human responses to the revelation of the Divine, of course. The 'degree' is the adequacy or otherwise of the nature of such a response, obviously.

This way of looking at *themselves* – Christ as the 'fullest' revelation and Christianity as the most 'adequate' response – and at the 'others' in function of their self-image is hardly novel. We have already had an occasion to note this with respect to St. Augustine's idea of the true religion. However, what makes it new is the constellation of the development sketched in chapter #3, *viz.* the enlightenment and Romantic views on religion. The other relevant factor to us is that this 'school' would very soon get *academic* recognition in the 'secular' universities in Europe.

Speaking of religion in these terms meant an explicit recognition that even Christianity is historical. This was their *second* claim. Again, what makes it new is the form in which it gets articulated. As I have noticed earlier on, the Enlightenment thinkers and the Romantic scholars periodised *human* history. A primal religion and its decay, and its subsequent degeneration constituted the recognisable landmarks of such a history. What the *Religionsgeschichtliche Schule* did was to carry this orientation one-step further and one-step sideways. Religion itself has a history and it is a part of human history. The history of religion *evolves,* and this history is the story of the evolving human responses to the revelation of the Divine. In short, religion itself evolves as humankind does. In this way, it transcends the idea that religion was an error – after all, if it is an error, why does it continue to flourish? – while recuperating the developmental ordering of human history.

Their *third* claim is consistent with the above two. Religion is one. They tried to argue this not by looking at this or that theological claim but by focusing upon the human *response*. That is, they looked at the 'living' religion in its various manifestations. By doing so, on the one hand, they rejected the attempted reduction of religion to morality alone. In its trajectory, 'Natural Religion' had landed up somewhere in the vicinity of such a view. They rejected this position, on the other hand, by accepting the Enlightenment contribution to the Christian thought, *viz.* the belief in the universality of the domain of religious experience. The human response to the revelation of divine – which constitutes the domain of religious experience or religiosity – is universal and cross-cultural. This is what religion is. The difference among religions, as a first approximation, is the variety in the responses. As these responses get articulated, the variety gets its Gestalt. Articulations of different responses, in their turn, are non-trivially dependent on the nature of the divine revelation. The tension between the revelation of the Divine and human responses to it defines the dynamics of the evolution of religion and its history.

In sum, this is the contribution of the *Religionsgeschichtliche Schule* to the twentieth-century scholarship. In the latter, a discerning student will find more than mere echoes of this school and its influence. Yet, very little scholarly work is done about this school. I have no explanation for this neglect; I am not even sure that such an explanation is relevant for my purposes. What I will do in these two chapters is to trace the importance of the claims of this school through different authors: in Schleiermacher, their spiritual teacher; in Söderblom, their contemporary; in Otto, an independent thinker; in Eliade, who founded the journal *History of Religions;* in Durkheim, who tried to build a 'scientific' theory of religion; and among some proponents of the idea of 'atheistic' religiosity; and in an argument about the nature of our secular world. While the themes of the *Schule* constitute the background of my textual analyses, the latter are meant as answers to other questions and concerns. Now is the time to talk about these as well.

### 6.1.2. Grouping the Concerns

If we look back at the drift of my argument over the last four chapters as a whole, we see that some questions not posed at the beginning have come to the fore. I would like to identify them because in seeking solutions to them, I can also traverse the ground I need to cover.

*Firstly,* there is the standard textbook story about the Enlightenment and its consequences to the European culture. Beginning with the *phi-*

*losophes'* critique of religion, a new movement of 'Free Thinkers' has found its Gestalt. Over a period, this resulted in the loosening of the grips of religious ideologies and frameworks on the social life. Today, one speaks of 'secular' as against 'religious' thought and, more often than not, correlates 'scientific' investigation with extending the sway of 'secular' thinking over social life.

My story, however, has attempted to sketch another plot to the Enlightenment. I have accused the figures of this period of extending Protestant themes and charged them guilty of generalising the Christian themes in a secular garb. In that case, the obvious challenge I face is to account for the post-enlightenment phase of 'secularisation'. How can I consistently extend my story to incorporate the post-enlightenment period as well? Could I redescribe even this movement as drawing nearer to Jerusalem and going farther away from Athens? These two questions constitute the *first* concern of these chapters, *viz.* that of adding plausibility to my claims by making implausible claims.

There is a consequence to the above standard textbook story, which is the *second* question I must tackle. If a secularisation process has been active for over two hundred years – a process, which is as deep and wide as its champions maintain – then the West itself should be an exemplar of a culture without religion. Where such a claim is made, and it is made very often in response to my theses, then we face a remarkable state of affairs: the western social scientists make the claim that religion is a cultural universal. That is to say, they tell us that *cultures* without religion do not exist. They say that while being situated in a culture that is allegedly an example of a culture without religion!

In the process of telling my story further, I need to see whether I can illumine this state of affairs without appealing to *ad hoc* hypotheses. That is, I need to answer the question 'is the West itself a culture without religion?' in the *negative* without being *ad hoc* or inconsistent. This, then, constitutes the *second* concern of these two chapters.

*Thirdly*, it is often suggested that understanding religion is inherently a comparative enterprise. Knowledge of other religions has allowed students of religion to develop a scientific approach to the study of the phenomenon of religion.

My story, with respect to India in any case, is at loggerheads with this suggestion. I have argued that 'religions' were *created* in India by the West and that such is the compulsion of a religious culture. The compulsion to create religions everywhere is strengthened by an endless translation of 'religious' texts. This reinforcement can only have disastrous effects on executing a 'scientific' study of religion. That is to say, I have to establish the case that the study of religion takes place within the framework of religion. My *third* concern will indeed be to do so.

These are the three issues as they have emerged during the course of the second, third, and fourth chapters. In this and the subsequent chapters, we shall see where a settling of the issues is going to take us.

## 6.2. A Pagan Prosecution of Christianity

*Christian Forgetfulness*

In an extremely stimulating book, a Jesuit scholar, Michael Buckley (1987) develops an interesting historical argument demonstrating the parasitic relationship between atheism and theism. (See also Kors 1990 who argues for similar conclusions from a different point of view.) With the development of Christian theology into a theism, whose beginnings he locates at the Louvain University in the hands of Lessius, he argues that atheism became inevitable. Christology became subordinated to the problems posed by the 'pagan' authors. Henceforth, establishing the existence of God by the light of natural reason took precedence over the nature and person of Jesus Christ as the fulcrum of Christianity.

> (T)he arguments which Lessius uses and the evidence to which he alludes are...from the classical philosophers. To deal with a putative atheism, Lessius steps back over almost fifteen hundred years of Christian theology as if these centuries had left no mark upon European consciousness, and revives the arguments of ancient, pagan masters.
>
> The typical atheists are the ancient philosophers. So atheism in the sixteenth and seventeenth centuries is treated as if it were a philosophic issue, rather than a religious one; this shift characterizes Catholic apologetics for the succeeding four hundred years...Atheism is taken as if it were simply a matter of retrieving the philosophical positions of the past, rather than a profound and current rejection of the meaning and reality of Jesus Christ. Christology has become irrelevant in establishing the reality of god (Buckley 1987: 47).

In this history of the transformation of Christianity into a theism, he traces several moments: the presupposition of the existence of God for the existence of Self (Descartes); the order in the world as an evidence for the existence of the Creator (Newton); the nature of man and so on. That is to say, neither Christology nor a mystagogy of experience was reformulated by the theologians to present *vestigia et notae* of the reality of god – as if Christianity did not possess in the person of Jesus a unique witness to confront the denial of god or as if one already had to believe in order to have this confrontation take place. In the rising attacks of atheism, Christology continued to discuss the nature of Christ, the unity of his freedom and his mission...but the fundamental reality of Jesus as the embodied presence and the witness of the reality of god within human history was never brought into the critical struggle of Christianity in the next three hundred years...In the absence of a rich and comprehensive Christology and a pneumatology of religious experience Christianity entered into the defence of the existence of the Christian god without appeal to anything Christian (*ibid*: 66-67).

Atheism followed on the heels of such arguments only to demonstrate that they were susceptible for alternate interpretations that are more coherent. Theism was to flee from pillar to post haunted by a spectre it had raised: atheism. One such moment was the refuge in man's subjectivity: the 'religious' experience. I will not summarise Buckley's book, nor will I continue the story from where he left off. Therefore, let me allow Buckley to tell the end of the story as well:

(The) shift in theological foundations evoked, carried, and even shaped its corresponding atheisms. If nature was not at issue human nature was. And for every philosopher or theologian who asserted god as a necessity if human life were to be consistent, appropriated...another rose up who argued just the opposite: that human life was not enhanced but infantilized by god; that god was not human appropriation but human projection; that human beings could only be free when religious belief had been superseded. The area of evidence advanced by the great upheavals of Kant and Schleiermacher became, not the final moment, but a formative influence in the evolution of atheistic consciousness...Whereas the theological appeals to nature had generated an atheism founded upon the adequacy of nature, similar calls upon human nature for theological assertions now generated the demands of Feuerbach, that human nature be recognized as infinite, of Marx that it be freed from social alienation wrought by religion, and of Freud that it be free to live without these theological illusions.

...Argue god as the presupposition or the corollary of nature; eventually natural philosophy would dispose of god. Argue god as the presupposition or the corollary of human nature; eventually the denial of god would become an absolute necessity for human existence (*ibid*: 332-333).

I am not a Christian; my knowledge of Christology and other aspects of Christian theology is limited. Despite this, I want to join issue with

Father Buckley. Better said, I want to dispute a point about Christology precisely because I am not a Christian, and because this disputation constitutes *the* most crucial point in Christology itself.

Before I do so, let me give my assent to the basic argument of the book: Christian theology brought forth atheism in the West because it ceased being distinctively Christian. Admittedly, this is a crude formulation; how else could one summarise a book of over four hundred pages in half-a-sentence? In all probability, he is right in discerning the presence of the pagan masters from the Antiquity in defining the question. However, I think he is fundamentally wrong in assuming that either Lessius, or the later Christian theologians, took over the questions posed by the Ancients. As I have suggested earlier on, both the questions and the answers changed fundamentally when Christianity appropriated pagan problems. The problem lies within Christology itself even if many other historical events were required to bring it to light.

## A Christological Dilemma

The understanding and interpretation of the person and acts of Jesus Christ – which is the broad domain of Christology – involve an extraordinary attitude (see also chapter #2). It not merely conceptualises the multiple pasts of human groups as one common history of humankind, but it also claims that Jesus is the historical fulfilment of a promise made to a people, *viz.* the Jews. In Jesus, God not only reveals Himself, but also does so *uniquely*. The emphasis of Christology accordingly is and should be not so much on God's revelation as much as Jesus Christ *in whom* God reveals himself. Unfortunately, contrary to the expectation of the early Christians, the world did not end immediately or even a bit later.

Judaism did not disappear in order to become one with the Greek and Roman 'religions', but instead continues to survive to this day: as a tradition and as a practice of a people. Neither Christology nor Christianity has a leg to stand on, as the pagan critics of Christianity noted long ago, without considering itself as a fulfilment of Judaism. Despite several attempts during the centuries, the "Jews are neither dead, nor close to dying, nor even dangerously ill" (paraphrasing Lyall's description of Hinduism; see chapter #3).

Condemning them to eternal damnation is one option, but a serious Christology – which has to talk about the continued action of a resurrected Jesus Christ in human history as its agent – has to do more than that if it has to understand human history after Paul. The *past* that Christianity claims is the past of another people, another group. Judaism is not in the past; if it were, Christianity could easily consider itself as its heir very much the way the western culture calls itself the inheritor of the Graeco-Roman civilization. Judaism has a past, whereas the past of Christianity begins with Jesus. In this sense, Judaism appears as a problem within Christology: why did not history go the way it was supposed to? Alternatively, if you prefer a less suggestive formulation, what is revealed of God's plan in the empirical history of the last nineteen hundred years or more?

The internal divisions and schismatic movements raise a parallel problem in Christology as well. The person of Jesus Christ is *the* way for humankind; in him, humanity finds its oneness. Precisely this claim has been the ground for *dividing* not merely the humankind into believers and non-believers but also the very Christian community itself.

Other cultures and groups in the world – with their real or imagined pasts – pose other kinds of challenges to Christology. There is the daunting and the as yet unaccomplished task of assimilating the parallel and different pasts into *one history;* and then, even more importantly, there is the task of communicating the exclusivity of an 'all-inclusive' Christ (see Moule 1977; especially the fine debate between Wilmer and Moule therein). The Christian missionaries confronted the latter problem repeatedly, already at the level of translating the concept of (Christian) God into other tongues (*e.g.* Loewe 1988; Kors 1990 to get a flavour of the problem in early China). This is not just a 'translation' problem but also Christological. If this is one horn of the dilemma, which arises from the Christ-centred approach, another arises from a God-centred orientation. Let us look at that as well.

Suppose that you put the emphasis on God's revelation in Jesus. Because the focus shifts to the One who reveals Himself and not to the one in whom such a revelation occurs, it enables 'us' to speak of multiple revelations of the 'divine' in human history. The world becomes, literally, a "universe of faiths" (Hick 1973, 1989; see also Surin 1990 for a 'materialist' critique). Such a 'liberal' stance allows one to acknowledge the possibility of the knowledge of God outside Jesus even if, as Father Schillebeeckx does, one appeals to the particularity of the figure of Jesus:

Al kunnen we Jezus in zijn volheid niet bereiken, tenzij we daarbij zijn unieke, eigen-aardige relatie tot God mede in rekening brengen, dit betekent toch niet dat Jezus de enige levensweg naar God is. Ook Jezus *openbaart* niet alleen God, hij *verhult* Hem ook, daar hij in niet-goddelijke, schepsellijke menselijkheid verschijnt. En zo, als mens, is hij een historisch, contingent of beperkt wezen, dat op geen enkele wijze de volle rijkdom van God kan representeren… tenzij men de realiteit van zijn mens-zijn loochent… (Schillebeeckx 1989: 28).

[Although we cannot grasp Jesus in his fullness, unless we reckon with his unique and specific relation to God, this cannot possibly mean that

Jesus is the only way in life to God. Jesus does not only *reveal* God, but he *conceals* Him as well; because he appears in the non-divine, in the human, and in creaturehood. Consequently, as a human being, he is a historical, contingent or limited being that can in no way represent the full richness of God...unless one dismisses the reality of his being human.]

The price, the Christological price, paid for this admission is evident: the *uniqueness* of God's revelation in Jesus will have to be sacrificed. In such a case, the *Christ figure* becomes the problem of Christianity – the relation, that is, between Jesus and the Christ. In his poignant book, Father Schillebeeckx notices the problem in this way:

> We worden hier geconfronteerd met enerzijds het moeilijke, haast para-doxale idee van Jezus' particuliere, onbeschrijflijk bijzondere verhouding tot God en anderzijds met het feit dat hij als historisch verschijnsel een 'contingent', beperkt proces is, dat andere wegen naar God niet kan uit-sluiten of negeren...Dit...impliceert ook dat we theo-logie niet kunnen herleiden tot een christologie...(*ibid*: 29).
>
> [On the one hand, we are confronted here with the difficult, almost para-doxical idea of the particular, indescribably special relation of Jesus to God and, on the other, with the fact that, as a historical appearance, he is a 'contingent' and limited process which cannot either neglect or close-off other roads to God...This...also implies that we cannot reduce theo-logy to a christology.]

Not only will such a stance sacrifice Christ, but also the 'divine'. Because this divine – when looked at cross-culturally – refers to differ-ent entities in different traditions. That is to say, 'God' itself will be-come a *Christian* God; he will find his place among other gods; or he will be assimilated in these cultures by becoming yet another member of the 'heathen' pantheon. This assimilation may enable one to talk in the languages of other peoples and cultures but the 'theo-logical' and not merely the Christological price is also in proportion: who is this 'God' that is supposed to reveal Himself? Rama? Shiva? Shakti? The 'Brahman'? Perhaps, none of these and the Devil himself in person?

The alternative, of course, is to deny multiple revelations and empha-sise the uniqueness of the God-Christ relationship. Such a Christology, as I have already noted earlier on, poses the problem of the exclusiv-ity of the 'all-inclusive' Christ. With respect to other cultures, as said before, the situation is one of being unable to *say* what the 'all-inclus-iveness' is about.

Of course, an implicit presupposition is at work in my argument. Revelation must be accessible to all and this contributes to its unique-ness as well. I do believe that this must indeed be the case and that the nature of religion demands it. However, I need to have developed other arguments before showing why this must be the case. Therefore, I shall postpone tackling this issue to a suitable place (#9.3.3). For now, let me just say this: either you emphasise the 'Catholicity' of Jesus, and you can only do that by sacrificing the specific nature of Christianity; or you emphasise the specific nature of Christianity, then your discourse becomes radically unintelligible to others, in exactly the same way it was to the pagans of the Antiquity.

In the course of western history, many solutions have been worked out. One such, I want to claim, was the philosophical theism, and the transformation of the question of atheism into a philosophical one. That is to say, this is one solution to the problem of Christology. Such a theism could talk about God in terms understandable to others only by eschewing a Christ-centred approach. In the first place, it meant that a philosophical theism tried to develop a 'universal' language. Doing so entailed a sacrifice of local colours, cultural variations, *etc.* To talk about religion and God across cultures required a general and abstract theism. By sacrificing a Christ-centred approach, theism became more of a philosophy of religion (*e.g.* MacGregor 1973; Nielsen 1982; Morris, Ed., 1987). However, Buckley is wrong in not seeing that the movement towards theism is a solution to a Christological problem, *viz.* the nature of God's revelation in Jesus Christ.

To those who are believers and theologians, this may constitute the most challenging problem of Christology and Christian theology. Being neither, and speaking from outside, it appears to me that this Christological dilemma sums up the problem of Christianity: with the emphasis on the uniqueness of God's revelation in Jesus Christ, Christianity can never become truly 'Catholic' (in the sense of 'universal'), but must remain content with being one conglomeration of sects among others. This, of course, means giving up its universalistic pretensions to being the 'true religion' even if, paradoxically enough, it cannot but claim universality precisely on the grounds of its exclusivity. Alternatively, it does not put that emphasis, in which case it could become universal; the cost, however, is that it will cease being specifically Christian. Such then is how the pagan world of today is 'prosecuting' Christianity. What we need to know is how Christianity punishes the pagans for this prosecution.

### 6.3. A Christian Persecution of Paganism

Beginning with Schleiermacher, the liberal Protestant tradition laid a new accent on the subjective aspect of religion: the religious experience. This 'experience' is supposed to constitute the religious domain, demarcating and distinguishing it from all other domains of human experience.

This approach is characteristic not only of other liberal Protestants like Rudolf Otto, Nathan Söderblom, and William James, but also of phenomenologists like Mircea Eliade and sociologists like Emile Durkheim. Custom clubs all these names together. As though this congregation is not alarming in itself, a similar approach is taken over by a loose confederation of 'atheistically religious' scholars – suggesting, as a first approximation, the great popularity of this approach.

### 6.3.1. Delineating Some Protestant Themes

If you look at the history that Buckley sketches and the authors I want to talk about very briefly, it will look as though the transformation of Christianity into theism was a mere prelude to what was to come. It now appears possible to talk about religion – specifically and including Christianity – without even having to appeal to a Christian God, even if He is a "philosopher's God". A Christian God appears to have become increasingly irrelevant to being religious to such an extent that atheistic Christianity and atheistic religiosity appear as reasonable options.

I should like to proffer an apology in advance. None of the authors will be treated in any detail in the pages to follow. Even more regrettably, I look at some others in a perfunctory manner. This cannot be helped, given my concerns. I shall look at these authors in terms of one issue *as* it relates to the theme of the book. Specifically, I want to explore the relation between 'religiosity' (conceived of as the subjective experience of an individual), a religion and the notion of God or divinity. Let us begin with Schleiermacher.

### Reden über die Religion and the Contemporary Readers

I will use the text from the first edition of Schleiermacher's famous set of five speeches *On Religion*. (In the subsequent editions of this work, the author introduced many changes, distancing himself from some of his early 'radical' formulations. See the translator's introduction to the text: Crouter 1988.) A rhetorically powerful text, it does not lend itself to a kind of critical examination that one could subject a theory to. Nevertheless, or perhaps because of it, this work enjoyed an enormous popularity in many circles.

The reason for choosing the text from the first edition has to do with the idea, which Schleiermacher was to soften in the later editions of that work, that God has nothing to do with religion and that there could be religion without God:

> From my standpoint and according to my conceptions that are known to you, the belief "No God, no religion" cannot occur...one religion without God can be better than another with God. (Schleiermacher 1799: 136-137)

This flat assertion, together with his emphasis on intuition and feeling, has led many to see in Schleiermacher a possible source not only for developing a characterisation of religion that serves the purposes of

(i) demarcating 'religion' from 'non-religion';

(ii) guiding cross-cultural investigation into the religion;

but also for

(iii) defending forms of 'religiosity' independent of any beliefs.

Proudfoot's excellent book on *Religious Experience* (1985) is an extended discussion of the possibility of severing religious experience from concepts. Predictably enough, one of the main targets of his critique is Schleiermacher. He locates the context of the latter's work in the aftermath of the havoc wreaked by Kant's *Critiques*. He sees a fundamentally apologetic move in Schleiermacher's attempt. To safeguard the religious domain from Kantian attacks, says Proudfoot, Schleiermacher created a new domain, which was neither practical nor theoretical. This was to be the domain of religious intuition and taste.

> (Schleiermacher)...is motivated in this project by two goals. The first is to present an accurate description of the religious consciousness...
>
> The second goal is more theoretical and apologetic. Schleiermacher hopes that by presenting religion in its original, characteristic form he will demonstrate the inapplicability of Enlightenment criticisms of religious belief, particularly of the Kantian critique of speculative metaphysics, to the actual phenomena of religion. Religion is a sense, a taste, a matter of feeling and intuition. Consequently, it remains unscathed by Kant's contention that our experience is structured by the categories and thoughts that we bring to it and thus that we produce rather than reproduce the world we think we know. As a sense that precedes and is independent of all thought, and that ought not to be confused with doctrine or practice, religion can never come into conflict with the findings of modern science or with the advance of knowledge in any realm. It is an autonomous moment in human experience and is, in principle, invulnerable to rational and moral criticism (Proudfoot 1985: 2).

The brunt of Proudfoot's thesis is that this project fails on conceptual grounds: a religious experience of the kind that Schleiermacher accurately describes is an intentional state, which requires a specification of the object of thought. Personally, I find that Proudfoot's general points are extremely well taken. In so far as contemporary authors use

Schleiermacher for the ends they do, namely to provide an autonomous domain to religion on the grounds of some alleged experience or another, Proudfoot's critique of Schleiermacher is well-grounded. However, my problem is with his Schleiermacher and, by extension, with all those who use Schleiermacher to speak of a religious experience, or a kind of religiosity, which is not supposed to depend on concepts that structure them. That is to say, what was Schleiermacher doing in that book?

### Reden über die Religion and Schleiermacher's Public

To begin with, let us remember that Schleiermacher presents his book as a set of lectures. Who is his audience? As the subtitle indicates, and indeed as he repeatedly makes it clear throughout, the book is a set of speeches to the *cultured despisers* of religion. His audience is a cultured public. It is 'cultured' in the sense that it is cultivated and, therefore, has achieved a stage of development beyond that of the 'common', 'uncultivated', and 'lower' class of people.

> (D)o not relegate me without a hearing to those whom you look down upon as common and uncultivated as if the sense for the holy, like an old folk-costume, had passed over to the lower class of people...You are very well disposed to these our brothers...But, I ask you, do you then turn to them when you want to disclose the innermost connection and the highest ground of those holy sanctuaries of humanity? Do you turn to them when concept and feeling, law and deed are to be traced to their mutual source, and the real is to be exhibited as eternal and necessarily grounded in the essence of humanity?
>
> ...I wish to show you from what capacity of humanity religion proceeds, and how *it belongs to what is for you the highest and the dearest*...Can you seriously expect me to believe that those who daily torment themselves most tiresomely with earthly things are the most preeminently suited to become intimate with heaven? That those who brood anxiously over the next moment and are firmly chained to the nearest objects can raise their eyes furthest to the universe? And that persons who have not yet found themselves in the uniform succession of dead industriousness will most clearly discover the living deity? Therefore, I call *only you to me, you who are capable of raising yourselves* above the common standpoint of humanity, you who do not shrink from the burdensome way into the depths of human nature in order to find the ground of its action and thought. (Schleiermacher 1799: 86-87; my italics.)

This long citation and others like its kin (*ibid*: 95) clearly indicate that Schleiermacher speaks to a specific audience. That is to say, only the 'cultivated' people are able to understand Schleiermacher.

What is he saying so that his audience may understand? He is saying that "Religion's essence is neither thinking nor acting, but intuition and feeling" (*ibid*: 102). Religion is "an insolent enemy against the gods" (*ibid*). Because religion is neither art the way praxis is nor speculation the way science is, but a sensibility and taste for the infinite, Schleiermacher's questions carry a punch:

> Without religion, how can praxis rise above the common circle of adventurous and customary forms? How can speculation become anything better than a stiff and barren skeleton? Or why, in all its action directed outwardly and toward the universe, does your praxis forget to actually cultivate the humanity itself? It is because you place humanity in opposition to the universe and do not receive it from the hand of religion as a part of the universe and as something holy (*ibid*: 103).

He entreats his audience to become familiar with the formula of an intuition of the universe (*ibid*: 104), which is the highest and most universal formula for religion. Kant and Schleiermacher's use of 'intuition' partly overlap, but this is not the place to discuss it.

> (T)o accept everything individual as a part of the whole and everything limited as a representation of the infinite is religion (*ibid*: 105).

In other words, as we work our way through the second speech, "On the Essence of Religion", we begin to realise that this religious 'intuition' and 'feeling' is, in fact, quite well-structured. It tells you what your object of experience is and how you should experience that object; how you should experience what you are experiencing as...That is to say, you cannot have this experience if you do not already have the concepts that help you structure it:

> But persons who reflect comparatively about their religion inevitably find concepts in their path and cannot possibly get around them. In this sense, all these concepts surely do belong to the religion, indeed, belong unconditionally, without one being permitted to define the least thing about the limits of their application (*ibid*: 132).

Further, these concepts (*nota bene,* he is talking about such specific concepts as miracles, inspirations, revelations, feelings of the supernatural, and the like)

> indicate in a most characteristic manner human consciousness of religion; they are all the more important because *they identify not only something that may be in religion universally, but precisely what must be in it universally (ibid:* 134; Italics mine).

He is talking about religion as an intuition and is explicitly identifying the presence of the above-mentioned concepts as an identifying mark of religion.

Not only must his audience have these concepts, but it must also have already experienced the universe in such a way that

> the universe is one pole and your own self is somehow the other pole between which consciousness hovers. The ancients certainly knew this. They called all these feelings "piety" and referred them immediately to religion, considering them its noblest part. *You also know them...*(*ibid:* 130; my italics).

This then is the *second sense* in which Schleiermacher's audience must be cultured. There is also a *third sense* in which his public requires to be cultured and cultivated. To speak of this, Schleiermacher indulges in historical comparisons. The following long citation shows the extent to which Schleiermacher is a child of his culture:

> To the *unrefined person* who has only a confused idea and only a dim instinct of the whole and of the infinite, the universe presents itself as a unity in which nothing manifold is to be distinguished, as a chaos uniform in its confusion, without division, order, and law, and from which nothing individual can be separated except its being arbitrarily being cut off in time and space...With this impulse his God becomes a being *without definite qualities,* an idol or a fetish, and if he accepts several of these, such beings can only be distinguished by the arbitrarily established limits of their realms. At *another level of formation (Bildung),* the universe presents itself as a multiplicity without unity, as an indeterminate manifold of heterogeneous elements and forces...If the idea of a God is added to this universe, it naturally disintegrates into infinitely many parts...gods arise in infinite number, differentiated by the various objects of their activity, by different dispositions and inclinations. You must admit that this intuition of the universe is infinitely more worthy than the former; *Now let us climb still higher* to the point where all conflict is again united, where the

universe manifests itself as totality, as unity in multiplicity, as system and *thus for the first time deserves its name.* Should not the one who intuits it as one and all thus *have more religion,* even without the idea of God, *than the most cultured polytheist?* Should Spinoza not stand just as *far above a pious Roman, as Lucretius does above one who serves the idols?* (*Ibid*: 137; italics mine.)

These are the different levels of cultivation or culture. In general, those at the lower level are unable to grasp the higher. The higher is not only better but it also expresses the 'most holy', the highest unity:

However fortunate you may be at deciphering the *crude and undeveloped religions* of the distant peoples or at sorting out the many types of individual religions that lie enclosed in the beautiful mythology of the Greeks and the Romans is all the same to me; may their gods guide you. *But when you approach the most holy, where the universe is intuited in its highest unity,* when you want to contemplate the different forms of systematic religions – *not the exotic or the strange but those that are still more or less present among us* – then it cannot be a matter of indifference to me whether you find *the right point from which you must view them* (*ibid*: 211; my italics).

When one reads ideas like these, one really wonders how commentators could possibly ascribe the idea that religion is some kind of 'unstructured' experience to Schleiermacher. Even this level of culture and cultivation is not enough to belong to Schleiermacher's public. One must find a right point of view. Which religion has achieved this highest unity without having the right point of view? Why, Judaism of course. Here, then, is the *fourth* sense in which you have to be cultured, if you want to be the public of Schleiermacher's speeches. You must neither be a polytheist, though he is better than an idol worshipper, nor a 'primitive'; it is not even sufficient that you are a monotheist, because Jews are that as well. You need to be a Christian. As he puts in *The Christian Faith* (1830: 37-38)

On the highest plane, of Monotheism, history exhibits only three great communities – the Jewish, Christian and the Mohammedan; the first being almost in process of extinction, the other two still contending for the mastery of the human race. Judaism, by its limitation of the love of Jehovah to the race of Abraham betrays a lingering affinity with Fetichism...And so, this comparison of Christianity with other similar religion is a sufficient warrant for saying that Christianity is in fact the most perfect of the most highly developed forms of religion (cited in Eilberg-Schwartz 1990: 74-75).

Of any colour perhaps? No, doctrines and beliefs that Christians hold have little to do with being 'religious'. Who holds dogmas central to religion? The Roman Catholic Church, obviously. Consequently, it is not even enough to be a Roman Catholic in order to belong to Schleiermacher's group of *cultured* despisers: you must be a *Protestant.*

In other words, Schleiermacher makes no bones about the fact that the public in whom he hopes to find that feeling are Protestants. Those who can have this experience, who have had such experiences, are the Protestants as well.

That this is the case with Schleiermacher will become obvious if we reflect on two further considerations. Schleiermacher does recognise that Christianity is a tradition with a history and that, for example, it is different from Judaism. If indeed religion was merely, and only, a question of the experience of an individual then there is no way on earth that there could be such a thing as Christianity or Judaism or whatever else. After all, that they exist and do have a history is dependent upon the fact that they are transmitted. If religion were to be identical to some intuition or some experience of the universe alone, then such a transmission is impossible. One can transmit doctrines but that alone is not religion. That is why you cannot 'teach' religion, as Schleiermacher says (*e.g.* 144-145).

There is a second consideration as well. If you cannot teach this sense to others, how can anyone, whoever he may be, ever have this experience? No problem, says Schleiermacher, every human being has an innate religious sense (*ibid:* 146).

However, this alone is not enough. This 'inborn religious capacity' requires training; it requires formation. It can be nurtured or destroyed depending on the tradition one is born into. From what I have said above, it is obvious that not all traditions can nurture it. Only some can do this. This does not imply that a tradition, which nurtured such a feeling a thousand years ago, can continue to do it even today. The second Protestant theme resurfaces here: the corruption and degeneration of the religion into dogmas, rituals, priesthood, and the laity.

As though this is not enough, Schleiermacher keeps insisting that religious experience can be had *only* within a religious tradition. In fact, his most famous assertion on this score goes like this:

> (R)eligion can be understood only through itself and its special manner of construction and its characteristic distinction will not become clear to you until *you yourself belong to some one or other of them.* (ibid: 210-211; italics mine.)

These lines are immediately followed by the previous citation (see above) making it clear that when he speaks about understanding religion through itself, he is *not* talking about some experience which can be understood only by having that experience. Nevertheless, many have seen in this an attempt at immunising religion against the criticism made by, say, atheists. Even worse, it is alleged that he wants to make religion immune to any scientific investigation.

However, I have gathered enough citations from Schleiermacher to propose another, more attractive, and yet a very simple interpretation. Schleiermacher claims that one can have a religious experience only within a religion; he argues that religiosity is an internal aspect of a religion; and suggests further that one can be religious only within a religious tradition. That is to say, Schleiermacher is not providing us with a tradition-independent concept of 'religiosity' and 'religious experience', which one could use to classify some *sui generis* experience as 'religious'. He is telling us what it means to be a religious person by presupposing a specific religion. In short, it is not an inter-traditional, comparative concept, which picks out a phenomenon like 'religion' by speaking about the experiential state of an individual. Rather, it is an intra-traditional concept that picks out a 'truly' religious person. It distinguishes such a person from someone who merely believes a set of doctrines or from someone who merely observes the practices of his tradition.

Nothing of what I say need be said if you are willing to recognise that Protestant theologians have seen Schleiermacher as a Protestant. Until Karl Barth's withering criticisms of Schleiermacher, the latter was the most influential theologian in the German Protestant tradition. Even as I write now, his star is once again raising in Germany.

*Nathan Söderblom: Archbishop and Scholar*

This is how Eric Sharpe, a professor of religious studies, titles the eighth chapter of the biography (Sharpe 1990) of Nathan Söderblom. From 1914 to his death in 1931, Söderblom was the archbishop of Uppsala and primate of the Church of Sweden. He was, of course, religious – deeply and devoutly religious. He wrote as a Christian, but this does not disqualify him from writing about religion. Many of his books are not translated into English, but most students of religion are familiar with his justly famous entry in the *Encyclopedia of Religion and Ethics*, under the heading "holiness":

> Holiness is the great word in religion; it is even more essential than the notion of God. Real religion may exist without a definite conception of divinity, but there is no real religion without a distinction between holy and profane. The attaching of undue importance to the conception of divinity has often led to the *exclusion* from the realm of religion of (1) phenomena at the primitive stage, as being magic, although they are characteristically

religious; and of (2) Buddhism and other higher forms of salvation and piety which do not involve a belief in God. The only sure test is holiness. From the first, holiness constitutes the most essential feature of the divine in a religious sense. The idea of God *without the conception* of the holy is not religion (F. Schleiermacher, *Reden über die Religion*, Berlin 1799). Not the *mere* existence of divinity, but its *mana*, its power, its holiness, is what religion involves. This is nowhere *more obvious than in India*, where men of religion, through their art of acquiring holy power, became dangerous rivals of the gods, who, in order to maintain something of their religious authority, were obliged to adopt ascetic holiness themselves (Sat. Brahm. ii.2.4, ix.1.6, 1ff.). The definition of piety (subjective religion) runs thus: 'Religious is the man to whom something is holy.' The holy inspires awe (religio). The original idea of holiness seems to have been somewhat indeterminate, and applied to individual things and beings...(731; my emphases).

The liberal intentions are impeccable, as the Actress teased the Bishop, but is the clerical habit so easily disposed of? Söderblom's problem is to consider 'magic' and the Indian traditions (Buddhism, Jainism and Hinduism) as religions. A careful reading of the entry makes clear that the author does not make an experience coextensive with religion. An experience is seen as an experience of 'something': 'something' has to be holy, 'something' has to inspire awe, 'something' has to be sacred. Belief in the 'mere' existence of divinity does not suffice; one must 'experience' its powers in order to be properly called religious.[1]

Of course, in one trivial sense, merely believing in the existence of God does not make one into a religious figure: after all, as the Bible tells us, the devils believe in His existence too and tremble at His name. The belief in His existence does not transform the devils into 'religious' figures; 'something' more is required to become a believer. Several figures from several periods have characterised this 'something' differently. The closest thing that one could describe as the common denominator is the notion of *trust:* to be religious one must trust Him, have trust in Him and so forth.

The relation between faith and belief is an important issue and I shall take it up later (see #9.3). For now, just as an example, see how the Roman Catholic Bishops of Belgium address themselves to the question 'what is it to believe?' in a book of faith directed to their flock:

---

[1] Drobin (1982) does not agree. He splits the Protestant-Kantian subjective, emotionalistic, and idealistic way from the Roman Catholic-Thomistic, 'realistic' ('objective') and intellectualistic way, and places Söderblom in the first camp.

Niet...ik geloof *dat iets* waar is, dat er een God bestaat...(Maar) ik geloof in *Iemand*, ik geloof *in* God...geen geloof (de inhoud) zonder geloven (de houding). (*Geloofsboek*, De Bisschoppen van België, Tielt: Lannoo, 1987: 12.)

[Not...I believe *that something* is true, that there is a God. (But)...I believe in *Someone*, I believe *in* God...No belief (the content) without believing (the attitude).]

The word 'believing' could as well be replaced by 'to have faith in', or 'to trust' in this context. A Protestant philosopher-theologian (Plantinga 1983: 18) puts it thus:

One who repeats the words of the Apostle's Creed "I believe in God the Father Almighty..." and means what he says is not simply announcing the fact that he accepts a certain proposition as true; much more is involved than that. Belief in God means *trusting* God, accepting God, accepting his purposes, committing one's life to him and living in his presence.

With this qualification in mind, let us look at Söderblom's entry to investigate the extent to which this description could make the question of the 'origin of religion' an intelligible one. After all, he himself talks about the 'original idea' of holiness, the phenomena at the primitive stage, *etc.*

Suppose we go along with the fairy tale recounted earlier (chapter #5) about the origin of religion. Caught in a situation of tension, stress and fear, the early man postulates invisible powers to account for the chaos of his phenomenal world. Could we say that the primitive man had religion? We can go either way with our answers. Yes, the primitive man experienced 'awe'; no, he did not. What are we to think of one of the common representations of Epicureanism? Divinities might exist, but man had no contact with them. Again, if we take recourse to the experience of 'holy' in order to ascribe religion to all cultures, we are faced with the problem of making this experience itself intelligible. From whence the origin of this experience of the holy? In terms of which experience shall we explain the emergence of the 'sacred'?

If we follow the proponents of these ideas, we cannot. The experience is *sui generis:*

Religion is, first of all, an experience *sui generis,* incited by man's encounter with the sacred. (Eliade 1969: 25)

This is not merely Eliade's own ideas on the subject, but Söderblom's as well. As Sharpe, his biographer puts it:

Religious experience to Söderblom was an experience sui generis, to
which human beings had always been open. It had begun, so far as our
records are capable of knowing, with notions akin to those of *mana* and
*tabu*. (Sharpe 1990: 213.)

If it is not a derived experience but a fundamental one instead, there is
only one possibility: the primitive man (wherever he lived) encountered
that 'object' which induces this experience. That is to say, God must
have revealed Himself to all human beings at sometime during history. Indeed so, as Söderblom repeatedly states. In 1899, while applying for a professorial chair at Uppsala, the scholar said – speaking of
Schleiermacher's views – that

> religion is not anything we do, nor is it anything we might think about
> God, but what God does with us; also that we can know God only to the
> extent he reveals himself to us. (In Sharpe 1990: 81.)

In 1910, speaking of *The Problem of Religion in Catholicism and Protestantism*, Söderblom wrote:

> Something of revelation is to be found everywhere. In the higher religion
> it is purer (*ibid*: 157).

Not only does he quote Luther and Kierkegaard in support of this view
but also the Gita. This belief is underpinned by the Old Testament, or at
least in some of its interpretations. Put differently, this characterisation
of religious experience is parasitic upon accepting some truth or another with respect to what is commonly accepted as religion. Consequently,
this will not help us to find out what religions are but only what they are,
if we presuppose a religious tradition.

In other words, what is true for Schleiermacher is true for Söderblom as well. That religious experience which so many appeal to, the
'holy' or the 'numen', is not some conceptually unstructured experience
but a well-structured one. In fact, Söderblom talks about his 'perception' of the holy (in 1893) in the third person thus:

> One Sunday, he had held his service as usual. When he returned with
> a close friend to his room, there came over him what might be called a
> direct perception of the holiness of God. He understood what he had
> long felt indistinctly, that God was far stricter than he could imagine or
> than anyone can really comprehend. God is a consuming fire. This ap-
> prehension was so powerful, so shattering, that he was unable to stay on

his feet. Had he not collapsed into a chair with his head on the table, he felt that he must have fallen to the floor. He moaned and groaned under this mighty grasp. Slowly he recovered and calmed down. But for the rest of his life, for decades these two experiences have been firm points of departure or, rather, irrefutable experiences, fundamental to spiritual life, incomparable in their meaning, the incomprehensible means of mercy: the cross, the miracle of God's mercy. Man's nothingness, broken-heartedness, trembling, his faith *quand même*. Since then he has been unable to doubt God in spite of everything (*ibid*: 44).

Söderblom's Protestantism – as well as the typically Augustinian themes – are as much presuppositions of this experience as the manifestation of the 'mana' of the Divine.

## Otto and his Das Heilige

The third of the trio that I will look at – even more briefly than the other two – is Rudolf Otto. His *Das Heilige* (1917), which formulated and popularised the phrase *'mysterium tremendum et fascinans'*, begins with the following *warning* to the reader of his work in the English translation:

In this book I have ventured to write of that which may be called 'non-rational' or 'supra-rational' in *the depths of divine nature*...The 'irrational' is to-day a favourite theme of all who are lazy to think or too ready to evade the arduous duty of clarifying their ideas and grounding their convictions on the basis of coherent thought...

Before I ventured upon this field of inquiry I spent many years of study upon the *rational* (italics in the original) aspect of that supreme Reality we call 'God', and the results of my work are contained in my books...*And I feel that no one ought to concern himself with the 'Numen ineffabile' who has not already devoted assiduous and serious study to the 'Ratio aeterna'*... (xxiii: italics, unless otherwise indicated, mine).

Even if one does not read the English translation, the first paragraph of the first chapter sets out clearly what Otto is talking about: Christianity, the Christian God and the experience of this deity (or the 'non-rational' but not the 'irrational'):

It is essential to every theistic conception of God, and most of all to the Christian, that it designates and precisely characterizes the deity by the attributes spirit, reason, purpose, good will, supreme power, unity, selfhood...Now all these attributes constitute clear and definite *concepts:* they can be grasped by the intellect; they can be analyzed by thought; they even admit of definition...Only on such terms is *belief* possible in contrast to mere *feeling*...We count this the very mark and criterion of a religion's high rank and superior value – that it should have no lack of *conceptions* about God; that it should admit knowledge – the knowledge that comes by faith – of the transcendent in terms of conceptual thought, whether those already mentioned or others which continue and develop them. Christianity not only possesses them in unique clarity and abundance, and this is, though not the sole or even the chief, yet a very real sign of its superiority over religions of other forms and at other levels. This must be asserted at the outset with the most positive emphasis (1917: 1).

If this is not enough, Otto continues to speak throughout his book in developmental terms as well. From the 'primitive religion' through the 'most perfect', the 'most advanced' *etc.* religion, *viz.* Christianity (in its Protestant version). The experience – *mysterium tremendum et fascinans* – is an experience of the Deity, of God, of the Numinous. Other cultures and other religions have vaguer conceptions and some kind of experience of this Numen because that is what, as we know by now, the Bible claims. And Otto does not characterise religion on the basis of the 'non-rational' elements of personal experience, but identifies such elements in religion and their relation to the 'rational', *i.e.* he relates the conception of the deity to its experience.

In the justly famous beginning of the third chapter, which speaks of the elements in the 'Numinous', Otto is both clear and categorical:

> The reader is invited to direct his mind to a moment of deeply-felt religious experience, as little as possible qualified by other forms of consciousness. *Whoever cannot do this*, whoever knows no such moments in his experience, is *requested to read no farther;* for it is not easy to discuss questions of religious psychology with one who can recollect the emotions of his adolescence, the discomforts of indigestion, or, say, social feeling, but cannot recall any intrinsically religious feelings. We do not blame such an one, when he tries for himself to advance as far as he can with the help of such principles of explanation as he knows, interpreting 'aesthetics' in terms of sensuous pleasure, and 'religion' as *a function of the gregarious instinct and social standards*, or as something more primitive still. (Otto 1917: 8; italics mine.)

In the next paragraph, it is clear who 'the reader' is. Speaking of the 'state of the soul' in solemn worship, says Otto

> As Christians we undoubtedly here first meet with the feelings familiar
> enough in a weaker form in other departments of experience, such as feel-
> ings of gratitude, trust, love, reliance, humble submission, and dedication
> (*ibid*).

The book appears liberal in tone because it is tolerant of 'other religions', and does not dismiss them as 'Devil's worship'. This is indeed
true, but what of it? When you allow an innate sense of divinity, peri-
odise human history in terms of the development of this sense of divinity, characterise your religion as the most perfect, most advanced form
of expression, and on the grounds of its theology you have allowed God
to reveal Himself to all men, what is difficult about being both liberal
and tolerant?

Sharpe (1990: 99) remarks, while commenting on the liberalism
of Söderblom, that this attitude was very typical of the liberal Protestantism of the time. As an illustration, he cites James Moulton – an
English Indo-European philologist of that time – as saying:

> We may claim that Christianity has proved its claim overwhelmingly. Our
> study of Comparative Religion has made us thankful for the truth under-
> stood by those who have not yet received the Gospel, and has removed the
> reproach which narrower views of God brought upon religion. He has not
> left Himself without witness anywhere, nor allowed a small proportion
> of His children to monopolize the life-giving knowledge of Himself. But
> the more carefully and sympathetically we study other religions, the more
> clearly does it appear that Christ completes and crowns them all.

Just because you call other cultures and human beings primitive, it does
not commit you to denying humanity to them.

In this sense, depending on the extent to which *secular* values like
toleration, pluralism *etc.*, are allowed to enter one's appreciation of others and their traditions, one may or may not want to call the Hindus
(who challenge their Gods), Buddhists and the Jains (who deny the
existence of any such entity), as 'religious' peoples. But it is important
to note that this presupposes (i) identifying these traditions as religions;
(ii) fitting them in some kind of developmental framework; (iii) ranking
them in a hierarchy which includes Judaism, Islam and Christianity.

In fact, as Söderblom says at a later stage of the entry in the *Encyclopedia of Religion and Ethics,* the conception of the 'Holy' disappears
in Hinduism over a period of time to be replaced by the notions 'clean-
liness' and 'uncleanliness', *i.e.* by hygienic concepts. This theme is familiar to us from the earlier chapters as well. The growth of non-Christian
religions has always been in a one-way street, which terminates in de-

generation. To use the eighteenth-century terms, 'popular Hinduism' is a degeneration of 'philosophical Hinduism'. So, what is new?

## A Simple Argument

The reason for speaking about these various attempts has to with the popularity of the strategy of characterising religion on the grounds of some kind of experience. Should this experience be characteristic of religion, as Eliade and some others aver, it is not a correct representation of the thoughts of those who have spoken of such an experience. One cannot have this experience without there being some object that induces or causes this feeling. In fact, these liberal Protestant thinkers accept their Biblical histories, and that is why they spoke of the experience of the Divine. Yet, we have 'atheists' speaking of an 'atheistic religiosity' by appealing to the 'definitions' of Otto, Söderblom, and Schleiermacher. In Schleiermacher, Söderblom and Otto, we do not have a concept of religiosity that is independent of the tradition to which they belonged. "An absolute dependence on the totally other"; "*mysterium tremendum et fascinans*" "a sense of being a part of the whole", *etc.* are not independent of the Christian Protestant tradition.

The above consideration can further be motivated at two levels. *Firstly,* the way Schleiermacher, Söderblom, and Otto, explicate, describe, and indicate the nature of these experiences presupposes the truth of a whole arsenal of theological ideas. Schleiermacher, Söderblom, and Otto accept this explicitly and emphatically assert it as well. *Secondly,* having a religious experience – as they describe it – presupposes that one belongs to a religion as well. Belonging to which religion? None of the authors leaves an attentive reader with any doubt: the Protestant Christian tradition.

All my previous points can be summarised in the form of a simple argument. Only on the presupposition that the divine has revealed itself in the Universe; only on the presupposition that this revelation has been understood differently by different peoples; only on the presupposition of some definite conception of divinity; and hence, by consequence, only on the presupposition that some one standpoint is more adequate and fuller than the others; only on these presuppositions could one speak of the religious experience of different cultures. These, as we know by now, are *all* Biblical themes. Without presupposing the truth, in other words, of the Bible you cannot speak of the 'religious experience' of the Hindus, of the Buddhists, of the Africans and of the American Indians, *etc.* Schleiermacher, Söderblom, and Otto accept this. The same awareness, however, cannot be predicated of those indefinitely many scholars who speak of 'religiosity' independent of a specific religion. They see in it a 'neutral' or 'universal' experience.

One is free, however, to see what one feels like. However, the result of my claim is that religiosity (seen as an experience) requires the background presence of some definite religion. That is to say, one must be a part of a religion in order to be a 'religious' person. Further, the subjective experience of an individual can make a person religious but this does not distinguish religion from other phenomena. In the next chapter, I will return to this point at greater length. Therefore, let me leave it here to look at another aspect of the issue.

### 6.3.2. Tracing the Themes Further

There is an analogous point with respect to 'religiosity' when we view it as a concept that picks out an experience. Using this concept would involve accepting the background presence of Christian themes as well. That is, discussions about religiosity will have to be conducted within the framework of a religion. Formulating it in 'neutral' or 'scientific' terms does not lead to a 'neutral' or 'scientific' understanding of this experience. Instead, it will simply smuggle in religious categories. One way of illustrating this claim is to look at the conceptual difficulties that two secular characterisations of religion face in their 'quest' to provide precisely such a 'neutral' (*i.e.* nonreligious) description of the 'religious experience'. The authors are Durkheim and Eliade.

### The 'Sacred' and the 'Profane'

Earlier on (in chapter #1), I already had an occasion to draw your attention to Durkheim's definition. Let us recall what that definition is:

> A religion is a unified system of beliefs and practices relative to sacred things, that is to say, things set apart and forbidden – beliefs and practices which unite into one single moral community called a Church, all those who adhere to them.

I do not intend to enter into the controversy of the adequacy or otherwise of Durkheim's theory of religion. (See Pickering 1984 for such an overview.) Instead, I want to draw attention to the tension inherent in this definition. Durkheim relates religion to 'sacred things', that is, to 'objects set apart and forbidden'. Set apart from whom? Forbidden by whom? Or, what makes objects sacred? This 'sacredness' and 'setting apart' is not a part of religious belief and practice; it does not arise from the moral community that the Church is, because beliefs and practices are constituted relative to these 'sacred' objects. The moral community itself results from the adherence of individuals to these beliefs and practices. In other words, 'sacred' and 'profane' do not belong to a religious vocabulary but are 'neutral' or 'scientific'.

If all cultures had set apart the same set of objects, or if they constantly treated some set of objects as sacred, one could argue that we may call these sets of objects 'sacred' irrespective of the word the other cultures used. This, however, is not the case. Neither of the two invariants exists. As though this is not enough, the claim itself exhibits three distinct steps: first, sacred objects come into being; and then relative to it beliefs and practices congeal; subsequently, there is the crystallisation of the moral community called the Church.

To be sure, Durkheim does not see these three stages chronologically. Nevertheless, as the definition makes it clear, they are distinct from each other. My purpose in focusing on them is not to draw the obvious parallel between these steps and the history of either Judaism (Durkheim was a Jew, and was expected to become a Rabbi; see Lukes 1972) or Christianity as the believers tell them. Rather, it is to point out more clearly that the 'sacred' of Durkheim is not constituted by religious beliefs and practices.

Because the set of 'sacred' objects varies across cultures and is not constant within a culture, one has to suggest that 'sacred' objects themselves are constituted. That is to say, the distinction between 'sacred' and 'profane' is drawn within a religion. In that case, it cannot be used to distinguish between religion and something else. Not being prior to religious beliefs and practices, a person inducted into a religious community learns to draw the distinction between the sacred and the profane accordingly as he is initiated into his religion.

At least in the case of Durkheim, the problem can be posed sharply. The same, however, cannot be said of the extremely prolific writer –Mircea Eliade. He also uses the separation, the sacred and the profane, without alluding to Durkheim. (Apparently, this is a standard practice: Freud casually refers to Durkheim; Durkheim hardly speaks of Marx; Eliade does not refer to Durkheim.) The problem with this greatly influential and enormously respected writer is that it is extremely difficult to find out what his 'theory', if any, is of the phenomenon whose history he chronicles. It is, of course, possible to postulate a framework based on archival work (Saliba 1976 is one such attempt); or do a half-philological work to excavate the meaning of this distinction as a doctoral dissertation (Farace 1982); or take an article and discuss it at length, as indeed many have done. I will issue a promissory note, which will be redeemed in the near future, to treat Eliade with the care and attention he deserves. For the moment, permit me just to note that:

> Religious man assumes a particular and characteristic mode of existence in the world and, despite the great number of historic-religious forms, this characteristic form is always recognizable. Whatever the historical context in which he is placed, *homo religiosus* always believes that there is an absolute reality, *the sacred*, which transcends this world but manifests itself in this world, thereby sanctifying it and making it real. He further believes that life has a sacred origin and that human existence realizes all of its potentialities in proportion as it is religious – *i.e.* participates in reality (Eliade 1961: 202).

Despite the talk of history and the independence of human beings from their contexts, I am perfectly willing to grant that the *homo religiosus believes* in all these things and more. Given my personal distaste for fruitless controversies, I would even allow him to entertain all these beliefs. All I ask in return is that we accept that this is how such a creature experiences the world. That is to say, you grant me that the way you experience the world is structured by your categories – especially when you start seeing "manifestations of the sacred", which is "totally the other" and yet "transcendent", in mundane day-to-day objects like stones and pigs. One may want to call 'the sacred' a force, an energy, which is at the foundation of life, universe, and what-have-you. All these do not matter as long as one sees energy, a force, *as sacred* and not just as energy and force. The *homo religiosus* has these categories and I do not; which is why he is the "religious man" and I am not. That means that the 'sacred' and the 'profane' are not distinctions drawn from within a language and vocabulary common to us both, but one which belongs exclusively to this *homo religiosus*. This might be my personal misfortune, but I doubt whether this is any greater a calamity than is the case: as an unrepentant pagan, my soul is lost to the Devil anyway.

If categories like 'sacred' and 'profane' are internal to a religion or to the *homo religiosus,* how can they help us distinguish between religion and other phenomena? If the 'sacred' and the 'profane' distinction is drawn *within* an initiation ritual, then the initiation ritual cannot be seen as drawing the distinction between the 'sacred' space and the 'profane' space. Quite apart from this, how can this 'sacred' and 'profane' dichotomy help us distinguish one religion from another? The latter question can be easily answered in one way: religions form a hierarchy – with some having "extra dimensions", whereas other have to make do with bare necessities. Sounds a familiar theme, does it? Listen now to Eliade:

> (F)or the entire Paleo-Semitic world...a sacrifice...was only custom...in Abraham's case it is an act of faith. He does not understand why the sacrifice is demanded of him; nevertheless he performs it because it was the

Lord who demanded it. By this act, which is apparently absurd, *Abraham initiates a new religious experience,* faith. All other (the whole oriental world) continue to move in an economy of the sacred that will be *transcended* by Abraham and *his successors*...Abraham's religious act *inaugurates a new religious dimension*...(1959: 109-110; italics mine.)

Of course, it is possible for a person from within a religion to make a distinction between his tradition and other phenomena – including other religions. However, the claim of Eliade and Durkheim is that they are providing a characterisation of religion without using categories specific to any particular religion. My disputation is about this claim.

Let me sketch the state of affairs in the following way. On the one hand, some particular religion becomes the framework to describe other cultures. On the other hand, neither of these two thinkers could be accused of perpetrating a fraud on their readers. How can we make this state of affairs intelligible where gifted and brilliant authors are blind regarding the theological nature of their claims?

## 6.4. "J'ACCUSE"

Though the milieu in which Christianity grew was fundamentally pagan in nature, it never really understood paganism. Confronted by an 'other', it did the only thing it could, *viz.* transform the 'other' into a variant of itself – albeit an erring variant. It was successful in its attempts, if for no other reason than the disappearance of the Graeco-Roman civilization. The opponents were vanquished.

Nevertheless, the 'other' of today, call it pagan too if you like, refuses stubbornly either to disappear or to be vanquished. All evangelical attempts notwithstanding, the pagans continue to remain the 'other'; the traditions of cultures and peoples from elsewhere resist description and defy analyses in terms that would make them mere erring variants of Christianity.

In the previous section, I suggested that the pagan world was prosecuting Christianity by formulating a Christological dilemma. One horn of the dilemma was that Christianity could become universal, only if it ceased being specifically Christian. That is to say, the more the secular world of today becomes Christian, the less Christian it will look. If we look at the pagan world, we see that there is yet another description to be given of the same process but from another point of view.

The secular, pagan world of today is not merely a problem *to* Christology but is, actually, a problem *in* Christology itself. That is to say, the more it becomes a Christological problem, the less will the world continue to remain pagan. Christianising the pagan world falls together with the de-christianising of Christianity. It must be clear by now how Christianity is persecuting its pagan prosecutors: the 'sacred' has entered the domain of the 'profane'.

The twin movements of Christianising the Pagan world and the de-Christianising of Christian beliefs help us understand what is 'really' going on: the secular world is itself under the grips of a religious framework. What we observe is not the "illusion of religion", but an illusion of being free from it. I make this charge. What we now need to find out is whether the secular world is really...

CHAPTER SEVEN

# "GUILTY AS CHARGED, MY LORDS AND LADIES?"

In the previous chapter, we saw the *Religionsgeschichtliche Schule* arguing that we have to study religiosity (*i.e.* the experiential aspect of religion) to understand religion. One of their concerns was the living religion as experienced by people. They radically historicised religion by claiming that religion developed along with human culture. This constantly evolving human response to the revelation of the divine constituted the *living* religion. Bereft of this, religion would freeze into a fixed set of dogmas and doctrines. The *Religionsgeschichte* was not a history of *religions* but the *history* of religion, *i.e.* the history of the varying manifestations and forms of religiosity.

What evolves in the course of human history is the human response. However, what makes the response religious is that it is a response to the revelation of the divine. Several Christian themes are present in this conceptualisation. The multiple pasts (real or imagined) of peoples become parts of a single human history. God reveals himself in history and human beings respond to this revelation (instead of going to sleep, for instance) because they can do nothing else (*i.e.* the sense of divinity is innate in us). These presuppositions allow them to speak of 'religiosity' as a characteristic property of religion – something that distinguishes this response from the responses to ecological, social, economic, and aesthetic problems.

In the course of the previous chapter, I looked at three Protestant thinkers – Schleiermacher, Söderblom, and Otto – to show their explicit acknowledgement of the tradition they work in. I also looked at two other thinkers – Durkheim and Eliade – who make no such acknowledgement, but are constrained by a religious framework. In other words, I have tried to provide a brief exegetical support for the contention that the notion of religiosity does not provide a 'neutral' description of some experience, which we could identify, but that this label makes sense only within a religious framework.

Not many would agree with such a claim. Most assuredly not those who fancy themselves 'atheistically' religious. They believe, as Proudfoot (1985) shows, that religiosity can be detached from its conceptual moorings – so that the Christian presuppositions can be neutered and its implications neutralised – and applied to the experiential state of any Tom, Dick, and Harry. Why cannot one's feeling of absolute dependency have 'Nature' as its object? Why cannot one experience the Cosmos as *mysterium tremendum et fascinans?* Why may one not experience events such as birth, death, *etc.*, as sacred? In all these cases, the theistic foundations are not necessary; one can continue to be an atheist while deriving all the benefits of being religious at the same time. Why not?

Answering this challenge requires splitting it up into two issues: is atheistic religiosity logically possible? We will take up this question once we have a better grasp of religion. Consequently, I will postpone the question to a later chapter (see #9.4.1). The second issue: is it possible to build a case for the charge that 'religiosity' is part of a religious vocabulary and framework? I believe it is. I will go even further and argue that the *notion* 'religion' is a part of a religious framework. The 'scientific' investigations into religion are conducted within a religious framework, which is not even noticed by these 'scientists'. This religion is a de-christianised Christianity, secularised to suit the modern tastes, but no less religious because of that. That is my brief.

## 7.1. THE PROSECUTION'S CASE

In the course of the previous chapter, two different types of questions admitting two different types of answers have constantly interfered with each other. I would like to emphasise that their difference is one of *types:* each question is of a different logical type.

Consider the following question: "who is a religious person?" A moment's reflection, or a quick look-up in a dictionary, will tell you that this question does not have a single correct answer. The aptness of the answer depends upon who is asking the question to whom, the context of the dialogue, and so on. The question can be about a member of an office (member of a cloister or a bishop) or his subjective state or that of the laity. At the other extreme, if we are answering a Martian, the question will have a different scope.

The 'aptness' of the answer has to do with logical types. The question, which our hypothetical Martian asks and that of Schleiermacher's public belong to two different levels. Consequently, what is apt in one case is a category mistake if conceived as an answer to another.

### 7.1.1. "Tell Me, Sonadanda, Who is a Brahmin?"

By way of establishing this case, let me take you back to a previous chapter. We have seen the West claiming that the Buddha rebelled against the caste system, rejected Brahmanism, *etc.* You have also had the occasion to see that the Christian missionaries rejected the caste system because they found it revolting. One of the common descriptions of Buddhism is that it is a 'universal religion'. Hence, it is often put in the exalted company of Christianity and Islam (*e.g.* Whitehead 1926) because it does not discriminate between human beings. In that case, your minimal expectation (assuming that you are a competent language speaker) regarding Buddha's teachings must be to find an *unequivocal* rejection of the caste system there. Of course, the terminology of Buddha's criticisms will be different from that of the Christian missionaries. However, the message must nearly be the same. Such is our expectation if 'rejection' and 'revolution' should mean anything at all.

Let me take two texts from the early Buddhist tradition at random: *The Dhammapada*, a major text ascribed to the Buddha himself and *Sonadanda Sutta*, a minor text recording Buddha's dialogues. The last chapter of the *Dhammapada* (Carter and Palihawardana, Trans., 1987) is about the Brahmins. Here are three from the fifty-odd verses on the issue:

Not by matted hair, or by clan,
Or by birth does one become a brahmana
In whom is truth and dhamma,
He is the pure one, and he is the brahmana (§393; 78)
Again,
And I do not call one brahmana
Merely by being born from a [brahmana] womb,
Sprung from a [brahmana] mother.
He is merely a "bho-sayer"
If he is a possessor of things.
One who has nothing and takes nothing,
That one I call a brahmana. (§396; 78)
Or again,
Who, here, having abandoned the human bond,
Has transcended the heavenly bond,
Who is released form all bonds,
That one I call brahmana. (§417; 81)

In tenor, theme, and substance, all the verses are of the same nature: Buddha tells us who or what a 'true' Brahmin is. He does not say that being a Brahmin is to be a fraud, cheater, or a liar; he does not call Brahmanism or caste system an abomination; he does not do any of the things that Christian missionaries were to do centuries later.

Would we expect this from someone who rejects the caste system? Before you answer this question, consider the following: Marx rejected capitalism and revolted against the bourgeois society. He did this not by suggesting that his society was not 'truly' capitalist. Calvin did not reject Catholicism by saying that the Roman Catholic Church was not 'really' Catholic but by calling it the 'Devil's church'. However, Calvin defended Christianity by telling us who a 'true Christian' is. It was in the name of Christianity that Calvin rejects Catholicism. So is it with apologetics of either 'capitalism' or 'socialism': the present form of capitalism is not 'true' capitalism or that some society is not 'really' socialist.

If this is how we *use* these words, Buddha appears *not* to be revolting against the caste system. Before we ask what else he was doing, consider the following dialogue with a Brahmin named Sonadanda about who a Brahmin is:

11. (The Buddha) said to him: 'What are the things, brahman, which the brahmans say a man ought to have in order to be a brahman, so that if he says: "I am a brahman," he speaks accurately and is not guilty of falsehood?

12-13. Then Sonadanda...drawing his body up erect, and looking round on the assembly,...said to the Master: 'The brahmans, Gotama, declare him to be a brahman able to say "I am a Brahman" without being guilty of falsehood, who has five things. What are the five? In the first place, sir, a brahman has to be well born on both sides, on the mother's side and on the father's side, of pure descent back through seven generations, with no slur upon him, and no reproach in respect of birth.

'Then he must be a scholar who knows the mystic verses by heart, one who has mastered the three Vedic samhitas and other scholarly subjects...

'He must be handsome, pleasant in appearance, inspiring trust, with great beauty of complexion...He must be virtuous, very virtuous, exceedingly virtuous.

'Then he must be learned and wise...'

14. 'Of these five things, Brahman, is it possible to leave one out, and to declare the man who has the other four to be a brahman, so that he can, without falsehood, claim to be a brahman?'

'Yes, Gotama, that can be done. We could leave out colour. For what does colour matter? If he has the other four...

15. 'But of these *four* things, brahman, is it possible to leave one out, and to declare the man who has the other three to be a brahman...?'

'Yes, Gotama, that could be done. We could leave out the verses. For what do the verses matter? If he has the other three – good birth, virtue and wisdom...'

16. 'But of these *three* things, Brahman, is it possible to leave one out, and to declare the man who has the other two to be a brahman...?'

'Yes, Gotama, that could be done. We could leave out birth. For what does
birth matter? If he has the other two – virtue and wisdom – brahmans
would still declare him to be a brahman...'

21. 'Then', said the Master, 'of these two things, brahman, is it possible
to leave one out, and to declare the man who has the other to be a brahman...?'

'Not so, Gotama!...Where there is morality, there is wisdom, and where
there is wisdom there is morality...'

22. 'That is so, brahman. I,.too, say the same...' (Ling, Ed., 1981: 42-45)

This Brahmin begins with the five necessary criteria, which a Brahmin should possess and, in the course of the dialogue, ceases considering some of them as necessary properties. This could be the result
of a "Socratic method of dialogue, which the Buddha adopts", as
Weber (1958: 225) remarked once; but such was also the opinion of
several Brahmin friends, who were present there. During the dialogue,
Sonadanda turns around to his fellow-Brahmins in order to justify or
explain himself. The Brahmin friends of his are consternated by the
ease with which Sonadanda gives up the three criteria; they feel that
their colour, learning, and birth are being deprecated. In order to put
them at ease and to make them understand the reasonableness of his
own argument, Sonadanda argues:

19. 'My venerable friends...I do not depreciate our colour, nor our scholarship, nor our good birth.'

20. 'Venerable friends, you see this Angaka, our nephew?'

'yes, sir, we see him.'

'Well! Angaka is handsome, pleasant in appearance, inspiring trust...

'And Angaka, sirs, is a scholar who knows the mantras by heart, he has
mastered the three Vedic samhitas...

'And Angaka, sirs, is born well on both sides...of pure descent back
through seven generations...

'Now, sirs, if Angaka should kill living things, and take what has not been
given, and become an adulterer, and tell lies, and drink liquor, what then
would his colour be worth? what the verses? what his birth?' (Ibid.: 44-
45.)

## "Objection, Your Honour!"

At this stage of the argument, some readers of an earlier version of this
essay took objection to the claim that Buddha was not rejecting the
caste system. This objection appealed, among other things, to similar

or parallel developments in European history. Criticism and rejection of the nobility (as a class) went hand-in-hand with an attempt to speak of nobility (as a virtue) of human beings. I shall accept this portrayal as true and, in order to avoid fruitless controversies, I will even accept that the Buddha is criticising both the Brahmins of his time and Brahmanism. However, the question is: was Buddha *rejecting* the caste system?

Before proceeding to answer the question, perhaps it is relevant to point out why this issue is important. I want to show that 'being a Brahmin' picks out individuals belonging to a determinate domain. Even if the criteria for being a Brahmin are formulated in terms of moral virtues, the range of application of these criteria is not the domain of *all* human beings but only the domain of persons constituted by the 'caste' system. Even if all 'true' Brahmins are both moral and wise, not all moral and wise human beings are Brahmins – 'true' or otherwise. The reason is that not all human beings belong to the domain of the 'caste' system but only some do. I want to argue that there are specific pragmatic presuppositions to Buddha's dialogues one of which is their "universe of discourse". The latter is the 'caste' system and, therefore, Buddha (if he is to remain intelligible at all) could not be rejecting the 'caste' system. In other words, the conditions of intelligibility for Buddha's dialogues involve identifying their pragmatic presupposition, *viz.* Buddha's public: to whom was Buddha talking?

Textbook histories (*e.g.* Warder 1971) tell us, I have no option but to accept them, that two traditions coexisted in India for a long period: the Sramana and the Brahmana. Seeking the truth (Sramana translates as 'strivers'), the former group opted out of social life. One could call them 'world-renouncers' (although, see the warning in Collins 1988; see also Silber 1985). It is important to note that the Sramanas was not a protest movement, or one that rejected some or another form of social order. To them, renunciation of social life was the condition for achieving the enlightenment. To seek it, one had to be free from personal, ethical, and social obligations that bound an individual to earthly life. From this stream grew the Ajivikas (see Basham 1951), the Jain tradition, and, much later, the Buddhist tradition.

In addition, there was the Brahmana tradition. This was oriented towards social life and developed an elaborate structure of rituals over a period. It also regulated the social institutions, the structure of social interactions, and did not see opting out of society as the only means to enlightenment. From this tradition too grew many 'philosophical' schools, elaborate ritual practices, and the 'caste' system.

The Indian culture evolved as an interaction between these two traditions: while the Brahmana tradition recognised – in its own way – the legitimacy of opting out of society as a way to enlightenment (see the interesting attempt by Kaelber 1981), the Sramana tradition began to address itself to those who lived in society. In doing so, they had to face the question of the possibility of living in society and seek enlightenment. Among other things, this meant paying the required attention to the issue of social regulation. (Hall 1985 tries to locate the failure for the development of indigenous capitalism in India, among other things, in the lack of adequate attention paid by Buddhism to social regulation.)

By virtue of having opted out of society, the Sramanas were outside the 'caste' system. They were not outcast and, thus, not outcastes; they did not belong to the domain of the 'caste' system. However, when they turned towards social life and began to build up followers in society, its members faced two possibilities: either one renounced society to become a 'monk' or one continued to live in society – as a householder, as a Brahmin, as a king, *etc.* – and strive for the enlightenment. Because the Sramana tradition was neither a reformist nor a revolutionary movement, it did not propose blueprints for an alternate social order. Their concerns were different: given what exists, how can individuals (in the socio-psychological position they found themselves in) achieve liberation?

Such were the terms of the dialogue of the Sramana with the Brahmana tradition. Buddha, as he emerged out of the former, is faithful to this tradition. He tries to persuade people that they too can follow the eightfold path. They can do so in the position they are in. Which positions were they in? They were within the positions assigned by the 'caste' system. One of the pragmatic presuppositions of Buddha's dialogues was this audience, as the history books tell us, divided into the four varna's: the Brahmins, the Kshatriya's, the Vaisyas, and the Sudras.

Such, in brief, is a rather caricatured sketch of the context of Buddha's dialogues. I shall now allow different people to testify that this sketch is not very much off the mark. First, the word will be given to a hostile critic of the Indian religion, the late Max Weber:

> So far as it actually took place, the disregard of Buddhism for status differences meant no social revolution. That members of the lowest strata were to be found among the adherents of early Buddhism is not traditional and very improbable. For it was precisely *Sramana* who came predominantly from distinguished circles of lay culture recruited from the city-dwelling Kshatriya patricians, somewhat as in the case of our Humanists, who constitute its membership. In fact, it appears certain that originally *Buddhism, exactly like Jainism, first firmly adhered to the conviction that only one born in the Brahman or Kshatriya castes was qualified for full gnosis...*

A "struggle" against the Brahmans somewhat in the manner of Christ against the Pharisees and scribes cannot be traced in Buddha's preaching. He left aside the question of the Gods as well as *the meaning of the castes...*
...(T)o change the social order in this world neither early nor later Buddhism has attempted to do. (Weber 1958: 226-227; italics mine.)

Next, we shall allow a hostile critic of Brahmanism and a sympathetic admirer of Buddhism to testify:

According to the Buddha all four classes are equally 'pure', and what matters is their conduct. Although the Buddha thus rejected their special claims and sought to reform their entire ideology, he wished to do so by conciliating the Brahmins, by restoring them, according to his version of history, to their original condition. In effect his idea was to assimilate the brahmans to the sramanas: to establish that anyone could become a brahman by adopting a simple life of meditation and virtuous, tolerant and gentle conduct. (Warder 1980: 180.)

At first sight, this is a very ambiguous claim. To reduce the ambiguity, we need to expand on at least one thread. Warder refers not only to the four classes, all of which Buddha apparently found equally pure, but also to Buddha's version of the history of the four classes.

In *Agganna Sutta,* also called the 'Buddhist Book of Genesis', Buddha discusses the matter with two disciples: Vasittha and Bharadvaja. As usual,

both were brahmans and belonged to wealthy families; the former is said to have been an expert in Vedic lore, and to have renounced great wealth when he became a Buddhist bhikku. (Ling, Ed., 1981: 101.)

One day, discussing the claims of the Brahmins (*viz.* that they were born from the mouth of Brahma and that "the Brahman class is the best"), the Buddha remarks that "the Brahmans have certainly forgotten the past when they say that sort of thing" (*ibid.*: 103). "There are four social classes", continues the Buddha, "the nobles (Kshatriya's), brahmans, tradespeople (the Vaisyas), and work-people (the Sudras). Amongst all of them moral qualities are often to be found." So begins this dialogue. The first thing to note is that the Kshatriya's come first, followed by the Brahmins. Secondly, it is equally important to bear in mind that the Buddha himself was a Kshatriya. The importance of these two statements will become clearer as we work our way further into the dialogue.

Buddha begins to tell a story about one evolutionary cycle of the world. After the previous world had disappeared, aeons later, earth formed again. Many cycles later, human and other beings appeared too. As the world evolved further, more events took place, including the appearance of rice. Having discovered its edibility, human beings cultivated rice; stored the harvest in granaries; and, finally, divided the rice fields among themselves. Each distinguished his own plot from those of the others by marking its boundaries. A greedy person from the community, while guarding his own plot, stole the rice plot of another and made use of it. The others in the community took note of this and severely reprimanded the greedy person, who, despite punishment and warnings, continued to repeat the act. These people, continues the Buddha,

gathered themselves together, and lamented what had happened; they said:

"Our evil deeds have become obvious; stealing, censure, lying, punishment are now known among us. What if we were to select a certain person who should be angry when indignation is called for, who should censure whatever be censured, and should banish anyone who deserves to be banished? We will give him a certain proportion of the rice in return for these duties."

'Then,...they went to the one among them who was the handsomest, the best favoured, the most attractive, the most capable, and said to him: "We wish you to be the one who will be indignant at whatever one should be rightly indignant at, censure whatever should rightly be censured, banish him who deserves to be banished. And we will contribute to you a certain proportion of our rice."

'He consented, and did so, and they gave him a portion of their rice.

21. '"Chosen by the whole people"...this is what is meant by Maha Sammata; [the Great Elected One]; this was how the name arose. "Lord of the Fields" is what is meant by "kshatriya"; *so kshatriya [noble] was the next title to arise...*(R)aja was the third title to arise.

'This...was the origin of this social circle of the nobles...Their origin was from among those same beings as themselves, and no others; and *it took place according to dhamma, fittingly.*' (*Ibid*: 109-110; italics mine.)

As a 'caste', kshatriya is the first and the king comes from this group. Not only does Buddha elevate the kshatriya but also declares that this took place according to 'dhamma' (not the Buddhist dharma, but the 'universal dharma'; for a discussion of the concept 'dharma' see Creel 1977), and that it is appropriate. Surely, an interesting claim about heraldry. However, let us not draw conclusions yet, and let Buddha continue the story.

22. Now it occurred...to some of them as follows. "Evil deeds have become manifest among us: such as stealing, censure and lying. Punishment and banishment are also common. Let us put away evil and immoral customs." So they put away evil, immoral customs, and...thus it was that 'brahmans' became the earliest title for those who did so...

23. '...Such...was the origin of this social circle of brahmans. Their origin was from just those people [above referred to]; *[and it took place] according to dhamma [according to what ought to be]*' (*ibid.*: 110-111; italics mine).

The origin of the second group is also appropriate. Among them, Buddha distinguishes further subgroups: those who meditated; those who took to writing books because they were unable to meditate; and those who learnt the Vedic lore having been unable to accept the discipline the other two activities demanded of them. It is the last group, says the Buddha ironically, which now claims to be the best. Having thus completed the story of this social group, the Buddha speaks of the emergence of the next two 'caste' groups, *viz.* the Vaisyas and the Sudras. Both of them took place according to 'dhamma' as well:

24. 'Now...there were some others...who, adopting the married state, took up various trades. The origin...of the social group called the vaisyas... took place in accordance with dhamma [according to what ought to be, justly].

25. 'Now...those of them who were left took to hunting...Thus...is the origin of this social group called sudras...[and took place] according to dhamma [according to what ought to be]' (*ibid*: 111).

Apart these four 'castes', Buddha speaks of the Sramanas thus:

26. 'Now there came a time...when some kshatriya, misprising his own dhamma, went from home into the homeless life, saying "I will become an ascetic." Some brahman did the same; likewise some vaisyas and some sudras, each finding some fault in his particular dhamma. Out of these four groups the company of the ascetics came into being. Their origin was from just these beings like unto themselves, not different. And it took place according to dhamma, that is, fittingly' (*ibid*: 111-112).

In other words, the Buddha finds that each of these 'caste' groups and the Sramanas came into being correctly, appropriately, and according to dharma. This alone would be enough to reduce the ambiguity concealed in Warder's testimony. After all, he too speaks of the same story (Warder 1980: 158-163).

There is still something more to this story. The dialogue ends on a verse, which Buddha attributes to Brahma. After having first recited it, the Buddha says:

> 32. 'Now this stanza...was well sung by Brahma the ever-youthful, well said, and full of meaning. And I too...say:
> *The kshatriya is the best among this folk*
> Who put their trust in lineage.
> But one in Wisdom and to virtue clothed
> Is best of all 'mong spirits and men.' (*Ibid*: 113; my italics.)

Buddha leaves little room for doubt, here, whether he is *rejecting* the 'caste' system or not.

After recounting this story, but without referring to this verse, Warder (1980: 163) concludes:

> It should be noted that the Buddha's opposition is not total: rather he seeks to conciliate and win over the brahmans of his day to his new way of thinking. He flatters them that their class was formed originally from good motives and had good traditions. It is only more recently that it has become degenerate and its way of life harmful...

The message must be clear by now. Buddha's criticisms of the Brahmins should not be seen as a *rejection* of the 'caste' system.

Finally, I shall now ask a 'sceptic' to come to the witness box. He is Frits Staal, Professor at the University of California, who has put in a lot of effort in "seeking out the Buddha". He will now tell us something about the results:

> If he preached that the true brahman is not he who is born in the highest caste, but who is fearless, controlled, free from sins, etc. – *the Upanishads had already stated that a brahman is only he who speaks the truth, or knows brahman*...and the Jaina Uttaradhyayana-sutra had declared: "He who is exempt from love, hatred and fear, and who shines forth like burnished gold, purified in fire, him we call a brahman..." (Staal 1989: 406-407; italics mine.)

In other words, whatever Buddha might or might not have been doing in these dialogues, it is difficult to suggest that he was *rejecting* the 'caste' system. If he did not presuppose the 'caste' system and its continued functioning, his question would not make sense at all.

On these grounds, I would like to suggest that the objection is *not* well taken. Buddha is not rejecting the 'caste' system; 'Brahmanism' is not identical to the 'caste' system in Buddha's dialogues; consequently, even if he rejected 'Brahmanism', he was not doing the same with respect to the 'caste' system. 'Who is a Brahmin?' picks out an individual belonging to the 'caste' system, and its range is not the domain of all human beings.

*"Objection Overruled. Proceed Mr Prosecutor..."*

Let us now bring both the dialogues of the Buddha and the speeches of Schleiermacher sharply into focus to see what their analogy consists of. Sonadanda picks out Angaka, who is a Brahmin, to say that 'being a Brahmin' does not consist of either colour, or birth, or knowledge of the Vedic samhitas. His fellow-Brahmins agree that if this Brahmin were to indulge in certain actions, and be devoid of certain 'properties', he would cease being a Brahmin even if he possessed the other three properties.

Schleiermacher talks to a Protestant audience. He tells them that 'being religious' does not consist of believing in this or that doctrine (*e.g.* the existence of God), or in going to this or that celebration in the church. It involves having a particular kind of experience. The word 'God' in Christian vocabulary designates merely a particular kind of experience, one of being "absolutely dependent on the totally other". As he expresses this point in *The Christian Faith:*

> As regards the identification of absolute dependence with "relation to God" in our proposition: this is to be understood in the sense that the *whence* of our receptive and active existence, as implied in this self-consciousness, is to be designated by the word "God," and that this is for us the really original signification of the word. (In Proudfoot 1985: 20.)

His audience agrees that they, the Protestants, would not be religious without such an experience even if they were born into the religious tradition in question.

The question 'Who is a Brahmin?' makes sense to a Brahmin. The question 'Who is religious?' makes sense to a Protestant. Are these questions also intelligible to others? If yes, to *which* others?

In the case of Buddha, the question makes sense to his audience, which consisted not only of Brahmins but also of the other 'caste' groups. His public could make sense of this question if, and only if, 'Brahminhood' and 'being a Brahmin' were experiential categories to them. That is to say, even though 'Brahmins' are different from the other 'caste' groups, this 'otherness' cannot be alien. It must be the case that the constitution of Brahmins also constitutes the other 'caste' groups in such a way that they, together, experience this constitution as a tradition.

The same holds good for 'religiosity' as well. The concept makes sense to those who are not alien to the Protestant tradition. The Protestant religiosity of a Schleiermacher must be an experiential category to them as well. The Protestants are different from the Catholics but cannot be totally the *other*. Indeed, several of my Catholic friends have no difficulty at all in accepting Schleiermacher's position. This, of course, is understandable: they are both constituted by the same tradition, *viz.* Christianity.

Could either of these questions make sense to yet others as well? That depends on the nature of this 'otherness'. Could a Catholic make sense of the question 'are you a Brahmin?' It does not make sense to ask where the Belgians or the Germans fit with respect to Buddha's position or the Brahmin's answer: they do not. They fall outside and beyond the scope of both the question and the answer. To ask such a question to a Belgian Catholic or a German Protestant is a category mistake.

Why would it be so? One commits a category mistake whenever terms and concepts, which are appropriate to some domain, are misapplied elsewhere. Decisions about appropriateness or otherwise of categories are the result of ontology (*i.e.* beliefs about what there is in the world), linguistic practices, and knowledge about the relevant domains. The category of 'Brahmin' has individuals constituted by the 'caste' system as its domain of application. The dispute about either its meaning or its use reflects a lack of unanimity about its application within a domain: which of the individual members within some given domain are Brahmins? Irrespective of the answers, to use this category elsewhere is to commit a category mistake. Belgian Catholics and the German Protestants do not belong to the domain of individuals to whom the category 'Brahmin' is applicable.

What about religiosity? It appears to make sense to atheists because, after all, they do talk of an atheistic religiosity. Without feeling that they are committing a category mistake, western anthropologists, philosophers, theorists of religions, all and sundry in fact, talk of religiosity of the Hindus, of the Africans, of the Native Americans,...*etc.*

Confronted with the latter situation, you can choose one of the two routes: either defend this practice on grounds of its 'truth', or try to reflect about the considerations and arguments I have put across so far. In the former case, you are in the absolute majority – during the last four hundred years and more, this is the received knowledge. If you choose the second path, reflect once more upon the point: you do not feel the category mistake because both your language (the Christian language), and your ontology (the Christian faith) have 'become' the universal language and ontology of humankind. If, as an atheist, you talk of 'religiosity', consider the possibility that your atheism is the 'atheism' of Schleiermacher. The 'others' in the world are neither irreligious nor antireligious; it is a category mistake to use the concept of religiosity to describe their worlds.

### 7.1.2. "Tell Me Again, Brother Jacob, Who is Religious?"

Here is where the twain meets. Not the East and the West but the Christian and Secular worlds. In the previous chapter, I spoke of the extent to which Christian ideas became so secular that one does not realise how Christian they are. One does not have to be a Brahmin or even endorse the 'caste supremacy' in order to make sense of the question 'who is a Brahmin?' Equally, one does not have to be a Christian, or a theist, to make sense of the question 'who is a religious person?' Nevertheless, one has to be a part of these cultures – a Brahminical culture in one case and a Christian in the other – for these questions to become intelligible. In the case of India, it seems obvious: the entire society, we are constantly reminded, is dominated by the 'caste' system. In the case of the West, alas, it does not appear so. The reason for this appearance, as I have tried to show, has to do with the universalistic pretensions of Christianity, which has compelled it to secularise its ideas. The long currency it has had in its religious form, the self-evidence it has acquired by virtue of this and its current secular guise have made the situation opaque. 'Who is a Brahmin' is a question internal to a culture and a tradition, which requires that the interlocutors share a set of presuppositions. This is also the case regarding 'who is religious?' Take the 'caste' system away from the one's context, the first question does not make sense; take the religion away from the other's context, the second becomes unintelligible as well.

In India, *two* distinct kinds of individuals have problems with the question 'who is a Brahmin?' The first are among the Brahmins themselves: educated, literate, reflective Brahmins, who, rightly or wrongly, think that the caste system is an evil in Indian society. Under the influence of some or another doctrine about society, be it Marxism or Classical liberalism or whatever else, the first thing they often do is to renounce their own Brahmanism. Normally, it involves two steps: giving-up some rituals and practices; and assume an explicit stance that the 'caste' system is an evil monstrosity that ought to be abolished. However, despite this, many are driven to confess, as a famous writer from a South Indian state once did: "even though I have renounced Brahmanism, the latter will not renounce me".

This is also how Brahmins are experienced among individuals from the second group: educated, literate, and reflective members of the 'lower caste groups'. Even though many from this layer never progress beyond the mantric repetition of hackneyed criticisms from the eighteenth-century Europe, exactly the same realisation pervades their perception as well. A vague sense that 'rejection' of this or that practice and an endorsement of this or that belief does not suffice – either with respect to themselves or with respect to the Brahmins.

Do not misconstrue this point as an argument in favour of "cultural determinism". It has an entirely different purpose, which is to draw attention to the situation in the West. In this culture too, there are two steps involved for someone brought up as a Christian to cease being one. The first step involves rejecting a set of beliefs (mostly, it involves just one belief, *viz*. the existence of God); the second step is to stop going to the church. Neither the individuals who take these steps nor those outside and around them seem to realise that they have an unresolved problem. No, they are now 'atheists' (or 'agnostics' or whatever else), who are free of religion. Atheism or agnosticism is seen as a solution to the problem they had.

The world is also set up in such a way that it can teach individuals how to structure the problem: experientially, they are taught to displace the issue. If someone has a problem with Christianity while being located in that tradition, the world around him tells that his dissatisfaction arises from having accepted the wrong solution hitherto. His problem with Christianity, he is led to believe, has to do with the fact that it is an unsatisfactory solution to another problem, *viz*. does God exist? The solution is unsatisfactory because it is wrong, unscientific, or whatever else. Both atheism and the different religions (including his own) are so many answers to the question of divinity, or meaning of life...Therefore, if an individual experiences some problem with respect to his religion, his world encourages him to choose the right answer to a question, which he always had. That is why after a short, initially painful, 'transition' period, such individuals thrive in a secular world.

How could they really do this? How, if the secular world is really the 'other' of the religious world, could they adapt themselves so easily? How could they find their points of reference with such ease, if the 'secular' world of theirs was alien to the religious world they once inhabited? If religion is an attitude, a feeling, a way of life – as everyone keeps insisting it is – how could you navigate yourself with such skill in an entirely new world? You know my answer: the 'secular', atheistic, world is a solution to the Christological dilemma. It is not the other; it is not an alien world to Christianity. The religious world creates the secular world in its own image.

Thus, we can now better understand the dissatisfaction that many people feel with respect to 'atheism', and their vague unease in the secular world. Their feeling, often inarticulate, has to do with an unfulfilled expectation: they had expected to find another world, which was different from the world they once knew. Instead, they find the 'same world'; but then, not quite the same either because the familiar reference points appear to have taken another form. Yet, they feel that they have come from one religious world into another. I claim that their unease is justified: they have moved from one religious world into another. When you encounter such individuals, and there are many of them, you can interpret their unease and search in at two different ways.

One is that they are seeking a new religiosity, a new spirituality, outside their churches. The Christian churches, you might want to say, have failed in their self-proclaimed (or God-ordained) task of satisfying the 'religious need' of human beings. If you do this, do not forget to keep in mind what you assume: human beings have a specific 'need' that is not satisfied by anything other than religion. Churches might be the wrong answers in your eyes, but you are saying that they were answers nonetheless. There is no unbridgeable chasm between the Churches that failed and your position: man has an innate sense of divinity, say the churches; man has an innate 'religious' need, you say; man searches for God, say the churches; man searches for a 'religious' experience, you say.

Then there is also a second way of looking at such individuals and their unease. You localise it at two levels at least. Firstly, you suggest, they are moving away from their religion in search of an alternative to religion; secondly, what they thought they would find in the secular world is not what they in fact find, *viz.* a world without religion. They merely encounter religion in a new guise.

### 7.1.3. *"Who is Religious, Dear Reader, Who Secular?"*

I will now touch on one facet of the rapprochement between the Christian and the secular world. This should be enough to highlight the issue. We have already seen how one could be a Brahmin or a religious person in their respective traditions even without satisfying the criterion of being born as a Brahmin or believing in God, the creator. As Christian beliefs begin to dominate the world, they do so by appearing increasingly less Christian.

It seems to me that this process can be described in the following terms: some beliefs are detached from the set of religious beliefs and practices with which they were intimately bound. Because this interdependency gave them depth and significance, the detached beliefs become progressively devoid of their biting force and specificity in direct proportion to their 'universal' acceptance. This, however, does not make them secular: they remain religious – no matter how one twists and turns.

Consider Apostel's (1981: 28) claims about atheistic religiosity. He tries to provide some room for this experience by referring to the etymology of the *word:*

> The well-known etymological remark that brings 're-ligion' in connection with 're-ligare' (to tie together, to link) makes us see religious phenomena as instruments of connection, as modes of union.

That this sentiment helps the author to see religion the way he wants to see it or that the remark is well known (implying, therefore, that it is also true) – neither of these issues is worth disputing about. To what extent is this only an etymological point?

In the literature, one comes across *two* attempts at deriving the Latin word *religio* from some or another root. Neither of the proponents of either of the two etymologies was a trained linguist. The first etymological attempt is by Cicero in *De Natura Deorum* and the second derivation is by Lactantius in his *Institutiones Divinae* (*e.g.* Cook 1913: 692; n. 2). Cicero lived about half-a-century before Christ; Lactantius was a Christian theologian, who lived around two hundred and fifty years after Christ. Balbus, the Stoic partner in the Ciceronian dialogue, argues thus:

> For religion has been distinguished from superstition not only by philosophers but by our own ancestors. Persons who spent whole days in prayer and sacrifice to ensure that their children should outlive them were termed 'superstitious'...Those on the other hand *who carefully reviewed and so to speak retraced all the lore of the ritual* were called 'religious' from *relegere* (to re-trace or re-read), like 'elegant' from *eligere* (to select), 'diligent' from *diligere* (to care for), 'intelligent' from *intellegere* (to understand); for all these words contain the same sense of 'picking out' (*legere*) that is present in 'religions'. (*De Natura Deorum,* II: 72; italics mine)

This etymological derivation of Cicero, in its turn, appeals to his culture and tradition. Given what we have seen about Roman *religio* (see chapter #2), this stance appears both sensible and acceptable. As I argued there, *religio* was almost synonymous with *traditio.* The ideas of *carefully* reviewing, or retracing, and 'picking out' do make sense when religion is the tradition handed down by your ancestors.

About three hundred years later, Lactantius – who thought of himself as a Christian Cicero – in explicit opposition to his pagan counterpart reflected upon the etymology of *religio* in these terms (*Institutiones Divinae,* IV: 28):

We are fastened and bound to God by this bond of piety, whence religion itself takes its name. The word is not as Cicero interpreted it from 're-reading', 'or 'choosing again' *(relegendo)*....We can know from the matter itself how inept this interpretation is. For if superstition and religion are engaged in worshipping the same gods, there is slight or rather no differ-ence...because religion is a worship of the true; superstition of the false. And it is important, really, why you worship, not how you worship, or what you pray for...We have said that *the name of religion is taken from the bond of piety, because God has bound and fastened man to Himself by piety, since it is necessary for us to serve Him as Lord and obey Him as father...They are su-perstitious who worship many and false gods; but we, who supplicate the one true God, are religious.* (Trans. Sister McDonald 1964: 318-320; italics mine.)

This remark of Lactantius makes sense as well. Christianity sees man as the servant of God; he is tied and bound to Him as His creature. After all, it is not sufficient that one merely worships – one has to worship God not the Devil. It is, therefore, perfectly plausible that Lactantius would speak of the bond between the individual worshipper and God as the defining trait of religion.

Lactantius' derivation, hardly surprisingly, became well known and famous. Many authors during the Renaissance, like Vico for example, reflected upon the nature and origin of religion and further popularised the etymology of Lactantius.

The contrast between the 'etymological' derivations of *religio* of the pagan Cicero and the Christian Lactantius is far too important to note only in passing. We are, therefore, justified in standing still for a mo-ment in order to appreciate some of the differences between these two writers, and evaluate the implications of their standpoint regarding our theme.

Cicero suggests that *'superstitio'* refers to excesses: "spending days in prayer and sacrifice in order that one's children outlive their parents". This is contrasted with *religio*, where one *carefully* selects from the in-herited tradition. (It does not matter where you put the emphasis: be it on 'selecting' or on doing it 'carefully'.) The function of criticism was to restrain excesses, *i.e.* the function of reason was to criticise *'superstitio'*.

In Lactantius, we already see the extent to which paganism had be-come incomprehensible to Christianity. The distinction between *religio* and *superstitio* is now the opposition between the 'true' and the 'false'. He complains that this distinction – which, note well, paganism does not make – disappears if one focuses merely on the modes of worship. He is both right and wrong. *Superstitio* was also *religio* to the pagans, but carried to extremes. Excessive smoking and drinking are excess-es; but they do not cease being smoking and drinking because of that. Abstaining completely from alcoholic drinks and non-smoking are opposed to drinking and smoking, and this is how Lactantius sees *religio* and *superstitio*. In this sense, he is right that the opposition disappears in Cicero, but he is wrong to imply that pagans saw this distinction as an opposition.

Consequently, the focus of *religio* shifts to whom you worship: God. Not any God, if you please, but the One who is your Maker, Master, and to whom you are tied by bonds of obedience, piety, and so forth.

If, as Lactantius observes, the word *religio* is derived from such ideas as the above, then the very concept of *religio* itself depends on other theological concepts. The difference between the Pagan Cicero and the Christian Cicero is indeed one of 'theologies': Although both use the same word, its sense and reference shifts. The difference between them is not one of emphasizing the 'subjective' and the 'objective' aspects as Smith (1962) maintains, because this is Lactantius' position. To accept it, we need to assume the truth of Christian theology. If we do not accept this theology, we cannot accept this representation of the difference between these two writers either.

The foregoing reflection is sufficient for us to draw two interesting conclusions. First, with respect to the way theological ideas get detached from their context and yet remain recognizably theological; the second with respect to the very concept of 'religion'.

When we come to appreciate the relationship between *re-ligare* and Christian theology, the 'etymology' of Lactantius and his problems with Cicero become perfectly intelligible. What happens when this "well known remark" gets detached from its context and penetrates the secular world? How does it become 'universal'?

It becomes 'universal' in the sense that one can now speak of the other *relatum* of this relationship (Man is one *relatum* and God is the other in Lactantius) in whatever terms one feels like without feeling restricted by Christian theology. It can be the 'finite' or the 'infinite'; the 'cosmos' or the 'universe'; 'humanity' or 'life'; 'individual' or the 'society' *etc.* Yet, the idea that the experience of being tied or linked is a religious experience is recognizably Christian. The background of Christian theology makes it intelligible; otherwise, it is not.

To appreciate this point in all its poignancy, consider the oft-made (partially true) claims about the Indian traditions. These 'religions' (let us continue to use this word until its inappropriateness is pointed out), it is said, aim at liberating men from their bondage, *i.e.* from the ties and bonds that link men to the world. These religions do not aim at severing this or that bond, but all links, bonds and connections, men have in the world, with the world, and with the Cosmos. As a consequence, if religion is *re-ligare,* Indian religions cannot be 'instruments or modes of connection' either. A religion whose explicit aim it is to free you from links cannot possibly provide you with that experience, whose zenith consists of developing precisely this feeling of dependence.

You cannot say that Indian religions are different: you have no other conception of religion when you are discussing 'atheistic' religiosity. What, in other words, sounds perfectly absurd to Indian (Asian) ears sounds perfectly sensible in the western culture. That such a typically Christian theme becomes the cornerstone of 'atheistic' religiosity tells you of the distance that separates a Christian, religious world from a pagan, secular one. Let us turn our attention to the second point.

Although several hypotheses could render this state of affairs intelligible, I would like to opt for one that appears as a logical extension of the argument thus far developed: *the concept 'religion' is itself tradition-bound; it is theological; it is intra-traditional and not inter-traditional.* I should like to reiterate once again that I am not discussing the word 'religion'. For all you like, call it 'boom boom'. My thesis is this: the word 'boom boom' expresses some concept; this concept, enunciated by the word 'boom boom', is Christian-theological. It is not, it cannot be, an inter-traditional concept.

This thesis appears false: after all, as Smith (1962) argues convincingly, but at times confusingly, even the Christians very rarely used the word *religio* with respect to themselves. Besides, he makes an extremely interesting and well thought-out case (Smith 1977, 1979) that both the frequent use of the word *religio* and its association with beliefs is an Enlightenment legacy. This is a disputed thesis (Sharpe 1973; Wiebe 1979; replies in Smith 1973, 1980 respectively), but which thesis is an undisputed truth? As though this is not enough, many Christian theologians from Teilhard de Chardin to Karl Barth are behind him. 'Piety' or 'faith' best summarises, says Smith, the Christian self-description. What arguments do I have against this? Furthermore, how, according to my thesis, is a science of religion (say, a comparative science of religion) possible?

Formidable objections, these. My answers, however, will be very brief. 'Religion', I claim, is how Christianity (to speak only of this tradition) described itself when demarcating itself from the traditions of other peoples and cultures. It is a self-description of Christianity but one directed against the others. It is the outer-boundary of Christian self-consciousness and not its internal core. Christians, when they talk to each other, may or may not talk in terms of their religion. Externally, when they talk to the 'others', it is their self-identity. In fact, Smith himself says as much (1962: 24-25) without realizing its significance:

> The Christian group, to verbalize the new life that they were experiencing and proclaiming, introduced in addition to *ecclesia* other elements of a new vocabulary...In addition, however, they of course took over also a great many terms from the older religious life ... Among these was the

word *religio,* which *appears richly in the Christian writing in Latin from the beginning.*

Actually, until the fourth century it was used more than later. It would seem that there is perhaps a correlation between the frequency of the usage of this word and the historical situation of religious pluralism and rivalry ... *By the fifth century, when the Christian church had virtually eliminated its rivals, the term was less actively in use, and in fact almost disappeared* (my italics).

Of course, they took over the word. They did so by radically shifting its reference. Contra Smith, as I have argued, it is not a mere 'taking over' of a vocabulary. Christianity fashioned a new vocabulary. *'Religio'* lost its roots in paganism when the Christians took over the word. Henceforth, it would grow in a new soil until the only connection between it and the old concept would be the 'word' alone. 'Religion', in this sense, is rooted in the Christian appropriation of the Old Testament.

Yes, a science of religion (whether comparative or otherwise) is possible but as theology (if you allow theology as a science). It is possible to the same extent you can have a science of revelation, a science of trinity, or a science of piety. Religion, I repeat, is a theological concept – at the boundaries, to be sure, but theological nonetheless.

Yet, religion can be studied scientifically: on condition that we do not use theological concepts as our 'theoretical' or 'observational' terms. One such that we should not use is the concept 'religion' itself. What other concepts should we use then? I will address myself to this question in subsequent chapters (chapter #9 and #10). For now, let us see where we have arrived.

At the beginning of the chapter on the Roman *religio,* I reflected upon the fact that we all share a Christian world. "Our (intellectual) world happens to be a Christian world", I wrote there, "whether a Jew, a Dinka or a Brahmin; whether a theist, an atheist or a Muslim, our questions have a common origin". It must be obvious what I had in mind then, and how true it is. *In the name of science and ethnology,* the Biblical themes have become our regular stock-in-trade: that God gave religion to humankind has become a cultural universal in the guise that all cultures have a religion; the theme that God gave *one* religion to humanity has taken the form and belief that all religions have something in common; that God revealed himself to humankind is sanctified in the claim that in all cultures and at all times there is a subjective experience of religion which is fundamentally the same; the idea that God implanted a sense of divinity in Man is now a secular truth in the form of an anthropological, specifically human ability to have a religious experience...And so the list goes on, and on, and on. Theme after theme from the pages of the Bible has become the 'but of course!'

of intellectuals – whether Jew, Muslim, Dinka, or Brahmin. One *has* become a Christian precisely to the degree Christianity has become less Christian in the process of its secularization. We may not have had our baptisms or recognise Jesus as the Saviour; but this is how we prosecute the Christians. The retribution for this is also in proportion: the pagans themselves do not know how pagan they really are. We have, it is true, no need for specifically Christian doctrines. But then, that is because all our dogmas are in fact Christian.

We might as well stop here, but we cannot. The tragedy, or is it the Divine retribution, goes deeper. Far, far deeper.

## 7.2. "THE PROSECUTION RESTS, M'LORDS ..."

At the risk of emasculating the force of the argument, I would like to re-formulate the point made so far by reminding you of our discussions in chapter #1. I pointed out to an inconsistency there. Either creeds, be-lief in God, *etc.*, are necessary for some tradition to be a religion or they are not. One cannot affirm both. Nevertheless, as we also observed in that chapter, our authors affirm both. This posed a problem: why have not these gifted authors seen the inconsistency in their reasoning? Let us see whether we are able to understand this situation any better now.

Let us look afresh at the following two questions: (i) what distinguish-es religion from phenomena like philosophy, literature, caste system, and so on? (ii) What distinguishes one religion, say, Christianity from another, say, Islam?

Let us begin with the second question, and accept the following an-swer: Islam claims that Muhammad was the last prophet of God, and that Jesus was an earlier prophet. While this specific claim, let us agree, distinguishes Christianity and Islam as specific religions, what is com-mon to them both is a belief in the prophets. Claims that are even more specific may distinguish one Christian group from another; one Muslim group from another; but the more general our categories become, the more general are the common properties we attribute.

As you will have noticed, answer to the lower level question – in our case, the second question – contains an implicit criterion from a higher level. Our problem was: are the properties like belief in God, presence of the Churches, existence of the priests and holy books, and such like, which are common to Islam, Christianity, Judaism also the properties that distinguish religion from other phenomena? At the stage of the argument we were in (in chapter #1), I provided a positive answer by inviting you to indulge in a thought experiment: bracket away the above properties (*e.g.* no Koran, no Bible; no Imam, no Pope, no priest...) from these traditions, we will not be able to distinguish them as religions anymore. There might still be differences between individuals of these groups, but we would not be able to specify them as religious differences.

Though this is an extremely convincing argument as far as I am concerned, it may not have appeared thus to others' eyes. Because we are moving from a lower level to a higher one, one could always suggest that there was an intermediate level: what is common to Judaism, Christianity and Islam need not be what distinguishes religion from other phenomena. That is to say, one could argue that between this group of Semitic religions (common to which are these group-specific properties like belief in God, *etc.*) and Hinduism, Greek religion, *etc.*, there is another property shared by all the members of the class.

One such candidate was religiosity: a particular, subjective experience. This could be common to all religions, distinguishing religion from other phenomena. I hope to have shown how this concept presupposes theology and, consequently, why this property does not distinguish between religions and something else. To put it a bit technically, 'religiosity' is an individuating criterion and not a condition of identity: given a group of individuals who belong to a religion, it can distinguish a characteristic or exemplary specimen of that religion from those others who are not. However, it cannot do so across traditions.

The last remark requires a qualification. Suppose, as I have argued, that this theology is presupposed. What then? Then, religiosity cuts across all traditions because one theology becomes the universal frame of reference. In the rest of what follows, I will try to show what it means to make the above suggestion.

### 7.2.1. Raising a Problem

Discussions about other religions are mostly conducted within the framework of Christian theology. Almost all the concepts that I have come across reflect this: 'prophetic', 'sacramental' and 'revelatory' religions; 'liturgy', 'worship', 'sacrament'; 'eschatology', 'soteriology'; 'sacred', 'profane', 'God' and 'Devil'; 'transcendent', 'immanent', 'holy' and 'absolute'; 'faith', 'piety', 'blasphemy'; 'apocalyptic', 'salvation' and 'sin'; and so on and so forth.

As anybody will recognise, these groups of concepts form a cluster and, together, pick out practices: directly they pick out linguistic practices of a community of believers (and not merely that of the researchers), and indirectly refer to the cultural practices of a community with a history. The issue is not so much about the meaning of specific words. In the absence of a background set of beliefs, is it possible to pick out what they are referring to, something, which is constituted as a 'totality' due to the interrelationship between these concepts? The 'totality' of those practices, which these concepts presuppose for an 'intelligible' interpretation of the individual words, is what a religious theology or, better still, Christian religious life in this case, is all about. In cultures where these words have made a house for themselves ('sacrament', 'liturgy', *etc.*) or where native terms have been introduced at the level of daily language (such that people are able to pick out incidents and episodes from their own history to explicate the meaning of these words), it does not present a problem. That is to say, where there is a shared history of practices there these concepts are readily intelligible.

When we transport these terms to a culture lacking these practices and a language lacking these words, our problems are self-evident. Personally, I have had the greatest difficulty in understanding what these terms refer to. I have come across books and articles by their hundreds, which speak of "Buddhist Soteriology", "Hindu Eschatology", "Taoist Liturgy", "Sacrament of the Vedas", and so on. These writers do not question the presumption of sameness: Jewish eschatology and its Hindu counterpart stand in the same relation as driving rules in Israel do with those in effect in India. This, of course, has a double advantage: such writers sound terribly profound in the ears of those not trained to speak in a theological language; after all, how many Indians are trained in Christian theology? The effect is exactly like using a technical vocabulary – from some or another specialised domain – while having a perfectly normal conversation in English with a nonprofessional. Such profundity rests on the unintelligibility of the discourse to the public. This generates the second advantage, which is pernicious to any intellectual enquiry: the very possibility of questioning such a writer is excluded. You cannot challenge these writers unless you master this way of describing but the very process of acquiring this language is also to make these descriptions your own.

Even though this is a personal point, its implications are not limited to exhibiting my intellectual inadequacy. It should draw your attention to two problems. In the first place, the mere use of theological concepts in describing traditions like, say, Hinduism, does not establish that Hinduism is a religion: after all, each of these concepts faces those very problems that the concept 'religion' faced. How can you argue that the Veda's are 'scriptures'; that the Indian temples are akin to churches; or that Bhakti is piety? Besides, we are still to agree that using such concepts is 'fruitful'.

There is a second problem, which is more damaging. Consider, for example, the way Sharma (1986: xii-xxiii) talks of *The Bhagavadgita*: the commentaries on this text have laid bare, he says, its 'theological contradictions', 'soteriological ambiguity', 'liturgical inconsistencies', 'canonical ambivalence', *etc.* Each of these concepts has been coined by Christian priests (or appropriated from elsewhere) to talk about Christianity. These are theological concepts and parts of the Christian religious life. If you use this framework to talk about either Hinduism or the Gita, then you are using it the way we use scientific theories and their categories. That is, you are identifying Christian theology as the 'science' of religion – something that not all Christian theologians them-selves would consent to. This could turn out to be true but one cannot assume its truth beforehand.

Why, then, have those indefinitely many writers not seen what they have been doing? A part of an answer to this question has already been given: the assumption that all cultures have religion is a historical legacy. Due to its long currency, it has become an unexamined *trivium*. In the previous part, I examined how this religious belief became progressively secular. I have extended this consideration not merely to concepts like 'holy' and 'religiosity' but to concepts like 'liturgy', 'sacrament' and such like. However, we have not quite seen the import and significance of the suggestion that 'our' secular world is a Christian world. What I will do now is to outline the contours of this argument.

Suppose that one defines religion (*i.e.* one explicates our pre-theoreti-cal intuition about 'religion') as involving a belief in the existence of God. Our intuitions tell us that Buddhism and Jainism are religions, which, as we well know, deny the existence of any such entity. Consequently, Buddhism and Jainism are 'counter examples' to this definition of reli-gion. Hence, it is said, this definition is not a 'good' one.

This counterintuitive consequence is easily blocked simply by deny-ing that it is counterintuitive – this tells us what goes wrong here. It requires that we all share exactly the same pre-theoretical intuition. (If you dislike the word 'intuition', you are free to use the word 'notion' in its stead.)

What does it mean when one speaks of a pre-theoretical notion? By it is meant that the notion in question is no part of a theory (as is obvi-ous), and that it is no term-of-the-art because of not being explicitly (or otherwise) defined in a theory. That is to say, it is a notion that you and I have. Not being part of a theoretical discourse, it is part of our ordinary language use.[1] Our definitions, then, are 'good' so long as they explicate the intuitions (or notions) underlying our use of the word 'religion'.

To paraphrase the above in more neutral terms, so as to avoid the philosophical problem of 'meaning' and 'use', the argument comes down to this: an explication will have to rest on the ultimate authority of our linguistic practice. A counterexample, consequently, would show that the given explication runs counter to our linguistic practice.

Pray, *whose practice* and *which language?* Shall we say the practice of the West and languages like English, Dutch, German, French…and such like? Or, are we willing to cast our nets wider?

---

[1] Ordinary languages are contrasted with specialised and/or artificial languages of our scientific theories.

Linguistic practices are those of a community that speaks *this* way and not *that* or *another* way. It is thus that practices have a cultural history. The cultural history of the West has happened to be, among other things, a history of Christianity as well. Are we to say that all cultures have a religion simply because the linguistic practice of one cultural community, the West, allows that all cultures have a religion?

If it is merely a dispute about using the word 'religion', the problem is easily settled: none of the Asian languages has the word 'religion'; therefore, one cannot use that word in identifying Hinduism through Shintoism. If Asians do not have that word (or any other word from the concept cluster), they do not have a pre-theoretical intuition related to the use of that word or any other word from the concept cluster either.

At this point, to recount my experience, the discussion tends to shift grounds abruptly: Asians may use another word but they do have the concept of religion. The task of a good definition would be to explicate this concept. The answer to the question, 'how does one know whether other cultures do have this concept?' reveals the presupposition: it is inconceivable that Asians do not have religions.

Why is it inconceivable? What makes it inconceivable *to whom* to say that Buddhism, Shintoism, *etc.* are not religions?

### 7.2.2. A Problem Illumined

#### Religious Practice and Linguistic Practice

As I have suggested in the previous part (chapter #7.1), religion is simultaneously two things: it is both the outer boundary of Christian self-consciousness and a part of the religious/theological vocabulary of the Christian life. This is one of the reasons why we need a way of referring to what the believers call 'religion' without ourselves using this word because the explication of this term rests non-trivially upon theological vocabulary. I am not going to explain the 'why' of this now (see chapter #9), but I want to suggest that thinking about religion takes place within the framework of a linguistic practice, which is itself religious. The network of practices referred to by 'religion', in the deepest sense of the term, moulds the pre-theoretical notion of what religion is. That is to say, one learns to use the word 'religion' accordingly as one participates in, and becomes a member of, a linguistic practice of a community. It is important to realise that this 'linguistic' practice refers not to the practice of using a natural language (like French, German, or Dutch) but to that of using a theological language.

I am using the term 'linguistic practice' well advisedly. Not because religious life involves using some or another natural language, but because the concept cluster which gives Gestalt to a religious life has taken the status of being an integral part of a natural language-use.

Let us leave aside some of our philosophical stances regarding 'meaning', 'proposition', etc., to look at the issue more closely. Consider such sentences as 'It is raining', 'Het regent', 'Es regnet', from English, Dutch, and German respectively. We believe that these sentences are saying the same thing, i.e. that they express the proposition that it is raining. (If you prefer, these sentences mean that it is raining.) Whenever they are enunciated, such natural language sentences are understandable by those in whose language such sentences are utterable. The reference (or the meaning) of such a sentence is guaranteed by its background, viz. a particular linguistic practice.

Not only do speakers of a particular language understand such sentences in their language, but the possibility of translation depends on the fact that these concepts (or propositions) expressed in these different languages are the same. The 'how' and the 'what' of it is a hotly debated issue; let me just notice this situation as a fact.

Just for the sake of clarity, if you allow that such sentences as the above are a way of talking about the weather, then my point is this: the Christian way of talking about itself (viz. as a religion) appears as natural a way of talking as talking about the weather. To say that 'it is hot', 'it is dry', 'it is raining', etc., do not appear to presuppose any specific vocabulary but merely a shared, common world. The world we live in, the experiences we have therein, a competence in some natural language, are the requirements to utter and understand such sentences. Exactly the same status is being accorded to concepts like 'religion', 'sacrament', 'liturgy',...etc., whenever one speaks of other cultures and their religions. Without problem, people say Shintoism involves ancestor 'worship'; speak of the 'theology' of Buddhism; 'gods' of the Hindus; and so on. Having a religion is as natural as rains and harvest – both being the preconditions of human existence.

We must take very seriously the fact that the western culture has been *dominated* by the Christian religion for over eighteen hundred years and reflect about its implications. With respect to language, it is this: the theological vocabulary does not appear tied to a specific religion. Religious language does not seem to possess a recognisable Gestalt because it has faded into the background. This 'naturalness' of a theological, religious language has taken such grotesque proportions that both the 'theists' and the 'atheists' discuss the possibility and the necessity of the existence of God using modal logic. That is to say, they use modal logics (which formalise the concepts of 'necessity' and 'possibility') to talk intelligibly to each other about a concept from the Old Testament theology. What makes this situation hallucinatory is their absolute lack of realisation that their discourse about God is totally *unintelligible* to those others (like me, for example) who do understand modal logics (see #9.5.1). And then, people inform me, they are 'atheists' and, therefore, not religious.

In part, this is what it means to say that Christianity has gone secular. Its language, its vocabulary, its concepts, are all part and parcel of the daily language, daily practice, daily vocabulary of even those in the West who have been brought up as 'atheists', 'free thinkers', 'heathens', or however else one feels like describing them. In a subsequent chapter (chapter #10), you will come to appreciate this situation from another perspective. I have said enough here to propose another fragment of an answer to the question I started out with, *viz.* Why is it so counterintuitive for people in the West to believe that there are cultures that do not know of religion?

*The Linguistic Inconceivability*

Relative to a given discourse, philosophers often draw a distinction between an 'object' and a 'meta' level: an 'object level' discourse refers to the discourse about an object, and the 'meta-level' discourse refers to the way we talk about the object. Theories about, say, the functioning of a refrigerator or the structure of the Universe could be seen as object level discourses – their objects being the refrigerator and the Universe. We could also discuss about these theories. In that case, *relative* to the object of these theories, we are talking at a meta-level. As must be clear from the emphasis I have put, this is not an absolute but a relative distinction.

Religion, as I said earlier on, is both the outer boundary of Christian self-consciousness, and refers to the totality of Christian life. To formulate this in terms of the above distinction, religious language has become its own meta-language. That is to say, today, it is not possible to talk about religion without using the language and vocabulary of a religion talking about itself. In the same way when we talk about the English language in English, English is both the object and meta-language, so is it with religious language. There is no problem about this situation when we communicate in English. However, how can you talk to me about the English language, if I do not understand English?

The answer is simple: you can talk in another language about English assuming, of course, that we both know this language. Let us now extend this argument.

Suppose you believe that there are other languages besides your own in the world, and you come to my part of the world. You see us making gestures, you hear us producing sounds, and you notice us reacting to the gestures and the sounds. Because of your belief that there exist other languages besides your own, you assume that we too have a language. You will no doubt think that we are speaking merely in another language with a different syntax and semantics, and a distinct phonology, and so on.

Suppose you believe that your language is the only language on earth. As a visitor, or as an anthropologist, you now come to my part of the world. What do you see? You hear us producing sounds but not being part of the vocabulary of a language, they appear to have little resemblance to any human language; you see us making signs and gestures but, because we do not seem to have a language, there is no obvious connection between these and the sounds we produce. In other words, because of your assumption that your language is the only human language, our actions must be so radically unintelligible to you that you will have to deny that we speak a language too. Let us recollect a citation we have already come across before:

> Max Müller quotes Sir Emerson Tennent to the effect that the Veddahs of Ceylon have no language: "they mutually make themselves understood by signs, grimaces, and guttural sounds, which have little resemblance to definite words or language in general." In fact they speak Sinhalese (an Indo-European tongue). (In Evans-Pritchard 1965: 106.)

Suppose that you are a traveller or a missionary from sixteenth, seventeenth, or eighteenth century Europe, visiting my part of the world. You share the assumptions of your contemporaries and fellow-discoverers, which we have identified elsewhere (chapter #3). As a Thomas Bowrey, or a Ludovico Varthema, or as an Abrahamus Rogerius, you come to my part of the world – to Calicut, to the Malabar coast, to Goa, or wherever else your ship may be anchored. Your religious language grants that we are idolatrous people, worshipping stones and animals, images and icons. What do you see? You see heathenish practices and Devil's worship. You see our 'priests' and our heathen immorality.

Now, you should be able to see where we are heading: towards the twentieth century. With the legacy of centuries of description of religions of other cultures behind you, you are an atheist nonetheless. You do not know much about your Bible and still less of its theology, but your daily language is saturated with the theological terms we already spoke of. Not only does this language allow you the assumption that other cultures have religions, but it also threatens to make some set of practices radically unintelligible if they are not described as religions. Chinese, English, etc., are all different languages, but they are not other than languages. Thus also in the case of religions: Buddhism, Hinduism, etc., appear as different forms of religion. To say that they are not religions appears to make these practices radically unintelligible. Their apparent unity is itself threatened. It is only by linking up practices and

The questions 'who is religious person?' and 'who is a Brahmin?' raise issues of identification. I say 'issues' because these questions raise at least *two* such. Firstly, there is the problem of providing criteria for religiosity' or 'Brahminhood' that answer the question: under what conditions is someone, anyone, religious? Here 'religiosity' is used as the general, repeatable, or universal property. For the sake of convenience, let us call this the issue of identity.

There is also a second issue. Given a domain of individuals, the answer to the question 'who is a religious person?' or 'who is a Brahmin?' individuates. That is to say, it distinguishes between two individuals who belong to that class. Let us, again for the sake of convenience, call this the issue of individuation. Both issues are tied to one another, but they are also distinct from each other as Munitz (1971: iii-iv) rightly notes:

> The distinction between what it is to be an individual or a particular instance on the one hand, and what it is to be general, repeatable, or common on the other, is as fundamental as any distinction in philosophy. It is central to the conceptual scheme with which the human mind operates... Involved in the attempt to work out this distinction is another central pair of concepts, namely, sameness and difference. To be able to identify an individual requires that we be able to say that it is the very same individual and no other...(T)he problem of establishing the identity of an individual involves...differentiating that individual from other *coexisting* individuals...
>
> Meanwhile, in the other direction, as we seek to bring out what constitutes the common or the repeatable, again we inevitably fall back on the notions of the 'same and different'. To say what distinguishes one kind or type from another and makes it the very kind or type that it is calls for a criterion of identity that would apply to that which is repeated. (Italics in the original.)

I have tried to argue that from Schleiermacher's speeches to Buddha's question, the issue has been one of individuation. 'Given a religious tradition, who is religious amongst them?' asks one; 'Given the caste system', asks another, 'who is a Brahmin?' There is no one *unique* Brahmin any more than there is a *uniquely* religious person. Consequently, neither 'Brahminhood' nor 'religiosity' can be an individuating concept. The argument can only be pragmatic in nature, *i.e.* it must appeal to the context of the dialogues and the nature of the public.

I have done so with respect to the authors I have treated. You and I are having a dialogue too. Hence, I have also appealed to the context of our dialogue. In our case as well, the religious person is the subset of all those who belong to a religion. However, as I have argued, this

construing them as a unity – as 'Hinduism', as 'Buddhis
phenomena are saved from the apparent threat of total u

The threat, as I say, is only apparent. In exactly the s
gion is but one kind of linguistic practice, there could exi
of practices in other cultures. The members in these cultur
be able to describe their traditions differently without ha
intelligibility or unity to their traditions. From within on
a Japanese is simultaneously a Buddhist and a Shintoist. F
point of view, a different description of the Japanese may
ing which provides an alternate unity. Whether such des
forthcoming or not is a question that neither you nor I can
any degree of certainty. That is not at issue here. What is a
ever, is the extent to which this argument helps to make
unargued and deeply rooted belief, which the West has, tha
know of religion in some form or the other.

When you look at a Japanese bowing before the graves
raits of his ancestors; or at a Thai putting garlands on the s
Buddha; or at a Hindu prostrating himself on the ground
the only way you can save these phenomena from the threa
ligibility and lack of unity is to call them religious obser
need to tie such practices with other ones, and these with
and so on, until you can see them constituting a unity. Hov
well: the unity you create, the descriptions you provide are
for you and to those others who share your religious lan
those who do not share your language, in all probability, the
you generate will appear chaotic; your intelligibility conditior
opacity; your 'obvious' and 'self-evident' truisms are their es
the exotic.

In other words, we can better understand why you have
ate Hinduism, Buddhism, Shintoism, and all those other relig
language, the practice of the community you are part of, th
render phenomena chaotic if they are not construed *this* wa
way or *another* way. At the same time, you also feel that the w
quite how you have described it: hence the unease, the incon
and the dilemmas that we took note of at the very beginnir
essay (chapter #1).

*7.2.3. "What Say You, The Jury, Guilty or Not Guilty?"*

It is time for us now to look back at the last two chapters, recol
our questions were, and see what answers we have on our hand
stage of the journey. Let me begin by closing the argument
chapters on a philosophical note.

religion has secularised itself. The Biblical themes have become secular and our stock-in-trade. Therefore, 'religiosity' now individuates – or so it appears – across different religions, and across religious and secular life. However, this situation does not make 'religiosity' any less of an individuating criterion than it was in the hands of a Schleiermacher or a Söderblom or an Otto. It merely shows that religion has spread wider and deeper than its champions maintain or its critics dream.

The continuity of this story with those of the earlier chapters is now obvious. Our 'secularised', modern world is closer to Jerusalem than it is to Athens. We are indeed travelling further and farther away from that grand old pagan city.

Now I can answer the question 'is the West itself a culture without religion?' in the negative and yet qualify it. When religious themes have secularised themselves as 'scientific' certainties, indeed, how is it possible to claim that one of the constituting moments of the western culture is not continuous with religion? Yet, the qualification is there: the de-Christianised Christianity gives the impression that the themes are not typically religious.

Now I can argue further that the creation of religions in India has to do with the conceptual compulsion of a religious culture. If one is already (quite independent of conceptual and empirical enquiries) certain that Buddhism and Jainism are religions even when they deny the existence of God, or even a plurality of 'gods', what is one talking about when one talks of religions? How, if belief in God is utterly irrelevant to being religious, are we to begin making sense of all those centuries of bitter struggle between atheists and theists (which included, at the centre of its dispute, the existence or nonexistence of God), all those tortures, persecutions and executions, in the West itself? Are we supposed to take seriously that this was a linguistic, etymological misunderstanding? Could you, without feeling sick to your stomach, imply that the horror of religious persecution could have been avoided if only the participants knew their Latin well and had sat down with each other to discuss the meaning of 're-ligare' instead of chopping each other's head off? How is it possible to consider one set of structures where the existence or nonexistence of God is an intelligible question and another where such questions cannot even be formulated as identical (or even similar)?

The question "Do you believe in Vishnu?" makes no sense in the Indian context: *it cannot even be put.* (Burghart and Cantile, Eds., 1982: viii; my italics.)

Further, I have begun to argue that a 'scientific' study of religion will be 'scientific' only in the sense that theology is a science. I have provided considerations to the effect that theology has been the framework for studying religion. It may be interesting to note that Söderblom appears to have seen this, and had little or no problem with it:

> The scientific approach to the study of religion...does not rest on the absence of personal conviction, least of all on the absence of a religious conviction...The requirement that the theologian should possess a feeling for religion or a definite religious conviction or belong to a religious community is implied...in the general scientific requirement of familiarity with the object [studied]...Therefore science cannot recognize any difference in principle between the science of religion and theology. (Motto in Sharpe 1990.)

I submit, in other words, that the three concerns that grouped the last two chapters together have found some kind of resolution.

## 7.3. About One Half of An Argument

Our agenda has become cluttered. Some initial questions with which we began this journey have been partially answered, and new ones have arisen to take their place. Some well-known landmarks have become alien, whereas exotic drinks have begun to taste familiar. Given that I have completed one stage of the journey, it is time for us to look back to where we started from, the place we are at now, and chalk-out the road we need to travel.

"Is religion a cultural universal?" We started out with this question. Because the consensus today is an affirmative answer to this question, our query took the form: what grounds do the intellectuals have to argue that religion is a cultural universal? My argument has been to the effect that, with respect to the Indian religions in any case, empirical investigation has not been the ground for making the claim. As far as theoretical grounds are concerned, it is Christian-theological: because the Bible tells us that religion is God's gift to humankind, religion is a cultural universal. This is where we are now. However, let us notice the souvenirs we have collected during the journey. Let us do so chronologically.

In chapter #1, I raised several questions. To answer them, we had to go through the theoretical arguments for believing in the universality of religion (chapter #5), and the history of the knowledge of 'other' religions (chapters #2 through #4). Let us see what answers we have to some of them.

*First,* it has become abundantly clear that the question of the existence of religion was never a problem for empirical investigation. It was a belief whose truth was taken for granted and the discussions about the origin of religion proceeded from this assumption. The Testament theology lay at the basis of this idea and it has been popularised in its secular form ever since the Enlightenment. Theories which claim to explain religion by appealing to the structure of the human brain, the biological or genetic makeup of human beings, the original patricide, *etc.,* could not possibly do a credible job because (at this stage of the argument) it is not so evident anymore that they do have a 'universal' phenomenon to explain.

*Second,* my hypothesis that the concept of religion underlies and pervades all theory-formation about religion must now appear more credible. I argued that if the concept of religion is pre-theoretical, then the claim about the universality of religion rests on grounds other than empirical ones. If my narrative holds water, this implication appears true: there has been no empirical investigation, and the grounds are theological in nature.

*Third,* this circumstance also illumines the reason why we do not appear capable of spelling out the empirical consequences to our 'theories' of religion, if we come across cultures that do not have religion.

*Fourth,* we understand the situation that struck us forcibly in the fifth chapter: the theoretical edifice meant to account for the origin of religion appeared shaky and it seemed to generalise European history to encompass the multiple pasts of other groups in the world. A lesson, surely, for those who believe that theology – if only it is secularised – will overcome its theological limitations.

*Fifth,* while discussing the inconsistent reasoning of modern authors on religion, we briefly looked at the Wittgensteinian answer. There I suggested that speaking of "family resemblance" is not sufficient because it is not an answer to our question. The last three chapters should have strengthened this case. The virtue of the Wittgensteinian answer lies in drawing our attention to the culture of the investigator: why are people influenced by the cultural history of Christianity convinced that other groups have religion too? There is no necessity, I trust, to underline the obvious.

Furthermore, in the present chapter I have tried to present some considerations in favour of the idea that concepts like 'religion' and 'religious experience', the 'sacred' and the 'profane', are part of a specific theological vocabulary. By saying this, I do not want to imply that they are theological by virtue of some property such that we can differentiate between the 'theological' and, say, the 'scientific'. Rather, my thesis has been that the explication of these terms appeal non-trivially to other theological ideas.

In chapter #1, I identified a cluster of questions, each of which has been partially answered. One such question was, 'is the existence of religion susceptible to an empirical enquiry?' I have answered it by saying that it is not, as long as we pose the question in this fashion.

Although we have come to see several things in a new light by now, the project of this essay appears even more obscure than before. While the Biblical stories might have held intellectuals from the sixteenth to nineteenth centuries in thrall, the same could hardly be said of their descendants – those several atheistic philosophers and anthropologists of the twentieth century. How shall we understand their deeply held conviction that religion exists everywhere? There are three facets to an answer: historical, linguistic, and conceptual. The historical and the linguistic aspects have been dealt with. The conceptual will occupy us during the course of the next chapters.

(see #9.5.1). And then, people inform me, they are 'atheists' and, therefore, not religious.

In part, this is what it means to say that Christianity has gone secular. Its language, its vocabulary, its concepts, are all part and parcel of the daily language, daily practice, daily vocabulary of even those in the West who have been brought up as 'atheists', 'free thinkers', 'heathens', or however else one feels like describing them. In a subsequent chapter (chapter #10), you will come to appreciate this situation from another perspective. I have said enough here to propose another fragment of an answer to the question I started out with, viz. Why is it so counterintuitive for people in the West to believe that there are cultures that do not know of religion?

## The Linguistic Inconceivability

Relative to a given discourse, philosophers often draw a distinction between an 'object' and a 'meta' level: an 'object level' discourse refers to the discourse about an object, and the 'meta-level' discourse refers to the way we talk about the object. Theories about, say, the functioning of a refrigerator or the structure of the Universe could be seen as object level discourses – their objects being the refrigerator and the Universe. We could also discuss about these theories. In that case, *relative* to the object of these theories, we are talking at a meta-level. As must be clear from the emphasis I have put, this is not an absolute but a relative distinction.

Religion, as I said earlier on, is both the outer boundary of Christian self-consciousness, and refers to the totality of Christian life. To formulate this in terms of the above distinction, religious language has become its own meta-language. That is to say, today, it is not possible to talk about religion without using the language and vocabulary of a religion talking about itself. In the same way when we talk about the English language in English, English is both the object and meta-language, so is it with religious language. There is no problem about this situation when we communicate in English. However, how can you talk to me about the English language, if I do not understand English?

The answer is simple: you can talk in another language about English assuming, of course, that we both know this language. Let us now extend this argument.

Suppose you believe that there are other languages besides your own in the world, and you come to my part of the world. You see us making gestures, you hear us producing sounds, and you notice us reacting to the gestures and the sounds. Because of your belief that there exist other languages besides your own, you assume that we too have a language. You will no doubt think that we are speaking merely in another language with a different syntax and semantics, and a distinct phonology, and so on.

Suppose you believe that your language is the only language on earth. As a visitor, or as an anthropologist, you now come to my part of the world. What do you see? You hear us producing sounds but not being part of the vocabulary of a language, they appear to have little resemblance to any human language; you see us making signs and gestures but, because we do not seem to have a language, there is no obvious connection between these and the sounds we produce. In other words, because of your assumption that your language is the only human language, our actions must be so radically unintelligible to you that you will have to deny that we speak a language too. Let us recollect a citation we have already come across before:

> Max Müller quotes Sir Emerson Tennent to the effect that the Veddahs of Ceylon have no language: "they mutually make themselves understood by signs, grimaces, and guttural sounds, which have little resemblance to definite words or language in general." In fact they speak Sinhalese (an Indo-European tongue). (In Evans-Pritchard 1965: 106.)

Suppose that you are a traveller or a missionary from sixteenth, seventeenth, or eighteenth century Europe, visiting my part of the world. You share the assumptions of your contemporaries and fellow-discoverers, which we have identified elsewhere (chapter #3). As a Thomas Bowrey, or a Ludovico Varthema, or as an Abrahamus Rogerius, you come to my part of the world – to Calicut, to the Malabar coast, to Goa, or wherever else your ship may be anchored. Your religious language grants that we are idolatrous people, worshipping stones and animals, images and icons. What do you see? You see heathenish practices and Devil's worship. You see our 'priests' and our heathen immorality.

Now, you should be able to see where we are heading: towards the twentieth century. With the legacy of centuries of description of religions of other cultures behind you, you are an atheist nonetheless. You do not know much about your Bible and still less of its theology, but your daily language is saturated with the theological terms we already spoke of. Not only does this language allow you the assumption that other cultures have religions, but it also threatens to make some set of practices radically unintelligible if they are not described as religions. Chinese, English, etc., are all different languages, but they are not other than languages. Thus also in the case of religions: Buddhism, Hinduism, etc., appear as different forms of religion. To say that they are not religions appears to make these practices radically unintelligible. Their apparent unity is itself threatened. It is only by linking up practices and

construing them as a unity – as 'Hinduism', as 'Buddhism', etc. – that phenomena are saved from the apparent threat of total unintelligibility.

The threat, as I say, is only apparent. In exactly the same way religion is but one kind of linguistic practice, there could exist other kinds of practices in other cultures. The members in these cultures might well be able to describe their traditions differently without having to deny intelligibility or unity to their traditions. From within one description, a Japanese is simultaneously a Buddhist and a Shintoist. From another point of view, a different description of the Japanese may be forthcoming which provides an alternate unity. Whether such descriptions are forthcoming or not is a question that neither you nor I can answer with any degree of certainty. That is not at issue here. What is at issue, however, is the extent to which this argument helps to make sense of the unargued and deeply rooted belief, which the West has, that all cultures know of religion in some form or the other.

When you look at a Japanese bowing before the graves or the portraits of his ancestors; or at a Thai putting garlands on the statue of the Buddha; or at a Hindu prostrating himself on the ground in a temple; the only way you can save these phenomena from the threat of unintelligibility and lack of unity is to call them religious observances. You need to tie such practices with other ones, and these with the texts,... and so on, until you can see them constituting a unity. However, note well: the unity you create, the descriptions you provide are necessities for you and to those others who share your religious language. For those who do not share your language, in all probability, the unity that you generate will appear chaotic; your intelligibility conditions are their opacity; your 'obvious' and 'self-evident' truisms are their esoteric and the exotic.

In other words, we can better understand why you have had to create Hinduism, Buddhism, Shintoism, and all those other religions. Your language, the practice of the community you are part of, threatens to render phenomena chaotic if they are not construed *this* way but *that* way or *another* way. At the same time, you also feel that the world is not quite how you have described it: hence the unease, the inconsistencies, and the dilemmas that we took note of at the very beginning of this essay (chapter #1).

### 7.2.3. *"What Say You, The Jury, Guilty or Not Guilty?"*

It is time for us now to look back at the last two chapters, recollect what our questions were, and see what answers we have on our hands at this stage of the journey. Let me begin by closing the argument of these chapters on a philosophical note.

The questions 'who is religious person?' and 'who is a Brahmin?'
raise issues of identification. I say 'issues' because these questions raise
at least *two* such. Firstly, there is the problem of providing criteria for
'religiosity' or 'Brahminhood' that answer the question: under what conditions is someone, anyone, religious? Here 'religiosity' is used as the
general, repeatable, or universal property. For the sake of convenience,
let us call this the issue of identity.

There is also a second issue. Given a domain of individuals, the answer to the question 'who is a religious person?' or 'who is a Brahmin?'
individuates. That is to say, it distinguishes between two individuals
who belong to that class. Let us, again for the sake of convenience, call
this the issue of individuation. Both issues are tied to one another, but
they are also distinct from each other as Munitz (1971: iii-iv) rightly
notes:

> The distinction between what it is to be an individual or a particular in-
> stance on the one hand, and what it is to be general, repeatable, or com-
> mon on the other, is as fundamental as any distinction in philosophy. It is
> central to the conceptual scheme with which the human mind operates...
> Involved in the attempt to work out this distinction is another central
> pair of concepts, namely, sameness and difference. To be able to iden-
> tify an individual requires that we be able to say that it is the very same
> individual and no other...(T)he problem of establishing the identity of an
> individual involves...differentiating that individual from other *coexisting*
> individuals...
>
> Meanwhile, in the other direction, as we seek to bring out what consti-
> tutes the common or the repeatable, again we inevitably fall back on the
> notions of the 'same and different'. To say what distinguishes one kind or
> type from another and makes it the very kind or type that it is calls for a
> criterion of identity that would apply to that which is repeated. (Italics in
> the original.)

I have tried to argue that from Schleiermacher's speeches to Buddha's
question, the issue has been one of individuation. 'Given a religious tradition, who is religious amongst them?' asks one; 'Given the caste system', asks another, 'who is a Brahmin?' There is no one *unique* Brahmin
any more than there is a *uniquely* religious person. Consequently, neither 'Brahminhood' nor 'religiosity' can be an individuating concept.
The argument can only be pragmatic in nature, *i.e.* it must appeal to
the context of the dialogues and the nature of the public.

I have done so with respect to the authors I have treated. You and
I are having a dialogue too. Hence, I have also appealed to the context
of our dialogue. In our case as well, the religious person is the subset
of all those who belong to a religion. However, as I have argued, this

religion has secularised itself. The Biblical themes have become secular and our stock-in-trade. Therefore, 'religiosity' now individuates – or so it appears – across different religions, and across religious and secular life. However, this situation does not make 'religiosity' any less of an individuating criterion than it was in the hands of a Schleiermacher or a Söderblom or an Otto. It merely shows that religion has spread wider and deeper than its champions maintain or its critics dream.

The continuity of this story with those of the earlier chapters is now obvious. Our 'secularised', modern world is closer to Jerusalem than it is to Athens. We are indeed travelling further and farther away from that grand old pagan city.

Now I can answer the question 'is the West itself a culture without religion?' in the negative and yet qualify it. When religious themes have secularised themselves as 'scientific' certainties, indeed, how is it possible to claim that one of the constituting moments of the western culture is not continuous with religion? Yet, the qualification is there: the de-Christianised Christianity gives the impression that the themes are not typically religious.

Now I can argue further that the creation of religions in India has to do with the conceptual compulsion of a religious culture. If one is already (quite independent of conceptual and empirical enquiries) certain that Buddhism and Jainism are religions even when they deny the existence of God, or even a plurality of 'gods', what is one talking about when one talks of religions? How, if belief in God is utterly irrelevant to being religious, are we to begin making sense of all those centuries of bitter struggle between atheists and theists (which included, at the centre of its dispute, the existence or nonexistence of God), all those tortures, persecutions and executions, in the West itself? Are we supposed to take seriously that this was a linguistic, etymological misunderstanding? Could you, without feeling sick to your stomach, imply that the horror of religious persecution could have been avoided if only the participants knew their Latin well and had sat down with each other to discuss the meaning of 're-ligare' instead of chopping each other's head off? How is it possible to consider one set of structures where the existence or nonexistence of God is an intelligible question and another where such questions cannot even be formulated as identical (or even similar)?

The question "Do you believe in Vishnu?" makes no sense in the Indian context: *it cannot even be put.* (Burghart and Cantile, Eds., 1982: viii; my italics.)

Further, I have begun to argue that a 'scientific' study of religion will be 'scientific' only in the sense that theology is a science. I have provided considerations to the effect that theology has been the framework for studying religion. It may be interesting to note that Söderblom appears to have seen this, and had little or no problem with it:

> The scientific approach to the study of religion...does not rest on the absence of personal conviction, least of all on the absence of a religious conviction...The requirement that the theologian should possess a feeling for religion or a definite religious conviction or belong to a religious community is implied...in the general scientific requirement of familiarity with the object [studied]...Therefore science cannot recognize any difference in principle between the science of religion and theology. (Motto in Sharpe 1990.)

I submit, in other words, that the three concerns that grouped the last two chapters together have found some kind of resolution.


## 7.3. ABOUT ONE HALF OF AN ARGUMENT

Our agenda has become cluttered. Some initial questions with which we began this journey have been partially answered, and new ones have arisen to take their place. Some well-known landmarks have become alien, whereas exotic drinks have begun to taste familiar. Given that I have completed one stage of the journey, it is time for us to look back to where we started from, the place we are at now, and chalk-out the road we need to travel.

"Is religion a cultural universal?" We started out with this question. Because the consensus today is an affirmative answer to this question, our query took the form: what grounds do the intellectuals have to argue that religion is a cultural universal? My argument has been to the effect that, with respect to the Indian religions in any case, empirical investigation has not been the ground for making the claim. As far as theoretical grounds are concerned, it is Christian-theological: because the Bible tells us that religion is God's gift to humankind, religion is a cultural universal. This is where we are now. However, let us notice the souvenirs we have collected during the journey. Let us do so chronologically.

In chapter #1, I raised several questions. To answer them, we had to go through the theoretical arguments for believing in the universality of religion (chapter #5), and the history of the knowledge of 'other' religions (chapters #2 through #4). Let us see what answers we have to some of them.

*First,* it has become abundantly clear that the question of the existence of religion was never a problem for empirical investigation. It was a belief whose truth was taken for granted and the discussions about the origin of religion proceeded from this assumption. The Testament theology lay at the basis of this idea and it has been popularised in its secular form ever since the Enlightenment. Theories which claim to explain religion by appealing to the structure of the human brain, the biological or genetic makeup of human beings, the original patricide, *etc.,* could not possibly do a credible job because (at this stage of the argument) it is not so evident anymore that they do have a 'universal' phenomenon to explain.

*Second,* my hypothesis that the concept of religion underlies and pervades all theory-formation about religion must now appear more credible. I argued that if the concept of religion is pre-theoretical, then the claim about the universality of religion rests on grounds other than empirical ones. If my narrative holds water, this implication appears true: there has been no empirical investigation, and the grounds are theological in nature.

*Third,* this circumstance also illumines the reason why we do not appear capable of spelling out the empirical consequences to our 'theories' of religion, if we come across cultures that do not have religion.

*Fourth,* we understand the situation that struck us forcibly in the fifth chapter: the theoretical edifice meant to account for the origin of religion appeared shaky and it seemed to generalise European history to encompass the multiple pasts of other groups in the world. A lesson, surely, for those who believe that theology – if only it is secularised – will overcome its theological limitations.

*Fifth,* while discussing the inconsistent reasoning of modern authors on religion, we briefly looked at the Wittgensteinian answer. There I suggested that speaking of "family resemblance" is not sufficient because it is not an answer to our question. The last three chapters should have strengthened this case. The virtue of the Wittgensteinian answer lies in drawing our attention to the culture of the investigator: why are people influenced by the cultural history of Christianity convinced that other groups have religion too? There is no necessity, I trust, to underline the obvious.

Furthermore, in the present chapter I have tried to present some considerations in favour of the idea that concepts like 'religion' and 'religious experience', the 'sacred' and the 'profane', are part of a specific theological vocabulary. By saying this, I do not want to imply that they are theological by virtue of some property such that we can differentiate between the 'theological' and, say, the 'scientific'. Rather, my thesis has been that the explication of these terms appeal non-trivially to other theological ideas.

In chapter #1, I identified a cluster of questions, each of which has been partially answered. One such question was, 'is the existence of religion susceptible to an empirical enquiry?' I have answered it by saying that it is not, as long as we pose the question in this fashion.

Although we have come to see several things in a new light by now, the project of this essay appears even more obscure than before. While the Biblical stories might have held intellectuals from the sixteenth to nineteenth centuries in thrall, the same could hardly be said of their descendants – those several atheistic philosophers and anthropologists of the twentieth century. How shall we understand their deeply held conviction that religion exists everywhere? There are three facets to an answer: historical, linguistic, and conceptual. The historical and the linguistic aspects have been dealt with. The conceptual will occupy us during the course of the next chapters.

# PART III

The three chapters that constitute this part enter the phase of building a theory about religion. They do that by transforming the facts noticed and the conclusions drawn in the previous chapters into problems requiring solutions. How can religious language be its own meta-language? How can a secular world be a religious world in disguise? How can religion and its dynamic account for the contestable claims of the previous chapters? If studying religion requires taking recourse to theology, is a science of religion possible?

In addition to these and similar questions, my hypothesis about religion is also subject to constraints. All of them have to do with the properties that are essential to religion, as the believers claim. This part will lend intelligibility to these multiple claims.

I argue that religion is an explanatory intelligible account of the Cosmos and itself; therefore, is reflexive in a particular way; thus, exhibits a double dynamic of proselytisation and secularisation. I call this the dynamic of the universalisation of religion. Not merely is this hypothesis sufficient to account for what we have seen; it is also productive enough to propel us further in the direction of seeking the relation between culture and religion – the focus of the last part.

CHAPTER EIGHT

# A HUMAN TRAGEDY OR THE DIVINE RETRIBUTION?

As we have noticed, the eighteenth- century discussions about the origin of religion hardly interest thinkers of today. Often, the question about the origin of religion is interpreted to mean a precise localisation, in both time and place, of the emergence of religion.

> ...(I)t is important to recognize that we are not concerned here with the origins of religion. For all practical scientific purposes it is safe to assume that the origins of religion are lost in Antiquity. We merely accept the fact that religion exists and affects human behaviour (Vernon 1962: 43).

This stance, more or less, summarises the general attitude prevalent in the intellectual community. Consequently, to most, the universal existence of religion is a fact – not a problem requiring a solution or a phenomenon in need of an explanation.

How could we characterise the interests of the twentieth-century thinkers regarding religion? In one sense, the answer is obvious: they want to explain and understand religion. This answer, however, is both too narrow and too broad. It is narrow because most are not interested in developing speculative reconstructions demonstrating the necessity of religion for human societies and individuals. It is broader than my characterisation of their endeavour because their interest also includes specific religions – their history, development, and structure – and not merely religion as such.

The characteristic form taken by the study of different religions in the twentieth century is that of comparative studies. As we have seen, the 'science' of religion – in the last quarter of the nineteenth century – came into being as comparative studies of religion. However, once the 'novelty' of the other religions wore off, this trend exhibited its barrenness, sterility, and vacuity of content. Instead of a rejection of this approach, however, what we see in the twentieth century is a super-imposition of further 'isms' with the hope of squeezing something out of it yet: structuralism, functionalism, symbolic interactionism, Marxism, phenomenology,...etc. Books, journals, articles, and societies multiplied by their hundreds, each doing comparative studies: a mega-comparison of 'science' with 'religion' and 'Magic' (*e.g.* Malinowski 1925); maxi-comparison of Buddhism and Christianity (*e.g.* Garbe 1914) or Confucianism with Christianity (*e.g.* Ching 1977); point-by-point local comparison of 'Trinity' with 'Trimurti', 'Dharma' with 'God' (Cantwell Smith 1966). Such comparisons are the lifeblood of domains like sociology of religion, for example. If you cannot compare the function of Dinka religion in their society with that of another religion of some obscure tribe, and these two with those of the Brahmins and the Taoists, what can you possibly say about the function of religion in human societies?

The different permutations and combinations within each of the above mentioned 'isms', the explosive growth of different domains of investigation into human phenomena, the accumulation of information and the sheer size of data – all these have made it impossible for any one individual to have a global view of the field of religious studies. In the introduction to the two-volume *Contemporary Approaches to Religion*, the editor, Frank Whaling contrasts the classical period (which refers to a period before the Second World War) to the contemporary one. Speaking of the latter, he says,

> Today,...there is an extraordinary ramification within the study of religion, a vast growth of academic knowledge of all kinds, a springing up of new seeds within the field, and a complexification and globalization of the context wherein religion is studied that make easy generalizations...and a one person treatment difficult if not impossible (Whaling 1983: 3).

To tell a story of this period requires a more thorough documentation than any I can provide now. Consequently, the wise and the prudent refrain from telling any kind of story – be it a potted history or a thematic narrative. Rushing in where angels fear to tread, I shall press ahead with my tale though.

Yet, it will be a different kind of story. Call it, for the sake of convenience, a conceptual story. I shall carry it from where we left off, and conclude it in the first subsection (#8.1). Being a conceptual tale, it will answer one single question: if the secular world of today is a religious world too, what consequences does it have to the field of religious studies? Even though the process of secularisation must have influenced other intellectual domains, I am going to restrict myself only to that of religious studies. In so doing, I hope to lend credibility to the narrative penned hitherto by drawing some implications and elucidating them further. The illustrations will be our contemporaries: their arguments, their positions and, of course, their definitions. I will be telling a story about them while arguing with them at the same time. Alternating between these two modes of discourse will enable us to switch our tracks smoothly when the time is ripe for it, *viz.* in chapter #8.2.

In #8.3, I shall identify Christianity as an exemplary instance of 'religion'. The formulation and its context could give birth to some misunderstandings and several confusions. Consequently, I shall spell out what I am not even implicitly suggesting, and what we must definitely avoid. This turns out to be a timely warning because, as I elaborate on it in a discussion with Frits Staal and approach the end of the chapter, the problem involved in identifying an exemplary instance of 'religion' gets deepened.

Introducing the fifth chapter, I said that I was going to use a way of speaking about religion as an entry point to study religion. Further, I suggested that the multiple descriptions of religion in other cultures have their roots in the nature of religion itself. What we will see in this chapter is their meeting point. Until such a stage, I suggest you lean back, put your feet up, and listen...

## 8.1. BECAUSE THE STORY MUST GO ON

I have argued in the previous chapters that investigations into 'religions' in other cultures were carried out within a religious framework. I have suggested that Christian theology is the theoretical framework within which investigations into religion have taken place. This is how I have tried to account for the 'discovery' and creation of religions in India. Further, I have argued that this theological framework has universalised itself under a secular guise. In the process, it has faded into the background. The secular world of today is a religious world. Such a characterisation is not without consequences. In this subsection, I shall endeavour to demonstrate the truth of some of these consequences. I hope thereby to strengthen the case that just as a religious framework secularises itself to guide the twentieth-century investigations into religion, this framework itself becomes increasingly de-Christianised. I have also argued in the previous chapter (#7.2) that this framework has ended up becoming a part of natural language-use. In chapter #5, I proposed that the claim regarding the universality of religion undergirds theory-development about religion. Here, I spell them out a bit more in detail.

*The Structure*

More concretely, the structure of this section is as follows. If religion is a pre-theoretical concept, the disputes about the concept will exhibit

certain problems. In each subsection, I shall identify a different problem. In #8.1.1, I will argue that disputations about the nature of religion are carried out without the disputants having a clear idea of what
they are disputing about or even why. This is one of the consequences
of not having a theory, especially when the object is something as 'abstract' as religion.

Whenever we have a theory about an object, not only does it help us
decide whether or not some newly discovered entity belongs to its domain, but also, more importantly, how to go about settling the dispute
when it arises. In the absence of a theory, however, it is not obvious how
to arbitrate conflicts where and when they arise. In #8.1.2, I show that
the dispute about whether 'Hinduism', 'Buddhism', etc., are religions is
very much like a conflict of tastes.

A theory helps us in settling disputes because there are several
strategies for testing its claims. One such strategy is that of providing
counter examples. Though rather oversold and often much abused, its
method (e.g. see Schlesinger 1984) can be briefly formulated as follows:
given a domain of objects identified by some theory, by giving an example – real or imaginary – of an object from that domain which behaves
differently, one can refute the theory in question. In the absence of a
theory about religion, counter examples will have to target a definition.
I argue that not only is it empty to speak of giving counter examples to
definitions but also that it would lead us to an interminable discussion.
This is the subject of #8.1.3.

There is also another reason why disputes about the definitions – in
the absence of a theory about an object – are interminable. That has
to do with the fact that, in such a case, discussions about definitions
take the form of classificatory problems. In #8.1.4, I spell this problem
out by introducing an *ad hoc* distinction. This distinction has only a
pedagogic function. In the same subsection, I identify two different
problems in a debate about definitions: a referential problem and a classificatory problem.

In #8.1.5, I return to the referential problem and the consequences
that the absence of a theory has in answering it. One of the consequences is that a referential problem ends up getting a classificatory answer.

However true this portrayal may be, it makes authors – both contemporaneous and those from yesteryears – appear silly and stupid. I
am not willing to accept this description. In fact, making their actions
intelligible has constituted one of the dominant concerns of this essay.
Therefore, in each subsection, I provide an alternate description, which
makes their attitude consistent and reasonable by appealing to my
claim: in the background, and guiding their investigations, is the presence of a Christian theological framework.

There is a tension and a problem latently present in the argument.
Having developed the problem during the earlier chapters, its explicit

formulation in #8.1.6 enables us to switch tracks and go further in our attempts to understand religion.

Before I address myself to any of these questions, a warning requires to be borne in mind. Even though the discussion does involve definitions and the definitional questions, I am *not* addressing these issues in an abstract, methodological manner. That is to say, the arguments do not constitute a philosophical treatment of the nature and function of definitions. Instead, I look at the question of giving a definition of religion. Methodological lessons are relativised to the theme of the essay and general philosophical points help us come to grips with the subject-matter. Therefore, when I ask 'why give a definition?' this question is *contextualised.* I cannot emphasise this enough.

## 8.1.1. What is the Dispute About?

Consider a scientific theory, say, the theory of black holes. Such a theory is able to tell (a) what object(s) it is talking about; (b) what distinguishes black holes from white dwarfs and pulsars; (c) what properties do black holes have; (d) how black holes come into being; and many such things. That is to say, in such a theory you can ask several knowledge-seeking questions which are both precise and can be answered.

## A Thought Experiment

Suppose that, I am inviting you to do a thought experiment, there is not a single black hole physicist tomorrow morning and none of us is able to read what the textbooks say.[1] However, the use of concepts continues: singularity and the event horizon; black holes and quasars; and Chandrasekhar's limits and Schwartzchild's radius.

One generation passes. Then two. And then three. Some old disputes remain; some others disappear due to lack of intelligibility. The disputes are considered important, even though nobody knows any more why. Some groups remain adherents of the first cosmic law of censorship ("Thou shalt see no naked singularity"); others deviate to another position ("There shall be no naked singularity"); and yet others do not see why naked singularity should not be possible. And so on. Each group comes up with its own reasons – using some new terms and using some old ones – as to why their position is right. However, it is

---

[1] After composing this subsection, it struck me that MacIntyre (1981) uses a similar imagery. In order to record his priority in this matter, I shall make use of his description in the subsequent subsection.

not obvious either to them or to the bystanders *why* they are disputing or even what it is about.

Because the theory has disappeared but the debates continue, the disputed questions make sense only as differing positions as they are expressed in different formulations. Consequently, the attention shifts to terminological issues.

*An Illustration*

At first glance, the dispute in the field of religious studies appears to take this form. The discussions appear purely terminological. Nevertheless, there is a feeling that disputes are not at that level either. O'Toole, a sociologist (1984: 10), has this so say:

> It is apparent that a universally useful "all-purpose" definition is difficult if not impossible to attain, its intellectual desirability being, in any case, by no means self-evident. Secondly, it is clear that religion may logically be defined from any number of specific vantage points, none of which need presuppose the ontological accuracy or inaccuracy of religious knowledge in general or particular terms.

Having said this, he spends the next 30 pages discussing various 'definitions' of religions. Yet another sociologist, (Vernon 1962: 43) declares that

> (an) adequate definition of anything as complex and variable as religion is, however, difficult to provide. Some prefer not to make such a definition, feeling that religion can be described more adequately than it can be defined.

Nevertheless, a chapter on a 'sociological definition of religion' is indispensable to his book.

Thus we can go on and on literally building a huge list of authors who (i) insist on being unable to give an 'adequate' definition; (ii) provide their own definition; (iii) accept the permissibility of other definitions; and yet, (iv) spend a great deal of time and effort in criticising others' definitions.

Some philosophers even make a *virtue* of such disputes by tracing their roots to the characteristic property of our concepts. By calling some concepts 'essentially contested', they render the dispute senseless and sensible at the same time. It is sensible because our disputes appear 'normal' – after all, the concepts are 'essentially contested'; it is also senseless because, being essentially contested, there is no possibility of a resolution. Why not simply stipulate a definition and get on with the more serious job of building a theory? Kolakowski, a philosopher by training, begins his book on *Religion* (1982: 9-12) with these words:

> I am never sure what religion...is, but whatever religion is, it includes the history of gods, men and the universe...
>
> Still, I cannot avoid using the word 'religion'...In the investigation of human affairs no concepts at our disposal can be defined with perfect precision and in this respect 'religion' is in no worse position than 'art', 'society', 'culture', 'history', 'politics', 'science', 'language' and countless other words. Any definition of religion has to be arbitrary to a certain extent. Various definitions are thus permissible...
>
> The socially established worship of the eternal reality: this formulation comes perhaps closest to what I have in mind when talking of religion. It does not pretend to be a 'definition'...

*An Alternate Description*

Could we write such disputes off so easily? Are they meaningless disputes, which gifted and brilliant authors do not see, because they have not learnt their philosophies well enough?

The questions about what religion is, whether such entities as 'Buddhism', 'Hinduism', etc., are religions too, and so on are extremely important issues within a religious tradition like Christianity. If Jesus were to be no different from Buddha; or that God in Christianity were to be the '*Atman*' of the Hindus; or even that it made no difference to human salvation (as Christians see the latter) whether Christianity is true or Jainism (which denies gods and 'God') is; the threat that a religious tradition like Christianity faces is obvious. The same consideration, with appropriate modifications, applies to Islam and Judaism as well. Therefore, the questions about what religion is, whether religions of all other cultures exemplify 'religion', etc. are substantial questions for theological and empirical enquiries.

Such a cluster of questions, appreciation of their centrality and the importance of the problems and their answers invariably indicate the presence of a theory, whose questions they are. Without the presence of such a theory, these questions would cease making sense. In the imaginary example I just gave, the second and the third generation would lose interest about questions that were once important in black hole physics, because of at least two reasons. (A) Because the theory, using which one could raise some questions (the required mass of a star before it turns into a black hole; the question of the 'virtual' particles becoming real particles *etc.*) disappears, these questions disappear as well. (B) Yet other questions would cease to exhibit their 'cluster property', and end up (where they remain) as isolated problems. That is to say, one could recognise the continued persistence of some problems and nevertheless not realise their importance.

In other words, the disputants in the debates about the definitions continue to feel that some sets of questions hang together, that they are important, and that one must try to find resolutions to them. The importance they attach to issues like what religion is, whether 'Hinduism', Marxism, *etc.* are religions, testify to this state of affairs. The importance they attach suggests the presence of a theoretical framework.

However, this theory has faded into the background. One does not accept this theory explicitly. Consequently, they act as though they do not have a theory. The result is that they *feel* that their issues are important; but unable to find reasons for this feeling, they end up trivialising them.

*A Further Illustration*

Both the importance they attach to the questions and the way they end up trivialising the problem can be illustrated further by letting a sociologist (Vernon 1962: 43) tell us why it is important to say what religion is.

> If you cannot define something, how do you know what the "something" is? A definition is essential, in any meaningful discussion and to avoid confusion and argument.

There are three points that Vernon is making, and it is useful to keep them separately in mind. There is, first, the claim that in order to "know" something, one needs to define it. Both the context and the wording allow us a charitable interpretation: to identify some phenomenon X as "something", we need to say what it is. This is why we need a definition. Second, when we say what some phenomenon is, we avoid confusion with respect to the *reference* of the term. Thirdly, this prevents "argument". Of course, without argument (*i.e.* criticisms and disputations) there is little possibility that science could progress. Again, a charitable interpretation is to suggest that Vernon is saying that arguments about definitions should be avoided.

Eminently reasonable suggestions, one might feel inclined to say. Look at his definition:

> Religion is that part of culture composed of shared beliefs and practices which not only identify or define the supernatural and the sacred and man's relationships thereto, but which also relate them to the known world in such a way that the group is provided with moral definitions as to what is good (in harmony with or approved by the supernatural) and what is bad (contrary to or out of harmony with the supernatural) (*ibid*: 55-56).

This hardly helps us understand what phenomenon Vernon is talking about. Religion is a shared set of beliefs and practices (Is a founder of a religion or a religious movement ever religious then?); and abounds in terms like 'supernatural' and 'sacred'; 'harmony' and 'out of harmony'; 'known' and 'unknown' worlds, *etc.* The problem with this definition is that it is even vaguer than the term 'religion' as we use it in our day-to-day intercourse with people. Instead of eliminating confusion about the reference of the term, this 'scientific' definition makes it cloudy: a group of philosophers of science united by a platform, which is critical of 'paranormal' sciences answers this description as well. Further, it is not even clear whether only 'religion' does these things or whether other things do them too.

The same considerations hold good elsewhere in the literature. Geertz, the famous anthropologist, defines religion (1966: 4) as:

> (1) a system of symbols which acts to (2) establish powerful, pervasive, and long-lasting moods and motivations in men by (3) formulating conceptions of a general order of existence and (4) clothing these conceptions with such an aura of factuality that (5) the moods and motivations seem uniquely realistic.

While Geertz spends the rest of the article in 'unpacking' this definition, Williamson concludes his with a 'universal' definition:

> Religion is the acceptance of...a set of beliefs that exceed mundane matters and concerns; the commitment to a morality or the involvement in a lifestyle resulting from these beliefs; and the psychological conviction which motivates the relation of belief and morality in everyday living and consistent behaviour (1985: 30-31).

These examples, not exceptions to but illustrative of 'theorising' about religion in the twentieth century, are symptomatic of fetishes about definition. Let us, by all means, strive to provide clear and unambiguous definitions. But let us do so only when our discussions threaten to get sidetracked and derailed; or when we are unable to formulate questions for scientific enquiry because we are not sure what we are talking about; or when the ambiguity of certain terms becomes the foundation for asserting philosophical theses about the world. That is to say, it is recommendable to provide explicit definitions when we can improve upon our day-to-day discourse. None of the three definitions cited above do this. One would have thought this is hardly a way "to avoid confusion and argument". Such 'definitions' invite article after article on 'definitional' questions, like, for example, Spiro (1966) on definitions of religion, Southwold (1978) on the definition of religion and its consequences for Buddhism, Bianchi's (1972) on the relation between definitions and methodology, and Asad (1983) on Geertz's definition, and so on. This might be a good way to make a living, but it hardly takes us closer to a scientific understanding of religion.

### 8.1.2. ...De Gustibus Non Disputandum Est

Let me now describe another possible world, the one MacIntyre sketches, which talks of the disappearance of all sciences.

> Imagine that the natural sciences were to suffer the effects of a catastrophe. A series of environmental disasters are blamed by the general public on the scientists. Widespread riots occur, laboratories are burnt down, physicists are lynched, books and instruments are destroyed. ...Later still there is a reaction against this destructive movement and enlightened people seek to revive science, although they have largely forgotten what it was. But all that they possess are fragments: a knowledge of experiments detached from any knowledge of the theoretical context which gave them significance; parts of theories unrelated either to the other bits and pieces of theory which they possess or to experiment; instruments whose use has been forgotten; half chapters from books, single pages from articles, not always fully legible because torn and charred. Nonetheless all these fragments are reembodied in a set of practices which go under the revived name of physics, chemistry and biology. Adults argue with each other about the respective merits of relativity theory, evolution theory and phlogiston theory, although they possess only a very partial knowledge of each...
>
> In such a culture men would use expressions such as 'neutrino', 'mass', 'specific gravity', 'atomic weight' in systematic and often interrelated ways which would resemble in lesser or greater degrees the ways in which such expressions had been used in earlier times before scientific knowledge had been so largely lost. But many of the beliefs presupposed by the use of these expressions would have been lost and there would appear to be an element of arbitrariness and even of choice in their application...What would appear to be rival and competing premises for which no further argumentation could be given would abound. Subjectivist theories of sci-

ence would appear and would be criticised by those who held that the notion of truth embodied in what they took to be science was incompatible with subjectivism (MacIntyre 1981: 1-2).

Alasdair MacIntyre's description appears to pick out the twentieth century field of religious studies unerringly. Capriciousness would guide discussions about what religion is.

*An Illustration*

If we look at the procedures the authors adopt in the course of formulating their definitions of religion, we see that they are tailored to accommodate the personal choices and tastes of the author himself. He believes that certain practices are religions and seeks a definition that will do 'justice' to what he accepts as true. Durkheim, for example, is dissatisfied with the 'minimal' definition of Tylor ("Religion is a belief in supernatural beings") because he sees that Theravada Buddhism falls outside the scope of such a definition. Consequently, he provides a definition that would make Buddhism into a religion, while excluding magic. Söderblom feels that magic is also 'religious' and looks around for a definition that would include the former. There are those who think that baseball (*e.g.* Cohen 1946) and Nationalism (*e.g.* Nottingham 1954) are religions too; thus, they fish around for definitions that will include them. Yet others, more conservative or less imaginative as the case may be, are quite satisfied to provide a definition that would grant 'religious experience' or 'religiosity' or just plain old 'religion' to groups and cultures both well-known and almost forgotten: from the Apaches to the Kayapo Indians; from the Hindus to the Maoris; from the Bantus to the Bhils. And so the story goes on.

Such plenitude must thrill you to the very soul. As a Kantian, you will perhaps be touched to the marrow of your bones by the freedom with which each man defines his own terms; as a free-market advocate, you are no doubt in a consumer's paradise where you shop around, consume, but are under no obligation to buy; as a democrat, you cannot but marvel at this republic of learning where men of letters disagree with each other and agree to disagree; and if you are none of the above, why, you can take heart just by thinking of the number of articles you can write...And thus can *this* story go on as well.

However charming such stories might be, I think it is both wise and prudent to avoid telling them. The end of neither of these stories being in sight, we face a problem: what 'morals' could one draw from a story that does not end? Mine is this: do not narrate such stories, if you can help it.

If you see in these an attempt to state explicitly what one's tastes and preferences are, perhaps you will find it laudable. By virtue of this, conflicting definitions are very much like conflicts of tastes: you find that magic is also religion, I do not; so what do we do about it? You may find it unpalatable that I call baseball a religion, but, quite obviously, I find it extremely apt. How do we go about arguing?

## An Alternate Description

Even though the picture is true, it appears to make brilliant and reputed thinkers appear silly and stupid. One description makes them reasonable and consistent. I have tried to tell such a story where the religious themes are secularised and become a part of the background; where the religious framework becomes the general theory within which these authors work. Let me render the discussion more manageable by restricting our attention to traditions like Judaism, Islam, Hinduism, Confucianism, Christianity, *etc.* Methodologically, our writers consider these as religions before seeking an 'adequate' definition. The belief that such traditions are religions in one form or another (a pervasive idea found to be current with the corner-store grocer too), is backed up by the enormous literature produced about them. That is to say, the writer's acceptance of this commonplace belief is based on the studies undertaken by his contemporaries or predecessors. How have they studied them? As religions, of course.

In other words, his belief that Hinduism, Shintoism, Confucianism, etc., are religions is supported by the belief (held by both his predecessors and contemporaries alike) that they are religions. Convinced of the correctness of this belief, he then tries to find some definition that would be 'adequate' to the task of showing how he was right after all.

If we look at these thinkers in this fashion, we can see how they appear both reasonable and consistent. Because we already know that Buddhism and Hinduism are religions, as are Christianity and Taoism, our definitions of 'religion' must be adequate to the task of grouping these practices under one category. Counter examples take the form of counterintuitive consequences. The latter, in their turn, falsify some attempts as explications of our notions. Because such intuitions are unreliable in border cases, there is a vague feeling that disputes about the applicability of the word are arid.

In other words, my labour and its results in the previous chapters (#6 and #7) are not in vain. Nor are they far-fetched. Thus, we arrive at the conclusion that was textually demonstrated in the previous chapters. These theorists assume beforehand that their common-sense ideas of 'religion' are also what religion is.

We are now in a position to account for the preoccupation of contemporary authors. Their endeavour is sensible because they are elaborating upon accumulated knowledge. Of course, I have argued, this accumulated knowledge is based more on theology and less on empirical investigation. However, this does not render their efforts meaningless.

### 8.1.3. Interminable Disputations

In the next two subsections, I will not sketch any other possible world or invite you to conduct a thought experiment. Nevertheless, I shall keep to the structure of the previous subsections. Therefore, instead of a thought experiment, I would like you to consider...

### A Theoretical Point

Consider, for example, the field of Black hole physics and, say, Darwin's *The Origin of Species*. Both are about some specific phenomenon: one speaks of and describes the origin, growth, role, and properties of Black holes – a stellar object – and another speaks about the origin, growth, and development of biological life on our planet. In so far as both the physicists and biologists have some kind of theory, both 'black hole' and 'species' are concepts therein. Further, we could also discuss whether some biological specimen belongs to a particular species or whether a particular stellar object can be considered a black hole. This presupposes, however, that the participants accept the theories about the phenomena. That is to say, the interlocutors must accept some or another theory of black holes and some or another variant of evolutionary biology in order to have a sensible discussion.

Suppose we come across a stellar object which 'behaves' like a black hole – distortion of light and gravitational field, for example – but does not turn out to be one. Such an event will not be a counter example to the 'definition' of black hole, but it will challenge a specific theory of black holes. That is, to put it succinctly, 'definitions' do not allow of counter examples – only theories do. (That is why I suggested that the 'definitions' of religion are explications of 'our' common-sense knowledge of the phenomenon in question.) The reason for this is simple: definitions have no consequences, but the theories that embed them do. That is why substantial problems cannot be *solved* (but can be dissolved) by definitional means.

*An Illustration*

What happens if disputes occur in the absence of a theory? A counter example might not have the same force to those who provide the definition. The only counter examples for an explication of a pre-theoretical intuition are the counterintuitive consequences. How to settle the issue when *intuitions* conflict?

Melford Spiro (1966: 91) explicitly relates definitions to intuitions. Let me look at his definition in order to illustrate my point.

> Since 'religion' is a term with historically rooted meanings, a definition must satisfy not only the criterion of cross-cultural applicability but also the criterion of intra-cultural intuitivity; at the least it should not be counter-intuitive. For me, therefore, any definition of 'religion' which does not include, as a key variable, the belief in superhuman...beings who have power to help or harm men is counter-intuitive.

Spiro suggests that the task is one of providing a 'consensual ostensive definition' and settles for another "minimal" definition. Whose consensus though? To begin with, 'religion' is not a term of art, *i.e.* it is not a technical word coined by this or that theorist intended to standardise usage by all those who work in the same domain. Consequently, the 'consensus' cannot be about the use of the word by a group of theorists. There can be no consensus among the majority of human kind either, because most people on earth have never heard of the word 'religion'. Nor, for that matter, could we rest content with a 'consensus': after all, I want to know why we classify Buddhism as 'religion' and not as pornography.

His minimal definition, as we see above, is the following: "Belief in super-human beings". It is as easy to criticise this definition as it is for him to meet the criticisms. Consider the following objection: suppose that I believe in the existence of extra-terrestrial beings, whose physical chemistry is not carbon-based, who have abilities that human beings do not have. I believe further that they do have power to help or harm human beings. According to Spiro's definition, I am religious because of this belief. I could suggest that it is a 'counter example' to his definition; but all Spiro has to do is deny that this is a counter example. He could simply agree with the consequence and call me religious because of this belief. Given that neither of the participants has a theory, the only court of appeal left to both of us is our intuitions as language speakers. Why should the intuitions of either of us be wrong? Why should the 'intra-cultural intuition' of Spiro count for either more or less than my intuition? Spiro appeals to the "historical rootedness" of meanings of the word 'religion'. One assumes, with a very great certainty, that both the meaning of religion and the meaning of the word 'religion' have changed over the course of the last two thousand years. As I have argued, the reference of *religio* shifted when Christianity appropriated the term from the Romans. If I am right, some of the connotations were retained when the denotation (or reference) of *religio* shifted.

Quite apart from the truth-value of my claims, there is a weightier matter at hand. The "intra-cultural intuitivity" that Spiro talks of is neither constant nor homogeneous (chapter #7). Thus, for example, Smith (1962) argues that equating religion with belief (be it in "superhuman beings" or whatever else) is a relatively recent development dating from the Enlightenment. Which 'intuition' – if Smith is right, many think (*e.g.* Harrison 1990) that he is – should count? One with a history of eighteen hundred years, or one with a history of less than a hundred and fifty years? On what possible grounds could one propose a resolution of this question? In other words, all we can say about this dispute is that what is counter-intuitive to me, and thus a counter example, need not be so to Spiro.

*An Alternate Description*

Suppose that one accepts the description I have provided and entertains the idea that religion has secularised itself to become our common background. Then, discussions about whether Marxism is a religion, Hinduism and Buddhism are one, are disputes about whether these practices are religions too. Whether science or not, Christian theology is some kind of theory. In this sense, 'religion' is a concept in theoretical (or systematic) theology analogous to the way 'species' and 'black hole' are terms within theoretical biology and black hole physics. As a concept within theology, which presupposes such a theory, using it involves us in doing theology as well. That is to say, discussing whether some star is a black hole involves us in doing physics. The same consideration holds good regarding religion. In one case, it is transparent; in another case, as I have chronicled it at length, it is opaque.

However, the opacity does not mean that such a theory is absent in the background. With respect to Christianity's status as a religion, several theological positions are possible: from the position that all others worship the Devil through granting the vestiges of the 'primal' religion to other cultures to the multiple revelations of the divine. Therefore, disagreements about whether 'Hinduism' is a religion, whether or not magic is also religious, express ongoing discussions of an unsolved problem. The fact that it is unsolved makes the discussion appear interminable. However, the debate itself need not be futile. In our case, one is not giving a counter example to a definition but refuting a claim of a theory however 'intuitive' such a theory might be.

### 8.1.4. Classificatory Problems

If we use a theory to talk about the world, inter-subjectivity considerations require that others know what we are talking about. There are several such considerations: hermeneutic; the testability or falsifiability of one's theory; the communicative perspectives; *etc*. Therefore, when one discusses the 'problem' of definition within a theory, one is concerned about *identification*: 'what is one talking about?' In this sense, one of the functions of a term within a theory is to provide an answer to a *referential problem*.

Consider the disputes about the definition of religion. Is Voodoo magic or religion? Is Confucianism a religion or not? Is magic an earlier form of religion or a phenomenon of a different kind? In each of these cases, the disagreements could also be about the ways of classifying the facts at our disposal. Such a disagreement is interminable, because it is endemic to the classificatory activity. Why is that?

### A Theoretical Point

Consider the distinction of the following sort: (a) the way the world is; (b) our knowledge of the world; and (c) the way we order our knowledge of the world. While the distinction between the first two aspects may not appear in need of clarification, that between the last two might. When I speak of 'knowledge of the world', I would like to include both our theories about the world and those indefinitely many facts about it. Hence, we need to allow the possibility for a classificatory system that orders facts, concepts, and theories without itself being part of any specific theory. For example, an encyclopaedia classifies concepts of a domain (an encyclopaedia of bioethics or religion) for which no single theory exists; a natural language dictionary classifies words following this or that rule or heuristic; an ethnographic study classifies several facts about a culture without being guided by a theory, whose facts they are...and so on. In this sense, ordering or classifying our knowledge is distinguished from acquiring knowledge of the world.

This distinction does not entail that there is no relationship at all between knowledge and classification. Classification could help us systematise our knowledge and suggest questions and problems that one has to pursue. Thus, classificatory activity could be a heuristically important device in acquiring knowledge, even if it does not directly provide us with knowledge. In the process of developing theories and hypotheses, one may have to rely tentatively upon some or other kind of classificatory system. The point at which classificatory activity coincides with knowing is the limiting case of this distinction. To reach such a stage, however, *i.e.* the stage where classification of knowledge is also an extension of our knowledge of the world, more is required. When we have a theory, which describes the universe in such a way that our theories about the world constitute a part of the *explananda*, then an identity between classification and knowledge will be an accomplished fact. Such a theory would order itself. We are far, far away from such a stage. Therefore, the distinction between the activity of gathering knowledge and that of systematizing it remains acceptable today.

Because what we classify in these disputes are not events and phenomena but their descriptions, our problem arises at the level of the facts we want to classify. Assembling these facts is dependent on the classificatory systems we use. One could have a classificatory concept of 'religion' that includes sub-concepts like 'initiation rites', 'burial practices', 'worshipping modes', and so on. Such a person might assemble 'facts' about the initiation and funerary rituals in other cultures; or about practices of going to temples, mosques, churches, and such like, and claim that 'religion' is a set of such practices. To him, both the bar mitzvah of the Jews and the 'sacred thread' ceremony of the Hindus are initiation rites; a Thai putting garlands on the statue of Buddha and a Muslim praying in a Mosque are different modes of worship, *etc.* In such a case, the dispute about the definition of 'religion' merely shifts grounds. Now it would involve these other sub-concepts and their use without, however, resolving the problem. Why not?

The reason must be evident. You can always question the legitimacy of considering puja – which is what the Thai is doing – as a mode of worship. You might want to claim – as I do – that puja has nothing to do with worship. In such cases, either the disagreement is about the choice of *words*, in which case the dispute is arid or it is about the 'facts'. To one, it is a 'fact' that the Thai is worshipping because he is garlanding a statue; to the other, it is equally a 'fact' that he is not worshipping precisely because he is garlanding a statue.

That is, there is no agreement about what constitute 'facts' in our case. If one is willing to allow 'facts' as knowledge-items, it is equivalent to suggesting that we have a disagreement about whether or not we have knowledge of the phenomena. One way of resolving this dispute is to raise it to a higher level such that our units of discussion cease to be individual facts but a theory. If both participants agree on accepting some theory of religion, the probability is greater that the dispute has a terminus. Precisely that is lacking when we talk to each other, when we indulge in classificatory discussions.

Consequently, disputes about definitions – when the latter are classificatory terms – are interminable in the absence of a theory that provides us with knowledge of the world.

*An Illustration*

Martin Southwold (1978), in order to *make* Buddhism into a religion,
appeals to Rodney Needham's (1975) notion of Polythetic classes.
Needham refers to the Wittgensteinian idea of 'language games' and to
the contemporary classificatory procedures in Zoology, to establish the
notion of a polythetic class.

Polythetic classes are formed by attributing a cluster of 'closely rela-
ted/associated' properties to individual members of a class. Monothetic
classes are equivalent to our notion of sets, where clear-cut criteria exist
either to include or exclude an item from a set.

Southwold's claim is that 'religion', as we use the term in our languages, is a polythetic class. No particular religion need have all the properties that the class 'Religion' has. Which are those properties? This is
his list:

(1) A central concern with godlike beings and men's relation with them.
(2) A dichotomisation of elements of the world into sacred and profane,
and a central concern with sacred.
(3) An orientation towards salvation from the ordinary conditions of
worldly existence.
(4) Ritual practices.
(5) Beliefs which are neither logically nor empirically demonstrable or
highly probable, but must be held on the basis of faith...
(6) An ethical code, supported by such beliefs.
(7) Supernatural sanctions on infringements of that code.
(8) A mythology.
(9) A body of scriptures, or similarly exalted oral traditions.
(10) A priesthood, or similar specialist religious elite.
(11) Association with a moral community, a church...
(12) Association with an ethnic or similar group (1978: 370-371).

This list is neither exhaustive nor complete. 'New properties' could be
added to the list or the older properties modified as the critics want
them, says Southwold in a footnote:

Among the advantages of using a polythetic concept is the fact that it is
not crucial to state the relevant attributes completely and precisely from
the outset. If a critic points out that *other attributes should be added to the list,*

or that attributes should be specified more precisely...we *can incorporate* his suggestions *without invalidating* what has already been done (*ibid*: 377-378; n. 11; my emphases).

The only thing of importance for my purposes is to draw attention to the fact that anything can be called a religion as long as it has some (at least one) of the properties enumerated in the list. Even if it has none of them, it could still be a religion since nothing prevents us from "adding new properties" to the list. He cannot precisely specify all the attributes associated with religion because it would require more analysis than undertaken hitherto. Analysis of *what?* One supposes – of religion. That is to say, one must analyse Buddhism (Hinduism, *etc.*) as religions before we can provide all the attributes of this polythetic class.[2]

Using these attributes, one can classify almost anything as 'religion' including scientific theories and practices. Abounding as the list does with terms like 'godlike beings', 'salvation', 'sacred' and 'profane', 'religious elite', 'church', 'supernatural sanctions', it is a mere child's game to transform all terms in natural languages into polythetic classes: the Bible can join pornography, a timepiece can be in the same class as living organisms, and so on. The most important motivation of Southwold is the following:

> We have shown that practical Buddhism does not manifest a central concern with godlike beings. Hence *either* the theistic definitions and conception of religion are wrong *or* Buddhism is not a religion. But the latter proposition is not a viable option. In virtually every other aspect Buddhism markedly resembles religions, and especially the religion prototypical for our conception, i.e. Christianity. If we declare that Buddhism is not a religion, we take on the daunting task of explaining how a non-religion can come so uncannily to resemble religions. Moreover, since the comparison of Buddhism with religions is so interesting and important, we should have to form a super-class, called say 'religion-plus', containing all religion plus Buddhism; and this may well seem a scientifically valuable category than that of religion simply Y In any case the basic conceptual problem and challenge remain, however we shuffle labels: what, confronted with the facts about Buddhism, are we to make of our conception, or prejudice, that central concern with godlike beings is fundamental to phenomena of this kind? (*ibid*: 367)

---

[2] Why consider Buddhism as religion at all? Because of language-use! (*ibid*: 370)

There is a genuine issue here: what is gained by classifying Buddhism as a non-religion? Would we not simply push the problem one-step further?

Let us now look at another proposal. The suggestion is to look at the issue 'behaviouristically'. If we were to look at the behaviour of a pious European mother with an ill child and an Indian mother with a similar problem, then a case could be made for the claim that both are religious: one goes to St. Anthony, and the other goes to Ganesha. (Not to these persons but to their images, of course.) This proposal, however, does not work. It begs all the questions it purports to solve. The first question that arises is, of course, why consider these two sets of behaviours religious at all? Why not call it a superstitious behaviour, a ritualistic behaviour or even a 'going to the statue and kneeling-in-front-of-it behaviour'? Alternately, why classify the behaviour of these two mothers as members of the same class? The only possible way of not being *ad hoc* is to say that these two mothers share the same set of beliefs regarding these two figures.

If this answer is given, it ceases being a 'behaviouristic' criterion because appeal is made to the mental states of these two women: they happen to believe in something about the statue, and the content of their beliefs is the same. That is why we classify these two behaviours as belonging to the same class. In this way, we arrive at the absolute minimum that we require: a religious action is one that expresses a religious belief. To go any further without appealing to their belief-states becomes impossible because it cannot be argued that only 'religious' behaviour expresses religious beliefs, much less that all human behaviours are expressions of some belief or the other. To argue that these two mothers share identical belief states is manifestly false too. Our problem remains: why are these two behaviours identical?

*An Alternate Description*

To this question, there is an answer: the similarity between the entities studied. Southwold, for instance, notices an "uncanny" similarity between Christianity and Buddhism. He is not either the first or the only one to do so. What the two mothers do appears extremely similar. Besides, as we know, drawing analogical relationships has proved a heuristically important device in the process of scientific discoveries. We do not know much about what analogies are, how they work, why they are useful, what distinguishes them from metaphors...Nevertheless, we do know that they do work some of the time. Drawing similarity relationships has something to do with analogies (*e.g.* Vosniadou and Ortony, Eds., 1989). It is this fact, I submit to you, which lends cognitive interest to drawing similarity relationships.

In light of this, we can make both Southwold and our hypothetical behaviourist appear credible. They are trying to generate interesting theories by using the heuristic of drawing similarity relationships.
Because it is a heuristic – a rule of thumb – and not an algorithm that
functions infallibly and mechanically, there is no guarantee that pointing out similarities is enough to provide us with an interesting theory.

It is true that drawing similarity relationships suffers from a double
drawback: not all analogies are heuristically fertile; nor are all similarity
relationships analogies either. Precisely this situation puts the classificatory discussions in a better and different light.

One of the ways of looking at the production of a theory is to see it
as a problem solving activity. In finding an answer, it would be of immense help to determine the direction in which one should look for an
answer. That is what a heuristic does: it narrows our search.

By looking for similarity relationships, and by proposing different kinds
of similarities, what classificatory discussions do in our case is to narrow the search even further. Uninteresting similarities are dismissed
and one is forced to look for other similarities. In other words, what appears interminable as a discussion can be redescribed as a progressive
narrowing down of the search-space. Such a focussed search is possible
because there is a background theory. In its absence, this heuristic is no
heuristic. One can show that some object is similar to any other object.

### 8.1.5. A Confusion of Issues

Consider now the following two citations, both of which speak of the
importance of definitions. I would like you to look at them in the light
of what I have said so far about classification.

### A Theoretical Point

John Hick is an extremely prolific writer and is said to have his own
'theory' of religion. Being more modest himself, Hick merely describes
it as 'an interpretation of religion', which is also the title of his recent
work. There Hick (1989: 5) says that a definition helps us in knowing
whether *"Marxism...(and) Christian Science...(are) religion(s)"*. Hardly
the bother of losing one's sleep, one would have thought. Alston (1967:
142), however, has deeper grounds for being concerned. However, his
argument exhibits a characteristic confusion present in the discussions.

> An adequate definition should throw *light on the sorts of disputes and per-
> plexities that typically produce a need to define religion,* such as disputes over

whether communism is a religion, and whether devotion to science can be called a man's religion (my italics).

There are two ways of interpreting the "disputes and perplexities". Either they involve difficulties with our classificatory systems or the perplexities have to do with our knowledge of the phenomenon. My point is that these two possibilities are not coextensive or identical.

Consider the discussion about classifying 'Science' or 'Hinduism' as religions. If we say, it depends on our definitions of religion then (at best) it is a debate about our classificatory systems. Such disputes are arid, because they nearly always suggest that there are no theories about the phenomenon.

The more reasonable response is to say the resolution of this perplexity depends on our knowledge. That is to say, what do we know about 'Science', 'Hinduism', and 'Religion'? If this question is settled, more often than not, our "disputes and perplexities" disappear as well. Resolution of this problem requires that we try to acquire knowledge, *i.e.* build a theory about these phenomena. If instead of doing this, were we to first classify any of the above three under the category of any of the other two (*e.g.* science as a religion; religion as a science; Hinduism as a religion or as a science), this decision is arbitrary.

Do we not need to study phenomena under one category or another so that we may have knowledge about them? This is correct (see Clarke and Byrne 1993), but not when conceived as an objection to the point I am making: we can study any such phenomenon under categories that are different from and other than those in dispute. In other words, to take our hypothetical dispute, 'Science', 'Hinduism', and 'religion' are all human practices; they can be studied under this category. When we have a theory about science, Hinduism, and religion, we could discuss our classificatory systems. Otherwise, a legitimate challenge would question the choices in classifying, *viz.* why call Hinduism a religion and not science, philosophy, or magic, *etc.*?

Because of this, let us interpret our authors as suggesting that their questions are about knowledge-claims. In that case, why do they speak of this problem while talking about the definitions?

Recollect, if you will, that discussions about definition involve a request for identifying the object spoken about (#8.1.4). I have called it the referential problem to distinguish it from the classificatory problem. To illumine the latter, I introduced a distinction for purely pedagogic reasons. Now we can drop the distinction (if we are so inclined) and still appreciate the three different problems: what is one talking about? – a referential problem; how to classify 'facts'? – a classificatory problem; what claims does a theory make with respect to some object? – a theoretical controversy. I have suggested that in the absence of a theory, disputes are interminable because they are about classificatory problems. Under these conditions, the referential and classificatory problems are mixed up so that one raises a referential problem but ends up giving a classificatory answer.

*An Illustration*

In this light, consider what Spiro does. In his article on the definition of religion (1966), he treats us to a digest of the different notions of definitions: with an apparent display of familiarity with the relevant literature, he speaks of 'real' and 'nominal' definitions; 'explicit' and 'implicit' definitions, and such like. Having done this, he ends up arguing:

> Does the study of religion become any less significant or fascinating – indeed, it would be even more fascinating – if in terms of a *consensual ostensive definition* it were discovered that one or seven or sixteen societies *did not possess religion*? (1966: 88; my italics.)

On the grounds of an 'ostensive' definition, one cannot say anything about whether other cultures have religion or not. An 'ostensive' definition will give a reference to the term ("this phenomenon is an instance of what I refer to"). Only a theory, where the term 'religion' is defined the way Spiro wants to, could tell us whether all cultures have religion or not. However, if the claim about the universality of religion is pre-theoretical, then we can understand what has gone wrong. The problem of definition is seen as a classificatory issue. That is why Spiro formulates this point in strikingly classificatory terms: "if according to this *definition,* these societies do not have religion, then..."

*An Alternate Description*

Does Spiro really have no theory? Could his conviction that religion is a cultural universal have its roots elsewhere? I have suggested that religion is the background framework. In that case, the 'consensual' definition must express the vengeance that a theory will take for being oblivious to its presence. Reconsider Spiro's claim (1966: 91):

> Since 'religion' is a term with historically rooted meanings, a definition must satisfy not only the criterion of cross-cultural applicability but also the criterion of intra-cultural intuitivity; at the least it should not be counter-intuitive. For me, therefore, any definition of 'religion' which does not

include, as a key variable, the belief in superhuman...beings who have power to help or harm men is counter-intuitive.

Now it is a matter of established consensus that the Hindus worship trees, serpents, various animals (cow, monkey, and condor), images and idols. Are we to consider these people religious? It all depends, one may want to retort, whether or not Hindus consider the animals as "super-human beings that have the power to help or harm men". In non-trivial ways, animals can help or harm human beings, but Spiro does not probably have this in mind. The problem might well be about the belief-states of the Hindus: do they believe that animals are 'superhuman' beings? This is a question about the hierarchy of life on earth. Humans are at the summit of 'creation' and animals are well below them in the ladder of life constituting the 'infra' or 'sub-human' species. Consequently, and only because of it, can gods be 'super-human'. Cultures do exist which recognise the differences between species, but do not recognise any hierarchy of life on earth. Even if human life is a desirable form of life, or even as a privileged form of existence, this does not imply that either goal or direction is attributed to the emergence and 'evolution' of life. One such culture is India and, in fact, one of the problems of the Christian missionaries with the Brahmins had to do precisely with this *issue*, as Rogerius (1651: 110) records it:

> Hier toe an zijn sy niet te brenghen datse souden toe-staen dat een Mensch, de Beesten overtreffe, end dat den Mensch een edelder Creatuere zy, dan de Beesten, om dat hy met een voortreffelijcker Ziele zy begaeft. VVant soo ghy dat haer voor hout, sy sullen segghen, dat oock dierghelijcke Zielen de Beesten hebben. Indien ghy dit wilt betuygen door de werckingen van de redelijcke Ziele, die in den Mensch, ende niet in de Beesten, haer vertoont: soo heb je tot antwoort te verwachten...dat de reden, waerom de Beesten niet soo wel reden, ende verstant, voor den dagh en brengen, ende soo wel als de Menschen, en spreken, zijn, om datse gheen Lichaem en hebben ghekregen, dat bequaem is, om de qualiteyten van haer Ziele te voorschijn te brengen...
>
> [You cannot make them admit that Man outstrips the beasts and that he is a nobler creature than the animals because he has a superior soul. If you try to remonstrate with them on this, they would say, animals also have a similar kind of Soul. If you try to demonstrate this by the workings of the rational soul, which is evident in Man and not in the beasts: you may expect an answer...that the reason why the animals do not exhibit the kind of rationality and understanding that human beings can show, why they cannot speak as man does, is because they are not given a body capable of exhibiting the qualities of their soul...]

In other words, to the Christians, Man was/is at the summit of creation. To the Hindus, it was/is not so. Where does this take us with respect to Spiro's definition? His definition cannot be 'useful' to us unless we presuppose at least some amount of (suitably diluted) Christian theology: gods are superhuman, which is why they are worshipped; humans are at the top of the hierarchy of life with animals well below them, and so on.

This 'minimal' definition, which appears reasonable, merely expresses a linguistic and historical intuition of a religious culture: how could a religion not acknowledge the existence of 'superhuman' powers? This is a secularised theology, as far from 'science' as anything could possibly be.

### 8.1.6. On the Nature of a Meta-Problem

It is time for us to sit up, take notice of what has happened in the course of this subsection, and what has been happening over the last seven chapters. I made a suggestion, presented some evidence in its favour and, in this process, an unexpected problem has come to the fore. It is by specifying the nature of this problem that we switch tracks.

*The Suggestion and the Evidence*

In the fifth chapter, I proposed that we look at the claim about the universality of religion as a pre-theoretical idea. If true, in one sense it explained our inability to say what precisely the consequences of finding a culture without religion were. However, the proposal entailed several consequences, and I identified four of them at that stage. (A) The belief about the universality of religion would rest on grounds other than a theoretical or empirical investigation into the question. (B) It must be possible to account for the presence of the "stubborn superstition" that religion was a cultural universal. (C) The criteria for judging some entity as religion would show inter and intra-generational variations. Finally, (D) the field of religious studies would include a cemetery of definitions.

In the course of the last chapters, I provided evidence for the first two; in this subsection so far, I have shown that the third consequence is true. Regarding the last, let me just say that as early as 1912, Leuba (1912, appendix; see also his 1909) listed forty-eight such definitions adding two more of his own. Today, even a perfunctory glance at a few books will give you as many.

*Developing the Problem*

Reconsider the proposal that the universality of religion is a pre-theoretical claim. One of its evidential supports is that neither theoretical nor empirical investigations are conducted into the existence of religions in other cultures. In the process of exhibiting the historical truth of this claim, in chapters #3 and #4, I *extended* it well into the modern period. This *also* accounted for the persistence of the idea that religion was a cultural universal without having to appeal to *ad hoc* hypotheses. The variability in judgements exists, as well as a multiplicity of definitions.

What, however, has been the nature of this evidence? It has shown that the Christian theological framework has secularised itself. That is, the evidence has suggested that the universality of religion is a theological claim, *i.e.* it is a part of a Christian religious framework. In other words, the evidence for the proposal that some idea is pre-theoretical is that this idea is part of a theory!

Of course, I have argued that this theory has faded into the background. Nevertheless, the fact that some theory is a part of the context does not make it into any less of a theory. Indeed, the various concepts used to explicate the meaning of 'religion' are themselves parts of a theological framework. I have even suggested that the concept of 'religion' is itself a part of a religious framework. In other words, I am supporting the contention that 'religion' is a pre-theoretical concept by providing evidence that this concept is a part of a theory in such a manner that the explication of 'religion' forces us to using a theory – in our case, theology.

This has been the drift of the argument so far. In this chapter, I have tried to show that religion is a pre-theoretical concept by pointing out the five consequences that follow when you *dispute* about its definition. At the same time, I have provided an alternate description that could shed light on these authors and make them consistent. This means that we see these authors functioning within a theoretical, theological framework.

Such has been my commitment to the story of secularisation of Christianity, that I have allowed the possibility of a science of religion on condition that we find theology admissible as a suitable candidate. This commitment has arisen in the process of trying to lend substance to the thesis that the claim about the universality of religion is not a part of any one theory of religion, but that it undergirds all theory formation.

In other words, there is a *prima facie* inconsistency in my story. It arises not because a pre-theoretical claim cannot be part of a theory; nor even because a pre-theoretical intuition cannot become a 'theoretical term'. The inconsistency lies in the fact of insisting that 'religion' exclusively belongs to a religious language and theory (the arguments in chapters #6 and #7 amount to something like this), while insisting, at the same time, that the concepts and the claims are pre-theoretical in nature. The attitudes and the position of our contemporaries are sensible if seen as governed by no particular theory; but the evidence for the latter consists of the fact that they are governed by a theory – a theological one to boot.

Christianity was and continues to be a religion (see #8.2); de-Christianised Christianity – as a secularised religion – continues to remain a religion as well. I have located the movement towards the secularisation of Christianity in the Christological dilemma. In the process of secularising itself, Christianity does not disappear. It continues to remain *a* religion, distinguishing itself from other religions and distinguishing itself from other entities including the secularised variant of itself.

Without doubt, indefinitely many empirical and historical elements were required for this process. The latter are not the foci of my enquiry whereas religion is. Consequently, the question is, from whence the dynamics of this double movement of Christianity? Is it an intrinsic dynamic of Christianity to retain its own identity as a religion and, simultaneously, secularise itself as its 'other'? Is it able to do so because it is a religion? That is, does the identity of religion consist not merely in remaining a distinct entity, nor even in just secularising itself but precisely in this double movement?

If we look at the earlier chapters, then we can better appreciate what is involved in the issue. A religion (in our case, Christianity) transforms itself to become the 'other' (chapters #2, #6 and #7), while remaining itself. Christianity is both itself, a religion, and the 'other' – a de-Christianised religion. An earlier point about the distinction between the secular and the profane becomes even more evident: religion is both the "encounter with the sacred" and a "profane" variant of itself. It is *in* religion, looked at from this higher level, that both the 'sacred' (itself as a religion) and the 'profane' (its own secularisation as the other) distinctions are drawn.

*Formulating the Problem*

The story that I have told so far draws attention to the two *antipodal* moments *as parts of a movement*. I am trying to argue that Christianity has exhibited this dynamic. To study religion requires studying both religion and its externalisation of itself as the 'other' and to study this process as constituting the very motor of religion.

The problem is now clear. Can we describe this movement? Is it possible to argue that certain kinds of questions can only be formulated in a *theory*, only by using the resources of the theory, and yet insist that these questions precede the emergence of that theory? Can we show how some claims are both absolutely 'religious' and, at the same time, 'pre-religious'? Could we establish that this is what religion is?

This is the challenge that requires to be met head-on. The evidence for the claim that religion exists everywhere is *precisely* the absence of evidence to that effect. The only argument for showing the pre-theoretical nature of the belief (*viz.* that religion is a cultural universal) is to show that it is a part of one specific 'theory'. The only way of doing this is to show that this theory is the rock-bottom intuition, and precedes all theory-formation *including itself.*

I need to demonstrate that such an entity exists, that it is consistent, and on these grounds make earlier attempts intelligible. By providing such a consistent description all along the line, only by doing so and in no other way, can I hope to make my own story consistent and appear credible.

Such are the terms of the problem as I have developed them. Such is the problem as I have formulated it. *Hic Rhodus, hic salta!*

## 8.2. SWITCHING THE TRACKS

This is a meta-level problem about my narrative. I shall continue with the object-level queries and seek answers to them. When these answers emerge, we shall switch to a meta-level. At that stage, we can assess both the significance of the meta-question and the answers. Until then (chapter #11.3), we shall proceed as though oblivious to the challenge.

Nevertheless, this meta-problem has been productive too. To begin answering it, I need to say what religion is. To do this, it would require that I give a definition of 'religion'. Yet, I have criticised disputes about definition as at worst sterile and at best theological.

I would like to emphasise that I find *disputes* about definitions sterile. This does not imply that I find the task of providing definitions unimportant. Indeed, where possible, it is advisable that one fixes the reference of the term as clearly as one can so that we may talk about the world. If we neglect doing this or, at the other end, overemphasise its importance, we might end up discussing the way we talk about the world to the detriment of acquiring knowledge of the world. Further, there are constraints operating on us even when we are at liberty to define the terms the way we want to. These constraints are inter-subjective but not arbitrary. In this sense, a reasonable question that anyone could ask prior to a theoretical and empirical inquiry is about identification.

Because we are looking at the task of defining the concept of religion as a referential and not a classificatory issue, the best way of providing a reference to the word is to point the entities that this word picks out.

That is to say, we begin our investigation of religion in exactly the same way we began this essay as well: using 'religion' in an intuitive way, the way in which we use the term in our daily intercourse, as it picks out entities from Christianity through Shintoism.

### 8.2.1. "Religion is...

The most important consideration for us is that we are located in a linguistic, historical, and cultural milieu (see also #9.1.1). The traditions to which we belong have already raised and answered these questions to a certain extent. Therefore, unless we have very good reasons, it is both reasonable and expedient to follow the linguistic practices of our communities.

### Some Objections

I have argued so far that the linguistic, cultural, or pre-theoretical intuitions are themselves Christian-theological. Based on this fact, I have criticised other writers in their attempts to provide a characterisation of religion. I have argued that our secular world is a religious world in disguise. Yet, I am proposing that we follow our linguistic, cultural, or pre-theoretical intuitions. Is this a consistent position?

In chapter #1, I suggested that the practices of a community are no justification for calling 'Hinduism' a religion; in chapters #3 and #4, I tried to show that 'Hinduism' is an imaginary entity. Our common-sense ideas not only assume that 'Hinduism' is real but also that 'religion' picks out this entity as well. Now, I seem to be suggesting that we persist in this usage because our milieu does so. Again, is this consistent?

To these reasonable objections, let me add a third. It has been an implicit idea in this essay, which is both a personal conviction and a claim about my arguments, that a scientific study of religion (or anything else for that matter) should begin with as few of domain-related prejudices as possible. An enquiry without presuppositions is not possible; but I believe that one should *begin* by presupposing nothing specific about the domain. Is this position not a compromise with the idea that we take our common sense as the starting point? To each of these questions, my answer is in the negative.

*The Objections Answered*

Everyday, we see the movement of the sun around the earth in terms of sunrise and sunset; our theories tell us, however, that the solar system we inhabit is heliocentric. Every time we immerse a stick in water, we see it bent; we know that it is not. Each one of us can think of many such examples, but the point is that none of the theories tells us that our experiences are illusory. Instead, they explain why we see the way we do. That is to say, they save the phenomena. It is also equally undeniable that theories also correct our experience, but we need to note that it is *theories* that do so.

With respect to our experiences, I find such a stance cognitively healthy. It is also an intellectually important mechanism, which checks arbitrariness at many different levels. My motivation for beginning with our intuitive use has to do with this stance.

I am not arguing that our linguistic practice is a 'holy' cow. We may criticise these linguistic intuitions and suggest that they are wrong. To do so, we better have a sound theory. In its absence, I see no reason why one should *not* do what one has been doing all along. It would be irrational to discontinue a practice, when it has not been shown wrong.

In fact, the basic question that has engaged our attention so far has arisen from such an attitude: why have intellectuals in the western world believed that religion is a cultural universal? One could easily dismiss them as wrong or stupid, but it is like dismissing our experience of sunrise and sunset. Any decent theory of religion must answer this question in a non *ad hoc* manner, in exactly the same way our theories of refraction explain the bent stick in water.

In other words, unless one has a theory about why our daily language-use with respect to 'religion' is *wrong* (I have no such theory; neither has anyone as far as I know), we should take this practice as our point of departure.

Thus, we begin with the way we use the word. However, we have seen that the definitional question involves a referential and a classificatory issue. I have argued that the former is a genuine issue and a legitimate demand. The latter either will disappear with the development of a theory or will lead to sterile discussions. Consequently, with the word 'religion' – as used in daily interactions – we merely *refer* to entities from Judaism to 'Shintoism'.

It is important to emphasise that we are *not* classifying 'Shintoism' as a religion by appealing to our practices. We are merely saying that the word 'religion' picks out entities like 'Shintoism' as well.

One of the accepted procedures for 'defining' a concept is by an ostensive gesture, *i.e.* one defines a category by pointing to its instance. This is both epistemically and psychologically acceptable: parents and teachers teach categories to children by pointing out instances of the category in question. A child acquires the category 'cat', for example, not by being taught, "Cat is a furry, four-legged feline...*etc.*" (the intension of the term), and much less by being exposed to all the instances of the term (the extension of the term). An ostensive definition of a class gives us neither its necessary nor its sufficient conditions, but picks out an instance of the class instead. I shall provide an ostensive definition to begin with.

A mother may be able to teach the category 'cat' to her child by pointing her finger at a cat. I can hardly do the same. I will have to pick out an instance of 'religion' with some form of description. The description will not be defining the term 'religion' in terms of either its necessary or its sufficient conditions but will be a surrogate for the act of pointing, *i.e.* it will merely help us fix the reference of the term. In exactly the same way the act of pointing is not the same as the cat pointed at, the description that fixes the reference of the term 'religion' is not the same as defining the category 'religion' either. In this sense, we are not back to the problem of classification.

Consequently, the question 'what is religion so that we may know what it is?' gets a satisfactory interpretation: it is merely a request for a description to help fix the reference of the term without suggesting that fixing the reference is the same as providing knowledge of the phenomenon. The 'is' in 'what is religion' is a request for identification; the 'is' in 'so that we may know what it is' is a plea for acquiring a knowledge of the object.

*Carrying the Argument Further*

Which instances of the category shall we choose? This problem appears to conceal two questions. Which would be an instance of the category 'religion'? Which religion shall we study in order to build our theories? To revert to the example of a mother teaching the category 'cat' to her child, the first of the problems is: which animal shall we choose to fix the reference of the term 'cat'? The second: which cat shall we pick? A grey one, a black one, or one with white streaks? A tomcat or a house cat? With a long tail, or a short one? The cat that has lost an eye, or the one that limps?

Let me begin with the first question. What instances the category 'religion'? The American Association for the Advancement of Science? Voodoo practice? Pop music? The linguistic and other constraints operating on us help us answer this question. The above could either or not be instances of 'religion' only by virtue of the fact that we have already learnt at least a few other instances of the category. Even if one wants to play Humpty Dumpty discussing with Alice in the wonderland

("When *I* use a word, it means what I choose it to mean – neither more nor less." See Gardner, Ed., 1960: 268-270), on pain of total unintelligibility, one will have to include a few other members in this category: Judaism, Christianity, and Islam; Hinduism, Buddhism and Jainism. In other words, whether the American Association for the Advancement of Science and Pop music are 'religions' or not, it is not possible that Judaism and Jainism are not. Even though, in principle, we can choose any object as an instance of the category 'religion' it is advisable to pick out a more characteristic instance of the term than a less obvious one. In a stronger formulation, one could go even further by arguing that our (referential or classificatory) discussions about whether or not Voodoo practice is an instance of the category of religion is predicated upon the fact that we are able to identify other instances of religion like, for example, the range of practices from Judaism through Jainism.

It is important to note what we have done. We started out with our linguistic practice and saw that it imposed restrictions on our stipulative freedom. We did not have to take any *epistemic* decision about whether Voodoo is a religion or not. Irrespective of the status of such entities, we use the concept to pick out Judaism to Jainism.

Now, we shall use the same argument with respect to even this restricted group. Irrespective of whether Hinduism or Buddhism are 'religions'; Judaism, Christianity and, perhaps, even Islam are religions if 'religion' means and refers to something at all. That is, we have to say that religion is...

### 8.2.2. ...What Christianity, Islam, and Judaism Are"

#### Prototypical Examples

These three entities are *exemplary instances, i.e. prototypical examples* of the category 'religion'.

Prototypes, a concept I am borrowing from cognitive psychology and cognitive linguistics (*e.g.* Lindsay and Norman 1977; Mayer 1983; Lakoff 1987; Taylor 1989), are individual instances of a term which are also seen as its best examples. Rosch (1977, 1978), who has done pioneering work on the subject, tries to explain the human ability of categorisation on grounds of the availability of precisely such typical examples. Most of our natural language categories are not defined the way mathematical sets are. There are no clear criteria for set-memberships, and being a member of a set is not an all-or-none affair. (Just think of the category of 'bucket' or 'human face', for example.) These natural language categories allow graded membership, and are uncertain in border cases. How, then, do we learn such categories, and use them with the ease (if not with infallibility) that we do? One of the answers has appealed to the notion of prototypical examples: we choose a characteristic – a very typical – individual and judge the membership of other individuals in relation to such an example.

Not everyone, of course, accepts this answer. It knows of several versions, and of many defenders and critics (*e.g.* Markman 1989; Keil 1989; Armstrong, *et al.* 1983; Osherson and Smith 1981). Many of the problems confronted by the prototype theory have to do with issues such as how prototypes are represented in the memory; how they are built up; whether the theory effectively accounts for all of categorisation ability, and such like. None of these criticisms, as far as I can see, damages the proposal I am making: let us pick out an exemplary instance of the term 'religion' in order to provide a reference for the term. Nor, it appears to me, does it affect the point that Judaism, Christianity, and Islam are prototypical examples of religions.

Notice that by fixing the reference of the term this way, no avenue or answer is foreclosed prior to an empirical enquiry: it does not rule out the possibility that there are many, many other religions, besides the above three, which are only less prototypical than these exemplars. On the other hand, it does not necessitate that there exist other forms and other kinds of religions either. All this 'definition' does is to help us begin our investigation with few prejudices. To the task of defending this proposal, I now turn.

*On the Problem of Variety*

At the very outset itself, it is important to realise what is not entailed by choosing Judaism, Christianity, Islam, as prototypes of the category 'religion'. Just because these three religions are considered as exemplary instances, it does not mean that there are no significant differences between them. Despite the fact that each is a distinct 'entity', it does not prevent us from seeing them as exemplary instances.

The last sentence is likely to generate protests and is a harbinger of some difficulties. Both have to do with the fact that Judaism, Christianity, and Islam are not monolithic entities, but are themselves differentiated internally. The variety within each of these three religions occasions the difficulty of finding out what 'Judaism' or 'Christianity' or 'Islam' refers to. Is a cosmopolitan Sunni as much of a Muslim as a rabid Shi'ite? How could we consider a cardholder of the Likud party of Israel and a thoroughly secularised individual, whose only title to being a Jew is that his mother was one, as members of the Jewish religion? What is common to a Unitarian, a Catholic and a Baptist that makes them into Christians? Which group shall exemplify these religions, and for what reasons? Besides, which representative from any of these groups shall speak for us and, again, what would our reasons for the choice be? I suggested that religion is what Judaism is; what Christianity is; what Islam is. However, what is Judaism, or Christianity, or Islam? That is, those, which should function as exemplary instances of the term 'religion' and provide us with reference, appear themselves in need of further clarification. I seem to have merely pushed the problem one-step further without doing anything to solve it.

In order to find out how genuine this difficulty is, and whether we can overcome it, it would be best if we specify what precisely our problem with this variety is. Consider, to begin with, three individuals: let us say that one of them attends the Catholic mass every Sunday in a church; the other is a member of the Unitarian church and participates in some activities (including dancing) on Sundays, and yet another calls himself a Baptist. Let us further grant that our Catholic believes that transubstantiation occurs during the mass; and that our Unitarian listens to political speeches only – which is why he goes to his church every Sunday; and that our Baptist believes that Jesus went to America. If religion is what 'Christianity' is, our problem in this example is to specify what Christianity is so that we may know what makes the above three into Christians. More generally put, given that each of the three has different sets of beliefs, and performs several activities according to these beliefs, it is not an easy task to say what the commonalities among them are. Therefore, it is not self-evident what 'Christianity' is. This, as I see, is the difficulty that we could face: what makes them into Christians?

There are several answers to this problem as they are relevant for my purposes. To *begin with*, I am not studying the nature of Christianity but identifying it as an instance of religion. Consequently, *second*, the internal question of Christianity, viz. "who is a 'real' or 'true' Christian?" is not a problem that I need to solve. Identifying which of these three individuals should be called 'Christian' and for what reason must one do so is an internal question of this tradition. Because, this is the *third* answer, neither you nor these individuals have any doubt that they are Christians. They do not call themselves Jews, and you are not likely to mistake them for Lingayats either. In fact, each one of them represents a movement within Christianity and this is how we describe them, when we write sociological and psychological tracts about these groups. Even where these individuals – whether perversely or due to genuine reasons –are not certain they are Christians, they are not likely to suffer from a 'religious identity crisis' by meeting a 'Hindu' or a 'Buddhist'. At the outer boundary of their religious self-consciousness, the internal theological dilemmas play no role. This being the case, what is the problem and whose problem is it? Thus, we come to the *fourth* answer. Each one of them is an instance of the term 'Christianity', they are that for both themselves and us, and we are not confronted with a classificatory but a referential issue. 'Who is a Christian?' can be construed, as we have already seen, either as a request for identification or as a demand for classification. There is no problem of identification, whereas the problem of classification is internal to Christianity. There is no single theology that all Christians accept; hence, they fight about classification internally. However, this is neither your problem nor mine. What is true for a Unitarian, a Catholic, and a Baptist is generalisable and thus I claim that the identification of Christianity, Judaism, and Islam as instances of the term 'religion' does not create referential problems.

In other words, variety and multiplicity do not create problems to an ostensive definition. It neither precludes nor necessitates several instances and, as such, is ontologically neutral. Consequently, I do not have to identify the 'common core' of any of these three religions in order to defend the suggestion that Judaism, Christianity, and Islam are exemplary instances of the term 'religion'.

### 8.2.3. Linguistic Constraints Elaborated

Having shown that the use of terms like 'Judaism', 'Christianity', and 'Islam' does not create any referential problems, let me turn my attention to justifying the choice of these three religions as exemplary instances. Consider a line of defence, which consists of the following three reasons:

1. Because we are investigating that which is designated by the term 'religion', to pick out entities as prototypical instances of the term from other cultures and languages where the term 'religion' itself does not exist is to take an epistemic decision. That is, one already assumes beforehand that objects from other cultures instantiate the term as well. Such a decision is not justifiable at this stage because that is what we have to investigate.

2. Each of the three traditions has described itself as a religion. One could come to better grips with the term by ascertaining the empirical reasons why they call themselves thus.

3. Historically, the battle against religion has been fought against these three traditions. Atheists have construed their fight against religion as a battle against these three religions. By isolating what they fought against, we would be taking one further step in studying religion.

Even though these are reasonable suggestions, they conceal several kinds of problems. Let us begin by noticing them.

If, indeed, calling entities from other cultures as 'religions' where the term itself does not exist is to take an epistemic decision, how could we consider Islam as a prototypical instance at all? Or, for that matter, even Judaism?

Secondly, in exactly the same way some Jews and some Muslims and some Christians have described their traditions as 'religions', some Hindus, some Buddhists, and some Jains have done that as well. Consequently, why place such a great weight on some descriptions and not on others?

Thirdly, the historical fact that atheists fought Christianity (mostly), Judaism (to some extent), and Islam (hardly) does not signal much on its own. After all, this fact is susceptible to many interpretations and capable of several explanations. How, then, can this ambiguity testify unequivocally?

The first line of defence, despite its plausibility, appears to generate problems. How shall we tackle them?

My answer must be evident. Let us apply the same restriction to our language-use that we accepted before. Whether or not Judaism and Islam are religions, at least our term picks out Christianity as a religion. When we use the category 'religion', we minimally refer to Christianity.

Why 'minimally'? What if someone refuses to recognise that Christianity is a prototypical instance of the category 'religion'? My answer is that this is the only option open to us, unless we make epistemic assumptions about the object before having studied it.

Suppose that someone denies the prototypicality of Christianity as a religion. Then, he has to (a) either deny that the concept 'religion' has any reference to any entity in the world; (b) or claim that it has some other reference. If he argues the first position, he is running counter to our linguistic practice where the word does have a reference. Of course, one is at perfect liberty to do so; but, then, one must also have some kind of a theory about what 'religion' is and what it is not. As I have already said, I do not yet have a theory of religion, but I am taking the first step towards constructing one. This requires that I make no domain-specific assumptions, *i.e.* I make no assumptions about what religion is and what it is not. I am putting across the following claim: If 'religion' refers to something at all, and our natural language-use does suggest that it does, it must at least refer to Christianity. Otherwise, it picks out a fictitious 'entity' – and this is a theoretical claim I cannot make at this stage of the argument.

Regarding the second point, I can be briefer. Indeed, the concept could have other references, but it minimally picks out Christianity. To argue that it refers to some other entity without also referring to Christianity is to take an epistemic decision. After all, Christianity has described itself as a religion, and the word has its home in the European languages. To go against either of these two facts is to have a theory about both.

## A Recapitulation

We have seen in the course of this chapter that the definitional issue knows of two sub-problems: a referential and a classificatory problem. I have argued that the former requires answering, whereas the latter does not. When and if we have knowledge of the object, we can see whether the classificatory issue continues to persist.

I have also argued that even though the terms in a theory are stipulatively defined, constraints operate on us by virtue of the fact that we are located in a socio-cultural and linguistic context. Precisely these constraints have helped us provide a reference to the term 'religion' without committing ourselves to any presuppositions or prejudices.

While these are the themes of this subsection, in #8.1, we came across a formidable set of problems. There is an inconsistency in my story. The narrative is not yet threatened by it; but will be, if I do not provide a coherent solution. At stake is that the tale, as I have told it, turns out to be "…full of sound and fury, signifying nothing".

## 8.3. "Thou Shalt Resist Temptation …"

It is important to note what I have *not* done: I am not defining explicitly what the concept 'religion' means; I am simply identifying an example, a prototypical example, of the category 'religion'. I am *not* making any assumptions about what religion is, or what makes Christianity into one. My only argument is: if Christianity is not an exemplary instance of 'religion', then we have no other examples of religion. If one wants to challenge our language-use in this respect, one better has a good theory. Despite this warning, there is room for misunderstanding. In this subsection, I should like to clear it up. Let me begin with the possible misunderstandings.

### 8.3.1. Misunderstandings and Temptations

## What is not Said

My statement about the exemplary nature of Christianity must be situated in the context of providing an ostensive definition of the term 'religion'. As I already said before, such an ostensive gesture – in the form of a description – does not make any claims about the nature of the object except to point out that, in our language-use, the word 'religion' refers at least to Christianity. That is to say, it does not mean that

Christianity is the best religion or the perfect one, or the only one. In fact, it is easily conceivable that Christianity is not even a religion and that our language-use is wrong. Of course, it is sensible to say this only when we have a theory of religion and not before. In other words, one's view about Christianity – whether it is a 'true' religion or merely a false consciousness – does not affect the definition I am putting forward. My claim at this stage has to do with registering a fact about a language-use and not with the entities that Christianity and religion are.

Given the dangers I have spoken of in the earlier chapters, it is also advisable that we are extremely careful about making domain-specific presuppositions. Therefore, I make no assumptions about the nature of religion or Christianity in beginning a study of religion. You could really say that this is an enquiry into the nature of religion without presuppositions – not in the absolute sense of making no presuppositions at all, but in the sense that I make no domain-related presuppositions. In fact, I do not even assume the existence of religion. Rather, I merely point out the fact that unless we can show that our language-use refers to an entity that does not exist *in our world* – in which case we need not study religion at all – we may not reject our linguistic practice. Further, by questioning the acceptability of our linguistic practice as a starting point for a scientific investigation, I have arrived at the minimal condition: the term 'religion' refers to Christianity at least.

This linguistic practice itself is not neutral. After all, it is the practice of a community that speaks this way and not that or another way. I do not deny this at all. This fact about the linguistic practices of a community having a cultural history reflects a general point, *viz.* that as socio-cultural entities, we function in a context. To be sure, it also underlines the fact that scientific enquiries do have a context too. However, these are the general presuppositions of any human enquiry not merely of this one.

To accept that, in our context, the term 'religion' refers at least to Christianity is to begin an enquiry into the nature of religion without presuppositions (in the above sense). Nothing more has been said. In order to find out what requires doing, it would be prudent to specify what we may not do. The best way of circumscribing the latter is to outline the temptation one could succumb to at this stage.

*What May Not be Done*

Once we accept that the term 'religion' refers to Christianity, the *definitional task is completed* because the referential problem is solved. From this stage on, our task consists of studying the entity that religion is and *not* studying the concept 'religion'. If you want to study the nature of cats, and you have identified at least one organism that you call 'cat', then you will have to study that organism which you have identified as a cat and not the concept 'cat'. In an exactly analogous fashion, we will be studying an exemplar of religion but not the concept 'religion'.

It is at this stage that a temptation rears its ugly head. It consists of the belief that one can answer the question about the existence or non-existence of religion by simply looking at the properties of Christianity. That is, one might think that because some properties characteristic of Christianity are absent from traditions elsewhere (like, say, in 'Hinduism' or 'Buddhism'), the latter cannot possibly be religions. This position is justified only if one is able to show that the properties of Christianity, which one has identified, are also the properties of religion. In the absence of such an argument, all that one can do is to notice that Christianity and some other tradition differ from each other.

Consider the distinction between Christianity as a historical movement and Christianity as a religion. Today, the former owns buildings, land, telephones, television studios, aircrafts, *etc.* These are the properties – in both the senses of possessions and predicates – of Christianity. Is it any more or less of a religion because of that? The only way you can answer this question either way is by postulating (or having a theory about) the relation between Christianity and religion. One may want to argue that Christianity has progressively become less of a religion and more of a something else because it is now more interested in earthly possessions or the other way round. Notice, however, that this argument can work only if you *know* what religion is. By looking at Christianity alone you can make no such claims.

Consider, in this light, those very many atheists who have criticised *religion* by criticising the history of Christianity. How could they possibly become *atheists* – atheists, mind you, not anti-Catholics, anti-Protestants or Anti-Anglicans – by criticising the politics of the clerics or the doctrines of the Nicene council? They could not, unless they assume that properties of Christianity are also the properties of religion.

One can think of many such examples. One such, which is even more important for our purposes, is the obverse of this argument. Because some or another tradition appears to share some of the properties of Christianity, people have argued, the former is also a religion. Think of how Southwold, for instance, argues: because Buddhism shares many properties of Christianity, the former is also a religion even if it does not believe in God. This argument is flawed for exactly the same reason as well: the properties that Christianity has by virtue of being a religion may or may not be identical to the properties that it has by virtue of being a historical movement. If Southwold can argue anything at all on grounds of his polythetic attributes, he would have to say: because Buddhism shares many properties of Christianity, the former is also Christianity minus belief in God. However, he does not say this, does he?

In more mundane terms: we are studying, let us say, a brown cat that limps, has one eye, a tail, one ear, a few teeth, and eats rats. Question: Is limping, having one eye, a tail, one ear, being brown, having a few teeth, eating rats, the properties of cats or merely of this specific cat? Answer: that depends on what knowledge we have of cats. Precisely.

### 8.3.2. From a Simple Answer to a Complex Query

In order to formulate the *next* obvious question, I would like to look at one author – Frits Staal. He is one of the very few thinkers in the West (of late), who has thrown doubts upon the contention that religions exist in Asia as well. It is worth our while to pause and look at his points briefly, if for no other reason than as a salutary exercise.

In several of his writings (*e.g.* 1988, 1989), Staal takes exception to the existing concepts of religion and their 'applicability'(!) in Asia. He motivates this stance on two grounds in his most extended considerations on the subject so far (1989). The first ground involves using a rather narrow concept of religion based upon the three western monotheisms, and seeing the extent to which such a concept is useful in Asia. What would this narrow concept be?

> (E)ven if we do not seek to provide a precise definition, it is not entirely unclear what would be involved in a concept of religion based upon Judaism, Christianity, and Islam. It would involve such notions as a belief in God, a holy book, and (at least in two cases out of these three) a historic founder. Taking our cue from this last exception (the fact that Judaism has no founder), we can meaningfully ask whether it is feasible to apply to Asia a concept of religion that requires the presence of at least two of these three characteristics. (1989: 397-398.)

What would we find in Asia were we to apply this narrow concept of religion?

> What we find, even with these relatively flexible characteristics, is that none of the so-called religions of Asia is a religion in this sense. Buddhism, for example, has a founder, but neither belief in God, nor a holy book. ...Taoism does not have a belief in God...Tantrism does not appear as an independent movement. It is allied with Buddhism or Saivism, and shares characteristics with the Yoga which enters into similar alliances. Shintoism lacks all three characteristics. Confucianism possesses only one: it has a founder. And so our conclusion can only be that any notion of religion that is based on the characteristics of the three Western monotheistic religions is inapplicable in Asia (*ibid*: 398).

There is, to be sure, a great deal of truth to his empirical description of the Asian traditions. However, it is not clear that these properties make the three western monotheisms into religions either. Could Jesus be considered a founder of Christianity? An 'orthodox' Christian would be hard put to answer the question unambiguously: there cannot be a Christ figure without there being a past to Christianity. The fulfilment of God's promise is the event of the coming of Christ in flesh, but that does not make Jesus into the founder of Christianity in any unambiguous sense. If Christianity is the continuation of the 'real' tradition, then it is no breakaway group with Jesus as its founder. If Judaism is the 'real' tradition, then Christianity is the splinter movement. This point is equally true for Islam. Again, a Muslim would be hard put to answer the question unambiguously: if the prophet Muhammad was not there, in all probability, there would be no Islam. However, the Muslim would continue, Muhammad was merely the last prophet of God in a line of other earlier prophets. In this sense, just as is the case with Christianity, if one sees Islam as the continuation of the 'real' tradition, Muhammad did not found a new religion. On the other hand, if Mohammed was no prophet at all then one could say that he founded a new religion. Equally, Christ need not have asked Peter to build the Church – would Christianity have been any less of a religion for that? As far as holy books are concerned, there were Christians before the gospels were codified after all. In other words, it can be plausibly maintained (to some extent) that Christianity itself need not necessarily have these properties in order to be a religion. Of course, as a matter of historical fact, we do describe (from the outside) Christianity in terms of its holy book, the figure of Christ, the Churches, and such like. How much of this is historical contingency, and how much by virtue of the fact that Christianity is a religion?

The same point could be made with respect to belief in God. Even though I have tried to argue that 'atheistic religiosity' is Christianity gone secular, and I have difficulty in comprehending how God could become irrelevant to being religious, this argument does not establish that such religions could not exist elsewhere or that they could not come into being. In this sense, even this possibility requires to be left open until that stage where we could show that belief in God is essential not to just these three religious traditions, but to the very nature of religion itself.

The reply to Staal, then, could be that this 'narrow' concept is inapplicable in Asia because its 'applicability' to the Western monotheisms is itself suspect.

His second argument involves using an 'extended' concept of religion, which includes or incorporates the categories of 'doctrine' (belief), ritual, mystical experience, and meditation. He argues (I will not summarise the points here) that because the last three consist of other categories more fundamental than the concept 'religion', an 'extended' concept of religion that comprises of these three is an incoherent concept. As such, the category 'religion' exhibits

> all the characteristics of pathological, if not monstrous growth, tumorous with category blunders. It is worse than a spider with a submarine, a burning bush, an expectation, and a human head. We have found that the trio of ritual, meditation and mystical experience consists of categories that are more fundamental than the category religion itself (*ibid*: 401).

Consequently, he suggests that we take a terminological decision and confine the term 'religion' to Western monotheisms.

Let us go along with Staal for a moment and take this terminological decision. What exactly does this imply? It could imply several things, depending on how we state the thesis. What I shall do now is to provide *three* versions of Staal's thesis — a weak version, a strong version, and a stronger version. Even though more variants are possible, these three are enough to appreciate the problem.

(a) Our conceptualisation of religion has been inadequate. We need to develop a more adequate, more sophisticated, and a more fine-grained concept of religion in order to satisfactorily account for different religions.

This is the *weak version* of Staal's thesis that would almost win universal consensus. No intellectual worthy of his name would resist a plea for developing subtler and richer concepts. Further, there is also a quasi-universal consensus that the 'Western' concept of religion is inadequate. Staal subscribes to this thesis as he explicitly states:

> A philosophy of religion worthy of its name should begin with a discussion of the concept of religion and an investigation into the status of a possible science of religion based upon *what is presently known about religions or so-called religions of mankind* (*ibid*: 418; italics mine).

However, as we have seen in chapters #6 and #7, this is precisely what people have been doing for over a hundred years. This weak thesis does not entail that we confine the concept of religion to western monotheisms. If we cannot use the concept 'religion', which other concept shall we use? Indeed, many would be willing to concur with Staal that

> the imposition of the Western concept of religion on the rest of the world illustrates how Western imperialism continues to thrive in the realm of thought (*ibid*: 419).

They would also add that one has to start somewhere, with the existing concept of religion for example, and appropriately extend it, modify it, enlarge it, refine it, by studying other cultures. Studying what in other cultures though? Why, religions of course. Staal would also agree with this point of view because, as he says, we should base ourselves upon what is presently known both about religions and the "so-called religions" of humankind.

Let us now look at the strong thesis.

(b) We cannot use our concept of religion to translate certain concepts in Asia, because both this concept and the concept cluster associated with it are absent in its culture.

This is the *strong* version of his thesis, which may or may not imply the weaker thesis. (That is to say, it is logically independent of the truth of the weak version.) It does entail that the 'western' concepts of religion are not applicable in Asia. Staal subscribes to this thesis as well:

> (T)erms for religion that *refer to its doctrinal content* are relatively rare in the languages of Asia and are invariably of recent date…In India, the term dharma has been used in the sense of "religion" in expressions like *Hindu dharma, bauddha dharma, jaina dharma* only during the last few centuries. The same holds for the Chinese *tsang-chiao* and the Japanese *shukyo*. The concept of "Hinduism", incidentally, came up in the thirties of the nineteenth century in English literature (*ibid*: 390; italics mine).

One of the reasons why this *strong thesis* might not entail the weaker version has to do with the italicised portion of the citation. If one uses the concept of religion to refer to 'doctrinal contents', then the point could hold. However, this concept is not the only one floating around. There are other 'western' concepts too such as those that refer to an 'experience of the Holy', the 'absolute', or of a *'mysterium tremendum et fascinans'*. Or, if the 'western' concept constitutes a 'polythetic' class, in which the 'doctrinal content' is but one property, the entailment that the 'western' concept of religion is inadequate does not hold. The clarion call to refine this concept further, being the platitude that it is, is not affected.

These remarks are sufficient to turn our attention to the stronger version of the thesis.

(c) The concept of religion is 'inapplicable' because that which is designated by the term 'religion' in the West is absent from the cultures of Asia.

This is the *stronger* thesis, the one I am arguing. It entails the strong thesis (b) by being its *explanans*. The *weaker* version is logically independent of this stronger thesis as well, for obvious reasons. To say that religions are absent in Asia is to say that they are unreal in that culture;

they are not products of Asia but creations of the West. Staal appears to subscribe to this thesis as well:

> The inapplicability of Western notions of religion to the traditions of Asia... is also responsible for something more extraordinary: the *creation* (Staal's emphasis) of so-called religions. This act was primarily engaged in by outsiders and foreigners, but is sometimes subsequently accepted by members of a tradition. The *reasons lie in the nature of Western religion* ...In most parts of Asia, *such religions do not exist*, but scholars, laymen and Western converts persist in searching for them. If they cannot find them, they seize upon labels used for indigenous categories, rent them from their original context and use them for *subsequent identification* of what is now called a "religious" tradition. *Thus there arises a host of religions*: Vedic, Brahmanical, Hindu, Buddhist, Bon-po, Tantric, Taoist, Confucian, Shinto, *etc.* In Asia such groupings are not only uninteresting and uninformative, *but tinged with the unreal* (*ibid*: 393; italics, unless otherwise indicated, mine).

Staal goes even further to emphatically state:

> Hinduism does not merely *fail to be a religion*; it is not even a meaningful unit of discourse (*ibid*: 397; my italics).

This is what I have argued on historical grounds (chapters #3 and #4), with the implication that religion is not a cultural universal but a conceptual compulsion of a religious culture. If Hinduism is not a meaningful unit of discourse, that is because (Staal notices this) it does not refer to a single unified phenomenon or even to a set of discrete phenomena. Simply put, it has no reference to anything in the world but a learnt way of answering the question, 'are you a Hindu?' (See chapter #1.) As we have seen, Staal also implies this.

If Staal subscribes to this version, how then could he argue or accept the following?

> The study of religion ought to play an important part in the human sciences, for while language provides the foundation for most intellectual activity of the human animal, religion hovers around the loftier realms of human expression and belongs to a domain that lies beyond language (*ibid*: 387).

He could not; yet he does. My thesis entails the negation of the above sentiment. It may be informative and illuminating, given what I have said during the last few chapters, to note that Staal does not argue for the truth of the above but presupposes it: it is the opening paragraph of his discourse into religion.

Let me provide a brief overview of the nature of the difference between Staal and me. I am investigating the object designated by the term 'religion'; Staal is talking about some or other concept of 'religion'. I am arguing that religion – as an entity – has not been shown to exist in all cultures; Staal assumes its universality and suggests that the 'Western' concept is incoherent. If I succeed in my aim, I will have argued that religion does not exist in Asia and, therefore, it is not a cultural universal; Staal pleads for a philosophy of religion whose task would involve, among other things, a 'conceptual analysis' of the concept 'religion' (or, in more pedantic terms, providing a 'good definition').

There is also a second theme to this difference. Staal is content to note Western imperialism and its continued operation. I think that it is a problem we need to understand. What compels thinkers of today and yesteryears in the West to see and create religions in other cultures? To call it 'imperialist' is to baptise it with a name and names, as we all know, do not explain anything or solve any problem.

## Christianity as a Religion

Anyway, it is time to draw our methodological lesson. A comparison of Judaism, Christianity, and Islam with each other in order to isolate their common properties will not give us much mileage in the absence of arguments to show they have these properties by virtue of being religions. At best, it will merely show that 'our' concept based on a comparison of these three traditions may (or may not) be applicable elsewhere, and that conclusion is what we need to avoid. We need to avoid this conclusion for the simple reason that it does not take us far in trying to understand religion. It is easy to observe that Asian traditions differ from the Western religions; it requires more courage and a deeper insight to argue that the 'Western' concept of religion may require to be jettisoned (*e.g.* see Smith 1962).

For my purposes though, neither of this will do. Let us say that in some phenomenon this or that property, or even a group of them, is absent; let us assume that these very same properties are present in Christianity. This situation does not tell us a great deal: it could be that the former is merely less prototypical than Christianity; or that the former is a 'truer' religion than Christianity; it could be that both have all the properties of religion; *etc.*

What, then, is our question when we take Christianity as a prototypical example of religion? Clearly, my concern is not to study the nature of Christianity, but to begin a study of religion. That is to say, to study Christianity as a religion so that we may make some headway in understanding the nature of religion. *How shall we go about studying religion, and not Christianity, by looking at one exemplary instance?*

In the earlier chapters, I argued that our common-sense ideas about religion are Christian-theological. Yet, in this sub-section, I argue that 'religion' must at least refer to Christianity – unless we have a theory capable of explaining why such is not the case. That is to say, I seem to be accepting Christianity's reference to itself as a religion. Indeed, I am. Nevertheless, this is not to accept the theological framework *yet*. At this stage, there is also an implicit question present: What *makes* Christianity into a religion? A search for answers to this and allied questions will determine the extent to which the background theology needs to be accepted.

In the coming chapters, which too form a unit, we shall seek answers to all our questions. Seek we must, whatever the results, because as we shall soon know...

# CHAPTER NINE

# "BLESSED ARE THOSE WHO SEEK..."

Today, it has become trite to observe that Christianity was an intolerant religion. Not many believers, whatever their denominational affiliations, would endorse the manner in which Christianity has persecuted both heretics and heathens; even more people believe that a prerequisite for a peaceful society is a toleration of other opinions, including different religious opinions.

Closely connected to its intolerance is the missionary activity of Christianity. Being a religion of and for the humankind, the portal doors of the Church are open to anyone who comes knocking. Again, not all people concerned about the missionary activity find this an event to be excited about; or, better said, not all get excited in the same way and for the same reason.

Intolerance and proselytisation were/are, of course, not the unique prerogative of Christianity alone. Islam shares these properties too, as did Judaism in the early centuries during the Common Era and in an extremely subdued form today. Whatever one's moral standpoint on intolerance and conversion might be, I would like to suggest that we could only be grateful to these two attitudes because they carry an *epistemological solution* to our problem. Like all interesting solutions, the present one suggests the next step of our investigation.

That step involves leaving both the *word* 'religion' and the associated *concept(s)* behind us, and embarking on building a theory about the object that religion is. As we all know, theory-construction is hypothesis generation under constraints. The constraints we face are twofold: historical and phenomenological. The chapters #2 to #4 specify the outlines of the questions, which a theory of religion should illumine. The first section of this chapter (#9.1) elaborates on this.

In the subsequent section (#9.2), I formulate my preliminary hypothesis about religion working under the constraints spoken of earlier. However, as is well known, given a set of 'facts' to account for, we could always come up with an *ad hoc* hypothesis that 'explains' just that set and nothing else besides. To prevent my hypothesis from suffering the same fate, I identify some additional adequacy conditions. They have to do with the experience of religion as believers have formulated it themselves. The rest of the chapter mostly devotes its attention to the phenomenological adequacy of the hypothesis. My description must satisfy the *intuitions* and claims of the practitioners of religion.

The sections #9.3 and #9.4 address the issue of investigating whether doctrines play a role in being a believer. Even though merely the first stage in exploring the issue, the preliminary description of religion generated in the previous section must show not only that 'doctrine' and 'faith' are interrelated but also what their relationship is. If we can do this without appealing to additional and *ad hoc* hypothesis, we can safely assert that the description has passed through its initial test. In the process, we come to appreciate the insights of the earlier generations. In one case, it refers to the insight of the enlightenment thinkers and to the promissory note given at the end of chapter #5. In the other case, in section #9.4, it refers to the early church fathers and other religious figures, who have continuously emphasised the importance of faith, at times, to the detriment of doctrines as the opponents have accused them. In showing how both the first and the second group are right, we meet Schleiermacher and Otto – an occasion to return to the problem of atheistic religiosity.

Once this is accomplished, I shall develop the hypothesis further in two directions is section #9.5. First, I shall shed light on the troubled encounter of the heathens with religion; second, I look at the relationship between my characterisation of religion and the paradigmatic case of religious practice, viz. worship.

In this way, the ninth chapter reproduces in itself the journey of the last eight. You could consider this chapter as having nine parts, eight of which you have read so far. The present chapter is itself a prologue to the tenth, which will carry the tale further.


## 9.1. The Epistemology of Intolerance

Christianity was intolerant of both heretics and heathens. That is, it persecuted beliefs and practices that ran counter to those of its own. Such an activity has been dependent on the spiritual and temporal power of the churches, which have varied in time and place. However, that the Church wanted to persecute at all signals the fact that Christianity saw these others as its rivals. Of *what* kind? As *rival religions* of course. That is to say, Christianity fought against those traditions, which it construed as rival and competing religions.

The Christian Church, and the mass of believers, met with several different kinds of competitors over the course of the centuries. The Catholic Church, for instance, was regularly embroiled in competing with the monarchy for political power. The same Church has also fought against authoritarianism and in favour of military dictatorships.

Nevertheless, it has not construed either democracy or monarchy as competing religions.

To avoid possible misunderstandings, it is important to note that the justification provided by the church is not at issue here. For instance, the competition between a monarch and the church – in the history of the Roman Catholic Church, for instance – was about who the Vicar of Christ was. Both parties specified the relation between the temporal power and the spiritual power as they saw them both. Yet, the church did not fight monarchy as a rival religion even if, as was the case in Britain, a monarch could only settle the issue in his favour by becoming the head of an alternate church.

In other words, the church has met with several rivals during its history but it has *not* construed all of them as rival religions. The same applies to the mass of believers: they fought the Roman *religio*, the Jews and the Muslims, the schismatic movement within Christianity as rival religions. They also fought for or against democracy, Fascism, *etc.*, as rivals but not as rival religions.

Christianity thought of itself as the true religion. All other religions were either misguided or false, or even downright diabolical. By calling them so, Christianity recognised these other traditions as *competing and rival religions.* In this sense, whatever this or that theologian thought or said 'religion' was, a surer way for us to begin studying the nature of religion is to identify those traditions and movements, which our exemplar saw as its competitors. For some reason or the other, Christianity (over the ages) saw the heretics and the traditions of the heathens as rival religions. They were combated as religions and this circumstance makes both intolerance and conversion so important for our purposes.

It requires emphasising that I am not discussing the reasons why, let us say, the Roman Catholic Church was justified in construing some of these rivals as rival religions. Protest movements and rebellions motivated by socio-economic dissatisfactions, as we might want to call some of them today, were often branded as heretical offshoots and accorded the status (or the punishment) of rival religions. Were they really 'religious' movements or was this label merely a pretext used by the church(es) to fight them? This is an interesting and important question, to be sure, but one that is irrelevant to my argument. To say that they were not 'religious' movements requires saying what a 'religion' is, and that is what we are investigating. Once we know what religion is, we can then either justify or explain why certain 'non-religious' movements were construed as rival religions and persecuted accordingly. My concern is *prior* to this issue and merely records the following fact: Christianity has met with several rivals over the course of its history and it has not construed *all* of them as rival religions, but only *some.*

This is a significant fact to us because it tells us that, throughout its history, Christianity has drawn a distinction between those who were its rivals *as religions* and other rivals. Whatever the motivations for drawing this distinction, Christianity has drawn it nevertheless. Because Christianity saw itself as a religion, the manner in which it drew the battle line *between religions* will tell us something about what Christianity thought religion was. Of course, what Christianity thought religion was, might or might not be what religion 'really' is; at this stage of our argument, the only way we can get to know the latter is through the former.

Here is where history imposes the first set of constraints. I shall develop my argument in distinct steps so that we may also appreciate the extent to which these historical constraints are also productive.

### 9.1.1. Historical Constraints Elaborated

While discussing the question of defining religion (#8.2.1), I suggested that we are constrained in our language-use because we are located in linguistic, cultural, and historical contexts. In a later subsection (#8.2.3), we also saw that the linguistic constraints provided us with a conceptual problem, to solve which the historical journey made in the earlier chapters came to our rescue. The very same history is now going to impose more restrictions on both the question and the answers. In other words, each step we take narrows our freedom to define the words the way we want to. Hence, I am not defining the concept 'religion'. Instead, I am building a theory about the object that religion is. As I have said before, definitions do not solve problems; theories that embed them do.

I have argued that if the word 'religion' refers to something at all, it refers at least to Christianity because the latter refers to itself as a religion (*i.e.* it uses the word with respect to itself). If Christianity refers to itself as a religion and recognises itself as one, then the terms in which it does so gives us 'its' *concept* of religion. This concept not only enabled Christianity to describe itself as a religion, but also helped it to recognise some of its rivals as religious rivals. Therefore, to study Christianity *as a religion* is to study those properties by virtue of which not only did Christianity think of itself as a religion but also confronted rival or competing religions. This is the *first step* of the argument. This step merely allows us to establish the terms of description.

Christianity is a historical movement. So are Judaism and Islam. The former has construed the latter as rival religions. Whatever goals they were/are competing for, they did/do so as religions. Christianity did not merely baptise Judaism and Islam as rival religions. The latter also saw Christianity as a rival religion under the same description.

The *second step* establishes that the terms under which Christianity recognised itself as a religion are also the terms under which Islam and Judaism recognise themselves as religions as well (using whatever word they use). That is to say, the concept used by Christianity to *call itself* a 'religion' is also the one which makes some who do not call themselves as 'religions' into religions (because it is also their self-description). Therefore, the 'Christian' concept is not just Christian. It cuts across the three Semitic religions. This is not *my* concept or *your* concept, but self-descriptions of these religions. Consequently, what we have on our hands is the only reasonable concept of religion that does not presuppose what religion is. At the same time, it suggests that the concept of religion is itself part of a religious framework and vocabulary. This lends a greater probability to the claim that whether or not Judaism and Islam use the word 'religion', they too are religions. That is, if Christianity is a religion, so are Judaism and Islam.

The third and the fourth steps establish this case as conclusively as we possibly can. The *third step* picks out two salient facts. One: the terms under which Christianity transformed Islam and Judaism into rival religions also make Judaism and Christianity rivals to Islam, and Islam and Christianity rivals to Judaism. Of course, it is possible that Judaism and Islam merely *reacted* to the attacks of Christianity and accepted Christianity's self-description. The second salient fact rules out this possibility. Each of these three religions singled out exactly the same rivals under the same description elsewhere *unerringly.* Judaism had singled out the Roman *religio* as its rival before Christianity was even born; Islam had picked out precisely those Indian traditions as its rivals, which Christianity was also to identify, centuries before the European Christians launched their major and massive evangelising activities.

The *fourth step* completes the argument by looking at their *response* to Christianity, Judaism, and Islam. These rivals, the Roman *religio* and the Indian traditions, did not recognise themselves in the description provided by Christianity, Judaism and Islam. Nor did they perceive religious rivalry between themselves and the latter. Incomprehension of the Semitic terms of description and indifference to the alleged rivalry characterise the reactions of *religio* and the Indian traditions. "There are different roads to heaven", said one shrugging its shoulders; "How could only your religion be true and ours false?" asked the other uncomprehendingly. Even under persecution, this tone did not change. The 'reasons' for the persecution of the Christians in the early Roman Empire had little to do with the arguments, which Christianity would use to persecute the pagans centuries later.

The third and the fourth step, together, establish the following case: the terms under which Christianity recognised itself and identified rival religions were also those that provided self-identity and rivals to Judaism and Islam. Precisely this description was incomprehensible to those in whose language the word 'religion' existed (the Romans) and to those who had no such word (the Indians). Neither recognised itself in this description; neither fought the others as rivals under this description.

These four steps constitute the historical constraints under which we must generate our hypothesis about religion. On the one hand, our hypothesis religion must capture the self-description of the Semitic religions; further, it must also exhibit why 'Hinduism', 'Shintoism', *etc.*, appear as religions to them. On the other hand, the very same hypothesis must also show *why* neither the Hindus nor the Romans were able to recognise themselves as 'religions'. Now, we can take the *fifth step* by identifying two problems, which we need to solve.

The *first problem* is the following: What is Christianity's concept of religion, and how is it possible to show that its concept is also that of Judaism and Islam? Let us appreciate the problem in its complexity, because doing so will enable us to realise why we have to move beyond the 'concept of religion'.

The obvious way of solving this problem is Herculean because, in all probability, the problem is not solvable. The task entails an inductive exercise of trying to find out what Christians have said about 'religion' over the course of the last two thousand years. Even a preliminary survey (like Smith has done in his 1962), which involves tracking the use of the *word* 'religion' – after all, that is the only way we can begin – in extant writings will lead us to the conclusion that the word was used in a variety of ways. Like Smith, we will discover that the word disappeared for centuries, emerged again much later in yet other ways...*etc.* In fact, one does not even have to do a survey to predict this finding. As though this is not enough, we have to do the same with respect to Judaism and Islam. Neither uses the word 'religion' – unless in modern writings on the subject.

There is another solution. If one can generate a description of religion and show that Christianity, Judaism and Islam recognise themselves in such a portrayal, then one has answered the question. That is to say, by developing a hypothesis about religion; by arguing that the presence of 'something' makes Christianity, Judaism and Islam into religions; by showing that this hypothesis captures their self-descriptions one can argue backwards to their concept of 'religion'.

This gives birth to the *second problem:* I need to argue for two conclusions. I need to make sensible (a) not only why these religions see religions everywhere but also (b) why neither *religio* nor the Indian traditions recognise themselves in the Semitic description. Needless to reiterate, one must do both without appealing to *ad hoc* hypotheses.

I have argued that, at this stage, we have to accept the self-descriptions of the Semitic religions. Is self-description a necessary property of all religions? Does the nature of religion entail that such an entity also describes itself as a religion? If I can provide a positive answer to this question, the claim that a science of *religion* can only be a theology becomes comprehensible.

The more problems we solve more are the problems that we need to solve. It is fit and proper; after all, is this not what science is, in at least one of its descriptions? (*e.g.* Laudan 1977)

### 9.1.2. Religion and Doctrine

Along what lines did Christianity draw the distinction between religious rivals and rivals of another kind? Here is where our early excursions into the Roman and European history begin to pay off. In chapter #2, we saw how the pagan 'other' became a domesticated and erring variant of the Christian religion. Christianity isolated a set of beliefs for critique and attacked the pagan religion by criticising this set of beliefs.

We saw the same feat repeating itself (chapters #3 and #4) in greater detail, in another continent more than a thousand years later. The 'Hindus' practised their own heathen 'religion', which was based on their sets of beliefs. We also saw that localising the source of these beliefs and locating the texts expressing these beliefs was no easy job. However, once accomplished, 'Hinduism' took on a recognizable Gestalt. The same allowed the emergence of 'Buddhism' in an accelerated fashion. Defining 'Hinduism' and 'Buddhism' around a core of beliefs allowed one to distinguish between these 'different' communities according to their beliefs. How could one possibly argue that the difference between religious communities resides in the different beliefs they hold? Only because human practices are embodiments of beliefs – a theme that Protestants made so much use of.

There is no necessity to cover this ground in any further detail. Therefore, let me state in a very succinct fashion the features by means of which the 'others' were seen as rival and competing religions by Christianity.

(a) There was, to begin with, rivalry with respect to *doctrinal aspects*. There were differences in beliefs, which included the nature and existence of God.

(b) The difference between individuals and communities had to do with these beliefs.

(c) The different *practices* of individuals – to the extent these were relevant to religious practices – were expressions of competing religious beliefs because the actions of the faithful are embodiments of such beliefs.

(d) Consequently, conversion from one religion to another meant a rejection of one set of beliefs and practices and embracing another on grounds of *truth* and *falsity*. That is, the believers not only believed in the truth of their beliefs, but it was also vital and necessary that they so believed.

Christianity construed the others as rival religions along these lines. What makes both Judaism and Islam into religions as well – *i.e.* exemplary instances of the term – is that they also transformed other traditions as rivals along the same lines. That is, these three religions did the same thing to each other and to traditions elsewhere.

The attitude of the others – both the Romans and, much later, the Indians – with respect to Judaism and Christianity in one case, and Islam and Christianity in the other, was fundamentally different. Galen compares the figure of Moses not with this or that priest but with Plato the philosopher. Lucian, the satirist from the second century, describes Christianity as a philosophical school competing with the Stoics, Cynics, Sceptics, and such others. However, the rivals of Christianity, as the Christians saw them, were not these philosophical schools but those several cults, which flourished in Rome and elsewhere. Judaism had arrived at an accommodation precisely with respect to the 'religious' ceremonies of the Romans; whatever wrangles Philo might have with Heraclites, the Jews felt that the cultic ceremonials were in conflict with their religious observances.

The Indian traditions accorded a reception to both Islam and Christianity that bordered on indifference. They were *indifferent* to the doctrines and practices of both these religions, answering, when pressed, that "there are different roads to heaven" (chapter #4). This indifference or, if you prefer, toleration shows that the Indian traditions did not see either Christianity or Islam as their rivals.

Thus, we arrive at a first stage in the characterisation of religion. It appears to involve an emphasis on beliefs, and looking at actions as their embodiments. Before we ask questions about the nature of the beliefs involved, it might be best to see exactly what is being said, and what is not.

We need to appreciate that what we have on our hands is merely an aspect or property of the three Semitic religions under consideration. We have isolated this element purely on historical grounds. We are not yet in a position to say whether this aspect is *specific* to these three religions or a property of religion as such. Nevertheless, in terms of defining the problem-situation, we can observe that an aspect of religion (if the Semitic religions are exemplary instances of the term) has to do with a set of doctrines. That is why one can map the differences between religions to the differences in doctrines.

Despite the overwhelming historical and contemporaneous evidence in support of this contention, one might still be besotted with doubts: how true is this claim with respect to Judaism? What would be the doctrinal core of, say, Christianity? Let me begin with the first question.

It is widely held that the practical observances are of greater importance to being a Jew than the beliefs that one holds. While there is a great deal of truth in this statement, it is also an exaggeration: when compared to Christianity and Islam, perhaps it is true that the beliefs are relatively secondary in Judaism. However, the presence of a doctrinal core is crucial to this religion. Such a core, for example, consists of beliefs that the Mosaic Law was handed down by God; that the anointed one will come to liberate the Jewish people; that the God of Abraham, Isaac, Jacob is the true God, and so on. The truth of the importance of doctrines should be also evident from the fact that no Jew could accept the view that Jesus was the Messiah. By contrast, there would be little problem in accepting Jesus as an *avatar* much like the other *avatars* in India.

Regarding the second question, my point is that I need not answer it at all. Because the differences within Christianity have to do with the doctrinal differences, each Christian group would have its own doctrinal core. However, these differences occur within a clear framework that includes beliefs about God, about Christ, and so on.

The last two paragraphs are incidental to my argument. In all probability, some theorist or another is likely to contest what *I* have identified as the doctrinal 'core' in Judaism and Christianity. My central point is simpler: in some way or another, a doctrinal core appears to be an important component of religion. Once we have a hypothesis about religion on our hands, we can see why doctrines are important/unimportant to religion (see #9.5.2). For the moment, we are only outlining the problem of studying religion by looking at prototypical instances of the term 'religion'. If doctrines are important to being a religion, what kind of doctrines is involved?

We can grant that religion has met several other groups and movements unified and differentiated from each other on the bases of some or another set of doctrines (*e.g.* fascism, Human rights movements). For some reason, the doctrinal differences are seen to constitute religious distinctions if in some way they have to do with God and His relationship to humanity.

In the struggle of the Semitic religions against the pagan or heathen 'religions', one of the doctrines in dispute involves the nature of the pagan gods. In their struggle against each other, Semitic religions disagree about the revelation of God. That is, we can empirically observe that these three prototypical religions dispute about God and that this issue distinguishes religions from each other.

In other words, our first step in characterising religion has provided us with the next problem: why have religions found only some kinds of doctrines relevant to distinguishing themselves from each other? Answering this issue does not involve finding out what this or that representative has said about it. Instead, our quest requires that we answer the following question: what makes some doctrines into 'religious doctrines'?

Let me recapitulate. We have observed that religious rivalry has allowed us to identify three (not just the one we started out with) exemplary instances of the term 'religion'. Historically, we have also noted that doctrinal differences and disputes about God have contributed towards crystallising the religious rivalry. Any hypothesis about religion must shed light on all these *three* aspects: religious rivalry, importance of doctrine, and the necessity of God to religion. These are the preliminary *constraints* on theory-generation. They tell us where to look; narrow down the search-space and hence, as I said before, productive. However, the aspects I have just isolated need not constitute the properties of religion. To revert to an analogy used in the previous chapter, we have succeeded in isolating three cats. It is time to develop a hypothesis about this animal and see which the properties of the species are, and which belong only to these three cats.

The best way of building such a hypothesis is to look at a problem that the social sciences of today confront in their quest to gain knowledge of human beings.

## 9.2. "Our Father, Which Art in Heaven"

Today, something is the matter with the social sciences. We have had our quota of geniuses in several domains studying both individual human beings and their societies. There is no lack of either sophisticated mathematical apparatus or specially designed instruments. Research funding and intellectual workers are not in shortage, even though one could always use more of both. Nevertheless, for some reason or the other, a strange disquiet reigns in these disciplines. There is the dissatisfaction that the rate of progress in acquiring knowledge about human beings is far too slow in proportion to the input. As proponents from these several disciplines formulate it in moments of honesty or despair, there is also the feeling that no progress is being made.

*Explanatory Accounts and Intelligibility Considerations*

Many hypotheses try to account for this state of affairs. One of the sub-issues spawned by this debate, which has spanned generations, concerns the relation between *reasons* and *causes*. The questions are these: what should the social sciences look for in their attempt to account for human behaviour? Should we admit only those that appeal to causes in explaining human behaviour, or are we satisfied with those that make human actions intelligible by appealing to reasons? In fact, the difference between natural sciences and human sciences has often been described along these lines. Natural sciences provide us with explanations by identifying the (contingent) causal laws; the social sciences render human actions (rationally) intelligible by appealing to the reasons (beliefs, desires, *etc.*) for actions.

Perhaps, a very simple example might help illustrate both the difficulty and the issue in the discussion. Consider a non-smoker who objects to the others smoking in the same room. Let us say that we need to account for this behaviour. Why does he object if others smoke in his presence? Let us consider the *two* kinds of accounts, an explanatory and an intelligible one, given in answer to the above question.

One could make the reaction of the non-smoker *intelligible* by appealing to the (reasonable and justifiable) beliefs held by him: he believes that smoking is injurious to health; passive smoking is a form of smoking; he does not desire to injure his health...*etc.* Hence, we can understand his behaviour by appealing to his belief-states (or intentional states). That is, we look at this behaviour as an intentional act. "Why does this non-smoker object to the others smoking in his presence?" "Because", so the intelligibility account goes on, "he believes that..." The above beliefs would fill-in the ellipsis. It is important to note that principle(s) of sound reasoning connect his beliefs to his actions.

Because I merely want to illustrate the difference between two kinds of account using the same example, let me introduce myself into this picture as a possessor of some piece of information. Let us suppose that I am his friend and that, in strict confidence (which I am, alas, breaking for the good of science), he informed me that he cannot withstand the smell of the smoke. He does not believe that the smell is injurious to health at all. Smirking smugly, I now tell you that the *cause* of his behaviour has nothing to do with his 'beliefs'. "Because", I say grinning from ear to ear, "he cannot withstand the smell of the smoke..."

On the one hand, it appears impossible to speak of human actions without appealing to desires and beliefs, but to do so reduces the predictive power (or the problem solving capacity) of the accounts we may give. On the other hand, the search for the underlying (contingent) causal laws governing human behaviour has not yielded fruits either.

While more could be said about the issue, it is neither central nor relevant for my concerns to do so. The only point is that we have two kinds of accounts, an explanatory account and an intelligibility one, each of which appears to focus on different kinds of questions.

### 9.2.1. No Gods, but Lord God Alone

Consider an account, which promises to give us both. It suggests or hints that some sets of actions are intelligible because they instantiate some sets of beliefs. It further suggests that the relationship between 'intending' and 'acting' is not only constant but also because nothing else interferes between the former and the latter, they virtually become identical. To those from the outside who only observe the actions, knowledge of these actions is sufficient to draw inferences about the reasons for actions. There is only one *proviso* attached. Because the observer's knowledge of these actions is always framed in some description or the other, one can only read-off the purposes of the actions exhaustively if the descriptions of these actions are themselves exhaustive. A complete and accurate description of the actions is required before we have a complete knowledge of the reasons for the actions.

Such an account, when it is forthcoming; of such sets of actions, if they are possible; of such a being, if it exists; these, together, will give us an *explanatory intelligible* account of that being and its actions. The reason for calling it thus must be obvious: the *causes* of the action are also its *reasons*. Further, because each type of action instantiates one and only one purpose, prediction becomes possible as well. The causal law will be general, predictive power is not reduced, and the causes are the intentions of such a being.

Suppose that we now have a doctrine, which says the following: such a being exists, such actions exist too, but we could never provide a complete description of the actions of such a being. At best, we could have a very fragmented and partial description of such actions. Further, we cannot possibly observe all the actions of that being. It adds that this being has communicated its purposes to us – our ability to understand of this message is restricted by the descriptive possibilities open to us. In such a case, we have *two sources* of knowledge: some sets of actions that we try to understand and the message, which we try to make sense of.

Suppose further that this being is God. His actions are the universe. His message is precisely the above doctrine. We now have on our hands what we call a 'religious doctrine'. This doctrine makes the Cosmos an *explanatorily intelligible* entity – not by providing us with a detailed explanation of all cosmic events, happenings, and phenomena nor even by showing, to take up an issue that we have already come across before (chapter #5), how the equal length of the eyelashes could instantiate the purposes of God. It does neither but claims, instead, that all there is, was, and shall be are expressions of a will that constitutes the cementing bond of the Cosmos. In a deep and fundamental sense (to be partially explored further in chapter #11), to grow up within a religious tradition is to grow up with this fundamental experience where the Cosmos has an explanatory intelligibility. To have a religion is to have this experience. Note well that this doctrine is not 'religious' because it provides us with an explanatory account, which is complete in such a way that it makes the entire Cosmos (including all events) intelligible to us. Rather, it merely affirms that the Cosmos is explanatorily intelligible.

However, this claim about the nature of the Cosmos is not a bare and simple statement but is itself couched in the form of an account. Which kind of an account? It is an account that not only says that the Cosmos is explanatorily intelligible but also one that makes the Cosmos into such an entity. Among other things, the latter step involves that the 'religion' itself exemplifies explanatory intelligibility.

Consider what religion does. Firstly, it imparts knowledge by saying that the world is the expression of the purposes of God. Because this is what the world is, the knowledge of the world will be an explanatory intelligible account. Since the religion in question is making a claim about the world, it is a knowledge-claim. It is not just any knowledge-claim but one that brings reasons and causes together in an extraordinary way. If it makes this particular claim about the Cosmos, the account must exemplify the property that makes the universe into that kind of a place. That is, a religious account must be an explanatory intelligible account.

Secondly, this knowledge of the world is also in the world. If the universe is explanatorily intelligible, so is knowledge about the world. Therefore, this knowledge must make itself explanatorily intelligible. Consequently, it is not enough that the doctrine 'says' that the world expresses the Will of God, but it must also 'say' that this very account expresses the very same will of God. Religion makes both the Cosmos and itself explanatorily intelligible. That is, it must not only tell us, say, why God made the world and us but also why He gave religion to humankind.

This, then, is what makes an explanation into a 'religious' explanation: it is knowledge of the Cosmos which includes itself. It is the explanation of the universe, which includes itself as an *explanandum*. There would have been a logical problem here, the threat of circularity perhaps, if this were to be the result of our (human) understanding or theory of the world. However, this problem does not arise, because God has revealed His purposes by speaking to us about them. 'Revelation', then, is the crucial component that breaks the possible circularity (see further #9.4). As religious figures would put it perhaps, religion need not prove the existence of God; the existence of religion is the proof for the existence of God. In this sense, as an explanatory intelligible account, religion is God's gift to humanity and not a human invention.

To accept this is to accept that everything in the universe has a purpose. Our birth and death occurs in the Cosmos. Consequently, both events have a purpose as well. To be part of a religion – as a first approximation – is to believe that human life and death have significance, a meaning, and a purpose. A religious doctrine need not specify the purposes of any individual life or death; it is enough that it merely says there is one. Consequently, to accept that life, including your life, has meaning and purpose is to accept this doctrine.

As an individual, you do not know what the purpose or meaning of your birth or death is. However, because you believe that your life itself is explanatorily intelligible, your actions appear as constituting (or exemplifying) the meaning of your life.

Clearly, the difference between religions will revolve around the specification of these purposes. What, then, makes them into rival religions is their characterisation of this explanatory intelligibility of human life and death (at a minimum). What makes them into religions is their affirmation that the Cosmos is such an entity.

As I have said, this does not imply that in any particular religion some or another statement need occur to the effect that the Cosmos is an explanatorily intelligible entity. What I am saying is that such is the claim or affirmation of religion; that it *makes* the world explanatorily intelligible *by structuring* its experience accordingly. How can an affirmation about the nature of the Cosmos also structure its experience? This is a question for a later stage of investigation. For the moment, we need to understand the claim itself better. Let me draw upon the Bible to illustrate the idea.

### "The World is Governed"

The creation of the world and all that is in it, as the Bible tells us, is the Work of God. As a being with goals and purposes, He brought forth everything for some purpose or another. The cosmic products and processes embody the Will of this God. What we human beings see are the phenomena; but underlying them, and expressed in them, is the Will of God. The same God, the Good Book further tells us, has manifested His Will to us in two ways: through revelation, as 'captured' in the scriptures; and in His products, *viz.* Nature. We can study His works and through such a study learn inductively about His Will. There is also the Biblical revelation. In a deep and fundamental sense, the Will of The Sovereign governs the world.

How can we know the will of an actor by studying his actions? From our experience in the world, we know that there is a hiatus between the actions we perform and our belief states. Even such a 'trivial' action as my opening a door could not be said to instantiate some or other belief unambiguously. Perhaps, I feel that the room is stuffy or that it is too cold; perhaps I want you to get out; or I sense an eavesdropper...You cannot read-off my intentions unambiguously by looking at my actions. You could also ask me about the reasons for my action: but I could deceive you by telling a plausible lie; or I forgot my own reasons; or I am not even sure that I have reasons...This being the case, how can we know (or even hypothesise about) God's Will by studying His actions?

The answer must be obvious. God is perfectly good, perfectly consistent. His actions perfectly express His intentions. The Sovereign's Will is not arbitrary, but perfectly constant. Because he is a Being who is *perfectly trustworthy, His works do not deceive us.* The ascription of predicates of perfection to God, which many authors use as an argument for the impossibility of His existence, I suggest, was a necessary condition for the emergence of knowledge about the natural world.

Consider, by contrast, the 'gods' of the so-called religions like those of the Greeks, the Romans, or the Hindus. What is constant about these gods is their capriciousness or unpredictability. They ceaselessly interfere with the affairs of humanity, but in ways that are both unpredictable and mysterious.

Let me reformulate the earlier paragraphs in the following way: the Bible inculcates an experience of the Cosmos as a particular kind of order, and this order consists of the fact that phenomena *express* a deep, underlying constancy. This constancy is the Will of The Sovereign. His Will governs the world.

*Order, Explanation, and Religion*

Now, we are in a position to appreciate the insight of Hume and some other enlightenment thinkers. They grasped the idea, even though they did not put it this way, that religions are fundamentally explanatory in nature. Under this construal, *the prototypical model* of an explanatory framework (or theory) is the phenomenon that we designate by the term 'religion'. It is *not* the case that religion explains this or that specific phenomenon. *Nor* is it the case that it is a class of explanations alongside and besides which exist other classes of explanation like, say, the 'scientific' and 'philosophical' explanations (see, *e.g.* Clayton 1989 for such an attempt). My argument is that religion is *the* basic model of explanation. All other explanations, including 'scientific' explanations, are inspired by and modelled after this explanatory model.

How then to understand the conflict between theories in natural sciences on the one hand and religious beliefs on the other? I shall take up the question elsewhere (chapter #11.2.2). For now, let us look at the problem in the social sciences that we started out with. If the Will of the Sovereign is the cement of the universe, this very bond tells us about the purposes of God. If religion developed this orientation, it has also provided us with a problem by contrasting the two kinds of accounts we saw earlier: the 'law governed' as against the 'will governed' actions of human beings.

What else is possible? Human beings are made in the image of God (their actions are *intentional*), but their will does not function the way the natural laws do. That is to say, 'our' (*whose?*) ubiquitous folk-psychology, which makes our actions intentional (in the narrow, philosophical sense: actions resulting from desires and beliefs, *i.e.* intentional states lead to a behaviour), is gifted with a problem and tantalised with an apparently impossible solution both of which derive from the same source, *viz.* religion.

I am aware that I need to do at least two more things in order to substantiate this claim. (A) I need to show that even in the West (because I have taken the stance that the Roman *religio* was different from Religion), the relation between beliefs, desires, and actions was not seen the way we do now in the folk-psychology of today, and that this issue gets formulated only within a religious tradition. (B) I need to provide an alternative account of human actions. Because I am still working on both questions, I will not answer them within the confines of this essay.

### 9.2.2. Seek, and Ye Shall Find

One of the oft-heard claims about religion is that it helps human beings to find meaning and purpose in their lives. Equally often heard claims suggest that one of the problems in the secularised societies of ours is that individuals experience 'anomie' or 'alienation' by virtue of not finding such a meaning; or by finding that life is meaningless; or, used often as a synonym in this context, as absurd. This question about the 'meaning of one's life' (or life *überhaupt*) is supposed to be *the* existential problem, to which religion provides answers.

However, it is not always clear what this claim amounts to. Are the diverse religions so many different attempts to find solutions to the question of meaning of one's life and death? Some would say 'no'. Yet others would say 'yes'. Gazzaniga, one of the founding fathers of cognitive neuro-science, speculates on the origin of religion by speaking about "the inevitability of religious beliefs". Basing himself on the work of anthropologists, he considers it a universal in human societies. Assuming that it has something to do with the structure of the human brain (!), he invites us to

> (c)onsider the world ten thousand years ago. Throughout the entire world there were at most only ten million people. Of these, half were under the age of ten and the oldest and wisest in the village was typically only thirty. There is no reason in the world not to think that this inference-capable human did not experience a dash of existential despair. "What," he might

ask, feasting on roast gazelle, "does it all mean?" His dilemma must have been grave. Everything this organism did had meaning. If he didn't get up and go hunt, he didn't eat. If he didn't build a hut, he was cold. If he didn't domesticate wild grain, his diet was boring. Finally he asked, "I know why I do all those things, but *why am I here?*"(1985: 169; my italics)

Some would find this 'explanation' of the origin of religion absurd. I belong to this camp for the simple reason that it is not evident that religion answers this question at all. What religions have done is to assert that life and death have a meaning and purpose. I know of no religion that has been able to answer a specific individual's 'existential question'.

In fact, if you talk to people who do believe that they have found their meaning and purpose in life, you get the following reply as an explication of the said meaning of their lives: they describe what they are doing, and inform you that this description is the meaning of their lives. That is to say, they merely reply that their lives have meaning and that the meaning of their lives is the lives they are leading. To see what happens in such a case, consider the following event and its account.

Suppose that you have a friend who attends parties or goes to dancing clubs very regularly. Equally regularly, he chases after women on such occasions and, let us say, he succeeds in picking them up – each time a different woman. Puzzled, you ask him one day why he does it. His answer goes like this: "I always want a woman I cannot get – that is why I go after women at the parties. As soon as I get them, I lose all interest, which is why I drop them." Even though what you have on your hands is a mere re-description of his action, which you yourself have observed, this account makes it intelligible. As Davidson (1963) formulates it:

> (T)here is no denying that this is true: when we explain an action, by giving the reason, we do redescribe the action; redescribing the action gives the action a place in a pattern, and in this way the action is explained (in Davis, Ed., 1983: 64).

That is, "a reason makes an action intelligible by redescribing it" (*ibid*: 67). A re-description of an action by giving reasons appears to place the action in a pattern – thus making it intelligible.

*Religion and the Meaning of Life*

Those who have found meaning in their lives do precisely this: redescribe the lives they are leading. "Where I can help people using my skills", said a doctor to me once, "I do so. This makes my life meaningful to me". Neither you nor I is any the wiser for this piece of knowledge but we can see that it has the structure of an intelligibility account. Your friend made his action of chasing after women intelligible not merely by describing the pattern *in* his actions. By redescribing the pattern, he also appears to place it in a bigger pattern accessible to you. The description of a pattern *in* one's life also redescribes the pattern in one's life; it also places such a life in a bigger pattern. To those from the outside, the bigger pattern appears absent, which is why this account of life does not appear intelligible. From the inside though, *i.e.* to those to whom their own lives appear meaningful, a pattern appears to be present. They feel that their lives are placed *in* a pattern and not merely that their lives have a pattern.

They cannot tell you what that pattern is, any more than your friend can tell you about the pattern where his women-chasing activity is placed. In this sense, it is not true to say that one cannot communicate the meaning one has found to one's life because it is some "intensely personal thing" or because such a deep 'personal' thing is not communicable. No. In fact, these people are able to communicate the meaning of their lives. From the outside, to someone who listens to such accounts, the intelligibility appears missing because the pattern where such lives require to be placed is not known.

Put in general terms, the answer to the question of the meaning of life is not to be sought in the answer to the question but elsewhere, namely, in that belief which enables the formulation of such a question. Consider why we do not come across answers in any of the religious tracts, if religion was really invented as an answer to such questions as 'Why am I born?', 'Where am I going?', 'What is the meaning or purpose of life?' and so on. Surely, we can imagine a philosopher addressing himself to these issues. In fact, some philosophers have done so. Why, if religion was an answer to these questions, have religious figures (like Christ or Muhammad) kept silent about it?

My answer is simple. Religion does not answer these questions nor has it ever answered them. However, what it does is to enable one to raise such questions because it is the only framework where such queries can be formulated. Religion was not invented to answer questions about the meaning and purpose of life. These questions come into being within the framework of religion. These problems do not antedate religion; religion generates them. Having done this, the framework tantalisingly hints that the problem is solvable. Take religion away, you will also take these questions away.

By saying this, I do not imply that life is either meaningless or that it is absurd. Even *this* answer is given within a framework, which makes either meaning attribution or its denial *sensible* with respect to individual or collective life. Rather, what I am saying is that the questions about the meaning of life are internal to religion. They are religious questions no matter what your answer is. They are not questions that a 'primitive' man raised 10,000 years ago. They are not the questions of the 'modern' man but those of a religious man – *a homo religiosus*. We shall further see what its implications are, but, here, let me summarise what I have said so far in very simple terms: religion makes the world intelligible to us, promises to relate us intelligibly to the world.

### 9.3. "Thy Kingdom Come"

The best way of finding out whether we are on the right track to investigate the phenomenon of religion, and whether my characterisation helps us go further in this quest, is to look at the extent to which we can accommodate some of the basic intuitions that believers and practitioners have. At this stage of the investigation, the task is not to explain any or all of these intuitions but to see whether we can accommodate them. For the sake of convenience, let us call this the 'phenomenological' test that any portrayal of religion has to meet. That is, the greater the phenomenological adequacy of an account, the more it can 'save the phenomena'. In our case, the phenomenon we should save is the way believers and practitioners both experience and describe religion. The more our descriptions approximate what they have said about both, the closer we are to outlining and delimiting the object of our study, *viz.* religion.

Let us begin with the following problem: is my characterisation of the nature of religion not too 'intellectualistic' or 'cognitive'? I have spoken of religion as an account. Therefore, has not the emphasis shifted in favour of an intellectual orientation to the detriment of the uniquely subjective moment of religious experience? While the doctrines contained in such an account may indicate the cognitive element in religion (Kellenberger 1985), does the account do justice to the experiential side as well (*e.g.* Leuba 1909)? Is my characterisation of religion able to capture the phenomenological dimensions of faith, religious experience and practice?

These questions constitute the adequacy tests, which my portrayal has to pass. In what follows, I will answer them by taking up the issue of faith first, turning my attention to religious experience subsequently, and tackling the issue of religious practice last. At the end of this chapter, we shall see whether my description of religion captures these dimensions, which many people have emphasised over several centuries.

### 9.3.1. "When the Son of Man Cometh...

Earlier on, we observed the empirical fact that religious rivalries crystallised around the issue of God. This dispute also distinguished religions from one another. However, it is also an empirical fact that some of the philosophical schools in the Graeco-Roman civilizations also disputed about the nature of gods. However, Christianity did not consider these philosophical schools as competing religions. Equally, disputations about God and gods constitute the dominant preoccupation of the philosophy of religion. By virtue of the fact that the dispute is about God, this domain is not a competitor to religions either.

Clearly, something 'more' is required before a dispute about God or gods becomes 'religious'. Religious figures from different periods have drawn our attention to a crucial component: the dimension of faith (*e.g.* Smith 1977, 1979). To be religious is not merely an act of assenting to the proposition that 'God exists' (see also Pojman 1986; Wiebe 1981). It requires seeing your life as a part of the purposes of God. In my terms, it means to experience the world as an explanatorily intelligible entity.

The New Testament, for example, says:

> What *doth it* profit, my brethren, though a man say he hath faith, and have not works? Can faith save him?...Faith, if it has not works, is dead, being alone...Thou believest that there is one God; thou doest well: the devils also believe, and tremble (James 2: 14-26).

Martin Luther was no different. "Observe," wrote Luther

> there are two ways of believing. In the first place I may have faith concerning God. This is the case when I hold to be true what is said concerning God. Such faith is on the same level with the assent I give to statements concerning the Turk, the devil and hell. A faith of this kind should be called knowledge or information rather than faith. In the second place there is faith in God. Such faith is mine when I not only hold to be true what is said concerning God, but when I put my trust in him in such a way as to enter into personal relations with him, believing firmly that I shall find him to be and to do as I have been taught...The word in is well chosen and deserving of due attention. We do not say, I believe God the Father or concerning God the Father, but in God the Father, in Jesus Christ, and in the Holy spirit (in Lenker, Trans., 1907, Vol. 1: 203).

The Catholic Bishops of Belgium address themselves to this problem in similar terms, in a book directed towards their flock:

> Heb je er al eens op gelet hoe onze geloofsbelijdenis begint? Niet met: ik geloof *dat iets* waar is, dat er een God bestaat. Zij begint met: ik geloof in *Iemand*, ik geloof *in* God. Als je *in* iemand gelooft, ga je ook geloven *wat* hij zegt, natuurlijk. Maar het geloven *in* hem staat voorop. Zo zal het ook tegenover God zijn: geen geloof (de inhoud) zonder geloven (de houding). (*Geloofsboek*, De Bisschoppen van België, Tielt: Lannoo, 1987: 12.)
> [Have you ever considered how our credo begins? Not with: I believe *that something* is true, that there is a God. It begins with: I believe in *Someone*, I believe *in* God. If you believe *in* someone, obviously, you also believe what he says. But believing *in* him is primary. Thus also with respect to God: No belief (the content) without believing (the attitude).]

This, then, is how Christianity has posed (see *e.g.* Niebuhr 1989; Penelhum, Ed., 1989) the issue of faith. It is not enough to merely give assent to the proposition 'God exists' but one must trust and believe in Him.

The issue involves a tension between a knowledge-claim (*viz.* the belief about God's existence), and a relation (personal, emotional, attitudinal, or however else you may like to formulate it) between a person and the entity talked about. Where is the tension located, and what is its nature?

Although I am going to be brief in discussing this question, it is important to emphasise at the outset itself that there are two dimensions to the theme: one involving the individuals within a religious tradition, and another oriented towards those outside of it.

*The Two Dimensions of Faith*

The first dimension points to the distance separating one individual from another, both of whom belong to the same religious tradition. For example, it could take the form of an exhortation that, say, Christians ought to have faith in God and that it is not sufficient for their salvation to merely believe in the proposition 'God exists'. As the Bible formulates it, the devils too believe and shudder – a statement that makes sense only within the Biblical context. The reason for contextualising this statement must be obvious: if the Bible does not belong to one's tradition, neither does this specific claim about the existence of God and the Devil. Consequently, the problem of faith to a Christian, or a Muslim, or a Jew takes the form of being a pious and devout practitioner of his religion, and in understanding what being such an individual entails.

By contrast, the second dimension of faith is relevant at the outer boundaries of contact between two traditions. Depending upon the kind of traditions we are speaking about, the problem may take several forms. A deeply devout Christian may look at a Jew and a Muslim and feel that even though all three of them worship God, the other two are deficient in their worship. Whether or not this Christian would be quite ready to formulate the religious difference in terms of 'degrees of faith', he would have no hesitation in using the notion 'absence of faith' when describing an unrepentant pagan like myself. Despite this, I submit, at the point of contact between two traditions – Christian and Jew; Christian and pagan – the problem of faith takes the form of the question of truth: Why would a Jew or I not accept the truth of the Christian doctrines? Our faith in Jesus is parasitic upon the truth of the status and nature of the claims about The Saviour.

By isolating the question of faith along these two dimensions, I do not want to suggest that these dimensions are independent of each other, and that answers to one question are irrelevant to the other one. We can appreciate the nature of their mutual dependence properly only when we appreciate the difference between these two dimensions. Therefore, let me begin with the issue of faith within a religious tradition.

### 9.3.2. ... Will he Find Faith on Earth?"

Consider, for instance, a baptised, church-going Catholic. He attends the mass regularly, participates in all/most activities organised by his parish priest, and such like. Despite these, his fellow-Christians suspect that he is not 'truly' religious and merely acts as though he is one. His actions appear mechanical, his assent to 'doctrines' formal, and he does not appear to be guided by the state of mind that the believers call 'faith'. As a result, this individual's fellow-Congregationalists suspect that he does not 'really believe'.

The tension between the acts of this Christian and his state of mind, I would like to suggest, arises not because there is some mysterious, additional something called 'faith', which only the 'truly' religious have and their less devout brethren miss, but because of the nature of religion itself.

Religion does not merely explain the origin of the Cosmos or of human life by postulating God as the cause. It also makes the world intelligible by making the Will of God into the cause of the universe in such a way that the world expresses His purposes. One cannot possibly accept that everything – including one's own life – has a purpose, which is God's purpose, and still be without faith in Him. Faith, as we have seen earlier on, involves accepting precisely His purposes. To accept such an account as true is to have faith in Him.

In the case at hand, this is how I would make sense of the individual Christian: indeed, he does not 'truly believe'. Maximally, he perhaps believes that God created the universe (*i.e.* sees God as the cause) and, in believing this, grasps religion as an explanatory account. However, he does not 'see' that it is also an intelligibility account. Believing that God exists and that He created the universe does not make some person religious or these doctrines into religious doctrines, any more than their denial makes someone into a nonreligious person. It is only when an indissoluble link is postulated between the cause of the world and the Will of the creator God that an explanatory intelligible account comes into being. I have argued that this makes some accounts religious.

Why does this Christian not 'see' the intelligibility of the religious account? Better put, what is involved in seeing it also as an intelligibility account? One has to appreciate a relation between reasons and actions. Our Christian is willing to accept the statement that God is the cause of the universe is true, but he is unable to see that this cause is God's purpose. That is to say, he does not see that God is a person. To him, God has become a vague entity, an abstract conception, some kind of an *Urkraft*. His God, if you like, is not Allah, the Holy Trinity, or Jehovah. It is the de-Christianised God, the truly 'universal' God, a God who progressively loses Gestalt as He is generalised to include and incorporate all the 'manifestations of the divine' across all cultures and at all times. His God is the answer to the Christological dilemma (chapter #6). This human being is a truly tolerant Christian, who is willing to concede that all religions are equally true. The price he pays for this admission is also in proportion: he ceases being a Christian. He does not anymore believe in God as a personal entity, as someone whose purposes are expressed in the Cosmos. In short, he does not 'believe'. To him, God has become a variable capable of different interpretations, all of which are equally true.

*The Poignancy of the Question*

Let us appreciate what is said: he ceases being a Christian, because he is a truly tolerant Christian. Am I suggesting that intolerance and Christianity are necessarily related to each other? My answer is both a 'yes' and a 'no'. The 'yes' is evident, but the 'no' is more important: intolerance is not a necessary property of Christianity as a historical movement but one that accrues to it by virtue of being a religion. That is to say, I am suggesting that one cannot be 'religious' without being intolerant of those who are not. I am claiming that 'faith' and 'intolerance' are two faces of the same coin, and that you cannot have one without the other. I do not need to refer you to historical records to argue that the best exemplars of faith in each of these three traditions, depending upon the milieu they lived in, have also been the most intolerant regarding other traditions. What I need to show is how the nature of religion requires intolerance.

To have faith in God, I suggested, is to accept His purpose. The doctrine, which makes the Cosmos into an expression of God's purpose, can do so only by saying what that purpose is. As an individual or as a community, located at some place and time, one accepts this purpose by becoming its part. However, God's purpose is not exhausted by the commitment of any one individual or group, because both the Cosmos and human life exemplify His purpose. That is to say, a religion can speak only in terms of God's purpose for human beings – and not just for Tom, Dick and Harry. Of course, the latter might believe that each one of them has a unique purpose in life but they have that by virtue of being a part of the general purpose of God for the humankind. As an explanatory intelligible account of the Cosmos, a religion can only be universal, unrestricted by space, time, or culture.

The three exemplary religions we are looking at specify these purposes differently. Not merely in the sense that God will send the faithless to Hell and the faithful to Heaven, but the likelihood of finding yourself in either of these two places depends upon having got His purposes right. You will not get that right because you are Bernstein, Thomas or Abdullah but because you are a human being. Your choice is the right one because it is the only right choice for human beings.

In other words, it is simply not possible to have faith in God and at the same time claim that all religions are equally true, and that each religion is a 'manifestation of the divine'. In this sense, intolerance of the others arises because of your acceptance of God's purposes for humankind, *i.e.* because you have faith in Him.

Intolerance, then, is necessary to being a religious person. One cannot be a Jew, Christian, or a Muslim and tolerate each other and other 'religious' groups. This does not mean that intolerance needs to express itself in persecution, even though it has often done so. The relation between intolerance on the one hand and persecution on the other is mediated by many different circumstances, including power. One may or may not want to 'evangelise' other groups; this is an issue partially about the psychology of the individual and partially about the interpretation of the religious doctrine in question. In this sense, intolerance does not entail that each believer must be either a missionary or a persecutor. However, it does entail that there is no question of tolerating other 'religious' views as equally true. Jesus or Muhammad might have spoken to those around them out of infinite love and compassion for the humankind but that does not suggest that they were 'tolerant' of other faiths. A believer who believes in the truth of his doctrine and thus in God cannot be a tolerant person with respect to religion. That is to say, religious tolerance is either a grotesque hypocrisy or an expression of an absence of 'faith', when so advocated by a believer. The question of Luke (18:8), "When the Son of Man cometh, will he find faith on earth?" surely takes on an added poignancy when we realise this interdependence between faith and intolerance.

Perhaps, this is the place to make a related point. The 'resurgence' of Islam in the Arab world is often described as the growth of fanaticism and fundamentalism. Clucking like hens, shaking their heads sadly, western commentators make the claim that the Arab world has yet to undergo its 'enlightenment' and learn 'religious pluralism'. There is an exquisite irony to this situation, where we see religious figures from the Catholic Church proclaiming this idea precisely when the current pope (John Paul II) has launched a crusade, *nota bene*, for a "second evangelisation" of the West. The irony must be evident: you can have 'religious pluralism' only when you have lost faith and do not believe. The ferocious attack against the Muslims, when launched by the Church functionaries, boils down to this feeling: Muslims have faith and we do not. How dare they believe, when we do not do so anymore? It could be true that the 'enlightened' person does not have faith in God and does not believe at all, but what has that to do with religious pluralism?

In other words, the fact that Christianity, Islam, and Judaism competed with each other as religions does not merely appear as a contingent property, which these three religions have. I would like to suggest that this is a necessary property of a religious account. To understand even better why this is so requires that we turn our attention to the second dimension of 'faith', *viz.* the philosophical/theological issue about faith.

### 9.3.3. "It is Absurd, Therefore I Believe..."

The controversy, again briefly formulated, involves the relationship between 'faith' and 'reason'. As these religions put it, human salvation depends upon accepting some doctrines as true. However, the evidence for accepting these doctrines as true is (at best) inconclusive. These doctrines include such things as the Covenant God made with the people of Israel or the resurrection of Jesus Christ or God speaking through Muhammad. These religions make it praiseworthy that one holds on to these beliefs in spite of, or precisely because of, the absence of justifying evidence. Yet, it is also the case that many (or most) of us believe that holding on to a belief in spite of lack of evidence indexes a kind of self-deception. Minimally, such a state of affairs raises questions about God himself: is the goodness of God compatible with the fact that He would make our salvation depend on the acceptance of beliefs whose truth is in doubt, and which we can reasonably question?

These issues have occupied theologians and philosophers over the centuries. Extremely ingenious attempts at answering the questions exist, and the continued interest and debate around these problems indicate that conclusive answers are not forthcoming. I do not intend to summarise these discussions here, but it might be interesting to note that the strategies chosen have been wide and variegated.

At one end of the spectrum, there are attempts to show that these doctrines are extremely reasonable. One strategy involves demonstrating that these claims are extensions of other kinds of beliefs for which arguments and evidence exists. (St. Thomas is the brilliant exponent of this approach; see, *e.g.* Penelhum 1977.) Yet others, mostly the Protestant philosopher-theologians of America, suggest that certain beliefs are "properly basic", which do not require further justification and that the existence of God is one such. (Alvin Plantinga is a notable thinker representing this tradition.)

At the other end of the spectrum, there are the early Christian figures like Irenaeus and Tertullian. The ringing battle-cry of the latter, reverberating through the corridors of time and to be heard through the mouths of people like Luther and Kierkegaard, makes it emphatically clear that Christianity is to be "believed because it is absurd", and that Christ was "buried and rose again; the fact is certain because it is impossible".

Even though there could be no room for misunderstanding, it might still prove useful to add a cautionary note. None of them is saying that the absurdity of a claim is an evidence for its truth or that one ought to believe in something because it is absurd. Rather, their point is that it is not a proper question to ask of faith that it be justified on grounds of evidence. Faith is not a matter of 'facts'; it involves something quite different altogether.

These different stances, both early and modern are as fascinating as any issue one could think of in the domain of religion. However, as I have suggested already, the dispute is relevant for my purposes from only one point of view. I need to show that I can capture and redescribe it in terms of my characterisation of religion.

Religion does not prove the truth of the proposition 'God exists'. Theologians have tried to do so. Religion is the explanatory intelligible account of the Cosmos. One may accept it; reject it outright; be sceptical towards it; or whatever else. Nevertheless, accepting this account makes one 'deeply religious'. There is no further religious issue involved, but only that of truth.

In which sense though? With us human beings, everything we believe as true of the world depends on other things we believe to know about the world. Consequently, all our explanations and theories about the world are tentative and hypothetical. They are tentative in the sense that other theories, at some future date, could turn up and replace those we accept today; they are hypothetical in the sense that even if we chanced to hit upon a true partial description of the world, we cannot know that it is true (at this moment). Perhaps, it is important to emphasise that I am merely making an epistemological point as it relates to our theories about the world. We cannot know whether our theories are true because we do not have a way of testing some thing for its truth, *i.e.* we lack a criterion of truth.

In our daily activities in the world, we assume that many of our beliefs and theories are true. One such candidate, for example, is the belief that the earth revolves round the sun or that we do not change shape while we sleep. Even though we do not know whether they are true, we have no reasons (yet) to presume their falsity. The assumption about the truth of these beliefs is strengthened by a whole number of other beliefs: some are biological theories, some are about the efficacy of medical practices, yet others help us send satellites to circle the earth. We do not really despair about the tentative and hypothetical nature of our theories. Commendable and necessary though such attitudes are, our indifference does not affect the epistemological point: any of our theories could turn out to be false.

Religion not only tells us about the Cosmos but it also makes itself explanatorily intelligible. The first thing to note is that, based on human knowledge and human cognitive abilities both of which are finite, we could never arrive at an explanatory intelligible account, which includes itself as an *explanandum*.

Religion, which claims to be the truth about the world, is radically independent of our prior theories about the world. Whether one believes in the existence of witches, ancestors, or quantum particles; whether one can understand Gödel's theorem or the mechanism of gene-splicing; whether one can read or drive a car; one's access to the 'message' of a religion is not affected. Grasping the truth of the religious account does not depend on our finite knowledge of the world and this truth, note well, is about the Cosmos. As I have said before, religion is God's gift to humankind. On our own, as these religions have explained themselves, we could only arrive at a 'vague' conception of God as the creator. However, this notion does not make the world explanatorily intelligible. God has to reveal himself and aid us in seeing *the truth* because this truth does not depend upon human knowledge and what we, at any given moment, believe to be true.

What we have on our hands, then, is an account that has no other parallels in the domain of human knowledge. We know of partial explanatory accounts; we think that our folk-psychology makes use of intelligibility accounts. Religion alone is both an explanatory and an intelligibility account not of this or that individual phenomenon, but of the Cosmos and itself.

Correspondingly, the question of truth takes a radical form. The problem is not whether religion is true the way my belief about Brussels is true. The truth about the capital city of Belgium depends on other beliefs being true as well. This is not the case with religion at all. If we use the predicate 'true' to describe a religion, it looks as though we cannot use it for anything else: what makes religion true cannot make anything else true. Religion is *the truth* in the specific sense of not being dependent on the truth of any other belief we hold about the world.

In the sixth chapter (#6.2), while discussing the Christological dilemma, I argued that the uniqueness of revelation is a problem in Christianity. I suggested further that revelation must be universally accessible, because the nature of religion demands it. We can now understand why: as the truth about the Cosmos, religion does not depend upon the truth of any antecedent belief we hold about the world. Because the truth of religion is not conditional in nature, *access* to it cannot be conditional either. Hence, the Christological dilemma.

### 9.3.4. Ye Shall be as Children

One can now appreciate how and why the problem of faith takes the form of the question of truth at the point of contact between two traditions, at least one of which is religious.

At a first level, we need to believe that we have a true explanatory intelligible account when we have no examples of a true theory about any finite slice of the world. At a second level, epistemically speaking, we have to accept the truth of this account on its say-so. The very existence of this account is the proof for its truth: the Cosmos expresses the Will of The Sovereign. In no other sphere of human thought could we possibly countenance such a move. Nevertheless, we need to do precisely that in the case of religion because its yardstick is not human. Elsewhere, one would find such an account absurd. Yet, here, we have to say, "it is absurd; therefore, I believe".

For someone from another culture, there are yet other 'absurdities' to contend with. There is, to begin with, the 'impossibility' that Tertullian makes so much of: the death and the resurrection of Jesus Christ. This 'impossibility' does not have anything to do with the event, but the location where it took place. An explanation of this statement requires a bit of a detour.

As I have said already, because what we believe to be true (possible) or false (impossible) depends upon other beliefs that we hold about the world, what appears 'impossible' given one set of beliefs might turn out to be a commonplace given a different set of beliefs. To Tertullian and other believers, the resurrection of Jesus might appear 'impossible'. How would it have appeared in India two thousand years ago, if Jesus died there and was resurrected subsequently? Let a European scholar report a discussion he had with a denizen of the twentieth-century India:

> A Tantric scholar, a man of shrewd intelligence and wide-ranging knowledge, made the following observations on the passion and resurrection of Christ. He explained the first by the evident fact that Christ, like many ascetics, has obtained *siddhi* (instanced both in his 'knowledge' and in his miracles), in consequence of which he suffered no pain on the Cross; and the second as a *typical example* of the burial and later disinterment of an ascetic in meditative trance, a *phenomenon of common occurrence throughout the subcontinent.* (Piatigorsky 1985: 211; italics mine.)

Note the emphasised portion well, and you can understand the 'absurdity' I am talking about. Generalising this point, the additional absurdity can be formulated this way: other cultures have to believe not only that religion is the truth, but also that God sought out some half-forgotten tribe in some (until then) godforsaken desert to reveal His will. Not once or twice or even thrice. No. He seems to reveal Himself only there; perform miracles only with them. We, from other cultures, are supposed to accept as true not one or two absurdities, but a whole pile of them. One is inclined to reply with a very reasonable cry: "impossible and absurd!" However, there is our Tertullian telling us, "Impossible and absurd; *therefore* certain and true".

Because of this relation between faith and truth, we understand better why religion is an intolerant account. Its truth is divinely inspired, not human at all. To countenance other claims as true in the same sense in which religion is true is to acknowledge the falsity of religion. Such an acknowledgement is, among other things, a destructive paradox.

Further, we can also understand why doctrinal content is so important to a religion. (We shall shortly explore the issue of doctrinal content in more detail in section #9.5). We need to accept that this account of the Cosmos is also the truth and some vague notion of a God is no substitute for it. Therefore, to be religious requires accepting this explanatory account as true. Further, it demands that it does not remain merely 'explanatory' but lends intelligibility to the Cosmos itself.

In my portrayal, which I believe captures several intuitions present among religious people over the centuries, the theological/philosophical problem of faith and reason becomes the question, 'is religion the truth?' We have an account that tells us how the world is. It also claims that we can see the world as it is. This knowledge is direct and unmediated by the other things we believe to be true about the world. We have access to the truth irrespective of what we know. That is why one has to go to the Lord as a child.

We shall see further (in the next chapter) how we could make some 'sense' of this situation. However, I have said enough, I trust, to shift my attention to the next, related question, *viz.* the question of religious experience.

## 9.4. ON RELIGIOUS EXPERIENCE

This characterisation of religion also enables us to come to grips with authors like Schleiermacher and Otto (chapters #6 and #7), who speak of religious experience. As we have seen, both argue that having a religious experience presupposes that one belongs to a religion. As an account, religion makes use of concepts. To accept such an account is to feel a part of the purposes of that being and depend on it. Without such an account, there is no possibility of experiencing the 'absolute dependency' that Schleiermacher talks about; at best, a kind of relative dependency upon each other is all we can experience. In such a case, the 'other' is not "The Totally Other" of Schleiermacher. To have the experience that Schleiermacher talks about, we need to accept the explanatory intelligible account of the Cosmos.

One cannot substitute 'world' or 'Cosmos' for God and generate an atheistic religiosity. The explanatory intelligibility of the Cosmos does not reside in the fact that one depends on the Cosmos. A person might feel "one with the Cosmos" or feel "totally dependent" on all objects that exist. Despite this, one cannot call such an experience 'religious' (whether atheistic or not) for at least two reasons.

The first has to do with the nature of dependency. Maximally, in the best of the cases, one might feel a part of the Cosmos. (I grant this with good will, even though I cannot imagine anyone feeling dependent on a quasar or a black hole present in another galaxy.) However, this is merely a generalised feeling of dependency that a peasant has on his cow or a dog on its master. We would call neither 'atheistically religious'.

The second reason is even weightier in my eyes, which takes the form of an objection: involved in the above substitution is both a distortion of the linguistic meaning of concepts, and an inability (or unwillingness) to pay heed to what the religious figures say.

Whenever we speak of 'the world' or 'the Cosmos', what do we refer to? Consider David Lewis' answer (1986: 1) to this question:

> The world we live in is a very inclusive thing. Every stick and stone you have ever seen is part of it. And so are you and I. And so are the planet earth, the solar system, the entire Milky Way, the remote galaxies that we see through telescopes and (if there are such things) all the bits of empty

space between the stars and galaxies. There is nothing so far away from us as not to be part of our world. Anything at any distance at all is to be included. Likewise the world is inclusive in time. No long-gone ancient Romans, no long-gone pterodactyls, no long-gone primordial clouds of plasma are too far in the past, nor are the dead dark stars too far in the future, to be part of this same world. May be, as I myself think, the world is a big physical object; or may be some parts of it are entelechies or spirits or auras or deities or other things unknown to physics. But nothing is so alien in kind as not to be part of our world, provided that it does exist at some distance and direction from here, or at some time before or after or simultaneous with now.

Speaking of the notion of the "actual world", Bradley and Swartz clarify what it signifies (1979: 4-5):

When we speak of "the actual world" we do not just mean the planet on which we live. Nor do we mean our solar system, or even our galaxy... (T)he actual world...embrace(s)...the universe as a whole.

"(T)he actual world"...(is) not...just the universe as it is now, in the present...(It) encompass(es) not only what exists now but also what once existed in the past and what will come to exist in the future. The actual world embraces all that was, is, or will be.

The world or the Cosmos (used interchangeably here, as elsewhere) is everything that was, is, and ever shall be. An 'atheistic' religiosity that would like to describe itself as a feeling of dependency on the world must be able to account for feeling dependent on all that was, is, and will be. With a generosity that breaks the limit of my imagination, I can conceive of a person feeling dependent on the 'past' that includes the primordial cloud of plasma and the 'present' that includes spirits if they exist. How to conceive of a similar feeling of dependency with respect to what does not yet exist?

Quick answers like 'if Christians depend on God, who does not exist, why cannot we?' will not do. The Christians do depend on God, who they believe exists. By contrast, an 'atheistically' religious person depends on things, which he knows do not exist yet. How then can he feel dependent on them? Nor will it do to point out that human beings are often dependent on events that are 'not-yet', like a pregnant woman whose baby is not yet born. This kind of dependency merely suggests that the future of such a person depends on what will happen in the future, and that the present is partially dependent on anticipations of the future.

The kind of dependency that religious atheism requires is not this kind of relative dependency, as my earlier point makes it clear. It must postulate an absolute dependency on the Cosmos – all that was, is, and will be – and claim that such an experience is possible without the individual being able (in any sense of the word) to anticipate what will be. Given what we know about human psychology, such people are described either irrational or psychotic. Such a person is just about as rational as someone who overdraws his bank account by depending on winning the first prize in a lottery, which is yet to be drawn. Such people do exist – now and then, we also follow reports about the tragic end to their lives...

This is what I mean when I say that a distortion of linguistic meaning of concepts is involved: in all probability, when they speak of the world, the proponents of religious atheism have a *time-slice* (the 'now') of the world in mind. However, such a notion is woefully inadequate to generate a religious experience because this is not what people in a religious tradition refer to by 'religious experience'. This is my first objection.

This brings me to the second objection. When a religion speaks of faith in God – or, as I characterise it, accepting an explanatory intelligible account of the Cosmos – it indicates faith in an entity that was, is, and will be. The Cosmos is an expression of the will of such an entity whose purposes include what will be, but not is. That is to say, eschatology is a necessary part of any explanatory intelligible account of the Cosmos. It appears to me that when atheistic religiosity speaks of a religious experience, it cannot speak of the Cosmos as the object experienced. If it focuses on a temporal slice of the Cosmos, the reference is probably to what one calls a 'peak experience'. Even if religious experience is one such peak experience, not all peak experiences are religious. An inability (or unwillingness) to differentiate between these two kinds of experiences would make one call every 'peak' experience a religious one including, as one such 'atheistically religious' philosopher once said to me in perfect seriousness, an orgasmic experience.

### 9.4.1. Atheistic Religiosity

Does this mean that an atheistic religion is impossible? No. It is logically possible though difficult to conceive of. Before exploring this issue further, let us draw together other related questions that we have come across in an earlier chapter (#8.3.1). While discussing Staal's thesis, I made several points about founders, holy books, belief in God, churches, *etc.* While discussing Christianity as a religion, I asked how many of its properties were due to the historical contingency and which were necessary to being a religion. The possibility of an atheistic religion is a sub-issue within this broader question, and this is how I shall tackle the problem.

The answer involves us in doing a thought-experiment. It consists of imagining a possible world populated with beings with a religion. That is, they have an explanatory intelligible account of the Cosmos. They are telepathic and thus are able to transmit this account to their babies as soon as they are born. Consequently, such creatures do not need holy books. Further, because this telepathic transmission is accurate and the account is not corrupted during transmission, there is no necessity for any church to safeguard the message. Their account makes the entire Cosmos – including their lives – explanatorily intelligible without ever appealing to God and this is how their story goes. The Cosmos became self-conscious. (After all, contemporary cognitive sciences tell us that consciousness is an emergent property of sufficiently complex systems. If the computers in our world could become self-conscious, why cannot the Cosmos or some possible world become conscious?) This self-conscious Cosmos 'looked' at itself, contemplated its imperfections in remorse, and planned the best of all possible worlds. Through a series of complex computations, it was able to discover the initial conditions for a perfect Cosmos. Then, it collapsed into itself in such a way that its collapse generated the initial conditions of that perfect Cosmos, where these beings live. Among other things, what makes their Cosmos perfect is that the knowledge of the Cosmos was innate in the first exemplars of the sentient species that evolved. It became explicit when such a species developed first signs of self-consciousness. Consequently, the prophets are eliminated from such a religion. Their Cosmos now exemplifies a plan and a purpose contained in the initial conditions. As such, these beings do not need God either. They are 'atheistically' religious. In this sense, it is logically possible that there could be an atheistic religion.

Of course, this is an imaginary world. Why did we have to indulge in such a thought experiment? It shows that one has to specify the conditions of the growth and transmission of a religion. That is to say, it is not enough that one removes the word 'God' in order to generate an 'atheistically religious' account. One has to make a series of assumptions about the nature of human beings, their modes of learning, their mechanisms of transmission, *etc.*, in the process of developing such an 'explanation'. The function of the thought-experiment was to draw your attention to what requires doing, if one wants to allow for an atheistic religiosity. The etymology of 'religion' is not sufficient.

There is a second reason, which is more relevant for our purposes. *In principle,* a religion could exist even if it lacked 'prophets', 'churches', 'belief in God', 'holy books', and such like. Consequently, it adds force to the argument that I made earlier on: one cannot say much about religion by looking at the properties of the Semitic religions, unless one could show that these properties accrue to them by virtue of being religions.

Our conclusion must be obvious: the above properties have to do with human limitations. That is to say, given the kind of beings we are, religion on earth will acquire these contingent properties. Put another way, for religion to exist in human cultures, some minimum adequacy conditions must hold. These conditions make assumptions about human beings, their modes of learning, and such like. Very soon, we shall see what these conditions are and what their implications will be (#9.5.2). All that is relevant for us to note here is that the idea of religious atheism is on par with the science-fiction story about those telepathic beings: both could be true, but not for us human beings – at least, not yet.

## Secularised Religion or Secular Faith?

Earlier on, I suggested that religion is a prototypical model of explanation and that this model inspires all other explanations we have. In the last few pages, I have taken a further step in elucidating this idea by speaking about the relation between religion and truth. This is what it means to suggest that religion is 'explanation pure and simple', an insight I attribute to the enlightenment thinkers. I should now like to look at the phenomenon of secularisation of religion (chapters #6 and #7) in the light of what I have said so far.

In religion, causes and reasons are fused together to such an extent that reference to one is also a reference to the other. What happens to the experience of the world – as an explanatorily intelligible entity – when a multitude of partial theories about the world comes into being?

One set of questions. These theories explain the world; or do they? What makes them into explanations of the world? What are the causes of phenomena? What is a causal relation actually? Do these theories appeal to the causal forces, or do they not? The Will of God guaranteed regularity by governing the phenomena. Today it is called the 'causal relation'. Does the notion of God name causes, or is 'cause' a secular variant of God? To those familiar with the literature in the philosophy of the sciences, nothing more need be said. To those who are not, an additional word might prove helpful. These questions are actual and current. Some argue that sciences (theories in the natural sciences) explain the world; yet others argue that it is a problem-solving activity and not explanatory at all. Some believe that our theories about the natural world identify causal relations; yet others dismiss talk about causes as doing metaphysics in the bad sense. Some think that sciences give us the truth about the world; yet others argue that we can get rid of the concept of 'truth' altogether and make perfect sense of scientific progress; and so on.

Let us consider an individual brought up within a religious tradition. He has become an atheist, or an agnostic, or whatever else, because he has lost his belief. In chapter #7, I raised the question how such an atheist could navigate himself so successfully in a secular world, if he had really switched worlds. We can now understand the phenomenon slightly better.

Such an individual would perhaps cease to believe in the existence of God. Nevertheless, the Cosmos retains its explanatory intelligibility. He might be indifferent about why some star went supernova, but such an event would not have perturbed him when he was religious either. After all, as I have said repeatedly, religion never makes any such phenomenon explanatorily intelligible; it merely structures the experience of the world that way. He might even deny that human life (as such) has any 'objective' purpose, but he believes that individuals can give meaning to their lives. As I have said, no religion ever gives meaning to any individual human life; all it does is to enable one to attribute (or find) meaning to one's life. He may argue that nothing in the universe has any 'intrinsic' worth or value and human beings make something valuable by considering it so. This is not a denial of religion, but merely a heresy: every human being is now transformed into God. An absolute denial of value can appear disorienting only in such a culture. However, nihilism denies absolutes only by making everything into an absolute.

Religion suggests the existence of a pattern, hints that an individual life fits a broader pattern. What that broader pattern is, or even how it fits, is not a question answered by religion. Other theories might come up with appropriate units, which incorporate entities just below them. As Marxism does, one could suggest that human history incorporates epochs of social production, which include the capitalist mode of production, social classes, bourgeois intellectuals, *etc.* It could also be about the 'destiny' of a people – as Nationalism suggests. However, neither becomes a religion by virtue of such a conceptualisation. These doctrines and movements, I suggest, do not generate the commitment that people have, but they merely serve to focus it.

God, human salvation through Grace, and such like may have become irrelevant to the secular world of the contemporary West. Even if such a talk fades into the background, the experience structured by it does not. Annette Baier (1980: 293) argues that

...the secular equivalent of faith in God, which we need in morality as well as in science or knowledge acquisition, is faith in the human community and its evolving procedures – in the prospects for many-handed cognitive ambitions and moral hopes.

I suggest that she is right in many ways, more than she herself real-
ises, and that we read her literally. Faith in God as a guarantor for the
regularity of the Cosmos, as a perfect being with a constant will, was a
precondition for objective knowledge of the world. Faith in the rationality of human community, in its abilities to evolve ways and procedures
that will make objective knowledge of the world possible is our secular
equivalent. In both cases, faith is related to knowledge in such a way that
faith makes knowledge possible. Seeing whether this is merely a secular
equivalent of faith, or a secularisation of faith depends upon answering
the question whether knowledge acquisition and moral progress are
possible without 'faith' – be it in God or in the 'human community'.

### 9.4.2. Controversies Illumined

Let us consider authors like Schleiermacher and Otto once again. Now
we can see conceptually what we only saw textually before (chapter #6).
A 'religious person' has to belong to a religion. We can also see how a
Schleiermacher – without fear of contradiction – can say that religion
without God could exist and that it could be better than one with God:
an atheistic religiosity is logically possible. However, we also appreciate
his profundity in this context: he ranks such a religion without God in
the lower rung of a *developmental* framework, where Christianity occu-
pies the summit. Because such an atheistic religiosity is not possible for
us human beings, an individual who intuits that the Cosmos is explanatorily intelligible – or even a tradition which has this 'sense' – is closer to
the explanatory intelligible account that religion is than someone who
merely postulates 'God' (as an *Urkraft* of sorts) to explain the universe.
This developmental ordering is only possible when we have an account,
which makes the Cosmos explanatorily intelligible. Protestantism was
such an account to Schleiermacher; after all, catholic religion degenerated and had become a 'heathen' religion.

Not only does my portrayal capture the self-description of Christianity but also those of Judaism and Islam. What makes them into religions also divides them, and this dispute is *unsolvable*. Each is a specific
religion, that is, each is an explanatory intelligible account; each makes
the Cosmos into an explanatorily intelligible entity to those who accept
this account. Some individual might switch from one to the other because one does it better than the other. Nevertheless, this religion succeeds better in making the Cosmos explanatorily intelligible to *him*. He
might even believe – and, indeed, he has to – that this superiority arises
from the fact that his religion is better than the other one. However, he
can only say this *after* another religion has made the Cosmos explanatorily intelligible to him but not *before that event*. That is to say, he can
judge that one religion is better than the other one, only after trading

places. A 'formal' conversion might (and often does) come later, but the point is that there is no vantage point for the human being to judge the superiority of one religion against the other. The reason is, of course, simple: religion must make the Cosmos intelligible to him.

My hypothesis, thus, captures both the inter-religious disputes and the relation between intolerance and faith. It also sheds light on yet another dispute.

Very often, believers make the claim that one cannot investigate the nature of religion, unless one is a believer oneself. Brilliant and reputed thinkers have tried to argue for this point of view. Their opponents accuse such people of 'bad faith', of dogmatism, and of harbouring apologetic motivations. The opponents have maintained that any phenomenon can be scientifically studied, including both religion and science. Why should one belong to a religion to discuss its nature? One does not have to be a stone to describe its fall, any more than one has to be a neurotic to discuss the nature of neurosis. Therefore, why should one have to be religious to investigate religion scientifically?

I just spoke of how a person could judge the superiority of one religion against another. One can only do so from within the framework of a religion. Only from within the framework of some religion could one judge the 'adequacy' of the other religion. To investigate religion – as an explanatory intelligible account of the Cosmos – one has to accept some or another explanatory intelligible account of the Cosmos. That is, religion can be investigated only by being religious oneself; religion is an object of investigation from within some or another religion. This position stands to reason because, as I have said, religion makes itself explanatorily intelligible too. The believers are not dogmatic when they say, as Söderblom did, that the only science of religion could be theology.

Again, it is important to note what I am saying and what I am not. Any specific doctrine within a specific religion – say, for example, the doctrine of trinity – is not either immune from criticism or beyond discussion. After all, those who do not accept it criticise and discuss this doctrine. In this sense, in all probability, every single doctrine of every religion has been discussed and criticised either by the believers or by others at one time or another. So, if a Jew can criticise the doctrine of Trinity, why not someone else, who denies the existence of God? Belonging to a religion is not equivalent to holding a party card.

We are not interested in finding out what makes some tradition into Christianity, but what makes Christianity into a *religion*. That is, investigating what makes something into an explanatory intelligible account of the Cosmos requires that one possesses such an account. From the outside, without having any such account, I cannot say *what* makes *this* account an explanatory intelligible account of the Cosmos; *why* it is this only to some and not to the others; *what* its explanatory intelligibility consists of; *etc.* These issues require investigation. To be sure, we can ask the believers to explain themselves. In such a case, we study what it means 'to believe' for these people. If we understand their answers to the 'meaning' of Cosmos and life (see the discussion about the meaning of life, #9.2.2), we will have some idea about what it means to be religious.

## 9.5. "HALLOWED BE THY NAME"

While discussing the constraints imposed by the historical facts on my hypothesis about religion, we saw that one of them had to do with the attitude of the Romans and the Indians towards the Semitic religions. Neither recognised their tradition in the description provided by these religions. Romans had *religio* but they thought that Christians were atheists; the Indians could not comprehend how they were all wrong and only Christians were right. We have noticed these facts, but not explained them. The question is this: is it possible to illumine their incomprehension using my hypothesis about religion?

There is an additional reason why the above question is important. A hasty reader of this chapter might be inclined to say that my story about religion is imprisoned within the Semitic framework; as a result, nothing is easier than argue the absence of religion elsewhere. The point I would like to make is this: according to the Semitic religions, 'Hinduism', 'Buddhism', *etc.*, are also religions (whether false ones or not). Loosely put, according to the 'Christian' concept of religion, Indians also have religions.

In the hypothesis under development, I have to account for two disjunctive facts: first, Semitic religions identified religions elsewhere; second, the others reacted in total incomprehension. If I can show how both are necessary (*i.e.* explain the 'why' of these facts), then the charge that my account is imprisoned by 'western monotheisms' loses its credibility. In the rest of what follows, I shall look at both these facts, beginning with the second.

### 9.5.1. "The Heathen in his Blindness...

In the historical chapters constituting this work, we have noticed that Christianity failed to understand the pagan traditions it encountered. I have had the occasion to trace the process of domestication of the heathens. There is a reverse side to the coin: did the heathen and pagan traditions understand the phenomenon they confronted? It is time to look at this question; doing so enables us to shed light on the vital theme of the *mechanism* of domestication.

## The Question of Symmachus

Written in the fourth century, the third *relatio* of Quintus Aurelius Symmachus, the last of the pagan prefects of Rome, is well known to the students of Antique history. Often, it is seen as an example of an early plea for religious tolerance. I would propose another interpretation, which is more in line with my story. My suggestion is that Symmachus is not pleading for *religious* tolerance. He is simply confessing to ignorance: he tells us that he does not understand religion at all. Let us listen to him again:

> Grant, I beg you, that what in our youth we took over from our fathers, we may in our old age hand on to posterity. The love of established practice is a powerful sentiment...*Everyone has his own customs, his own religious practices; the divine mind has assigned to different cities different religions to be their guardians.* Each man is given at birth a separate soul; in the same way each people is given its own special genius to take care of its destiny...If long passage of time lends validity to religious observances, we ought to keep faith with so many centuries, we ought to follow our forefathers who followed their forefathers and were blessed in so doing...
>
> And so we ask for peace for the gods of our fathers, for the gods of our native land. It is reasonable that whatever each of us worships is really to be considered one and the same. We gaze up at the same stars, the sky covers us all, the same universe compasses us. *What does it matter what practical system we adopt in our search for truth? Not by one avenue only can we arrive at so tremendous a secret.* (Barrow, Trans., 1973: 37-41; my italics.)

If we place the last two lines in its context, the drift of his argument is clear. To him, a human search for 'truth' is what *religio* is. It is a human product, an expression of human striving, and a 'practical' system. As we have seen before, it is *traditio:* the ways, customs, habits and ceremonies as developed by a people *as a people*. As there are different people, so are there different traditions. Hence, there cannot be only one avenue for arriving at a tremendous secret. Multiplicity of traditions indicates that *religio* is a creation of human communities (ancestral practices) to be venerated because of their antiquity. Each tradition is different from the other, because each is that of some people. One cannot arbitrate between traditions; every one of them belongs to a people. As an individual, who is part of a community, you continue the practice of your forefathers. However, because of the very reason that it is a human practice, you could always ask: what does it matter what practical system human beings adopt in their search for truth?

By speaking of 'divine assignment', Symmachus appears willing to grant the following: Christianity is the practice of a people. That is, he is prepared to accept that Christianity is also a tradition. However, if Christianity is also a tradition, he cannot understand why the Christians continue to deny the others their own tradition. Symmachus is caught in this quandary.

He is unable to see the gulf separating the two: *religio* as a tradition of a people; religion as God's gift to humankind. By expressing a willingness to classify Christianity as another practical system, as one more expression of the human striving after truth, Symmachus is doubly blind: to the claim that religion is the truth as revealed by God; as a consequence, to the very existence of religion.

How could the last pagan prefect of Rome, evidently an intellect of no mean standing, not understand what every Christian writer had been saying for nearly three centuries before the *relatio* was composed? A random citation, from the period of the Apostolic Fathers (from an epistle dated to have been composed about 124 C.E.), should give the reader a flavour of *how* the Christians were describing their own religion. In *The Epistle to Diognetus* (translated by Staniforth), purporting to be a "reply to an inquiring heathen's desire for information about the beliefs and customs of Christians" (*ibid*: 171), an anonymous writer explains thus:

> The doctrines they (the Christians) profess is not the invention of busy human minds and brains, nor are they, like some, adherents of this or that school of human thought...
>
> As I said before, it is not an earthly discovery that has been entrusted to them. The thing they guard so jealously is no product of mortal thinking, and what has been committed to them is the stewardship of no human mysteries. The Almighty Himself, the Creator of the universe, the God whom no eye can discern, has sent down His very own Truth from heaven, His own holy and incomprehensible Word, to plant it among men and ground it in their hearts...(*ibid*: 176-178).

Symmachus might have been willing to pay Christianity the greatest tribute his culture possibly could: recognise that Christians too had their own way, their own practical system. To the Christian ears, fittingly perhaps, any such pagan tribute would have sounded like blasphemy.

Nearly 1400 years later, in another place, another time, and by another people, such a tribute was paid. The recipient too had changed somewhat. The Hindu 'priests' of the coastal town of Malabar (*i.e.* the

Brahmins) assured Bartolomaeus Ziegenbalg, a Lutheran missionary during the early eighteenth century,

> For as Christ in Europe was made Man, so here our God Wischtnu was born among the Malabarians; and as you hope for Salvation through Christ; so we hope for Salvation thought Wischtnu; and to save you one way, and us another, is one of the Pastimes and Diversions of Almighty God. (*Ziegenbalg Papers*, excerpted in Young 1981: 23; under the heading, you guessed it, "Religious plurality".)

The heathen, as a famous hymn tells us, is blind. Blind to what? To *the truth*, of course. Not merely are they blind to the truth, as revealed by the scriptures and as announced by the coming of The Saviour, but to its very existence. If the Christians did not understand the Pagans, the latter were defective too; they were blind. What you see in my hypothesis about religion is this: why people like Symmachus had to be blind and talk the way they did.

As I have argued before, religion is the truth, its own foundation. It exists by itself, and its truth is not dependent on whether the other beliefs we hold are true. Being a reflexive entity, it is accessible only to those who are *part* of such an account. Heathens and pagans cannot testify to the truth of religion because this truth is not accessible to those *outside* it. Religion is what it says about itself and what it says about itself is the truth. That is to say, it is in the very nature of religion that those who do not have it in their midst are blind to its existence.

Because religion renders the heathens blind to its existence, it is obvious how they treat it: as merely one avenue to a 'tremendous secret'; as another tradition; as acceptable as any other system in search of truth. Both the Indians and the Romans were blind to religion, because they had no such phenomenon. Knowing only human certainties, how could they recognise an account that made both the Cosmos and itself explanatorily intelligible? Possessing only human knowledge, how could they recognise *the divine truth*? Having only human striving, how could they ever grasp God's gift to humankind?

### The Sight Restored

Religion cannot cause only blindness. If it did, it could not spread at all. It has spread and continues to spread. The empirical circumstances of conversion do not concern us. We need to identify the mechanism of conversion, as it is relevant to the story.

Though blind to the divine truth, the heathen is cognisant of human certainties. His certainties regarding his tradition reflect the character of traditions as such: customs handed down with their 'origin' lost in time; lore, legends and myths; *etc.* An individual located in a tradition is always fallible. There is no cognitive certainty that he is continuing the tradition. In the *first* moment, religion amplifies this uncertainty and fallibility. There is no 'guarantee' that the transmission was accurate; the accumulated stories and legends do not agree with each other... That is to say, religion plays upon the very nature of tradition to *efface* its *otherness* as tradition.

In which way is a tradition the *other* of religion? The predicates 'true' and 'false' are not applicable to a tradition because it is a set of practices (see #2.2.1). By thematising this as a belief-guided and theoretically founded set of practices, religion transforms the very terms of description. Practical certainties are provided with something they never had or ever needed: a theoretical foundation (see also further #11.3.3). This foundation, of course, is the set of stories, legends, *etc.*, that surround a group of practices collectively called 'tradition' by those who follow it.

Now comes the *second* moment. The otherness of the tradition is effaced by *transforming* it into *another.* Another what? Why, another religion of course. "Other people have other traditions; your tradition is other than mine"– such is the heathen perception of himself and others. However, when transformed into another religion, this tradition (which is both uncertain and fallible) acquires a property it never had: *reflexivity.* When religion confronts the transformed tradition as a 'mere another', it does so by providing it with a 'deeper' foundation. The inconsistent myths and legends, the relative 'novelty' of a practice that was alleged to have been preserved from times immemorial, express a deeper truth. Pagan traditions have retained intimations of their original nature. To put in a slightly different form, realising that one had hitherto entertained false beliefs is not merely to be aware of this fact but also to recognise it as an expression of the thirst for truth. If you believe in the Devil, that is because you want to believe in God. That is to say, the fallibilities of the transformed tradition are testimonials not only to its falsity but also to the awareness of its own falsity. In short, it is a false religion.

In the *third* moment, not only is one's own tradition made to appear false, but also those of others. All of them are false religions. They are that in exactly the same way. They do not see that their search for truth was never 'their' search; they seek truth because of a past when they had that truth; though forgotten, their erring ways have preserved the memory of this past; that is why they do not see that the search for truth was never 'their' search...

These are the abstract, logical moments of the mechanism of conversion. This is also how Christianity grew: by absorbing the Roman cultic deities by transforming them into demons (*i.e.* as minions of the

Devil); by disputing with the 'absurd tales of the poets'; by developing its theology; *etc.*

In simple terms, the basic mechanism in the spread of religion is its *effacing of the otherness of the other.* The other is transformed into an 'image' of the self. Otherness becomes another variant of the self. There is no 'other' to religion – but merely another religion.

Effacing the otherness is possible if and only if there is a framework, which does not allow an otherness. A universal human history is the framework, which makes it possible to deny the *other* to religion. Having transformed a real or imaginary past of a people (the Jews) into the universal history of the humankind, Christianity developed its own theology to enable the transformation of the other into another of itself. That is to say, the theology of Christian faith begins to take shape in polemics with the heathens because of the mutually reinforcing relationship between the creation of a universal history and transforming the other into another.

This is how the heathen and the pagan – peoples without religions – are incorporated into theology. They are members of the pagan religions. Religion is invisible to the pagan as long as *otherness* is a practical certainty. It is a practical certainty as long as he remains within the folds of a tradition. When he enters the process of 'conversion' – whose cognitive steps are described as the logical moments of proselytisation – then the otherness of all traditions becomes the same kind of 'anotherness'. When this happens, scales fall from his eyes, and his sight is restored. He is now a member of a religion, because he had formerly belonged to a false religion.

The otherness of the traditions thus disappears within the framework of the reflexive entity that religion is. Which 'other' could there be to an account that makes all that was, is, and will be, including itself, explanatorily intelligible? Having no 'other', religion merely postulates other religions.

It is impossible that India does not have religion; it merely has another religion. It is impossible that pagans do not worship; the "heathen in his blindness", as our Good bishop Reginald Heber's hymn continues,

### 9.5.2. ...*bows Down to Wood and Stone*"

Consider the image of a woman kneeling before the cross or even a statue of the Virgin Mary in an attitude of worship and supplication. This is a classic example of religious practice, if anything is. The most obvious question raised by this image is about the adequacy of my characterisation of religion. Is my description able to deal with such a practice satisfactorily? That is to say, can I capture a very vital dimension of religion, *viz.* the act of worship? Without introducing *ad hoc* modifications, can I embed a characteristically religious practice in my hypothesis about religion? Why have religions emphasised the worship of God so much and, equally importantly, decried idolatry? Why does faith in God express itself in worship? Why does accepting His purposes include worship? Is this a necessary property of religion or merely a contingent one? Put differently: why should worship be *a testimony of faith?*

A fair challenge. This is one of the phenomenological adequacy tests, which my hypothesis has to pass. In the pages to follow, I shall examine the extent to which it is possible to answer these questions. On the one hand, faith must express itself in worship. On the other, worship can be a purely outward manifestation without faith. What is the relationship between the two?

### Constraints on Religion

My characterisation of religion has so far been silent on two issues: who provides such an account? To whom is it provided? My science fiction story shows that religion could exist without God (doctrines, churches, prophets, *etc.*) and that the recipients need not be human beings. However, as soon as we speak of religion amidst human communities, several constraints come into operation. Let me call them the conditions for the existence of religion among human beings (see #9.4.1).

As human beings, we know of only one kind of intelligibility account, *viz.* that which appeals to reasons or purposes. Because religion makes both itself and the Cosmos intelligible, both embody the reasons or purposes of some entity or being, which is capable of having reasons or purposes and acting accordingly. For the sake of convenience, let us call such an entity 'God'. Consequently, as soon as we say that human beings have religion, we require that God has provided such an account. That is to say, existence of creatures like us with religion requires that God has provided such an explanatory intelligible account. In this sense, the *first* contingent property that religion acquires amidst human beings (but a necessary condition for the existence of such an account among us) is that God is such an entity.

It is important not to be confused by the previous sentences. As I have said earlier on (#9.4.2), why some set of doctrines makes the Cosmos explanatorily intelligible to some person and not to another is a question I cannot answer. It is a question internal to a religion. All I am saying is that to those who have such an account, it is obvious that God gave the doctrines, which make the Cosmos into such an entity. Their attitude stands to reason, human reason. To those who are religious, religion is the proof for the existence of God. That is why the notion of God is internal to a religion and not a concept that could be meaningfully discussed using modal logics (see #7.2.2).

The *second* contingent property that religion acquires among human beings is that some claim is made about the kind of beings to whom such an account is provided. Human beings are part of the purposes of God, *i.e.* they fulfil some purpose or another. The specification of these purposes says something about the kind of beings that humans are. That is, religion must specify the addressee of the message. Let us say, some kind of anthropology is required.

Further, this message also tells these beings what that purpose is. It must be possible for them to achieve that purpose – otherwise there would be no intelligibility to the doctrine. Therefore, accepting God's purpose is to seek and achieve the purposes that God has given to humankind.

God's purposes are not exhausted by the act of any particular individual or community at some place or time. Hence, an eschatology (because the purpose can be achieved), or a goal for humankind as a whole, is part of such a message.

In the above sense, religion in human communities postulates a relation between human beings and God's will. Human beings are there for a purpose; their nature is such that they can achieve the purpose. Accepting the purpose of God lends explanatory intelligibility to human life because human beings can find meaning to their lives only by trying to achieve that goal. Thus, the *third* empirical property of religion: in human communities, it must postulate a relation between God and human beings.

Not merely must religion speak of God's purposes, why human beings are there and what their goal is, but also *how* this goal can be achieved. That is, specifying God's purposes involves giving the reason for the existence of humankind; the goal it ought to pursue; and the means for achieving it. This, then, is the *fourth* contingent property: an explanatory intelligible account of the Cosmos must speak of the means through which such an account continues to be explanatorily intelligible. Such means must itself be part of that account.

*Worship*, I would like to suggest, is the *means* through which an explanatory intelligible account continues to retain its character to the believers. Worship sustains and expresses faith. True worship requires and strengthens faith. Without faith, one cannot truly worship. In worship, man expresses his faith in God; that is, affirms that he is using the means required to be a part of the purposes of God. In so doing, he is affirming himself as the kind of a creature who is capable of so doing.

Thus, we can also appreciate why *doctrines* are a crucial component of religion and why they are not that at the same time. It is a property that religion acquires, if it exists among human beings. This is the *fifth* contingent property. (Now we can appreciate the full force of the science fiction example.) Because the means through which God's purposes can be achieved is itself rooted in doctrines, my explication captures the attempt of the believers to find 'scriptural grounds' for worship. As Samuel Clarke expounds in *A Discourse Concerning the Being and Attributes of GOD, The Obligations of Natural Religion, and the Truth and Certainty of the Christian Revelation* (eighth edition, 1732: 288-297):

> In *what particular Manner,* and with *what kind of Service* he [God] will be worshipped, cannot be certainly discovered by bare reason...*what Propitiation* he will accept, and *in what Manner* this reconciliation must be made; here Nature stops, and expects with impatience the aid of some particular Revelation. The God will receive returning Sinners, and accept Repentance instead of perfect Obedience. *They* cannot *certainly know,* to whom he had not declared that he *will* do so. (Excerpted in Pailin 1984: 175-76; italics in the original.)

The concrete specification of the purposes of God (consequently, the means for fulfilling the purposes of God) depends on the doctrine in question. Each explanatory intelligible account defines that for itself.

We can see why worship is a concept internal to religious life and religious doctrines. Worship involves seeing the Cosmos as explanatorily intelligible; and doing what is necessary – as the doctrine in question specifies it – in order to continue to experience the Cosmos in this way. It is the means for the reproduction of religion because it links anthropology, eschatology, *etc.*, to each other. Without such a link, each would fall apart from the other. Further, what it links are doctrines, *i.e.* messages about each of the above aspects.

At the same time, worship appears as an attitude and a feeling: an expression of trust. One who worships is being religious within a tradition, carrying out the act, as his religion requires it.

If we now return to the image of the woman kneeling in an act of worship, we can see how my description is able to account for her attitude. She is affirming the relationship between herself and God by using the means provided by her religion. That is, she is reproducing what Cosmos is to her: an explanatorily intelligible entity.

### The Sin of Idolatry

We are now in a position to tie one or two loose threads together. We have seen how religion effaces the otherness of tradition by transforming it into another religion. Such a false religion, gifted with a pseudo-reflexivity, is also said to have a god. I need not tell you who or what that god is; Luther can do it for me.

(R)eason never finds the true God, but it finds the devil or its own concept of God, ruled by the devil. So there is a vast difference between knowing that there is a God and knowing who or what God is. Nature knows the former...it is inscribed in everybody's heart; the latter is taught only by the Holy Spirit. (*Luther's Works* 19, 55; cited in Harrison 1990: 8 and note 13 to that page.)

A pseudo-mechanism is provided to enable the false religion to reproduce itself. Needless to say, Devil's worship was castigated as idolatry. In the early periods, it connoted false worship, *i.e.* the worship of the false god. However, as Christianity expanded, so did the concept: it now incorporated many things including the worship of animals and images.

In a way, the last sentence is preposterous. Despite what is and was written about other people, it is always difficult to write-off other cultures as stupid: I mean, which Indian *worships* (as I have just explained the notion) the cow? Which pagan ever worshipped images? How did he ever 'bow down to wood and stone'?

Many before me have thought about this issue too. Brian Morris tells us (1987: 102), surely an exaggeration, that anthropology had to wait until the beginning of the twentieth century to realise that

no people worshipped material objects simply as material objects; that animals, plants, and inanimate objects were simply symbols. Thus Taylor initiated a symbolic approach...to magico-religious phenomena.

Exaggeration or not, this exhibits the problem I have tackled at length in the seventh chapter. 'God', 'worship', 'prayer', 'eschatology', *etc.*, are concepts internal to religion. Use them and you are forced to do theology because you are forced to accept that the heathen does worship cows, monkeys, serpents, their images, and such like. In the twentieth century, it is difficult to sing Bishop Heber's hymn openly in the Church. Hence, a 'symbolic' approach seems necessary to explain *as* worship, an act that is, perhaps, not worship at all...

In this context, another intriguing question arises. We could almost rewrite the history of Christianity, Judaism and Islam in terms of their hatred of idolatry. Given their theology, such an attitude is perfectly understandable. Is my account able to explicate the notion of idolatry as well?

The answer is both a 'no' and a 'yes'. No, because the notion of what constitutes false worship is specific to a given set of theological doctrines. A hypothesis about religion, which talks about the object that religion is, cannot attempt to explain idolatry.

Nevertheless, the answer is also a 'yes'. By appealing to the dynamic of religion, I shall show that idolatry has another dimension as well. It too can be illumined the way religious practice of worship has been. Because the Semitic religions fought their alleged religious rivals on grounds of false worship as well, our question becomes: how is battle against idolatry involved in the spread of religion? I shall return to this issue at the end of the eleventh chapter (#11.4.2), once we have seen more about both the mechanism of the spread of religion and the consequences attached to it. For now, let us see where we are and what we have achieved.

## A Summary

At the beginning of this chapter, I invited you to look at it as a conceptual reproduction of our earlier journey. Without doubt, the account of religion provided here is the first phase in building a theory about this object. That is why it had to pass through some adequacy tests.

By using the history of rivalry between Christianity and the others, I argued that Christianity recognises itself as religion – not merely as Christianity – and considers some others as rival religions by placing emphasis on some kinds of doctrines. These doctrines have 'something' to do with God. Factually and historically, Judaism and Islam have done the same.

The argument, simplistically put, takes the form of a conditional: if Christianity is a religion, so are Judaism and Islam. The rule of inference *modus ponens* will prove the consequent true, if the antecedent is true and the conditional holds.

The problem, of course, is to show the truth of the antecedent and argue that the conditional holds. I have done it by characterising religion as an explanatory intelligible account; by showing that this portrayal is sufficient to account for the multiple descriptions given by people belonging to different groups within Christianity. The *prima facie* opposition between 'faith' and 'belief' is overcome, as well as the apparent inconsistency in the Schleiermacherian claim about the possibility of religion without God. The same description allows us to derive the necessity of religious rivalry along the lines historically observed by us. If this characterisation helps us both to capture the self-description of Christianity and derive the lines along which religious rivalry should proceed; and it is the case that the rivalry between Judaism, Islam, Christianity has crystallised along these lines; and, if, furthermore, both Judaism and Islam have identified exactly the same rivals as Christianity has done and along the same lines; all these, together, lend credibility to the truth of the conditional even where neither Judaism nor Islam have the word 'religion' in their vocabularies.

Thus, I can suggest that the conditional holds. Because religion is an explanatory intelligible account, Christianity is a religion. All religions must identify their rivals along certain lines suggested by the above account. Judaism, Islam, and Christianity have done this both with respect to each other and with some others. Christianity has described this rivalry as *religious* rivalry. Therefore, whether or not the word exists in Judaism and Islam, they are religions too. In this manner, the antecedent is shown to be true as well. Even though our starting point was language-use, the basis of my argument has been subject to adequacy tests that have little to do with language-use.

My portrayal has brought together both the emphasis on doctrines and the importance of faith by showing what their interrelationship is. This tight connection is not at just one level, but at several different levels. I have been able to explain the sense in which religious language is its own meta-language; capture the insight of the enlightenment thinkers regarding the connection between religion and explanation; exhibit both the necessity of religious rivalry and the *drive* towards ecumenism.

I have taken up the challenges posed to my characterisation of religion too: I have argued that my hypothesis is not intellectualistic by showing how it can account for faith, religious experience, worship – all three typically 'subjective' dimensions of religion. I have explained too why heathens could not recognise themselves in the descriptions provided by Christianity, Judaism and Islam. In the early chapters, I had argued that concepts like 'worship', 'God', 'religion', *etc.* were part of a religious language and vocabulary. With respect to worship, we can see why: it links doctrines and is embedded in them. The same must also be evident with respect to the other concepts referred to earlier.

If all the notions that one uses to study religion belong to the self-description of religion, what does it entail? Does it mean, then, that we cannot 'scientifically' study religion at all unless we are believers ourselves? There might still be a way to study religion without being religious. Drobin puts it this way:

> Philosophies and theologies are explicit logical systems. They can be studied in the same manner as mathematical propositions and their consequences. *Religions are implicit world views. They can be studied only through implicit world views* (Drobin 1982: 273; italics mine).

If we take this citation at its face value, it might be possible to study religion without being a believer, if one can show that religion can be studied under the description of a worldview. To show this is to argue that one can legitimately replace the concept 'religion' by the concept 'worldview', because the description that picks out a worldview also picks a religion out. This is what I shall look at in the next chapter.

At the beginning of the fifth chapter, I asked you to imagine a doubly hypothetical situation where we would stumble across a culture (either living or dead) without religion. In the next chapter, I will try to argue that such a situation is not hypothetical. As a preparatory exercise for the next stage of our journey, let me invite you to...

# CHAPTER TEN

# "IMAGINE, THERE IS NO RELIGION..."

We have come to appreciate why one cannot study religion *as* an explanatorily intelligible account of the Cosmos without entering that framework. If you cannot study some object at one level of description –in our case religion, and the level of description is its own self-description – it does not mean that you cannot study that object at all. Any object can be described at various levels, *i.e.* different kinds of true descriptions are possible. A human being, to give but one example, can be studied at different levels: at the level of cell-biology, at the level of physiology and anatomy, at the psychological level, social level, *etc.* At each of these levels, we could give a true description of the creature that a human being is, without being clear about the relation between these different levels of description.

Exactly the same point could hold for religion too. Using its self-description and study religion *as* religion forces us to be religious ourselves. Consequently, it would be better if we could look at the same object from another level of description, *viz.* as worldviews. In the first section, I will argue that we can indeed do so. To do that, it must be possible for us to show that the concept 'worldview' is a description of the same object that religion is. In section #10.1, I argue that substituting 'worldview' for 'religion' is defensible. In the first part (#10.1.1), I show that religions are good examples of worldviews by arguing that such a substitution of terms does make a fundamental difference to some of the definitions of the concept of religion. In the second part (#10.1.2), not only do I show additional advantages of the substitution, but also suggest that religions are the best examples of worldviews. I make this suggestion by briefly describing the properties of worldviews. At that stage, we discover that the property of religion is carried over in a description of worldviews. In this sense, Drobin is right: religion can be studied as a worldview because religion is also a worldview. We realise that even though religion is 'more' than a worldview and worldview is different from religion, we have difficulties in identifying worldviews that are not religions.

At this juncture, the two central themes of this essay get picked up. Our enquiry into the nature of religion is motivated by the failure to find empirical and theoretical support for the claim that religion is a cultural universal. Given that we now have a preliminary characterisation of religion as (a) an explanatorily intelligible account of the Cosmos and itself and (b) as a worldview, we can look at the question of religion in India. In section #10.2, the burden is to show that Indian culture cannot be characterised under either of these two descriptions. I argue this on grounds of two impossibilities: a metaphysical and sociological impossibility.

The second of the two central themes, 'why have the western intellectuals believed that religion is a cultural universal?' is taken up in the third section (#10.3). Consistent with the earlier arguments in the previous chapters, I speak of the secularisation of religion. Now, however, I take the first step to shed light on this process by locating it in the dynamic of religion. Thus, slowly, but surely, the object-level argument and the meta-level track begin converging once again. In the subsequent chapter, they meet: at that stage, we shall see what answers we have to our meta-problem.

## 10.1 ON THE VERY IDEA OF A WORLDVIEW

In the definitions and/or explications of the concept of religion, one appeals to notions that belong to the domain of theology: 'belief in God or gods', 'experience of the divine', 'faith' and 'worship', *etc.* It is religion that tells us what 'God' is and who the 'gods' are; what it is to experience the divine; and what constitutes 'faith' or 'worship'. Consequently, to use these concepts as explications of the concept of religion, I have suggested, is to accept some or another variant of theology as the general framework for the study of religion. While there is no objection to the study of religion within the confines of, say, a Christian theology, it does not solve the problem of whether religion is a cultural universal.

Could we solve the problem if we address ourselves to the task of describing religion in terms of worldviews? There are two issues here. The first issue is whether the concept of worldview could legitimately replace the concept of religion. Secondly, because we now have a characterisation of religion, we need to ascertain whether the word 'worldview' refers to religion. In this section, I shall tackle both these issues. In #10.1.1, I will look at the first; in #10.1.2, we shall see what the answer to the other entails.

### 10.1.1. A First Line of Defence

To what exactly does the proposal to replace 'religion' with 'worldview' amount? Should we define religion in terms of worldviews? There are several reasons why it does not make much sense to see 'worldviews' as an explication or *definiens* of the term 'religion'. The *first* of them has to do with the objection that one will then be defining the obscure in terms of the more obscure. *Second,* our arguments should not depend on any one particular definition of religion since changes in the *definiens* make the investigation and the results useless. *Third,* as I have been at pains to argue, we should avoid the terminological and definitional disputes as much as we possibly can. Debates about these issues are at best sterile and at worst counterproductive at this stage. *Fourth,* the task is to study religion and not the concept 'religion'. *Fifth* and finally, all we need (at this moment) is a way of referring to what the believers call 'religion'. Whatever the truth may be, that is, whether religion is God-given or fabricated, whether divinely inspired or neurotically induced, we merely need a general term to pick out this object without having to take recourse to theology.

For these reasons, 'worldview' is not an explicit definition of the concept of religion. Nevertheless, this does not mean that the introduction of this term is a fiat. There are several adequacy tests we can subject this concept to. The first is to find out whether 'worldview' and 'religion' do refer to the same entity. The second is to see whether any additional clarity or advantage accrues to us by virtue of this substitution.

To say what these tests are and show what may be gained by a replacement would justify our decision to allow 'worldview' to substitute for 'religion'.

*Religion and Worldview: A Preliminary Foray*

Not only is the notion of worldview vexed, so is the relation between it and 'religion' (see, *e.g.* the articles in Marshall, *et al.,* Eds., 1989). The German concept *Weltanschauung,* apparently first coined by Kant (Wolters 1989), became popular in the tradition of German Idealism and Romanticism. The same author claims that the anglicised equivalent, 'worldview', has a recorded usage since 1858 which indexes the relative novelty of this notion. Since then, it has gained currency in many social sciences (Griffioen 1989) winning popularity, if not any additional clarity. Ninian Smart, one of the most prolific writers in the field of comparative religious studies, has been championing (see his 1981, 1983, 1987, 1989) the idea that we need to view both secular ideologies (like Marxism and nationalism) and religions as different species of the genus worldviews. In this sense, many have suggested that there is an intimate connection between worldviews and religions, and that we may profitably use the notion of worldview even in religious studies.

A partial solution to the vexation lies in not defining religion in terms of worldview but the latter in terms of the former. That is to say, I want to suggest that a most perspicuous way of saying what worldviews are is to pick out an example, *viz.* religion. It is not that some specific web of religious beliefs constitutes a worldview, but that the best way of saying what it is for something to be a worldview is to pick out a religion. That is to say, we can get-by with the assumption that religions are good examples of worldviews.

At this stage of our argument, doing so merely entails accepting the idea that religions are also worldviews, whatever the status of the latter might be. Before something can be accorded the exalted and edifying position of being a religion, it must wear the more lowly and mundane garbs of a worldview. Therefore, this terminological decision does not have any great theoretical repercussions. Consequently, we are now entitled to take the second step and see whether the replacement of concepts creates any special difficulties.

*Religion and Worldview: A Secondary Foray*

Let us begin by considering what Paul Tillich, a Christian theologian of some stature, has to say about the nature of religion. Speaking to the lay public (1958: 41-42), he addresses himself to characterising the "predicament of western man" as one of having lost depth by losing religion.

> The decisive element in the predicament of western man in our period is his loss of dimension of depth...What does it mean?
>
> It means that man has lost an answer to the question: what is the meaning of life? Where do we come from, where do we go? What shall we do, what should we become in the short stretch between birth and death? Such questions are not answered or even asked if the "dimension of depth" is lost...I suggest that we call the dimension of depth the religious dimension in man's nature. Being religious means asking passionately the question of meaning of our existence and being willing to receive answers.

Consider now what Olthuis (1989: 26), another Christian theologian of a somewhat lesser stature, has to say when he waxes eloquent on the subject of the "ultimate questions of life":

> The ultimate questions of life lie deep within the heart of everyone. Who am I? Where am I going? What's it all about? Is there a god? How can I live and die happily? Everyone formulates some answer to these questions about the human condition, if only partially and implicitly. The answer

we give may be referred to as our worldview, or vision of life. It may or
may not be thematized or codified, but it makes up the framework of
fundamental considerations which give context, direction, and meaning
to our lives.

From this citation, it would appear as though these 'fundamental' questions – including whether there is a God – are innate species-specific
questions, which human beings ask. Because the answers constitute a
worldview, the ultimate questions must be prior to and independent of
the worldviews. The differences in worldviews appear to reside in the
different answers they give to this set of questions. When he warms to
his subject, the claims take a more radical form:

> A worldview (or vision of life) is a framework or set of fundamental beliefs
> through which we view the world and our calling and future in it. The
> vision need not be fully articulated: it may be so internalised that it goes
> largely unquestioned; it may not be explicitly developed into a systematic
> conception of life; it may not be theoretically deepened into philosophy;
> it may not be even codified into creedal form; it may be greatly refined
> through cultural-historical development. Nevertheless, this vision is a
> channel for the ultimate beliefs which give direction and meaning to life. It
> is the integrative and interpretative framework by which order and disor-
> der are judged; it is the standard by which reality is managed and pursued;
> it is the set of hinges on which all our everyday thinking and doing turns.
>
> Although a vision of life is held by individuals, it is communal in scope
> and structure. Since a worldview gives the terms of reference by which
> the world and our place in it can be structured and illumined, a worldview
> binds its adherents together into community. Allegiance to a common vi-
> sion promotes the integration of individuals into a group (*ibid*: 29).

The invitation to contrast these two writers has less to do with the literary merits of their respective styles than with their subject matter. One is
talking as a believer about the religion and the other, again as a believer,
about worldviews. Important for us to note is that we could switch the
word 'religion' or 'worldview' in both these descriptions without noticing the difference. Even the *ambiguity* in their characterisations is of the
same kind. It is not clear in Tillich whether religion is an answer to the
'fundamental questions' or whether these could only be raised within
the framework of religion. (For an illuminating discussion of Tillich's
characterisation of religion, see Clayton 1980.) The same ambiguity is
also retained in Olthuis' description of a worldview.

Moving from theologians to anthropologists and sociologists merely
reinforces this impression. Consider how Clifford Geertz, an anthropologist of some stature, defines (1966: 4) the subject:

(1) a system of symbols which acts to (2) establish powerful, pervasive, and long-lasting moods and motivations in men by (3) formulating conceptions of a general order of existence and (4) clothing these conceptions with such an aura of factuality that (5) the moods and motivations seem uniquely realistic.

Talcott Parsons, the American sociologist, introducing Max Weber to the English-speaking audience, describes Weber's vision on the issue in terms of

a pattern or programme *for life as a whole*, which is given meaning by an existential conception of the universe, and within it the human condition in which...action is to be carried out. (Parsons 1963: xxxiii; italics in the original.)

As Roland Robertson expresses it, Weber was interested in

the basic perspectives around which a group or a society of individuals "organise" their life – their basic orientations to human and social life, conceptions of time, the meaning of death: in fact the basic cosmological conceptions in relation to human existence. (Cited in O'Toole 1984: 22.)

Geertz is defining 'religion'; Parsons is introducing Weber's *Sociology of Religion* and, in the process, talking about the latter's conception of religion. Again, for all the difference it makes, both could be talking about worldview.

As last examples, suppose I say that building a worldview involves a "quest for unity in a disordered life" (Gordon Allport); or that having one entails "a conviction of harmony between ourselves and the universe at large" (John McTaggart). Would you find it particularly disturbing? Most probably not. However, the *explicatum* in these cases, as both authors would have it, is 'religion' but not 'worldview'. This situation is indicative of the probability that we are talking about the same phenomenon whether we use the concept 'religion' or 'worldview'.

As I see it, the only reason for doubting whether 'religion' and 'worldview' refer to one and the same phenomenon has to do with the possibility that there could be worldviews which are not religions (like, for example, a 'scientific' worldview) and that religion is 'more' than a worldview. The first possibility requires further examination, whereas the second can be looked into immediately.

## 10.1.2. A Second Line of Defence

In a way, I have already admitted the possibility that the concept 'religion' could mean more than the concept 'worldview': explicating the
former requires making use of theological concepts and the same cannot be said of the latter. Further, I have suggested that we need to find
a way of talking about what the believers call 'religion' without having
to subscribe to its self-description. I do not know what religion "really"
is (*i.e.* whether or not it is God's gift to humankind), but to speak about
this entity from the outside, I need a concept. If religion is a good example of worldview, it merely means that 'religion is *also* a worldview'
and *not* that 'religion is nothing but a worldview'.

As a further strengthening of this case, consider attempts like those
of Eliade and Durkheim. As we have seen, the one defines religion as an
"encounter with the divine"; the other does it relative to the "sacred and
the profane". While this might appear an obvious characterisation of
religion, many will not subscribe to a similar description of worldview.
There is no plausibility whatsoever to the claim that "worldview is an
encounter with the sacred" or that it is "an experience of the *mysterium
tremendum et fascinans*".

The difference between these two concepts appears less of a handi-
cap and more of an advantage: one cannot smuggle in theology without
much ado; one has to be more explicit about such moves.

Despite these considerations, there is a problem. What does the
claim that religion is more than a worldview amount to? It could suggest that worldviews are the more fundamental entities from which
religions emerge; or it could suggest that worldviews describe an object partially, whereas religion describes itself more fully *etc.* Let us see
whether talking of what we know about religion and worldview helps
settle the problem.

### Reflexivity in Religion

Recollect my earlier suggestion that religion is both the outer-boundary
of the Christian (Islamic, Judaic) self-consciousness as well as the entity
designated by that term. I said that religious language is both the object
language and its own meta-language. At that stage of the argument, we
were not in a position to understand why this should be so or even what
it indicated. Now is the time to explicate the suggestion further.

I have argued that religion is an explanatory intelligible account of
both the Cosmos and itself. It must make itself explanatorily intelligible
because it makes the Cosmos into such an entity, and avoids a crippling
circularity by placing the origin of this account outside those who ac-

cept it. In simple and simplified steps, both the problem and its solution are as follows:

    *step 1:* Created by God, the Cosmos exhibits His purpose;

    *step 2:* We know this because God has revealed it;

    *step 3:* God's revelation consists precisely of both the previous steps including this step.

As an account, religion tells us what the Cosmos is like (step 1); makes itself into an object by telling us how we could know that such is the case (step 2); characterises both itself as an account and the account of the Cosmos as true (step 3). What is paradoxical, perhaps even impossible, when viewed from the standpoint of finite individuals with finite knowledge and abilities, ceases being so when claimed to instantiate the infinite knowledge of some 'totally other' kind of being. The problem we could have with respect to such knowledge is not epistemic but hermeneutic in nature: our interpretative abilities are finite; therefore, the sense that we could make of this knowledge is fallible. Unless, of course, this Divine Being also helps us out in this case. Candour requires me to add: rumour has it that this Being is known to do precisely that, even if His criteria for selecting individuals remain rather vague and mysterious.

Looked at in terms of what human beings do and what they think of it, Religion involves a peculiar kind of reflexivity. It is its own justification, its own truth, founded on nothing that is human. Given the nature of this object, we need not wonder anymore that we have to take recourse to religious/theological vocabulary in order to explicate the concept of religion.

As I said then, I reiterate now, we could nevertheless begin a study of what the believers call 'religion'. This object will get its Gestalt and form the way we human beings see it. The concepts, the categories, the methods we use in such a study will appeal to the *merely* human, the *merely* fallible, and the *merely* conjectural. One cannot claim that our object of investigation is also what "religion really is" because what religion "really is" includes what religion (as an explanatory intelligible account of the Cosmos) says about itself.

With this in mind, let us now turn our attention to worldviews. What do we know about them? To what extent would we be able to recognise the object of our study?

*Worldviews*

Consider a doctrine that claims to be a worldview. *First,* as a view of the world, it is also knowledge of the world. *Second,* being knowledge of the world, it claims to be the view of the world. It is both decidable and undecidable: it is decidable because it is knowledge and, therefore, we can know whether it is 'true' or 'false'; it is undecidable because we could never view the world. We can only have a perspectival relationship within the world and with respect to a finite slice of the world. Consequently, a worldview is possible only for that being which is outside the world but not to those inside it. Therefore, either that being outside the Cosmos (or the world – I am using these two terms synonymously) or those who have received it directly from such a being could have a worldview. It follows from this, that if there is only one such being, there can only be one worldview. Furthermore, because it is knowledge, only one view could be true. *Third,* because of these properties, a worldview can only be universal. That is to say, what is true for a perspective and what is required for some perspective to be true (time, space and a cultural location give us a perspective – which is 'true' only under these restrictions) is not applicable to a worldview. *Fourth,* the borders of a community can be drawn along the lines of those who have this knowledge and those who do not. *Fifth,* we can now appreciate both why revelation is crucial to religion (receiving the view of the world from the 'transcendent' entity), and why religions are intolerant of each other. A worldview cannot be anything else. *Sixth,* the attitude of a culture having a worldview is understandable as well. As the Roman Catholic Bishops of Belgium tell us, other cultures (like, say, India) do have "rays of lights" in their midst but not the truth. This is understandable because a worldview can explain a perspectival relationship and not the other way round.

In other words, those properties that appear to be true of worldviews are also those of religions. Further, as we have seen while discussing Tillich and Olthuis, even the ambiguity with respect to worldview is applicable to religion: that is, whether they answer the "ultimate questions of life" or whether they enable you to formulate them. It appears to me that we have more than sufficient ground to argue that religion is not merely a good example of a worldview but also the *best* one.

*On the Nature of the Best Example*

At this stage, one might be inclined to protest: some inadequately defended empirical assumptions are made in the above paragraphs. Those have been that, as human beings, we can never view the world but could only have a perspectival relationship to it; and that a worldview is the truth. Why could we never view the world? Why can we not have a hypothetical, tentative, conjectural worldview? I will treat these questions as objections before answering them.

The first question does not weaken our ability to recognise that, in worldviews, we are indeed given the object that religion is. In fact, the history of religion is constituted by the questions and their answers.

Recollect that consequent to the schisms within Christianity, a new theoretical attempt to make sense of these divisions came into being. Seeking commonalities among the different Christian communities, some of the proponents of "natural religion" argued that religion was an endowment of man that did not necessitate any 'revelation'. Man's natural reason was sufficient and it did not need any 'extra' knowledge (see Byrne's illuminating 1989). In this sense, the claim that we can view the world has its correlate in the claim that we do not need revelation by a transcendent entity in order to have religion. One says that we have innate ideas – be they the "ultimate questions of life" or whatever else – that enable us to have a worldview and that a being outside the world need not reveal it to us. The other says that religion is what human beings (everywhere) come to, unaided by revelation and aided only by their natural reason. Objections are the same as are the answers; the very possibility of raising this question strengthens my claim about the relationship between worldview and religion.

How is the claim strengthened? Defenders of 'natural religion' raised questions about identifying religion itself: in their description of religion, it ended up as a set of moral codes together with a vague conception of a creator. Those who were religious (irrespective of their affiliations) rejected that this was 'true' religion, because it made a system of ethics together with an affirmation of the existence of a creator into religion. Exactly the same argument holds in this case as well. Because a religion is also a worldview and we pick out religions to talk about worldviews, if we have a difficulty in identifying the first, we will also have a difficulty in identifying the second.

Further, religious people felt (and continue to feel) that there is a crucial difference between religion and other things in the world. I submit that this is also true in our case. Worldview is not simply a theory – though it could *also* be one – about some arbitrary object in the world. If it were, it would not be fundamental to our existence. To signal the dissimilarity between our theories about the world and worldviews, we have to specify their differences at the level of epistemic predicates.

*On Epistemic Dissimilarities*

Consider the two following answers to the question why worldviews are not hypothetical or conjectural entities. Because worldview is the basic framework from within which both our theoretical enquiries and practical actions are executed, we cannot possibly say that we test the worldview as a worldview. When we test knowledge-claims, our individual units are entire theories at the minimum. We do not test isolated statements of a theory. Hence, the *first* epistemic dissimilarity: because we cannot say that we test an entire worldview, even though we do exactly that for all other knowledge-claims, the epistemic status of the latter is different from the former. Further, what counts as knowledge and what does not, and what does and does not count as hypothesis; what does and does not count as an interesting problem and an acceptable solution; *etc.*, are all constrained by the nature of the worldviews. This, then, is the *second* epistemic dissimilarity between worldview and knowledge-claims.

Even if one decided to call a worldview 'hypothetical' and 'tentative', and even if one believes that one is ever ready to change, modify, and revise one's worldviews, the first epistemic dissimilarity draws attention to the fact that the way a worldview is all of these differs in non-trivial ways from our theories about some aspect of the world. We can test theories about a finite slice of the world in several different ways; we are unable to say the same with respect to testing a worldview *as a worldview.*

This has to do with the second dissimilarity. Because worldviews are the overarching frameworks within which everything else occurs, it depends *on* the worldview to specify what has been tested. Assume, for instance, that one comes across an individual who has problems of navigating himself in the world. What does this show? Does it mean that he has wrong ideas about how people function? Is it the case that he has not learnt the required social skills? Does it show that his worldview is not adequate or that it is time he revises his ideas about some or another aspect of the world?

In a way, similar problems confront us when we test our theories too. Dubbed the "Duhem-Quine thesis" in the literature (*e.g.* Harding, Ed., 1976), it points to the fact that even our theories about the world are embedded in a context and that they face the tribunal of experience collectively.

Assume, for the sake of argument, that this is true – at least, in the sense that we are unable to epistemically *specify* the relevance of some evidence to a given theory. This inability tells us that we face difficulties in localising precisely which part of our theory is suspect in the face of recalcitrant evidence.[1] Is this also not the case with our hypothetical individual? A part of his worldview is obviously defective, even if we have trouble in identifying which part requires modification.

This could be true, but only conditionally: if we can establish that the relation between our theories about the finite slices of the world and the worldview is a part-whole relationship. When we face negative evi-

---

[1] In fact, we are able to distinguish between relevant and irrelevant evidence. None of us believes that the evidence for claiming that this essay is not plagiarised is the fact that the grass is green, or that Freud's first name was Sigmund. See Glymour's interesting book (1980), where this problem is discussed very well.

dence to some or another theory, it is because there is a logical relation-ship between this 'fact' and the theory that made the prediction. Even if the theory is tested together with its background context, there is some or another logical relationship between the theory, its context, and the 'fact'.

This is not shown to be the case with worldviews. As it is with Drobin, it is often assumed that our worldviews are mostly *implicit* and that there is a part-whole relationship between our claims about the world and the worldview. It could be the case that there is a dependency relationship; it could be that there is no relationship at all; it could be that some ideas are closely knit and yet are unrelated to other ideas; *etc.* That is to say, we cannot establish that we test our worldviews *as* worldviews. Equally, it is not possible to show that our worldviews are not tested as worldviews either. Hence, I suggest that between our theo-ries and worldviews there is an *epistemic* dissimilarity. We cannot *say* that we test our worldviews the way we test our theories. Therefore, if we characterise our theories as conjectural, hypothetical, *etc.*, on these epistemic grounds, it is not possible to use the same predicates regard-ing our worldviews.

There is also a *third* epistemic dissimilarity between our theories about some slice of the world and worldviews. We have difficulties in saying when one has changed one's worldviews, unless by pointing to 'unambiguous' cases. When a Jew becomes a Christian, he appears to have changed his worldview. When a Catholic becomes a Mormon, he seems to have modified his Christian worldview. In both cases, we can say what is entailed (up to a point). Thus, we can explicate what it means to switch worldviews.

What do these dissimilarities establish? At the least, that there are important and non-trivial differences between our theories about the world and our worldviews. These differences are significant enough to warrant our reserving certain categories for the one and not use them for the other. This is what I have tried to signal by reserving the notion of 'the truth' to worldviews. I want to distinguish worldviews from the hypothetical and tentative entities our theories are.

We need to note that there is an additional reason to see religion as the best example of worldview. The additional reason is simply this: the kind of difference between religions and our theories closely parallel the difference between worldviews and theories in yet another way.

Even though religion is an explanatory intelligible account of the Cosmos, the 'truth' in this sense, it does not mean that doctrines of any given religion are not susceptible to modification. After all, recollect that our 'interpretation' of the divine message received – unless aided by this Being Himself – is fallible, finite, and subject to revision. This does not make religion any less of 'the truth'. Exactly the same con-sideration holds for worldviews as well. Even if we change this or that aspect or part of a worldview (assuming, counterfactually, that all our beliefs about objects and events in the world are parts of a worldview), it need not affect the epistemic status of the worldview.

Consider, finally, the following minimal argument (contrasted with a maximal argument, see section #10.3), in defence of the position that religion is the best example for something to be a worldview. Until the advent of secular ideologies, scientific theories, *etc.*, the only candidates for the term 'worldview' were religions. For more than 1600 years, religions fulfilled the role of worldviews. Therefore, the decision to take the latter as the best example of the former is not a fiat. The argument will have to go the other way: if religions were not the best examples of worldviews, what else would be?

### 10.1.3. Religion and Worldview

Where have these ruminations brought us? It has not led us to doubt whether religion is the best example of worldview but whether these two are different descriptions at all. Not merely do both concepts appear to pick out the same object but, more importantly, the properties of religion are carried over into a description of Christianity, Judaism and Islam as worldviews as well. One of the reasons why we decided to try this description – instead of subscribing to the self-description of religion – was that one could not talk about religion without being religious. Now, it appears as though we cannot speak about worldviews without ourselves having one.

> Philosophies and theologies are explicit logical systems. They can be studied in the same manner as mathematical propositions and their consequences. *Religions are implicit worldviews. They can be studied only through implicit worldviews.* (Drobin 1982: 273; italics mine.)

Is this merely a disguised way of saying that one cannot study religion without being religious oneself? Are there really religious as against secular worldviews? Should one study the religious worldview from within a 'scientific' one?

I have been talking about worldviews as it is relevant to these questions: religions are the best examples of worldviews. Outside of religions, we have great difficulties in identifying a worldview: Is 'nationalism' or Marxism a *worldview*? Are they merely a set of beliefs or theories about a part of the world? Is humanism a worldview?

An 'example' is something about which there is a consensus of sorts. Choosing any of these secular theories as examples of worldviews can be justifiably contested, as they have been. In that case, it would seem as though religions are not only the best examples of worldviews but also the only ones.

## A Human Dilemma

On the one hand, we seem to think that each one of us has a worldview; on the other, we are hard put to identify any entity other than religion as an example of worldview. We are almost intuitively convinced that worldviews differ from religions; yet, their differences are not where we expect them to be, *viz.* at that level which makes something into religion or worldview. The properties of religion are retained in the description of a worldview. It appears possible to study religion without subscribing to the religious self-description; yet, to say that one can study a worldview only from within a worldview is hardly what we expect. From whence the dilemma?

There is, *first,* the intuitive conviction that a successful navigation of individuals in the world requires a worldview, which is adequate for that task; there is, *second,* the equally intuitive conviction that there is something wrong about the situation where we are unable to successfully identify a nonreligious worldview. The conflict, then, is between an intuition about the kind of beings we are and an intuition of wrongness arising out of our epistemic inability. If we identify the nature of this conflict, perhaps we can then solve the dilemma.

So, let us look at the intuition about the kind of beings we are. To navigate themselves in the world, human beings need a worldview. A successful navigation requires an adequate worldview; a fractured, tortured, and unhappy life of an individual indicates a fragmented, incoherent or even a wrong worldview.

To investigate this intuition and appreciate its implications, let us formulate it as a problem: Does each one of us have a worldview? Do we need a worldview to navigate ourselves in the world? This formulation of the problem does not help us solve it. Let us, therefore, reformulate the problem in terms of a unit higher than individuals and see whether it helps.

(a) Do all cultures have worldviews?

(b) Do all cultures and all individuals need a worldview?

(c) Could one describe a community and its boundaries by describing the outlines of a worldview?

As soon as we reformulate the problem this way, we see that we are back to one of the central questions of this essay: Is religion a cultural universal? This time though, the question is sharper: we have a preliminary characterisation of religion; we have identified the latter also as a worldview. Consequently, we are better equipped to tackle the issue now than we were before. This shows that our journey was not wasted;

it also shows that this process is one of building a theory. Our questions are relatively well defined (only relative to the starting point!) and, more importantly, they restrict the space where we look for answers. They do the latter by telling us where not to search: those mountains of books which speak of religions in other cultures. Better still, it helps us to sift through them with a critical eye and a question or two, which we did not have before.

Let us turn our attention to answering these questions. The culture that we will be looking into is India.


## 10.2. WORLDS WITHOUT VIEWS


Does India, the land of many 'religions', have either religions or worldviews? One might be wondering how I am going to answer this question in anything but the affirmative when the accumulated ethnographic facts about 'religious' practices and the multiple worldviews in India are truly staggering in size. First, I need to make a few crucial philosophical points about the nature of evidence, both accumulated and the ones I am going to present.

To begin with, I am going to let the facts stand as they are, *i.e.* I shall not call the truth of any ethnographic work into question. Secondly, I shall accept the constraint imposed by most works in Indology, anthropology, and so on, and limit myself to a few texts in order to develop one strand of my argument. Thirdly, I shall provide you with the strongest species of argument that one could ever use in scientific discussions (used often, almost exclusively, in logic and mathematics), *viz.* the *impossibility argument*. I shall argue that no matter what the facts are, there could simply be no 'religion' in India (under some conditions – to be specified later on). After this is accomplished, I shall formulate a proposal that might help us see the 'facts' in a different light.

*An Epistemological Point*


Let me solicit your agreement on a general epistemological point: whenever we distinguish things and phenomena from each other, we could use one kind of a test. It consists of taking some exemplar or paradigmatic instance of a class and testing it for necessary properties. That is to say, if this member could not possibly belong to some class (or could not be an exemplar) in the absence of some properties, then those are necessary properties.

This is a neutral formulation allowing for differing ontological commitments. For instance, one might want to consider it either as an essential property of the object, or as a criterion used in our classificatory systems. This test works for both fuzzy sets and standard sets, *i.e.* it works for sets where degrees of membership with indeterminate boundaries are allowed, and for those well-formed sets with unambiguous criteria for set membership.

No collection can be a beard, to take the famous example of Plato's beard, unless it is a collection of hairs (human, synthetic or animal). You could say that it is the essential property of a beard that it has hairs, or say that we call some collection a 'beard' by using the criterion whether or not it has hairs. While 'having hairs' is an empirical property of a beard, it is not any more or any less important (ontologically) than any other property that one might wish to consider.

However, like all epistemological points, the ability to execute such a test depends on our knowledge of the world. There is no guarantee that we would be able to specify a set of such properties in all cases. However, if and where we can, it would be useful to do so. Again, there is no guarantee that what we consider as a necessary property at any given moment will always remain so. That is because we are talking about our knowledge of the world today so that we may improve upon it. Consequently, our claims are tentative, capable of revision and improvement. This is no drawback but a strength instead.

If you agree with this epistemological point as it is relativised to our knowledge of the world today, I can now take the step to applying this test to our knowledge of religions. That is to say, we shall make use of both what has been said about religion so far, and what we know about those we have identified as religions, *viz.* Christianity, Islam, and Judaism.

*Religion and Worldview: A Disjunction*

In the previous chapter, we have come across a number of constraints imposed on religion, if it has to exist in human communities. As an explanatory intelligible account of the Cosmos and itself, it makes a series of claims about the message (*i.e.* itself), the author, the addressee and the relationship between all three. Even though these properties are contingent to religion, they are its necessary conditions: given the kind of beings we are, religion *must* incorporate these dimensions ere it gains a foothold among us.

The most exhaustive discussion about religion in India, ideally speaking, would test candidates ('Hinduism' through 'Jainism') for each of these conditions. The size of the present study, however, makes me foreswear such a task; besides, I shall use a species of argument, which does not require it.

Yet, it might not be amiss to indicate how such an exhaustive discussion should look. I will do that by focusing on *two* conditions that should be met by an explanatory intelligible account.

The *first* is that religion must make claims about the origin of the world. If the Cosmos is an expression of the purposes of the entity called God, and if these purposes are causal relations, the form that such an account should take is obvious. It must take the form of a *creation* account that speaks not merely of the 'how' but also of the 'why'. In the three religions, which are our prototypical examples, such is the case: God gives religion by telling us that He made the world, and that it embodies His purposes.

The *second* is more general and is applicable to everything said by religion: the message must be true; or, better put, it must be believed to be indubitably true. That is, religious claims must be seen as knowledge items. (We have seen that these items instantiate not human but divine knowledge.)

For the sake of identification, I shall call the conjunction of these two conditions 'metaphysical'. After all, the claim is about the creation of the Cosmos and absolute truth-value is ascribed to the claim. While it is acceptable to speak of the metaphysical conditions when discussing about religion, it is not obvious whether one could do the same with respect to worldview. It is not very clear whether there is a disjunction between religion and worldview on the issue of the 'origin' of the world.

I should very much like to argue that there are some compelling reasons why a worldview 'ought' to talk about the origin of the world. At the same time, there are good reasons why this might not be a necessary property of a worldview. That is to say, it is difficult to demonstrate the truth of either of the two claims today.

(a) Let us look at the reason why a worldview needs to make claims about the origin of the world. As I have already suggested, 'the world' which one has a view of is unrestricted by both temporal and spatial considerations. Both the past and the future, the near and the farthest, belong to the world as much as the 'here' and the 'now'. Because the 'here' and the 'now' are indexical terms, they require temporal and spatial coordinates in order to have a truth-value. A view of a spatio-temporal slice of the world is a perspective but not a candidate for the position of a worldview. To argue this point further, an illustration might be of some help.

Suppose I say the following: "my worldview is exactly five seconds true"; "I have a worldview of the last fifty years of the European civilization"; "I have a worldview of the Moon", *etc*. Clearly, there is something both funny and ridiculous about these claims. Ordinarily, we would not take such statements seriously. The suggestion that one has a worldview of the 'here' and the 'now' is just as acceptable as the above statements.

Further, if we were to countenance perspectives of the spatio-temporal slices of the world as world-views, then every partial description of the world would count as a worldview. Every isolated statement itself will count as a worldview. The very notion of 'worldview', under such a permissive attitude, becomes trivial.

It must be obvious, therefore, that we need a way of distinguishing theories about some aspect of the world from entities worldviews are. Because our world is such an all-inclusive thing, worldviews will have to make claims about the beginning (the absolute beginning) of the world. It is, however, important to note that making statements about the origin is necessary but not sufficient to consider such a group of statements as part of a worldview. That is why, for example, this property does not transform the super string theory (or the 'big bang' hypothesis) into a worldview. These theories or speculative hypotheses advance a series of assertions with respect to a finite slice of the Cosmos, *viz.* its initial conditions.

(b) Yet, there are equally good reasons for suggesting that this might not be the case. No logical intuition is violated when we talk or think of incomplete or evolving worldviews. This is partly because of the consensus that human beings create worldviews. Hence, the believers refuse the reduction of religion to worldviews; hence also the attempts of 'atheists' *etc.*, to do precisely that.

Given, however, that we have difficulty in identifying entities other than religions as worldviews, and that our task involves precisely an explication of our intuitions about worldviews, it is counterproductive to take a stance at this stage. Therefore, despite my own inclination, I shall restrict the scope of the 'metaphysical' argument. We shall restrict ourselves to religion, while considering this argument.

I can now spell-out the structure of this section. In #10.2.1, I shall focus on the question of *religion* alone: the argument will be that Indian traditions could not possibly be religions because one cannot properly raise the issue of the origin of the world. Though I would like to, I cannot argue the absence of worldviews on these grounds because our problem is that it is not clear what worldviews are.

In #10.2.2, by contrast, my arguments will be applicable to both religions and *worldviews*: whatever worldviews and religions might be, they could not possibly survive in the absence of certain conditions of transmission. Therefore, I conclude, Indian traditions are neither religions nor worldviews.

## 10.2.1. A Metaphysical Impossibility

### Primal Myths?

To begin with, consider the following 'creation' hymns from the Rig Veda: There is, first, the hymn (10.121) about the golden embryo, which is itself born. The waters appear to have been there before the embryo, while it is also suggested that the latter generated the former:

> In the beginning the Golden Embryo arose. Once he was born, he was the one lord of creation. He held in place the earth and the sky...When the high waters came, pregnant with the embryo that is everything, bringing forth fire, he arose from that as the one life's breath of the gods...
> Let him not harm us, he who fathered the earth and created the sky... who created the shining waters (O'Flaherty, Ed., 1981: 27-28).

Second, there is the hymn (10.90) about the 'sacrifice of the primal man': from the Purusa comes the world. Again, the gods, the sages, and some other creatures exist before him.

> It is the Man who is all this, whatever has been and whatever is to be... When the Gods spread the sacrifice with the Man as the offering...With him the gods, Sadhyas, and sages sacrificed (*ibid*: 30).

There is also the 'original incest'. Here, the father lusts after his own daughter and commits incest, which might account for the creation. However, other creatures exist before this act: among others, Agni, the lord of fire. Fourth, there is the hymn (10.72) that becomes another creation story about the birth of gods, as O'Flaherty remarks:

> It is evident from the tone of the very first verse that the poet regards creation as a mysterious subject, and a disparate series of eclectic hypotheses (perhaps quoted from various sources) tumbles out right away...(*ibid*: 37-38).

Finally, there is the hymn (10.81-2) about the artisan of the gods, who is

> imagined...as a sculptor, a smith, or as a woodcutter or carpenter, but also as the primeval sacrificer and the victim of the sacrifice, assisted by the seven sages. Finally, he is identified with the one who propped apart

sky and earth, the one who inspires thought and answers questions but is himself beyond understanding (*ibid*: 34-35).

The 'origin' stories thus go on. Some recur in several contexts and are retold in different ways. However, the point is their multiplicity: one could speculate as much as one wanted to about the 'beginnings' of the world. In the ultimate analysis, as the following Rig Vedic hymn (10.129) makes it clear, it does not appear to matter all that much:

> There was neither non-existence nor existence then; there was neither the realm of space nor the sky which is beyond. What stirred? Where? In whose protection? Was there water, bottomlessly deep?...
>
> Who really knows? Who will here proclaim it? Whence was it produced? Whence is this creation? The gods came afterwards, with the creation of universe. Who then knows whence it has arisen?
>
> Whence this creation has arisen – perhaps it formed itself, or perhaps it did not – the one who looks down on it, in the highest heaven, only he knows – or *perhaps he does not know* (*ibid*: 25-26; my italics).

Consider now some stories from the Brahmanas and the Upanishads, where some of the earlier motifs reappear in a rather characteristic form:

> Prajapati approached his daughter; *some say* she was the sky and *others* that she was the dawn. He became the stag...as she had taken the form of a doe. *The gods saw him* and they said, 'Prajapati is now doing what is not done.' They wished for one who would punish him, but they did not find him in one another. Then they assembled in one place the most fearful forms, and these, assembled, became the deity Rudra. (O'Flaherty, Ed., 1975: 31: my italics.)

This deity kills Prajapati and from this body many other things, including man emerge. This story, told in the *Aitareya Brahmana*, takes a different form in the *Kausitaki Brahmana*. The latter text says that Prajapati desires progeny and practices asceticism (*tapas*). During this process, he heats up and thus fire is born. Following it, the wind, sun, moon and the dawn are also born. He instructs his children to practice asceticism too and while they are doing it, the daughter assumes a seductive form. Looking at her, the brothers have an orgasm. They beg their father to save their seed, which he does. From this is born the thousand headed god, and so on. The *Satapatha Brahmana* tells another story altogether: Prajapati does penance, begets *agni* (the fire) from his mouth as a result. The hungry fire wanted to devour him. He gives oblation to the fire, and from this oblation many things are born. How was Prajapati himself born? (XI, i, 6)

> Verily, in the beginning this (universe) was water, nothing but a sea of water. The waters desired, "How can we be reproduced?" They toiled and performed fervid devotions, when they were becoming heated, a golden egg was produced. The year, indeed, was not then in existence: this golden egg floated about for as long as the space of a year.
> In a year's time a man, this Prajapati, was produced therefrom; and hence a woman, a cow, or a man brings forth within the space of a year; for Prajapati was born in a year. He broke open this golden egg. There was then, indeed, no resting place: only this golden egg, bearing him, floated about for as long as the source of a year. (Sproul, Ed., 1979: 184-185.)

In the *Brihadaranyaka Upanishad,* a mortal, the primal man, creates the world, which includes the immortal gods. In the *Chandogya Upanishad,* the idea of the origin takes the following forms. First,

> (i)n the beginning this was non-existent. It became existent, it grew. It turned into an egg. The egg lay for the time of a year. The egg broke open. The two halves were one of silver, the other of gold. The silver one became this earth, the golden one the sky, the thick membrane (of the white) the mountains, the thin membrane (of the yoke) the mist with the clouds, the small veins the rivers, the fluid the sea. What was born from it that was aditya, the sun...(Müller, Ed., 1879: 54-55.)

Second, this apparently is not how it went at all. As a father instructs his son:

> 'In the beginning', my dear, 'there was that only which is, one only, without a second. Others say, in the beginning there was that only which is not, one only, without a second; and from that which is not, that which is was born.
> 'But how could it be thus, my dear?' the father continued. 'How could that which is be born of that which is not? No, my dear, only that which is, was in the beginning, one only, without a second.
> 'It thought, may I be many, may I grow forth. It sent forth fire. That fire thought, may I be many, may I grow forth. It sent forth water....
> 'Water thought may I be many, may I grow forth. It sent forth earth (food)....(*ibid*: 93-94).

The stories go on, from the epic Mahabharata through the Puranas, in a similar fashion. The Jains deny any creation of the universe or the possibility of a creator god, as the following ninth century piece from the Mahapurana (4.16-31, 38-40) shows:

> Some foolish men declare that Creator made the world.
> The doctrine that the world was created is ill-advised, and should be rejected....
> No single being had the skill to make the world –
> For how can an immaterial god create that which is material?
> How could God have made the world without any raw material?
> If you say he made this first, and then the world, you are faced with an endless regression.
> If you declare that this raw material arose naturally you fall into another fallacy,
> For the whole universe might thus have been its own creator, and have arisen equally naturally.
> If God created the world by an act of his own will, without any raw material,
> Then it is just his will and nothing else – and who will believe this silly stuff?...
> Know that the world is uncreated, as time itself is, without beginning and end,
> And is based on the principles, life and rest.
> Uncreated and indestructible, it endures under the compulsion of its own nature, divided into three sections – hell, earth, and heaven. (Embree, Ed., 1988: 80-82.)

The Buddhists are not far behind either. In the *Digha Nikaya* (3.28), a discourse attributed to the Buddha, we read:

> There are some monks and brahmans who declare as a doctrine received from their teachers that the beginning of all things was the work of the god Brahma. I have gone and asked them whether it was true that they maintained such a doctrine, and they have replied that it was; but when I have asked them to explain just how the beginning of things was the work of the god Brahma they have not been able to answer, and have returned the question to me. Then I have explained it to them thus:
> There comes a time, my friends, sooner or later...when the world is dissolved and beings are mostly reborn in the World of Radiance. There they dwell...for a long, long time.
> Now there comes a time when this world begins to evolve, and then the World of the Brahma appears, but it is empty. And some being, because his allotted span is past or because his merit is exhausted, quits his body

in the World of the Radiance and is born in the empty World of Brahma, where he dwells for a long, long time. Now because he has been so long alone he begins to feel dissatisfaction and longing, and wishes that other beings might come and live with him. And indeed soon other beings quit their bodies in the World of Radiance and come to keep him company in the world of Brahma.

Then the being who was first born there thinks: "I am Brahma...the All-seeing, the Lord, the Maker, the Creator, the Supreme Chief, the disposer, the Controller, the Father of all that is or is to be. I have created all these beings, for I merely wished that they might be and they have come here!" And the other beings...think the same, because he was born first and they later....

That is how your traditional doctrine comes about that the beginning of things was the work of the God Brahma (*ibid*: 1988: 127-128).

There are many 'creation' stories present among those many tribes that populate India too.

The mere presence of this multiplicity of stories and claims in India is not what makes the case interesting. After all, they could all be believed by different groups severally, giving us a picture of the Indian culture as one constituted by distinct communities. Rather, it is the case that each individual believes (or most individuals believe) in all of these ideas! That is to say, it is neither abnormal nor exceptional to hear the same individual repeating each of the above-mentioned ideas with respect to the origin of the Cosmos in different contexts. Taken together, these ideas allow one to say just about anything and everything – one could even dismiss the question about the origin of the Cosmos as an illegitimate problem. That is to say, depending on the context, an individual may refuse to advance claims about the origin of the Cosmos, or consider it a purely speculative exercise lacking all truth content, or argue that all claims are equally true, or even that the Cosmos has no origin at all – thus as always present.

*An Objection and an Illustration*

At this stage of the argument, the following objection could possibly arise. Does not this belief about the Cosmos (as something that was always there) itself count as an answer to the question of the origin? One might believe that God created the world, or that big bang was at the origin, or even that the world was, is, and will always be there. Is not each one of them an answer to the question?

I would like to emphasise once again that the issue of the origin of the Cosmos is only a necessary property. It requires more than a single belief about the beginning to transform something into a religion. What we are talking about now concerns one of the building blocks of such an entity, *viz.* the question of the origin of the Cosmos.

There is, however, a second response. Religion is impossible in a culture where the question about the origins is an illegitimate one. Because of this, the answers to this problem do not count as contributing to the advancement of knowledge. One does not say that human beings are unable to answer the question; it would merely express an epistemological stance with respect to the limitations of our knowledge capabilities. Instead, what one suggests is that there are no questions to be asked. The claims about the origin of the Cosmos – be it involving the Golden Embryo, a primal man, even several primal men, or whatever else – are as legitimate as any other claim or even none. I want to draw your attention to this stance.

As a further illustration, consider the experience of an association of science teachers in the south-Indian state of Kerala. Overwhelmingly Marxist, this association has been busy carrying science to the people. It believes that India is in the grips of centuries-old prejudice and superstition. Social change in such an archaic society, consequently, could only be brought about by spreading scientific theories and scientific attitudes among wide segments of the populace.

One of the ways in which this association has tried to utilise *Science for Social Revolution* is to organise a series of lectures at the grass-roots. In the course of summarising their experience of the lecture campaigns of 1973-76, two authors speak about the first lecture in the following terms:

> In the first lecture...the question on the origin of the universe is presented as an absurd problem. Origin means prior existence and "prior" (i.e. time) cannot exist without matter, it is stated that universe always existed. The presentation gave no place for the creator (Issac and Ekbal 1988: 23).

At the risk of underlining the obvious, I would like to draw your attention to the curious fact of teachers in natural sciences thinking that the origin of the universe is an absurd question, and claiming that the world always existed. Intrinsically, no problem is either absurd or sensible, but can become so only in relationship to other ideas and opinions. To these Indians, Marxists and scientists though they might be, the origin of the universe appears an absurd question.

Why does such an incredible multiplicity of 'creation' stories exist? One of the reasons has to do with the nature of this event. Creation of the world, as told in the so-called creation stories, is neither a unique nor a radical event. It is not unique because several creation stories are attributed to several epochs because of which all creation stories turn out to be 'true'; it is not radical because creation is not *ex nihilo* and, properly speaking, no creation at all. Consider the following story from the *Visnu Purana:*

> Maitreya: 'Tell me, mighty sage, how, *in the commencement of the kalpa,* Narayana, named Brahma, created all existent things.'
>
> Parasara: 'At the close of the *past kalpa,* the divine brahma...awoke from his night of sleep...(and) concluding that *within the waters lay the earth, and being desirous to raise it up,* created another form for that purpose; and, as, *in preceding kalpas,* he has assumed the shape of a fish or a tortoise, so, in this, he took the figure of a boar' (Sproul, Ed., 1979: 185; italics mine).

As Shulman (1980: 75) puts it:

> Creation in India is not a unique event at the beginning of time, but an ever-recurring moment, a repetition of something already known.

Why have the Indian intellectuals not found the issue of the origin of Cosmos either interesting or important enough to require systematisation? (See Sinha 1985 for the kind of 'synthesis' that comes out when such attempts are made.) Why have many origin stories proliferated without being subject to censure?

*On the Truth of the Stories*

Regarding both itself and the Cosmos, the claims of religion have to be true. This does not mean that some religion does not consider the other as wrong or false. However, as we have seen, this can be said only within the framework of an explanatory intelligible account and not outside of it. Furthermore, given both the reflexivity of religion and the kind of beings we are, one has to accept the absolute truth of the claims made by religion in order to be religious. With respect to Indian culture, I want to advance the following thesis: it is a category mistake to ascribe the predicates 'true' or 'false' to the epics and mythologies. That is to say, it is an ill-formed question to ask, "Do you believe that Ramayana (or whatever) is true?"

There is not very much 'proof' I can provide in defence of this claim, unless it be by adducing two conceptually significant facts and elucidate a bit further on how an average Indian looks at the issue.

By common consent, neither atheism nor rival 'religious' traditions are absent from the Indian history. It is only when we contrast the western religious history with that of the East that an absence becomes significant and striking: in the last three hundred years, the intellectual landscape in the West is littered with the battered corpses of literature dealing with the truth and historicity of the Bible, Biblical events, and its figures. This intellectual graveyard – in size and scope – is what is new. Nevertheless, a space was marked out for a cemetery long, long ago. It has always been important that at least some of the Testament 'stories' are true, known to be so, and indubitable. This attitude towards the scriptures, and issues generated thereby which grip the intellectuals of the West to this day, hardly disturb or excite their counterparts in India. That is to say, the questions about the 'truth' or 'falsity' of their holy books are irrelevant within the Indian intellectual tradition.

There are, of course, several possible 'explanations' for the near absence of such literature in India and the total absence of such an intellectual tradition. From amongst the many, let me focus on two of the very best.

The first is the 'explanation' current in the common sense of the West. It argues that this lack has to do with the absence of a scientific tradition and scientific theorising. This will not work for the simple reason that religious controversy was responsible (to a great extent) for the growth of scientific theorising in the West. The discussion about the age of the earth (*e.g.* Rossi 1979), the first man, *etc.*, to take but one example, was not a controversy between religious believers and the scientists of the sixteenth- and seventeenth-century Europe. It was a controversy within the religious discourse itself. The threat of atheism, religious schism, and the Damocles' sword of heresy fuelled these debates about the age of earth, *etc.*, which was to ultimately provide us with geology, palaeontology and so on. In India, by common consent again, neither atheism nor 'religious schism' was unknown. What was unknown and remains unknown to this day is the notion of "heresy" as understood in the religious traditions of the West. Without "truth", there can be no heresy either.

The second explanation, which continues along the lines of the former though less bold in scope, localises it in the absence of a sense and science of history in India. You will not find a single book (in all probability) about India that does not bemoan the absence of historical records. As Arthur Macdonell put it in his *History of Sanskrit Literature* (1929: 10):

History is the one weak spot in Indian literature. It is, in fact, non-existent. The total lack of the historical sense is so characteristic, that the whole course of Sanskrit literature is darkened by the shadow of this defect, suffering as it does from an entire absence of exact chronology (in Donald Brown 1988: 21).

More recently, Paul Hacker in his *Grundlagen Indischer Dichtung und Indischen Denkens* (1985: 47) formulates the general difficulty in this way:

> Es hat in Indien keine eigentliche Geschichtsschreibung gegeben. Das gilt nicht nur für politische Geschichte, sondern auch für die Geschichte der philosophischen und religiösen Schulen (in Puttanil 1990: 1).
> [There was never any real history writing in India. This applies not only for political history, but also for history of philosophical and religious schools.]

I do not want to enter into polemics with this claim, so let me draw another Asian culture into the fray whose science of history has generated admiration in the West, *viz.* China. The anthropologist Donald Brown (1988: 47) speaks of the Chinese historical consciousness in these terms:

> For its combination of depth, comprehensiveness, accuracy, and continuity, Chinese Historical writing has no peer...The Chinese...are so historically minded that for them history takes the place of myth...History was the "queen of the sciences" for the Chinese.

He is not the only one, as the references and the citations in his text make it clear.

Having seen that India does not have a science or sense of history, and China has one, let us draw the West into the picture as well. Literally, the first question that the western intellectuals asked, when they encountered Buddhism, concerned the historical Buddha. If the historicity of the Buddha was a question raised by a culture (the West) that has a science of history, one would expect to find similar questions in the Chinese intellectual tradition as well. After all, Buddhism went out from India, confronted rival 'religious' traditions in China (if we follow the standard textbook trivia), and, therefore, the Chinese intellectuals ought to have been interested in doing 'historical' research about the Buddha. To be sure, they do ask the question: 'why did the Bodhidharma come to the East?' However, they ask it *not* as a historical question, but as a Zen *koan* (*e.g.* Reps, Ed., 1957: 125). Why did the Chinese not analyse the claims of Buddhism the way the West did? Neither anti-Buddhist sentiments nor atheism is alien to China. Why did they not produce tracts along the lines of the European intellectuals?

These are interesting and important questions, and not merely rhetorical ones. One has to undertake empirical research to answer it. For my purposes though, the answers do not matter as much as the possibility of raising the question with respect to the Chinese culture. It is to an absence of a particular kind of questioning that I want to draw your attention. If neither scientific theorising nor the sense or science of history are responsible for raising questions about the 'truth' or 'falsity' of claims of the 'holy books', what is? Here is one answer: the nature of these 'holy books' themselves. That is to say, the attitude of a culture towards the 'scriptures' generates such questions or fails to do so.

This then is my first conceptually significant fact: argument from a cultural absence. The absence of some particular genre of enquiry and literature in a culture is indicative of the fact that such a genre is not considered important in that culture. That is, it is an 'uninteresting' exercise to the members of such a culture. This way of formulating the issue is a bit dangerous because it might suggest that the members of a culture have sat and deliberated over the issue at some time or another. I do not want to suggest anything like that. Therefore, one could say that the intellectual constraints of this culture are such that some lines of enquiry do not occur to them or, where they do, die out due to the lack of intelligibility.

Literature that investigates the truth-value of the claims made by the 'religious texts' is absent in India. This lack indicates that the question of truth is not the right kind of question to ask with respect to these texts.

What kind of 'texts' are we talking about? Most of them are stories – if we were to restrict ourselves to texts that parallel the Bible – or, as scholars are wont to call them, mythologies. It makes sense to ask whether the story of Genesis is true, but it is nonsensical to ask whether the story about one of the 'incarnations' of Vishnu is true. It makes sense to ask whether the New Testament references to Jesus Christ – in the stories about Jesus of Nazareth – are to a 'historical Jesus'. To ask a parallel question about, say, Rama is to betray an absolute ignorance of what the story is...namely, *a story*.

This, then, is the second conceptually significant fact that I want to adduce: in India, an incredible multiplicity of stories makes claims about the world. I hesitate to use the word 'mythology' because 'myth' is contrasted with 'reason' or 'fact', and is most often mapped onto the predicate 'false' (see Puhvel 1987). The Indian epics (or the Jataka tales, or whatever) are not fictions; neither are they facts. To ask whether they are true or false is to exhibit a profound ignorance of the culture whose stories they are. To question their truth status is to assume that they are knowledge items, which they are not.

*A Dialogue Transcribed*

How does an average Indian look at the issue? Let an Indonesian, discussing with a German writer (Bichsel 1982), do all the talking for me:

> Als ich entdeckte, oder als mir erklärt wurde, daß der Hinduismus eine pädagogische Religion sei, nämlich insofern, als die beste „gute tat" eines Hindus darin besteht, einem anderen etwas zu erklären, da verlor ich meine Hemmungen und begann mit Fragen...
>
> Ein junger Balinese wurde mein Hauptlehrer. Eines Tages fragte ich ihn, ob er denn glaube, daß die Geschichte vom Prinzen Rama – eines der heiligen Bücher der Hindus – wahr sei.
>
> Ohne zu zögern, antwortete er mit „Ja"
>
> „Du glaubst also, daß Prinz Rama irgendwann irgendwo gelebt hat?"
>
> „Das weiß ich nicht, ob der gelebt hat", sagte er.
>
> „Dann ist es also eine Geschichte?"
>
> „Ja, es ist eine Geschichte."
>
> „Und dann hat wohl jemand diese Geschichte geschrieben – ich meine: ein Mensch hat sie geschrieben?"
>
> „Sicher hat sie ein Mensch geschrieben", sagte er.
>
> „Dann könnte sie ja auch ein Mensch erfunden haben", antwortete ich und triumphierte, weil ich dachte, ich hätte ihn überführt.
>
> Er aber sagte: „Es ist gut möglich, daß einer die Geschichte erfunden hat. Wahr ist sie trotzdem."
>
> „Dann hat also Prinz Rama nicht auf dieser Erde gelebt?"
>
> „Was willst du wissen?" fragte er. „*Willst du wissen ob die Geschichte wahr ist, oder nur, ob sie stattgefunden hat?*"
>
> „Die Christen glauben, daß ihr Gott Jesus Christus auf der Erde war", sagte ich, „im Neuen Testament ist das von Menschen beschrieben worden. Aber die Christen Glauben, daß dies die Beschreibung von der Wirklichkeit ist. Ihr Gott war wirklich auf der Erde."
>
> Mein balinesischer Freund überlegte und sagte:"Davon hat man mir schon erzählt. Ich verstehe nicht, warum es wichtig ist, daß euer Gott auf der Erde war, aber mir fällt auf, daß die Europäer nicht fromm sind. Stimmt das?"
>
> „Ja, es stimmt", sagte ich. (13-14, my italics.)
>
> [When I discovered, or when it was explained to me, that Hinduism is a pedagogical religion, namely, that the best "good deed" of a Hindu consisted of explaining something or the other, I lost my inhibitions and began with questions...
>
> A young Balinese became my primary teacher. One day I asked him if believed that the history of Prince Rama – one of the holy books of the Hindus – is true.

Without hesitation, he answered it with "Yes".

"So you believe that the Prince Rama lived somewhere and somewhen?"

"I do not know if he lived", he said.

"Then it is a story?"

"Yes, it is a story."

"Then someone wrote this story – I mean: a human being wrote it?"

"Certainly some human being wrote it", he said.

"Then some human being could have also invented it", I answered and felt triumphant, when I thought that I had convinced him.

But he said: "It is quite possible that somebody invented this story. But true it is, in any case."

"Then it is the case that Prince Rama did not live on this earth?"

"What is it that you want to know?" he asked. *"Do you want to know whether the story is true, or merely whether it occurred?"*

"The Christians believe that their God Jesus Christ was also on earth", I said, "in the New Testament, it has been so described by human beings. But the Christians believe that this is the description of the reality. Their God was also really on Earth."

My Balinese friend thought it over and said: "I had been already so informed. I do not understand why it is important that your God was on earth, but it does strike me that the Europeans are not pious. Is that correct?"

"Yes, it is", I said.]

Consider carefully the claims of this young Balinese. (A) Even though the narrative of events could have been invented and written by a human being, his 'holy book' remains true. (B) He does not know, and is not interested in knowing, whether *Rama* really lived but this does not affect the truth of Ramayana. (C) He draws a distinction between a story that is true (not just any story, nota bene, but his 'holy book') and the issue whether it is a chronicle of events on earth. (D) Finally, it remains his 'holy' book despite, or precisely because of, the above.

That is to say, he is indifferent to the historical truth and suggests, in the italicized part of the dialogue, that it is not a proper question; even if the invention of a human being and historically untrue, the story is true. He correlates impiety with believing in the truth of the Biblical narrative. As I would like to formulate it, not only is the young Indonesian drawing a distinction between a story and a history but also suggesting that the historicity of Ramayana is irrelevant to its truth.

In a way, in the West and elsewhere, we do talk about stories in an analogous fashion. When the Sherlock Holmes Society disputes whether the famed detective ever really said "Elementary, my dear Watson", the dispute is not whether Sir Arthur Conan Doyle wrote such a sentence but whether Sherlock Holmes ever said such a thing. In this sense, we do talk about the 'truth' or 'falsity' of stories (the way the Indonesian does), where we do know that there is no historical truth to them.

In the case of this Indonesian, or the Asian, who believes in his 'holy books', the situation is more complicated: in his culture, Ramayana is as 'true' though it is not clear what the status of the book is. Perhaps it is fiction perhaps it is not. He neither knows nor cares. To *know* that the Bible is *true*, suggests this Balinese, makes the Europeans impious. Impiety is to believe that one's 'religion' is true!

We can say that Sherlock Holmes did not exist, and still argue that it is true that he lived in 221B Baker Street. When we discuss the truth of fictional objects, we *know* that we are talking about fictions. The question about how we can analyse our disputations about the truth of an object or an event *in* a story is different from an indifference regarding the status *of* the narrative itself. The first is familiar to us; there are interesting attempts (*e.g.* Lewis 1978) to analyse them as well.

I want to draw attention to the second: whether Ramayana is true or not; whether it is fiction or fact, its epistemic *status* is irrelevant to its truth.

How similar is this stance with respect to the Bible? In the last decade, a "narrative criticism" (as Moore 1989 describes it) is observable in the theological circles. Many advocate that we look at the Bible in its entirety (*e.g.* Ricoeur 1969; Munson 1985) as a series of stories; yet others focus on the New Testament in an analogous fashion (*e.g.* Tannehill 1986). Especially under the influence of the 'deconstruction' movement (*e.g.* Culler 1983), and of 'post-modern theology' (*e.g.* Taylor 1984), the Greek distinction between *mythos* and *logos* has come under attack and criticism. Are the theses I am advancing comparable to these and allied tendencies (see also Warner, Ed., 1990) within some segments of the western theological discussions?

Because much more requires to be said in this context than I can possibly do now, let me rest content with making just two points. Whatever the intellectual fashion in the Biblical scholarship (or even New Testament theology), we must not forget that they are responses to the historical problems posed by the Biblical exegesis. The 'narrative turn' is one answer to the problem of the historicity of Jesus and the truth of the Gospels. Even these narrativists, today in any case, would not dream of taking the stance (as Christians, *nota bene*) that the existence of Jesus on earth is irrelevant to the truth of the Bible. As Moore (1989: 5) suggests, while discussing an early article of Tannehill, this turn is predicated on the historical veracity of the New Testament Bible:

There is little in Tannehill's study that might startle a more traditional scholar. He is especially on the lookout for reliable indications of the overarching purpose of Luke-Acts. He finds such indications in previews of future events and reviews of past events that interpret the overall course of the story, in Old Testament quotations that express a divine purpose to be realized, in accounts of the various commissions given to Jesus, the twelve, Paul, and so forth, and in statements by reliable characters within the story (*e.g.* Jesus, Peter, Stephen, Paul) that interpret events and disclose God's purpose.

Suppose one says the following: Jesus might or might not have existed; he might be The Saviour or he might not be; he might have asked Peter to found the Church or he might not have; the Gospels might be the fictitious invention of some four people or it might not be. As far as he is concerned, any of the above possibilities could be true, and the truth or falsity of none affects his belief in the truth of the Gospels. How could we understand such a person? Probably, The Holy Bible is not 'holy' to him; perhaps, he sees the Bible as a moral tract or a story-based philosophical treatise on the human condition. Whether or not such an attitude is justified, it is not enough to make him a Christian.

There is a second point. Even where the Gospel is seen as a story, it becomes an object of investigation as a text. Only as a text can the Bible provide 'knowledge' (of whatever kind). Such an attitude dovetails into a point made earlier on (see chapter #3) that knowledge is primarily textual in nature in the West. Consequently, even the narrative turn – if and where it does turn radical – requires knowledge of the text. Further, it will look at the text of the Bible as a story, and will talk about the way the Gospels talk about the world, *etc.*, without, however, being able to look at stories in other ways. That is to say, stories are treated as knowledge-claims.

The difference, with respect to the Indonesian, lies along these two lines: to him, the story of Rama does impart knowledge without being a knowledge-claim. Stories are 'true' not because they are 'fictions' and even less because they are historical facts. These raise several intriguing questions about the nature of stories and the attitude of those who make these stories their own (see Balagangadhara 1987).

Let me conclude this subsection by drawing your attention to a dominant metaphor current in the Indian culture. Used by the literate and the illiterate alike, it is about our relation to the Cosmos: ten blind men, while touching and feeling ten different parts of an elephant (tusk, tail, snout, ear, trunk, leg, toenails, skin, back and underbelly) carry on maintaining that an elephant is that part which he happens to be touching. Such, the wise tell us, is our disputation about the world.

Indian culture could not possibly have religion because it knows of no unique and radical creation of the Cosmos. The many origin stories, which do talk of the origins, are neither true nor false. They are not 'epistemic' candidates for knowledge-claims by virtue of these two crucial reasons. These mythologies, epics, puranas could not possibly be construed as accounts of the world, whatever else they might be. They lack an object, and they lack the status for being knowledge-claims.

### 10.2.2. The Sociological Impossibility

Until now, I have accepted a possible disjunction between a worldview and a religion. Consequently, I spoke exclusively of religion while tackling the issue of the origin of the world and the truth-value of the claims about the origin. However, from now on, we could indiscriminately talk of either religion or worldview. Therefore, I shall continually use the notion 'worldview' in what follows.

So far, I have treated the problem statically by looking at some texts written during the different periods to see whether it is sensible to talk of religions with respect to the Indian culture. Irrespective of what any text does or does not say, if we have to speak of societies and cultures in terms of their religions or worldviews, we have to look at the issue diachronically as well. Because the entities under consideration are 'Hinduism', 'Buddhism', 'Jainism', *etc.*, we need to consider them as historically continuous, even if evolving and changing over time. That is to say, we have to look at the *sociological conditions* that are the absolute prerequisites for guaranteeing the identity of these entities. Such is their nature that in the absence of some conditions, there could be no talk of a continued existence of a worldview or a religion across any two generations.

What are these conditions? Primarily, they are the preconditions of transmissions – be it of a worldview or whatever else. Consequently, they are empirical in nature. Taken together, they make claims about human beings, given certain facts about their biological constitution. I shall enumerate some of these conditions and briefly defend them first. Afterwards, we can look at whether these conditions hold in the Indian culture.

### The Conditions of Possibility

If we want to speak of the transmission of worldviews across generations, the *first condition* is that *there is a worldview*. We can reasonably assume that 'Hindu', 'Buddhist', 'Jain' and other worldviews will have been textually codified, if they exist. The reasonableness of this assumption must be self-evident: even if the 'Hindus', the 'Buddhists' and the 'Jains' had an 'oral' worldview that was not committed in writing, the last few centuries of empirical work would have brought it to light.

Therefore, we are entitled to assume that these worldviews have been codified. Such codifications, of course, constitute the 'holy books' or 'scriptures' of these traditions. Quite obviously, it is not enough that these worldviews are ensconced in the scriptures. The 'Hindus', the 'Buddhists', the 'Jains' need to have them as well. Because these two points are interdependent, let us agree that the first condition requires not merely that scriptures exist, but also that the worldviews are known to the members of that tradition. Otherwise, there could be no question of transmission.

Transmission of meaningful information across generations undergoes transformations. Consequently, if a culture transmits some sets of distinct worldviews, it will also have evolved mechanisms to constrain the extent to which some worldview can undergo transformation. A *standard worldview* must thus be present – a standard against which transformations are measured. This, then, is the *second condition*.

This brings us to the *third condition*. Each individual or each generation interprets a given worldview in some particular way, depending upon accumulated knowledge and the prevailing conventions. Of necessity, therefore, there will be a conflict of interpretations. That might involve a dispute about the identity of the standard worldview or the direction of its growth. Consequently, in a culture where worldviews are transmitted over generations, there is a need for resolving these disputes. That is, there must be some or another kind of *authority to settle disputes*. Note well, however, that this sociological condition does not require that this 'authority' is also effective in resolving these conflicts. Nevertheless, it entails the need for such an authority.

What kind of an authority could it be? This brings us to the *fourth condition*. The first possibility is that it is a doctrinal authority, *viz.* a textual source. However, what to do if the conflict involves interpretative difficulties with respect to this textual source? We need some kind of an organisational authority in that case. The problem with any such authority is that it will be manned by human beings and, consequently, could always be challenged by other human beings. Of course, whether or not such challenges emerge depends upon other empirical factors prevalent in a culture. Nevertheless, this challenge is always latently present. Therefore, in such a culture, the issue of legitimation of the organisational authority – as the authority – would always be an actual question. Consequently, an organisational authority denounces those who challenge its legitimacy. A plurality of such mutually denouncing authorities is neither foreclosed nor necessitated by this sociological condition. In short: there must be (at least) one *source of excommunication*.

This brings us to the *fifth* and the last sociological condition. There must be some kind of an *organisation to transmit* and propagate the worldviews. This is the mechanism to ensure that the worldview is not totally lost or transformed in its entirety in the process of transmission. Minimally, such an organisation must be bigger than an individual family; maximally, it could include an entire community that shares a worldview. Otherwise, we could not speak of entities like 'Buddhism' *etc.*, either inter-generationally or intra-generationally.

My contention is that these five sociological conditions are individually necessary but jointly sufficient to allow the transmission of worldviews across space and time. My argument will now be that none of these conditions are fulfilled in India and, therefore, no matter what the 'facts' are, there could simply be no worldview in India. That is to say, it is sociologically impossible that the Indian culture could transmit worldviews like 'Hinduism', 'Buddhism', 'Jainism', *etc.*

*On Unfulfilled Conditions*

As we have already seen elsewhere (chapter #1), 'Hinduism' has no single (or multiple) authoritative scriptures or texts. Despite everything written about the canonical texts, the same applies to Buddhism and Jainism. Shintoism and Taoism join the same group. It is important to realise what I am arguing for, when I suggest that there are no authoritative scriptures or texts.

One of the oft-heard claims made by others over the 'Hindus' is that the Veda's are their ultimate authority and that these constitute their holy texts. Most 'Hindus' might talk about 'the message' of the Vedas but their knowledge of the Vedas is limited. What kind of evidence can prove this claim? The best, perhaps, would have been statistical in nature. Unfortunately, I have not come across any statistical enquiry about exactly how many 'Hindus' know what is written in the Vedas and the Upanishads. Therefore, let me draw upon two authors, both of whom are British but separated by more than 150 years, prefacing them with my own personal experience.

The first confession has to do with my own upbringing. I was brought up a very 'orthodox' Brahmin (when compared to my other Brahmin friends) and, to this day, I do not know what is said in either the Vedas or the Upanis.ads. I was as 'orthodox' as they come but I read more of the *Sacred books of the East* while working on this essay than ever before in my life.

In 1808, Chatfield was expressing the *consensus* of his time in the following words:

> If...(we consider) the general ignorance of the Brahmins of the present age, the force of their prejudices will be found the more difficult to subdue...

In confirmation of this opinion of the general ignorance of the Brahmins, it is recorded, *that they cannot even read the books which contain their sacred records,* but are altogether immersed in such deep sloth and depravity, that immoral practices, which the most barbarous nations would have feared to adopt, are at this hour, openly allowed and sanctioned, in the most public places and polished cities of Hindoostan. Of the people, the description is generally degrading; *uninformed,* and only careful of their ablutions and the particular customs of their caste, they are said to *have as little acquaintance with the moral precepts of their Sastras,* as the Samoeides, and Hottentots, with the elegant arts of sculpture and painting. (Chatfield 1808: 212-13; italics mine.)

To illustrate the ignorance of the 'Hindus' about the Vedas, consider the following story I was told as a young child: science, technology and the concomitant prosperity of the West have to do with their theft of the fourth Veda, *viz.* the Atharva Veda. Apparently, there was only one manuscript available in India which the British stole. Having ingested all the knowledge in it, they built their machines and instruments and became rich. To my question as to why we could not ask the British to give our manuscript back, I received answers that satisfied the curiosity of a young child. The British (at times it was the Germans) dumped the manuscript into the sea or they refuse to give it back to us and we cannot force them because they are very powerful, or some such thing. As I grew up, I never thought about this story any further until I recently came across a piece of ethnographic work by the British anthropologist Jonathan Parry. Describing the result of his fieldwork in Benares this is what he had to say:

In Benares I have often been told – and I have heard variants of the same story elsewhere – that Max Müller stole chunks of *Sama Veda* from India, and it was by studying these that German scientists were able to develop the atom bomb. The *rishis,* or ancient sages, not only knew all about nuclear fission, but as (what we would call) mythology testifies, they also had supersonic aeroplanes and guided missiles (1985: 206).

Such tales exhibit a very deep ignorance on the part of the 'Hindus' (the 'Hindu' Brahmins, *nota bene,* in a city like Benares!) about the content of their "sacred books". If such is the ignorance of the Brahmins, the 'priests' of the Indian culture, what could we say about the knowledge of other 'Hindus' regarding their 'sacred texts'? The picture, I believe, will substantially be the same. In this sense, the foregoing is enough, I trust, to show why using texts like the Vedas or the Upanishads to make claims about the 'Hindu' (or Brahmanic) worldviews is a grotesque exercise. The same, *mutatis mutandis*, applies to the Buddhists, the Jains and so on.

It is not as though western ethnography of Indian culture is ignorant of this state of affairs. They describe it in terms of their cultural assumptions: lay Buddhists as distinguished from *Sangha* Buddhism, popular Hinduism as distinguished from philosophical Hinduism, *etc.* (chapter #4). One could fill books and articles with these distinctions, as is indeed the case, but they do not tell us anything except the following: texts *ought* to be central to a religion but they are not so in Hinduism, Buddhism, *etc.* One could go either of the two ways when confronted with this fact: either Hinduism, Buddhism, *etc.*, are no religions (the route I have chosen) or they are religions and the 'popular' religion is a corrupted version of a purer one to be found in secret enclaves and dusty tomes.

However, one might object to this argument on two grounds. Firstly, by appealing to the popularity of the Bhagavadgita and the epics Ramayana and Mahabharata among the 'Hindus'; secondly by pointing out the similar absence of scriptural knowledge among the Jews, Christians, and the Muslims. Let me begin with the first objection.

To be sure, Gita is better known among certain layers – but its 'popularity', I suggest, has to do with the western efforts and little with the indigenous tradition. Even then, it is hardly considered a sacred text – it is a deeply moving, melodious song, which imparts some 'metaphysical' and 'moral' advice. On the other hand, what exactly is the worldview in the Gita? Let us recollect how Sharma summarises the consensus about it. The commentaries on this text have laid bare, he says (1986: xii–xxiii), its "theological contradictions", "soteriological ambiguity", "liturgical inconsistencies", "canonical ambivalence", *etc.* I shall take up the question of the epics shortly, when I discuss the third sociological condition.

Regarding the second objection, I can be equally brief. I am not claiming that a member of a religion must have a direct acquaintance with his holy text. Rather, it has to do with the fact that a total ignorance of the 'holy texts' is compatible with being a 'Hindu' and even being a Brahmin. There is a contrast between this situation and that of a Jew, a Christian, and a Muslim with respect to their sacred texts. One could not belong to these religions if one (directly or through the mediation of a rabbi, a priest, an imam, or even one's parents) is ignorant of what their scriptures are about.

In either case, the point is this: transmission of a 'Hindu', 'Buddhist', or a 'Jain' worldview requires the existence of such a view in a textual source, and knowledge about it. So far, the argument has been that this sociological condition is not fulfilled in India.

Let me look at the second condition. Texts, however, require interpretations. For someone to be a Hindu or a Buddhist, it is necessary that there is a standard interpretation. Even if we were to use this notion in the broadest possible sense, *viz.* as constraints on interpretations, we are hard put to identify any such within these traditions. The reason for this absence lies in the very nature of these texts: the Rig Veda itself, to take but one example, provides us with different creation stories (to restrict ourselves to one idea). If you consider the more widely disseminated puranas, you will find that it is next to impossible to speak of any one standard interpretation of any one idea.

Why do we need standard interpretations? How, otherwise, is it possible to transmit worldviews (or religions) across generations? Again, drawing a contrast will highlight the problem. How could there be Islam, Christianity, and Judaism if there was no transmission of one specific view? After all, we are talking of entities like the Hindu, Brahmanic worldview, the Buddhist and Taoist worldview, and so on. If we cannot identify one stable entity (*i.e.* a standard interpretation), how could we maintain that Buddhism, Taoism, Hinduism are 'distinct entities' with a history of 2000 years or more?

One might be tempted to compare the fragmentation within Christianity, Islam or Judaism with the state of affairs that I am sketching. It will not work. The reason is simple. Religious schism involves conflict of interpretations but not a denial of a common constraint on interpretation. There are constraints on the interpretations of a Catholic mass; Jesus was not the son of the Devil; Idolatry is forbidden; one cannot be a Muslim and say that Muhammad was not a prophet of God but a charlatan instead; one cannot be a Jew and believe that Jesus was the Messiah...and so on. No such constraints operate for Buddhism, Hinduism, *etc.* Consequently, one cannot delineate them as worldviews at all.

Let us look at the problem of conflict of interpretations and speak of the third sociological condition: in the case of conflict of interpretations, we need some kind of authority to settle the disputes. Some kind of authority is required, because its absence is equivalent to removing all constraints on interpretation.

The first possibility is a doctrinal authority. That is, some text or a doctrine puts a purely semantic constraint on the interpretation of a text. Such a text is the last court of appeal, so to speak. This requires a hierarchy of texts, a sort of theology. Absent from the 'religious' traditions of Asia is precisely such a hierarchy. One could take any text or even none at all, and remain a 'Hindu', 'Brahmin', 'Buddhist' or whatever else.

To realise its significance, a citation from an ethnographic work might help. Conducted in Tamil Nadu, India, the author is after the worldview of the villagers:

(T)he following creation myth, told to me by an elderly villager in the presence of a number of other villagers *who threw in their own versions, connections and modifications as the narrative unfolded...*

God (Kat.avul.) was everything. In Him were the five elements of fire, water, earth, and ether [*akasam*], and wind. These five elements were uniformly spread throughout [the three humors] phlegm [*kapam*], bile [*pittam*], and wind [*vayu*]. They were so evenly distributed that even to say that they were phlegm, bile, and wind would be wrong. Let us say that they were in such a way that one could not tell the difference between them. Let us say they were nonexistent...Even the question as to their existence did not arise. Then something happened. The five elements started to move around as if they were not satisfied, as if they were disturbed. Now, as to who disturbed these elements or why they were disturbed, no one knows.

At this point, a second villager interrupted the narrator to suggest that the one who caused this mysterious disturbance was Kamam, the god of lust. The narrator *found his suggestion unacceptable, because Kama had not even come into existence at that time.* But his friend insisted...*After considerable debate, it was agreed that it did not make sense to speak of Kamam existing* when he was as evenly distributed throughout Kat.avul.'s body as floating atoms...(Daniel 1984: 3-4; italics mine).

Imagine, if you will, a discussion like this about the 'creation myth' in the Bible, conducted by devout villagers in religious cultures!

This is very typical within the Indian culture with respect to the transmission of the epics as well. One of the English translators of the Mahabharata speaks about its transmission in these terms:

The text of *The Mahabharata* itself gives us some idea of how we should picture its authorship. In its present form it is recited by the bard Ugrasravas, who recites it after Vaisampayana, who was one of the pupils of Krisna Dvaipayana. In other words, we have right here three generations of reciters through whom the text had been transmitted. One cannot expect that this transmission was a literal one, as it has been in the case of the Veda. A reciter's reputation was based on his skill in bringing the old stories to life again. Successive generations would add, embellish, digress: but also understate what might have been emphasized before...All this creates the impression that what would come down from generation to generation were, first, the summaries, and, second, the technique of spinning out a tale to please the listeners. The reciter was thus also a creative poet, within the idiom of his craft. (van Buitenen 1973: xxiii-iv)

We need to appreciate that changes that occur in telling the story is not as important as the fact that transformations of a text are considered both desirable and necessary.

The second possibility for adjudicating when there is a conflict of interpretations is the presence of an organisational authority to judge disputes. In the case of Hinduism, it is evident that no such authority exists. The same consideration holds for Taoism. Could we say the same for, say, Saivism, Vaisnavism, Buddhism with its *Sangha*, and the Jains? To show that it is true for these groups as well, we need to examine the next sociological condition.

What happens when two interpretations collide? Does each become heretic in the eyes of the other? If so, who decides? There exists no organisational authority to recognise someone as a Buddhist or denounce him/her as a heretic. None of these traditions constitutes a Church. The Buddhist *Sangha* is an association of a group of people who decide to live in one particular way within the Buddhist tradition. They are not the focal points of the laity; they are an association within a community. The members of a community might respect the Buddhist monks, heed their words where useful but they have no spiritual power granted to them by virtue of being monks.

This brings me to the final sociological condition: not only is there no source for 'excommunication' but there is also no source for the 'communication' of one worldview. That is, there is no organisation to propagate such views. The transmission of these traditions takes place through families and friends. Local characters and customs modify the transmission in innumerable ways. How, then, could we possibly speak of a Brahmin from South India sharing the same worldview as a Brahmin from the North, or a Buddhist in Tibet sharing the same worldview as a Buddhist from China? We simply cannot. Nor could we call them 'Buddhist', unless *we* specify a 'standard' worldview called 'the Buddhist worldview', which is precisely what the West did. It took a road familiar to it because of its own culture: identification of texts as the unifying element.

Let me summarise. The above-mentioned sociological conditions are necessary if we have to speak of entities like worldviews, which preserve their identity in the course of their transmission over generations. My claim is that these conditions are unfulfilled in India with respect to Hinduism, Buddhism and so on. From this, it follows that whatever these traditions might be, they could not possibly be either worldviews or religions.

Because of the metaphysical impossibility and the sociological impossibility, I can now argue, Indian culture could know neither religions nor worldviews. I have argued for this without contradicting ethnographic 'facts' but making some use of them instead.

*By Way of a Summary*

This long argument requires a summary now that we have reached the end of another phase in the argument. I have suggested that my characterisation of religion exhibits the reflexivity involved in a religious account. Further, I have argued that the concept 'worldview' is not an explicit definition of religion, but that the latter is the best example of the former.

In the second section, I provided a very strong species of argument in support of my contention that India knows of no religions or worldviews. It has taken the form of identifying the metaphysical and sociological conditions required to speak of the existence of religions and worldviews in a culture. The metaphysical impossibility has to do with the fact that the candidates for knowledge-claims are stories and, as such, are neither true nor false. It also has to do with the fact that they lack the object, *viz.* the world, which they have to make explanatorily intelligible. Because we are talking about historical entities handed over the centuries, the sociological conditions specify the constraints on any such transmission. I have argued that these conditions are systematically absent in India. These arguments strengthen the basic contention that India knows of no worldviews or religions.

It must be evident why one cannot describe the Indian culture (or, as I believe, the Asian culture) by outlining its worldview. *There is no worldview to outline* in India. What then have the anthropologists been studying all the while? Whatever they might be studying, the second subsection went in search of an answer to the problem whether each of us has a worldview and whether we need one to navigate ourselves in the world. The answer is in the negative: there exists at least one culture, which knows no religion or worldview. Better formulated, if religion is a constitutive element of all cultures, then the claim is empirically false. Religion is not a cultural universal.

One of our central preoccupations has an answer. However, it lends a greater urgency to the second preoccupation, *viz.* that of making the western intellectuals and their common sense intelligible.

To carry this task to its successful conclusion, let us pick up the question posed in an earlier section of this chapter (#10.1). The intuition that without a worldview we cannot navigate ourselves in the world is not empirically true. From whence this intuition then? What lends strength and credibility to this feeling?

## 10.3. Views Without the World

Wendy Doniger O'Flaherty, currently the Mircea Eliade professor in the history of religions at the University of Chicago, is a world-renowned expert on Indian religions and their texts. By virtue of her superior mastery of the texts and myths of the Indian traditions, it is no wonder that she has also acquired a 'deep' insight into the culture of a people. One such penetrating observation, which cuts right into the core of a culture, is in a book where structural method is applied to a corpus of mythological tales of India:

> ...(C)ompromise is never the Hindu way of resolution, which proceeds by a series of oppositions rather than by one entity which combines the two by sacrificing the essence of each. There are, in fact, scattered epigrams closely akin to the Greek *meden agan*...'Excesses must be avoided in all things'. But this is not the prevalent Hindu attitude, nor is it the attitude underlying the mythological texts, which by their very nature tend to exaggerate all polarities, including potentially dangerous excesses.
>
> Hinduism has no 'golden mean'; it seeks the exhaustion of two golden extremes...Hinduism has no use for Middle paths; this is a religion of fire and ice (1973: 82).

As a Hindu, I shall strive to be true to her description. The best way of doing this right now is to extend the scope of my claim even more radically: religions are not only the best examples of worldviews, but also the only examples we have because that is how religion has secularised itself. That is to say, what makes several of our dilemmas understandable is the dynamic of religion itself. In this subsection, I shall not only defend this position but also show how many interesting things can happen in the world if only we give up our desire to seek the "golden mean".

*About the Conditions of a Defence*

Earlier on (chapter #1), I argued that how contemporary writers talk about 'religions' in other cultures is an example of inconsistent reasoning. If religions were the only examples of worldviews, one would hope to find a similar kind of inconsistency – with necessary modifications – in arguments about worldviews. Second, I argued that Christianity has been secularised (chapter #6) and that the belief in the universality of religion is a biblical theme (chapter #7). Both themes will recur, if my argument is plausible. Third, I have shown that missionaries described the differences among people along the lines of their religion (chapter #6). I shall show that this is not merely an archaic practice.

These three arguments, in conjunction with those developed earlier on, will provide the required defence for the position that religion is the only example of worldview. Because each is intertwined with the other, I shall address them as a block by providing, at the same time...

### 10.3.1. A Conceptual Fragment of the Answer

In the process of accounting for the stubborn persistence of the idea that all cultures have a religion, I have provided two fragments of an answer. One fragment was historical in nature: the belief about the universality of religion is a religious thesis about an original religion (whether as *Urmonotheismus* or as *Urpolytheismus*). Even though religion slowly lost its hegemonic control over the intellectual life that it once exercised, this religious belief became common currency and joined the unexamined trivia. The association between 'having a religion' and 'being civilized', an understandable relation within the context of Roman '*religio*', persisted with an added moral, evaluative dimension. In chapter #7, I provided a linguistic fragment of the answer: religious language has become part of the ordinary language-use. The Gestalt has faded into the background in such a way that it appears linguistically normal to use theology to understand religion.

These are aspects of the answer. I also hinted in the direction of another, more conceptual fragment of the answer. By now, it must be obvious what it will be and why it is even more intriguing.

One of the most strongly held beliefs amongst intellectuals of the western world today concerns the necessity and indispensability of worldviews. Amongst anthropologists, this idea takes on two forms: to study a worldview (or a fragment of it) is to understand the people whose worldview it is. Consequently, to compare cultures is to compare different worldviews. Among other social scientists, including philosophers, there is a very firmly rooted belief that no individual or group could survive in the world if not endowed with a worldview.[2] Analogous to all (or most) firmly held beliefs, arguments and evidence for the necessity of worldviews are inversely proportional to the strength of the belief.

In starkest terms, we could formulate this diffuse idea thus: all organisms react depending on the representations they have built up of the world. Without some representation of the world, one cannot survive in the world. Therefore, it is almost evolutionarily necessary that there are worldviews.

---

[2] In the hands of some, all systems require 'worldviews' to function and not just human beings.

Many who subscribe to the following general diagnosis of the western culture also entertain the very same sentiment: there is a crisis in this culture, which is best described as a crisis in its worldview. During the Middle Ages, Christianity provided us with a worldview, which is inadequate for the contemporary world. One of the most important tasks facing a philosopher or a theorist of society is to build an adequate, scientific worldview.

The first thing, which ought to strike anyone, is the incompatibility between the above two paragraphs. In the first, a claim is made that no individual could survive without possessing a worldview; in the second, the thesis is advanced that the old worldview has disintegrated in the western culture and that a new worldview does not (yet) exist. If this thesis is true, the first claim is empirically false. In the western culture, many (most) individuals go about the world without possessing a worldview.

If the first claim is true, there could never be a crisis in worldview. All individuals, at all times, do need and effectively do possess a worldview. That is to say, the thesis advanced in the second paragraph is false. Furthermore, the first claim effectively rules out any possibility of a culture-specific worldview. If each individual builds up a representation of the world, how could you understand the culture of the Dinka, the Hopi Indians, the Chinese, *etc.*, by studying a fragment of a 'worldview' as provided by an informant or two?

Despite the manifest incompatibility between these two positions, there is also a relation of dependency. The only argument that lends depth, poignancy, and urgency to the call for building an adequate worldview today is that without worldviews, individuals cannot orient themselves in the world. Their survival depends non-trivially on their ability to navigate themselves in the world, and this is what they have lost in losing their worldview.

Lost since when? Since Christianity ceased being (a) either the worldview of the West, or (b) an adequate view of the world. When did these momentous events take place? This question does not require an answer that localises a precise time, date, or place. Instead, it reveals both the depth of the tragedy and the shallowness of the farce.

One could argue that the 'scientific revolution' inaugurated the process of disintegration of the religious worldview, and continues to this day. What does this scientific revolution consist of? Let a respected scientist, approvingly citing a hackneyed theme, do all the talking in this case.

Sigmund Freud remarked that each major science has made one signal contribution to the reconstruction of human thought – and that each step in this painful progress had shattered yet another facet of an original hope for our own transcendent importance in the universe:

"Humanity has in course of time had to endure from the hand of two great outrages upon its naive self-love. The first was when it realized that our earth was not the center of the universe, but only a speck in a world-system of a magnitude hardly conceivable...The second was when biological research robbed man of his particular privilege of having been specially created and relegated him to a descent from the animal world."

(In one of history's least modest pronouncements, Freud then stated that his own work had toppled the next, and perhaps last, pedestal of this unhappy retreat – the solace that, though evolved from a lowly ape, we at least possessed rational minds) [Gould 1987: 1].

To read such bloated references of Freud to the western Christian-Jewish people as "Humanity" is as nauseating as Gould's pompous characterisation and identification of the biblical beliefs with the "thought of humanity". Nevertheless, let us leave polemics aside and concentrate on the idea instead. This disintegration, then, has been going on for at least three hundred years now. What has happened in the West during this period? It has colonised the world, accumulated incredible wealth, decimated other cultures and people, exported capitalism, science and technology, democracy, and, as many say, its own 'worldview' to all other parts of the world. Whatever your moral verdict on this state of affairs, I thought these feats index the flourishing of a culture and not its disintegration.

On the other hand, if this 'worldview' is slowly disintegrating as the view of a culture, at least a few generations have lived in the West without any worldview whatsoever. That is, in the last three hundred years or more, some people have given up embracing the Christian worldview and have brought up their children in the same fashion. Why, then, can others not follow suit?

It must be obvious that the force of the argument about the crisis in western culture does not derive from an answer to these questions, but from the idea that without worldviews one cannot survive. Precisely this belief is in contradiction with the projects for building 'scientific worldviews'.

Before we try to answer the question why evidently gifted and brilliant minds do not appear to see this incompatibility, let us see whether the claim about the relation between individuals and worldviews is plausible. Because a universal statement is made, falsification is easy. Not all representations of the world are worldviews. The court of appeal in this case, given the absence of any explicit theorising, is our language-use: we cannot speak of the worldview of an ant, the worldview of a fish, the worldview of a thermostat, the worldview of a mountain-gorilla and so on, except as a joke. For example, the statement, "according to the worldview of my trained flea..." could make us laugh because of the category mistake, *viz.* ascription of the property of 'possessing a worldview' to your trained flea. Consequently, we do not countenance all representations of 'the world' as worldviews. One reason is that while such creatures might have a representation of a fragment of the world, we are not willing to admit that they have a representation of 'the world'. From this, it merely follows that organisms require some representation of the relevant slice of the world.

For the claim about the worldviews to remain plausible, we need to restrict its scope. Could we suggest that only human beings require worldviews? Again, consider the following ascriptions: the worldview of those above 50, a childish worldview, *etc.*, do not make any sense unless relativised to a specific individual (Tommy's worldview, Peter's worldview, and such like). Of course, we do speak of the 'worldview of a child', 'children's worldviews', *etc.* Even in these cases, the reference is either to an individual or to a set of beliefs common to a group of people. Alternately, it picks out a class of beliefs present in the worldview of one group but absent in the other.

However, the statement about Judaic, Christian, Brahmanic and Marxist worldview appears sensible. That is to say, either the notion 'worldview' is associated with a doctrinal core and/or refers to a community unified by a doctrinal core. This situation further confirms the relationship postulated between 'religion' and 'worldview' but does not tell us why worldviews are either crucial or indispensable.

If the term 'worldview' is a secular term for 'religion' then the theological belief that all cultures, peoples, nay, even all individuals have either a sense of divinity implanted in them or have a religion takes the secularised form that all cultures, peoples, nay, even all individuals have a worldview. I claim that this is exactly what has happened: the necessity and indispensability of worldviews is the secularised version of a theological belief.

Now we can understand why gifted minds do not see incompatibilities when advancing such flatly inconsistent ideas. Not only have they taken over a religious idea but they also believe that it is 'scientific' or 'empirically true' due to its familiarity. To claim that cultures without religion exist is to claim that there exist cultures without worldviews. This is almost inconceivable within the confines of a culture dominated to this day by religion.

We can also understand why foes and friends alike often perceive the humanists and Freethinkers (a typical European phenomenon) as "priests on their heads". They are priests: they carry on religious discourse in secular terms. Who needs a religious terminology if the same idea can be said without being explicitly religious? Who indeed but the secularly religious? We can also further understand why claims about the universality of religion among cultures find sympathetic echoes in the hearts of even diehard atheists or secular-thinking people: they cannot conceive of peoples without worldviews.

If we hold on to this insight and look afresh at the anthropologists, we can appreciate how and in what sense they are successors to their Christian (or other religious) ancestors: communities and cultural groups are distinguished along the same lines as the heathens and the pagans. One believes that to understand a people or their practices, one has to understand their beliefs. In order to understand the latter, one either elicits information about the 'worldviews', reads the texts of a culture, or provides a 'symbolic interpretation 'of cultural practices in terms of 'worldviews'!

If the greatest part of western ethnography and knowledge of other cultures is based on studying the worldviews of other cultures, and if there are cultures which do not have worldviews, what 'knowledge' does the West have of other cultures? What, precisely, are the western anthropologists studying when they study nonexistent entities?

### 10.3.2. The Depth of the Deep Questions

The above questions make sense if worldview is merely a secular equivalent of religion and, consequently, even the grounds for arguing the universality of religion has spread wide and deep into the commonsense wisdom. The idea of an innate sense of divinity in man must have received its secular translation. I have suggested that it has. Does this suffice to account for the intuition that one needs worldviews to navigate oneself in the world? It does not. This intuition is reinforced by another idea about what worldviews do.

Consider the following sketch of an argument: everywhere, human beings ask some questions. These are the 'deep' questions regarding the meaning and purpose of life; questions about the continuity between the past that earlier generations were, and the future that the coming generations will be, mediated by the present that we are. There are many different answers to these questions. Religion is one such. Worldview could be another. Our inability to identify a non-religious worldview does not show that such an entity cannot exist, or that there is no difference between religion and worldview. Our inability underlines the urgency of building a scientific worldview.

I believe these arguments for building a scientific worldview torpedo the task.

*Religion and Worldview: A Maximal Argument*

While presenting the minimal argument, I have said that religion was also a worldview during, let us say, the Middle Ages. If religion is also a worldview, any secular worldview must share a minimal set of common properties with its religious brethren. Otherwise, we would have a religious worldview and a secular 'something else'.

What would/could distinguish worldviews from each other and other things? It cannot be the fact that they ask/answer different questions. Rather, the fact that they give different answers to the same questions distinguishes them from each other. The difference between the different religious worldviews, and the difference between religious and secular worldviews, depends on the answers they share in common.

Their answers should be answers to their common questions. The latter must be general enough to allow different answers. They must be common across both the different religions and between religious and secular worldviews. I do not think it is necessary to defend this proposal, because I have already done so elsewhere (chapter #9.1): the rivalry between different religions is a historical fact and I am simply re-describing it as a rivalry between the worldviews. Worldviews are each other's rivals because of their identity and difference: they share some set of questions and some set of answers, and they differ regarding interpretations of both. If this were not the case, they would be indifferent to each other: one's questions would not be those of the other.

At this stage, one must be very careful in describing the kind of rivalry that exists between religions and worldviews. The temptation is great to treat them on par with other intellectual products of the human mind like, for example, cosmological, philosophical, or scientific theories and speculations. That is to say, one could carelessly describe religions or worldviews as answers to some problems, which predate a worldview or a religion. I believe this is a fundamental mistake: neither a religion nor a worldview has come into being as answers to questions raised prior to and independent of having a religion or worldview. Religions or worldviews do not solve any cognitive, emotional, or existential problems. Instead, such problems can only be formulated given the existence of a worldview or a religion.

I have argued this point on two grounds so far: the difference between religion's claim to truth, and the cognitive claims of our intellectual products (chapter #9); the difference between the way we test our theories about the world and the difficulty of testing a worldview as a worldview (section #10.1). These draw attention to the epistemic dissimilarities between theories about some object in the world, and the status of entities like religions and worldviews. These dissimilarities reinforce the suggestion that worldviews are unlike theories in that the latter come into being as answers to some or another problem. By contrast, in entities like religion or worldview, certain kinds of question arise.

I will now pursue this suggestion indirectly. I will do so by seeing whether the argument of the proponents of a 'scientific' worldview makes their task a plausible one.

## Two Possibilities

Let us assume that there are some 'deep' questions, which human beings ask everywhere. These species-specific questions relate to the meaning and purpose of human life (or the place of man in the universe or whatever else). Today, one could argue, we need scientific answers to these basic, existential questions. This position can be true either (a) as a conclusion of an argument, whose other premises are also true, or (b) as a hypothesis. Let us look at both possibilities.

(a) *As a conclusion:* That people have always and everywhere asked 'deep' questions could be the conclusion of an argument, which makes at least the following two assumptions: (i) religions have existed in all cultures and at all times; (ii) religions have always and everywhere answered these questions. If these two premises are true, and the rules of inference used in drawing these conclusions are valid, then the conclusion is also true. Are these premises true?

We do not know whether the first premise about the existence of religions in all cultures is true. With respect to India in any case, I have argued that none has done an empirical enquiry to find out whether India knows of religions. Consequently, at the minimum, its truth-value is uncertain: it could be true or false.

The second assumption shares the same fate: no recognised religious figures or texts have formulated or answered the question of either the meaning or purpose of an individual life, or that of a spatio-temporally restricted group. To be sure, you can read the Bible with these questions. However, from this, it does not follow that these are the queries to which the Bible is an answer.

Consequently, even if you do not follow me in saying that both the premises are false, I have provided you with enough evidence and arguments to shed doubt on its truth. That is, today, we can reasonably claim to be uncertain about the truth-value of both these assumptions.

Therefore, the conclusion that some 'deep' questions are asked by everyone, everywhere, is – at best – a conclusion drawn from premises, which are not known to be true. The conclusion could still be true; but we cannot affirm its truth on logical grounds. The least we can do is deny the self-evidence or the obviousness of its foundations. More, much more is required to argue that we need a 'scientific' worldview.

(b) *As a hypothesis:* One could argue the need for a 'scientific' world-view on the hypothesis that there are some 'deep' questions, which human beings ask. In this case, if we can show that one or more false implications follow, we can conclude that something is wrong with the argument (assuming, once again, that valid rules of inference are used). We cannot say that the hypothesis itself is false, because we need to use other hypotheses in conjunction with the above in order to derive some conclusions.

One such additional hypothesis that we need is the answer to the question, 'why have people asked these questions?' Presumably, they find the answers important – so important that they cannot live in their absence. The 'presumption' suggests the additional hypothesis I want to propose: persistence of some questions among human beings indicates the importance of these questions. Under such a hypothesis, the claim of the proponents of a 'scientific' worldview is false. Cultures exist where even no answers – or any answer you feel like giving – would do. The answers are not important nor are the questions.

It is possible that my additional hypothesis is not accepted. It could be true that we are genetically programmed to ask silly questions – some people find them 'deep', yet others do not find them comprehensible –even though they are not (depending on the culture) considered cog-nitively important. In that case, the argument for building a 'scientific' worldview undermines its own plausibility. Why provide the answers, when the task is not urgent or important? Let people ask away all the questions they want – both silly and deep. Why answer them? People are genetically programmed to keep asking them in any case!

However, at this moment, to the best of my knowledge, this is not shown to be true. In fact, human socio-biologists (the term is from Kitcher 1985) and cognitive neuroscientists, in their speculative mo-ments, do not show how or why we are genetically disposed to create religion. What they do, in fact, is just the opposite: because there is overwhelming ethnographic and archaeological evidence for the exist-ence of religions in all cultures, they argue, there must be genetic or cerebral grounds for religion.

Neither as a premise nor as a conclusion is it evident that religion answers a pre-religious question. Consequently, it is not possible (on these grounds) to argue that a 'scientific' worldview is needed or that it would be different from a 'religious' worldview.

This, then, is my maximal argument: the questions that a 'scientific' worldview could possibly answer are those, which can only be raised within a religion. Should a 'scientific' worldview ever be built up, a prospect that I doubt, either it will supplement a religion or it will sup-plant a religion. It will either not be a worldview but a mere theory about some slice of the world or it will merely be a rival to a religion and, thus, a religious rival.

### 10.3.3. Proselytisation and Secularisation

Let us reconsider what I have said so far. The belief about the universality of religion has been secularised in the guise of the universality of worldviews. There is an innate sense of divinity in man, which makes him search for God, said religious figures of yesteryears. Man seeks passionately to find the meaning of life and is open to receiving answers to it, say some modern theologians. Secular-thinking people agree with the latter-day theologian: one calls it 'religion' and the other calls it 'worldview'. One looks at the Bible without neglecting sciences; the other looks at the sciences without neglecting the Bible. Because of this, we are to suppose that one speaks of a religious worldview and the other of a 'scientific' one.

In the earlier chapters of my story, we have repeatedly come across the same movement. Biblical themes become an intellectual inheritance of a group – not just an intellectual inheritance, it is even genetic according to yet others – and a few generations later, it is not even realised that they are claims made within a religion. Long familiarity gives these ideas the cloak and mantle of respectability, and they fade into the background.

Thus far, my units of description are individual beliefs, even though they are connected to each other. Consequently, I have described secularisation – at one level – as a process where some beliefs from a specific religion become commonplace from the grocer to the Guru. Except very briefly in the sixth chapter (#6.2), I have not spoken of what secularisation signifies or how it happens. The time has come to expand on this theme.

The conditions under which religion could universalise itself in human cultures are also the restrictions imposed upon it. Consequently, universalisation does not imply the absence of restrictions. It requires only their reduction, if not in the number then in kind: local variations and culture-specific constraints require overcoming. Religion reaches its pristine form (as much as it is possible in human cultures) when encumbrances are reduced. One such encumbrance is that religion is couched in some or another doctrine.

### Universalisation of Religion

Religion, however, is always *a* religion – some or another specific configuration. Universalisation of religion does not merely mean a geographical and spatial extension of some religious movement; such an extension would merely generalise a particular configuration. Instead, universalisation of religion implies that religion, as the explanatory intelligible account of both the Cosmos and itself, becomes pristinely 'simple' and becomes as formal as possible. That is to say, the proselytising drive of some specific religion (in our case Christianity) does not only mean that it wins converts. It also means that Christianity universalises itself as a religion by becoming increasingly less Christian. That is, its doctrines must spread in two distinct ways: conversion of people into Christianity and a widespread acceptance of its account by non-Christians, because the account itself spreads in a de-Christianised form. This double aspect of religion (a) of being tied to a specific explanatory intelligible account (because religion is always some religion or another); and (b) being, at the same time, *the* explanatorily intelligible account of the Cosmos (each tradition is a religion precisely because of this property) enables the double movement of the universalisation of religion.

This double movement expresses itself in the double relation that religions have towards each other: they are, it is true, intolerant of each other; but there is also inter-religious dialogue and the gut-level feeling that "all religion is one". Doctrinal differences are both extremely important and, at the same time, the feeling persists too that these differences are, somehow, at some level, rather unimportant. In those who 'really believe', both feelings are simultaneously present. Hence the urgency for an 'interfaith' dialogue and ecumenism felt by the believers. At the same time, it is impossible to have a real dialogue because tolerance (as a religious, not a secular stance) is simply not possible.

In the West, Christianity tried to universalise itself on a massive scale. Even though it underwent modifications and changes as it won converts, the first phase merely universalised a specific religion. However, its evolution and development laid the seeds for the universalisation of *religion* – not Christianity.

If religion has to be decked in one set of clothes, and it can be changed over the years, different clothes could deck religion too. Protestant reformation was the signal that sent many to hurry to their tailors. The tailoring profession prospered, the sartorial elegance spread, and religion could now be clothed in many different ways.

What we see after the reformation is the first phase in the universalisation of religion – unrestricted by space, time, culture or *ideational clothes*. As I have told it, this is the story of the French enlightenment: the thinkers from this period fought Christianity, attacked its doctrines –though not openly – and made fun of its beliefs. They were fighting religion, but only to free it from recognisably Christian clothes. The victory thereafter was the victory of religion in another set of clothes.

I would like to suggest that 'worldview' is that set of clothes. It was brought forth by a specific religion, *viz.* Christianity. The emergence of a worldview might seem to signal a halt to the march of Christianity both as a historical movement and as a specific religion. However, this does not mean that religion is not being universalised. It does so as a worldview, as something other than and different from Christianity, Judaism and Islam. A secular or scientific worldview will be different from these three religions. These religions make the Cosmos into an explanatory intelligible entity. A worldview does exactly the same, but in different ideational clothes. Thus, it will also be religion.

In this sense, the universalising drive of a religion involves a double movement: proselytisation and secularisation. This movement expresses itself in a religion that continues to remain itself, *viz. a* religion while *creating* another at the same time. The latter does not appear as 'religion'; it is, after all, the secular worldview. They oppose each other differently than those historical grounds on which the three religions confront each other. The shifting of grounds in our context merely means a shifting of historical constellations. Nevertheless, the rivalry between a religion and a secular worldview will still be along the old lines: religious rivalry.

In section #8.1, I raised the question whether religion remains both itself and the other. I have answered this question in the affirmative. As the explanatory intelligible account of the Cosmos, religion must universalise itself because every concrete form is a restriction on its universality.

If this argument holds water, let us see how it illumines the situation, which brought us thus far. The acceptance of religious beliefs in secular terms has occurred because religion has secularised itself – one aspect of its universalisation – while remaining a distinct religion that seeks to proselytise and convert (the other aspect of its universalising drive). Should this be true, we can indeed better appreciate why the belief in the universality of religion has such strong roots. Its roots are religious, and religion itself has very deep and very wide roots in the western culture.

If that is the case, what is the difficulty in identifying a non-religious worldview in the West? Why is there a feeling of an absence of a secular worldview while being guided, at the same time, by the conviction that there is one?

It has to do, I will propose in the next chapter, with the new clothes that religion has assumed over the centuries. Parallel and alongside proselytisation, Christianity has also been secularising itself. It is not a movement from yesterday, or from the Enlightenment or even from the Protestant reformation. Religion has constantly expressed this double movement. In fact, religion constitutes one element of the identity of the western culture as a culture. The belief that religion is one of the constitutive elements of culture is true only because the culture, which believes in this, is constituted by religion. The West, as a culture, was not given 2000 years ago; even today, it is not a finished entity as no culture is. The West has grown into a culture, the western culture, as religion has universalised itself. The West is a culture partly through the very story of religion itself. To tell such a story is to tell the story of a people in terms of one thread, an aspect, a theme, and of how, in fact, they became a people.

# PART IV

Taken together, the next two chapters bring us to our destination. In the previous part, I developed and tested my hypothesis about religion in chapter nine. The tenth chapter related it to the theme of the universality of religion. Here, however, the ambition is to develop an overarching hypothesis that should relate culture to religion.

More specifically, I characterise human cultures as configurations of learning and distinguish cultures accordingly. This enables me to expand the hypothesis about religion and relate its dynamic to the formation of western culture. The enlarged hypothesis not only enables a tentative characterisation of Indian (Asian) cultures, but also illumines ethnographic facts in a new and different light. This chapter embeds the last three parts in an explanatory framework as well.

However, such an exercise as this requires scrutiny from the perspectives in philosophy of the sciences. The last chapter assesses the status of my arguments and concludes on an answer to an epistemic question in anthropology, *viz.* the impossibility of describing the 'other' in language.

In the previous ten chapters, I have taken you through a journey. It constitutes an attempt to present and represent a process in the becoming of a people. My narrative is naked and threadbare, potted and impoverished. The tale is not about how a people and its culture came into being; but it hints, instead, in the direction of how such a story must be told. This is no blemish; nor is the recognition of inadequacies a confession of modesty. It is neither one nor the other, because such tales, including the one I have told, count merely as...

# CHAPTER ELEVEN

# PROLEGOMENA TO
# A COMPARATIVE SCIENCE OF CULTURES

Why "prolegomena"? That is because of the absence of what makes a science of cultures possible. Multiple descriptions given by members from different cultures of both themselves and others against the background of their own cultures are absent. Such (partial) descriptions that do not trivialise the nature of cultural differences are not many. I have tried to problematise both the existence of religion as a cultural universal and the belief about its universality by trying to catch them together in the same movement. In this chapter, I will explore some further implications of talking about the western culture in terms of the double dynamic of religion.

In the first section, I try to spell out my general argument. In the process, I pick up the unanswered and the vexed question of the relation between science and religion. In the second section, I look at the issue of describing the other: does my proposal help us speak of other cultures differently than before? In the third section, I look at India again and suggest how this proposal also lends a greater intelligibility to what we have seen of the Romans. Further, I describe the meeting of two cultures and touch upon the problem of migration of learning.

The treatment of the problems will be brief, as I do not have worked-out solutions. Yet, I cannot avoid looking at them not only because they are important, but also because my description raises these questions. Therefore, consider this treatment as an appetiser for another meal, a promise, but no more than that. To serve the main course as a dessert would not only violate all gastronomic conventions, but also elementary ideas of hospitality. In this sense, the dessert in this menu hints at the main course elsewhere – and this chapter introduces you to it: a comparative science of cultures. Together with the last two, this chapter enables us to answer the problems raised in the subsection #8.1.6. That concludes the second half of an argument.

## 11.1. Cultures As Configurations of Learning

In the previous chapter, I spoke of the double dynamic of religion in terms of secularisation and proselytisation. The West emerged as a culture and became a distinct cultural entity through, among other things, this movement. To speak of the western culture, it is no requirement that one defines "the West" first. As I have tried to tell the story, the West is the becoming of a people. In his brilliant book on the formation of the western legal tradition, Berman formulates the idea thus:

> The West...is not to be found by recourse to a compass. Geographical boundaries help to locate it, but they shift from time to time. The West is, rather, a cultural term, but with a very strong diachronic dimension. It is not, however, simply an idea, it is a community. It implies both a historical structure and a structured history...
>
> ...The West, from this perspective, is not Greece, and Rome and Israel but the people of Western Europe *turning* to the Greek and Roman and Hebrew texts for inspiration, and *transforming* those texts in ways that would have astonished their authors. (Berman 1983: 2-3; italics in the original.)

In many ways, the above paragraphs capture what I have done. Nevertheless, unlike Berman, I am obliged to do more. As it is relevant to my concerns, I need to provide a partial synchronic snapshot of the western culture as well. In #11.1.1, I tackle this question and describe cultural differences along the lines of culturally specific ways of learning. Subsequently, in (#11.1.2), I go deeper into the issue by touching (but not solving) the issue of the relationship between religion and science.

### 11.1.1. Learning Processes and Cultural Differences

In broad terms, learning is the *way* an organism makes its environment *habitable*. That is, learning is an activity of making a habitat. When compared to other animals, the human species suffers from disadvantages from several points of view: it takes a (relatively) long period before the human infant is able to fend for itself; its physiology is unsuited for living unaided under extreme climatic and weather conditions; it has no natural preys; and so on. Such a species, if it has to survive at all (it has survived for so long, whatever the future may bring), will have to place an enormous premium on its ability to make the environment(s) habitable, *i.e.* learning is extremely crucial to its survival.

Evolutionary theory further tells us that the sexual act is an inefficient way of guaranteeing human progeny. Coping with groups has been as important as coping with nature in the survival of our species. Human groups, thus, constitute the second environment of the human infant.

When we look at human beings and their learning processes from the point of view of these two environments, the activity of making a habitat assumes complex proportions: one has to *learn* to live with the group; one has to *learn* to live in the natural environment.

Human beings are socialised in the framework of groups. I am using 'socialisation' in the broadest possible sense, *i.e.* as living with others. When socialised, an organism learns who these others are and what it means to live with them. What the human organism learns depends largely on the content of transmission. If we look only at the transmission, the process of socialisation involves transmitting knowledge from the reservoir of a group. The resources of a group, *i.e.* its customs, myths, traditions, and what-have-you, constitute the reservoir from which the organism learns.

The same reservoir puts constraints on the content and the mechanisms of transmission. Child-rearing, formal and informal schooling, *etc.*, are the mechanisms of transmission from one generation to another. These socialisation mechanisms have evolved through either deliberation or reflection or through unintended discovery processes. They are further constrained by the content of transmission.

What is a learning process, when looked at from the point of view of the organism that is being socialised, is also a teaching process if looked at from the vantage point of those who socialise this organism. These teachers also draw upon the resources of the group to which they belong.

Methods and ways of teaching an organism will teach if, and only if, they dovetail into the processes of learning. Are we genetically compelled to learn in any one particular way? Evolutionarily speaking, I believe the answer will have to be in the negative because of the great diversity of environments: not only have human beings structured their groups differently during the course of history but they have also occupied diverse regions of the earth. The argument from diversity does not establish conclusively that we are not programmed to learn in any one specific way. It could be the case that there is one learning process, which can be applied flexibly in a variety of ways. Nevertheless, given the diversity of human achievements, it is more attractive to speak of different kinds of learning processes. The creation of complex societies and forms of social interaction over the centuries; the creation of rich and subtle theories and speculations; the creation of wonderful forms of music, dancing, and such others – all of these lend a greater plausibility to the idea that they are the results of different kinds of learning processes. At some future date, it might be possible to show that these products are the results of applying one method of learning. Until such time, we can work with the idea that human beings are born equipped with an ability or capacity to learn, but not with any species-typical learning process.

For a human infant, learning involves going-about in the world. That is to say, it learns to go-about in the natural and in the social environments. It learns these goings-about from its group. The broader environment is accessible through the social environment and the latter forms the going-about in the world. In this way, the organism develops a structured way of going-about in the world. Both the nature and extent of this structuring depend on the social environment: what the environment transmits and how it does so.

One of the differences between human groups lies in the way they are structured. That is, human beings have created different kinds of social environments. In so far as goings-about in the world constitute an aspect of culture, the difference between cultures have something to do with the differences in social environments. Thus, cultural differences between human groups will have 'something' to do with the different ways of going-about in the world. Because learning involves going-about in the world, it is plausible to suggest that cultural differences will have something to do with differences in learning processes.

*Cultural Difference and Configurations of Learning*

I am making two different suggestions in the above paragraphs. Firstly, there are many kinds of learning processes; secondly, there are differences in learning processes as they relate to cultures. As I treat the issue, these two do not fall together. Present across cultures are several kinds of learning processes: the kind that is required to build societies and groups; the kind that creates poetry, music and dance; the kind required to develop theories and speculations, *etc.* As I see them, these different kinds of learning processes are the common adaptive strategies developed by each human group that has survived as a culture. Cultures transmit these learning processes to their members. The latter, in their turn, learn them to a different degree and in different combinations. If we characterise the product of learning as 'knowledge', we can rewrite the above proposal thus: by producing knowledge, human beings manage to live in the world; there are different kinds of knowledge; in each culture, different kinds of knowledge are present. They constitute the reservoir of cultures and teaching involves transmitting them.

As a *first* approximation, the difference between cultures is the presence of these several kinds of knowledge in different degrees. Learning processes produce knowledge and the former are constrained not only by the content of the transmission, but also by how the transmission takes place. Therefore, as a *second* approximation, cultural differences can be chalked out according to the constraints placed on the learning processes.

These constraints pattern or structure the goings-about of an individual in the world. That is, there are patterns or structures to our learning activities. Therefore, as a *third* approximation, we can plot cultural differences along the lines of how our goings-about in the world are structured.

Each culture uses something or the other to structure the goings-about of its members. The teachers draw upon the resources of their groups to do this; so does the individual. As an individual organism is socialised and goes-about, it also learns to structure the further goings-about.

The goings-about are of different kinds – whether we look at them socially or at an individual level. As said earlier, minimally there are two kinds: going-about in the natural environment, and going-about in the social environment. The varieties of going-about in each of these environments depend upon the different kinds of knowledge present in a culture. Therefore, the structuring of these goings-about also structures them *as* different kinds of goings-about in the world. Thus, we have a *fourth* approximation: the patterning of the goings-about into different kinds indicates cultural differences. This process uses something or another to do the patterning.

How can something, any thing, do this? If the processes of learning also involve a meta-learning, *viz.* a learning to learn; if what is used to form or structure learning also brings about this meta-learning; then, indeed, as teachers teach so the individual learns. He not only learns some knowledge but also learns to produce this knowledge. The extent to which any given individual does this is not at issue. I am not talking about inter-individual differences within a culture but about inter-cultural differences. Consequently, we have a *fifth* approximation to plotting inter-cultural differences: they can be described in terms of that which structures the different goings-about in the world by generating the process(es) of learning to learn.

The above paragraphs answer the question of what is specific to cultures. That is, some group is a culture because of what it uses to structure the different goings-about in the world. Because the process of structuring configures different kinds of learning, one kind of learning is *dominant* in such a configuration. Other kinds of learning are *subordinate*. I call such configurations of learning processes as culture-specific ways of learning.

Therefore, as a *sixth* approximation, my suggestion amounts to this: one can partially describe cultural differences in terms of culture-specific ways of learning. Specific to each culture is a configuration of learning, where one kind of learning is *dominant* and the others subordinate. This emphasis entails that one kind of learning to learn (or meta-learning) dominates all other learning process (together with their meta-learning). Consequently, typical to each configuration of learning is a type of learning to learn. This meta-learning depends on the kind of learning dominant in the configuration.

To summarise, specific to each culture is its configuration of learning and meta-learning. Therefore, we can partially study cultural differences in terms of the entity that brings about a configuration of learning.

Three caveats. Even though abundantly clear, I would still like to emphasise that I am talking about a configuration of learning processes as a culturally specific way of learning. This does not entail that in each culture only one kind of learning process is present. Nor am I suggesting that subordinate learning processes are not taught or learnt. I merely claim that the relationship between the dominant and subordinate learning processes varies across cultures.

Secondly, even more importantly, one must see this process in developmental terms. Over a period, the configuration of learning comes into being slowly by coordinating different kinds of learning processes. It is stable only to the extent cultures are, and finished only the way cultures could be.

Thirdly, because we can study a culture by studying the entity that brings about a culture-specific way of learning, one can also describe a culture in terms of a culture-specific knowledge. Even though the knowledge produced by each learning process is present in all cultures, even though each configuration of learning contains learning processes present in all cultures, knowledge produced by a configuration of learning (*i.e.* a culture-specific way of learning) is culture-specific.

With respect to the theme of this essay, here is my suggestion. In the West, a root model of order brings about a configuration of learning. This root model is religion, which configures learning processes by structuring the experience of the world. Typically, this specific way of learning is a "knowing about". It produces a culture-specific knowledge, a species of knowledge, *viz.* theoretical knowledge, that we call sciences.

### 11.1.2. Religion as the Root Model of Order

As we have seen, religion claims that the world is explanatorily intelligible. As I have said repeatedly, it does not just claim it; it *makes* the world into such an entity. How does it do the latter? By being an exemplification of precisely that order, which the Cosmos is supposed to be.

To accept the account of religion is to experience the Cosmos as an explanatorily intelligible entity. To experience the Cosmos this way is to preserve the account because the latter exemplifies that order. The structure of its account mirrors what it claims to be the structure of the world. Because of this relation, religion is *the* model of the order the world is supposed to be.

Religion is also the root model of order. It generates an attitude and an orientation; it puts constraints on the intellectual and practical energies of a culture; it forms the sense and feeling of relevance and importance; and so on. It is able to do this because it is the ultimate example for something to be an account: the structure of its description mirrors the structure of the object described. In this sense, it is the basic model, which inspires the other explanations.

Religion, thus, generates or forms a culturally specific way of learning: going-about in the world requires knowledge about the world. Orientation and successful navigation in the world require knowing what there is in the world.

This meta-orientation comes about because religion claims that the Cosmos expresses God's purposes. To act in the world requires knowing (to the extent it is possible for us to know this, of course) what that purpose is. Therefore, knowledge about the world – knowing what there is in the world – is a prerequisite for *properly* going-about in the world.

Knowing what there is in the world is to seek and decipher God's Will as it is expressed in the world. It is both revealed and hidden: His Will is revealed in the phenomena, and is their hidden regulator. Discovering these regularities focus the intellectual and practical energies of this culture. Because knowing what there is in the world is the prerequisite for acting properly in the world, knowledge about the world guides proper activities. That is to say, all actions in the world are 'proper' in so far the knowledge-about *guides them*. In order to be a friend or a father, one should know what it is to be a friend or father; to build a good society, one should first know what a good society is; to build human relationships, one should know what they are...*etc*. A rational action is an execution of a rational decision, which is itself the result of a rational deliberation using rational criteria about rationally gathered information. Human goings-about in the world begin to mirror the Divine in many ways. God's Will and His Actions are different from each other but difficult to distinguish. Human intentions and human actions appear to share the same fate. Actions are individuated according to the intentional states they instantiate; the very identity (or existence) of actions depends upon specifying the agent and his intentions.

What makes this "knowing about" into the dominant way of learning is its extension to all other goings-about in the world. To know a people or a culture is to know their 'beliefs'. Because all human actions are expressions of beliefs, to know cultures is to have knowledge about the beliefs of these cultures. These beliefs, of course, will have to do with what they think about the world, what they think about what there is in the world, *etc*. In other words, a culture-specific way of learning is also expressed in the way a culture seeks to understand other cultures.

God has revealed His Will not merely in the world. There is also His message. The message does several things in this culture: as a message, because *oral*, it is not only a source of knowledge but also *the* form of knowledge. All knowledge is *sayable*. Not everything said is knowledge – of course not – but, if something is knowledge, it can be said. Otherwise, it is a hunch, an intuition, perhaps even a skill. In liberal or tolerant moments, one might speak in terms of "artistic", "poetic" and such other "knowledge". However, the bottom-line is this: knowledge is what can be said. If we cannot, it shows that we do not have knowledge.

Even though this message is *oral*, it is knowledge because it is constantly accessible as a text. As the form of knowledge, knowledge is *textual*. Not merely in the sense that one sees accumulation of knowledge as a possibility only when it is written down (see Staal's wonderful critique in his 1986b), but also in the sense that one can know only by textualising the items. Stories, sagas, myths, *etc*, become *texts*, studying which one can find out what they are saying. This *interpretative* orientation can be carried as far as one likes: actions can be interpreted in terms of beliefs or in terms of symbols; cultures can be interpreted in terms of their worldviews; and, further, one could even see cultures as texts and oneself as the hermeneutist. The possibilities are truly endless and giddying.

In such a culture, both inter-cultural and inter-individual problems begin to shift to the level of messages. The problem of inter-cultural understanding tends to become one of inter-cultural *communication* and this is thematised as verbal communication. Not that 'nonverbal' communications are not cognised; but they are seen in terms of the sent 'messages' and the 'interpretative' difficulties. Inter-individual problems get resolved by talking *about* them. Sophisticated psychological jargon ends up as clichés in the daily language.

Art, architecture, poetry…become subordinate modes as a culture-specific way of learning grows and gains in strength. They too are embodiments of ideas; they too tell us about the world. The artist tells us about his perception of what there is in the world; he expresses 'abstract' ideas (I wonder what a 'concrete' idea looks like!); he does 'conceptual' art and, through his chosen medium, enters into *debates* with contemporaries. Art is thinking about; art makes you think-about too. The distance between a critic of art and an artist begins to narrow. What counts are one's ideas, irrespective of whether one can paint or sculpt. After all, so one could *argue*, a book about boredom, properly speaking, should exemplify the subject matter by being extremely boring.

Thus the story can go on, tracing the impact of this way of learning as it courses through the veins of a culture. Thinking – a component of this way of learning – is common across cultures. What distinguishes the West from all other cultures is the culturally specific way of learning. It makes knowledge-about the only form of knowledge and learning becomes the seeking of this knowledge.

Knowledge about what? Of what there is. What is there? An explanatorily intelligible entity. That is to say, the Cosmos becomes a *place* where you can ask different kinds of questions. One such pertains to 'meaning'; the other is explanation seeking. It is possible to ask and answer both kinds of questions.

As the root model of order, religion enables one to pose the "meaning problems": does the Cosmos have a meaning? What is the meaning of man? What is the meaning of life? What is the meaning of my life? So on *ad infinitum*. The foundation or the presupposition of these questions can and does vary: then it was the Bible, now it could be biology; then it was the infinite God, today it is our finitude, *etc.*

What makes the West into a culture, among other things, is this: the gradual emergence of religion as the root model of order. This is the process of the universalisation of religion: proselytisation by the Christian communities and the secularisation of religion as the root model of order. I suggest we have difficulty in identifying a secular worldview because of this situation: 'worldview' picks out what I am calling the root model of order.

Let me summarise. This way of learning, seeking knowledge about, has generated *theoretical knowledge*: the natural sciences – a species of knowledge that grew out of a religious culture. If you are willing to entertain these suggestions, we can take a further step in characterising 'religion' or worldview as the root model of order, which forms a way of learning that produces a specific kind of knowledge, *viz.* theoretical knowledge. If this distinguishes cultures from one another, having religion or worldview characterises the West as a culture.

More than once, I have related the development of science to religion. Most history books tell another story. It is time, therefore, that we touch upon this issue.

*A Dialogue Concerning Religion*

Let me describe the moments involved in the kind of experience that religion structures. The best way of doing this is to return to the primitive man and the question of the origin of religion (chapter #5). Recollect, if you will, that one of the reasons for the origin of religion – as people argued – had to do with the alleged experience of the primitive man, who experienced nature as 'chaotic'. As I said then, I reiterate now, there is no way the primitive man could have confronted chaos. If anything, he would have been impressed by the orderliness of the world. Besides, why should he assume that it is in the nature of the divine being(s) to impose order and, furthermore, why should these be "hidden, causal forces" – as Hume put it? Let us reconsider these issues in the light of what has been said about the Biblical structuring of the experience of the world (chapter #9), and my suggestion about religion as the root model of order for the West.

The Bible conveys that the Will of The Sovereign governs the world. If religion – to the extent the Biblically inspired movements are religions – shapes the basic experience of the world-as-an-order, how could we describe such an experience? Let me distinguish *three* conceptually distinct moments in this experience by taking our primitive man as an example.

To begin with, he has a naive experience of order. This naive experience is merely that of the regularities of his world: seasonal, astronomical, natural, and biological. Let us further suppose that he comes across unfamiliar (unanticipated, unexpected) events. Now his world consists of two groups of events: the familiar and the unfamiliar. The group of unfamiliar events, generally speaking, undergoes reduction in size as time progresses. Regular encounters with the strange and the unfamiliar transform them into the familiar, even if they remain unexpected and unanticipated. Thus he would have gone to his grave, had he not had the fortune of meeting a member from a religious culture, a certain Mr. David Hume by name.

"Look here, old fellow", as an imaginary *Dialogue Concerning the Necessity of Religion* might have gone on, "why do you think there was thunder when the sky was cloudless, and there is no rain on the plains?"

Our primitive, let us not dignify him with baptism yet, scratches his head, looks up at the blue sky, blinks in puzzlement, and admits that it never really struck him to ask this question.

"I forgive you for this lapse, not being Scottish and all that", continues our Mr. Hume, "but tell me, dear chap, why the sky is blue, why do pigs have no wings, or even why your father died the other day?"

Our primitive gapes at the extraordinary acumen of the interrogator and replies that things have always been that way ever since he was a young boy. The sky is blue when there are no clouds on the horizon; many people he has known have died; and as to why the pigs do not have wings, well, there is this story his grandmother told him...

"Yes, yes, I know all that", interrupts Mr. Hume impatiently. "But why, my dear fellow, Why?"

Without waiting for an answer, Mr. Hume goes on:

"You see, thunder strikes from a cloudless sky, the sky itself is blue, people die, pigs do not have wings...and you do not even know why. There is no rhyme or reason to any of these things. In fact..." Pausing ominously for a moment, Mr. Hume lowers his voice to a dramatic whisper. "Don't you see, old man, the world is a chaos. Things just happen..."

In other words, the second conceptual moment must deny the naive experience of order, focus attention on the unexpected, unanticipated, and the unfamiliar. Having done this, it must then *reinterpret* the familiar and the expected in terms of the unfamiliar and the unexpected. (For a description of science as an activity of reducing the known into the unknown, see Popper 1972, 1979.) At this stage, the world does appear chaotic in the light of an account that has re-described the world.

The third conceptual moment reintroduces order into this chaotic world. This too is part of an account: the ordering force is invisible; it is hidden below the surface. It is not an empirical given, but one which manifests itself in the form of the 'order' the world has or appears to have. As David Hume put it:

> The order of the universe proves an omnipotent mind; that is, a mind whose will is *constantly attended* with the obedience of every creature and being. (Hume 1740: 633, n. 1; Hume's italics.)

Perhaps, this 'omnipotent mind' was in Hume's mind when he wrote to a friend in 1754 (cited in Davies 1982: 77):

> But allow me to tell you that I never asserted so absurd a Proposition as *that anything might arise without cause*: I only maintain'd that, our Certainty of the Falsehood of that Proposition proceeded neither from Intuition nor Demonstration; but from another Source.

These, then, are the conceptual moments involved in the experience of the world-as-an-order in a religious culture: the bracketing away of a naive experience of order, postulation of chaotic phenomena, and rediscovery of an underlying force to account for the apparent phenomenal order. Hume's description of the origin of religion is not an account of how religions came into being, but an expression of his own and his culture's experience of the world. It involves the postulation of a hidden force to reduce the 'chaos' the world is. Precisely this account makes the world appear chaotic in the first place.

Such an experience of the world (*i.e.* the world as an entity governed by rules) requires that the experience is structured by an account. It has to be an account, linguistic in nature, because both 'chaos' and the underlying 'order' are "theoretical" notions and not any part of a naïve experience of the world. The *concepts* of chaos, randomness, and regularities that connect descriptions of phenomena are meta-concepts relative to a given theory or used while contrasting theories about the world. (See, *e.g.* Kuntz, Ed., 1968.) That is to say, one experiences the world-as-an-order in terms of a particular *kind* of order. No experience without categorisation, as the slogan goes. That is why the world is alleged to be a "bloomin', buzzin' confusion" to a child that has not yet learnt to categorise.

In this sense too are these explanations about the origin of religion, as I said in chapter #5, "the results of the development of religion" but not its "experiential presuppositions". Religion *makes* the world into an explanatorily intelligible entity, and does so as an account.

In other words, religion structures the experience of the world so that, in the absence of deeper and underlying laws, the phenomenal world seems chaotic. Human beings have never experienced a chaotic world, outside and independent of an experience of the world-as-an-order. Yet, those who belong to a religious culture are convinced that such is the case. Consequently, they attribute an experience of chaos to the primitive man, who could order his world only by postulating an invisible set of powers to regulate chaos and provide order.

### 11.1.3. Science and the Root Model of Order

One of the most familiar stories regarding the growth of scientific thinking in the West, regarding its early stages at least, is about the conflict between the Church and science. The religious institutions consistently impeded the investigation of nature; religious doctrines lost out to the triumphant, if at times troubled, march of scientific theories; religious persecutions created martyrs in the cause of science and freethinking; *etc.* While there is a great deal of truth to all of these, the basic thrust of this story – *viz.* the conflict between religion and science – can be put in a different light.

I would like to claim that this conflict is not due to any inherent antagonism between science and religion. As suggested earlier on (chapter #9), religion was a necessary condition for the development of scientific thinking and, as I suggest now, religion generates a culturally-specific way of learning. Before explicating this proposal, however, let me note that many before me have perceived the important role religion has played in the growth of science. Most notable of them is the Dutch historian of science, R. Hooykaas (Hooykaas 1972). But their arguments (see also Whitehead 1925; Burtt 1932; Shapiro 1983) are not mine – I shall suggest a different thesis.

*Firstly*, religion related phenomena to each other: the Cosmos to the individual; actions to beliefs; individuals to society, and provided the ground for all of these in one single postulate. In its conflict with the 'philosophical schools' of the Graeco-Roman period, one of the virtues of the Christian doctrine was its simplicity: the God of the Bible was the fountainhead of everything. *Secondly,* this doctrine provided an explanatory link – appealed to the invisible ordering force – between phenomena apparently unconnected otherwise. As I have said already, this explanatory link is the purpose of God. The explanatory 'unification' of Cosmic processes, the dissemination of this belief among all layers of the population for more than a thousand years, is absolutely unique to religion. For my purposes at hand, it does not matter how exactly this belief was expressed. Even though these details are extremely important for a better understanding of both science and religion, I cannot provide them here lacking both the required competence and knowledge. Nevertheless, I make the claim I do because no matter whether the belief in the explanatory intelligibility of the Cosmos was due to the 'desacralisation of nature'; no matter whether the notion of 'scientific law' had its analogue in the idea of divine legislation (as Zilsel 1942 and Needham 1951 argued) or it had independent roots (as Ruby 1986 convincingly shows); no matter whether other 'philosophical schools' of the Graeco-Roman period had developed doctrines that Christianity absorbed and transformed; the typical belief that pervaded and grounded the basic attitude of the West for centuries long was the explanatory intelligibility of the Cosmos. *Thirdly,* this was not a surface intelligibility – it was deep, neither manifest nor evident to the senses – but one that required a search for the underlying explanatory units.

In other words, what one calls a 'scientific' attitude today is continuous with the religious attitude. Religion formed it, nurtured it, and gave birth to science as a result. In its absence, as I have suggested, there would have been no science. (For a weaker version of this thesis, see Funkenstein 1986; hints in Smith, H. 1972.)

Religion, then, provides us with the basic model, the most fundamental one in fact, of what it is for something to be an explanation. It links parts of the world to each other by postulating necessary and intelligible connections between them. This is the reason why, I would like to suggest, "sciences" (as we know the natural sciences) emerged in religious cultures: among the Jews, Christians, and the Muslims. And why they failed to emerge in, say, China (this is the famous "Needham question"). As I say, this is not sufficient to explain the extraordinary growth of sciences. I am simply identifying one of the conditions for their emergence in the West. However, to make this claim stick, several other questions require to be answered: what about the sciences in the Antiquity? How are we to understand the conflict between science and religion? How about the development of the science of language and ritual in India?

I cannot adequately answer these questions today. My answers, much like those given by others, are fragmentary. Nevertheless, I shall try to trace one thread of an answer, as it is relevant to two of these questions.

## Religion and Science

With respect to the growth and development of science, I think that the following condition requires to be fulfilled. There must be a fertile cognitive soil, where speculations and theories can take root and grow. In Antiquity, to be sure, we do see the emergence of sciences (geometry, hydrostatics, *etc.*). Their growth was constrained by the extremely limited social group within which they arose. What religion (specifically Christianity) did was to generalise the attitude required for the growth of sciences. It cut the link, so to speak, that had tied sciences to a small social group. Now sciences could really develop and expand, luxuriously growing in the soil prepared for it, while helping to farm the ground further.

That is to say, religion transformed science into a social process by slowly universalising itself and through the proselytising drive of a religion. It formed a way of learning through which sciences could emerge and enabled their emergence by making the Will of the Sovereign constant, His works trustworthy, in an absolutely perfect way. There is, in other words, a qualitative difference between the sciences in the Antiquity and the sciences of today.

This dynamic of religion also helps us to understand the conflict between religion and science. The universalisation of religion, as I have said, is through the proselytising drive of a religion. Proselytisation of a religion also meant a secularisation of religion (in the sense of a crystallisation of the root model of order). The secularisation of religion, however, limits its other aspect, *viz.* proselytisation of a religion. Consequently, a religion, Christianity, is limited by itself, *i.e.* in its character as religion. Hence, in the initial stages, we witness hostility against the growth of sciences and scientific theories. These theories challenged the doctrines of a religion. Until then, only rival religions formulated such challenges. The consequence of the challenge by the scientific theories was that Christianity ended up treating them as rivals.

However, scientific theories express knowledge – human, fallible and tentative. They cannot challenge the 'totally other' kind of knowledge that religion claims to be. The emergence of this human knowledge, however, is due to religion bringing forth a culturally specific way of learning. Consequently, both appear related and human knowledge seems to challenge the Divine Knowledge.

Nevertheless, a religion recognises itself, even in the 'other' of religion, in a secularised religion. Hence, the ambiguous attitude of Christianity had towards scientific theories. It did not appear a religious rival, yet there was something recognisable about it. Science may or may not challenge the doctrines of a specific religion. However, that does not give us a 'religion versus science' controversy. Ideally, religion is tied to no doctrine, but religions are always tied to doctrines.

In other words, it was not clear, even today it does not appear so to some, whether science itself was a worldview; or whether it fleshed out an existing worldview; or whether it could lead to a new worldview; and so on. That is to say, the hostility between religion and science had to do with determining the identity of the latter: What kind of a thing was this 'science'? To be sure, it uncovered some order in a finite slice of the world and it provided accounts, but what precisely did these indicate?

I have tried to argue that the 'knowledge' that religion is can never be claimed by finite human beings. Our knowledge is hypothetical and tentative, whereas religion lays claim to the truth. There are basic epistemic dissimilarities between religion and science.

There is yet another dissimilarity, which the received wisdom of today bemoans, between a worldview and the scientific theories, if we look at the latter in their evolutionary dynamic. I have suggested that, as human beings, we can only have a perspectival relationship with *the world*. Growth of knowledge – theoretical knowledge, that is – implies (in this framework) knowledge of increasingly more slices of the world. The more we slice the world, the more slices there will be to the world; the more we are able to slice the world, the more we know how to slice, which leads to more slicing...That is to say, specialisation increases in leaps and bounds. Increase in knowledge can only take the form of increasing specialisation.

This view has two important consequences. The so-called 'fragmentation' of human knowledge is no fragmentation of *human* knowledge at all. This is what human knowledge is like – and this is how it grows. In this sense, such a 'fragmentation' is highly desirable, if theoretical knowledge is desirable at all.

The second consequence is with respect to the relation between human knowledge and "the truth" that religion is. I suggest that the former is indifferent to the latter, *i.e.* any kind of human knowledge is indifferent to "the truth". As human beings slice the world up in many different ways, and the knowledge of these slices combine and recombine in different ways, human knowledge moves away from – neither against nor for, but totally indifferent to – religious knowledge.

To sum up: the conflict between science and religion, as I see the issue, is both historical in nature (see also Brooke 1990, 1991) and a case of mistaken identity. A controversy between, say, evolutionary theory and Creationism is a conflict between two different claims about the world but not any 'science vs. religion' discussion.

I do not know whether these suggestions will bear scrutiny or not. That is something, which only further empirical research into the history of sciences and further theory building with respect to religion can solve.

*Slicing a Problem*

Let us now take stock of a problem as it has been growing throughout this section. Religion forms a culturally specific way of learning, which gives birth to science, and it does so by allowing a particular kind of learning to dominate. (As suggested, any configuration of learning has dominant and subordinate learning processes. What is particular to the West is that 'knowledge-about' – or theoretical learning – dominates.) As the root model of order, religion is the worldview of the West. After all, it structures nothing less than the experience of *the world* itself. As something that generates a configuration of learning, its attitude seeps into every walk and facet of human life in the West. When the West looks at other cultures it looks at them in its own terms. As the dominant mode of learning, theoretical learning *founds* other modes of learning. It is, however, its own foundation.

What are its limits? At first sight, theoretical learning – or theoretical knowledge – appears unlimited. Firstly, only knowledge can draw the limits to knowledge (ignorance is not the limit of knowledge); secondly, the dominant way of learning subordinates other knowledge producing processes to itself, these other knowledges cannot draw that limit; thirdly, as a consequence, theoretical knowledge draws its own limit. Hence, it appears as though there are no limits to this configuration of learning.

There are, however, limits. Limits are postulated both from the outside and from the inside. The heathens and the pagans limit religion; other cultures limit some particular culture; the boundary to knowledge is drawn by knowledge and within knowledge.

Our knowledge about the world itself draws the first limit: by pointing out other configurations of learning present in cultures elsewhere. This is the result of our knowledge about the world. Up to a point, this very same knowledge also helps us describe the contours of other kinds of knowledge. Here, it runs up against itself. Other kinds of knowledge – as products of other configurations of learning – are as much knowledge as theoretical knowledge is. In other configurations of learning, other kinds of learning have subordinated the learning process that dominates here. Such configurations constitute the limits of this culturally specific way of learning in exactly the same way the latter constitutes the limits to the former.

In the next section, therefore, let me draw the limits to a configuration of learning, a culture-specific way of going-about in the world, from within itself. It is sufficient that we pick out an alternate configuration – show how such a configuration could possibly generate knowledge. More is not required at this stage. After all, I want to draw a limit and show that it can be done within the descriptive possibilities opened up so far. My example, again, is India.

## 11.2. Conceptualising Cultural Differences

We can say that cultural ways of learning are the adaptive strategies of human beings that not only enable them to survive, but do so as human cultures. Our access to the broader environment, where we survive as a species, is through the social environment that our cultures are. Therefore, we survive as a species by developing ways of learning that not only give birth to our cultures but also sustain them. In this sense, we could see configurations of learning as cultural answers to the biological problem of our survival. That is, they answer the question: 'How to live?'

One answer to this question is to find out what there is in the place we live in. This is a simplified way of formulating the issue but it is sufficient to indicate a second possible simplified answer. Another answer to the question treats it as a problem of *how* to go-about in the world. That is, both the question and the answer become *performative* in nature.

In such a case, a practical or performative learning process will dominate the configuration of learning. As a culturally specific way of learning, it would also evolve and give identity to a culture. Such a culture exists, I would like to suggest, and it is an Asian culture, *viz.* India. Its way of going-about solves the problem of 'how to live' not by building a worldview but by developing among its members *an ability* to try to live the best way they can. That is to say, such is their way of learning that it teaches them *how to live*. This is not done by imparting knowledge *about* the world but by imparting *practical knowledge*.

If Indian traditions have to impart this knowledge to their members, the latter must be capable of learning this 'how to' ability. At the same time, this culture itself must be an embodiment of this 'how to' knowledge. This is to say two things:

(a) The most dominant unit of teaching does *not* impart any knowledge about the world, *i.e.* it does not tell you much about what the world is like. If it does not do this, such units of knowledge do not explain. Where they do not, these teaching or learning units, which impart knowledge to the members of this culture, are neither explanatory nor are they *true or false*. Stories, as I said earlier (#10.2), are neither true nor false and they are not explanatory.

(b) If this way of learning is specific to a culture, then its dominant
mode of learning must be deeply connected to *practices*. That is,
goings-about in the world must itself be experienced in *performative* terms.

In this section, I will give a staccato description of this configuration
of learning to illustrate both the idea and the title of this chapter. In
this process, the hope is that the central theme and arguments become
more perspicuous.

### 11.2.1. Another Configuration of Learning

Let us try to envisage a culture-specific way of going-about, where practical or performative knowledge (seen as a 'how to' ability) dominates.
This is a purely hypothetical construction. It is generated under the
constraints imposed upon us by a particular kind of knowledge, *viz.*
theoretical knowledge. I should like to identify these constraints.

*First*, let us specify the domain of such knowledge. It will have to do
with building and sustaining groups and societies; creating and sustaining inter-individual relationships both as inter-personal ones and
as relationships between social beings; and so on. More broadly put,
practical knowledge has the social environment as its domain.

*Second*, if this knowledge has to be the dominant one in a culture,
it has specific implications with respect to the first point. The growth,
development, differentiation, *etc.*, of the social environment must proceed without being guided by the knowledge about the social or natural
environment. This alone would not be sufficient, of course: all human
societies have evolved without their individual members knowing about
any of these aspects. Let us, therefore, strengthen the condition: the social environment must exhibit an extraordinary degree of stability and
cohesion, integration and differentiation, complexity and dynamism.
Individual members should be able to reproduce such an environment
without knowing about the rules of its reproduction. Even this is not
enough, but this suffices for our present purposes.

*Third*, performative knowledge must subordinate other kinds of
knowledge. That is to say, the 'object' of thinking about must be the
activities of going-about; the purpose of thinking about is to improve
these activities; but because these activities are the dominant ones in
the configuration, thinking about these actions does not provide the
foundation to going-about the world, but functions as its critic.

*Fourth*, theoretical speculations about what there is in the world
must be coloured by the goings-about in the world. That is to say, such
hypotheses must be formulated in recognisably performative terms.

Configurations of learning, as suggested earlier on, are brought
into being by 'something' that structures our goings-about. Analogous

to what is said about the West, in a configuration of learning where practical or performative learning dominates, the entity that structures the configuration must itself be a structured set of goings-about in the world. While this is the *fifth* constraint that goes into our visualisation of such a configuration of learning, there is also a *sixth* one.

We have seen that the structuring of goings-about in the world must enable an individual to continue to give form to all his further goings-about in the world. That is to say, this structured set of goings-about, which structures the learning processes, must also generate a meta-learning, a way of learning to learn.

*Seventh,* and finally, not merely must this way of learning to learn itself be performative; it is not even enough that one learns to structure learning processes performatively. More is required if this configuration of learning has to be stable enough to become a culturally specific way of learning. Both the structure of the entity that forms the configuration of learning and the structure of this way of going-about the world should be seen (by us) as a possible answer to the problem of survival.

These seven parameters merely enable us to think more concretely about a different configuration of learning. Even though, in principle, one does not have any objection to the idea that learning processes are connected to the culture of an organism, it is difficult to say more about what a 'different' configuration of learning processes looks like.

Even though it is now possible to see how another configuration could exist, our question is whether it does exist on earth. If it does, why has it not been seen so far? Much as I would like to answer both questions exhaustively and single-handedly, I am afraid I cannot build a comparative science of cultures on my own and so easily. Nevertheless, I will try to take a step towards answering both. That is to say, I will put down a few points, which appear to indicate the existence of such cultures; this essay as a whole gives one strand of an answer to the second question.

## On the Nature of the Configuration

I would like to approach the first problem by talking a bit more about the entity that could structure the configuration of learning where performative learning dominates. What kind of an entity is it?

Such an entity is a structured set of actions. What it must do is enable different kinds of goings-about in the world. The best way an entity could do this is by being a structured set of actions that belongs to no specific kind of going-about in the world. (We can conceive our actions in the world in terms of *kinds:* teaching, acting as a father, doing logic, visiting friends, *etc.* For our purposes, it is sufficient to know that 'kinds of activities' merely group similar or identical actions together.) That is to say, if this entity were to be a set of *generic* goings-about, activities pure and simple, action *simpliciter*, then it could indeed structure our different goings-about by enabling different kinds of going-about.

It would be useful to look at what this entity has to do if it has to structure actions. Let us do so by drawing a parallel between this entity and religion on the one hand, and looking at the way we talk about actions on the other.

Let us begin with the latter. Actions are individuated according to the intentional states of an actor they instantiate. That is, actions are what an *actor* does; what he *believes* to be doing; what he hopes (desires, anticipates, *etc.*) to achieve thereby. You could also speak of the means he uses, why he believes these are useful to what he intends to bring-about, what he knows about either the means or the ways of achieving the goals...*etc.* but these refinements are not necessary for us.

Minimally, we need at least two things to identify an action: an actor and his intentions. Why do we need either of the two? In one way of going-about in the world, actions are expressions of belief-states. Because belief-states are always of someone or another, we need an actor.

We are now talking *about* another configuration of learning where this is not the case. How could we describe generic actions, actions as such, actions *simpliciter*, from within the framework of a configuration of learning where actions are expressions of belief? The answer is obvious: generic actions are those that do not instantiate any belief-states; therefore, *a fortiori*, actions that are agent-less; hence, actions that are goal-less too. Therefore, that entity which must structure the goings-about of individuals, whose learning is predominantly performative, must be a set of actions without 'agents', without 'goal' and without 'meaning'.

This way of formulating a description is itself indicative of the fact that we are reaching the limits of our ability to conceptualise another configuration of learning, while remaining within the framework of the one we are using. At this stage, the easiest solution is to fall back on un-examined trivia of one's own culture and say, "Because all human beings do act with goals, purposes...quite obviously, such an entity could not exist in human cultures".

It would be wise to avoid complacency, because we are not discussing human actions as they are *conceptualised* in the western configuration of learning. We are trying to think of another configuration of learning which structures human goings-about differently. As I have said repeatedly, people think, dream, hope, *etc.* in every culture. People reason everywhere too. 'Actions are intentional' is one specification of a relation between thought and action. Other relations between action and thought are possible, including the one where thought merely limits action from the 'outside' as it were.

Therefore, let us press ahead with the issue at hand by drawing a parallel with religion. Religion has generated a way of going about the world that is recognisably religious. Similarly, the entity which produces performative knowledge must also generate a way of going-about, which is recognisably practical.

We can now take the crucial step towards *identifying* the entity that could structure another configuration of learning. It is a structured set of generic actions; it could be described as a-intentional, agent-less, and goal-less. Does such an entity exist? Yes. Where? In Asia. What is it? *Ritual.*

Ritual, just like religion, brings about a culturally specific way of going-about in the world. In a configuration of learning generated by it, performative learning dominates. Learning to *do* rituals is performative; the way in which members of this culture go-about in the world is itself recognisably ritualised. Finally, the configuration of learning generated by ritual is stable because the ritual structure is a recursive structure. Performative or practical knowledge is the ability to act recursively in the world. The social environment created in such a culture will itself be recursive, exhibiting the properties of recursive systems. The history of this culture, the coming-to-be of a people, just like the way it is with the West, is the story of the emergence, crystallisation, and development of a recursively structured learning configuration.

### 11.2.2. A Different Kind of Knowledge

I do think that we have at least partially succeeded in getting hold of the idea of different configurations of learning. I will show that there is sufficient *prima facie* evidence for us to take the proposal seriously.

#### Evidences at Face Value

1. Are all rituals recursively structured? Or only some? This is like asking the question whether all religions are explanatorily intelligible or only some. I think the recursive structure makes a set of actions into rituals. There is some evidence for the above claim in the works of Frits Staal (see the references). Over the last decade or more, he has done pioneering work in the study of some Indian rituals and their structure. One of the results of his analysis is that rituals exhibit a recursive structure. Even though his work is one of the indicators, his explanation and my proposal do not meet.

2. Because rituals are what they are due to their structure, they are 'meaningless' actions. Again, as far as I know, Staal is the only one who argues for this point of view. (In fact, one of his articles is titled "The

Meaninglessness of Rituals". For criticisms, which miss the point, see Penner 1985, Lawson and McCauley 1990.) However, one must be careful about saying what is 'meaningless' about rituals.

Perhaps the most common description of rituals within the West is that they are "mechanical, repetitive, and stereotyped". As far as I know the literature, there is no distance between scholarship and common sense in this case. The only exception is Staal, who has investigated rituals and their structures with earnestness and seriousness, for which posterity can only be grateful. In any case, this common description (which has very clear religious roots) is not that far-off the mark, if you re-examine it in the light of what I have said so far. 'Repetitivity' is our description of a recursive structure, when we do not recognise it as a structure. It is 'stereotyped' because configurations of actions appear to return constantly. It is 'mechanical', because it appears difficult to specify it in terms of 'intentional' states. Remember, even opening a door is an intentional act – and that is so in the common-sense psychology of the West. In exactly the same intentional psychology, rituals appear 'so mechanical' that one hesitates to individuate rituals *as* rituals under an intentional description. That is to say, the point (or the goal) of rituals does not appear evident or manifest.

Now the theoreticians of the West step in, wearing ridiculous hats. Of course, there is a purpose to rituals. Its function, you guessed it, is to reduce anxiety and tension; to act as a cementing bond of the community ('*re-ligare*' perhaps)…and so on. It is far from me to deny that ritual does any or all of these things, but, surely, this is a bit silly. The same is also said of religion, of dancing in Africa (see Arnaut 1988), of anything one does not know much about, which is just about everything regarding human beings and their societies: war does it, sex does it, ideology does it, worldviews do it, magic does it, religions do it…So, Why cannot rituals do it too? This is the reason why one performs (what appears like) a 'repetitive, mechanical, stereotyped' activity.

Many recognise that, on their own, rituals are 'meaningless'. They do that by referring to a parasitic relation between the rituals and something else. Rituals enact a myth; or they are 'symbolic' actions, which signify or rehearse important events; or whatever else takes your fancy. (See Doty 1986 for a useful overview and bibliography.) The motivation is the same in both cases: ritual appears meaningless, but it is not. Why ever not? 'Because all our actions are meaningful'.

If every 'mechanical' *etc.* action is a ritual, there is the difficulty of distinguishing an obsessive or pathological action from a ritualistic one. To Freud, this was no problem: both religion and ritual were neurotic behaviours. Further, one could identify culture itself with neurosis.

The same common-sense description also implicitly severs the relationship between rituals and agency. It is not that actions float in the air, or that people do not perform them. Because intentional descriptions do not either specify or individuate ritual actions, human beings are not seen as *agents*. For good or for bad, ritualised 'behaviour' exhibits something else: our neurosis, our 'bestiality' (because animals have rituals too, as is unfailingly pointed out), or even a biological need we are born with. Whichever the option, ritual is not seen as an agent-centred activity. The so-called religious 'rituals', like the Catholic mass, are considered important by those who participate in them because of the liturgy. Some actions are allowed because they are textually guided and interpreted. They are better called liturgical actions, not rituals. However, that is another story.

Let me summarise. The common-sense characterisation of the West recognises that rituals are somehow different from the intentional activities of human beings. Because of this, there is the recognition that one may perform rituals believing in whatever one may want to believe in. The persistent idea is that rituals appeal to a 'need for rituals' – the way 'religious experience' appeals to a 'need for a religious experience' – which is either anterior to our intentions or other than it. Even more simply put, there is a feeling even in the western common sense that rituals appeal to our need to *act*, the way food appeals to our hunger. They are acts pure and simple, acts as such, acts *simpliciter*. To act, that is, independent of the 'meaning' of these actions. Even in the West, if you accept my portrayal of its intentional psychology, rituals have no meaning. As Lewis (1982: 19) puts it:

> What is clear and explicit about ritual is how to do it – rather than its meaning.

Such a 'meaningless' set of actions, in a society and culture where meaning questions predominate, appear best given-up. After all, performing meaningless actions knowingly is irrational, childish, or pathological.
3. In a culture where ritual forms a configuration of learning, the way its members go-about in the world must itself be recognisably ritualistic. (In a religious culture, as I have tried to show, the way its members go-about in the world is recognisably religious.) The entire social process itself would look ritualised,

> from the way the emperor opens the doors of the temple of Heaven on great ceremonial occasions right down to the way one entertains the humblest guest and serves him tea (Smith, H. 1972: 10).

4. Because rituals generate a way of learning whose domain is that of building societies, the insight about the 'cohesive' function of the rituals is preserved. This sheds further light on my proposal.

In China, Japan, and India, people have reflected on rituals much more extensively than in the West. They have suggested that a correct performance of rituals is an absolute presupposition for the continued existence of society. It is possible to preserve their insight as well. A random example from the Chinese culture ought to suffice. As the *Book of Rites* (the *Li Chi*) puts it:

> Ceremonies are the bond that holds multitudes together, and if the bond be removed, those multitudes fall into confusion. (Citation by Radcliffe-Brown in Schneider, Ed., 1964: 67.)

This is not merely the opinion of the early writers. Modern mind shares the same impression too. As Watson (1988: 10-11) formulates his opinion on the subject:

> By enforcing orthopraxy (correct practice) rather than orthodoxy (correct belief)...it (was) possible to incorporate people from many different ethnic or regional backgrounds, with varying beliefs and attitudes, into an overarching social system we now call China.

And further:

> If anything is central to the creation and maintenance of a unified Chinese culture, it is the standardization of ritual...What we accept today as 'Chinese' is in large part the product of a centuries-long process of standardization (*ibid*: 3-4).

While Watson believes that this makes China unique (*ibid*: 10), Staal repeats the same sentiment (in 1983, 1986a) with respect to India. Assuming that both the Ancient and the Modern mind have the intuition that rituals were somehow responsible for the creation and reproduction of societies, our problem is to explain this intuition.

In my story, performative knowledge is responsible for the creation and reproduction of societies, whether in the East or the West. Neither religion nor ritual is the 'cohesive' bond, which enables the creation of communities. Ritual generates a configuration of learning, whose *dominant* learning process builds societies. Religion generates another configuration of learning whose *subordinate* learning process builds societies. Adherence to a 'worldview' no more creates a community than adherence to some or another ritual creates societies. Empirical histories of human cultures with religions in fact show the opposite: religion *divides* communities; it does not unite them. As to the idea of rituals uniting societies by being present across a culture, recall what Weightman (1984: 191-192) said of Hinduism:

> (no) practice can be held to be essential to Hinduism. It is...possible to find groups of Hindus whose respective faiths have almost nothing in common with one another, and it is also impossible to identify any universal belief or practice that is common to all Hindus.

It must be obvious what has gone wrong. Many correctly identify that religion dominates one culture and ritual the other. Because both are societies too, they conclude, both religion and ritual are 'cohesive' bonds. My proposal is attractive because it captures the insights of other thinkers, while shedding light on their confusions at the same time. In the process, without violating the 'facts' at our disposal, avenues for further research open up. If intolerance is necessary for religion, how could it create communities? As my discussion of the sociological conditions of the transmission of religion or worldview (#10.2.2) must have made clear, the possibility of multiple interpretations and the necessity for a single authority mean that the schism and division in society are always latently present. Further, individuals perform rituals. How can a community come into being even if every individual, congregated in one geographical area, was to perform exactly the same ritual thrice a day at home?

If performative knowledge is a product of this alternative configuration of learning, which we are trying to conceive of, then it must also leave its mark on other domains and other walks of life. That is to say, there will be a recognisable analogy between the influence of this knowledge on such a culture and that of 'knowledge-about' on the western culture. I will pick up three areas to illustrate the case: the experience of going-about in the world, the problem of the meaning of life and the world, and speculative thinking.

5. Remaining within the western culture, consider what it would mean to have rituals structuring the goings-about in the world. In the western culture, we experience ourselves as agents. Our hopes, desires, and frustrations appear to guide our activities. Whatever its status, deep down, the belief is that we are 'selves' or 'persons' with ambitions, longings, and projects.

What would happen to such an experience if ritual structured the activities? Recollect that a 'mechanical, stereotyped, repetitive' activity structures not only the goings-about, but also the experience of such goings-about. These actions are 'agent-less' (in the sense described above). If ritual brings forth a configuration of learning, maximally, it must engender an absence of the experience of self, agency or personhood; or create a weak sense of self at the minimum. Is this the case?

An anthropologist, two social psychologists, and a psychoanalyst (all of
them from the West) are asked to speak.

Agehananda Bharati (1985: 189), an anthropologist, puts it thus:

> None of the scholastics of the Hindu tradition was concerned with the
> empirical self in any manner resembling that of the psychologists, anthro-
> pologists, sociologists, and even poets in the west. All Hindu traditions
> talk about the self either in order to reject its ontological status...or to as-
> similate it to a theological and metaphysical construct, which is a Self with
> a capital 'S'. When any of the Hindu traditions speak about what might
> look like the individual, like an empirical self, it is not to analyze but to
> denigrate it...The self as the basis of such important human achievements
> as scholarship, artistic skill, technological invention, *etc.* is totally ignored
> in the Indian philosophical texts.
>
> One might think that such abstruse thoughts could only have been rel-
> evant or exciting to an intellectual or religious elite...that would not affect
> Hindu India at large. Common sense and intelligent intuition might sug-
> gest that the non-scholarly Hindu had a down-to-earth notion of some-
> thing very much like the subject-matter of an 'empirical self'. Such an
> intuition, however, would be wrong. Hindu thoughts and perceptions,
> Hindu values – *all* Hindu values – have been thoroughly informed by
> these...concepts.

And again:

> Hindu concepts of self and Buddhist concepts of self and non-self...share
> family resemblances so strong that they cannot be juxtaposed except by
> radical contrast to western notions...Western notions of self are systemati-
> cally unrelated to Indian notions, Hindu, Buddhist, and Jaina (*ibid*: 204).

Finally:

> The empirical self, the ego as actor surrounded by other egos, is syste-
> matically marginalized in the Indian tradition...the lack of sense of his-
> toriography, the lack of sense of humor...are some of the consequences
> (*ibid*: 226).[1]

---

[1] Ernest Renan attributed a "complete lack of the faculty of laughter", a total
absence of humour, to the Semites. This was caused by their 'monotheistic
instinct', which is not a human invention but a 'special gift' (Olender 1989:
66-67).

Shweder and Bourne (1982: 172-73), two psychologists, are more re-strained in their observations. Speaking about the differences in the concept of person between the Americans and the Indians, they say:

> It is by reference to "contexts and cases" that Oriyas (in Orissa, India) de-scribe the personalities of their friends, neighbours, and workmates. These personal accounts…are concrete and relational…The concrete-relational way of thinking about other persons differs from the abstract style of our American informants. Americans tell you what is true of a person's behav-iour (*e.g.* he is friendly, arrogant, and intelligent) while tending to overlook the behavioral context…(T)he striking tendency of Oriyas (is) to be more concrete and relational than Americans.

Further:

> …(T)he concept of an autonomous, bounded, abstract individual exist-ing free of society yet living in society is uncharacteristic of Indian social thought.
> What makes Western culture special…is the concept "autonomous dis-tinctive individual living-in-society". What makes Indian culture special is the concept "autonomous non-distinctive individual living-outside-soci-ety" (*ibid*: 190-191).

Alan Roland, a practising psychoanalyst, tries to show the same thing too. Contrasting the "familial self" of the Indians and the Japanese to the "individualised self" of the Americans, he says (1990: 8) of the for-mer:

> (T)he experiential sense of self is of a "we-self" that is felt to be highly relational in different social contexts. (The) narcissistic configurations of we-self regard that denote self-esteem (derive) from strong identification with the reputation and honor of the family and other groups…from non-verbal mirroring throughout life…(A) socially contextual ego-ideal…care-fully observes traditionally defined reciprocal responsibilities and obliga-tions, and a public self (that looks after) the social etiquette of diverse hierarchical relationships, in complexly varying interpersonal contexts and situations…These inner psychological organizations, structures, and processes of the familial self underlie the great variety of group character throughout the Indian subcontinent…

6. Speculations about the universe would also take on a characteristic tinge. The famous Karmic doctrine could be seen as an attempt to thematise rituals in this way.

One of the creation stories from the Rig Veda speaks of the world in these terms: the gods created the world by sacrificing the primal man. By sacrificing, they were sacrificing to sacrifice. Commenting on this, Wendy O'Flaherty speaks of the typical Vedic paradox, which is very "subtle". I cannot judge its subtlety, but a paradox it certainly is not: it is simply describing the world in terms of ritual. The act of creation was a performative rite; the emergence of the world is a ritual; the act of performing a ritual is a ritual; and ritual is all there is to the world.

7. When speculations about the world and human beings are formulated in action terms, one of the conceptual problems will be about the *actor-action* relationship. In fact, this problem should become important in a culture, where the sense of 'self' is either absent or weak. The reason need not be the 'intuition' that action without an agent is impossible. It could well be to say something about actions; whether 'something' acts; whether this something is acted upon by the action; whether action-less agents could also exist as much as agent-less actions, *etc.*

As *prima facie* evidence, again, the above relationship is conceptualised in many different ways. These different answers partially distinguish traditions from one another. Two examples must suffice. The Buddhists polemical formulation of the issue:

> The view that movement is identical with the mover is not proper. The view that the mover is different from the motion is not proper.
>
> If the movement were to be identical with the mover, it would follow that there is identity of agent and action.
>
> If the discrimination is made that the mover is different from motion, then there would be movement without the mover, and mover without the movement. (2, 18-20; Kalupahana, Trans., 1986: 128-129.)

Therefore,

> An agent proceeds depending upon action and action proceeds depending upon the agent. We do not perceive any other way of establishing them.
>
> Following this method of rejection of agent and action, one should understand grasping. The remaining existents should be critically examined in terms of the concepts of action and agent. (8, 12-13; *ibid*: 186-187)

Again,

A sentient being…as an experiencer is neither identical nor different from the agent.

…an agent is like a created form and his action is like his creation. It is like the created form created by another who is created. (17, 28, 32; *ibid*: 258-260.)

The agent and his action come into being simultaneously, said some among the Buddhists. What kind of an 'agent' were they discussing about? It was not the empirical agent but the *atman*: who, as some others said, did not act but was nevertheless the only agent. This is present in everything, has all properties and no properties, and so on and so forth. (See Sharma 1972 to get an overview of the Upanishadic conceptions.)

In the *Brihadaranyaka Upanishad*, for instance, there are descriptions of this *atman*. He dwells in the earth, the water, fire, sky, air, heaven, sun, space, moon and stars, ether, darkness, light, all beings, breath, tongue, eye, ear, mind, skin, knowledge, *etc*. How does he dwell in all these things? What is he? Here is an example of a verse (each of the verses has the same structure):

He who dwells in the seed, and within the seed, whom the seed does not know, whose body the seed is, and who pulls the seed within, he is thy Self, the puller within, the immortal; unseen, but seeing; unheard, but hearing; unperceived, but perceiving; unknown but knowing. There is no other seer but he, there is no other hearer but he, there is no other knower but he. This is thy Self, the ruler within, the immortal. (III, 7, 23: Müller, Ed., 1879: 136)

This *atman* does some interesting things:

And as a caterpillar, after having reached the end of a blade of grass, and after having made another approach (to another blade), draws itself together towards it, thus does this Self, after having thrown off this body and dispelled all ignorance, and after making another approach (to another body), draw himself together towards it.

And as a goldsmith, taking a piece of gold, turns it into another, newer and more beautiful shape, so does this Self, after having thrown off this body…makes unto himself another newer and more beautiful shape…

That Self is indeed Brahman, consisting of knowledge, mind, life, sight, hearing, earth, water, wind, ether, light and no light, desire and no desire, anger and no anger, right or wrong, and all things. (IV, 4, IV-V: *ibid*: 175-176.)

In case you feel like identifying this entity with the 'soul', because the above paragraph seems to suggest the idea of 'reincarnation', a warning might prove useful. The Buddhists criticised the idea of *atman*, but spoke of 'reincarnation'.

8. There is at least one way in which even the idea of 'rebirth' becomes a possible evidence for the claims I am putting forward. How is it possible to talk about the 'significance' or 'meaning' of actions without taking recourse to intentional states? By determining an action with respect to what went before and what comes after. If the 'empirical self' is either not experienced or is only weakly experienced, then the significance of such an entity lies in its relationship to its predecessors and to its successors. The question about the 'meaning' and 'purpose' of the *life of some person* is either an unintelligible question or is intelligible only by referring to what went before this life and what comes after this life. If what went before this life and what comes after it were also lives, the meaning of 'life' of some person would be the life before this life and the life after this life. 'Life' would be an unbroken movement of 'lives'; by the same token, there could be neither a unique or a radical beginning, nor a unique or a radical end to a person.

I am not interested in either defending or criticising these positions. Before undertaking either, we need to understand them. All I am trying to do now is to tie some known 'facts' about the Indian culture as possible evidences for my proposals. Though not conclusive, evidence would look like this, if India has another configuration of learning generated by a set of actions.

## 11.3. How A Difference Makes The Difference

In the previous section, I attempted to conceptualise cultural differences in terms of configurations of learning. The focus was on our ability to conceptualise the 'otherness', while remaining within a culturally specific way of going-about in the world. This theme is problematised, among other things, in anthropology in terms of 'relativism' and 'universalism'. The necessity and/or the desirability of either of these two positions have been an unending source of debate as a meta-theoretical problem, *i.e.* as a problem about our descriptions of the world.

When so many intelligent people from the twentieth century so passionately discuss a theme, the likelihood is that there is a genuine issue somewhere (at least for us, the twentieth-century people). However, the ways these disputes take place indicate with a greater likelihood that it is a pseudo-debate. The possibility or the impossibility of knowing the 'other' is cast in such general epistemic terms that one can be sure that the discussion is not about understanding *cultural otherness* but some totally other kind of otherness. "How can we be ever certain that we have really and truly understood other cultures?" asks one; "But then", says the other, "when can we be certain that we have really and truly understood ourselves?" The epistemic insight about interesting facts being those of a theory turns out to be an ontological hurdle. "Because everything is said is in our cultural framework, we can never understand the other". Hence, 'the other' becomes an invention. Of anthropology says one (McGrane 1989); of Mankind says the other (Mason 1990). We are to believe that when an Indian or an African comes to Europe, what he experiences is an anthropological fiction. During all these centuries, Indians thought another culture and another people had colonised them. It now transpires that there never was a cultural 'other'. Perhaps, very soon, we will hear that there was no 'colonisation' either: after all, 'nations' are fictitious entities anyway.

There is, as I said, a genuine issue somewhere. In this section, like the previous one, I shall trace one facet of this problem at an object-level, as it is relevant to the theme of the essay. In the concluding chapter, I attempt a meta-level analysis.

### 11.3.1. Raising a Naive Question

Let us recollect an example (chapter #8) about the two mothers (one in Asia and the other in Europe) with sick children. One goes to the image of Ganesha and the other to that of St. somebody or the other. "How could you consider both behaviours as members of the same class?" I asked there, suggesting they were not. Now, I would like to treat this question in detail by generalising it as a problem, which confronts any observer or student of religion.

### Denying a Rhetorical Question

Several actions and observances (like pilgrimage, fasting, *etc.*) of the multitudes appear common across both India (Asia) and Europe despite their divergences and differences. Am I denying their commonalities, because they reflect local colours and flavours, thus missing the forest for the trees? Am I denying the existence of such facts as a Catholic visiting Rome, the Muslim going to Mecca, the Jew to the wailing wall, and their obvious similarities to, let us say, a 'Hindu' going on a pilgrimage (*e.g.* Gold 1988)? If I am not, what exactly am I claiming?

However natural and obvious such questions might appear, one must be careful while asking them. Before answering them, I would like to deflect the implicit rhetorical force contained in these questions.

The first thing that should strike anyone with any acquaintance of logics and/or rhetoric is the fallaciousness of these questions. Depending on how they are interpreted, either the suggestion is that one has to be a fool or an eccentric to deny their 'obvious' similarities or that one has to answer a question that takes the form "when did you stop beating your wife?"

The only 'obvious' thing about similarities is that one can draw such a relationship between any two objects (chapter #8). Besides, things can have something in common in one particular description of the world and not in another (Putnam 1988). Regarding 'facts', we know all too well that they are always facts of a theory. Facts are neither unequivocal nor do they have a privileged epistemological status. These general points, made in excruciating detail throughout the essay, are not answers to the questions raised by a naive questioner but merely serve to neutralise their illicit rhetorical force when formulated as objections.

There is, however, a more substantial issue lurking in the background, which is not so much an objection as a request for a further clarification of my arguments.

## A Substantive Answer to a Naive Question

Consider, for example, 'devotional' movements like the *Bhakti* movement in India (*e.g.* Turner 1969: 154-164; McDaniel 1989). If one looks at the attitudes, orientations, and thoughts expressed in their devotional songs (*e.g.* Peterson 1989; Heifetz and Narayana Rao, Trans., 1987), one cannot but be struck by their closeness to attitudes, orientations, and thoughts considered characteristically 'religious' in the West. Now the general problem appears to be this: how to understand the closeness between, say, *Bhakti* and the characteristically religious feeling in the West, if India (Asia) does not indeed know of religions? There are three answers to this question, two of which are methodological in nature and the other more substantive.

My substantive answer begins with the following observation: even though the question "what distinguishes cultures from one another?" constitutes the most fundamental preoccupation of every anthropologist, anthropological theory has not formulated it as a problem. If I may be allowed a caricatured representation, ethnological field work and theoretical anthropology part ways precisely around this question and pursue opposite paths: while doing field work, the ethnologist focuses upon details and differences; while attempting to build a theory, the anthropologist is on the lookout for a grand unifying theory of human culture. This internal opposition is within the breast of each anthropologist. Consequently, it does not come as a surprise to see groups polarised around the issue of the relative importance of theory and fieldwork to anthropological practice.

An ethnologist might give a very precise answer to the question, "what are the differences between the *Holi* festival in North India and the New Year celebrations in Sicily?" He may even be willing to follow us into saying that these differences are those between cultures. However, answers are not forthcoming if we ask whether these differences constitute cultural differences or are merely their expressions. His fieldwork results do not answer the question. Ethnological practice does give birth to certain problems: discovering striking similarities or dissimilarities where one had expected to come across the opposite often leads to a search for the causes. Whatever the ultimate result of such an enquiry, its goal is to explain the unexpectedness of the encountered.

A theoretical anthropologist, in search of a theory of culture, merely sees similarities. New Year celebrations are part of each culture, or so he might reason, and thus arrive at the question: why is New Year celebration a necessary component of human culture?

Admitted, my characterisation is crude. I merely need a background to suggest the following: we need a theory about cultural differences in order to build a theory of human culture. The former is a middle-range theory that enables us to put the right weight while sifting through differences.

Religion is the only example of a worldview and, as an explanatorily intelligible account of the Cosmos, it is also the root model of order. I have argued that it forms a culture-specific way of learning. A mode of learning dominant in one culture is found as a subordinate mode in other cultures. The relationships between the dominant and subordinate processes of learning, among other things, give Gestalt to a culture. This makes the latter a form of life, distinguishing it from other forms of life. In this sense, religion or worldview is absent in Indian (Asian) culture. However, this does not imply that the elements present in a religion are absent elsewhere.

*Methodological Answers to a Naive Question*

There is a further problem, and this brings me to the first methodological answer. The presence of elements in cultures, which resemble each other very closely, does not tell us much in and by itself. These elements could be the products of different processes or of the same process. What we need is some kind of theory to tell us more about the unity and the differences among cultures. What I am trying to do is precisely that: take a first step in building a *theory* of religion, so that we may see what differentiates cultures from each other.

Let me take an example to illustrate the bias of my story. Both a castle and a cathedral make use of some basic elements: wood, cement, bricks, iron, stones, *etc.* Depending on our focus of research, we could go two ways: either argue that all elements of one culture are present in the other or say what their differences are. In this sense, one can consider a culture as a set of elements, or as a structured and structuring way of going about the world. My story is oriented towards the second.

With respect to the theme of the essay, these two approaches take the following forms. (1) Postulate a set of elements ('the religious phenomena') and account for the differences among cultures by characterising the different relationships between the elements. This may or may not be a feasible approach. At the moment, we can only observe that there exists no theory capable of undertaking such a task. Even though this is the received wisdom, why has such a theory not taken off the ground despite immense labour? Because the discussion does not get beyond the first level, *viz.* the level of identifying the members of a class, no answers are forthcoming. That is, it is not evident whether Ganesha and God are members of the same class or belong to different classes; it is not clear what makes some statement into a religious and not a scientific statement, *etc.* In other words, as I have repeatedly pointed out, the discussion does not go beyond classification.

(2) The other approach, the one I have favoured, takes the alternate route. This is a minority view to the best of my knowledge. This attempt characterises religion as a structured and structuring unity, and sees cultural differences as differences in *patterns* of life.

This brings me to the second methodological point. In the first stages of building a theory about some phenomenon, the theoretical claims are highly abstract. Often called the method of "idealisation" in the philosophy of sciences (*e.g.* Krajewski 1977a, 1977b; Nowak 1980), it moves through successive concretisations in the process of treating the empirical phenomenon in question. Many objects of natural sciences are 'idealised' entities such as ideal gases, perfectly rigid bodies, inertial systems, material points, and so on. The more the descriptions approximate the object or phenomenon in question, the more concrete they become by taking other aspects of the phenomenon into account. My description of religion and ritual is abstract: it is capable of capturing some, but not all, details of religions like Judaism, Christianity, or Islam. Though the choice of such a methodology was not deliberate, I found myself working in an analogous fashion as my enquiry progressed.

*Three Answers to a Naive Question*

Now, what have these three answers to do with our naive questioner? In a culture where performative knowledge dominates the theoretical, worldviews may try to emerge but the cultural soil does not nourish them. Very soon any such attempt falls apart as a worldview and is subordinated to the dominant mode of learning. It survives only as a fragment of yet another partial speculation of a finite slice of the world. Put more accurately perhaps, ideas that could grow into a worldview do not do so in such an environment. Consequently, what one recognises in India (Asia) -- when looking from the West -- are fragments and pieces. Not of Indian (Asian) worldviews, note this well, but those which are parts of a worldview *in the West*. These 'pieces' are part of a different pattern in India (Asia); they have entered into different relationships with other parts; and they have an entirely different hue as a result.

Just to get the idea across, a contrasting description might be of some help. In one culture, the West, where the 'symbolic' dominates the performative, the latter itself becomes the 'symbolic' ('ritual is a symbol'). In the other, India, where the relation goes the other way, the symbol itself is performative ('symbol is a ritual').

Perhaps, we can get a better grip on the issue if we were to examine the way each looks (and has looked) at the other with respect to learning itself.

### 11.3.2. An Encounter of Cultures

Reconsider the *prima facie* evidence presented in the previous section. By speaking about the 'law' of Karma, the belief about the *atman*, and 'reincarnation', I appear to describe the worldview or religion of the Indians. Yet, I am presenting them as evidences for the absence of worldview or religion! As far as I am concerned, there is no great puzzle to this state of affairs. It merely confirms (at a meta-level) what I have tried to argue.

Each culture, as I have just said, contains many building blocks: theories, social groups, music, *etc.* Among other things, a culture is a configuration of learning. Religion has generated a configuration of learning in the West by universalising itself. The way this culture looks at others is partially determined by the way it has become a culture: namely, through religion and worldview. Consequently, in this culture, understanding another culture involves describing the other in terms of its worldview. The 'other' has been the 'other worldview' to this culture. Why? The answer to this question exhibits both the weakness and strength of the western culture.

Let me begin with its strength. As I said earlier (#10.2), a worldview can explain a perspective but not the other way round. If we know what there is in the world and what the world is like, we can generate descriptions of multiple perspectives. Religion is *the* explanatorily intelligible account of the cosmos. Nothing falls outside it.

The same strength is also its weakness. That is to say, the divinity of the message is the weakness of the message: its audience are limited beings. As finite creatures with finite abilities, our ability to understand the message is itself finite. Unless divinely inspired, one cannot speak with certainty about this divine knowledge. This strength and weakness of religion also characterise the western culture. Much like religion, which constitutes one element of its identity, the West is limited by itself.

Consider the question: why do Indians have the worldview they have? Why do they talk in terms of the *atman* or Karma? The answer exhibits the conceptual weakness of the western culture: these different beliefs, as they belong to the different worldviews, constitute cultural differences.

To appreciate this as a conceptual weakness of a culture, look at what Christianity did. The 'others' were pale and erring variants of itself, *the* explanatorily intelligible account of the world. If, indeed, God came to the Arabian Desert several times and gave religion to a people, "why did God do so" is a question neither you nor I can answer. Its exact correlate is our inability to answer why different cultures have different 'worldviews'. The West sees the differences between cultures only in *its* terms, *viz.* as having another (different) worldview.

The pagan cultures have their strengths and weaknesses too. A religion or a worldview, the explanatorily intelligible account of the Cosmos, ends up becoming a mere perspective in their hands. Not having received the message from God, they look at such messages as human beings do. Having worldviews is not how *the* human being goes-about in the world. It is merely *a* way of going-about. Some culture claims to have *the* worldview (be it a 'scientific' one or a 'religious' one); the pagans acknowledge the possibility and merely say that it is not their way of going-about.

Keeping the logic of this situation in mind, let us review the contact between the West and Asia.

*A Contrasting Description*

Consider the following two cultures. There is one culture so obsessed with chaos and order that it channels all its intellectual energies towards 'discovering' the order buried underneath the postulated chaos. This culture produces philosophers, theologians, and scientists (both natural and social). Theories are destined to break away from *practical life* because they deny any experiential order. Not only do these theories move away from experience in the sense that they have less and less to do with the experiential units, but they also oppose *theories* to practical life. Given a good set of principles, good rules, and good statutes, the emergence of a good society and a good human being appear as logical consequences. As the intellectual energies of this culture focus on locating the rational bases of social and human life, the transmission of practical or performative knowledge is arrested, impeded, loses all significance and becomes secondary. The practical life and interactions of a people, correspondingly and over time, become impoverished. Theories grow rich and sophisticated, whereas daily life becomes barren and poor.

Then, there was (is?) another culture. All its intellectual energies went towards creating, sustaining, and continuously modifying a social/practical order. One could see and experience the order in the society. Practical actions became sophisticated, patterns of interaction wide and variegated. Theoretical disquisitions *about* imagined orders were neither essential nor very much encouraged. A peculiar kind of theoretical poverty emerged as a result – again, over a period.

These two cultures met in the most unhappy of circumstances. One was willing to learn, the other thought that it could only teach. In any case, the gift was made:

It is, I believe, no exaggeration to say that all the historical information that has been collected to form all the books written in the Sanskrit language is less valuable than what may be found in the most paltry abridgements used at preparatory schools in England. In every branch of physical or moral philosophy the relative position of these two nations is nearly the same...

The question before us is merely whether...we shall teach languages [Sanskrit and Arabic] in which, by universal confession, there are no books on any subject which deserve to be compared to our own; whether, when we can teach European science, we shall teach systems which, by universal confession, whenever they differ from those of Europe, differ for the worse; and whether, when we can patronize true philosophy and sound history, we shall countenance, at the public expense, medical doctrines which would disgrace an English farrier – astronomy, which would move laughter in girls at an English public school – history, abounding with kings thirty feet high, and reigns thirty thousand years long – and geography, made up of seas of treacle and butter (cited in Keay 1981: 77).

This is Sir Babbington Macaulay speaking, in his famous minutes concerning the need for a British education system in India.

I am using the word 'gift' advisedly, because, in India, knowledge – theoretical knowledge in a very broad sense of the term – is not a product of learning. It is not so much a result of the effort put in by an individual, as it is a gift given by the teacher. Acquisition of knowledge requires, maximally, a peculiar kind of receptivity on the part of the pupil – a readiness to receive the gift from the teacher.

Being a pupil in this culture implies preparing oneself to *receive*. This is true not just of stories: figures like the Buddha and others become knowledgeable people – they literally have a dawning of knowledge – when they achieve this state of mind.

There is something utterly mysterious, or so it appears when you look in the direction of the MIT from Bombay, about scientific knowledge, which is received mostly by European scientists and, now and then, by the half-mythic figures from one's own culture. Choudhuri (1985: 489) calls this the 'schoolboy conception of science', transmitted in the Indian centres of learning:

> A good scientist must be a genius, intellectually much superior to the (student's) best professors. He is fully equipped with all the technical tools, which may possibly be necessary for any kind of research he may wish to undertake. He usually spends his time pondering over the fundamental issues of his discipline and when this divinely inspired individual happens to have a brilliant idea, he works it out in a straightforward way without much trouble, like a smart schoolboy solving his test problems.

## The Story Continued

The contrasting description is true, though deliberately *biased*. However, there is something else going on too, to understand which we need to look at this situation in terms of my proposal.

In a culture like Asia, where performative knowledge dominates the theoretical, the above cultural contact raises the following question: how to do science? Given what this culture is, the question has a practical answer. Hundreds of thousands of its members take to learning how to *do* science; to learn *about* science; to learn *about* the culture that produced (and produces) science; to learn 'about' this culture by going and living there; to try and do science in the West and in the East…

That is to say, this culture begins to 'mutate'. Its specific way of going-about in the world begins to shift, evolve and change shape: *a new way* of going-about in the world begins to emerge. However, a cultural way of going-about in the world is not a shirt to change at will. Asia encountered sciences from within its way of going-about. However, sciences are the products of a different way of going-about in the world. To what extent is doing sciences *tied* to having a worldview? One answer is to see whether it is possible to *do* science within the old way of going-about. In the old-way of going-about, theory was subordinated. Consequently, the relationship between the elements in the configuration begins to shift. Yet, they shift *within* the culture-specific way of going-about in the world, as determined by the latter.

What is happening in Asia, what has been going on for the last 150 years or more, is the emergence of a new configuration of learning. It is taking place in an accelerated fashion over the last fifty years. Asian cultures are *doing* a massive experiment in shifting and altering the relationship between different learning processes until a newer, stable configuration comes into being.

From the outside, it does look as though they are taking over a worldview. That is exactly what they are *not* doing. Their old ways are changing; but they are changing into a new way in conformity with their old way of going-about in the world. Doing sciences is a practical or performative problem to them. Whether or not migration of sciences is *tied* to worldviews will be answered practically too – will the Asians learn to do science? Will they evolve a way of learning that will allow science to grow? Once more, pagans will testify in a battle about religious truth.

The contrast cannot be sharper from the other side. When one culture (as a culture) is busy learning to evolve a new way of going-about in the world, the other (as a culture) is smug and satisfied as though it does have God's truth. When, literally, millions from one culture spend their time, energy, *etc.* learning from the other, the other cannot even raise the symmetric question.

As of this moment, this story has not yet reached its resting phase. My hope is that this proposal has at least drawn attention to a hitherto unsuspected dynamic. Asia might be becoming 'westernised'; but that is happening in an Asian way. No culture is static, least of all theirs. The 'dream' of hundreds of thousands of Asian intellectuals to come up with a 'synthesis of the East and the West' is not just the result of the wounded ego of a 'proud' civilization. It is more. Much, much more. It is as much a longing as a portent. It is as much a wish as a shaping force. It is as much wish-fulfilment as it is an expression of what is happening. In my proposal, what you see is how one is related to the other.

### 11.3.3. *Traditio, Knowledge, and the Religious Culture*

In an early chapter (chapter #3), while discussing the Reformation polemics within Christianity, I compared the growth of Christianity in a pagan milieu to the growth of an embryo in its mother's womb. In the way the growth and development of an embryo involve complex interactions between genetic factors and the environment nourishing and nurturing it, Christianity (Judaism and Islam as well) was both influenced by its own characteristics as a religion and the milieu it operated in.

It is undoubtedly true that Christianity absorbed several aspects of the Hellenic intellectual (philosophical) culture and doctrines. However, this absorption made Christianity grow not merely as a historical movement but also as a religion. If both Christianity and Judaism absorbed doctrines, that is because they were 'predisposed' (as one might want to put it) to absorb doctrines. That they took over some doctrine is not the point as much as what they made of that act. The doctrines elaborated and fleshed out a worldview. That is to say, the predisposition of Judaism, Christianity, and, at a later stage, Islam, to try to assimilate the Greek philosophical thought has to do with the nature of religion. Consequently, it is no great insight to blame the Greeks (as some deconstructionists do) for the doctrinal orientation among these three religions. Equally, it is as difficult to separate out the Greek contribution to the development of Christianity, as it is to say what is 'truly' Christian. Christianity is a result of both. Of course, it is trivially true that given another environment, Christianity would have evolved differently. However, that does not take us closer to the 'purer' or 'original' Christianity but to a Christianity-in-a-different-milieu.

If we look at the Roman cults and the Greek 'religion', the above consideration is reinforced. For some reason or the other, neither of the two felt inclined to integrate the philosophical doctrines the way Judaism or Christianity did. Philosophising was one kind of activity, whereas cults, their ceremonials, *etc.*, were another kind of activity. Philosophers, to be sure, criticised many 'religious' beliefs and put across several different kinds of doctrines regarding the nature, origin, existence or non-existence of gods. This is not at issue. What is at issue, however, is that these cults did not feel impelled to spin out their own theology as a response to these philosophical stances. Both Judaism and Christianity felt compelled to do what the Roman *religio* did not do. These two religions could have followed the example of the cults, which they did not. This is an additional reason why Judaism and Christianity are religions and, as I have tried to argue, the Roman *religio* was not.

Both in chapter #3 and in the above paragraphs, the suggestion is that the cultic ceremonials, rituals, festivals of the cities, and such like, which go under the rubric of *religio,* are different from discoursing about the nature of divinity, the existence of the gods, and the importance of the ceremonies and rituals. I suggested there that practising *religio* was not opposed to theorising and that the Roman *religio* was practised because it was *traditio.*

## 'Religio' as 'traditio'

To put it in a very compressed form, my suggestion is to look at the Roman *religio* more in terms of the notion of performative knowledge than in terms of the worldview that religion is. *Religio* is performative knowledge – if not identical to it, at least a variety of it – and, as such, it is not in need of any theoretical justification. As a collection of ceremonies, festivals, civic functions and rituals, *religio* was not merely transmitted from generation to generation, but it was also *experienced* as something crucial to social interaction. Though I cannot argue for it here in any detail, performative knowledge (whose exemplification is in rituals) is required to build societies and sustain social interactions. This is the 'how to live' ability I spoke of earlier. To speak of 'traditions' is to speak of (a) accumulated performative knowledge and (b) the mechanisms of transmission of such knowledge. The Roman *religio* was very close to this performative knowledge and it was practised because this practical knowledge was *traditio*.

What belongs to *traditio* or performative knowledge? Is, for example, the transmission of architectural secrets and skills (from father through son) also tradition? Is it therefore *Religio* by result? When we speak of traditions, the point is not one of defining the term by enumerating its contents. Tradition merely transmits the practical knowledge of living together. In so far as 'being an architect' not merely meant a skilled worker but, say, a Roman citizen who moved around as an architect, undoubtedly the architectural skills were part of the *traditio* too.

Hence the reason why many philosophers of different persuasions, especially during the Roman empire, strenuously argued against having to found *traditional practices* on rational arguments. These philosophers include not merely the Cynics or the Stoics but, above all, the Sceptics. In fact, the scepticism of Antiquity (both the Pyrrhonian and the Academic) was not – as we understand it today – an epistemological position with respect to the limits of human knowledge, but a way of living. Their 'argument' was that it was neither necessary to found *practices* on theoretical arguments, nor was it possible. It was not necessary because practical knowledge itself was knowledge, and human practices do not require foundation in reason. It was not possible, because the kind of certainty one falsely attributed to reason was illusory. The sceptical 'challenge', in one sense, was to philosophy but only to the extent that philosophers believed there was a 'rational' way of living (*i.e.* a way of living founded on theoretical principles). In the words of Hiley (1988: 9; see also Burnyeat 1983), one of the very few authors who seems to be aware of the point:

(Pyrrhonism)...did not seek to call into question the appearance and customs of daily life but instead opposed the philosophical attempt to get behind the appearances and ground them in something foundational or ahistorical. Its goal in opposing philosophy was to live tranquilly in accordance with instinct, custom and tradition; in that sense, its attack on philosophy aimed to restore the appearances of common life as guides for

> conduct...(T)he moral thrust of Pyrrhonism was to restore the reliability
> of the appearances and values of common life as a guide to action.

Even though Hiley is correct, the formulation is a bit misleading. I do
not think that Pyrrhonism tried to restore reliability of the 'values' of
common life as a 'guide' to action. After all, 'values' are normative statements, and to suggest that such statements 'guide' human action is to
say that actions are justified by referring to the normative statements.
In turn, such normative statements themselves require justification and
the sceptic did not justify them by saying that they were 'derived' from
daily life. Rather, the sceptic must be understood as saying that actions need not be 'guided' by anything other than tradition and custom,
which are themselves kinds of actions.

To conduct the affairs of daily life, to conduct the affairs of social
life, to live a human life amidst other human beings, argued the sceptics, one does not need knowledge *about* any of these actions. All these
activities are themselves a species of knowledge, transmitted from generation to generation, collectively called 'tradition' and 'custom'.

Such an attitude, it has often been charged, is conservative. In *which
way though*? Practical knowledge essentially *conserves;* it is accumulated
knowledge of and for living with other human beings. This charge of
'conservatism' is hardly a critique but a very trivial consequence of the
fact that human beings do not change dramatically every other day. A
culture dominated by theoretical knowledge misunderstands such 'conservatism'. Such critics see the attitude of the sceptics as acquiescence
to old ideas, values, rules of behaviour, and the slavish submission to
authority. Because of the notion that human action is an execution of
an idea or a belief, it appears impossible to conceive of knowledge that
is not theory or belief, but practical in nature.

The arguments of the sceptics with those who tried to give a foundation to human praxis (one kind of knowledge) in reason (another kind of
knowledge) were twofold: the former itself is knowledge and therefore,
needed no foundation in the latter; in any case, theoretical knowledge
is ill equipped to take over the role of practical knowledge. To show
this, they argued against those who championed the cause of only one
kind of knowledge by showing that we could not *know* anything with
certainty. Therefore, the argument that 'theories' could found human
goings-about the world becomes unacceptable. Hence, if one believed
that one needed to know in order to act, one could not act at all.

Within the western culture, the sceptical argument against confusing
theoretical knowledge with performative knowledge is misunderstood.
The sceptical position *in defence* of performative knowledge is seen to
lead, of all things, to inaction. The sceptic says, I do not need to 'know
about' actions in order to act; the 'modern' sceptic accuses him that be-

cause he does not 'know about' actions, he cannot act. Listen to Hume, the 'modern' sceptic.

> A Pyrrhonian...must acknowledge, if he will acknowledge anything, that all human life must perish if his principles universally and steadily to pre-vail. All discourse, all action would immediately cease; and men remain in total lethargy, till the necessities of nature, unsatisfied, put an end to their miserable existence. (Hume 1777: 160)

If the point I am making holds, a sceptic was arguing for *practical knowl-edge* – not ceasing to act, but in order to act – as a separate kind of knowledge that is *not based* on human theoretical reason. Hume could not understand a sceptic any more than his successors could. To both, scepticism merely posed an epistemological problem to human theoreti-cal knowledge: the impossibility of ever being certain about anything.

Ancient scepticism, of course, is quite a complex phenomenon. In these few pages, I do not intend to provide a radically 'new' interpreta-tion but merely want to throw a different light. We shall have to wait and see whether this approach is capable of further development.

Let me summarise. *Traditio* is best conceived as a variant of per-formative knowledge and *religio* did not require any theoretical justifi-cation. What Christianity did, something that Judaism had done much earlier, was to try to absorb practical or performative knowledge into the theoretical and see human activity as the execution of an idea or a plan.

## 11.4. THE DYNAMIC OF RELIGION

As the story has evolved thus far, the challenge raised in an earlier chap-ter (#8.1) has only been partially met. To meet it completely, it is advis-able to recollect both the terms of the problem and the nature of the answer.

In the narrative penned during the first eight chapters, I argued the following: the belief about the universality of religion is pre-theoreti-cal in nature. I alleged that this pre-theoretical idea undergirds theory-formation about religion. In the process of exhibiting the truth of this hypothesis, it turned out that all these beliefs were very much part of a theory – the Christian (or Old Testament) theology. Though inconsist-ent, what made the inconsistency interesting was that the latter is an evidence for the former.

In chapter #10 (#10.3.3), the dialectically formulated challenge ("Could religion be both itself and the other, while being constituted as such precisely due to this relation?") found an equally dialectical answer: religion universalises itself by the process of secularisation and proselytisation. Religion is both itself (a religion) and the other (the worldview), and this double movement constitutes it as religion. While dialectical formulations help capture a historical movement in terms of the dynamic of the structures, they also create a slight air of mystification. Because the focus lies on the dynamic, the tendency is to speak as though the object of description (in our case, religion) is also the subject of history. That is, by describing how religion universalises *itself*, the narrative centre of gravity shifts to religion as the subject.

A prosaic description of the same process could help us get rid of this mystification. However, it should be complemented by the dialectical one too lest we get a history without the dynamics of history. If a dialectical description errs on the side of the dynamic – tending to give us a dynamic without empirical history -- a more prosaic description errs on the side of history giving us a history without any dynamic. An empirical historian is right in accusing a dialectician of discerning 'grand patterns' in history and of seeing human history as the *way* in which some dynamic or another works itself out. The dialectician is right too, when he accuses that, without such a conceptualisation, human history becomes a collection of fortuitous facts and does not exhibit any intrinsic connection between events. "That is because no such empirical connections exist", says the empirical historian. "But that is no empirical but a philosophical claim", says the other...

I do not want to resolve the issue here even if I could, which I cannot; nor do I want to claim that I have 'synthesised' both points of view, which I have not. I merely want to draw attention to the fact that we need both, if we want to understand the constitution of a culture both ?s a *self*-constitution and as a process of coming-to-be of a culture.

### 11.4.1. Proselytisation and Secularisation

The spread of Christianity was a highly differentiated process. It retained some elements of the pre-Christian Germanic culture (for instance) and eliminated some others. Even here, it retained them in a transmuted form. Further, the spread of its doctrines and practices was neither uniform nor constant. Its doctrines were evolving and there was a differential transmission of these doctrines. Pockets of highly literate circles (mostly in theological centres, and even they came into being slowly) existed; there were pockets where the parish priests transmitted these doctrines to a populace barely literate or semi-illiterate; there were larger pockets of rural population who were hardly Christian or even untouched by the evangelising process. In other words, Christianisation of the West was not anywhere near what this phrase conjures up: an unstoppable and triumphant march of the message of the gospels and the victory of the servants of God against the followers of the Devil.

The story that I have told does not neglect that Christianisation was a complex or a differentiated process. On the contrary, it requires that the spread of Christendom is such a process. My story enables us to come to grips with the differentiation and complexity in *two different* ways: by speaking about the evangelising process and by speaking about the secularisation process. Both are linked together in the process of universalisation of Christianity.

If the Christian doctrines and practices had spread everywhere equally wide and deep (an impossibility for any process in human history), then every human being would be a Christian to the same extent. I have no idea what such a state of affairs could look like but it appears to me that if it had occurred, it would have imploded Christianity from within a long, long time ago.

What I am suggesting is this: the spread of Christianity was a differential one along two lines. Firstly, there is a differential degree of evangelisation; secondly, there is a staggered and differentiated spread of the attitudes brought forth by the former. If we agree that certain kinds of questions and orientations index the second, my claim is that the 'meaning questions' and the emphasis on 'knowledge about' spread differentially even as this religion itself expanded at an uneven pace. Communities and individuals, who were barely Christian, began to shift and change their attitudes and questions. These alterations shadowed those that Christianity created among its followers. The process of secularisation of Christianity followed the process of evangelisation.

Three events in the narrative penned by me index the extent to which this process of universalisation has spread: the Protestant Reformation, the Age of Reason, and the growth of sciences.

The popular nature of the Protestant Reformation indexes, among other things, how rooted the Christian doctrines were; the Enlightenment indexes, among other things, the extent to which the secularisation had taken place; the development of sciences, once again among other things, shows how a configuration of learning had already taken on a recognisable form.

The process of secularisation, as contrasted with that of evangelisation, gives us a clue about the kind of issues that some people in the West confront. People accept questions and adopt attitudes that a religion has brought forth. These do not presuppose the acceptance of or even familiarity with the doctrines of this religion. Nevertheless, a religious attitude has spread.

Christianity, as a religion, made the world explanatorily intelligible. It made the Cosmos into a particular kind of place by making it into an object of experience. The secularisation consists in having the Cosmos as an object of experience without being dependent on one particular kind of account. It is like possessing the structure of an account without accepting some particular interpretation of the variables. Different religions are the empirical interpretations of such an account; that is why we unhesitatingly pick out religions as the best examples of worldviews. Religions give sense to the 'formal' account the worldview is. That is why people feel that a worldview is *implicit* in each one of us. Because religion is always some or another religion, there is a drive to build a 'scientific' worldview. It appears as though one has a worldview even though one does not have a worldview. We all have worldviews, the feeling goes, but none an 'adequate' one.

If the West did not have religion or worldview, its members would not have the attitudes they have now. To ask meaning questions in the Cosmos requires that your theory has made the Cosmos *into* such a place. Therefore, the belief is completely *theoretical*. Without such a theory, without using the resources of such a theory, you could never formulate these kinds of questions.

## 11.4.2. Idolatry and the Sin of the Secular

Thus far, I have spoken of the universalisation of religion in terms of doctrines. I have spoken about the process where themes from a religion become low-level facts about human beings and their cultures as secularisation. Evangelisation, I have further claimed, has received a secular translation in terms of an experience of the Cosmos.

These constitute the *dynamic* of religion. That is, religion itself is a process and a movement (not merely a movement of people). My question in the eighth chapter (#8.1.6) was the following: could we not only exhibit the movement of religion but also show that this movement constitutes religion? I shall answer this question by looking at it from the perspective of idolatry.

From the days of its inception, one of the questions of Christianity is the following: who is a true Christian? What is it to be a Christian? Over the centuries, answers to these questions have evolved and changed – a circumstance, which counsels one to be wary of talking about 'the' Christian doctrine, 'the' Christian faith, and so on. Yet, because I am guilty of doing exactly that, I would like to defend my stance.

Remember, if you will, the suggestion made in the ninth chapter (#9.5.2): worship is the *means* through which the Cosmos retains its explanatory intelligibility to those to whom the world has such a character. We might also reformulate this idea, so that it is applicable not merely to the individual believer but also to the religious dynamic itself. Worship is the means for the reproduction of religion. That is, religion reproduces itself through worship. Note that this is different from both proselytisation and secularisation: they refer to the expansive dynamic of religion. We are talking about the daily or simple reproduction of religion, *i.e.* how believers continue to sustain their faith.

Such a reproduction of religion is at the same time a reproduction of the boundary of the religious world, as it is in contact with the non-religious or the secular world.

Let us step back in time and visit the Roman Empire during the early days of Christianity. Taking a synchronic slice of the Roman world, we observe Christian religious communities living *within* the pagan society. Worship and prayer enable Christianity to reproduce itself in a simple form. The Christian communities continue to survive as religious communities by praying, worshipping God, following the liturgy, *etc.*

Impelled by its nature as religion, Christianity had to proselytise and win converts. Continuing with our synchronic analysis of the slice of the Roman world, we can observe that the mechanism of effacing the otherness of the other enabled Christianity to expand. However, this expansion must occur obeying the dynamic of the simple reproduction of religion. That is, not merely must religion expand, but it must also make (and continuously remake) the Cosmos explanatorily intelligible to all believers, including the new converts.

However, worship is the means for the reproduction of religion, which also reproduces the boundaries between Christian communities and others. Further, the expansion of Christianity is also an expansion of the means for reproducing religion on an extended scale. From these two observations, it follows that the boundary between Christian religion and everything else is coextensive with the means of the reproduction of religion itself. In more simple terms, worship and prayer would separate the believers from the non-believers, Christians from the pagans and the religious world from the 'secular' world. Both induction of people into the community of the Christians and their exclusion from it will have to be drawn in terms of worship.

With respect to the mechanism of evangelisation, I can afford to be briefer because we have already been through this before. The pagan 'other' became a mere 'another' because Christianity attributed certain properties to paganism it never had: reflexivity, worship, *etc.* As pseudo-properties, they ended up becoming false predicates. *Religio* was false religion because its worship was false worship. That is, 'idolatry' – as a concept – domesticated the pagans, absorbed them into the Christian framework, while demarcating them from the community of true believers.

'Worship' and 'idolatry' are two descriptions of the twin aspects of the same process: the first refers to the reproduction of the community of believers; the second refers to the reproduction of the boundary of the community of believers as seen from within such a community. A congregation also segregates. 'Idolatry' does not just demarcate; it also domesticates and absorbs the other. Religion does not merely distinguish; it also expands by denying the 'otherness' to the 'other'. 'Idolatry' belongs to that arsenal of concepts which are crucial to the mechanism of proselytisation of religion.

Shifting into a diachronic mode, we notice that Christianity confronted a problem when it expanded within the pagan world. From among all the practices of that society, which were truly pagan practices and which merely those performed by the pagans? Which practices were idolatrous and which 'civic' or indifferent? As to be expected, this question has its twin: *Quid sit christianum esse?* What is to be a Christian?

> The trichotomy which had prevailed before...– of Christian (or sacred), secular (neutral, civic), pagan (profane) – vanished, to be replaced by a simpler dichotomy: sacred or profane, or, simply, 'Christian' and 'pagan' (Markus 1990: 134).

About what kind of practices are we talking? Like honouring the martyr on his feast day by getting drunk; attending circus games and enjoying spectacles; banquets, giving presents, *etc.*, during the New Year (*i.e.* the first of January); honouring an important person (like the emperor) by holding races and games; 'secular' festivals and banquets; attending shows in the theatres and hippodromes...the list is practically endless. If the pagan world is that because of the pagan practices, the practices are pagan because they are idolatrous and idolatry is the worship of the Devil, what must a Christian do in order to remain one?

Tertullian found the shows in theatres an expression of idolatry; Augustine found them more neutral. Christians thought that celebrating the New Year was not wrong; Churchmen like Ambrose and Jerome were unanimous in attacking it virulently. The former said,

> 'we commit no sacrilege, these are only games...– it is the gladness over the new, rejoicing over the start of a new year; it is not the falsehood of the [pagan] past, nor the sin of idolatry' (*ibid*: 104).

But the bishops thought otherwise: "he who would play with the Devil cannot rejoice with Christ" (*ibid*: 104-105). Christian emperors repealed prohibitions imposed by the local Christian authorities on local festivals and theatrical shows so long as decency, modesty and chaste manners were preserved; the Christian authorities had thought that all of these were associated with the pagan rites.

What one ate, how one dressed, what jewellery one wore...these too were matters for theological reflection.

Pope Nicholas I (858-67), for example, was asked about such matters by the recently converted Bulgars. Some of their queries received categorical answers: necklaces given to the sick for healing are 'demonic phylacteries' and their users are condemned by 'apostolic anathema'; the death penalty for negligent sentries is contrary to the example – a significant choice! – of Saul's ferocity abjured by St Paul on his conversion; but their king's habit of dining alone was 'not against faith, though it offends good manners', so in this matter they were offered 'not commands, but persuasion'. But when it came to anxiety as to whether Bulgarian women might wear trousers, not even advice was offered, for this was a matter of indifference (supervacuum): 'for what we desire to change is not your outward clothing but the manners (mores) of the inner man'. Here is a spectrum of practices, from what the pope considered as indifferent to what he regarded as supremely relevant (*ibid*: 6).

In other words, as Christianity expanded within the pagan world, this also meant a growth of a Christian-religious world. The 'other' now confronted this religious world as well: the pagan-secular world.

What kind of 'otherness' could there be to an account which makes everything explanatorily intelligible? The same mechanism of effacing the otherness of the other comes into operation here: the pagan world required domestication through absorption and thus denied its otherness. That is to say, as Christianity gained political recognition and economic power, the fate of the pagan world was sealed. It had to be absorbed into the Christian world.

The pagan world was the totality of all pagan practices including what we would today call the 'secular' ones. With the expansion of Christianity, what we see in the first place is a *contraction* of this 'secular', pagan world. Markus, in his brilliant book, calls this process a 'desecularisation' of the Roman world.

As Christian discourse shrank to the scriptural, so the world of which it spoke shrank to the sacred. The secular became marginalised, merged in or absorbed by the sacred, both in discourse and in the social structure and institutions. Corresponding to the 'epistemological excision' of the secular from the Christian discourse a 'de-secularisation' of its society took place on a variety of levels (*ibid*: 226).

'Idolatry' is a theological concept. While rooted in the Christian theology, it also looks outward into the non-Christian world. It enables the assimilation of the secular world into the Christian world. The 'desecularising' process in the Roman world, as Markus remarks, is not simply the gradual collapse of 'secular' culture and institutions; nor is it...the progressively wider and deeper 'christianisation' of Roman society and culture. Accompanying these...was a change in the nature of Christianity itself: a contraction in the scope that Christianity...allowed to the 'secular'...one of the forms in which this change in the nature of Christianity manifested itself was in the tendency to absorb what had previously been 'secular', indifferent from a religious point of view, into the realm of the 'sacred'; to force the sphere of the 'secular' to contract, turning it either into 'Christian', or dismissing it as 'pagan' or 'idolatrous' (*ibid*: 16).

It is time to be rhetorical, if only to understand that the questions and answers of Christianity – which appear straightforward when confronting the Roman *religio* – carry a bite and a sting when it expands.

Where did early Christianity live? Why, in a pagan world of course. What makes a world into a pagan one? Pagan practices, obviously. What was the nature of these practices that made them pagan and not Christian? Idolatry and Devil's worship, naturally.

*Quid sit christianum esse?* This is not a question that requires or requests an ahistorical answer. This is not a problem, which could be solved by enumerating the properties of a 'true' Christian. It is a question that is asked within a religious tradition (see also #7.2.3) by those belonging to it. Because this religion is itself a process, the answers have exhibited the same character. This question was and is raised incessantly. This circumstance should signal us that it is an issue about the *relation* between the 'religious' and the 'secular' world and not about criteria for set membership.

Let us return to the story, both diachronically and synchronically, in order to complete it. As western Christianity expanded, so did the Christian-religious world. The earlier civic, pagan world contracted and marginalised in this process. 'Idolatry', a theological concept, drew the boundaries. After having gone through purgatory and neutralised of its sin, once a practice was admitted into the Christian world, it could find a place in this world. It is thus that a 'secular' world was to emerge later, but within the Christian world. It is a Christian-secular world that came into being, as generated within a religious world. That is why the secular world is under the grips of a religious world (chapters #6 and #7).

The problem that the Semitic religions have with respect to idolatry is not *merely* theological. The immense importance attached to fighting it does not derive *merely* from the commandments of God. The virulent and vehement attacks are sustained by the very nature of the religious dynamic: to absorb the 'other' world – the pagan, civic world – into itself and generate another world – a 'secular' world – but as defined by the religious world. I have said many times (section #1.2; #8.1.6) that the distinction between the 'sacred' and the 'profane' is drawn by a religion and within it. If we look at religion in its dynamic, we can appreciate the added dimension to this claim.

If this process is indeed a description of the dynamic of religion, we can better understand how members from this culture would experience cultures elsewhere. There is the typical missionary experience: the other *culture* is idolatrous. However, another, equally typical, experience is important to us today.

To the early Christians, it was evident that they lived in a world dominated by false religion, which permeated all walks of life. Contrast this experience with a modern-day description of the same pagan world:

> While there is...an abundance of evidence that the Romans were even obsessively convinced of the need to placate the gods, belief in the gods seems to have had little effect on their conduct...If it were not for the descriptions of ritual a reader might conclude that the Romans of the late republic lived in *as secular a world as our own*...(Liebeshuetz: 1979: 3; my italics).

In that case, what are we to make of the experience of the Christians of the pagan world? Were all the Christians merely hallucinating for nearly five hundred years then? Not quite, I submit. If the religious world dominates 'our' secular world, then the other worlds and cultures are experienced the way the early Christians experienced the pagan Rome. That is, religion must be seen to dominate all walks of life. I will not refer you to the German Romantic description of India, but to a modern-day writer on Asia.

> There can never be a clear-cut understanding of the East on the part of the West until Westerners realise that *all* Asian thought is religiously conditioned. ... I can think of no single department of human activity in Asian lands that is not encompassed by religious concepts (Abbot Sumangalo 1972: 19-20).

If you replace 'religious' with 'secular', you are also closer to Liebeshuetz's description of Ancient Rome. You are also closer to understanding the nature of Asian cultures. In other words, I suggest to you, the western experience of other cultures (as evidenced by the above citation) is no different from that of the early Christians. It is not called 'idolatrous', to be sure, but that is because the 'secular' world of ours is also a de-Christianised religious world.

## 11.5. About the Other Half of An Argument

Now I can be extremely brief, as there is no point to repetition. We can begin to appreciate why people in the West believe that religion is a constitutive element of all cultures. That is because their culture *is* constituted by religion. Because going-about in this culture requires knowing-about, to go-about with other people requires knowing-about them. That is why one needs to know about what the latter know-about the world. That is the reason too why one creates religions in other cultures. Religion is necessary, so says this culture, because all human beings need to know about the world in order to go-about in the world.

This is one culture's way of going-about in the world. Religion has brought forth one configuration of learning; other things have brought forth other configurations of learning as well. Reconsider, within this framework, the question of the universality of religion and two authors. Raymond Firth in his *Elements of Social Organization* (1951: 216) says:

> Religion is universal in human societies. This is an empirical generalization, an aggregation of a multitude of specific observations (cited in Smith 1962: 203; n. 2).

Or, as Saliba (1976: 22) puts it:

> Since religion is a universal phenomenon, any study of a society or a culture which aims at taking a holistic approach cannot ignore it.

I have argued that religion is *not* a cultural universal but that one can explain why the West thinks so. Both have to do with religion: what religion is to *a* culture, namely, its constitutive element. Need more be said? Reasonably speaking, perhaps not. Nevertheless, in my interminable discussions with my friends in the West, I have often wondered... Need more be said?

CHAPTER TWELVE

# AT THE END OF A JOURNEY

Now that we have reached the end of our journey, it is time to look back. Not only do we need to see how far we have come but also assess the nature of the arguments put across. In the first section, I shall provide a quick overview of the former. Here, I shall retrace the route very briefly through the signposts of the titles of the individual chapters. I will not summarise the arguments, but presuppose them instead. In the second, I will summarise the basic thrust of the story and make a proposal regarding the epistemic status of the arguments. Together, they should help one take a stance with respect to the essay as a whole. In the third section, I shall relate the story of my book to a meta-theoretical argument in anthropology about the possibility of ever describing the other.

## 12.1. The Different Rest Houses

The essay begins with the following observation: both the western intelligentsia and the western-trained intellectuals from other cultures hold firmly that religion is a cultural universal. This belief is both part of the commonsense and a claim in the theoretical and empirical literature on the subject. Furthermore, the proponents of this idea are not practitioners of any one particular field but, instead, represent a consensus that cuts across social and human sciences: from anthropology through sociology to human socio-biology.

The belief in the universality of religion does not merely imply that there are believers in different parts of the globe or that there are religious communities in different cultures. When people say that religion is a cultural universal, be it as an empirical generalisation or as a claim about the nature of human beings, they do not just say, for instance, that there are Christian communities in all cultures. In the twentieth century world we live in, the claim does not mean that every human being has a religion either. These theorists notice the existence of atheism, agnosticism, or indifference to religious matters. They also notice that secular ideologies play a dominant role in the social life of most countries in the West.

If religion is a *universal,* it means that some or another religion is native to human cultures. That is to say, all cultures must have an indigenous, as against imported, religion (at least one). To the extent that religion is a *cultural* universal, the claim is not merely that native religions exist in all cultures but also that religion is constitutive of human cultures. That is, some or another religion lends identity to a culture, or that it is indispensable to a culture. Again, it is important to notice that both scholars and non-professionals hold this belief in the twentieth century. When socio-biologists and cognitive neuroscientists ask questions and put across speculative hypotheses about the genetic or neural basis of religion; or when the Europeans try to understand the immigrant communities in their midst (mostly from Turkey and Morocco) by talking about Islam; the presupposition is that cultures can be described (partially but not exhaustively) by relating religion to culture.

The burden of this essay is two fold. It argues that religion is *not* a cultural universal while clarifying at the same time why one believes in its universality. The philosophical and scientific merit of the essay consists in the fact that the argument about the nature of religion captures both foci. I do not put forward a*d hoc* explanations and the argument is amenable to empirical and logical control. Together with their heuristic potential, these two aspects lend credibility to the reasonableness of the argument.

The entire essay constructs *one* argument and develops two themes: is religion a cultural universal? Why do people think so? Each chapter signals a shift in the argument to come and, for the sake of convenience, I have dubbed each theme as 'half of an argument'.

"Some Puzzles and Problems", as the *first* chapter is titled, is intended to show that the way contemporary authors speak about religion in other cultures is rather puzzling. On the one hand, they appear unsure that what they speak about, "properly speaking", is a religion at all. Hinduism, Buddhism, Taoism, the religion of the Greeks and the Native Americans, they tell us, do not look like religions. On the other hand, and this is the puzzle, having recorded this observation, they proceed to describe and give account of these "religions". The several citations show the puzzles these authors pose. My arguments show that these puzzles confront us with several problems. I formulate the theme of the next seven chapters by suggesting that there is a *prima facie* inconsistency in their reasoning and by asking the question why these authors have not seen it. Exploring the ways open to render them consistent provides us with the questions that the subsequent chapters answer. From chapters #2 through #7, the essay looks at the two possible grounds for the belief that religion is a cultural universal. One is a theoretical ground and the other is an empirical ground.

The second, third, and the fourth chapters constitute a group and have two different functions. On the one hand, they explicitly address themselves to answering the question whether the belief about the universality of religion is a result of empirical enquiries. On the other, they lay the groundwork for looking into the theoretical grounds for this belief in chapters five, six, and seven.

The *second* chapter, "Not by One Avenue Only...", sets the scene for what is to follow. The title alludes to the famous *relatio* of Symmachus. More importantly, by looking at the matrix in which Christianity grew, it signals the gulf separating the last pagan prefect of Rome from the first Christian one. By contrasting the Roman *religio* with the religion of the Jews and the Christians, this chapter suggests that we should seek the origin of our problem in the emergence of the Christian world.

"The Whore of Babylon and Other Revelations" picks up the story around the sixteenth century. The European culture encounters other cultures elsewhere in the world for the second time. The first occurred during the Greek and Roman civilizations. Empirical investigations, if any, into the universality of religion will have to begin here – if anywhere. Indian culture is the 'other' now.

The travel reports of this and the subsequent periods assume that religion exists in India too, except that it is the religion of the heathens. Before long, in Europe itself, heathens and pagans were to become very important. That is the first obvious reference to Protestantism in the title: we meet the whore of Babylon in the book of revelations and the former, said the Protestants, is what the Roman Catholic Church is.

This leads to the second reference to Protestantism: the schism within Christianity, between the Protestants and the Catholics, determines how one approaches the question of religion. The opposition between 'false' religion and the 'true' one – the drama from the times of the Romans – is replayed with new actors.

The third, but not so obvious reference of the title has to do with the 'revelation' that a group called the *philosophes* are amongst the new actors. The Enlightenment thinkers, I argue, not merely reproduced protestant themes but did so energetically. The secular sons of the Age of Reason extended Christian themes in a secular guise.

'Revelations' do not stop here. They go further – into and beyond the fourth chapter, whose title 'reveals' the truth about Hinduism and Buddhism, "Made in Paris, London, and Heidelberg". It shows where the Indian religions are made and plots the trajectory of the manufacturing process: it begins in Paris, the cultural centre of the Enlightenment Europe. This suggests that one must understand the creation of religions in India in terms of the compulsion of a culture. The process then shifts to London, the administrative and the political centre of colonial India. The British administrators lay the foundation for "the Oriental Renaissance". The product, the religions of India, is finished and reaches wholesale distribution centres under the expert guidance of the Germans, especially the German Romantics. While this is the obvious significance of 'Heidelberg', there is something more. Between whole-sale distribution and the consumer, other phases intervene: packaging, advertisement, attractive discount rates, promotion and publicity, and so on. Heidelberg, a provincial town, houses a university of interna-tional repute staffed largely by the *gründlich* intellectuals of Germany.

The fifth chapter sings a "Requiem for a Theme". Here, I look at the most influential idea – which knows of several versions – that the origin of religion has to do with our experience of the world and our responses to it. This chapter discredits the proposal by showing that, on the same grounds, one may argue with equal plausibility for the oppo-site conclusion. I show that neither the experience of the world nor our responses to it need be the same and, therefore, that which is supposed to account for the origin of religion in human societies can do no such thing. The ease with which one can reverse the conclusion tells us that we do not have a theory on our hands but merely some kind of a pre-theoretical idea. This argument reinforces the suggestion made earlier in this chapter that the belief about the universality of religion is not a part of any one theory but that it underlies theory-formation.

The sixth chapter, "Shall the Twain ever Meet?", continues the story further. It is a thematic narrative of the nineteenth century, which car-ries us well into the twentieth century. It explores the theme of religious experience. An experience of the 'holy', of a *'mysterium tremendum et fascinans'*, is alleged to characterise religious experience. To show that this description cannot pick out a universal cross-cultural experience, the chapter briefly analyses the texts of Schleiermacher and the ideas of Söderblom and Otto. These experiences presuppose that an individual is located in a specific religion, and that speaking of religious experi-ence in these terms is parasitic upon being located in, and accepting the truths of a particular religion, in our case, the Protestant religion. In two 'secular' theorists, Eliade and Durkheim, who speak about religion in terms of experiences of the sacred, I trace the subsistence of these themes.

The seventh chapter, "Guilty as Charged, My Lords and Ladies?", builds a case for the charge I made in the earlier chapter that the secular world is a secularised religious world. (These are the twain, which the title of the earlier chapter speaks of.) It argues that the question 'who is a Brahmin?' presupposes a society where the 'caste' system exists, in exactly the same way 'who is a religious person?' makes sense within a culture where religion exists. Thus, we are acquainted with those who speak of atheistic religiosity. The chapter ends by showing how some anthropological facts are merely secularised claims from the Bible.

Taken together, these seven chapters argue the theme that the belief about the universality of religion is a theological idea, and that its per-sistence indexes the secularisation of religious themes.

In the next four chapters, I try to make sense of this process of secularisation. Now, the manifest theme is what was latent hitherto: why, then, have reputed thinkers in the West not seen what they have been doing? Answering this question requires that one studies what religion is. To do so, it appears, we need to begin with a definition of the concept of religion.

"A Human Tragedy or the Divine Retribution?", the eighth chapter, tackles this issue. It shows that we need not define the concept of religion at this stage, but merely accept constraints on the way we use the word 'religion'. Thus, we restrict the reference of the concept of religion. Our object of study is religion, not its concept.

"Blessed are Those Who Seek ..." gives a preliminary characterisation of religion. It does so by building upon the results of the earlier chapters. The ninth chapter conceptually reproduces the journey of the previous ones in order to say what religion could be. The question, of course, is whether we know we are studying religion and not some other object. The answers to this question are the adequacy tests: does the characterisation capture the different intuitions about religion and the several descriptions of religion? What is faith? What is its relation to doctrines? What is religious experience? What is worship? Because we can answer these questions without *ad hoc* modifications of the hypothesis, one can show that religion is the object of study. My hypothesis also makes sense of the questions about the meaning of life and the possibility of atheistic religiosity.

"Imagine, There is no Religion...", the obvious allusion to the famous song, is the tenth chapter. It shows that a great deal of imagination is not necessary to do so. There are cultures without religions, because certain necessary conditions required for their existence and propagation are systematically absent. By arguing that studying religion *as* religion forces us to do theology, it shows that we could try to investigate religion as worldview. Religion may be *more* than a worldview, but it is also a worldview. This shift in concepts tells us *why* it is interesting to ask the question whether religion is a cultural universal. If it is not, then cultures and individuals exist who do not need worldviews to go-about in the world. The argument tries to establish that India is one such culture.

"Prolegomena to a Comparative Science of Cultures" tries to take the first step in making sense of the possibility that cultures exist without worldviews. This chapter shows why the West believes in the universality of religion. Both the themes come together here: it is in the nature of religion to generate the belief that religion is a cultural universal. This chapter shows how religion has been a constitutive element of the West, and suggests how to thematise cultural differences.

The eleventh chapter conceptually reproduces the previous chapters. It does so without modifying the hypotheses in an *ad hoc* manner.

## 12.2. About the Argument

In a way, one could also describe the entire argument of the book in the following way. A culture, the West, believes that all cultures are constituted (partially) by religion; it further believes that individuals and cultures require worldviews to orient and navigate themselves in the world. These beliefs are those of a culture and I show that they partially constitute the West. To show this, I specify how cultures differ from each other. Relating learning processes to cultural differences help us here.

What is the epistemic status of my proposal and the arguments that have brought us so far?

As I have been at pains to emphasise throughout, this essay does not pretend to provide a theory about religion. It is the first phase in such a process. What you have on your hands is a partial description of a people and their culture as provided by someone from another culture.

Despite this, the description is not mere 'ethno-graphy'. Nor does it merely plead the case that people from different cultures could provide different partial descriptions of the world. It does more; better put, it is forced to do more.

The essay shows that the belief in the universality of religion is false. Because this belief is pervasive in the common sense of the West and among intelligentsia in cultures other than the West, it is not enough that I appeal to pluralism in descriptions and rest content with it. More is required on my part. That 'more' is simply this: provide you with good reasons, why my description is more acceptable than the received wisdom of the last three hundred years. These reasons, quite evidently, are meta-theoretical arguments.

*Constraints on a Description*

My proposals are cognitively productive. Many, many new problems have come to the fore; solution to each problem has generated newer questions. If science is a problem-solving activity, surely, my approach is scientific.

The competitor theories are both barren and unproductive. Hume's 'theory' from the mid-eighteenth century and the Euhemerian 'theory' antedating the birth of Christ are still in vogue today. That is to say, more than two hundred years of theoretical and empirical enquiry has *not* gone beyond the question: 'why does religion exist in all cultures?' Because it is 'God-given' says one camp; because it is 'man-made' says the other. The question is the same, and the answers do not generate any new problems for enquiry. One runs where one is standing, which is a healthy exercise; but it does not bring us far.

One could also judge scientific theories in terms of their explanatory power. Should one use this criterion, the essay does not disappoint. It is able to bring together beliefs about religion with the nature of the object. It connects these with the experience of 'self' and the discussion about personhood, relates social organisations to ritual, *etc.* in a tightly interlinked and a minimal number of hypotheses. Consequently, the hypotheses are promising; they indicate how theory formation should proceed. One cannot say the same of other 'theories' or ethnographic descriptions.

Thus, one could take up each philosophy of science and show that this essay is a more promising candidate than the others are. To do so would be irrelevant to my purpose. It is irrelevant not only because I have no theory, but also because of the status of my description and the context of the dialogue. I shall begin with the former first.

*Status of a Description*

History of natural sciences has taught us that many scientific theories, which we believed were true, have turned out to be false. Consequently, it would be nothing short of a miracle if all my claims turn out to be true. Even though it is not obvious to me now, and I believe that my claims are true, the probability is high that many/some of them are not. Because of this, it is important to know how treat my claims.

Though contested, an interesting distinction in the philosophy of sciences ties our theories to two contexts: the context of discovery and the context of justification. The former broadly picks out the relevant context(s), socio-psychological ones, of the origin of a theory; the latter refers to the relevant epistemic context(s) of theory appraisal. Like all interesting distinctions, it draws our attention to different problems: how does a theory come into being? Why accept it at all? One does not have to endorse a rigid distinction between these two contexts (discovery and justification) in order to appreciate that the scientific theories confront us with different kinds of problems.

One such, applicable to the phase of theory-formation my proposal is in, is about the context of acceptance. The ideas in this essay require further exploration and development before it can become a theory. Such explorations involve a collective effort. The latter presupposes that you take these proposals as candidates for testing and elaborating. However, how can I persuade you to take my claims seriously?

One strategy would draw attention to the counterintuitive character of my stance. However, every eccentric argument is also counterintuitive. The second strategy would show that, if true, the proposal has immense and important consequences. Many other claims can do the same: things might disappear when no one is looking; we are really robots programmed by Martians; our memories are false; we are figments of a dream...Each one of these, if true, has immense and important consequences. Nevertheless, we do not take them seriously, do we? The third strategy would demonstrate the truth of my hypotheses. That is precisely what building a theory would enable us to do: test the truth of a theory.

The only way is to combine all these three strategies (suitably diluted) and compare my proposal with those that exist in the marketplace. I have tried to do this. My proposal could be true (there are some indications); it appears to be cognitively productive and heuristically fertile; it promises to deliver us an empirically testable theory. In each of these aspects, it fares better than its rivals do. Therefore, shall we try to see what this will give us?

Maximally, in other words, I can extend an invitation. Present a reasonable case for the interesting nature of the endeavour. More, I cannot.

Therefore, let me bring the case to a completion. I have been battling constantly not against a well-articulated theory or even a set of them, but against a deeply entrenched commonsense idea, which is a hydra-headed monster. While true of a culture whose commonsense it is, it has also prevented the emergence of an understanding and appreciation of other cultures.

The previous statement, however, is controversial for more reasons than one. In the last and concluding section of the book, I want to look at one such reason. In fact, it takes the form of a challenge issued by some versions of contemporary anthropology. My previous paragraph, they might suggest, runs directly into...

## 12.3. Epistemic Questions

Questions: how could we ever describe the other? How could one ever break out of one's conceptual framework to describe the 'otherness' of the other? Could one describe the other without using one's own categories?

Let me begin with a 'naïve' formulation of the convictions behind these questions. Our theories about the world and its concepts determine our experiences of the world. Consequently, in describing the otherness of the other, we use our categories. Even if we use the categories of the other, the problem of translation guarantees us that we end up describing a *variant* of our experience of the world. Hence, it is not possible to describe the other. This is an epistemic dilemma for all cultures: they cannot describe the otherness of the other. The other is beyond language.

## A Simple Formulation

Let us look at a simplified version of the naive formulation first: we project our categories upon other cultures. Thus, what we describe as the other is merely a variant of ourselves.

This is hardly a problem. Assume that the only way we could ever begin describing the other is by projecting our own categories. In that case, let members from other cultures project their categories upon the social world as well so that we have multiple descriptions. When we have such multiple descriptions, we can ask the Kantian question: how should the social world be so that it allows multiple descriptions? The answer to this question will be the beginning of a comparative science of cultures. It is comparative in the sense that it begins – from its very inception – by taking multiple descriptions as the facts it must account for.

In my book, I have tried to exhibit what the 'projection' actually consists of. Here, I have tried to identify two phases. In the first, there is a secularisation of theological themes and this generates some facts. In the second and subsequent phase, meta-level reflections develop theories, which retain the facts of theology and try to explain them. That is to say, one does not begin by projecting some concept of religion. Instead, one generalises themes, generates facts, and accounts for them.

Theology was the first theory of religion. Secular theories transformed theological facts into their *explananda*. These facts are low-level themes from theology: for instance, all cultures have religion. In other words, the European intellectuals did not project their own categories in the process of understanding other religions.

My opponent might not agree that my portrayal of history is veridical. However, that does not matter. The dispute is not any more about the epistemic possibilities of human beings. Instead, it takes on an empirical character.

The same conclusion holds with respect to the more general questions as well. I will argue that the convictions supporting them are not epistemic but empirical in nature.

## On Equivocation and Suppression

Consider the two cultures I have talked about: India and the West. Because we are talking about the 'other' in anthropological terms, it means that (a) Indian culture is the other of the West; (b) The West is the other of the Indian culture. Let us examine the claim that it is impossible to describe the otherness of the other.

If we grant that cultures experience the world differently and that their descriptions reflect this difference, it follows that: (c) the otherness of India, as the westerners experience it, depends on the western culture; (d) the otherness of the West, as the Indians experience it, depends on the Indian culture. Therefore, it follows: *if these cultures are different*, so are their experiences of each other. Hence, one cannot logically infer that it is impossible to describe the otherness. It is a matter of empirical research. Into what? Into *how* each of these cultures succeed or fail in describing the otherness of the other culture. In other words, it is a logical fallacy to claim that one could never describe the otherness: may be one can; may be one cannot.

Of course, one could challenge the truth-value of the assumptions I have made. It might be the case that cultures do not experience the world differently; it might also be the case that their descriptions do not reflect their experiences. Again, this is an empirical issue about two cultures, not an epistemic point about human beings.

Suppose that one is willing to grant the truth-value of the above premises, and still insist that it is impossible to describe the otherness in language. We need a further premise to argue the epistemic impossibility: *each culture is the other in exactly the same way*. This too is an empirical premise. After all, cultures could be the others of each other in different ways. To argue that this is *not* the case requires recourse to language. That is, one has to argue that the difference between cultures is of the same *kind*. In that case, one cannot any more argue that the otherness is not expressible in language. Alternately, the assumption about the otherness is of uncertain truth-value: the 'unsayable' otherness of the other may or may not distinguish cultures from each other. Perhaps, it is typical of one specific culture that the 'otherness' of the others disappears from its descriptions of cultures.

Given the argument of my book, the last point requires elaboration. Western culture has brought forth anthropology and ethnography, as we know them both. This fact makes the empirical premise transparent. *Each culture (as the West has described them) is the other (of the western culture) in exactly the same way*. What is the 'otherness' in the Western description? It is merely '*anotherness*'. That is, the western description has effaced the otherness. It has transformed the other into another – a variant of self. This means that the Indian, the African, *etc.* cultures – as the West has described them – is the 'other' of each and of the West in exactly the same way.

The western cultural descriptions of both itself and other cultures make each one of them the other in the same way. The other of each is merely another – this is how the West has described the world. This situation gives raise to the feeling that the otherness has disappeared (which it indeed has) from the western descriptions.

In other words, one has to assume that each culture experiences the other the way the West describes (and experiences) the other. Now the empirical nature of this assumption is more transparent: one has to assume that the way the West experiences and describes itself and the other is the way all cultures experience themselves and others. This assumption could be true, but it is a matter for empirical demonstration. For the same reason, it could be false as well.

## From a Dilemma to a Problem

Let me reformulate the above paragraphs very succinctly: we do have an epistemic dilemma of the 'other' on our hands, if the West is the Cosmos of all cultures and if cultures do not differ from each other in different ways but only in the way the West imagines it to be the case. However, if the West is but one culture *in* the universe of cultures; if it is typical to the way in which the former has looked at itself and the others; then it is not a dilemma at all.

In fact, that is how I have tried to make sense of the western culture: why does the 'otherness' disappear from the western descriptions of other cultures? Why does everyone shine in the splendour of mono-chromatic dullness? I have answered these problems partially but *not by blaming the big bad wolf,* viz. religion. After all, it is my argument that religion has produced both western culture and science. What I have tried to do is something other than apportion blame. I have argued that the otherness of the western culture, *when viewed against the background of mine,* lies in its transformation of the other into another.

There are two independent tasks here. First, there is the task of providing a description of the mechanism of transforming the other into another. Subsequent to this, one has to argue that this constitutes the *otherness* of the western culture.

With respect to the former, my description is subject to multiple constraints: accessibility, intelligibility, and objectivity (see #12.2). Because I am describing the western culture, my description must be accessible to the members of this culture; it must make their experience of the world intelligible. However, in order to prevent the description from becoming *ad hoc,* it must be possible for me to bring together hitherto unconnected phenomena, pose new problems, be falsifiable, *etc.* That is, my description must satisfy the multiple conditions of rationality and scientificity. Such a description is hypothetical – as all our theories about fragments of the world are. This is no weakness but an epistemic strength. Regarding the second task, the situation is more complicated. With respect to the theme of the book, this is a meta-level question about my experience of the world. The description of the West is located within my experiential world. The object-level description suggests that the West has the truth about the world and that it has the view of the world. From the meta-level (or from my experiential world), this description has the following import: this is typical of the western culture; it is the western way of going-about in the world and not mine. In other words, I have merely located my description of the western culture in an experiential context. However, the task involves an explication of the experiential context as well. Completion of this task requires further theorising. That is, one has to describe the Indian culture as that culture sees itself. This is a task for the future; the flag-waving with respect to ritual in the previous chapter hints in a possible direction.

The choice for the title of the eleventh chapter is motivated on these grounds. What we need today is some kind of a theory about cultural differences. However, the prerequisite is that we break the shackles of a descriptive straightjacket, which is centuries old.

In any case, what appeared as an epistemic dilemma is not destructive because it is actually a combination of two questions, each applicable only to one level. The first is an object-level question: how can one describe the other? The second is a meta-level question: how to accommodate such descriptions in one's experiential world?

The answer to the first question is obvious. One describes the other in such a way that the other recognises the description of his own world. One's description is constrained here by different notions of rationality, scientificity, and objectivity. This is theory generation under constraints and it is never a finished job. Such a description is hypothetical; it is partial; it merely describes one kind of difference – and even that at a very high level of abstraction. In other words, it exhibits the dynamic of scientific theorising. All scientific theories face analogous problems. How could we ever falsify a theory, when the facts at our disposal are theory-laden? How could we ever generate an alternate theory, when imprisoned by the received theory? In the case of science of cultures, the job is easier and less mysterious. There are different cultures and, therefore, different partial descriptions of self and other are possible. Hence, one can generate different theories. Theories could compete with each other, whatever the epistemic status of the facts might be.

Regarding the second question, the answer emphasises differences. As human beings, we have been living with all kinds of differences for centuries long. No culture imprisons anyone.

*A Note*

What have I done in this book then? I hope to have shown *why* the existence question of religion is cognitively interesting. It is not a definitional question. It requires developing a theory about religion, culture, and their mutual interrelationship. Conceiving it in this fashion has enabled me to raise many interesting problems for enquiry. I do not know the extent to which I have persuaded you to take my ideas seriously; at least I hope to have made plausible why I think that a serious discussion about this issue will require a rethinking of the entire problematic. The ideas proposed in this essay could turn out to be wrong, but that is hardly the problem. There is wrong and there is wrong. It is better to be wrong in an interesting way than to recycle and peddle barren ideas that everyone *wrongly* believes to be right.

With these remarks, I have reached the end of this essay. Even though the journey – in which this particular book has the position of a resting place – is far from complete, the feeling is that one has at least come some way. Perhaps, this is the best one could say about any essay, any journey, and not merely this particular one.

# REFERENCES

AARSLEFF, HANS
  1967    *The Study of Language in England 1780-1860.* London: The Athlone Press, 1983.
  1982    *From Locke to Saussure: Essays on the Study of Language and Intellectual History.* London: The Athlone Press.

ABBOT SUMANGALO
  1972    "Common Denominators of Asian Thought." In JOHN BOWMAN, (Ed.), *Comparative Religion.* Leiden: E.J. Brill, 19-34.

ACHINSTEIN, PETER
  1983    *The Nature of Explanation.* Oxford: Oxford University Press.

ADKINS, A. W. H.
  1969    "Greek Religion." In E. JOUCO BLEEKER and GEO WIDENGREN, (Eds.), *Historia Religionum: Handbook for the History of Religions, Vol. 1, Religions of the Past.* Leiden: E. J. Brill, 377-441.

AGEHANANDA BHARATI
  1985    "The Self in Hindu Thought and Action." In ANTHONY J. MARSELLA, GEORGE DEVOS, and FRANCIS L. K. HSU, (Eds.), *Culture and Self: Asian and Western Perspectives.* London: Unwin, 185-230.

ALMOND, PHILIP, C.
  1988    *The British Discovery of Buddhism.* Cambridge: Cambridge University Press.

ALSTON, WILLIAM, P.
  1967    "Religion." In PAUL EDWARDS, (Ed.), *The Encyclopedia of Philosophy,* Vol. 7. New York: MacMillan Publishing Company, 140-145.

APOSTEL, LEO
  1981    "Mysticism, Ritual and Atheism." In APOSTEL, PINXTEN, THIBAU, and VANDAMME, (Eds.), *Religious Atheism?* Gent: Story Scientia, 7-55.

ARMSTRONG, S. L., GLEITMAN, L. R. AND GLEITMAN, H. G.
  1983    "On what Some Concepts might not be." *Cognition,* 13, 263-308.

ARNAUT, KAREL
  1988    "Africans Dance in Time: Kinaesthetic Praxis and the Construction of a Community." *Cultural Dynamics,* 1(3), 252-281.

ARRIAN

> *History of Alexander and Indica.* Translated by P. A. BRUNT. The Loeb Classical Library. London: William Heinemann Ltd., 1933, 1983.

ASAD, TALAL
1983    "Anthropological Conceptions of Religion: Reflections on Geertz." *Man,* (n.s.), 18(2), 237-59.

ATHENAGORAS

> *A Plea for the Christians.* In Rev. ALEXANDER ROBERTS and JAMES DONALDSON, (Eds.), *The Ante-Nicene Fathers: Translations of the Writings of the Fathers down to A.D. 325, Vol. 2, Fathers of the Second Century.* American reprint of the Edinburgh edition (n.d.). Michigan: Wm. B. Eerdmans Publishing Company, 1978.

AUGUSTINE

> *Of True Religion.* Translated by J. H. S. BURLEIGH. Chicago: Henry Regnery Company, 1968.

BADGER, GEORGE PERCY (ED.)
n.d.    *The Travels of Ludovico DiVarthema in Egypt, Syria, Arabia Deserta and Arabia Felix, in Persia, India and Ethiopia, A. D. 1503 to 1508.* Translated into English in 1863 by J. WINTER JONES. The Hakluyt Society, Series II, Vol. XXXII. Reprinted: New York: Burt Franklin, Publisher.

BAIER, ANNETTE
1980    "Secular Faith." *Canadian Journal of Philosophy,* 10(1), 131-48. Now reprinted as Chapter 15 in her *Postures of the Mind: Essays on Mind and Morals.* London: Methuen and Company Ltd., 292-308, 1985.

BALAGANGADHARA, S. N.
1987    "Comparative Anthropology and Action Sciences: An Essay on Knowing to Act and Acting to Know." *Philosophica,* 40(2), 77-107.

BALDAEUS, PHILIPPUS
1672    *Nauwkeurige en Waarachtige Ontdekking en Wederlegging van de Afgoderye der Oost-Indische Heydenen, Malabaren, Benjanen, Gentiven, Bramines, ....* ALBERT JOHANNES DE JONG, (Ed.), 's-Gravenhage: Martinus Nijhoff, 1917.

BARNES, TIMOTHY
1968    "Legislation Against the Christians." *Journal of Roman Studies,* 58, 32-50.

BARROW, R. H. (TRANS.)
1973    Prefect and Emperor: The Relationes of Symmachus. A.D. 384. Oxford: The Clarendon Press.

BARTH, A.
1881    The Religions of India. Translated by Rev. J. WOOD. Fourth Edition. London: Kegan Paul, Trench, Trübner & Co. Ltd, 1906.

BASHAM, A. L.
1951    History and Doctrines of the _j_vikas: A Vanished Indian Religion. London: Luzac and Company Ltd.

BEDFORD, R. D.
1979    The Defence of Truth: Herbert of Cherbury and the Seventeenth Century. Manchester: Manchester University Press.

BENKO, STEPHEN
1980    "Pagan Criticism of Christianity During the First Two Centuries A. D." In HILDEGARD TEMPORINI and WOLFGANG HAASE, (Eds.), Aufstieg und Niedergang der Römischen Welt: Geschichte und Kultur Roms im Spiegel der Neuren Forschung, 23.2. Berlin: Walter de Gruyter, 1055-1118.
1985    Pagan Rome and the Early Christians. London: E. T. Batsford Ltd.

BENZ, ERNEST
1959    "On understanding Non-Christian Religions." In MIRCEA ELIADE and JOSEPH M. KITAGAWA, (Eds.), The History of Religions: Essays in Methodology. Chicago: The University of Chicago Press, 115-131.

BERMAN, HAROLD, J.
1983    Law and Revolution: The Formation of the Western Legal Tradition. Cambridge, Massachusetts: Harvard University Press.

BIANCHI, UGO
1972    "The Definition of Religion: On the Methodology of Historical-Comparative Research." In U. BIANCHI, C. J. BLEEKER, A. BAUSANI, (Eds.), Problems and Methods of the History of Religions. Leiden: E. J. Brill, 15-34.

BICHSEL, PETER
1982    Der Leser, Das Erzählen: Frankfurter Poetik-Vorlesungen. Darmstadt und Neuwied: Hermann Luchterhand Verlag.

BODIN, JEAN
1857    Colloquium of the Seven about Secrets of the Sublime. Translated by MARION KUNTZ. Princeton: Princeton University Press, 1975.

BOENDERS, FRANS, AND COPPENS, FREDDY
1981    *De Goden uit het Oosten*. Hasselt: Heideland-Orbis.

BRADLEY, RAYMOND, AND SWARTZ, NORMON
1979    *Possible Worlds: An Introduction to Logic and its Philosophy*. Oxford: Basil Blackwell.

BRATA, SASTHI
1985    *India: Labyrinths in the Lotus Land*. New York: William Morrow and Company, Inc.

BREAR, DOUGLAS
1975    "Early Assumptions in Western Buddhist Studies." *Religion*, 5(2), 136-159.

BROOKE, JOHN HEDLEY
1990    "Science and Religion." In R. C. OLBY, G. N. CANTOR, J. R. R. CHRISTIE, and M. J. S. HODGE, (Eds.), *Companion to the History of Modern Science*. London: Routledge, 763-782.
1991    *Science and Religion: Some Historical Perspectives*. Cambridge: Cambridge University Press.

BROWN, DONALD, E.
1988    *Hierarchy, History, and Human Nature: The Social origins of Historical Consciousness*. Tucson: The University of Arizona Press.

BROWN, PETER
1982    *Society and the Holy in Late Antiquity*. Berkeley: University of California Press.

BRUCE, STEVE
1990    *A House Divided: Protestantism, Schism, and Secularization*. London: Routledge.

BUCKLEY, MICHAEL J., S.J.
1987    *At the Origins of Modern Atheism*. New Haven: Yale University Press.

BURGHART, RICHARD, AND CANTILE, AUDREY (EDS.)
1985    *Indian Religion*. London: Curzon Press.

BURKERT, WALTER
1977    *Greek Religion*. Cambridge, Massachusetts: Harvard University Press, 1985.

BURNYEAT, MYLES
    1983    "Can the Skeptic Live His Skepticism?" In MYLES BURNYEAT,
            (Ed.), *The Skeptical Tradition*. Berkeley: University of California
            Press, 117-148.

BURTT, E. A.
    1932    *The Metaphysical Foundations of Modern Science: The Scientific
            Thinking of Copernicus, Galileo, Newton and their Contemporaries.*
            New Jersey: Humanities Press, 1980.

BYRNE, PETER
    1989    *Natural Religion and the Nature of Religion: The Legacy of Deism.*
            London: Routledge.

BYRNES, JOSEPH, H.
    1984    *The Psychology of Religion.* New York: The Free Press.

CALAND, W. (ED.)
    1926    *Ziegenbalg's Malabarische Heidenthum.* Amsterdam: Koninklijke
            Akademie van Wetenschappen.
    1929    *De Remonstratie van W. Geleynssen De Jongh (1625).* De Linscho-
            ten-Vereeniging, Vol. XXXI, 's-Gravenhage: Martinus Nijhoff.

CALVIN, JOHN
            *Institutes of the Christian Religion.* Translated by HENRY BEVERIDGE
            in two volumes. Michigan: William B. Eerdmans Publishing
            Company, 1983.

CAMERON, AVERIL
    1991    *Christianity and the Rhetoric of Empire: The Development of
            Christian Discourse. Sather Classical Lectures, Vol. 55.* Berkeley:
            University of California Press.

CARTER, JOHN ROSS, AND PALIHAWADANA, MAHINDA (TRANS.)
    1987    *The Dhammapada.* Oxford: Oxford University Press.

CHADWICK, HENRY
    1966    *Early Christian Thought and the Classical Tradition: Studies in
            Justin, Clement, and Origen.* Oxford: Oxford University Press.

CHATFIELD, ROBERT
    1808    *An Historical Review of the Commercial, Political and Moral State
            of Hindoostan.* Reprinted as *Social, Political, Historical and Com-
            mercial Review of Hindoostan from the Earliest Period to the Present
            Time.* Delhi: Bimla Publishing House, 1983.

CHING, JULIA
    1977    *Confucianism and Christianity: A Comparative Study.* Tokyo: Kodansha International.

CHOUDHURI, ARNAB RAI
    1985    "Practising Western Science Outside the West: Personal Observations on the Indian Science." *Social Studies of Science,* 15, 475-505.

CHRISTIE MURRAY, DAVID
    1976    *A History of Heresy.* Oxford: Oxford University Press, 1989.

CICERO
            *De Natura Deorum.* Translated by H. RACKHAM. The Loeb Classical Library. London: William Heinemann Ltd., 1933, 1979.

CLARKE, PETER, B. AND BYRNE, PETER
    1993    *Religion Defined and Explained.* London: The Macmillan Press Ltd.

CLAUSEN, CHRISTOPHER
    1975    "Victorian Buddhism and the Origin of Comparative Religion." *Religion,* 5(1), 1-15.

CLAYTON, JOHN, P.
    1980    *The Concept of Correlation: Paul Tillich and the Possibility of a Mediating Theology.* Berlin: Walter de Gruyter.

CLAYTON, PHILIP
    1989    *Explanation from Physics to Theology: An Essay in Rationality and Religion.* New Haven: Yale University Press.

COHEN, MORRIS, R.
    1946    "Baseball as a National Religion." In LOUIS SCHNEIDER, (Ed.), *Religion, Culture and Society: A Reader in the Sociology of Religion.* London: John Wiley and Sons, 1964, 36-38.

COLLINS, STEVEN
    1988    "Monasticism, Utopias and Comparative Social Theory." *Religion,* 18, 101-135.

CONTRERAS, C. A.
    1980    "Christian Views of Paganism." In HILDEGARD TEMPORINI and WOLFGANG HAASE, (Eds.), *Aufstieg und Niedergang der Römischen Welt: Geschichte und Kultur Roms im Spiegel der Neuren Forschung,* 23.2. Berlin: Walter de Gruyter, 974-1022.

COOK, STANLEY, A.
   1913      "Religion." In JAMES HASTINGS, (Ed.), *Encyclopedia of Religion and Ethics*, Vol. 6. New York: Charles Scribner's, 662-693.

COOKE, J. A.
   1927      "Euhemerism: A Medieval Interpretation of Classical Paganism." *Speculum*, 2, 369-410.

CORTESÃO, ARMANDO (ED.)
   1944      *The Suma Oriental of Tomé Pires: An Account of the East, from the Red Sea to Japan, Written in Malacca and India in 1512-1515.* London: The Hakluyt Society, Series II, Vol. LXXXIX.

CREEL, AUSTIN, B.
   1977      *Dharma in Hindu Ethics.* Calcutta: Firma KLM Private Ltd.

CROOKE, WILLIAM (ED.)
   1909      *A New Account of East India and Persia being the Nine Years' Travels, 1672-1681, by John Fryer.* London: The Hakluyt Society, Series II, Vol. XIX.

CROOKE, WILLIAM
   1913      "Hinduism." In JAMES HASTINGS, (Ed.), *Encyclopedia of Religion and Ethics*, Vol. 6. New York: Charles Scribner's, 686-715.

CROUTER, RICHARD
   1988      "Introduction" to *On Religion*. In FRIEDRICH SCHLEIERMACHER, 1799, 1-73.

CULLER, JONATHAN
   1983      *On Deconstruction: Theory and Criticism after Structuralism.* London: Routledge and Kegan Paul.

D'COSTA, GAVIN
   1990      "'Extra Ecclesiam Nulla Salus' Revisited." In IAN HAMNET, (Ed.), 1990, 130-147.

DAMES, MANSEL LONGWORTH (ED.)
   1812a     *The Book of Duarte Barbosa: An Account of the Countries Bordering on the Indian Ocean and their Inhabitants written by Duarte Barbosa, and Completed about the year 1518 A. D. Vol. 1.* London: The Hakluyt Society, Series II, Vol. XLIV, 1918.
   1812b     *The Book of Duarte Barbosa: An Account of the Countries Bordering on the Indian Ocean and their Inhabitants written by Duarte Barbosa, and Completed about the year 1518 A. D. Vol. 2.* London: The Hakluyt Society, Series II, Vol. XLIX, 1921.

DANDEKAR, R. N.
1969    "Hinduism." In E. JOUCO BLEEKER and GEO WIDENGREN, (Eds.), *Historia Religionum: Handbook for the History of Religions, Vol. 2, Religions of the Present*. Leiden: E. J. Brill, 237-345.

DANIEL, VALENTINE, E.
1984    *Fluid Signs: Being a Person the Tamil Way.* Berkeley: University of California Press.

DAVIDSON, DONALD
1963    "Action, Reasons, and Causes." *The Journal of Philosophy*, 60, 685-700. Reprinted in STEVEN DAVIS, (Ed.), *Causal Theories of Mind: Action, Knowledge, Memory, Perception, and Reference*. Berlin: Walter de Gruyter, 1983, 58-72.

DAVIES, BRIAN
1982    *An Introduction to the Philosophy of Religion.* New edition. Oxford: Oxford University Press, 1993.

DAWEEWARN, DAWEE
1982    *Brahmanism in South-East Asia: From the Earliest Times to 1445 A. D.* Delhi: Sterling Publishers.

DAWSON, CHRISTOPHER
1951    "The Christian View of History." Reprinted in MCINTIRE, (Ed.), 1977, 28-45.

DE STE. CROIX, G. E. M.
1963    "Why were the Early Christians Prosecuted?" *Past and Present*, 26, 6-38.
1964    "Why were the Early Christians Prosecuted? – A Rejoinder." *Past and Present*, 27, 28-33.

DE WICK, E. C.
1953    *The Christian Attitude to Other Religions.* Cambridge: Cambridge University Press.

DODDS, E. R.
1965    *Pagan and Christian in an Age of Anxiety: Some Aspects of Religious Experience from Marcus Aurelius to Constantine.* Cambridge: Cambridge University Press.

DOTY, WILLIAM, G.
1986    *Mythography: A Study of Myths and Rituals.* Alabama: University of Alabama Press.

Dow, Alexander
1768    *The History of Hindostan*. Partially in P. J. Marshall, (Ed.), 1970.

Drobin, Ulf
1982    "Psychology, Philosophy, Theology, Epistemology: Some Reflections." *Scripta Instituti Donneriani Aboensis*, XI, 263-274.

Dubois, Abbé
1816    *Hindu Manners, Customs and Ceremonies*. Third Edition. Delhi: Oxford University Press, 1906, 1985.

Duff, Alexander
1839    *India and India Missions: Including Sketches of the Gigantic System of Hinduism Both in Theory and Practice*. Delhi: Swati Publications, 1988.

Dulles, Avery
1971    *A History of Apologetics*. London: Hutchinson and Co.

Dumont, Louis
1966    *Homo Hierarchicus: The Caste System and its Implications*. Complete revised English edition. Chicago: The University of Chicago Press, 1980.

Durkheim, Emile
1912    *The Elementary Forms of Religious Life*. In W. S. F. Pickering, (Ed.), *Durkheim on Religion*. London: Routledge and Kegan Paul, 1975.

Eilberg-Schwartz, Howard
1990    *The Savage in Judaism: An Anthropology of Israelite Religion and Ancient Judaism*. Bloomington: Indiana University Press.

Eire, Carlos, M. N.
1986    *War Against the Idols: The Reformation of Worship from Erasmus to Calvin*. Cambridge: Cambridge University Press.

Eliade, Mircea
1959    *Cosmos and History: The Myth of Eternal Return*. New York: Harper Torchbooks.
1961    *The Sacred and the Profane: The Nature of Religion*. New York: Harcourt, Brace, and Co.
1969    *The Quest: History and Meaning in Religion*. Chicago: The University of Chicago Press.
1978-85 *A History of Religious Ideas. (3 Volumes)*. Vol. 1, 1978; Vol. 2, 1982; Vol. 3, 1985. Chicago: The University of Chicago Press.

ELISON, GEORGE
    1973    *Deus Destroyed: The Image of Christianity in Early Modern Japan.*
            Council on East Asian Studies, Harvard University, 1988.

EMBREE, AINSLIE, T. (ED.)
    1988    *Sources of the Indian Tradition, Vol. 1, From the Beginning to 1800.*
            Second Edition. New York: Columbia University Press.

EUSEBIUS
            *Praeparatio Evangelica.* Translated by E. H. GIFFORD. Oxford,
            1903.
            *The History of the Church.* Translated by G. A. WILLIAMSON.
            Harmondsworth: Penguin Books, 1965.

EVANS-PRITCHARD, E. E.
    1965    *Theories of Primitive Religion.* Oxford: Oxford University Press.

FALLDING, HAROLD
    1974    *The Sociology of Religion.* Toronto: McGraw-Hill Ryerson
            Limited.

FARACE, DOMINIC JOHN
    1982    *The Sacred-Profane Dichotomy.* Doctoral Dissertation. Utrecht:
            Rijksuniversiteit Utrecht.

FEUERBACH, LUDWIG
    1841    *The Essence of Christianity.* New York: Harper Torchbooks,
            1957.

FINLEY, SIR MOSES
    1985    "Foreword" to P. E. EASTERLING and J. V. MUIR, (Eds.), *Greek*
            *Religion and Society.* Cambridge: Cambridge University Press,
            xiii-xx.

FOX, ROBIN LANE
    1986    *Pagans and Christians.* London: Viking Books.

FRASER, WATTS, AND WILLIAMS, MARK
    1988    *The Psychology of Religious Knowing.* Cambridge: Cambridge
            University Press.

FREDRIKSEN, PAULA
    1988    *From Jesus to Christ: The Origins of the New Testament Images of*
            *Jesus.* New Haven: Yale University Press.

FREND, W. H. C.
    1965    *Martyrdom and Persecution in the Early Church: A Study of Con-*
            *flict from the Maccabes to Donatus.* Oxford: Basil Blackwell.

FREUD, SIGMUND
   1913      *Totem and Taboo.* In *The Origins of Religion, Pelican Freud Library,*
             *Vol. 13.* Harmondsworth: Penguin Books, 1985.
   1927      *The Future of an Illusion.* In *Civilization, Society, and Religion,*
             *Pelican Freud Library, Vol. 12.* Harmondsworth: Penguin Books,
             1985.
   1939      *Moses and Monotheism: Three Essays.* In *The Origins of Religion,*
             *Pelican Freud Library, Vol. 13.* Harmondsworth: Penguin Books,
             1985.

FUNKENSTEIN, AMOS
   1986      *Theology and the Scientific Imagination from the Middle Ages to the*
             *Seventeenth Century.* Princeton: Princeton University Press.

GAMBLE, HARRY, A.
   1979      "Euhemerism and Christology in Origen: *Contra Celsum,* III 22-
             43." *Vigiliae Christianae,* 33(1), 12-29.

GARBE, RICHARD
   1914      *Indien und das Christentum: Eine Untersuchung der Religions-*
             *geschichtlichen Zusammenhänge.* Tubingen: J. C. B. Mohr (Paul
             Siebeck).

GARDNER, MARTIN (ED.)
   1960      *The Annotated Alice.* Revised Edition. Harmondsworth: Penguin
             Books, 1970.

GASKIN, J. C. A.
   1988      *Hume's Philosophy of Religion.* Second Edition. London: Mac-
             millan.

GAY, PETER
   1973      *The Enlightenment: An Interpretation, Vol. 1, The Rise of Modern*
             *Paganism.* London: Wildwood House.

GAZZANIGA, MICHAEL, J.
   1985      *The Social Brain: Discovering the Networks of the Mind.* New York:
             Basic Books.

GEDEN, A. S.
   1913      "God (Hindu)." In JAMES HASTINGS, (Ed.), *Encyclopedia of Reli-*
             *gion and Ethics,* Vol. 6. New York: Charles Scribner's, 282-290.

GEERTZ, CLIFFORD
   1966      "Religion as a Cultural System." In MICHAEL BANTON, (Ed.),
             *Anthropological Approaches to the Study of Religion.* London: Ta-
             vistock Publications, 1-46.

GIBBON, EDWARD
    1776    *The Decline and Fall of the Roman Empire*. In *Great Books of the Western World, Vol. 40*, London: Encyclopædia Britannica, 1952.

GILL, SAM
    1987    *Native American Religious Action: A Performance Approach to Religion*. Columbia: University of South Carolina Press.

GLOVER, T. R.
    1909    *The Conflict of Religions in the Early Roman Empire*. London: Methuen and Co.

GLYMOUR, CLARK
    1980    *Theory and Evidence*. Princeton: Princeton University Press.

GOLD, ANN GRODZINS
    1988    *Fruitful Journeys: The Ways of the Rajasthani Pilgrims*. Berkeley: University of California Press.

GOMBRICH, RICHARD, AND OBEYESEKERE, GANANATH
    1988    *Buddhism Transformed: Religious Change in Sri Lanka*. Princeton: Princeton University Press.

GOULD, JOHN
    1985    "Making Sense of Greek Religion." In P. E. EASTERLING and J. V. MUIR, (Eds.), *Greek Religion and Society*. Cambridge: Cambridge University Press, 1-33.

GOULD, STEPHEN JAY
    1987    *Time's Arrow, Time's Cycle: Myth and Metaphor in the Discovery of Geological Time*. Cambridge, Massachusetts: Harvard University Press.

GRANT, R. M.
    1973    "Porphyry among the Early Christians." In W. DEN BOER, P. G. VAN DER NAT, C. M. J. SICKING, and J. C. M. VAN WINDEN, (Eds.), *Romanitas et Christianitas*. Amsterdam: North Holland Publishing Company, 181-187.

GREENLEE, WILLIAM BROOKS (ED.)
    1937    *The Voyage of Pedro Álvares Cabral to Brazil and India from Contemporary Documents and Narratives*. London: The Hakluyt Society, Series II, Vol. LXXXI.

GRIFFIOEN, SANDER
    1989    "The Approach to Social Theory: Hazards and Benefits." In PAUL A. MARSHALL, et. alii., (Eds.), 1989, 81-118.

GRISLIS, EGIL
1971    "Calvin's use of Cicero in the *Institutes* 1: 1-5. A Case Study in Theological Methods." *Archiv Für Reformationsgeschichte*, 62, 5-37.

GUTERMAN, SIMEON, L.
1951    *Religious Toleration and Persecution in Ancient Rome*. London: Aiglon Press Ltd.

GUTHRIE, W. K. C.
1955    *The Greeks and Their Gods*. Boston: Beacon Press.

GUTTING, GARY
1982    *Religious Belief and Religious Skepticism*. Notre Dame: University of Notre Dame Press.

HALBFASS, WILHELM
1981    *India and Europe: An Essay in Understanding*. New York: State University of New York Press, 1988.
1985    "India and the Comparative Method." *Philosophy East and West*, 35(1), 3-15.

HALHEAD, NATHANIEL BRASSEY
1776    *A Code of the Gentoo Laws*. Partially in P. J. MARSHALL, (Ed.), 1970.

HALL, JOHN, A.
1985    *Powers and Liberties: The Causes and the Consequences of the Rise of the West*. Oxford: Basil Blackwell.

HAMNETT, IAN (ED.)
1990    *Religious Pluralism and Unbelief: Studies Critical and Comparative*. London: Routledge.

HANSON, R. P. C.
1980    "The Christian Attitude to Pagan Religions up to the Time of Constantine the Great." In HILDEGARD TEMPORINI and WOLF-GANG HAASE, (Eds.), *Aufstieg und Niedergang der Römischen Welt: Geschichte und Kultur Roms im Spiegel der Neuren Forschung, 23.2*. Berlin: Walter de Gruyter, 910-973.

HARDING, SANDRA, G. (ED.)
1976    *Can Theories Be Refuted? Essays on the Duhem-Quine Thesis*. Dordrecht: D. Reidel.

HARRÉ, ROM (ED.)
1988    *The Social Construction of Emotions*. Oxford: Basil Blackwell.

HARRISON, PETER
1990    *'Religion' and the Religions in the English Enlightenment.*
        Cambridge: Cambridge University Press.

HEIFETZ, HANK, AND NARAYANA RAO, VELCHERU (TRANS.)
1987    *For the Lord of the Animals – Poems from the Telugu.* Berkeley: University of California Press.

HERMAN, A. L.
1983    *An Introduction to Buddhist Thought: A Philosophic History of Indian Buddhism.* Lanham: University Press of America.

HICK, JOHN, AND MELTZER, EDMUND, S. (EDS.)
1989    *Three Faiths – One God: A Jewish, Christian and Muslim Encounter.* London: The Macmillan Press Ltd.

HICK, JOHN
1973    *God and the Universe of Faiths: Essays in the Philosophy of Religion.* London: The Macmillan Press Ltd.
1989    *An Interpretation of Religion: Human Responses to the Transcendent.* New Haven: Yale University Press.

HILEY, DAVID, R.
1988    *Philosophy in Question: Essays on a Pyrrhonian Theme.* Chicago: The University of Chicago Press.

HILL, CHARLES, E.
1992    *Regnum Caelorum: Patterns of Future Hope in Early Christianity.* Oxford: Clarendon Press.

HODGEN, MARGARET, T.
1964    *Early Anthropology in the Sixteenth and Seventeenth Centuries.* Philadelphia: The University of Pennsylvania Press.

HOLWELL, JOHN ZEPHANIAH
1767    *Interesting Historical Events Relative to the Provinces of Bengal and the Empire of Indostan.* Partially reprinted in P. J. MARSHALL, (Ed.), 1970.

HOOYKAAS, R.
1972    *Religion and the Rise of Modern Science.* Michigan: William B. Eerdmans Publishing Company.

HULEN, AMOS BERRY
1938    *Porphyry's Work Against the Christians: An Interpretation.* Scottdale: Mennonite Press.

HUME, DAVID
   1740    *A Treatise of Human Nature.* Selby-Brigge Edition. Second edition edited by P. H. NIDDITCH. Oxford: Clarendon Press, 1978.
   1757    *The Natural History of Religion.* In THOMAS HILL GREEN and THOMAS HODGE GROSE, (Eds.), *The Philosophical Works of David Hume.* Reprint of the 1882 London Edition, Vol. 4. Aalen: Scientia Verlag, 1964.
   1777    *Enquiries Concerning Human Understanding and the Principles of Morals.* Selby-Brigge Edition. Second edition edited by P. H. NIDDITCH. Oxford: Clarendon Press, 1975.

ISSAC, THOMAS, T. M., AND EKBAL, B.
   1988    *Science for Social Revolution: The Experience of Kerala Sastra Sahitya Parishat.* Trichur: Kerala Sastra Sahitya Parishat.

JAMES, WILLIAM
   1902    *The Varieties of Religious Experience.* New York: The New American Library, 1958.

JAMES, E. O.
   1969    "Prehistoric Religion." In E. JOUCO BLEEKER and GEO WIDENGREN, (Eds.), *Historia Religionum: Handbook for the History of Religions, Vol. 1, Religions of the Past.* Leiden: E. J. Brill, 23-39.

JANSSEN, L. F.
   1979    "'Superstitio' and the Persecution of the Christians." *Vigiliae Christianae,* 33(2), 131-159.

JOHNSON, JEFF
   1984    "Inference to the Best Explanation and the Problem of Evil." *The Journal of Religion,* 64(1), 54-72.

JONES, SIR WILLIAM
   1789    *The Concept of Gods in Ancient World.* Delhi: Eastern Book Linkers, 1983.

KAELBER, WALTER
   1981    "The Brahmacharin: Homology and Continuity in Brahmanic Religion." *History of Religions,* 21(1), 77-99.

KALUPAHANA, DAVID, J. (TRANS.)
   1986    *Nagarjuna: The Philosophy of the Middle Way.* New York: State University of New York Press.

KEAY, JOHN
   1981    *India Discovered.* London: Collins, 1988.

KEIL, FRANK, C.
1989    *Concepts, Kinds, and Cognitive Development.* Cambridge, Massachusetts: The MIT Press.

KELLENBERGER, J.
1985    *The Cognitivity of Religion.* London: The MacMillan Press Ltd.

KERESZTES, P.
1979a   "The Imperial Roman Government and the Christian Church. I. From Nero to Severi." In HILDEGARD TEMPORINI and WOLFGANG HAASE, (Eds.), *Aufstieg und Niedergang der Römischen Welt: Geschichte und Kultur Roms im Spiegel der Neuren Forschung, 23.1.* Berlin: Walter de Gruyter, 247-315.
1979b   "The Imperial Roman Government and the Christian Church. II. From Gallienus to the Great Persecution." In HILDEGARD TEMPORINI and WOLFGANG HAASE, (Eds.), *Aufstieg und Niedergang der Römischen Welt: Geschichte und Kultur Roms im Spiegel der Neuren Forschung, 23.1.* Berlin: Walter de Gruyter, 375-386.

KITCHER, PHILIP
1985    *Vaulting Ambition: Sociobiology and the Quest for Human Nature.* Cambridge, Massachusetts: The MIT Press.

KLEIN, RICHARD, G.
1989    *The Human Career: Human Biological and Cultural Origins.* Chicago: The University of Chicago Press.

KLOSTERMAIER, KLAUS, K.
1989    *A Survey of Hinduism.* New York: State University of New York Press.

KOENTJARANINGRAT
1975    *Anthropology in Indonesia: A Bibliographical Review.* The Hague: Martinus Nijhoff.

KOLAKOWSKI, LESZEK
1982    *Religion.* London: Fontana.

KOPF, DAVID
1969    *British Orientalism and the Bengal Renaissance: The Dynamics of Indian Modernization 1773-1835.* Berkeley: University of California Press.

KORS, ALAN CHARLES
1990    *Atheism in France 1650-1729, Vol. 1, The Orthodox Sources of Disbelief.* Princeton: Princeton University Press.

KRAJEWSKI, W.
 1977a *Correspondence Principle and the Growth of Science.* Dordrecht: D. Reidel.
 1977b "Idealization and Factualization in Science." *Erkenntnis,* 11(3), 323-39.

KRIEGER, LOENARD
 1989 *Time's Reasons: Philosophies of History Old and New.* Chicago: The University of Chicago Press.

KUMARAPPA, BHARATAN
 1933 *The Hindu Conception of the Deity.* Delhi: Inter-India Publications, 1979.

KUNTZ, PAUL, G. (ED.)
 1968 *The Concept of Order.* Published for Grinnell College at London: The University of Washington Press.

KUPER, ADAM
 1988 *The Invention of Primitive Society: Transformations of an Illusion.* London: Routledge.

LACH, DONALD, F.
 1965 *Asia in the Making of Europe, Vol. 1, The Century of Discovery.* Chicago: The University of Chicago Press.
 1977 *Asia in the Making of Europe, Vol. 2, A Century of Wonder.* Chicago: The University of Chicago Press.

LACTANTIUS
   *The Divine Institutes.* Translated by Sister Mary Francis McDonald. *The Fathers of the Church, Vol. 49.* Washington, D. C.: The Catholic University of America Press.

LAKOFF, GEORGE
 1987 *Women, Fire, and Dangerous Things: What Categories Reveal about the Mind.* Chicago: The University of Chicago Press.

LATOURETTE, KENNETH SCOTT
 1949 "The Christian Understanding of History." Reprinted in MCINTIRE, (Ed.), 1977, 46-67.

LAUDAN, LARRY
 1977 *Progress and its Problems: Towards a Theory of Scientific Growth.* Berkeley: University of California Press.
 1990 *Science and Relativism: Some Key Controversies in the Philosophy of Science.* Chicago: The University of Chicago Press.

LAWSON, THOMAS, AND MCCAULEY, ROBERT, M.
  1990    *Rethinking Religion: Connecting Cognition and Culture.* Cambridge: Cambridge University Press.

LENKER, J. N. (TRANS.)
  1907    *Luther's Catechetical Writings. 2 Volumes.* Minneapolis: Luther Press.

LEUBA, JAMES, H.
  1909    *The Psychological Origin and the Nature of Religion.* London: Archibald Constable and Co. Ltd.
  1912    *A Psychological Study of Religion: Its Origin, Function, and Future.* London: Macmillan.

LEWIS, DAVID
  1978    "Truth in Fiction." *American Philosophical Quarterly,* 15, 37-46. Reprinted together with "Postscripts" in his *Philosophical Papers, Vol. 1.* Oxford: Oxford University Press, 1983, 261-280.
  1986    *On the Plurality of Worlds.* Oxford: Basil Blackwell.

LEWIS, GILBERT
  1982    *Day of Shining Red: An Essay on Understanding Ritual.* Cambridge: Cambridge University Press.

LIEBESCHUETZ, J. H. W. G.
  1979    *Continuity and Change in Roman Religion.* Oxford: Clarendon Press

LINDSAY, PETER, H. AND NORMAN, DONALD, A.
  1977    *Human Information Processing: An Introduction to Psychology.* Second Edition. London: The Academic Press.

LING, TREVOR (ED.)
  1981    *The Buddha's Philosophy of Man: Early Indian Buddhist Dialogues.* London: Everyman's Library.

LIPTON, PETER
  1990    "Contrastive Explanation." In DUDLEY KNOWLES, (Ed.), *Explanation and Its Limits.* Cambridge: Cambridge University Press, 247-266. Also reprinted in RUBEN, (Ed.), 1990.
  1991    *Inference to the Best Explanation.* London: Routledge.

LIVINGSTONE, DAVID, N.
  1987    "Preadamites: The History of an Idea From Heresy to Orthodoxy." *Scottish Journal of Theology,* 40, 41-66.

LOCHER, GOTTFRIED, W.
  1965    "The Change in the Understanding of Zwingli in Recent Research." *Church History*, 34, 3-24.

LOEWE, MICHAEL
  1988    "Imperial China's Reactions to the Catholic Missions." *Numen*, 35(2), 179-212.

LORENZ, KONRAD
  1971    *On Aggression*. New York: Bantam Books.

LOTT, ERIC, J.
  1988    *Vision, Tradition, Interpretation: Theology, Religion, and the Study of Religion*. Berlin: Mouton de Gruyter.

LUKES, STEVEN
  1972    *Émile Durkheim. His Life and Work: A Historical and Critical Study*. Harmondsworth: Peregrine Books, 1975.

MACGREGOR, GEDDEN
  1973    *Philosophical Issues in Religious Thought*. Boston: Houghton Mifflin Company.

MACINTYRE, ALASDAIR
  1981    *After Virtue*. Second Edition. Notre Dame: University of Notre Dame Press, 1984.

MACMULLEN, RAMSAY
  1981    *Paganism in the Roman Empire*. New Haven: Yale University Press.
  1984    *Christianizing the Roman Empire, (A. D. 100-400)*. New Haven: Yale University Press.

MAJOR, R. H. (ED.)
  n.d.    *India in the Fifteenth Century: Being a Collection of the Narratives of Voyages to India in the Century Preceding the Portuguese Discovery of the Cape of Good Hope*. London: The Hakluyt Society, Series I, Vol. XXII. New York: Burt Franklin, Publisher.

MAJUMDAR, R. C. (ED.)
  1960    *The Classical Accounts of India*. Calcutta: Firma K. L. Mukhopadhyay.

MALINOWSKI, BRONISLAW
  1925    "Magic, Science and Religion." In *Magic, Science and Religion and Other Essays*. New York: Doubleday Anchor, 1955, 17-92.

MANUEL, FRANK, E.
    1959    *The Eighteenth Century Confronts the Gods*. Cambridge, Massachusetts: Harvard University Press.
    1983    *The Changing of the Gods*. Published for Brown University Press by London: University Press of New England.

MARKHAM, C. (ED.)
    1877    *Book of the Knowledge of all the Kingdoms, Lands, and Lordships that are there in the World, and the Arms and Devices of Each Land and Lordship, Or of the Kings and Lords who Possess them. Written by a Spanish Franciscan in the Middle of the XIV Century*. London: The Hakluyt Society, Series II, Vol. XXIX, 1912.

MARKMAN, ELLEN, M.
    1989    *Categorization and Naming in Children: Problems of Induction*. Cambridge, Massachusetts: The MIT Press.

MARKUS, ROBERT
    1990    *The End of Ancient Christianity*. Cambridge: Cambridge University Press.

MARSHALL, PAUL, GRIFFIOEN, SANDER, AND MOUW, RICHARD J. (EDS.)
    1989    *Stained Glass: Worldviews and Social Science*. Lanham: University Press of America.

MARSHALL, P. J. (ED.)
    1970    *The British Discovery of Hinduism in the Eighteenth Century*. Cambridge: Cambridge University Press.

MASON, PETER
    1990    *Deconstructing America: Representations of the Other*. London: Routledge.

MASSARELLA, DEREK
    1990    *A World Elsewhere: Europe's Encounter with Japan in the Sixteenth and Seventeenth Centuries*. New Haven: Yale University Press.

MASSIE, J. W.
    1840    *Continental India, 2 Volumes*. Delhi: B. R. Publishing Company, 1985.

MAURICE, THOMAS
    1795    *The History of Hindostan; Its Arts and Sciences*. Delhi: Navrang, 1973.
    1800    *Indian Antiquities or Dissertations of Hindostan, 7 volumes*. Delhi: Concept Publishing Company, 1984.

MAW, MARTIN
1990    *Visions of India: Fulfilment Theory, The Aryan Race Theory, and the Work of British Protestant Missionaries in Victorian India.* Bern: Peter Lang Verlag.

MAYER, RICHARD, E.
1983    *Thinking, Problem Solving, Cognition.* New York: W. H. Freeman and Co.

McDANIEL, JUNE
1989    *The Madness of the Saints: Ecstatic Religion in Bengal.* Chicago: The University of Chicago Press.

McGRANE, BERNARD
1989    *Beyond Anthropology: Society and the Other.* New York: Columbia University Press.

McINTIRE, C. T. (ED.)
1977    *God, History, and Historians: Modern Christian Views of History.* New York: Oxford University Press.

MEREDITH, A.
1980    "Porphyry and Julian Against the Christians." In HILDEGARD TEMPORINI and WOLFGANG HAASE, (Eds.), *Aufstieg und Niedergang der Römischen Welt: Geschichte und Kultur Roms im Spiegel der Neuren Forschung, 23.2.* Berlin: Walter de Gruyter, 1119-1149.

MINUCIUS FELIX
*The Octavius.* In Rev. ALEXANDER ROBERTS and JAMES DONALDSON, (Eds.), *The Ante-Nicene Fathers: Translations of the Writings of the Fathers down to A.D. 325, Vol. 4.* American reprint of the Edinburgh edition (n.d.). Michigan: Wm. B. Eerdmans Publishing Company, 1978.

MLECKO, JOEL, D.
1982    "The Guru in Hindu Tradition." *Numen*, 29(1), 33-61.

MOLSBERGEN, E. C. G. (ED.)
1916    *Reizen in Zuid-Afrika in de Hollandse Tijd. Eerste deel, Teksten naar het Noorden 1652-1686.* De Linschoten-Vereeniging, Vol. XI. 's-Gravenhage: Martinus Nijhoff.

MOMIGLIANO, ARNALDO
1963    "Pagan and Christian Historiography in the Fourth century A. D." In A. MOMIGLIANO, (Ed.), *The Conflict Between Paganism and Christianity in the Fourth Century.* Oxford: Clarendon Press, 79-99.

MONIER-WILLIAMS, SIR MONIER
1891    *Brahmanism and Hinduism, Or, Religious Thought and Life in India, as Based on the Veda and Other Sacred Books of the Hindus.* Fourth Edition. London: John Murray.

MOOR, EDWARD
1864    *The Hindu Pantheon.* A New Edition by Rev. W. O. SIMPSON. Delhi: Indological Book House, 1968.

MOORE, STEPHEN, D.
1989    *The Literary Criticism and the Gospels: The Theoretical Challenge.* New Haven: Yale University Press.

MORRIS, THOMAS, V. (ED.)
1987    *The Concept of God.* Oxford: Oxford University Press.

MORRIS, BRIAN
1987    *Anthropological Studies of Religion.* Cambridge: Cambridge University Press.

MOULE, C. F. D.
1977    *The Origin of Christology.* Cambridge: Cambridge University Press.

MÜLLER, MAX
1883    *India, What can it Teach us?* New Delhi: Munshi Ram Manohar Lal, 1961.

MÜLLER, MAX (ED.)
1879    *The Upanishads. 2 Volumes.* New York: Dover Publications, 1962.

MUNITZ, MILTON, K (ED.)
1971    *Identity and Individuation.* New York: New York University Press.

MUNSON, THOMAS, N.
1985    *The Challenge of Religion: A Philosophical Appraisal.* Pittsburgh: Duquesne University Press.

NAKAMURA, HAJIME
1980    *Indian Buddhism: A Survey with Bibliographical Notes.* Tokyo: KUFS Publication.

NEEDHAM, RODNEY
1975    "Polythetic Classification: Convergence and Consequences." *Man* (n.s.), 10, 349-369. Now reprinted as chapter 3 in his *Against the Tranquillity of Axioms,* Berkeley: University of California Press, 1983.

NEEDHAM, JOSEPH
   1951     "Human Laws and Laws of Nature in China and the West."
            *Journal of the History of Ideas,* XII(1), 3-30; XII(2), 194-230.

NEILL, STEPHEN
   1984     *A History of Christianity in India, Vol. 1, The Beginnings to A. D.
            1707.* Cambridge: Cambridge University Press.

NIEBUHR, RICHARD, H.
   1989     *Faith on Earth: An Inquiry into the Structure of Human Faith.* New
            Haven: Yale University Press.

NIELSEN, KAI
   1982     *An Introduction to the Philosophy of Religion.* London: The Macmil-
            llan Press Ltd.

NITECKI, MATTHEW, H. (ED.)
   1989     *Evolutionary Progress.* Chicago: The University of Chicago
            Press.

NOCK, A. D.
   1933     *Conversion.* Oxford: Oxford University Press.

NOTTINGHAM, ELIZABETH, K.
   1954     *Religion and Society.* New York: Random House.

NOWAK, L.
   1980     *The Structure of Idealization.* Dordrecht: D. Reidel.

O'FLAHERTY, WENDY DONIGER (ED.)
   1975     *Hindu Myths.* Harmondsworth: Penguin Books.
   1981     *The Rig Veda.* Harmondsworth: Penguin Books.

O'FLAHERTY, WENDY DONIGER
   1973     *Siva: The Erotic Ascetic.* Oxford: Oxford University Press, 1981.

O'TOOLE, ROGER
   1984     *Religion: Classic Sociological Approaches.* Toronto: McGraw-Hill
            Ryerson Limited.

ODEGARD, DOUGLAS
   1982     "Miracles and Good Evidence." *Religious Studies,* 18, 37-46.

OLENDER, MAURICE
   1989     *The Languages of Paradise: Race, Religion, and Philology in the
            Nineteenth Century.* Cambridge, Massachusetts: Harvard
            University Press, 1992.

OLTHUIS, JAMES, H.
1989    "On Worldviews." In PAUL A. MARSHALL, et. alii., (Eds.), 1989, 26-40.

ORIGEN
Contra Celsum. Translated by HENRY CHADWICK. Cambridge: Cambridge University Press, 1965.

OSBORN, ERIC
1981    The Beginning of Christian Philosophy. Cambridge: Cambridge University Press.

OSHERSON, D. N., AND SMITH, E. E.
1981    "On the Adequacy of Prototype Theories as a Theory of Concepts." Cognition, 9, 35-58.

OTTO, RUDOLF
1917    The Idea of the Holy. Oxford: Oxford University Press, 1923, 1950.

OUVRY, JAN
1979    "Open Deure tot het Verborgen Heydendom": Perceptie van de Indische Maatschappij en Religie in Engelse, Franse en Nederlandse Reisverhalen uit de 17de Eeuw. Unpublished Licentiate Dissertation. Gent: Rijksuniversiteit.

PAILIN, DAVID, A.
1971    "Some Eighteenth Century Attitudes to 'Other Religions'." Religion, 1(2), 83-108.
1984    Attitudes to Other Religions: Comparative Religion in Seventeenth and Eighteenth-century Britain. Manchester: Manchester University Press.

PARRY, JONATHAN
1985    "The Brahmanical Tradition and the Technology of the Intellect." In JOANNA OVERING, (Ed.), Reason and Morality. London: Tavistock Publications, 200-225.

PARSONS, TALCOTT
1963    "Introduction" to MAX WEBER's The Sociology of Religion. Boston: Beacon Press, xix-lxvii.

PELIKAN, JAROSLAV
1971    The Christian Tradition, Vol. 1, The Emergence of the Catholic Tradition (100-600). Chicago: The University of Chicago Press.
1984    The Vindication of Tradition. New Haven: Yale University Press.
1985    Jesus Through The Centuries: His place in the History of Culture. New Haven: Yale University Press.

PENELHUM, TERENCE
1977    "The Analysis of Faith in St. Thomas Aquinas." *Religious Studies,*
        13, 133-154. Also reprinted in TERENCE PENELHUM, (Ed.), 1989,
        113-133.

PENELHUM, TERENCE (ED.)
1989    *Faith.* New York: Macmillan Publishing Company.

PENNER, HANS, H.
1968    "Myth and Ritual: A Wasteland or a Forest of Symbols?" *History
        and Theory, Beiheft 8, On Method in the History of Religions,* JAMES
        S. HELFER, (Ed.), 46-57.
1985    "Language, Ritual and Meaning." *Numen,* 32(1), 1-16.

PERELMAN, CHAIM
1977    *The Realm of Rhetoric.* Notre Dame: University of Notre Dame
        Press, 1982.

PETERSON, INDIRA VISWANATHAN
1989    *Poems to Siva: The Hymns of the Tamil Saints.* Princeton: Princeton
        University Press.

PHILOSTRATUS
        *The Lives of Appollonius of Tyana.* Translated by F. C. CONYBEARE.
        The Loeb Classical Library. London: William Heinemann Ltd.,
        1927.

PIATIGORSKY, A.
1985    "Some Phenomenological Observations on the Study of Indian
        Religion." In RICHARD BURGHART and AUDREY CANTLIE, (Eds.),
        *Indian Religion.* London: Curzon Press, 208-258.

PICKERING, W. S. F.
1984    *Durkheim's Sociology of Religion: Themes and Theories.* London:
        Routledge and Kegan Paul.

PIETZ, WILLIAM
1987    "The Problem of the Fetish, II: The Origin of the Fetish." *Res,*
        13, 23-45.

PITT, JOSEPH, C. (EDS.)
1988    *Theories of Explanation.* Oxford: Oxford University Press.

PLANTINGA, ALVIN
1983    "Reason and Belief in God." In ALVIN PLANTINGA and NICHOLAS
        WOLTERSTORFF, (Eds.), *Faith and Rationality: Reason and Belief
        in God.* Notre Dame: University of Notre Dame Press, 16-93.

POJMAN, LOUIS, J.
1986     *Religious Belief and the Will.* London: Routledge.

POPKIN, RICHARD, H.
1979     *The History of Scepticism from Erasmus to Spinoza.* Berkeley: University of California Press.

POPPER, SIR KARL
1972     *Conjectures and Refutations: The Growth of Scientific Knowledge.* Fourth revised edition. London: Routledge and Kegan Paul.
1979     *Objective Knowledge: An Evolutionary Approach.* Revised edition. London: Routledge and Kegan Paul.

PREUS, SAMUEL, J.
1977     "Zwingli, Calvin, and the Origin of Religion." *Church History,* 46, 186-202.
1987     *Explaining Religion: Criticism and Theory from Bodin to Freud.* New Haven: Yale University Press.

PROUDFOOT, WAYNE
1985     *Religious Experience.* Berkeley: University of California Press.

PRUDENTIUS
         *Against Symmachus.* In *The Poems of Prudentius, Vol. 2.* Translated by Sister M. CLEMENT EAGAN. *The Fathers of the Church, Vol. 52.* Washington: The Catholic University of America Press, 1965.

PUHVEL, JAAN
1987     *Comparative Mythology.* Baltimore: The Johns Hopkins University Press.

PUTNAM, HILARY
1988     *Representation and Reality.* Cambridge, Massachusetts: The MIT Press.

PUTTANIL, THOMAS
1990     *A Comparative Study on the Theological Methodology of Irenaeus of Lyon and Sankaracharya.* Bern: Peter Lang Verlag.

QUINE, W. V. O.
1951     "Two Dogmas of Empiricism." In his *From an Logical Point of View: Logico-Philosophical Essays,* Second revised edition. New York: Harper Torchbooks, 1953, 1961, 1963, 20-46.

RADCLIFFE-BROWN, A. R.
1952     "Religion and Society." In LOUIS SCHNEIDER, (Ed.), *Religion, Culture, and Society: A Reader in the Sociology of Religion.* London: John Wiley and Sons, 1964.

RAITT, THOMAS, M.
1987    "The Ritual Meaning of Corn Pollen Among the Navajo Indians." *Religious Studies*, 23, 523-30.

REARDON, BERNARD, M. G.
1985    *Religion in the Age of Romanticism: Studies in the Early Nineteenth Century Thought*. Cambridge: Cambridge University Press.

REPS, PAUL. (ED.)
1957    *Zen Flesh, Zen Bones*. Harmondsworth: Penguin, 1971.

RICOEUR, PAUL
1969    *The Symbolism of Evil*. Boston: Beacon Press.

RIST, J. M.
1972    *Epicurus: An Introduction*. Cambridge: Cambridge University Press.

ROGERIUS, ABRAHAMUS, D.
1651    *De Open-Deure tot het Verborgen Heydendom ofte Waerachtigh vertoogh van het Leven ende Zeden, mitsgaaders de Religie, ende Godsdienst der Bramines, op de Cust Chormandel, ende de Landen daar ontrent*. Leiden. Reprinted by De Linschoten-Vereeniging, Vol. X, 's-Gravenhage: Martinus Nijhoff, 1915.

ROHNER, RONALD, P., AND CHAKI-SIRCAR, MANJUSRI
1988    *Women and Children in Bengali Village*. Published for the University of Connecticut by London: University Press of New England.

ROKEAH, DAVID
1982    *Jews, Pagans and Christians in Conflict*. Leiden: E. J. Brill.

ROLAND, ALAN
1988    *In Search of Self in India and Japan*. Princeton: Princeton University Press.

ROSCH, ELEANOR
1977    "Human Categorization." In N. WARREN, (Ed.), *Studies in Cross-Cultural Psychology*. London: The Academic Press.
1978    "Principles of Categorization." In ELEANOR ROSCH and B. B. LLOYD, (Eds.), *Cognition and Categorization*. Hillsdale, New Jersey: Lawrence Erlbaum Associates.

ROSSI, PAOLO
1979    *The Dark Abyss of Time: The History of the Earth and the History of Nations from Hooke to Vico*. Chicago: The University of Chicago Press.

RUBEN, DAVID-HILLEL, (ED.)
1993    *Explanation.* Oxford: Oxford University Press.

RUBY, JANE, E.
1986    "The Origins of Scientific 'Law'." *Journal of the History of Ideas,*
XLVII(3), 241-359.

RUSSELL, BERTRAND, AND COPELSTON, F. C.
1948    "The existence of God – A Debate." In PAUL EDWARDS and
ARTHUR PAP, (Eds.), *A Modern Introduction to Philosophy: Read-
ings from Classical and Contemporary Sources.* Third Edition. New
York: The Free Press, 1973, 473-490.

SALIBA, JOHN, A.
1976    *'Homo Religiosus' in Mircea Eliade: An Anthropological Evaluation.*
Leiden: E. J. Brill.

SCHAFF, P. AND WACE, H. (EDS.)
1896    *A Select Library of the Nicene and Post-Nicene Fathers of The Christian Church. Second Series, Vol. 10, St. Ambrose: Select Works and
Letters.* Grand Rapids: Wm. B. Eerdmans Publishing Company,
1979.
n.d.    *A Select Library of the Nicene and Post-Nicene Fathers of The
Christian Church. Second Series, Vol. 13, Part 2, Gregory the Great,
Ephraim Syrus, Aphrahat.* Grand Rapids: Wm. B. Eerdmans
Publishing Company, 1979.

SCHILLEBEECKX, EDWARD
1989    *Mensen als Verhaal van God.* Baarn: Uitgeverij H. Nelissen.

SCHIPPER, KRISTOFER
1982    *Tao: De Levende Religie van China.* Amsterdam: Meulenhoff,
1988.

SCHLEIERMACHER, FRIEDRICH.
1799    *On Religion: Speeches to its Cultured Despisers.* Translated by
RICHARD CROUTER. Cambridge: Cambridge University Press,
1988.

SCHLESINGER, GEORGE
1984    "The Method of Counterexample." In JAMES H. FETZER,
(Ed.), *Principles of Philosophical Reasoning.* Totawa, New Jersey:
Rowman and Allanheld, 151-171.

SCHNEIDER, LOUIS (ED.)
1964    *Religion, Culture and Society: A Reader in the Sociology of Religion.*
London: John Wiley and Sons.

SCHNEIDER, LOUIS
    1970    *Sociological Approach to Religion.* London: John Wiley and Sons, Inc.

SCHWAB, RAYMOND
    1950    *The Oriental Renaissance: Europe's Rediscovery of India and the East 1680-1880.* New York: Columbia University Press, 1984.

SCHWEINITZ, JR., KARL DE
    1984    "John Stuart Mill and India." *Research in the History of Economic Thought and Methodology,* 2, 47-61.

SEZNEC, JEAN
    1940    *The Survival of the Pagan Gods: The Mythological Tradition and Its Place in Renaissance Humanism and Art.* Princeton: Princeton University Press, 1972.

SHAPIRO, BARBARA, J.
    1983    *Probability and Certainty in Seventeenth-century England: A Study of the Relationships between Natural Sciences, Religion, History, Law, and Literature.* Princeton: Princeton University Press.

SHARMA, BALDEV
    1972    *The Concept of _tman in the Principal Upanis.ads.* New Delhi: Dinesh Publications.

SHARMA, ARVIND
    1986    *The Hindu Gita: Ancient and Classical Interpretations of the Bhagavadgita.* London: Duckworth.

SHARPE, ERIC, J.
    1965    *Not to Destroy but to Fulfil: The Contribution of J. N. Farquhar to the Protestant Missionary Thought in India before 1914.* Uppsala: Swedish Institute of Missionary Research.
    1973    "Dialogue and Faith." *Religion,* 3, 89-105.
    1990    *Nathan Söderblom and the Study of Religion.* Chapel Hill: The University of North Carolina Press.

SHERWIN-WHITE, A. N.
    1964    "Why were the Early Christians Prosecuted? – An Amendment." *Past and Present,* 27, 23-27.
    1966    *The Letters of Pliny: A Historical and Social Commentary.* Oxford: Oxford University Press.

SHULMAN, DAVID DEAN
    1980    *Tamil Temple Myths: Sacrifice and Divine Marriage in the South Indian _aiva Tradition.* Princeton: Princeton University Press.

SHWEDER, RICHARD, A. AND BOURNE, EDMUND, J.
1982    "Does the Concept of the Person Vary Cross-culturally?" In
        R.A. SHWEDER and R.A. LEVINE, (Eds.), *Culture Theory: Essays
        on Mind, Self, and Emotion.* Cambridge: Cambridge University
        Press, 1984.

SILBER, ILANA FRIEDRICH
1985    "'Opting Out' in Theravada Buddhism and Medieval Christian-
        ity: A Comparative Study of Monasticism as Alternative Struc-
        ture." *Religion,* 15, 251-277.

SINHA, K. P.
1985    *Indian Theories of Creation: A Synthesis.* Varanasi: Chaukhambha
        Orientalia.

SMART, NINIAN
1981    *Beyond Ideology: Religion and the Future of Western Civilization.*
        San Francisco: Harper and Row.
1983    *Worldviews: Crosscultural Explorations of Human Beliefs.* New
        York: Charles Scribner's.
1987    *Religion and the Western Mind.* New York: State University of
        New York Press.
1989    *The World's Religions: Old Traditions and Modern Transformations.*
        Cambridge: Cambridge University Press.

SMITH, MORTON
1968    "Historical Method in the History of Religion." *History and
        Theory, Beiheft 8, On Method in the History of Religions,* JAMES S.
        HELFER, (Ed.), 8-16.

SMITH, HUSTON
1972    "Accents of the World Religions." In JOHN BOWMAN, (Ed.), *Com-
        parative Religion.* Leiden: E.J. Brill, 1-18.

SMITH, WILFRED CANTWELL
1962    *The Meaning and End of Religion.* London: SPCK, 1978.
1966    "Religious Atheism? Early Buddhist and Recent American." In
        JOHN BOWMAN, (ED.), *Comparative Religion.* Leiden: E.J. Brill,
        53-81.
1973    "On Dialogue and Faith: A Rejoinder." *Religion,* 3, 106-114.
1977    *Belief and History.* Charlotsville: The University Press of
        Virginia.
1979    *Faith and Belief.* Princeton: Princeton University Press.
1980    "Belief: A Reply to a Response." *Numen,* 27(2), 247-255.

SNELL, BRUNO
1982    *The Discovery of Mind in Greek Philosophy and Literature.* New
        York: Dover Books.

490 REFERENCES

SÖDERBLOM, NATHAN
1913 "Holiness." In JAMES HASTINGS, (Ed.), *Encyclopedia of Religion and Ethics*, Vol. 6. New York: Charles Scribner's, 731-741.

SOUTHWOLD, MARTIN
1978 "Buddhism and the Definition of Religion." *Man* (n.s.), 13, 362-379.

SPIRO, MELFORD, E.
1966 "Religion: Problems of Definition and Explanation." In MICHAEL BANTON, (Ed.), *Anthropological Approaches to the Study of Religion*. London: Tavistock Publications, 85-126.

SPROUL, BARBARA, C. (ED.)
1979 *Primal Myths: Creating the World.* New York: Harper and Row.

STAAL, FRITS, (ED.)
1983 *Agni: The Vedic Ritual of the Fire Altar, 2 Volumes.* Berkeley: The Asian Humanities Press.

STAAL, FRITS
1986a *Over Zin en Onzin in filosofie, Religie en Wetenschap.* Amsterdam: Meulenhoff.
1986b *The Fidelity of the Oral Traditions and the Origins of Science.* Mededelingen der Koninklijke Nederlandse Akademie van Wetenschappen, Afdeling Letterkunde. Nieuwe Reeks 49(8). Amsterdam: North Holland Publishing Company.
1988 "De Godsdiensten van het oosten zijn niet oosters en ook geen godsdiensten." In his *Een Wijsgeer in het Oosten.* Amsterdam: Meulenhoff.
1989 *Rules Without Meaning: Ritual, Mantras, and the Human Sciences.* New York: Peter Lang Verlag.

STANIFORTH, MAXWELL, (TRANS.)
*Early Christian Writers: The Apostolic Fathers.* Harmondsworth: Penguin Books, 1968.

STEPHENS, W. P.
1992 *Zwingli: An Introduction to His Thought.* Oxford: Clarendon Press.

STRABO
*The Geography* of Strabo. Translated by H. L. JONES. The Loeb Classical Library. London: William Heinemann Ltd., 1930.

SURIN, KENNETH
    1990    "Towards a 'Materialist' Critique of 'Religious Pluralism': An Examination of the Discourse of John Hick and Wilfred Cantwell Smith." In IAN HAMNET, (Ed.), 1990, 114-129.

TACITUS, CORNELIUS
    *The Histories.* Translated by KENNETH WELLESLEY. Harmondsworth: Penguin Books, 1964, 1975, 1986.

TANNEHILL, ROBERT, C.
    1986    *The Narrative Unity of Luke-Acts: A Literary Interpretation, Vol. 1, The Acts of the Apostles.* Philadelphia: Fortress Press.

TATIAN
    *Address to the Greeks.* In Rev. ALEXANDER ROBERTS and JAMES DONALDSON, (Eds.), *The Ante-Nicene Fathers: Translations of the Writings of the Fathers down to A.D. 325, Vol. 2, Fathers of the Second Century.* American reprint of the Edinburgh edition (n.d.). Michigan: Wm. B. Eerdmans Publishing Company, 1978.

TAVERNIER, JEAN-BAPTISTE
    1676    *Travels in India, 2 Volumes.* Edited by WILLIAM CROOKE. New Delhi: Oriental Books Reprint Corporation, 1977.

TAYLOR, MARK, C.
    1984    *Erring: A Postmodern A/theology.* Chicago: The University of Chicago Press.

TAYLOR, JOHN, R.
    1989    *Linguistic Categorization: Prototypes in Linguistic Theory.* Oxford: Clarendon Press.

TEMPLE, SIR RICHARD CARNAC (ED.)
    1905    *A Geographical Account of Countries Round the Bay of Bengal, 1669 to 1679, by Thomas Bowrey.* Cambridge: The Hakluyt Society, Series II, Vol. XII.

TERTULLIAN
    *The Prescription Against the Heretics.* In Rev. ALEXANDER ROBERTS and JAMES DONALDSON, (Eds.), *The Ante-Nicene Fathers: Translations of the Writings of the Fathers down to A.D. 325, Vol. 3, Latin Christianity: Its Founder, Tertullian.* American reprint of the Edinburgh edition (n.d.). Michigan: Wm. B. Eerdmans Publishing Company, 1978.

THEOPHILUS OF ANTIOCH

    *Theophilus to Autolycus.* In Rev. ALEXANDER ROBERTS and JAMES DONALDSON, (Eds.), *The Ante-Nicene Fathers: Translations of the Writings of the Fathers down to A.D. 325, Vol. 2, Fathers of the Second Century.* American reprint of the Edinburgh edition (n.d.). Michigan: Wm. B. Eerdmans Publishing Company, 1978.

THOMAS, TERENCE

    1988    "The Impact of Other Religions." In GERALD PARSONS, (Ed.), *Religion in Victorian Britain, Vol. 3, Controversies.* Manchester: Manchester University Press, 281-298.

THOULESS, ROBERT

    1961    *An Introduction into the Psychology of Religion.* Cambridge: Cambridge University Press.

TILLICH, PAUL

    1958    "The Lost Dimension in Religion." In WILLIAM WILLIAMSON, (Ed.), 1985, 41-47.

TURNER, VICTOR

    1969    *The Ritual Process: Structure and Anti-structure.* Ithaca: Cornell University Press, 1977.

TYLOR, SIR EDWARD, B.

    1873    *Primitive Culture, Vol. 2, Religion in the Primitive Culture.* New York: Harper Torch Books, 1958.

URWICK, W.

    1885    *India 100 years Ago: The Beauty of Old India Illustrated.* London: Bracken Books, 1985.

VALENTINE, DANIEL

    1985    *Fluid Signs: Being a Person the Tamil Way.* California: University of California Press.

VAN BUITENEN, J. A. B.

    1973    "Introduction" to *The Mahabharata, Vol. 1, The Book of the Beginning.* Chicago: The University of Chicago Press, xiii-xliv.

VAN FRAASSEN, BAS

    1980    *The Scientific Image.* Oxford: Oxford University Press.

VAN BAAL, J.

    1971    *Symbols For Communication: An Introduction to the Anthropology of Religion.* Assen: Van Gorcum.

    1981    *Man's Quest for Partnership.* Assen: Van Gorcum.

VERHELST, THIERRY
1985    Cultures, Religions and Development in India: Interviews Conducted and recorded by Thierry Verhelst, 14 to 23-1-1985. A.P.H.D. working group on Religions and Cultures. Brussels: Broederlijk Delen, Mimeo.

VERMES, GEZA
1984    "The Gospel of Jesus the Jew III." In his Jesus and the World of Judaism. Philadelphia: Fortress Press.

VERNON, GLEN, M.
1962    Sociology of Religion. New York: McGraw-Hill Book Company.

VOSNIADOU, STELLA, AND ORTONY, ANDREW (EDS.)
1989    Similarity and Analogical Reasoning. Cambridge: Cambridge University Press.

WACH, JOACHIM
1944    The Sociology of Religion. Chicago: The University of Chicago Press.

WADE, IRA, O.
1977    The Structure and Form of the French Enlightenment, 2 Volumes. Princeton: Princeton University Press.

WALZER, RICHARD
1949    Galen on Jews and Christians. Oxford: Oxford University Press.

WARDER, A. K.
1971    Outline of Indian Philosophy. Delhi: Motilal Banarasidas.
1980    A History of Buddhism. Second Revised Edition. Delhi: Motilal Banarasidas.

WARDY, B.
1979    "Jewish Religion in Pagan Literature during the Late Republic and Early Empire." In HILDEGARD TEMPORINI and WOLFGANG HAASE, (Eds.), Aufstieg und Niedergang der Römischen Welt: Geschichte und Kultur Roms im Spiegel der Neuren Forschung, 19.1. Berlin: Walter de Gruyter, 592-644.

WARNER, MARTINE (ED.)
1990    The Bible as Rhetoric: Studies in Biblical Persuasion and Credibility. London: Routledge.

WATSON, JAMES, L.
1988 "The Structure of Chinese Funerary Rites: Elementary forms, Ritual Sequence, and the Primacy of Performance." In JAMES L. WATSON, and EVELYN S. RAWSKI, (Eds.), *Death Ritual in Late Imperial and Modern China.* Berkeley: University of California Press.

WEBER, MAX
1956 *Economy and Society, Vol. 1.* GUENTHER ROTH and CLAUS WITTICH, (Eds.). Berkeley: University of California Press, 1978.
1958 *The Religion of India: The Sociology of Hinduism and Buddhism.* HANS G. GERTH and DON MARTINDALE, (Eds.). New York: The Free Press, 1967.

WEIGHTMAN, SIMON
1984 "Hinduism." In JOHN R. HINNELLS, (Ed.), *A Handbook of Living Religions.* Harmondsworth: Penguin Books, 191-236.

WENEGRAT, BRANT
1990 *The Divine Archetype: The Sociobiology and Psychology of Religion.* Lexington, Massachusetts: Lexington Books.

WHALING, FRANK
1983 "Introduction: The Contrast between the Classical and Contemporary Periods in the Study of Religion." In FRANK WHALING, (Ed.), *Contemporary Approaches to the Study of Religion, Vol. 1, The Humanities.* Berlin: Mouton Publishers, 1-28.

WHITEHEAD, SIR ALFRED NORTH
1925 *Science and the Modern World.* New York: The Free Press, 1953.
1926 *Religion in the Making.* London: The Macmillan Company.

WHITTAKER, MOLLY (ED.)
1984 *Jews and Christians: Graeco-Roman Views.* Cambridge: Cambridge University Press.

WIEBE, DONALD
1979 "The Role of 'Belief' in the Study of Religion." *Numen,* 26(2), 234-249.
1981 *Religion and Truth.* The Hague: Mouton.

WIEDEMANN, THOMAS
1990 "Polytheism, Monotheism, and Religious Co-existence: Paganism and Christianity in the Roman Empire." In IAN HAMNET, (Ed.), 1990, 64-78.

WILKEN, ROBERT, L.
  1970 "Toward a Social Interpretation of Early Christian Apologetics." *Church History*, 39, 437-458.
  1984 *The Christians as the Romans Saw Them*. New Haven: Yale University Press.

WILLIAMSON, WILLIAM, B.
  1985 *Decisions in Philosophy of Religion*. Buffalo: Prometheus Books.

WILLSON, LESLIE, A.
  1964 *A Mythical Image: The Ideal of India in the German Romanticism*. North Carolina: Duke University Press.

WILSON, EDWARD, O.
  1978 *On Human Nature*. Cambridge, Massachusetts: Harvard University Press.

WILSON, FRED
  1985 *Explanation, Causation and Deduction*. Dordrecht: D. Reidel.

WILSON, BRYAN
  1982 *Religion in Sociological Perspective*. Oxford: Oxford University Press.

WOLFSON, H. A.
  1947 *Philo: Foundations of Religious Philosophy in Judaism, Christianity, and Islam, 2 Volumes*. Cambridge, Massachusetts: Harvard University Press.

WOLTERS, ALBERT, M.
  1989 "On the Idea of Worldview and Its Relation to Philosophy." In PAUL A. MARSHALL, *et. alii.*, (Eds.), 1989, 14-25.

WUTHNOW, ROBERT, J.
  1988 "Sociology of Religion." In NEIL J. SMELSER, (Ed.), *Handbook of Sociology*. London: Sage Publications, 473-509.

YOUNG, RICHARD FOX
  1981 *Resistant Hinduism: Sanskrit Sources on Anti-Christian Apologetics in Early Nineteenth-Century India*. Leiden: E. J. Brill.

ZILSEL, EDGAR
  1942 "The Genesis of the Concept of Physical Law." *The Philosophical Review*, LI(3), 245-279.

# NAME INDEX

Adkins A. 13
Agehananda Bharati 420
Agrippa 32
Almond Philip 129-130, 132-133, 135, 137-138
Alston William 263-264
Apostel Leo 222
Aquinas Thomas 54-56, 60
Arnold Edward 133
Asad Talal 252
Ast Friedrich 126
Athenagoras the Athenian 33
Augustine 48, 52, 54-55, 60-65, 114, 139, 177, 442
Augustus 32
Badger G. P. 72
Baier Annette 323
Balbus Quintus Lucillus 40, 43-44, 61, 222
Baldaeus Philippus 106, 123
Barbosa Duarte 70-72, 76, 78, 105
Baxter Richard 104
Bayle Pierre 92
Benz Ernest 16
Berman Harold 160, 396
Bernier François 115, 123
Bianchi Ugo 252
Bodin Jean 121, 144, 147-148, 172
Bopp Franz 123
Bossuet 99
Bourne Edmund 421
Bousset Wilhelm 175-176
Bowrey Thomas 72, 76-77, 234
Bradley Raymond 319
Brown Donald 364
Buckley Michael 90, 159, 180-2, 185-6
Buddha 18, 129, 132-136, 160, 207-8, 210-219, 249, 259, 360, 365, 432
Burnouf Eugène 132-133
Cabral Francisco 117
Caecilius 34, 42, 45
Calvin John 60, 62-64, 81, 83, 86, 140, 209
Cameron Averil 56, 58
Celsus 45, 51-52
Chatfield Robert 109, 115, 118, 132, 373-374
Childers Robert 137
Choudhuri Arnab Rai 432
Cicero 35-39, 42, 61, 81-82, 89, 94-95,

222-224
Clarke James Freeman 135
Clarke Samuel 334
Clement of Alexandria 48
Colebrooke H. T. 119, 123
Collins Steven 15, 211
Columbus 27, 63, 153
Comte Auguste 147
Conti Nicòlo 71, 76
Copelston F. 98
Cotta Gaius 35, 39-40, 61
Ctesias of Cnidus 67
Dandekar R. 13-14
Dapper 26, 106, 123
Darwin Charles 255
Davidson Donald 305
de Chardin Teilhard 225
de Castro João 86
Democritus 159
Diderot D. 36-38
Dodds E. 31, 164
Domitian 32
Drobin Ulf 194, 337, 339, 350-351
Dubois Abbé 113-114, 118, 128
DuBose H. C. 134
Duff Alexander 104, 132
Durkheim Émile 16, 144, 147-148, 152, 174, 186, 201-202, 204, 206, 253, 335, 450
Eliade Mircea 94, 120, 174, 178, 186, 195, 200-204, 206, 345, 380, 450
Ennius 54
Epicurus 35, 37, 39, 61, 163-164
Euhemerus 54
Eusebius 46, 48, 51
Evans-Pritchard 96, 145, 234
Ferreira Christovão 100
Feuerbach Ludwig 147-148, 152, 181
Finley Sir Moses 11-12
Firth Raymond 2, 6, 446
Fontenelle Bernard 96-97, 147
Forster Georg 125
Foucaux Philippe Édouard 133
Fox Robin Lane 31-32, 164
Freud Sigmund 144, 147-148, 150, 152, 172, 181, 202, 349, 382-383, 416
Fucan Fabian 100
Galen 163-164, 296
Gaskin J. 161
Gay Peter 36-37, 42, 83

Gazzaniga Michael 3, 304
Geden A. 110
Geertz Clifford 251-252, 343-344
Gibbon Edward 31, 36, 95
Gill Sam 11, 19, 27, 153
Goethe 124
Gould John 12-13
Gould Stephen Jay 383
Gunkel Hermann 175-176
Hacker Paul 365
Hastings Warren 119
Hegel 127
Heitmüller Wilhelm 175
Heraclitus 44
Heber Reginald 331, 335
Herbert of Cherbury 120-121, 147
Herder 124-125, 128
Herodotus 67
Hick John 57, 152, 183, 263
Hiley David 435-436
Hodgen Margaret 67
Holwell John 115, 123
Hooykaas R. 406
Hume David 6, 36, 97-97, 108, 144, 1147-148, 154, 161, 166-168, 172, 303, 404-405, 437, 452
Ignatius of Antioch 50
Irenaeus 314
Jones Sir William 94, 119, 122-123, 125, 138
Justin 48
Kant 181, 187, 189, 341
Kierkegaard 90, 196, 314
Kircher Anastasius 123
Knighton William 136
Kolakowski L. 249
Kors Alan 92, 94, 181, 183
Kuper Adam 98
La Peyrère Isaac 100
Lach Donald 67, 84, 87-88, 116
Lactantius 222-224
Lafite Joseph 93-94
Lancilotto 117
Laudan Larry 153, 295
Le Comte Louis 93
Lessius 159, 180, 182
Leuba James 267, 307
Lewis David 318, 369
Lewis Gilbert 417
Linschoten 72
Lott Eric 154
Lucian 35, 296
Lucretius 35, 163, 191
Luke St 49, 313, 370
Luther Martin 58, 134-135, 196, 308, 314, 334-335

Macaulay Sir Babbington 431
Macdonell Arthur 364
MacIntyre Alasdair 247, 252-253
MacMullen Ramsay 32, 35, 41-42
Markus Robert 442-443
Marshall P. J. 110, 115, 341
Marx Karl 127, 181, 202, 208
Massarella Derek 87, 117
Maurice Thomas 106, 132
Megasthanes 67, 70
Menucius Felix 33
Mill James 108, 135
Montesquieu 36
Moore Stephen 369
Morris Brian 3, 145, 185, 335
Moulton James 199
Müller Max 96, 134, 137-138, 234, 359, 374, 423
Munitz Milton 236
Needham Rodney 260, 407
Neill Stephen 75, 84, 113, 118
Nero 32
Noah 66, 68, 85, 100
Novalis G. 126
O'Flaherty Wendy Doniger 357, 422
O'Toole Roger 248, 345
Oldenberg 137
Olthuis James 342-343, 347
Origen 45, 48, 52
Otto Rudolf 6, 174, 178, 186, 197-198, 200, 206, 237, 290, 318, 324, 450
Pailin David 62, 104, 118, 121, 334
Parry Jonathan 374
Parsons Talcott 344
Pelikan Jaroslav 48, 51, 54, 60
Perelman Chaim 8-9
Philo of Alexandria 44, 296
Piaget Jean 99
Pires Tomé 71, 76
Plato 51, 59, 164, 296, 354
Pliny 67
Plutarch 35, 37-38, 40, 42, 81-82, 89, 163
Porphyry 46, 53
Preus Samuel 81, 121, 144, 146-148
Priest Joseph 76
Proudfoot Wayne 187-188, 206, 217
Ptolemy 66
Rhys-Davids 137
Rist J. 163
Robertson Roland 344
Rogerius Abrahamus 62-64, 123, 138, 234, 266
Rosch Eleanor 274
Ross Alexander 62, 364
Russell Bertrand 98

Saliba John 3, 202, 446
Schillebeeckx Edward 183-184
Schipper Kristoffer 17
Schlegel Friedrich 124
Schleiermacher Friedrich 6, 174, 178, 181, 185-193, 196, 200, 206-207, 217-219, 236-237, 290, 318, 324, 326, 450
Schwab Raymond 120, 123
Sharma Arvind 229, 375, 423
Sharpe Eric 104, 110, 112, 116, 175-176, 193, 195-196, 199, 225, 238
Sherring M. A. 111
Shulman David 363
Shweder Richard 421
Smart Ninian 145, 341
Smith Wilfred Cantwell 3, 10, 90, 145, 224-226, 244, 257, 287, 294, 308, 407, 417, 446
Socrates 51, 57, 140
Söderblom Nathan 6, 174, 178, 186, 193-197, 199-200, 206, 237-238, 253, 325, 450
Sonadanda 207-210, 217
Southwold Martin 252, 260-263, 281
Spiro Melford 149, 252, 256-257, 265-267
Staal Frits 133, 216, 245, 282-287, 320, 402, 415-416, 418
Strabo 66-67
Swartz Norman 319
Symmachus Quintus Aurelius 43, 59, 327-329, 449
Tacitus Cornelius 45
Tannehill Robert 369
Tatian 47, 59
Tertullian 48, 58, 89-91, 101, 314, 316-

317, 442
Theophilus of Antioch 48
Tiberius 32, 34
Tillich Paul 342-343, 347
Tinoco Antonio Velho 26
Titus 32
Troeltsch Ernst 175
Tylor Sir Edward 63-64, 147, 253
van Riebeeck 26
Van Baal J. 3, 155, 170
Varthema Ludovico Di 72-77, 79, 234
Verhelst Thierry 15
Vermes Geza 49
Vernon Glen 146, 243, 248, 250-251
Vico Giambattista 99, 147, 221
Virgil 51
Voltaire 37-38, 92, 122-123
Vygotsky V. 99
Warder A. 138, 211, 213, 215-316
Watson James 152, 418
Weber Max 128, 172, 210, 212-213, 344
Weightman Simon 14-15, 419
Weiss Johannes 175
Wesley John 118
Whaling Frank 244
Whittaker Molly 42-43
Wiedemann Thomas 32, 34
Wilkins Charles 119, 123
William James 186
Williamson William 48, 251
Wittgenstein Ludwig 20, 24
Wrede William 175
Xavier Francis 87, 113
Ziegenbalg B. 114, 121, 329
Zwingli 81

# SUBJECT INDEX

Absence of religion
consequences to our theories 149-151
Actions
as embodiments of beliefs 53, 85, 103, 296
Anthropologists
and their kinship to missionaries 70, 105, 106; as heirs to missionaries 116
Anthropology
and the travel reports 70
Apologetics
Christian 47; Jewish 44, 45
Asians
as the descendents of Noah 66, 85; ruled by a Christian king 66
Atheism
parasitic upon Christian theism 180-181
Atheistic religiosity 221-225
based on Christian themes 225; the possibility of 318-321
Atheist nation
China 92
Atheist nations
and the philosophes 92

Bible
as the history of humankind 56; as the history and chronicle 57
Brahmin
Buddha's citeria for 208
Brahminhood
as an experiential category 217; the nature of 210, 217
Brahmins
and their ignorance of religious texts 109; and their immorality 72, 76; and their impiety 114, 115; as an obstacle to evangelisation 113, 115; as priests 72, 76, 112
Buddha
as the Luther of India 134; the original and the fake 132
Buddhism
and the contexts of its creation 131, 132; as a creation of the West 129, 131-134, 136-138; as a reaction against

brahmanism 134, 136; as a solution to Evangelical quandaries 134, 136; as built around texts 133; as the Protestantism of India 134-135; popular and philosophical 136

Caste
as an obstacle to evangelization 111; as evil 116; inhibiting progress 127; moralised discourse about 116
Category mistake
involved in attribution of religions 207, 218
Catholicism
turned into paganism 82
China
as an atheist nation 92
Christianity
and heresy 52; and intolerance of rival religions 290-291; and its attitude to 'other religions' 54-55; and its development into a theism 180-182; and the alleged influence of pagan philosophy 58; and the construction of religious rivalry 295-296; and the defence of its antiquity 47; and the demarkation of the sacred and the secular 440; and the importance of theology 51; and the Roman complaints 46-47, 51; and true doctrine 50; as an obstacle to understanding non-Christian religions 15, 16; as a religion 287; as a religion and as a historical movement 281; as the fulfilment of all nations 50-51; as the fulfilment of Judaism 49-50; its schism and the context of evangelisation 120; reflexivity in 225; the schism and the context of evangelisation 83-85
Christians
and the Christian complaints against 117-118
Christological dilemma
accessibility of revelation 316; accessibility of the revelation 184; Christology and philosophical theism 185; a dilemma of 182-183, 185; the concerns of 182-183

Concept of religion
and Christianity 292; and Judaism and Islam 292, 294; its historical constraints 292, 294
Cultural difference
and configuration of learning 398-400; and the problem of similarities 425-425; cultural difference; as difference in patterns of life 428
Culture
its mutation in Asia 432-433

Definitions of religion
and classificatory problems 258-263; and linguistic practice 271-272; and problems with the prototypes 277-278; and prototypical examples 274-276; and the absence of a theory 247-248, 250, 253; and the referential issue 263-265; justifying accumulated knowledge 254-255; possibility of counter-examples 256; their nature 247-251; Staal's thesis 282-286
Doctrine
and its relation to practice 53; and the antiquity of Christianity 58; and the characterisation of religion 296-297; and the christian dispute with pagan philosophers 51

Emergence of Religion
and the Primitive man 155
Emergence of religion
as a reduction of uncertainty 157; as a response to mysteries 159; as being rooted in fear 161
Enlightenment
and human history 99; and the secularisation of Christian themes 101; as a confluence of several threads 89-91, 95
Ethnographic knowledge of India
based on texts 138; based on the Ancients 66-67
Ethnography
as a description of belief systems 86, 138; as a twentieth century farce 139; as knowledge about 85; and sources from antiquity 66; as geography 69-70; as knowledge about the natives 69
Euhemerism 55
European image of Asia 68
European history
equation with human history 99-100
European Miracle
as the framework for understanding the other 105

Evangelisation
conceptual problems in converting the heathens of India 104-106; social obstacles in converting the heathens of India 107-113
Explanations
religious and other 168-170

Faith 308
and intolerance 311-312; and its formulation within a religious tradition 310-311; and the problem of truth 313-316; expressed by worship 332; the two dimensions of 309-317
Fear
and gods 162
Fear theory of
the origin of religion 161-164

God
and the cosmological argument 98; His irrelevance to religion 186; relation to man 81; will of 163

Heathens
and their indifference to Christianity 117
Heresy
inevitability of 52
Hinduism 13-14
and Casteism 15; as an imaginary entity 108, 119; as an obstacle to evangelisation 108, 110; as pervading all aspects of religious life 109; as pervading all aspects of social life 128; its amorphous nature 107-108; its immoral nature 110, 116, 128; popular and philosophical 110
History
as the execution of the divine plan 56, 57
Holiness
the experience of 193
Human history
and Elightenment 99; and paganism 96; and the primitive 96; as a secularisation of Christian history 100; equation with European 165

Idolatry
and the worship of animals and images 335; as a false religion 334; Protestant attacks against 79, 86; varieties in India 75
Images of Asia
as exotic and wealthy 65

India
and the absence of authoritative scriptures 373-375; and the absence of a 'church' 378; and the absence of a doctrinal authority 376; and the absence of a standard interpretation of scriptures 375-376; and the multiplicity of primal myths 357-360; and the origin of the world as an illigitimate question 362; and the truth of the stories 363, 365-366, 368-370; as a culture without religion 357-363, 365-366, 368-370; as a culture without worldview 371-376, 378; as a static culture 127; as the cradle of human civilization 124, 126

Indians
and idolatry 75-76, 78; and their sexual mores 71-73, 75; and the deflowering of the virgins 71-72; and the immolation of widows 78; and wife-swapping 73-74; as licentious 71

Judaism
and its defence against the Romans 44-45; and traditio 44

Knowledge
and the meeting of cultures 429-432; and western culture 400-403; as knowledge about 401-403; as textual 68, 402; evidence for another kind 415-417, 419, 421-422, 424; performative 411; performative, and building societies as its domain 418, 435; performative, and its configuration of learning 412-414; performative, and scepticism 435-437; theoretical knowledge and its boundaries 410; as knowledge about 402

Learning
and cultural differences 398-399; and different kinds of learning processes 398; as a going-about in the world 398; as configurations of 400; as related to social environment 396-397

Linguistic practice
and cultural history 228-230

Missionaries
and their knowledge of India 84-85; and their report of India 78; unwilling to learn the Indian languages 83

Morality
and sexual mores 71, 79; grounded in religion 78

Nature
its experience structured by concepts 159; wild and hostile 161

Origin of religion
and primitive man 155; and the experience of the holy 178, 195; and the fear theory 161, 165; and the naturalistic paradigm 146; and the reduction of uncertainty 157; as a dead issue 144-146; as a responce to mysteries 158-159

Paganism
assimilation of the Ancients and the Indians as 94-95; as an erring variant of the true religion 56-57, 82; as an otherness 54; as a battle line 80; as a witness to religious truth 80, 91, 122; as the childhood of man 96; resurrected 82

Pagans
and their misunderstanding of religion 327-329

Philosophes
and atheist nations 92; and Tertullian's battle cry 90; and their critique of religion 101; and their imagination 96; and the Protestant critique of Catholicism 91

Practices (Cultic)
and doctrines 38; and Intellectuals 35-36, 39; and Roman intellectuals 36; as a cultural problem 38; as embodiment of doctrine 53; as opposed to beliefs 51; multiplicity of 32; participation of the Romans in 34; the legitimation of 40, 43, 327

Priests
protestant criticism of 112

Primitive
the myth of 96, 98

Primitive man
and abstract thinking 97; and his canonisation 98; and the chaotic world 156; as a logical thinker 98

Proselytisation
and the creation of religions 88; the eternal problems of 86-88;

Reflexivity in religion 225

Reformation
and Catholicism turned into paganism 82; and religious truth 82, 84; and the battle against idolatry 80; and the relation between man and God 81; and the terms of the discussion 79

*Religio*
and culture 43; and its reduction to religion 53, 57; and the Romans 39; as ancestral heritage 41; as a human search for truth 327; as a variant of performative knowledge 433-437; as *traditio* 42-43, 327, 434-437
Religion
Native American 11; Ancient Greek 11-13; and creation story 355; and definition 23; and doctrine 296-297, 333; and effacing the otherness of the other 330-331; and explanation 303; and its necessary conditions 355; and the absence of a definition 22; and the conditions for its existence among human beings 332-334, 354; and the development of the sciences 406- 409; and the dynamic of secularisation and proselytisation 389-390; and the experience of nature 157, 159; and the indifference of other traditions 296; and the issue of faith 308-316; and the meaning of life 304-305; and the mechanism of domestication 329-330; and the order of the Cosmos 302-303; and the production of theoretical knowledge 403; and the structuring of experience 302, 403; and worldview 340-341, 351; as an explanatory intelligible account 298-300; as a bond 222; as a feature of humanity 61-62, 81; as a pre-theoretical concept 231; as explanation 173; as more than a worldview 345; as the only example of worldview 381; as the root model of order 400-403; Dinka 12; misunderstood by pagans 327-329; properties of 227; reflexivity in 345; shift in its reference 226; the double dynamic of its universalisation 437-439; as a language game 24; its etymology 221-224
*Religionsgeschichtliche Schule*
and its themes 175, 177-178
Religion as a linguistic practice 230-232
implcations for studying other religions 234
Religion in other cultures
absence of 25-26; and the absence of empirical investigation 63, 79, 138; and the *philosophes* 92; an inconsistent reasoning 21; as a logical inference 63; as a substantial question within theology 249; four aspects to mystification 20; inadequate identification 10, 19-21; mystifying circumstances 18-19; problem of identification 19

Religiosity
as an individuating criterion 228, 236; as a theological concept 218-219
Religious crime 34
Religious experience
and belonging to a tradition 192; and Durkheim's definition 201-202; and Eliade's ideas 202-203; and sacred objects 201; and the *homo religiosus* 203; and the Numinous 198; as a cultural universal 178; as a Protestant theme 200, 201; as *sui generis* 196; Otto's arguments 197-199; Schleiermacher's speeches 187-193; Söderblom's claims 193, 195-197
Religious explanations
properties of 166-167
Religious language
as its own meta-language 233, 345
Religious texts
the problem of identification 106; sanctioning the social organisation 112; the problem of identification 109
Renaissance
Oriental, anticipations about 119
Ritual
and actor-action relationship 422-423; and their 'cohesive' function 417, 419; and the absence of intention 416; and the absence of the experience of self 419, 421; and the creation of the world as a performative rite 422; and the idea of reincarnation 424; as a recursive structure of actions 415; as meaningless actions 415-417; structuring a configuration of learning 415-417, 419, 421-422, 424
Romanticism
and its ideas about the origin of religion 126; and the childhood of man 125; and the legacy of Elightenment 124;

Science
and its dissimilarity with religion 408-409; and the conditions for its emergence in the West 408; and the fragmentation of human knowledge 409
Science of religion
as theology 229; the possibility of 226
Secularisation
and explanatory intelligibility of the world 322-323; of Christianity 218-221, 232, 237, 269; of religious themes 226, 389

Study of religion
  its complexity in the twentieth century
  243-244
*Superstitio* 223

Taoism 16
Theology
  as the framework for a science of religion 226, 228-229
The 'other' 204
  and its poor conceptualisation 102-103;
  as a transformation of the Christian 'self'
  269; and multiple descriptions 455; and
  the problem of his conceptualisation
  424; as an epistemic dilemma 454-455;
  effacing into another 456-457; the possibility of description as an empirical
  question 455, 457; the problem of description 454
*Traditio*
  and its transformation by Christianity
  48, 51; and Judaism 44; and the
  Christians 46; and the Romans 42-43
Travel reports
  and the domain of morality and religion
  70; and the structure of ethnographic
  knowledge 69; and the structure of ethnography 68
Universality of Religion
  as a pre-theoretical intuition 149-154

Universality of religion
  and the naturalistic paradigm 148; as a
  non-empirical claim 231; as a theological claim 200; as a theological theme
  226; as both a pre-theoretical intuition
  and a theological claim 267-270; the
  claim as the compulsion of a culture
  233, 235; the linguistic answer to a conceptual compulsion 233-235
Universal History
  the conceptual conditions for 99

Worldview
  and its difference from theories 348-
  349; and its disjunction with religion
  355; and religion as the only example of
  386; and the origin of the world 355-
  356; as an intuitive necessity 352; as a
  secular equivalent of religion 385; inconsistent descriptions 382-383; its necessity as the secularization of a theological belief 384, 389; religion as a good
  example of 342-344; religion as the
  best example of 346-347; the necessity
  of 381-384, 387; the sociological conditions for the transmission 371-372
Worship
  and idolatry 335; as an element of an
  explanatory intelligible account 333-
  334; sustaining faith 333